Cooking Light®

best ever test kitchen
secrets

Compiled and Edited by
Anne C. Cain, M.P.H., M.S., R. D.

Library of Congress Control Number: 2004115102

ISBN: 0-8487-2790-8
Printed in the United States of America
First printing 2004

Oxmoor House, Inc.
Editor in Chief: Nancy Fitzpatrick Wyatt
Executive Editor: Katherine M. Eakin
Art Director: Cynthia Rose Cooper
Copy Chief: Allison Long Lowery

Cooking Light Best-Ever Test Kitchen Secrets

Editor: Anne C. Cain, M.P.H., M.S., R.D.
Copy Editor: Diane Rose
Editorial Assistants: Jessica Dorsey, Shannon
    Friedmann, Terri Laschober, Dawn Russell
Senior Designer: Emily Albright Parrish
Publishing Systems Administrator: Rick Tucker
Director, Production and Distribution: Phillip Lee
Books Production Manager: Leslie Johnson
Production Assistant: Faye Porter Bonner

Contributor:
Indexer: Mary Ann Laurens

Cooking Light ®

Vice President, Editor in Chief: Mary Kay Culpepper
Executive Editor: Billy R. Sims
Art Director: Susan Waldrip Dendy
Managing Editor: Maelynn Chung
Senior Food Editor: Alison Mann Ashton
Senior Editor: Anamary Pelayo
Editorial Coordinator: Carol C. Noe
Food Editor: Krista Ackerbloom Montgomery, M.S., R.D.
Associate Food Editor: Ann Taylor Pittman
Assistant Food Editor: Susan Stone, R.D.
Assistant Editors: Cindy Hatcher, Rachel Seligman
Contributing Beauty Editor: Lauren McCann

Test Kitchens Director: Vanessa Taylor Johnson
Food Stylist: Kellie Gerber Kelley
Assistant Food Stylist: M. Kathleen Kanen
Test Kitchens Staff: Sam Brannock, Kathryn Conrad,
    Jan Jacks Moon, Tiffany Vickers, Mike Wilson

Assistant Art Director: Maya Metz Logue
Senior Designer: Fernande Bondarenko
Designer: J. Shay McNamee
Assistant Designer: Brigette Mayer

Senior Photographer: Becky Luigart-Stayner
Photographer: Randy Mayor
Senior Photo Stylist: Cindy Barr
Photo Stylists: Melanie J. Clarke, Jan Gautro
Digital Photo Stylist: Jan A. Smith
Studio Assistant: Celine Chenoweth

Copy Chief: Maria Parker Hopkins
Senior Copy Editor: Susan Roberts
Copy Editor: Tara Trenary
Research Editor: Dani Leigh Clemmons

Production Manager: Liz Rhoades
Production Editors: Joanne McCrary Brasseal,
    Hazel R. Eddins

CookingLight.com Editor: Jennifer Middleton
Online Producer: Abigail Masters

Office Manager: Rita K. Jackson
Editorial Assistants: Melissa Hoover, Brandy Rushing
Correspondence Editor: Michelle Gibson Daniels

Contents

PART 1: The *Cooking Light* Way to Cook 11

Eating smart starts with cooking smart—and these basic tools, skills, and techniques will help you do just that.

CHAPTER 1 **The Essential Kitchen** 13

What are the tools and pieces of equipment that you need for light cooking?

CHAPTER 2 **Cooking Basics** 33

We teach you the skills and cooking methods that are a vital part of light cooking: making stocks and sauces, roasting, grilling, oven frying, poaching, stir-frying, and more!

CHAPTER 3 **Baking Basics** 91

Cooking Light has fine-tuned the art of light baking, and we share the secrets of our success with you.

PART 2: The Guide to Essential Ingredients 181

Great cooking starts with great ingredients. Let us show you how to stock your kitchen with the best.

CHAPTER 4 **Stocking Up** 183

Use our *Cooking Light* guide to the ingredients you need to keep on hand.

CHAPTER 5 **Meats, Poultry, Fish & Shellfish** 193

Here's all you need to know about selecting beef, chicken, and fish—and how to prepare them the light way.

CHAPTER 6 **Dairy, Eggs & Soy** 233

As an alternative to meat, these foods play a key role in healthy cooking and eating.

18   151   108

266   426   424

Letter from the *Cooking Light* Test Kitchens Director

Dear Friends,

Step into our Test Kitchens on any morning, and the first thing you might hear is the whirring of a mixer or the sizzling of meat in the skillet. You might also hear what I call "counter conversation"—staffers gathering around the kitchen counter to discuss recipes. We test over 4,000 recipes a year, so there is plenty of conversation!

Our dream for *Best-Ever Test Kitchen Secrets* is that you will feel as if you have entered our kitchens and are a part of our cooking discussions. This book is a compilation of the tips, techniques, secrets, and shortcuts we've gathered as we test recipes for the magazine.

Much of light cooking is about trial and error—and we are acquainted with both! You'll find actual kitchen-tested and kitchen-tasted recipes, along with the light techniques that we've discovered and perfected. None of us even pretends to know everything there is to know about light cooking—we learn something new each time a story comes through. We learn a lot from each other, too, and we want to share that knowledge with you in this book.

Our Test Kitchens Staffers come to the table with a wealth of training and experience:

• We have five culinary school graduates and five home economists with degrees in food and nutrition.

• Our Food and Photo Stylists, Kellie Kelley, Kathleen Kanen, and Jan Smith, all spend time in the Test Kitchens preparing recipes and using their food knowledge to make our food photography the best it can be.

• Jan Moon, who has a wedding cake business on the side, shares her secrets for making perfect layer cakes (page 134).

• Kathryn Conrad, our resident baker, offers her best tips for making yeast breads (page 108).

• Tiffany Vickers gives you step-by-step instructions for making custards (page 52).

• Mike Wilson, whose reputation as a barbecue master has spread throughout the company, is our go-to guy for grilling questions (see page 62 for our Top 10 Grilling Secrets).

• Sam Brannock, a former California restaurant owner, brings us a unique perspective on food and his passion for fresh produce.

Light cooking has come a long way since 1987, when the first issue of *Cooking Light* magazine hit the newsstand. Food trends come and go, and nutrition information is always evolving, but one thing that has not changed is our staff's passion for good food and healthy living. Please join us in the kitchen, and let us share our secrets for making the best light food ever.

> Food trends come and go, and nutrition information is always evolving, but one thing that has not changed is our staff's passion for good food and healthy living.

There are certainly some undisputed "kitchen truths" regarding light cooking, but it's still an art and is subject to personal opinions. We often have lively discussions about the best skillet to use or how to keep a cheesecake from cracking—or whether a cracked cheesecake is even a bad thing.

Vanessa Johnson

How to Use This Book

Whether you're an experienced cook or a novice, you'll find this book to be a wealth of information that you'll want to keep handy as a kitchen reference.

Two features you'll see throughout the book are: "Test Kitchen Secrets"—the insider tips that we've decided to make public; and "Cooking Light Recommends," where we highlight particular brands or types of cooking equipment or products. The chapters are not arranged alphabetically as a glossary; rather, we've organized them in a functional way, starting with equipping your kitchen, basic cooking skills, and baking techniques.

Then we provide comprehensive information on the ingredients we use most often in light cooking. You'll learn how to select the best products, how to store them, and how to use them in recipes. We end with our "Global Kitchen," which allows you to bring the great flavors and dishes from around the world into your own kitchen.

Cooking Light Confidential

Test Kitchen SECRET

Three is a small number, a humble number. But at *Cooking Light*, it's a magic number. A rating of "3" means a recipe is the best it can be—it's incredible, a "Wow!" kind of dish.

Every Tuesday through Friday, members of *Cooking Light's* editorial team assemble in our kitchens to rate the recipes tested that day. Food Editors and Test Kitchens Staffers are always present; other tasters may include members of the copy desk or the art, food styling, and photo departments. Such a broad mix of palates guarantees lively—and often passionate—discussion about a dish.

All told, we test more than 4,000 recipes a year. To do that, we use a simple yet rigorous system. Some dishes simply fail, while those that pass receive a numerical rating:

1	OK recipe
1+	good overall
2	very good overall
2+	high-quality recipe
3	superior in all aspects

The majority of recipes in the magazine are rated 1+ or higher. We don't publish many 1s because they're usually reworked until they get a higher rating. Still, we're a demanding crew, so 3s are rare.

A "3" Is Born There are many indications that a recipe deserves a 3, one of which is that there's not much left by the time taste testing starts around noon. The first few recipes begin to appear at 7 a.m. each day, so when one of them is outstanding, it's usually nibbled on all morning, leaving just enough for the group to sample.

We ask ourselves a variety of questions about each dish we taste in order to come up with the rating:

- How could we make this better?
- If we had this at a restaurant, would we think it was superb?
- Would we make this tonight? Would we make it again and again?
- Is it better than other versions of the dish we've had?
- Can we tell it's light?
- Will we tell our friends to make this?
- Would we be proud to serve this to our guests?

Top 20 Reader Questions

Michelle Daniels, our correspondence editor, has received as many as 100 letters and e-mails in one day from *Cooking Light* readers. While she admits that she sometimes receives some "off-the-wall" queries, she also gets a lot of the same questions. According to Michelle, here are the most often asked questions from our readers.

1. My light cake turned out very moist and heavy and did not rise. What happened?

We know from experience that baking a light cake can be tricky. For every e-mail we've received from a reader who raved about a specific cake, we've received another from a reader who had trouble with it. For some recipes, the cake probably turned out well—just not as light as expected. Unlike cakes baked with full-fat ingredients and methods, light cakes tend to be a bit heavier and more moist. But there are several critical things to check.

- First of all, it is important to measure the flour correctly. See page 93.
- Another potential problem is the butter; it should be soft to the touch but not melted.

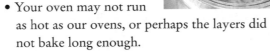

- Your oven may not run as hot as our ovens, or perhaps the layers did not bake long enough.

See Chapter 3, "Baking Basics," on pages 134-155 for detailed information about cakes.

2. Can I substitute applesauce for the butter/oil in a recipe? Do I substitute an equal measure? If not, what is the correct ratio of applesauce to fat?

While we don't typically recommend substituting applesauce for oil in recipes (we think it results in a gummy product), there are a few recipes in which this substitution works just fine. See page 149.

3. Why is my cake (or dough) dry and crumbly?

The culprit is almost always too much flour due to incorrect measuring. See page 93 for information on how to measure flour correctly. For additional information on making bread, cookies, and cakes, see the following sections in Chapter 3, "Baking Basics."

- Quick Breads, pages 96-103
- Yeast Breads, pages 106-121
- Cookies, pages 122-133
- Cakes, pages 134-155

4. Can I reduce the sugar in a recipe without changing the outcome?

In some recipes, you can reduce the amount of sugar slightly with only a minor change in flavor. But in other recipes, especially baked goods, the sugar contributes to the texture as well as the flavor, so your product might not turn out as desired. See page 91 for information about the role of sugar in recipes.

5. Can I use a sugar substitute instead of sugar in a recipe?

We don't recommend using sugar substitutes, especially for baking, because sugar substitutes don't contribute the tenderness and browning action that sugar does. If you need to use sugar substitutes for health reasons, we recommend that you contact the manufacturer of the specific sweetener for information on the best way to use that sweetener in recipes. See page 91.

6. What can I substitute for the heavy cream in a sauce recipe?

Many of our sauces and cream soups use a low-fat white sauce in place of heavy cream. See pages 40-41. And in some cases, we actually call for cream. See page 236 for information on using cream in light recipes.

7. How can I substitute olive oil for the butter in a recipe?

Whether or not you can substitute olive oil for butter in a recipe largely depends on the particular recipe. For example, in cakes and cookies, the olive oil would contribute a less-than-desirable flavor and texture if you used it in place of butter. But in some savory recipes, there wouldn't be a problem. See page 361.

8. I don't have buttermilk on hand. What can I use as a substitute?

Instead of 1 cup of buttermilk, add 1 tablespoon of vinegar or lemon juice to 1 cup of fat-free milk, and let it stand for 10 minutes. See page 466 for our ingredient substitution charts.

9. Can I substitute soy milk for the milk in a recipe?

It depends on the recipe. Soy milk has a distinctive flavor that might not be desirable in a particular recipe. See page 247 for information on using soy milk in recipes.

10. Can I substitute powdered egg substitute/liquid egg substitute for the eggs in a recipe?

Egg substitutes don't work in recipes such as custards, which need the egg yolk for thickening power. See pages 92, 144, 145, 174, and 242-244 for information on eggs.

11. How can I tell if a recipe (or a certain food) will freeze well?

There are a lot of factors that determine whether a recipe is suitable for freezing. And certain types of containers are better for freezing than others. See the Freezer Guide on pages 190-191.

12. How can I adapt recipes to work in a slow cooker?

Since recipes prepared in a slow cooker cook for a long time at a low temperature, the amount of liquid in the recipe is an important factor. For more information on cooking in a slow cooker, see pages 59 and 60.

13. So many of your recipes call for egg whites only. I hate to throw away all of those egg yolks. How can I save them or use them later?  You may store unbroken raw egg yolks, covered with water, for up to 2 days in an airtight container in the refrigerator. Or you can freeze them for up to 8 months. See page 242.

14. Can I substitute honey, molasses, or corn syrup for the sugar in a recipe?
Whether or not you can make a substitution really depends on the role of the sugar in the particular recipe. For example, honey and molasses do not contribute to the tenderness of a cake in the same way that sugar does. See pages 91 and 391-395 for information on sugars.

15. Can I substitute whole wheat flour for the all-purpose flour in a recipe?
Generally, you can substitute up to one-half of the all-purpose flour in a recipe with whole wheat flour. If you replace all of the all-purpose flour in a recipe with whole wheat, your product will probably be too dense. See pages 106 and 263.

16. Can I substitute a nonwheat flour such as soy for the all-purpose flour in a recipe? Soy flour does not contain gluten, so you cannot replace all of the all-purpose flour with soy flour. See page 246.

17. I don't use alcohol in cooking. What can I substitute? If it's just a splash of liqueur that's added for flavor, it's usually okay to leave it out. But if the alcohol is adding a significant amount of liquid to the recipe, you'll need to replace it with fruit juice, broth, or water. See the Alcohol Substitutions chart on page 469.

18. Many of your recipes call for coating a nonstick skillet with cooking spray. The instructions with my nonstick skillet state that cooking spray should never be used on this pan. Can you suggest any substitutes?
Heavy use of cooking spray over time can cause a residue to build up on the nonstick surface, thus decreasing its nonstick qualities. If you use a lot of cooking spray, you might consider rubbing a small amount of olive oil into the skillet before cooking, rather than adding cooking spray. If the recipe calls for sautéing the food in olive oil, the food probably won't stick, even if you don't use cooking spray. See pages 20-21 for information on nonstick skillets.

19. Many of your recipes call for toasted nuts. How do I toast nuts?
You can toast nuts in either a skillet, an oven, or in a microwave oven. See page 363.

20. What is the best way to calculate the nutritional information for my own recipes? Or is there a Web site or some software that will calculate the nutritional information for my recipes?
We analyze our recipes with a software program called Food Processor (ESHA Research), and we find it to be very easy to use and accurate. It's a PC-based software program, so it's fine for home use. There are a number of other acceptable nutrient analysis programs available.

We recommend that you shop around and see which program will give you the type of information you need. Almost all of them will do the basic function of calculating the nutrients in a recipe.

PART ONE

The Cooking Light® Way to Cook

At *Cooking Light*, we've pioneered and perfected a host of cooking techniques, kitchen strategies, and recipes to help you "eat smart, be fit, and live well." Eating smart starts with cooking smart—and there are skills and tools that will allow you do just that. Light cooking—it's easy, fun, healthy, and satisfying. It's the *Cooking Light* way to cook. And we want to show you how.

CHAPTER 1

The Essential Kitchen

Here are the tools and equipment that we believe
are necessary for healthy cooking.

Utensils

Whether you are stocking your kitchen from
scratch or paring down to just the basics, these
are the tools you need for healthy cooking.

Colanders/Strainers We use both metal and
plastic colanders in varying sizes. A large colander works well for draining pasta and salad
greens and rinsing vegetables. A small strainer is
great for separating fruit
juice or pulp from seeds.
Mesh strainers are the
most versatile because
nothing can get through
the holes except liquid.

**Most of us prefer plastic
strainers with handles.
They have more holes
and are great for
draining and rinsing.**

Cutting Boards We use both wood and plastic
cutting boards in the Test Kitchens. Whichever
you choose, wash thoroughly to avoid food
contamination. Use diluted bleach on wooden
boards, and wash thoroughly; sanitize plastic
ones in the dishwasher.

Food Scales Use a scale to measure the correct
amount of cheese or to make sure that pieces
of meat, poultry, and fish are the specified size.
The Salter digital scale is small, lightweight, and
accurate. The old-fashioned food service scales
by Pelouze also work well.

Kitchen Tools You'll *Really* Use
Cooking Light Recommends

We've given you a list of the essential tools for light
cooking in this section, but these are a few specific tools
we find ourselves using the most.

Chef's knife: Honestly, you just have to have one, and
you have to keep it sharp. It'll make almost everything
easier, and your food will look more attractive. (See pages
16-19 for more information on knives.)

Garlic press: This provides the easiest and most efficient
method of crushing garlic for recipes.

Kitchen shears: They can cut just about anything—from
herbs and chicken to canned tomatoes and pizza.

Multi-purpose scraper and chopper: Bash 'N Chop,
Graham Kerr's device (800-426-7101), scoops up chopped
ingredients so deftly that you'll use it constantly. It also
has handy inch markings on
the edge.

Silicone spatula: This tool by
OXO Good Grips (800-545-4411
or www.oxo.com) looks like a
regular rubber spatula, but its
600° heat resistance means
you can cook with it, too. It also
has a notch for scraping under
jar rims.

Garlic Press Use this tool when a recipe calls for crushed garlic because you'll be able to get both the garlic and its juice. **(A)**

Heat-Resistant Spatulas Choose an assortment of wide and narrow spatulas in silicone or nylon; they won't scratch nonstick cookware surfaces.

Instant-Read Thermometer Use an instant-read thermometer to check meringues, meat, and poultry to make sure they're cooked to the correct temperature. Don't leave it in the oven while the food is cooking, and remove it from the food after you read the temperature. **(B)**

Juicer Fresh juices, such as lemon, lime, and orange, add zesty flavor that you just can't always get with bottled juice. A juicer makes getting that juice supereasy. Electric juicers are available, but **for small jobs, such as squeezing one lemon or lime for juice, we use a handheld juicer.**

Kitchen Shears Keep kitchen shears handy to mince small amounts of herbs, chop canned tomatoes, trim fat from meat and skin from poultry, and make slits in bread dough. **(C)**

Measuring Cups Accurate measuring is crucial in light cooking. Dry measuring cups, available in metal or plastic, are flat across the rim. Fill cup to just above the rim, and scrape off excess with a knife. We use the standard 1, ½, ⅓, and ¼ nest of cups. Use dry measuring cups for ingredients like flour, grains, cereals, nuts, and seeds. If you measure liquid ingredients in dry measuring cups, the amount may not be accurate. Liquid measuring cups are available in clear glass or plastic so that you can see the level of liquid through the side of the cup. Liquid measuring cups come in various sizes from 1 cup to 4 cups.

> **We've found that the 1- and 2-cup liquid measuring cups are more accurate than the larger cups.**

Measuring Spoons Sometimes a "pinch of this" and a "pinch of that" results in a less-than-desired flavor. Use measuring spoons to make sure your recipes come out just right.

Having at least two sets of dry measuring cups and measuring spoons and a variety of sizes of liquid measuring cups is a great time-saver that will keep you from having to rinse in the middle of a recipe.

Oven Thermometer All ovens are equipped with internal thermostats, yet the actual temperature inside the oven may vary. Use an oven thermometer to find out if you need to calibrate your oven's thermostat. (Follow the directions in your owner's manual.) **(D)**

Peeler A peeler removes the skin from both vegetables and fruits. Select one with a comfortable grip and an eyer to remove potato eyes and other blemishes on vegetables and fruits.

Pepper Mill Give your food a bit of pungent flavor with a sprinkle of cracked or freshly ground pepper. **(E)**

Salad Spinner With just a few pumps or turns of the handle, you'll remove excess water from freshly washed salad greens. Some spinners have a lid so that you can use it for refrigerator storage.

Stainless-Steel Box Grater A box-style grater gives you a choice of hole sizes. Use the smaller holes for grating hard cheese or chocolate. For shredding an ingredient like Cheddar cheese or carrots, use the largest holes. **(F)**

Whisks Whisks in assorted sizes are ideal for beating eggs and egg whites, blending salad dressings, and dissolving solids in liquids. **We consider them essential for making creamy sauces.** Whisks are available both in stainless steel and nylon; the nylon ones won't scratch nonstick surfaces.

Measuring Up

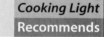
Cooking Light Recommends

You may be surprised to discover that all measuring cups are not created equal. *Cooking Light* contributor Jim Fobel was.

"One day while preparing a recipe, something didn't look right when I measured a quarter-cup of flour," he recalls. "Instinct told me to measure the same flour in another cup. The first measuring cup was off by a full tablespoon."

The culprit? The cup either had a misprinted measurement grid or an inaccurate cup mold." A standard cup should be 237 milliliters," says Test Kitchens Staffer John Kirkpatrick. "Not very many of them are, though."

In response to this quandary, we tested every measuring cup and spoon in our kitchens. You can get accurate and trustworthy sets from the following sources:
- Tupperware (www.tupperware.com)
- OXO Good Grips (www.oxo.com)
- Williams-Sonoma (www.williams-sonoma.com)

Top 3 Knives

You can cover an array of kitchen tasks with just three knives: a chef's knife, a serrated knife, and a paring knife. Each has functions unique to its shape and design. Learn to use them efficiently and safely to improve your speed and finesse in the kitchen and to make your food look more appealing.

> **"The best way to select a brand of knife is to see how each one feels in your hand."**
> Vanessa Johnson,
> **Test Kitchens Director**

Paring   Chef's   Serrated

Chef's Knife

The chef's knife (along with a cutting board) is the workhorse of the *Cooking Light* Test Kitchens. We use it for more tasks than any other. It works for almost all chopping: herbs, onions, garlic, fruits, and vegetables. It's also great for cutting boneless meats (it even cuts through small bones, such as those of chicken and fish), slicing and dicing, and general cutting tasks.

Many chefs choose a 12-inch-long chef's knife, but most of us are comfortable with an 8-inch knife. No one size is uniformly best—it's a matter of personal comfort.

The curved blade and heavy weight of the knife give it an advantage for chopping. With the tip of the knife on the chopping board, rock the knife back and forth with a subtle movement of the wrist and forearm. The weight of the thickest part of the blade, near the handle, adds force as it slices through food. A heavy handle does more of the work for you, reducing the amount of force with which your arm has to move the knife.

The Right Build

Most professional cooks use a high-carbon stainless-steel forged knife with a full tang, meaning the blade metal runs from the tip of the knife through the handle to the opposite end.

The blade should have a Rockwell hardness rating of at least 55, which indicates the knife sharpens easily and holds its edge. Look for this rating on the package.

The handle should feel comfortable and secure and have no gaps or burrs. Handle materials vary but should have enough weight to balance the blade.

A Good Chef's Knife for Every Budget

So which knife is the best? The "best knife" is a concept that's as unique as the person searching for it. Our staffers all have different preferences, but the top picks are Wüsthof, Henckel, OXO, and the Shun Classic. Here are six great 8-inch chef's knives for a variety of prices.*

Chicago Cutlery Centurion 8-inch chef's knife ($19.99): If you consider yourself a casual to average cook, go with this inexpensive knife. It has a forged blade, full tang, and sports a hardness rating of 52. It will take an edge quickly with a steel.

OXO Good Grips MV55-Pro 8-inch chef's knife ($30): This moderately-priced knife boasts a full tang and has a hardness rating of 55. The soft pressure-absorbing handle provides a comfortable grip.

Henckel's Professional "S" 8-inch chef's knife ($89.95): This is a solid, dependable knife with a hardness rating of 55 to 58. The weight, shape of the handle, and rocking action are great for everyone.

Kershaw Knives Shun Classic 8-inch chef's knife ($129): Our Test Kitchens staff went nuts over this knife, which boasts a hardness rating of 60. It has a razor-sharp, hard-yet-flexible blade that makes for effortless slicing.

New West Knife Works 8-inch chef's knife ($139): With a hardness rating of 57 to 59, this handcrafted knife is strong and durable. It's also beautiful, with colorful hardwood veneer handles.

Wüsthof Culinar 8-inch chef's knife ($160): The weight and balance of this knife are amazing, and we love the sleek look of the all-metal design. It has a hardness rating of 56.

*Prices listed are from manufacturers at publication date and may vary in retail outlets or at online sources.

Paring Knife

With its blade of 2½ to 4 inches, the paring knife looks like a miniature chef's knife, but its use is very different. The paring knife is great for peeling most fruits and vegetables; slicing a garlic clove or shallot; controlled, detailed cutting, such as cutting shapes or vents into dough; and scoring designs and patterns on the surfaces of food. It is also useful for precise work like removing ribs from a jalapeño or coring an apple.

Unlike the chef's knife, which is always used on a cutting board, you can cut with the paring knife while holding it aloft, as though it is an extension of your hand. The small handle gives the cook maximum control over the tip and the edge of the blade.

Serrated Knife

A serrated knife, with its scalloped, toothlike edge, is ideal for cutting through foods with a hard exterior and softer interior, such as a loaf of crusty bread. The principle behind a serrated knife is similar to that of a saw: The teeth of the blade catch and then rip as the knife smoothly slides through the food. It cuts cleanly through the resistant skin and juicy flesh of a ripe tomato without crushing it. It is easier and neater to cut crusty bread using a serrated knife because the crust will not splinter as much.

> "I use my serrated knife to slice cake. It's thinner than a chef's knife and doesn't tear up the tender cake. It's also easier than getting out the electric knife." Ann Pittman, Food Editor

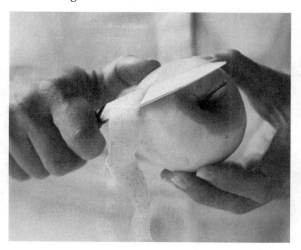

More Paring Uses

Test Kitchen
SECRET

Hull strawberries: Use the tip of the knife to remove the stem and carve out the white center core from the stem end of each berry.

Section an orange or lemon: Hold the fruit over a bowl to catch the juice that drips. Peel the fruit to the flesh, then cut between the white membranes to extract each section. Because you hold the fruit as you cut it, this job is much safer when performed with a paring knife than with a chef's knife.

Devein shrimp: Cut a shallow slit down the outside curve of the shrimp; remove the dark vein, and rinse the shrimp under cold water.

> "Is there really a difference between a $100 knife and a $20 one? Absolutely. The more expensive knives last longer, cut better, and just feel better in your hand."
>
> Mike Wilson, Test Kitchens Staffer

Buying the Right Knife
Cooking Light Recommends

An inexpensive knife wears out more quickly and doesn't hold its edge as well. How do you find the right one? First, look for one fits comfortably in your hand. Here are some other features to look for:

- A high-carbon stainless-steel knife so it won't corrode
- A grip with smooth—not sharp—edges so nothing scratches or rubs your hand as you hold the knife
- Rounded edges near the bolster (where the blade meets the handle)
- A balanced feel (when gripping the handle of the knife to cut, it should feel balanced without tilting on its own toward or away from the tip)

Take a knife for a test drive to see how the different brands feel in your hand as you go through the various cutting motions that you would use for each type of knife.

Storing and Cleaning Knives

Nothing makes a blade duller or ruins it faster than poor storage. We keep our knives in wooden blocks in the Test Kitchens. Or you can use a strong magnetic wall rack. **Never store knives loose in a drawer; banging against other metals is a surefire road to ruin.** Also, don't put your knives in the dishwasher—the heat affects the blades, and they won't sharpen as well. The dishwasher is bad for wooden handles, too.

Keeping Knives Sharp

It's important to keep knives sharp—a dull blade can slip and cause more injury than a sharp knife.

A sharpening steel straightens and sharpens the cutting edge of the blade. Frequent use of this tool will maintain a good blade edge for up to 2 years, at which point you may need to

Use a steel made by your knife's manufacturer to be sure that the metal used is harder than that of your knives.

resharpen your knives with a whetstone. To use the steel, grip the knife, sharp edge down, in one hand and the steel in the other. Cross them, place the blade against the steel at a 20-degree angle, and then pull it along the entire length of the steel. Repeat several times on both sides of the knife.

To use a whetstone (a small stone used for sharpening the edges of knives and other tools), draw the blade across at a 20-degree angle, alternating sides five or six times. Moisten the stone with water or oil if you wish.

To use a slotted stand or frame (which holds the whetstone in place), pull the knife blade, held perpendicularly, repeatedly through the slot in the frame until the blade is sharp. Electric knife sharpeners have whetstones mounted on two grinding pads, and you pull the knife through the pads.

Skillets & Saucepans

"When buying pots and pans, sometimes it's better to buy individual pieces rather than a whole set so that you can pick the few pieces that you really need."

Vanessa Johnson, Test Kitchens Director

Skillets

For healthy cooking, a nonstick skillet is essential because it requires little added fat. But sometimes, food needs to stick. If you want to leave browned bits behind for deglazing (see page 50) or achieve a dark brown surface on meats, use a heavy skillet without a nonstick coating, such as one made of copper, cast iron, or stainless steel. Is there one perfect skillet for everything? Not exactly—it depends on what you want to achieve. See the skillet comparisons chart below.

"In our Test Kitchens, we reach for a trusty heavy skillet almost as often as the nonstick variety."
Vanessa Johnson, Test Kitchens Director

Nonstick Skillets

Nonstick coatings are more durable than they were years ago, thanks to modern technology. Here's what to look for when selecting a nonstick skillet.

- Start out with a medium- to heavy-gauge skillet. This provides a sturdy base for the nonstick coating and helps prevent overheating, which can cause the coating to lose its nonstick properties.
- Check the packing box or manufacturer's pamphlet for a nonstick finishing process involving multiple-step application. Multiple coats suggest the base metal has been carefully

Nonstick and Heavy Skillet Comparisons

	Nonstick Skillets	Heavy Skillets *Stainless Steel or Cast Iron*
General Uses	quick sautéing and stir-frying meats, seafood, and vegetables	searing, sautéing, and stir-frying meats, seafood, and vegetables
Best for	cooking with very little fat, sautéing delicate foods like fish, or cooking recipes that have lots of liquid	browning and creating "crusts" on foods
Absolutely Necessary for	scrambled eggs, pancakes, and crêpes	deglazing (scraping off browned bits stuck to the pan to use in flavoring the sauce)
Limitations	doesn't brown foods or conduct heat as well as stainless steel; shouldn't be placed over high heat; many have plastic handles that can't go in the oven	can't cook completely free of fat (some oil must be added to the pan); delicate foods tend to stick

prepared and the nonstick layer is thick enough to be durable.

- Stick with reputable manufacturers and cookware lines that stand behind their products, or choose the toughest name-brand finishes, such as Excalibur, Autograph, SilverStone Professional, SilverStone Xtra, and Quantum.
- Manufacturers of nonstick coatings say their finishes work equally well and last just as long on all types of surfaces—smooth, rough-textured, or patterned. Surfaces with ridges, however, collect food and are harder to clean.

Care of Nonstick Skillets Although modern nonstick coatings are durable, there are some things you can do to maintain the surface for the long run.

- Take care not to overheat nonstick pans, especially when they're empty. These pans' coatings are made of fluoropolymer substances that are damaged by excess heat. So stay away from the HIGH setting on the cooktop dial.
- Use wooden or nylon utensils, and hand-wash pans so the coating performs better and lasts longer.

- Follow the manufacturer's instructions for care, as various coatings have different compositions and require different care.

The Most Versatile Nonstick Skillet

If you're looking for the best nonstick skillet to handle the widest variety of cooking tasks, we recommend either one of the following types of pans:
- $11\frac{1}{2}$- to 13-inch diameter nonstick sauté pan with 3- to 4-inch deep sides (sometimes called a sauté/Dutch oven combo pan or chef's pan, this type of skillet is deep enough for a pot roast or stew but is also fine for routine sautéing and browning; it can even serve as a large saucepan)
- 10- to 12-inch flat-bottomed nonstick skillet with 1- to $1\frac{1}{2}$-inch deep sides (an omelet-style pan with gently curved sides or a traditionally shaped skillet with slightly flared sides works well for all kinds of sautéing, browning, and pan-grilling tasks; the low sides, which ensure rapid evaporation, make this pan well suited for reducing sauces and pan juices)

What to Seek in a Skillet

If you're in the market for a skillet—either a nonstick or a heavy skillet, here are some things we consider when purchasing skillets for our Test Kitchens.

Size: While we have a variety of sizes in the *Cooking Light* Test Kitchens, we use 12-inch skillets most often.

Heavy-gauge bottom: This ensures consistent, uniform heat and reduces scorching and hot spots.

Lid: A lid isn't absolutely necessary because you'll use the skillet primarily to sear, sauté, and stir-fry. In a pinch, use a lid from another pan.

Handle: It's nice to have one that's heat resistant so your skillet can go in the oven—to finish a meat dish seared on the stovetop, for example. Many manufacturers produce "stay cool" or heat-resistant plastic handles, but check the handle's temperature tolerance before you purchase the skillet.

Our recommendations: We polled our food editors and Test Kitchens staff for their favorites.
- For nonstick skillets, Anolon (www.anolon.com) reigned, though we also liked the inexpensive Mirro skillet (www.onestopshopcatalog.com).
- For the heavy skillets, we preferred those by All-Clad (www.allclad.com) and Calphalon (www.calphalon.com).

> "Some of us prefer heavy stainless-steel skillets to nonstick pans because you get better browning and deglazing."
>
> Vanessa Johnson, Test Kitchens Director

Heavy Stainless-Steel Skillets

You don't have to have nonstick skillets for light cooking—several of our editors prefer to use heavy stainless-steel skillets, especially for searing meats, fish, and poultry, and for deglazing. If you use cooking spray or a small amount of oil in these skillets, the food won't stick.

Because stainless steel is not a good heat conductor, most of these skillets have another metal, such as copper or aluminum, in the core or on the bottom so that foods will cook quickly and evenly.

Most of these skillets are oven safe; check the manufacturer's information to see if the skillet handle is a "stay cool" handle. Some stainless-steel pans are dishwasher safe, but for others, washing by hand is recommended. Always check the manufacturer's instructions for care and cleaning.

heavy stainless-steel skillet

Cast-Iron Skillets

You can make an upside-down cake in a cake pan, but the gooey, caramelized edges won't turn out nearly so crunchy as when made in a cast-iron skillet. The same goes for corn bread. Everything browns better in cast iron.

cast-iron skillet

Seasoning a Cast-Iron Skillet Seasoning is the process of oiling and heating cast iron to protect its porous surface from moisture. The oil is absorbed, creating a rustproof nonstick surface. (See "How to Season a Skillet" on page 23.) Generally, you need to season your pan only once before using it.

The more you use it, the more nonstick the surface becomes. That's because cast iron is porous, and when it's heated, it absorbs a bit of the oil, protecting it against future moisture.

Care of Cast-Iron Skillets Cast iron can rust if neglected. By following some basic rules, your skillet should remain free of rust and last for generations.

- Cast iron can corrode when acidic foods are added, so remove acidic food, such as tomatoes, from the skillet as soon as the dish has finished cooking. If the skillet is well seasoned, corrosion is unlikely.
- As soon as food is removed, scrub the pan under hot water, then place on a warm burner for a few minutes to dry. After drying, dribble some vegetable oil in it. Rub the oil all over the inside of the skillet with a paper towel so that the skillet shines. Cool.
- If your pan is rusted, scour the rust away with fine steel wool. Scrub the pan with hot soapy water, then scour with fine steel wool again before drying and reseasoning.
- Never put a cast-iron skillet in the dishwasher because it's not good for the cast iron to be left in a moist environment.

"Because a well-seasoned cast-iron skillet requires little oil for cooking, it's ideal for light cooking."

Krista Montgomery, Food Editor

How to Season a Skillet

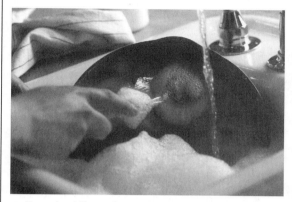

1. Rinse the skillet under warm sudsy water. Dry the skillet well.

2. Rub the skillet generously with vegetable oil.

3. Leave the skillet on a burner turned to low heat for about an hour, or bake it in a 350° oven for 2 hours. Let the skillet cool, then pour out any residual oil. Do this process two or three times before using to get it completely seasoned.

Saucepans

No single pan shape is ideal for all uses. Tall, narrow pots are great for simmering stocks and soups, but if you're making a sauce, a whisk cannot reach into the edges. Shallow, wider pans are better for whisking and usually are more balanced. Size is actually more important than the type or brand.

> "We like to call for the right size for the job, so we recommend that you have three different sizes: small (1-quart), medium (2-quart), and large (3-quart)." Jan Moon, Test Kitchens Staffer

Pans with heavy bottoms are the best. The heavy bottom is especially important when you're preparing custards, melting chocolate, and making sauces so the heat gets distributed evenly.

Heavy-Bottom Pan

Test Kitchen SECRET

stainless-steel saucepan

We've found that a heavy saucepan moderates temperatures as well as a double boiler. This works so well that we rarely use a double boiler. The key is to cook with low heat and to watch the food carefully.

Dutch Oven

A Dutch oven is neither Dutch nor an oven; rather, it's a deep pot with a tight-fitting lid that can go from cooktop to oven. It usually holds 3 to 6 quarts. Some versions come with a long handle, like a skillet.

Dutch oven

If you choose one with a long handle, make sure there's also a "helper handle" on the other side, since a hot Dutch oven full of food can be heavy. (For information on using a Dutch oven for braising, see page 55.)

> We frequently use Dutch ovens in our Test Kitchens for braising; making soups, stews, chili, pot roast, and pasta; and for cooking large amounts of greens, such as spinach.

"It's worth it to spend the extra money on heavy saucepans, especially if you're cooking a lot."
Kathryn Conrad, Test Kitchens Staffer

> "We use a variety of saucepans in our Test Kitchens, but our favorite pans are All-Clad stainless steel."
>
> Kathleen Kanen, Photo Stylist

Skillets and Saucepans: Metal Matters

Pans made of thinner metal are easier to lift and handle and are often cheaper than the heavy pans. But heavier-gauge pans generally perform better and last longer. So choose a metal that's appropriate for the specific job and for the way you cook.

Type of metal	Pluses	Minuses
Anodized Aluminum	hard, durable, and conducts heat extremely well	gunmetal-gray "industrial look" finish that can discolor; tends to be expensive
Aluminum or Enamel-Coated Aluminum	an excellent heat conductor; lightweight, reasonably priced, and comes in a range of colors	not as durable as other choices because aluminum is relatively soft unless it's anodized; pans without an exterior enamel coating can discolor
Copper	an excellent heat conductor that also cools rapidly; beautiful enough to use at the table	tarnishes rapidly, requiring frequent polishing; very pricey
Stainless Steel	hard and very durable, with a smooth, lustrous, stain-resistant surface	a poor heat conductor; most pans are layered with aluminum or copper on or within the bottom to boost conductivity
Enamel-Coated Carbon Steel	heats up rapidly and gets very hot (good for searing and blackening); durable (in better brands, the enamel is quite chip-resistant); comes in fashionable colors and is handsome enough to go from stovetop to table	somewhat heavy; may cook unevenly or have hot spots

Small Appliances

These are the appliances we consider necessities if you're doing a lot of cooking.

Blenders

A blender actually does a better job with liquid mixtures than a food processor and is especially great for pureeing soups, emulsifying salad dressings, and whipping up smoothies. **We've also found that recipes like dips and thick sauces, normally made in a food processor, work great in the blender, too.**

The blender can easily stand in for a food processor as long as the ingredients are tender enough to be chopped by its blade and there is enough liquid to keep the contents from clinging to the sides of the container.

When you're adding ingredients to the blender, the order in which you add them usually doesn't matter unless the recipe specifies otherwise.

Chocolate-Peanut Butter Smoothie

A blender is the best way to whip up smoothies for either a single serving or a whole batch.

- ½ cup 1% low-fat milk
- 2 tablespoons chocolate syrup
- 2 tablespoons creamy peanut butter
- 1 frozen sliced ripe banana
- 1 (8-ounce) carton vanilla low-fat yogurt

1. Place all ingredients in a blender; process until smooth. Yield: 2 servings (serving size: about 1 cup).

CALORIES 332 (29% from fat); FAT 10.8g (sat 3.2g, mono 4.5g, poly 2.3g); PROTEIN 12.7g; CARB 49.8g; FIBER 3.1g; CHOL 8mg; IRON 1mg; SODIUM 194mg; CALC 282mg

Blender Selection

Cooking Light Recommends

We have a variety of blenders in our Test Kitchens, and we like them all—Oster, Hamilton Beach, and Waring. But there are definitely some blender features that we prefer.

Not-too-deep base: The base is the section at the bottom of the container that connects with the motor. You'll want a base that is not deep for three reasons: It makes cleanup easier, food won't get caught beneath the blades during blending, and when you are blending a small amount of food, the food is mixed by the blades instead of being whirled to the sides.

Multiple speeds: If you're only going to make milk shakes or frozen drinks, a blender with one or two speeds will work fine. But for more versatility, choose a blender with several speeds (a pulse option is great, too). If you'll be making lots of frozen beverages, look for an ice-crushing mode.

Clear glass container: Stainless-steel containers look sleek and retro, but they don't allow you to see what you're blending. And although plastic containers won't break, they hold odors; blending a slushy drink after whipping up a garlicky sauce in plastic may not yield appetizing results.

Shallot and Grapefruit Dressing

A blender works great for liquid mixtures like this salad dressing because there's nothing that needs to be chopped—it just needs to be blended well. And this liquid mixture is thin, so you don't have to worry about anything clinging to the sides of the container.

1	teaspoon olive oil
½	cup chopped shallots
2	cups fresh grapefruit juice (about 3 grapefruits)
2	tablespoons chopped fresh cilantro
2	teaspoons sugar
¼	teaspoon freshly ground black pepper
2	tablespoons olive oil

1. Heat 1 teaspoon oil in a large nonstick skillet over medium heat. Add shallots; cook 5 minutes or until golden brown. Stir in juice. Bring to a boil over medium-high heat, and cook until reduced to 1 cup (about 6 minutes). Remove from heat; cool.

2. Place the grapefruit juice mixture, cilantro, sugar, and pepper in a blender; process until smooth. With blender on, slowly add 2 tablespoons oil; process until smooth. Serve over mixed greens. Yield: 1 cup (serving size: 1 tablespoon).

CALORIES 35 (51% from fat); FAT 2g (sat 0.3g, mono 1.5g, poly 0.2g); PROTEIN 0.3g; CARB 4.2g; FIBER 0.1g; CHOL 0mg; IRON 0.1mg; SODIUM 1mg; CALC 4mg

When you're blending hot liquids in a blender, be careful because the steam can increase the pressure inside the blender container and blow off the lid. Here are some tips.

- Don't fill the blender more than halfway. Blend in batches if necessary.
- Let mixture cool, uncovered, in a blender for a few minutes before blending.
- Hold a potholder or towel over the lid when blending.

Food Processors

A food processor can make speedy work out of slicing and chopping fruits and vegetables, blending ingredients, and kneading dough. (See pages 110-112 for yeast bread recipes that use the food processor for kneading.)

"Most food processors in our Test Kitchens are 7-cup machines, and that's adequate for most of the recipes we test." Susan Stone, Food Editor

They come in different sizes to accommodate different amounts of food, and most come with a set of blades for different tasks, such as shredding and slicing.

A mini food processor is sometimes handy for small food prep tasks, such as chopping onions, garlic, herbs, and nuts, and it doesn't take up much room on the countertop or in the kitchen cabinet.

Preferred Processor

Cooking Light **Recommends**

We use Cuisinart food processors in our kitchens and think they're the best. We actually still have some of the Cuisinarts we bought when we first moved into our new Test Kitchens in 1989, and

they're still going strong. Even though these food processors are more expensive than some of the other brands, we think they're worth it because they last so long.

We use food processors in a lot of recipes and always choose a processor over a blender for ingredients that are thick or dry, such as beans and flour.

If a *Cooking Light* recipe calls for a blender or a food processor, this means we've tested the recipe using both appliances and found that both give similar results.

Microwave Oven

Most people seem to use microwave ovens only to reheat leftovers or steam vegetables. The problem may be that preparing food in the microwave is perceived as not really cooking. But the microwave is just as good a way of applying heat as any other. Your microwave oven can cook great food the first time around, too. And speed is only one of its virtues.

What's the Wattage?

Test Kitchen SECRET

Microwave oven wattages range from 600 to 1,200 watts. Most new microwave ovens are 1,100 to 1,200, while the older ones are as low as 600 watts. Most of the microwaves in our Test Kitchens have wattages of 1,000 or less. If the wattage of your oven is higher, you may need to decrease the cooking time by 1 to 2 minutes.

If you don't know the wattage of your microwave oven, pour 1 cup of tap water into a 2-cup glass measure, and watch how long it takes to come to a boil at HIGH power. Then check your time and wattage below.

- less than 2 minutes ....850 to 1200 watts
- 2 to 3 minutes ....650 to 850 watts
- 3 to 4 minutes ....400 to 650 watts

Rosemary Potatoes

These potatoes taste as if they were roasted in the oven—but they take only half the time.

1	tablespoon butter
1	teaspoon bottled minced garlic
1	teaspoon dried rosemary
½	teaspoon kosher salt
¼	teaspoon pepper
1½	pounds red potatoes, quartered (about 4 cups)

1. Place butter and garlic in an 8-inch square baking dish. Microwave at MEDIUM-HIGH (70% power) 45 seconds or until butter melts. Add rosemary, salt, pepper, and potatoes; toss well. Cover and microwave at HIGH 15 minutes or until potatoes are tender. Yield: 4 servings (serving size: ¾ cup).

CALORIES 155 (18% from fat); FAT 3.1g (sat 1.9g, mono 0.8g, poly 0.2g); PROTEIN 3.9g; CARB 29g; FIBER 3.2g; CHOL 8mg; IRON 2.4mg; SODIUM 182mg; CALC 30mg

Foods cooked in the microwave retain nutrients. Because the food cooks rapidly and is usually in only a small amount of liquid, nutrient loss through evaporation or in the cooking liquid is minimal.

Microwave Accessories that *Really* Work

Cooking Light Recommends

We've found that most microwave-specific cooking gadgets are either unnecessary or don't work well, but we can suggest some that are worth purchasing.

- **Rock 'N Serve Containers (Tupperware):** These let you go from freezer to microwave to dishwasher. They're perfect for make-ahead meals. The prices vary per container, depending on the size, plus shipping and handling. Order online at www.tupperware.com, or call 800-366-3800 for more information.

- **PowerCrisp Microwave Bacon Cooker (Presto stock #05100):** This product makes bacon less greasy. Fat drips away, which means the bacon absorbs less grease than when pan-fried. It's available at retail stores or at www.presto-net.com

- **PowerPop Microwave Multi-popper (Presto, stock #04830):** Instead of using a popcorn air popper, this popper does the same thing in the microwave. It's available at retail stores or at www.presto-net.com

> "We discovered that you really can make good risotto in the microwave!" Sam Brannock, Test Kitchens Staffer

Italian Risotto with Shrimp

Classic risotto cooked on the stovetop takes about 30 minutes of constant stirring. This microwave version still takes about 30 minutes, but you don't have to stand at the stovetop and stir.

3½	cups fat-free, less-sodium chicken broth
½	cup dry white wine
1	cup chopped onion
2	teaspoons olive oil
1⅓	cups Arborio rice or other short-grain rice
1	pound shrimp, peeled and deveined
1	cup frozen whole-kernel corn
⅓	cup chopped bottled roasted red bell peppers
1	tablespoon chopped fresh basil
1	tablespoon chopped fresh oregano
¾	cup (3 ounces) grated Asiago cheese

1. Combine broth and wine in a 1-quart glass measure. Microwave at HIGH 5 minutes or until mixture boils. Remove from oven; keep warm.
2. Combine onion and oil in a 2-quart casserole. Microwave at HIGH 4 minutes. Stir in broth mixture and rice. Microwave at HIGH 15 minutes or until liquid is almost absorbed, stirring every 5 minutes.
3. Stir in shrimp and next 4 ingredients. Microwave at HIGH 4 minutes or until shrimp are done, stirring mixture every 2 minutes. Stir in cheese. Yield: 5 servings (serving size: about 1¼ cups).

CALORIES 409 (18% from fat); FAT 8.2g (sat 3.5g, mono 3g, poly 0.9g); PROTEIN 26.2g; CARB 55g; FIBER 2.2g; CHOL 121mg; IRON 4.3mg; SODIUM 722mg; CALC 233mg

Microwave Shortcuts
Test Kitchen SECRET

What do we really use our microwaves for most? Mainly to take shortcuts when we're doing the following:

Melting butter: Cut into small pieces, and place in a glass measure. For ¼ cup of butter, microwave, uncovered, at HIGH for about 55 seconds.

Melting chocolate: Place pieces of chocolate (about 1 ounce) in a glass measure, and microwave, uncovered, at MEDIUM (50% power) for about 1 minute or until melted. Stir well.

Melting jelly: Spoon the jelly or jam into a glass measure, and microwave at HIGH for about 30 seconds.

Cooking bacon: Place slices on a microwave-safe bacon rack or plate; cover with paper towels and microwave at HIGH until crisp. The rule of thumb is to cook about 1 minute per slice.

Heating milk: To heat ½ cup of milk, place it in a glass measure, and microwave, uncovered, at HIGH for 1 to 2 minutes or until thoroughly heated but not boiling. Add about 1 minute for each additional ½ cup of milk.

Steaming vegetables: Be sure to cover the vegetables in order to retain moisture.

Defrosting: Remove food from its packaging, and place in a microwave-safe dish. Foam trays and plastic wraps may melt and cause chemicals to migrate into the food.

Mixers

If you're doing much baking, you'll need a mixer to help with mixing, whipping, creaming, and kneading. All mixers come with beaters, and some come with other attachments, such as dough hooks. The two basic types of motorized mixers are stand mixers and handheld mixers. Which type you prefer is a matter of personal choice. We use both types for testing, depending on the recipe. For personal use, our staff is split between those who consider their KitchenAid mixer their most prized possession, and those who think a handheld mixer meets their baking needs.

> "The best testimony for a KitchenAid mixer is that it will last for a very long time. We really give them a workout, and we've never had to replace one."
>
> Vanessa Johnson, Test Kitchens Director

Stand Mixers

Stand mixers, also called stationary mixers, are good for mixing large amounts of batter and heavy batters. Heavy-duty stand mixers (such as KitchenAid) are designed like commercial mixers, with a single paddle and a powerful motor. "Heavy-duty" means they can handle thick doughs, such as cookie or bread doughs, without burning up the motor. The bowls on them are large, which helps when you have large amounts of batter or dough.

They usually come with multiple attachments, such as whisks for beating egg whites or whipping cream, a paddle for creaming butter and sugar, and dough hooks for kneading bread. An especially nice thing about these mixers is that the dough does not crawl up the beaters like it does with other mixers, especially when you have a thick dough.

A KitchenAid mixer can be a little intimidating if you've never used one, but you'll never want another stand mixer after you have a KitchenAid.

Handheld Mixers

Handheld mixers are fine for mixing most batters. They are small, easy to store, and offer great control. When you're using this type of mixer, you don't have to stop and scrape down the sides of the bowl. However, these small mixers will not be able to handle the kneading of bread dough or thick cookie batter. If you don't have a stand mixer, you'll be better off kneading the dough by hand.

Our Favorite Mixers

We think the best stand mixer is a KitchenAid. If we're making cakes, frostings, cookie doughs, bread doughs, and other thick-battered recipes, we call for a heavy-duty mixer because these mixers have larger motors and usually larger bowls that can handle big jobs. When a recipe calls for a heavy-duty mixer, we are talking about a KitchenAid stand mixer. However, most of us prefer to use a handheld mixer for most recipes just because it's quicker, lighter, and less messy. A hand-mixer works great for quick jobs, such as beating egg whites or mixing instant puddings.

Basic Inventory *Checklist*

Here is a list of the essential kitchen equipment that no kitchen should be without. The baking pans and dishes will be covered in more detail in Chapter 2, "Cooking Basics," and Chapter 3, "Baking Basics."

Cookware
Assorted baking pans
❑ Baking sheet
❑ Bundt
❑ Jelly-roll
❑ Loaf
❑ Muffin
　❑ miniature
　❑ regular
❑ Round cake
❑ Springform
❑ Square
❑ Tart (round, removable-bottom)
❑ Tube

Pots and pans
❑ Dutch oven: 3- to 6-quart
❑ Heavy saucepans
　❑ small (1 1/2-quart)
　❑ medium (2-quart)
　❑ large (3-quart)
❑ Nonstick skillets:
　❑ 10-inch
　❑ 12-inch
❑ Pasta pot
❑ Roasting pan
❑ Vegetable-steamer
　insert for saucepan

Assorted glass dishes
❑ baking dishes
❑ casseroles
❑ pie plate

Utensils
❑ Can opener
❑ Colander and strainer
❑ Corkscrew
❑ Graters: box and handheld
❑ Handheld juicer
❑ Heatproof spatula
❑ High-quality sharp knives
❑ Kitchen shears or scissors
❑ Measuring cups
　❑ dry
　❑ liquid
❑ Measuring spoons
❑ Thermometers
　❑ instant-read
　❑ oven
❑ Vegetable peeler
❑ Whisk
❑ Wooden spoons

Other Equipment
❑ Cutting boards
　❑ for meats and animal products
　❑ for nonanimal products
❑ Electric blender
❑ Electric food processor
❑ Food scale
❑ Glass mixing bowls
❑ Handheld electric mixer
❑ Pepper mill

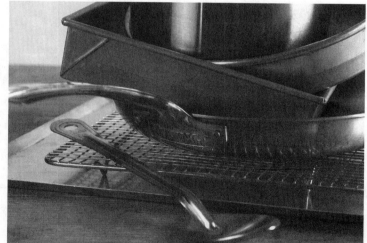

CHAPTER 2

Cooking Basics

Light cooking is all about getting the most flavor from the food while keeping an eye on fat and calories. With these basic skills and cooking methods, we'll show you how to do just that.

While we certainly don't claim these basic cooking techniques as our own, we can share what we've learned about using these methods to prepare light and healthy foods. Some of them are inherently "light," while others require that you make a few adjustments to keep calories and fat in line.

Knife Skills These skills are the foundation for food preparation. Learn how to use your knives just like the best of the chefs (see pages 16-19 for information on types of knives) . . . . page 34

Making Stocks Master the art of making stocks the light way . . . . page 37

Making Sauces Nothing gives you more confidence as a cook than knowing how to make a good sauce . . . . page 40

Braising You'll learn how to get the best flavor with this slow-cooking method and get a guide for using a slow cooker . . . . page 55

Grilling Be it burger, steak, seafood, or veggie, learn how to grill like a pro . . . . page 61

Oven Frying Yes, it's possible to get that deep-fried flavor the light way, and we'll share our secret techniques for crispy coatings . . . . page 70

> ## Our Favorite Flavor-Boosting Techniques
>
> **Test Kitchen SECRET**
>
> There are many ways to add flavor to foods, but if we had to pick a few favorites, these would be our top picks.
>
> **Braising:** Long, slow cooking is the ideal way to make inexpensive leaner meats melt-in-your-mouth tender.
>
> **Deglazing:** Take those browned morsels that stick to the bottom of the pan and turn them into a flavorful sauce. Just add wine or stock to the pan, scrape, and stir.
>
> **Indoor grilling:** Invest in a heavy-duty grill pan for smoky grilled flavors all year long.
>
> **Roasting:** This labor-saving method makes everything taste better and allows you to leave food unattended for a while.

Poaching See how easy this classic low-fat method can be . . . . page 72

Roasting This time-honored way of cooking just can't be beat because of its simplicity and flavor . . . . page 74

Steaming We share what we've learned about the best ways to steam foods . . . . page 82

Stir-frying This quick-and-easy technique works for all types of food . . . . page 86

Knife Skills

We just can't emphasize enough the fact that one key to easy food prep is having good knives and knowing how to use them. There's a reason that one of the first courses taught in most culinary schools is knife skills. When the prep work comes naturally and easily, you'll start having a lot more fun in the kitchen. (For more information on knives, see pages 16-19.)

How to Use Your Chef's Knife

Garlic

1. Begin by separating the head into individual cloves with your hands. Smash a garlic clove under the blade of the chef's knife by hitting it with the palm of your hand; this breaks the clove open and releases the peel.

2. To mince garlic, do this: Guide the garlic under the knife edge with your fingers, and rock the knife through the garlic until it is minced.

Herbs

Wash the leaves in cold water; nip off the stems, and pat dry in paper towels. Start by holding the herbs tightly together on a cutting board with one hand; as you cut, move the fingertips of this hand to the blade. Use your other hand to hold the blade on the cutting board, rocking the knife up and down and scraping the herbs into a pile as you cut.

Onion

Slice onion in half vertically, leaving the root end intact. Place each half, cut side down, on cutting board. Working from the root end, make several horizontal cuts through the onion. Turn the onion a quarter, and make even crosswise cuts through it.

> "When you chop with a chef's knife, your objective is to create uniform-size pieces that will cook evenly."
> Sam Brannock, Test Kitchens Staffer

Zucchini

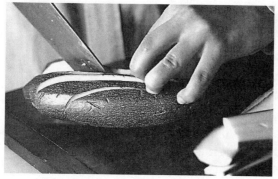

1. Cut off the blossom end. Then cut into ¼-inch lengthwise strips, cutting to, but not through, the stem end. Cut off the stem end, leaving 3 or 4 (¼-inch-thick) strips.

2. To dice zucchini, cut the stack of strips lengthwise down the middle. Turn the strips sideways, and cut them into large, medium, or small cubes.

Pepper

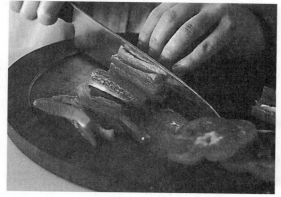

1. For ¼ x 1- or 2-inch julienne strips, start by cutting the pepper in half vertically and scraping out all the seeds and membranes. Place the pepper halves, skin sides down, on the cutting board. Cut the pepper halves into ¼-inch strips, then cut the strips into 1- or 2-inch pieces, making sure you keep the blade tip on the cutting board while pushing the blade through the peppers.

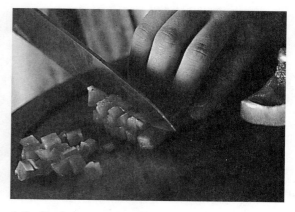

2. To dice the peppers, simply turn the julienne strips sideways so that they're at a right angle to the blade, and cut the strips into the size that is specified in the recipe.

Pitting Olives

Another great use for your chef's knife is pitting olives. Place an olive on a cutting board, and place the knife blade flat on top of the olive. Forcefully hit the blade onto the olive. The olive will pop open, exposing the pit for easy removal.

Cutting-Board Salsa

Here's a salsa recipe that lets you show off your chef's knife skills as you prepare the fresh herbs and veggies.

2	cups diced tomato
½	cup diced peeled jicama
½	cup diced onion
½	cup diced radishes
⅓	cup chopped seeded peeled cucumber
¼	cup fresh orange juice
2	tablespoons chopped fresh mint
2	tablespoons chopped fresh cilantro
2	tablespoons fresh lime juice
2	teaspoons chopped seeded jalapeño pepper (1 small pepper)
½	teaspoon salt

1. Combine all ingredients in a large bowl, and toss gently. Cover and chill. Serve with baked tortilla chips or as a topping for fish or chicken. Yield: 3½ cups (serving size: ¼ cup).

CALORIES 16 (11% from fat); FAT 0.2g (sat 0g, mono 0g, poly 0.1g); PROTEIN 0.5g; CARB 3.6g; FIBER 0.6g; CHOL 0mg; IRON 0.3mg; SODIUM 103mg; CALC 7mg

Ask the *Cooking Light* Cooks

What's the difference between something that's minced, diced, chopped, or cubed?

Mince To chop into very small pieces. Use your chef's knife in the same rocking motion used for chopping. Mincing herbs and garlic helps release their flavor throughout food.

Dice To cut into small ¼-inch cubes. Use a chef's knife to cut the food into slices of desired thickness, then cut the slices into strips of the same thickness. Stack the strips with the ends flush, and cut crosswise into small cubes.

Chop To cut into small irregular-size pieces. Use one hand to grip the handle of a chef's knife, and place the other hand on the blunt edge of the knife. Keep the knife tip on the cutting surface while rapidly lifting the handle up and down, cutting through the food. Continue chopping until the pieces are the desired size: coarsely chopped, chopped, or finely chopped.

Cube To cut into ½-inch or larger blocks. Use a chef's knife to cut the food into slices of the desired thickness, then cut the slices into strips of the same thickness. Stack the strips with the ends flush, and cut crosswise into cubes.

Making Stocks

Making stocks is a part of cooking that's as basic as it is classic. Here's how to master the art of stocks—the light way.

There are two basic stocks—white and brown—and we'll show you how to master them both. Both take about the same time to prepare, but the methods and the uses are slightly different.

White stock White stock is best to use when you need a mild flavor that won't overpower delicate ingredients, and it's also good to keep in the freezer for other recipes. Its light color suits risottos, mashed potatoes, and cream soups. White stock is prepared entirely on the stovetop.

Brown stock Brown stock has deeper flavor than white stock, and the procedure involves caramelizing chicken and vegetables in the oven for half the cooking time and then putting them in the stockpot so they can flavor the liquid during the second half of cooking.

Chicken Broth

Cooking Light Recommends

When our recipes call for canned chicken broth, we use fat-free, less-sodium chicken broth. Swanson's Natural Goodness is the brand we prefer—it's available in both cans and cartons.

Ask the *Cooking Light* Cooks

What's the difference between stock and broth? Although the products are similar, the difference is in the intent. A broth is the liquid that results from cooking vegetables, meat, poultry, or fish in water. For a stock, you add seasonings to the water when you're cooking vegetables, meat, poultry, or fish in order to get a flavorful liquid to use in soups and sauces. Also, in making stocks, you often brown the bones of the meat and the other ingredients before they're cooked in the liquid in order to get a richer flavor and darker color.

What do I do with the cooked chicken? To make stock, chicken is cooked for approximately 3 hours. You're left with great-tasting stock but exhausted chicken. For the best flavor, you'll want to add freshly cooked chicken to your soup. You can use the chicken from the stock in a pasta salad with olive oil, wine vinegar, and fresh herbs—these seasonings will perk up the meat.

What about storing all that stock? Cool up to 4 quarts of stock in the stockpot in the refrigerator. For a larger batch, place the pot in a bowl of ice water 30 minutes, stirring occasionally; then place the stockpot in the refrigerator. Stock will keep in the refrigerator up to a week and in the freezer up to 3 months.

White Chicken Stock

White stock has a light, clean flavor that provides a nice backdrop for more delicate ingredients.

- ½ teaspoon black peppercorns
- 10 parsley sprigs
- 8 thyme sprigs
- 3 celery stalks, cut into 2-inch-thick pieces
- 3 bay leaves
- 2 medium onions, unpeeled and quartered
- 2 carrots, cut into 2-inch-thick pieces
- 2 garlic cloves, crushed
- 16 cups cold water
- 6 pounds chicken pieces

1. Place first 8 ingredients in an 8-quart stockpot; add water and chicken. Bring mixture to a boil over medium heat. Reduce heat, and simmer, uncovered, 3 hours. Strain stock through a fine sieve into a large bowl. Reserve chicken for another use; discard remaining solids. Cover and chill stock 8 hours. Skim solidified fat from surface of stock, and discard. Yield: 10 cups (serving size: 1 cup).

CALORIES 28 (26% from fat); FAT 0.8g (sat 0.2g, mono 0.3g, poly 0.2g); PROTEIN 4.7g; CARB 0.4g; FIBER 0.1g; CHOL 15mg; IRON 0.3mg; SODIUM 18mg; CALC 4mg

Stock Tips

Put the vegetables and herbs in the pot first. Arrange the chicken pieces on top so the herbs don't float to the surface and interfere with skimming.

Start with cold water. If you pour hot water over the chicken, it releases specks of protein that make the stock cloudy.

Add only enough water to barely cover the chicken in the pot. More water dilutes the stock's flavor.

As soon as the chicken comes to a boil, immediately reduce to a simmer. As chicken cooks, it releases fat and protein, which float to the surface. If the stock boils, the fat and protein are churned into it and make it greasy and cloudy.

Cook noodles, rice, and matzo balls in water rather than stock so they don't muddy the stock.

Don't add salt to the stock because the stock concentrates during cooking. Add what you need to the final soup recipe so you can control the saltiness.

No Time to Chill

Chilling the stock overnight makes degreasing a cinch because the fat solidifies on top. But you can also proceed with a recipe right after making the stock.

While people have been known to use a paper towel, a slice of bread, or ice cubes to collect the fat, our favorite methods involve either a zip-top plastic bag or a fat-separator cup. The cup is

made of inexpensive plastic or glass with a spout at the base. When you pour out the stock, the fat floating on top stays behind. The bag works similarly. Pour stock into bag; let stand 10 minutes. (Fat will rise to the top.) Seal bag; carefully snip off 1 bottom corner of bag. Drain stock into a container, stopping before fat layer reaches opening; discard fat.

Making Brown Stock

1. Roasting the vegetables and chicken until browned creates a deep, rich caramelized flavor.

2. The browned bits from the pan add even more flavor. Deglaze the pan by adding water and scraping up the bits.

3. Simmer the stock ingredients for 1½ hours. Then strain through a fine sieve.

4. Skim the fat from the stock after the stock has chilled 8 hours or overnight.

Brown Chicken Stock

Use a pan large enough to roast the chicken and all the vegetables in a single layer. If the pan is too small, the chicken won't brown properly.

¼ pound fennel stalks, cut into 2-inch-thick pieces
3 carrots, cut into 2-inch-thick pieces
1 celery stalk, cut into 2-inch-thick pieces
1 medium onion, unpeeled and quartered
6 pounds chicken pieces
½ teaspoon black peppercorns
6 parsley sprigs
5 thyme sprigs
2 bay leaves
16 cups cold water, divided

1. Preheat oven to 400°.
2. Arrange first 4 ingredients in bottom of a broiler or roasting pan, and top with chicken. Bake at 400° for 1½ hours, turning chicken once every 30 minutes (chicken and vegetables should be very brown).
3. Place peppercorns, parsley, thyme, and bay leaves in an 8-quart stockpot. Remove vegetables and chicken from broiler pan; place in stockpot. Discard drippings from broiler pan, leaving browned bits. Place broiler pan on stovetop; add 4 cups of water. Bring to a boil over medium-high heat. Reduce heat; simmer 10 minutes, scraping pan to loosen browned bits.
4. Pour contents of pan into stockpot. Add 12 cups water; bring to a boil over medium-high heat. Reduce heat; simmer 1½ hours.
5. Strain stock through a fine sieve into a large bowl. Reserve chicken for another use; discard remaining solids. Cover and chill stock 8 hours. Skim solidified fat from surface of stock, and discard. Yield: 10 cups (serving size: 1 cup).

CALORIES 31 (32% from fat); FAT 1.1g (sat 0.3g, mono 0.4g, poly 0.2g); PROTEIN 4.7g; CARB 0.4g; FIBER 0.1g; CHOL 15mg; IRON 0.3mg; SODIUM 19mg; CALC 4mg

Making Sauces

Creamy, versatile, and delicious, sauces are worth making from scratch.

Don't get intimidated by the idea of making great sauces—they're surprisingly easy. Sauces can change everything in a recipe, drawing flavors together, melding ingredients, adding that final sense of unity—and tasting heavenly, too.

Béchamel Sauce (white sauce)

A béchamel sauce (pronounced "bay-shah-MEHL") is one of the foundations of creative cooking. It's traditionally made by stirring milk or cream into a butter-flour mixture called a roux. You can use this sauce on its own or to build other sauces. (Add cheese, for example, and you have a Mornay sauce.) Once you've learned to make it, you can use a béchamel sauce in many dishes.

An average béchamel sauce contains about 76 percent calories from fat; our lightened version has 46 percent. Yet all of the rich taste of a béchamel sauce is still there—that's because we've followed the traditional method of steeping savory flavorings, such as whole peppercorns, onion, and a bay leaf, in the warm milk.

Smooth White Sauce

Test Kitchen SECRET

The key to a smooth white sauce is to slowly but vigorously whisk the milk into the roux. A whisk is the "secret weapon" for making a good sauce.

Béchamel Sauce

This light white sauce is one of the most versatile sauces you can have. It's the secret to our reduced-fat cream soups, bisques, and chowders.

2½   cups 1% low-fat milk
8   black peppercorns
1   (½-inch-thick) slice onion
1   bay leaf
2   tablespoons butter
¼   cup all-purpose flour
¼   teaspoon salt
⅛   teaspoon ground white pepper
Dash of ground nutmeg

1. Combine first 4 ingredients in a heavy saucepan; cook over low heat to 180° or until tiny bubbles form around edge (do not boil). Remove from heat. Cover; let stand 10 minutes. Strain mixture through a sieve into a bowl; discard solids. Set aside.
2. Melt butter in saucepan over low heat. Lightly spoon flour into a dry measuring cup; level with a knife. Add flour to saucepan, stirring with a whisk until blended. Cook 1 minute, stirring constantly. Gradually add milk; cook over low heat 5 minutes or until thick, stirring constantly. Stir in salt, white pepper, and nutmeg. Yield: 2¼ cups (serving size: ¼ cup).

CALORIES 66 (45% from fat); FAT 3.3g (sat 1.7g, mono 1.3g, poly 0.1g); PROTEIN 2.7g; CARB 6.4g; FIBER 0.2; CHOL 9mg; IRON 0.2mg; SODIUM 120mg; CALC 86mg

"We've lightened a traditional béchamel sauce by replacing the cream with 1% low-fat milk and using a smaller quantity of butter." Jan Moon, Test Kitchens Staffer

How to Make a Light White Sauce

1. Steep peppercorns, onion, and bay leaf in the milk over low heat for about 5 minutes. This flavor combination infuses the milk with sweet and nutty tones.

2. Remove from heat; cool 10 minutes. Strain milk mixture through a sieve; discard solids.

3. Lightly spoon flour into a measuring cup, and level with a knife. Measure carefully. Too much flour will make the sauce too thick, while too little will leave it thin and watery.

4. A smooth roux is necessary for a creamy white sauce. Carefully whisk the flour into the melted butter, and cook 1 minute, stirring constantly. Watch carefully because an overcooked roux will make the white sauce taste burned.

5. Add the milk to the flour. This is where things can get tricky. If you pour all the milk into the flour at once, you'll get lumps. Add the milk to the flour gradually, whisking mixture vigorously after each addition—it'll stay smooth.

6. Heat the sauce over low heat until it is thick, stirring constantly. It should coat a spoon when ready. Don't worry if your sauce hasn't thickened after 5 minutes. Continue to cook it, stirring constantly.

Mornay Sauce (cheese sauce)

A Mornay sauce is a variation of a basic white sauce and can be made with a variety of cheeses, from sharp to mellow. Because it's a fairly mild sauce, it's typically served with eggs, fish, shell-

fish, vegetables, and chicken. We have two versions of cheese sauce: The first one starts with steeping peppercorns and a bay leaf in milk, much like we did in the Béchamel Sauce. (See page 40.) The second version, a "shortcut sauce," skips the steeping step. Both of these sauces are thickened by making a slurry (a mixture of flour and milk that is heated over low heat with constant stirring) instead of a roux.

"Steeping the milk with peppercorns and a bay leaf infuses great flavor into the sauce." Jan Moon, Test Kitchens Staffer

Classic Cheese Sauce

Try a mixture of Cheddar and Swiss for a great variation on this classic sauce. In fact, almost any cheese will work.

1⅓ cups 1% low-fat milk
3 whole black peppercorns
1 bay leaf
3 tablespoons all-purpose flour
1 cup (4 ounces) finely shredded extra-sharp Cheddar cheese

1. Combine first 3 ingredients in a medium saucepan; cook over low heat 5 minutes. Remove from heat; cool 5 minutes. Strain mixture through a sieve into a bowl, discard solids.
2. Place flour in pan; gradually add ¼ cup milk, stirring with a whisk until blended. Cook over low heat 1 minute, stirring constantly. Add remaining milk; cook until thick (about 5 minutes), stirring constantly. Remove from heat, and add cheese, stirring until melted. Yield: 1½ cups (serving size: about ¼ cup).

CALORIES 113 (55% from fat); FAT 6.8g (sat 4.3g, mono 1.9g, poly 0.2g); PROTEIN 6.8g; CARB 5.8g; FIBER 0.1g; CHOL 22mg; IRON 0.3mg; SODIUM 144mg; CALC 203mg

Adding Cheese to a Sauce

Test Kitchen
SECRET

Don't try to save time by cubing the cheese instead of shredding it. Shredding makes for quick, even melting.

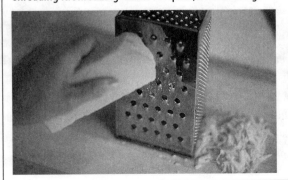

Add the cheese after you remove the sauce from heat so the cheese will not get too hot and coagulate.

"To give my cheese sauce a little 'punch,' I always use a strong-flavored cheese, such as extra-sharp Cheddar or a smoked cheese." Mike Wilson, Test Kitchens Staffer

Easy Cheddar Cheese Sauce

This easy cheese sauce is as creamy, delicious, and versatile as the classic version. Spoon it over fish or steamed vegetables, bake with a batch of cooked pasta, or use it as the base for a chowder.

¼   cup all-purpose flour
2   cups 1% low-fat milk
1¼ cups (5 ounces) shredded sharp Cheddar
     cheese

1. Lightly spoon flour into a dry measuring cup; level with a knife. Place flour in a medium, heavy saucepan; gradually add milk, stirring with a whisk until blended. Place over medium heat; cook until thick (about 8 minutes), stirring constantly. Remove from heat; add cheese, stirring until melted. Yield: 2 cups (serving size: ½ cup).

CALORIES 222 (53% from fat); FAT 13.1g (sat 8.3g, mono 3.7g, poly 0.4g); PROTEIN 13.6g; CARB 12.2g; FIBER 0.2g; CHOL 42mg; IRON 0.7mg; SODIUM 281mg; CALC 407mg

The Right Pan

Test Kitchen SECRET

Be sure to use a heavy saucepan for the Easy Cheddar Cheese Sauce. In a lightweight one, the sauce may lump or scorch more easily.

Variations:

Asiago Cheese Sauce: Substitute 1 cup (4 ounces) grated Asiago cheese for shredded Cheddar cheese. Proceed with recipe.

CALORIES 191 (41% from fat); FAT 8.7g (sat 5.5g, mono 2.5g, poly 0.2g); PROTEIN 14.9g; CARB 12.7g; FIBER 0.2g; CHOL 24mg; IRON 0.7mg; SODIUM 515mg; CALC 487mg

Smoked Gouda Cheese Sauce: Substitute ¾ cup (3 ounces) shredded smoked Gouda cheese for shredded Cheddar cheese. Proceed with recipe.

CALORIES 155 (42% from fat); FAT 7.2g (sat 4.6g, mono 2g, poly 0.2g); PROTEIN 10.1g; CARB 12.3g; FIBER 0.2g; CHOL 29mg; IRON 0.5mg; SODIUM 235mg; CALC 300mg

Gruyère Cheese Sauce: Substitute ¾ cup (3 ounces) shredded Gruyère cheese and ⅓ cup (about 1½ ounces) finely grated fresh Parmesan for shredded Cheddar cheese. Proceed with recipe.

CALORIES 209 (47% from fat); FAT 11g (sat 6.6g, mono 3.3g, poly 0.5g); PROTEIN 14.9g; CARB 12.2g; FIBER 0.2g; CHOL 35mg; IRON 0.5mg; SODIUM 303mg; CALC 492mg

Swiss Cheese Sauce: Substitute 1 cup (4 ounces) shredded Swiss cheese for shredded Cheddar cheese. Proceed with recipe.

CALORIES 186 (44% from fat); FAT 9.1g (sat 5.9g, mono 2.4g, poly 0.3g); PROTEIN 12.9g; CARB 12.7g; FIBER 0.2g; CHOL 31mg; IRON 0.5mg; SODIUM 135mg; CALC 424mg

Béarnaise Sauce

Béarnaise sauce is a classic French sauce made with a reduction of vinegar, wine, tarragon, and shallots, and finished with egg yolks and butter. It's usually served with meat, fish, eggs, and vegetables.

Our lightened version uses low-fat sour cream instead of egg yolks and butter, so the fat is significantly lower than that of a traditional Béarnaise sauce.

Béarnaise Sauce

Don't use fat-free sour cream in this recipe because it tends to curdle when it's heated.

½	cup thinly sliced shallots (about 2 ounces)
3	tablespoons dry white wine
2	tablespoons white wine vinegar
1	teaspoon dried tarragon

Dash of salt
Dash of pepper

⅔	cup low-fat sour cream

1. Combine first 6 ingredients in a small, heavy saucepan; bring to a boil, and cook 1 minute. Strain mixture through a sieve into a bowl; discard solids. Return liquid to saucepan; stir in sour cream. Place over low heat, and cook 1 minute or until warm, stirring frequently. Yield: ¾ cup (serving size: 3 tablespoons).

CALORIES 76 (60% from fat); FAT 5.1g (sat 3g, mono 1.6g, poly 0.2g); PROTEIN 2.4g; CARB 6g; FIBER 0.4g; CHOL 15mg; IRON 1.4mg; SODIUM 21mg; CALC 88mg

Alfredo Sauce

Alfredo sauce is best known in the traditional dish fettuccine Alfredo, where the pasta is coated in a rich sauce of butter, grated Parmesan cheese, and heavy cream.

In our lightened version, we use half-and-half instead of whipping cream and decrease the amount of butter and cheese slightly to lower the fat by about 10 grams per serving.

Alfredo Sauce

To get the best-tasting Alfredo Sauce, use fresh Parmesan cheese and freshly ground pepper. This sauce is traditionally tossed with fettuccine. For this amount of sauce, you'll need to cook 1 pound of uncooked pasta to get 8 cups cooked pasta.

1	tablespoon butter
1¼	cups half-and-half
¾	cup (3 ounces) grated fresh Parmesan cheese
½	teaspoon salt
¼	teaspoon freshly ground black pepper

1. Melt butter in a large skillet over medium heat. Add half-and-half, cheese, salt, and pepper; cook 1 minute, stirring constantly. Yield: 6 servings (serving size: about ¼ cup).

CALORIES 145 (68% from fat); FAT 11g (sat 6.7g, mono 3.6g, poly 0.2g); PROTEIN 7.2g; CARB 2.3g; FIBER 0g; CHOL 42mg; IRON 0.2mg; SODIUM 452mg; CALC 225mg

Fat-Free Half-and-Half
Test Kitchen SECRET

We don't recommend using fat-free half-and-half as a way to reduce the fat even more in Alfredo sauce. Fat-free half-and-half has a slightly sweet taste, which is often great for desserts but not so desirable for this savory sauce.

Clam Sauce

Most traditional Italian clam sauces are made by simply tossing tiny clams in their shells with hot olive oil and chopped garlic, then moistening them with wine or broth. Because Italian clams are so savory, little or nothing needs to be done to them to build up the flavor. **Since clams from other areas, including the United States, are blander, we've added tomatoes and basil for a flavor boost.**

Clam Sauce

Fresh tomato and fresh basil are perfect complements for mild-flavored clams. We think this sauce is best over fettuccine, spaghetti, or angel hair pasta. For this amount of sauce, use 8 ounces of uncooked pasta to get 4 cups cooked pasta.

3	(6½-ounce) cans minced clams, undrained
1	tablespoon olive oil
2	garlic cloves, minced
1⅓	cups chopped tomato (about 1 large)
2	tablespoons minced fresh parsley
1	teaspoon crushed red pepper
½	cup dry white wine
2	tablespoons chopped fresh basil

1. Drain clams in a colander over a bowl, reserving liquid.

2. Heat oil in a large skillet over medium heat. Add garlic; sauté 30 seconds. Add tomato, parsley, and pepper; cook 1 minute. Add wine; cook 30 seconds. Add reserved clam liquid; bring to a boil. Boil, uncovered, 12 minutes or until mixture is reduced to 1 cup, stirring frequently. Stir in clams and basil. Yield: 4 servings (serving size: ½ cup).

CALORIES 82 (41% from fat); FAT 3.7g (sat 0.5g, mono 2.7g, poly 0.4g); PROTEIN 7.5g; CARB 5.3g; FIBER 1g; CHOL 17mg; IRON 1.7mg; SODIUM 610mg; CALC 16mg

Pesto

Pesto is an uncooked sauce of fresh basil, garlic, olive oil, pine nuts, and Parmesan and Romano cheeses. It's typically tossed with hot *trenette* (wide, flat pasta similar to linguine) or cooked potatoes. *Pesto* means "pounded" and refers to the traditional preparation using a mortar and pestle.

To lighten a traditional pesto, we reduced the amounts of oil, pine nuts, cheeses, and butter usually found in a classic pesto, cutting 28 grams of fat per serving without losing any flavor.

Pesto

To keep from adding too much basil, don't pack the leaves when you measure them.

2	ounces fresh Parmesan cheese, cut into pieces
½	ounce fresh Romano cheese, cut into pieces
2	garlic cloves, peeled
4	cups fresh basil leaves
2	tablespoons pine nuts
2	tablespoons extra-virgin olive oil
2	teaspoons butter, softened
¼	teaspoon salt

1. Place cheeses in a food processor; process until finely grated. Add garlic; process until minced. Add basil and remaining ingredients; process until blended. Yield: 4 servings (serving size: ¼ cup).

CALORIES 192 (78% from fat); FAT 16.7g (sat 5.1g, mono 8g, poly 2.6g); PROTEIN 8.2g; CARB 3.6g; FIBER 1.8g; CHOL 21mg; IRON 2mg; SODIUM 417mg; CALC 260mg

---

Pesto and Pasta
Test Kitchen SECRET

When you're tossing pesto with pasta, add about 3 tablespoons of the pasta cooking liquid along with the pasta. The extra liquid helps the pesto thoroughly coat the pasta.

Marinara Sauce (tomato sauce)

As basic as it is, no one seems to have the true story on marinara. If you look it up in a dozen Italian cookbooks, you're likely to find as many different explanations of what marinara is and how it's made. Some say that marinara is a very simple fresh tomato sauce with garlic and olive oil. Other authorities say the name is derived from the Italian word *mare,* which means sea. **In America, to add to the confusion, the word *marinara* is used to refer to any tomato sauce made without meat.**

We've got two tomato sauces for you to add to your repertoire: one with fresh tomatoes and the other with canned. We think our Quick and Easy Tomato Sauce (page 47) with canned tomatoes will beat a jarred sauce any day.

> "Our homemade tomato sauces are lower in sodium than most commercial tomato sauces."
>
> Krista Montgomery, Food Editor

Marinara Sauce

This simple, fresh tomato sauce is great served over spaghetti. For this amount of sauce, you'll need to cook 1 pound of spaghetti to get 8 cups cooked pasta.

1	tablespoon olive oil
1½	tablespoons minced garlic
6	pounds coarsely chopped peeled tomato (about 6 cups)
¾	teaspoon salt
½	teaspoon pepper
¼	cup chopped fresh basil
¼	cup chopped fresh parsley

1. Heat oil in a large saucepan over medium heat. Add garlic; sauté 2 minutes. Add tomato, salt, and pepper; bring to a boil. Reduce heat; simmer 25 minutes, stirring occasionally. Stir in basil and parsley, and cook 1 minute. Yield: 6 servings (serving size: 1 cup).

CALORIES 128 (26% from fat); FAT 4.2g (sat 0.5g, mono 1.9g, poly 0.9g); PROTEIN 4g; CARB 22.2g; FIBER 5.2g; CHOL 0mg; IRON 2.3mg; SODIUM 337mg; CALC 30mg

Tomato Substitution — Test Kitchen SECRET

If fresh tomatoes aren't available for the Marinara Sauce recipe above, you can use a 28-ounce can of whole tomatoes, undrained and chopped, plus a 28-ounce can of diced tomatoes, undrained, instead. This will be the equivalent of 6 cups chopped fresh tomato. To balance the flavor and thicken the sauce, add 3 tablespoons of tomato paste and 1 teaspoon of sugar to the canned tomatoes.

Quick-and-Easy Tomato Sauce

Use this sauce anywhere you might use a store-bought sauce, such as on pasta, in lasagna, or over polenta.

  1   tablespoon olive oil
1½   cups chopped onion
  1   cup chopped green bell pepper
  1   teaspoon dried oregano
  4   garlic cloves, minced
  ½   cup dry red wine
  1   teaspoon dried basil
  ½   teaspoon salt
  ¼   teaspoon black pepper
  2   (28-ounce) cans whole plum tomatoes,
          undrained and chopped
  1   (6-ounce) can tomato paste
  2   bay leaves

1. Heat oil in a large saucepan over medium-high heat. Add onion, bell pepper, oregano, and garlic; cook 5 minutes or until vegetables are tender, stirring occasionally.
2. Add wine and remaining ingredients, and bring to a boil. Reduce heat, and simmer for 30 minutes. Discard bay leaves. Yield: 8 cups (serving size: 1 cup).

CALORIES 93 (23% from fat); FAT 2.4g (sat 0.4g, mono 1.4g, poly 0.5g); PROTEIN 3.3g; CARB 17.1g; FIBER 3.3g; CHOL 0mg; IRON 2.4mg; SODIUM 487mg; CALC 77mg

This sauce will freeze well for up to 3 months. Place it in an airtight container or zip-top plastic bag, label, and freeze.

Making Tomato Sauce

1. Chop the tomatoes in the can with scissors or a sharp knife. This will cut down on your mess.

2. Sauté the vegetables. Add the chopped tomatoes, tomato paste, and remaining ingredients. Simmer the tomato sauce for 30 minutes to blend the flavors.

"A lot of pasta dishes tend to be 'oversauced' in my opinion. If you thin out a thick sauce a little, it will coat the pasta nicely without completely overpowering the pasta." Mike Wilson, Test Kitchens Staffer

Mushroom Sauce

In the spring and autumn, markets throughout Italy are flush with all kinds of fresh mushrooms: morels, honey mushrooms, oyster mushrooms, porcini, and many other specimens. Dedicated foragers make a cottage industry of picking and selling mushrooms to Italian cooks who are crazy for them. The Mushroom Sauce below combines dried porcini and fresh cremini or button mushrooms; our Port Wine-Mushroom Sauce (page 49) features shiitake mushrooms.

Mushroom Sauce

The combination of mushrooms and red wine create a hearty, "meaty" flavor in this meat-free sauce. Toss it with cavatappi or any other short spiral pasta.

1½	cups dried porcini mushrooms (about 1½ ounces)
2	teaspoons olive oil
½	cup finely chopped prosciutto (about 2 ounces)
½	cup finely chopped onion
4	cups sliced cremini or button mushrooms (about 8 ounces)
½	teaspoon grated lemon rind
½	teaspoon salt
¼	teaspoon pepper
2	garlic cloves, minced
1	cup fat-free, less-sodium chicken broth
¾	cup dry red wine
1	tablespoon cornstarch
1	tablespoon water

For a genuine Italian mushroom sauce, we prefer using fresh, wild mushrooms like porcini because they have a strong woodsy, nutty taste. Because they're difficult to find in the United States, we call for dried porcini along with supermarket cremini mushrooms (baby portobellos) in this recipe.

Mushroom Combination

Test Kitchen SECRET

Fresh cremini mushrooms (below, left) and dried mushrooms (below, right) make our savory Mushroom Sauce.

1. Place porcini mushrooms in a bowl; add boiling water to cover. Cover and let stand 30 minutes. Drain; rinse and coarsely chop mushrooms.

2. Heat oil in a medium skillet over medium-high heat. Add prosciutto; sauté 1 minute. Add onion; sauté 3 minutes or until tender. Stir in mushrooms and next 4 ingredients; cook 4 minutes or until browned, stirring frequently. Stir in broth and wine, scraping pan to loosen browned bits. Bring to a boil; cook 3 minutes. Combine cornstarch and 1 tablespoon water in a small bowl. Add cornstarch mixture to pan; bring to a boil. Cook 1 minute, stirring constantly. Yield: 4 servings (serving size: 1 cup).

CALORIES 125 (32% from fat); FAT 4.5g (sat 1g, mono 1.9g, poly 0.4g); PROTEIN 9.2g; CARB 12.5g; FIBER 2.2g; CHOL 13mg; IRON 2.9mg; SODIUM 735mg; CALC 17mg

Port Wine-Mushroom Sauce

This deeply flavored brown sauce is reminiscent of the classic bordelaise sauce (a French sauce made with wine, brown stock, and bone marrow), only it's made in a fraction of the time. It's virtually fat-free—another plus. This sauce garnered our highest rating in the Test Kitchens. Try it with beef, lamb, venison, or pork.

1½ cups sliced shiitake mushroom caps (about 3½ ounces)
 1   tablespoon all-purpose flour
 ⅓   cup port or other sweet red wine
 ¼   cup minced shallots
 1   tablespoon balsamic vinegar
 1   cup beef broth
 2   teaspoons Worcestershire sauce
 1   teaspoon tomato paste
 ⅛   teaspoon dried rosemary
 ½   teaspoon Dijon mustard

1. Combine mushrooms and flour in a bowl; toss well.
2. Combine wine, shallots, and vinegar in a medium skillet. Bring to a boil; cook until thick (about 3 minutes). Reduce heat to medium. Add broth, Worcestershire, tomato paste, and rosemary; cook 1 minute. Add mushroom mixture; cook 3 minutes, stirring constantly. Stir in mustard. Yield: 1 cup (serving size: ¼ cup).

CALORIES 69 (3% from fat); FAT 0.2g (sat 0g, mono 0g, poly 0.1g); PROTEIN 3.8g; CARB 8.4g; FIBER 0.5g; CHOL 0mg; IRON 1mg; SODIUM 367mg; CALC 14mg

> When you toss the mushrooms with flour, it helps thicken the sauce.

Making Port Wine-Mushroom Sauce

1. Combine wine, shallots, and vinegar in a medium skillet. Bring to a boil; reduce liquid by cooking about 3 minutes until thick and syrupy.

2. Reduce heat to medium. Add broth, Worcestershire, tomato paste, and rosemary; cook 1 minute. Add mushroom mixture; cook 3 minutes, stirring constantly.

"Use any kind of fresh mushroom in place of the shiitakes, but stick with a strong, sweet red wine, such as port, to maintain the deep, rich flavor of the sauce."
Kathryn Conrad, Test Kitchens Staffer

Deglazing

It's easy to think that those brown, crunchy bits left behind in the pan after cooking your favorite meat are best scoured out and thrown away. But even for light cooking, these tasty morsels—well-done traces of that same meat—can become the foundation of a highly flavored sauce that will be the perfect complement for your entrée.

This technique is both classic and simple. It usually starts with searing meat quickly with a little oil in a hot skillet. Heat oil in the pan for 1 to 2 minutes. **When you add the meat, you should hear a loud sizzle or pop.** That means the temperature is sufficient to develop a caramelized brown crust that retains juices. Pieces of that crispy, seared shell are what stick to your pan when you take out the meat. You can also deglaze using the drippings left in the pan after roasting.

Deglazing turns these seeming scraps into powerful nuggets of flavor. While the pan is still hot, pour in a little wine, apple juice, tea, or other compatible liquid. Keep up the heat, and scrape the meaty bits loose. The liquid will start to cook away, but this is good because it

 intensifies the flavors. When you serve the resulting sauce you'll realize the importance of what you saved. And as a bonus, the pan will be a lot easier to clean.

No Nonstick	Test Kitchen
	SECRET

Nonstick skillets are a staple in our kitchen, but deglazing is a technique that calls for a skillet without a nonstick surface. Here's why: Only a hot skillet that allows for sticking will sear meat with a tasty crust during sautéing and capture those tidbits that add flavor during deglazing. As their name implies, nonstick pans don't fit the bill.

Gravies

A gravy is a sauce made with the juices or drippings from roasted meat or poultry. The juices are usually combined with broth, wine, or milk and thickened with flour or cornstarch.

Gravies can be high in fat if they're made from high-fat meats with fatty drippings. **The secret to low-fat gravy is starting with lean meats and using only a small amount of the drippings. You can keep the sodium low in gravy by using low-sodium or less-salt broth.**

Making Classic Giblet Gravy

1. Combine flour and reserved turkey drippings to keep the flour from clumping when you add it to the wine.

2. Whisking the flour-wine mixture constantly as it begins to cook ensures a smooth gravy with no lumps.

Classic Giblet Gravy

It takes about 1½ hours to make the stock for this gravy, so you'll need to start it about 2 hours before the turkey is done. That way, they'll be finished at the same time.

    4   cups water
    ½   cup parsley sprigs
    1   teaspoon black peppercorns
    2   medium carrots, each cut into 3 pieces
    1   large onion, cut into 8 wedges
    1   bay leaf
    1   (14-ounce) can fat-free, less-sodium
        chicken broth
Reserved turkey neck and giblets (from a
        12-pound fresh or frozen thawed turkey)
    ¾   cup dry white wine
    3   tablespoons all-purpose flour
    3   tablespoons reserved turkey drippings
    ¼   teaspoon salt
    ¼   teaspoon freshly ground black pepper

1. Combine first 8 ingredients in a large saucepan. Bring to a boil. Reduce heat, and simmer over medium-low heat until reduced to 2½ cups (about 1½ hours). Strain stock through a sieve into a bowl; discard solids.
2. Bring wine to a boil in pan until reduced to ½ cup (about 3 minutes). Combine flour and turkey drippings in a bowl, stirring with a whisk until smooth. Add to pan; cook over medium heat for 1 minute, stirring constantly. Stir in strained stock, salt, and ground black pepper; cook over medium heat 15 minutes, stirring occasionally. Yield: 2½ cups (serving size: about 3 tablespoons).

CALORIES 20 (45% from fat); FAT 1g (sat 0.3g, mono 0.4g, poly 0.2g); PROTEIN 0.7g; CARB 1.9g; FIBER 0.1g; CHOL 1mg; IRON 0.2mg; SODIUM 118mg; CALC 2mg

Brown Gravy

Adding vegetables to the beef broth gives a rich flavor without adding calories or fat.

    2   (14-ounce) cans less-sodium beef broth
    1   cup coarsely chopped onion
    ½   cup coarsely chopped fresh mushrooms
    ¼   cup coarsely chopped celery
    ¼   teaspoon dried thyme
    ⅛   to ¼ teaspoon pepper
Cooking spray
    2   tablespoons all-purpose flour

1. Combine first 6 ingredients in a medium saucepan. Bring to a boil; cook 15 minutes or until liquid is reduced to 2 cups. Strain mixture through a sieve into a bowl; discard solids.
2. Coat a medium skillet with cooking spray; place over medium-high heat until hot. Add flour, and cook 2 minutes or until browned, stirring constantly. Transfer flour to a large bowl, and cool completely.
3. Add ¼ cup broth mixture to flour; stir well with a whisk. Add remaining broth mixture, stirring well with a whisk. Pour mixture into pan; place over medium-high heat. Bring to a boil; reduce heat, and simmer 3 minutes or until thick, stirring constantly. Yield: 1¾ cups (serving size: ¼ cup).

CALORIES 20 (5% from fat); FAT 0.1g (sat 0g, mono 0g, poly 0g); PROTEIN 0.5g; CARB 2.6g; FIBER 0.1g; CHOL 0mg; IRON 0.2mg; SODIUM 4mg; CALC 1mg

"The key to smooth, creamy gravy is to stir, stir, stir."
Kathleen Kanen, Food Stylist

Custard Sauce

Custard sauce goes by all kinds of names: stirred custard, boiled custard, soft custard, and crème anglaise (which translates as "English cream"). Custard sauce is a rich liquid custard that's traditionally used for Bavarian creams and ice creams and for spooning over fruits and desserts. It's most often made from whole milk, cream, sugar, and whole eggs or egg yolks.

The creamiest custards are thickened with just yolks, which contribute fat. **With low-fat recipes, it's tempting to use cornstarch or flour to add body while replacing fat. That's not our approach. We switched to low-fat milk but kept the egg yolks because they're what makes custard sauce luscious and smooth.**

We cook our custard sauce on a gas stovetop. If your stovetop is electric, you'll need to cook the sauce about 4 minutes longer (for a total of 10 minutes).

It's important that some stovetop custards

stop cooking as soon as they become thick. In those cases, an ice bath is necessary: Spoon the hot custard into a bowl, then place the custard bowl into a larger ice-filled bowl.

Making the Perfect Custard

Test Kitchen SECRET

Tiffany Vickers, Test Kitchens Staffer, shares a few of her tips for making custards.

- Egg yolks can curdle in a heartbeat. Pay close attention when you heat the custard mixture, and stir it constantly with a wire whisk. Never stop stirring a sauce that calls for constant stirring—it can cause the custard to overheat. Some of our staff members stir in a figure-eight pattern to maintain constant heat; some claim a zigzag motion does the trick, and some use a simple circular motion. Whatever you do, keep the mixture moving away from the bottom of the pan.

- Use a heavy saucepan. While many custard sauce recipes call for a double boiler, we've found it unnecessary as long as you use a pan with a thick bottom. It tempers the heat and distributes it more evenly and slowly than a thin pan, reducing the chance of curdling. If you have only a thin pan, decrease the heat, and watch the process carefully because your sauce will cook more quickly.

- Test a stirred custard for doneness. It should coat the back of a spoon thickly enough so that when you run a finger across it, the mark remains. If egg particles show, the custard is overcooked.

"If you only have two dessert sauces in your repertoire, we recommend that you master custard sauce and fudge sauce." Vanessa Johnson, Test Kitchens Director

Custard Sauce (Crème Anglaise)

You can substitute 2 teaspoons vanilla extract for the bean, but the flavor won't be as good. You can find vanilla beans in your supermarket's spice section.

1¾ cups 1% low-fat milk
1 (3-inch) piece vanilla bean, split lengthwise
⅓ cup sugar
4 large egg yolks

1. Pour milk into a medium saucepan. Scrape seeds from vanilla bean; add seeds and bean to milk. Cook over medium heat 6 minutes (do not boil); discard bean. Remove from heat.
2. Combine sugar and yolks in a bowl, stirring with a whisk until blended. Gradually add milk mixture to bowl, stirring constantly with a whisk. Return mixture to pan. Cook over medium heat 6 minutes or until mixture coats the back of a spoon, stirring constantly with a whisk. Immediately pour mixture into a bowl. Cover and chill (mixture will thicken as it cools). Yield: 1¾ cups (serving size: ¼ cup).

CALORIES 97 (33% from fat); FAT 3.6g (sat 1.3g, mono 1.3g, poly 0.4g); PROTEIN 3.6g; CARB 12.6g; FIBER 0g; CHOL 127mg; IRON 0.4mg; SODIUM 35mg; CALC 88mg

Custard Sauce (Crème Anglaise) can be stored in the refrigerator for up to 3 days.

Making Custard Sauce

1. Because this is such a simple sauce, *quality ingredients are key*—that's why we've opted for a vanilla bean (the extra effort really makes a difference). Cook the milk mixture 6 minutes to bring out the bean's full flavor. If all the seeds don't come out at the start, they'll be released as they steep.

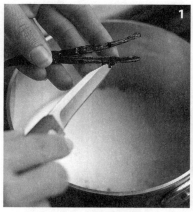

2. Gradually pour the hot milk mixture into the egg yolk mixture in the bowl, stirring constantly with a whisk. *By doing this, you eliminate the risk of cooking the egg mixture too quickly, which could result in scrambled eggs.*

3. Cook gradually over medium heat, stirring constantly, until the sauce thickens and coats the back of a spoon. Don't get impatient and turn the heat too high; the eggs could curdle.

4. Immediately pour the finished sauce into a bowl. *Curdling is possible as long as the sauce stays in the hot pan.*

Fudge Sauce

You can use a rich fudge sauce as an ingredient in other dessert recipes, or drizzle it over fresh strawberries, poached pears, cake, or low-fat ice cream or yogurt.

The key ingredients in our fudge sauce are unsweetened chocolate and cocoa. They contribute intense chocolate flavor with less sugar than semisweet or milk chocolate. (See pages 396-397 for more information on chocolate.)

Fudge Sauce

This sauce is lower in fat than a traditional chocolate sauce because it has only 2 tablespoons of butter and uses fat-free milk instead of whole milk or whipping cream.

2	tablespoons butter
2	ounces unsweetened chocolate
½	cup sugar
6	tablespoons unsweetened cocoa
1	cup dark corn syrup
½	cup fat-free milk
2	teaspoons vanilla extract

1. Combine butter and chocolate in a small saucepan; cook over low heat until chocolate melts, stirring occasionally. Combine sugar and cocoa in a medium bowl; add corn syrup and milk, stirring with a whisk until well blended. Add cocoa mixture to saucepan. Bring to a boil over medium heat, and cook 1 minute, stirring constantly. Remove from heat; stir in vanilla. Yield: 2 cups (serving size: 2 tablespoons).

CALORIES 125 (26% from fat); FAT 3.6g (sat 2.2g, mono 1g, poly 0.1g); PROTEIN 1.3g; CARB 24.4g; FIBER 0.1g; CHOL 4mg; IRON 0.6mg; SODIUM 45mg; CALC 17mg

Perfect Fudge Sauce — Test Kitchen SECRET

The secret to a good fudge sauce is melting the chocolate evenly over low heat so it doesn't scorch. In a small saucepan over very low heat, cook the butter and chocolate together. Melting the chocolate with butter helps the chocolate melt evenly, but it can still scorch easily, so be sure to watch the mixture closely.

"To prevent a skin from forming on a dessert sauce, cover it with plastic wrap. Press the wrap directly onto the surface of the sauce to seal completely."

Jan Moon, Test Kitchens Staffer

Braising

The lowest-fat cuts of meat lend themselves to braising, so you can have rich stews without resorting to fat-laden ingredients.

Braising—cooking with a small amount of liquid in a closed container over low heat—creates intensely flavored meats and sauces but keeps your hands-on involvement to a minimum. Preparation is quick. You brown the meat, add vegetables and liquids, such as tomatoes and wine, and then let everything simmer or bake while you go about your business, checking in only every 20 minutes or so.

> **"Different cuts vary in their tenderness, so cooking times may not always be the exactly the same time recommended in the recipes. Keep an eye on the timer, and have a fork ready."**
> **Kellie Kelley, Food Stylist**

Some of the best cuts of meat are tough. But when you cook them steeped in moist heat, their very nature transforms. They become remarkably tender and succulent as the gristly parts literally melt away to produce rich, delicious sauces.

A fricassee is a type of braised dish in which meat is browned before it's stewed with vegetables. Fricassees are traditionally made with white meats, such as veal or chicken, but they can also be made with lamb and pork. (The recipe for Coq au Vin, a classic example of a fricassee, is on page 58.)

Best Bets for Braising

Test Kitchen SECRET

Tough cuts of meat work best for braising because they tend to have plenty of hard-worked muscle and collagen. Over low heat, collagen melts into a flavorful natural thickener that helps make rich sauces.

Tender meats, on the other hand, tend to dry out in slow cooking. So for braising, look for cuts from lower legs, shoulders, necks, breasts, and rib cages, where strong muscles abound. For example:

Beef: Chuck (bone in or boneless), bottom round, rump roast, round steak, and eye of round
Lamb: Shanks, shoulder (roast, chops, or stew meat), neck, leg of lamb, and sirloin
Pork: Boston butt (pork shoulder butt), picnic shoulder, blade end of the loin, ham hocks, pork neck, leg, and shank
Veal: Cuts from the shoulder, breast, and shank

A Dutch oven is a must for braised dishes because the ingredients need to cook a long time in a pot with a tight-fitting lid. (See page 24 for more information on Dutch ovens.)

Perfect Braising

1. Before the meat is browned, it's usually coated with a spice rub. Spices add extra flavor to the meat and the sauce. Using a heavy pot, such as a Dutch oven, heat oil over medium-high heat. Add meat to the pan, and brown on all sides. This creates a flavorful caramelized crust and leaves bits in the pan that are incorporated into the sauce. Do not overcrowd the pot as this will prevent browning. If necessary, prepare the meat in batches.

2. Remove the meat from the pan, and set aside. Add the vegetables, and stir them with a metal or wooden spatula, scraping up the browned bits from the bottom of the pan.

3. Add the liquid, stirring and scraping up any remaining browned bits still stuck to the pan. Bring to a boil, and return the meat to the pan. Cover with a lid, and cook according to the recipe. For most braised dishes, the liquid should be no more than 1 or 2 inches deep, coming about halfway up the meat.

4. After the allotted time, check the meat with a fork for tenderness. If the meat shreds easily, it's ready. If it's still firm, continue to cook, checking periodically, until the meat is tender.

"Braised dishes offer a bonus for those of us with busy weeknight schedules: They taste better when prepared a day or two ahead, so that means you can refrigerate on Saturday and reheat on Monday." Jan Moon, Test Kitchens Staffer

Thai Braised Beef with Coconut Milk and Ginger

You can find light coconut milk in the Asian or Mexican section of most supermarkets. If yours does not carry it, ask your grocer to order it for you.

1	(2½-pound) boneless chuck roast
1	teaspoon salt
2	teaspoons ground coriander
1	teaspoon ground cardamom
1	teaspoon ground cumin
1	teaspoon ground red pepper
1	teaspoon ground turmeric
1	teaspoon freshly ground black pepper
2	teaspoons vegetable oil, divided
3	cups chopped onion
1	cup diced carrot
2	tablespoons minced peeled fresh ginger
4	garlic cloves, minced
1	(16-ounce) can fat-free, less-sodium chicken broth
1½	cups light coconut milk
2	tablespoons sliced peeled fresh lemongrass or 1 tablespoon thinly sliced lime rind
3	bay leaves
6	cups hot cooked Chinese-style egg noodles (about 12 ounces uncooked)
1	cup chopped fresh cilantro

1. Trim fat from beef. Cut beef into 2-inch pieces. Combine salt and next 6 ingredients in a small bowl. Sprinkle 2 tablespoons of spice mixture over beef, and toss to coat; reserve remaining spice mixture.
2. Preheat oven to 325°.
3. Heat 1 teaspoon oil in a large Dutch oven over medium-high heat. Add beef; cook 5 minutes, browning on all sides. Remove from pan. Heat 1 teaspoon oil in pan. Add onion, carrot, ginger, and garlic; sauté 8 minutes or until tender. Stir in broth, scraping pan to loosen browned bits. Return beef to pan. Add remaining spice mixture, coconut milk, lemongrass, and bay leaves. Bring to a boil. Cover and bake at 325° for 2 hours. Remove beef from pan using a slotted spoon; shred with 2 forks, set aside, and keep warm. Bring vegetable mixture to a boil over medium-high heat. Cook 10 minutes or until slightly thickened. Discard bay leaves. Serve beef and vegetable mixture over noodles. Sprinkle with cilantro. Yield: 6 servings (serving size: 3 ounces beef, ¾ cup vegetable mixture, and 1 cup noodles).

CALORIES 554 (29% from fat); FAT 18g (sat 7g, mono 6.4g, poly 2.4g); PROTEIN 40.5g; CARB 54.9g; FIBER 4.5g; CHOL 145mg; IRON 8.3mg; SODIUM 905mg; CALC 81mg

Coq au Vin

This classic fricassee cooks the whole time on the stovetop in a Dutch oven. It's essential to use a deep, heavy pot with a tight lid.

¼   cup all-purpose flour
¼   teaspoon pepper, divided
⅛   teaspoon salt
2   chicken breast halves, skinned
2   chicken thighs, skinned
2   chicken drumsticks, skinned
1   tablespoon olive oil
2   tablespoons diced shallots
1   pound small mushrooms
1¼   cups diced plum tomato
1   cup diced carrot
1   cup diced celery
1   tablespoon chopped fresh tarragon
1   bay leaf
⅔   cup dry red wine
½   cup fat-free, less-sodium chicken broth
¼   teaspoon salt
2   tablespoons finely chopped fresh chives

1. Combine flour, ⅛ teaspoon pepper, and ⅛ teaspoon salt in a shallow dish. Dredge chicken in flour mixture.
2. Heat oil in a Dutch oven over medium-high heat. Add chicken and shallots; cook 5 minutes until browned. Remove chicken. Add mushrooms; sauté 3 minutes. Add tomato, carrot, celery, tarragon, and bay leaf. Cook 1 minute, stirring constantly. Stir in wine and broth; scrape pan to loosen browned bits. Return chicken to pan. Bring to a boil. Cover, reduce heat, and simmer 1 hour, stirring occasionally. Stir in ⅛ teaspoon pepper and ¼ teaspoon salt. Discard bay leaf. Garnish with chives. Yield: 4 servings (serving size: 3 ounces chicken and ¼ cup sauce).

CALORIES 326 (26% from fat); FAT 9.4g (sat 2g, mono 4.2g, poly 1.8g); PROTEIN 40.8g; CARB 19.9g; FIBER 4g; CHOL 115mg; IRON 4.2mg; SODIUM 390mg; CALC 62mg

Making Coq au Vin

1. Brown chicken and shallots in a Dutch oven over medium-high heat. Browning sears in the chicken's juices and caramelizes the surface at the same time.

2. Remove chicken from pan. Sauté remaining vegetables until most of the moisture evaporates. Browning the vegetables gives the fricassee a deeper flavor.

3. Add wine and broth. Scrape all the browned bits on the bottom of the pan with a spoon. This mixture provides more flavor and works as a thickener as well.

4. Return chicken to pan; cover, reduce heat, and simmer 1 hour, stirring occasionally. Serve immediately, or refrigerate overnight.

Braising in a Slow Cooker

Nothing about a slow cooker will slow you down. This timesaving appliance can turn a few minutes of morning preparation into a flavor-packed dinner.

Cooking in a slow cooker is another approach to braising.

If your slow cooker has a removable insert, you are doubly blessed. For some recipes, you can assemble the ingredients in the insert the night before, refrigerate the whole thing, and go to bed. Next morning, set the insert in the slow cooker, turn on the heat, and head to work knowing that something delicious will be waiting for you at home at day's end. This appliance intensifies flavor with persistent, gentle heat, giving those few minutes of before-work prep time a payoff in taste that would seem to have required hours in the kitchen.

Though most popular for cooking stews and chilis, you can also use your slow cooker for dishes that are usually prepared in a Dutch oven or skillet, such as Caramelized Onions (right). In addition to caramelizing onions, we are fond of using the slow cooker for chili, spaghetti sauce, and pot roast because the long simmering time really makes the flavors better.

"Any recipe that requires long, slow, gentle heat is choice for a slow cooker." Sam Brannock, Test Kitchens Staffer

---

The Sweetest Onions	Test Kitchen SECRET

We discovered that the way to get the richest, sweetest flavor for caramelized onions is to cook them in the slow cooker rather than standing over the skillet. To get the maximum flavor, cook the onions the full 24 hours.

Caramelized Onions

Serve these delicate cooked onions as a side dish or as a pizza topping. Or toss them with pasta and Asiago cheese. You can use the skimmed onion-scented butter from the recipe to flavor soups and stocks or to spread over toasted slices of French bread.

½ cup butter
3 pounds Vidalia or other sweet onions (about 4 medium), peeled

1. Combine butter and onions in an electric slow cooker. Cover and cook on low-heat setting 24 hours.
2. Remove onions with a slotted spoon.
3. Pour cooking liquid into a bowl. Cover and chill.
4. Skim solidified fat from surface; reserve for another use. Discard remaining liquid. Yield: 4 servings (serving size: about 1 cup).

CALORIES 180 (32% from fat); FAT 6.3g (sat 3.7g, mono 1.8g, poly 0.4g); PROTEIN 4g; CARB 29.4g; FIBER 6.1g; CHOL 16mg; IRON 0.8mg; SODIUM 69mg; CALC 70mg

---

"Although cooking time is more flexible than with a stovetop method, overcooking and even burning are possible in a slow cooker, so test for doneness close to the time given in the recipe." Jan Smith, Photo Stylist

Pork Roast with Three-Mushroom Ragoût

Cooking a lean pork roast in a slow cooker helps the pork retain moisture, so the final product is tender and juicy.

1	(3½-ounce) package shiitake mushrooms
¼	cup all-purpose flour
1	cup canned crushed tomatoes, divided
2	tablespoons chopped fresh or 2 teaspoons dried thyme
2	(8-ounce) packages button mushrooms, cut in half
1	(8-ounce) package cremini mushrooms, cut in half
1	large onion, cut into 8 wedges
½	ounce sun-dried tomatoes, packed without oil, quartered (about 6)
1¾	pounds boned pork loin roast
½	teaspoon salt
¼	teaspoon pepper
5	cups cooked medium egg noodles (about 4 cups uncooked pasta)

1. Discard shiitake mushroom stems; cut caps into quarters.

2. Lightly spoon flour into a dry measuring cup; level with a knife. Combine flour, ½ cup crushed tomatoes, and thyme in an electric slow cooker; stir with a whisk. Add mushrooms, onion, and sun-dried tomatoes.

3. Trim fat from pork; cut pork into large chunks. Sprinkle pork with salt and pepper; place on top of mushroom mixture. Pour ½ cup crushed tomatoes over pork. Cover with lid; cook on high-heat setting for 1 hour. Reduce heat setting to low; cook 7 hours. Remove pork from slow cooker; cut chunks into slices. Serve over noodles. Yield: 5 servings (serving size: 3 ounces pork, 1 cup sauce, and 1 cup noodles).

CALORIES 460 (22% from fat); FAT 11.2g (sat 3.4g, mono 4.4g, poly 1.8g); PROTEIN 34g; CARB 56g; FIBER 6g; CHOL 117mg; IRON 5.6mg; SODIUM 444mg; CALC 62mg

---

Slow Cooker Safety
Keep It SAFE

The U.S. Department of Agriculture (USDA) recommends that no matter what type of meat or poultry you're cooking in a slow cooker, turn the heat to high for the first hour. It creates steam and gets the food cooking quicker. The strategy is aimed at bringing cooking temperatures up to levels needed to prevent the growth of bacteria.

Thaw frozen meats completely before cooking; don't cook meats from a frozen or partially frozen state. Thaw meats in the microwave if necessary.

Don't cook whole poultry (such as a roasting hen) or a whole roast in the slow cooker because they can't heat up fast enough, and some parts will be in the temperature range that is ideal for bacterial growth. If you're cooking a roast, cut it into several large pieces.

Use a instant-read thermometer to check the internal temperature of large pieces of meat. Here are the safe temperatures to reach:

- Beef: at least 155°
- Lamb: at least 155°
- Pork: at least 160°
- Poultry: at least 170°

Don't reheat leftovers in the slow cooker. They can't heat up fast enough, so there's a chance of bacterial contamination.

"We don't really have a preference in terms of brands of slow cookers, but having one with a removable insert is a must." Kathleen Kanen, Food Stylist

Grilling

Grilling is the ultimate high-flavor, low-fat cooking method. It intensifies the flavor of all sorts of foods without relying on extra fat.

As a whole, we spend an average of 5 or 6 hours at the grill each week, so we've really figured out what it takes for "grade-A" grilling. Here are our tips on how to get perfect results every time.

Grilling Basics

Charcoal or Gas? Our staff doesn't really have a preference for one type of grilling over the other. Some people claim to detect a taste advantage with charcoal, but we really haven't found that to be the case as long as the two fuels provide a similar temperature range. We've cooked on several good gas grills, and the results are always just as tasty as those from charcoal.

Firepower Advantage The main advantage of charcoal over other fuels is that it generates high heat, even with the lid open. This isn't normally true of the gas burners in grills; you have to shop carefully to find a gas grill with the same heat range as any inexpensive charcoal model.

Start with the Best
Test Kitchen SECRET

Start with quality ingredients. Because it's a dry, high-heat cooking method, grilling accentuates the natural flavor of food. No amount of seasoning will change the essential quality of the ingredients you use, so start with the best cuts of meat and the freshest vegetables.

Grilling: Fast vs. Slow

Fast (Direct): Direct grilling involves putting food on a grill rack directly over hot coals. The best candidates for direct grilling are firm-fleshed fish and shellfish such as salmon, tuna, swordfish, halibut, mahimahi, and shrimp; chicken breasts and thighs; chops; burgers; and steaks. Vegetables can also be grilled directly—just be sure to cut them large enough so that they don't fall through the rack (or use a grill basket).

Slow (Indirect): This method is similar to oven roasting. Both sides of the grill are fired up, then one side is turned off. If using a charcoal grill, push the hot coals to one side. A disposable aluminum foil pan (also called a drip pan) containing water (or wine, broth, or other liquid) is placed directly over the coals on the side of a gas or electric grill where the heat has been turned off. On a charcoal grill, the pan is placed on the side where the charcoal has been moved. The food is then placed on the rack over the pan. The pan serves two purposes: It creates a steamy environment in which the food can cook, and it catches drippings from the food, minimizing flare-ups. Good candidates for this type of grilling include whole chickens, roasts, turkey breasts, and other large foods.

To further intensify flavor, brown food over direct heat at the start or end of grilling.

Top 10 Grilling Secrets from the *Cooking Light* Cooks

1. Be organized. Have the food, marinade, sauces, and utensils grillside and ready to go before you start cooking. Make sure you have enough gas or charcoal before you start.

2. Take the chill off. If you take marinated meats out of the refrigerator and let them stand at room temperature for 10 to 15 minutes before grilling, you won't end up with a cold center.

3. Keep it clean. We recommend cleaning your grill twice: once after preheating the grill, and again when you've finished grilling. Use both a metal spatula and a wire brush to scrape the grates clean.

4. Oil the grate or coat it with cooking spray before placing food on it. Quickly run a paper towel that is moist with oil over the grates. This seasons the grill, helps clean it, and helps prevent food from sticking.

5. Know when to baste. Too many people ruin great food by basting it too early with sugar-based sauces, which results in charring. Add sugar-based sauces toward the end of the cook time to prevent burning. You can baste with yogurt-, citrus-, or oil and vinegar–based sauces throughout cooking. If you use the marinade to baste, stop just before the last 3 minutes of cooking.

6. Go light on the sugar in homemade sauces, and avoid those bottled sauces that are mostly sugar and salt. Sometimes all you need is a little salt and pepper.

7. Give it a rest. Meat will taste better and be juicier if given a chance to rest a few minutes after you take it off the grill.

8. Turn; don't stab. Use tongs or a spatula to turn the meat. Don't use a carving fork because it pierces the food and lets valuable juices out.

9. Don't overcook. Know in advance how long you expect to grill the food, and set a timer to alert you to check it. For large cuts of meat and poultry, use an instant-read meat thermometer to gauge doneness.

10. Control flare-ups, and don't let food burn. When dripping fat produces a flame in one spot, move food to a different area on the grill. Keep a spray bottle of water by the grill to put out accidental flare-ups. Also, you're less likely to have flames when you keep the oil in the marinade to a minimum.

"We've tested recipes on both charcoal and gas grills, and we like both equally well." Vanessa Johnson, Test Kitchens Director

> "If we're cooking over a charcoal fire, we prefer to use coal in lump hardwood instead of briquettes because it ignites more easily and burns hotter and cleaner."
>
> Mike Wilson, Test Kitchens Staffer

Covered or Uncovered? As a rule, **cover the grill when doing slow, indirect grilling with large pieces of food.** Resist the temptation to peek; you lose all the built-up heat and add 5 to 10 minutes to your cook time for each peek. **Leave the grill uncovered when doing fast or direct grilling with smaller items that cook quickly.**

The Two-Level Fire Many foods reach their peak when you grill them at two different temperatures, usually starting at a high level and then finishing at a lower level.

On charcoal grills that have an adjustable grate or firebox, lower the heat by increasing the distance between the coals and the food. If you don't have that feature, build two similarly sized cooking areas on opposite sides of the grill by stacking and spreading the charcoal differently. For the hot section, pile coals between two and three deep; for the medium area, scatter them in a single layer so that they're just touching one another. Doing this may seem a bit of a bother, but with many foods, building a two-level fire noticeably improves results.

On gas grills you can make temperature adjustments with nothing more than the turn of a knob. With smaller models that have one or two burners, simply turn down the heat at the appropriate time, and move food temporarily to a cooler edge of the grate to speed the temperature transition. **With gas grills that have three or more burners, you can usually keep a hot fire and a medium fire going simultaneously from the beginning.**

How Hot?

Test Kitchen SECRET

The best way to measure the temperature of an open fire is the time-honored hand test. Simply hold your hand (a cook's tool employed universally since antiquity) about 3 inches above the grate, then time how long you can keep your hand there before you're forced to withdraw it.

- 1 to 2 seconds—signifies a hot fire that's perfect for searing a steak or grilling shrimp
- 3 seconds—indicates medium-high heat, which is great for most fish
- 4 to 5 seconds—signifies a medium range, ideal for most chicken and vegetables
- 7 to 8 seconds—indicates the temperature is low and perfect for grilling delicate vegetables and fruit

Porterhouse and tuna steaks are two examples of foods that are best when you sear them first on a hot fire, then move to medium heat for cooking through.

Thermometer Readings Thermometers that come with most grills measure only temperatures inside the grill when the cover is closed.

If you cook with direct heat with the cover down, you get a measurement of the reflected heat that contributes to the cooking process, but you don't get the actual grilling temperature on the grate where the food sits. The top side of the food is cooked at the oven temperature indicated, while the bottom side directly above the fire is grilled at a higher temperature.

See the Test Kitchens Secret on page 63 for the best way to determine the heat of the fire.

Meat Safety	Keep It SAFE

Because you're working close to the heat source and dealing with an outside temperature, safety is always an issue when you're grilling. Here are our safety "musts."

- Marinate food in the refrigerator, not on the countertop.
- Never desert your post. Pay attention. Even though grilling is easy, it requires vigilance because of flame-ups and other potential problems.
- Don't baste foods with the same mixture in which the raw meat marinated; any contamination in the raw meat can be transferred from the meat to the marinade.
- Use an instant-read meat thermometer to gauge doneness for poultry and large cuts of meat to make sure they've cooked to a safe temperature. (For more information on safe temperatures for particular foods, see page 60.)
- Place grilled foods on a clean platter or cutting board.

The Right Fire for the Food

To get the best results when you're grilling, be sure to use the right level of heat for the food. Here's what we've found works best.

Medium Heat
- Bell peppers, corn on the cob (shucked), eggplant, and most other vegetables
- Chicken breasts and halves
- Duck breasts
- Pork chops and most other pork cuts
- Pork ribs (after baking in an oven or cooking on a covered grill until tender)
- Turkey fillets
- Veal chops (can also cook on medium-low)

Medium-High Heat
- Most fish and shellfish

High Heat
- Calamari
- Salmon fillets and steaks
- Scallops
- Shrimp (peeled)

Sear on high heat; finish on medium heat
- Beef and pork tenderloin
- Chicken thighs and drumsticks
- Hamburgers (switch to medium after searing each side 1 minute)
- Hot dogs (switch to medium when deeply browned all over)
- Lamb chops and butterflied leg of lamb
- Steak
- Tuna steaks
- Uncooked sausage
- Venison steaks

How to Grill Fish

The most important thing to know when grilling seafood is what kind to use. You want fish that has a thick, firm, meaty texture so that it won't fall apart while it's cooking. Although some firm-textured seafood tends to be higher in fat than other more delicate fish, it's the type of fat that's heart-healthy.

> "After plenty of fish disasters, we've figured out which types of seafood are the best for grilling. Our big discovery? Success depends on the fish's texture." Sam Brannock, Test Kitchens Staffer

Checking for Doneness To avoid overcooking the seafood, go with a medium-hot fire rather than a really hot one. You should start checking the fish several minutes before you think that it's done. There are a couple of ways to do this: There's the old standby method of testing for flakiness with a fork. Or you can also make a small slit in the thickest part of the fish with a sharp knife. Cooked fish will be firm to the touch and opaque; undercooked fish will appear shiny and semitranslucent.

Strategies for Seafood
Test Kitchen SECRET

- When you grill seafood, it's particularly important that the rack be very clean. Any residue on the rack could interfere with the seafood's delicate flavor; a clean rack also helps prevent sticking. Also, you should always place seafood on a hot grill rack and leave it there for several minutes before you try to move it. This way, a sear will develop between the fish and the grill rack, which will further help prevent sticking.
- Lightly spray the grill rack with cooking spray before placing it over the coals. This keeps the food from sticking and makes the grill rack easier to clean.

Seafood That Can Take the Heat

Here are some of the fish that are well suited for the grill.

Grouper: This white-meat fish is sold in fillets and steaks. If you can't find grouper, you can use sea bass or mahimahi.

Halibut: The meat of this fish is white and mild-flavored and comes in steaks and fillets. Although it's a firm fish, it's a tad more delicate than the other fish in this list, so be gentle when turning it on the grill.

Salmon: With a range of flavors from rich to mild, salmon can take on a char and still keep its distinct taste. Salmon's pink meat comes in steaks and fillets.

Scallops: This bivalve is usually classified into two groups: bay scallops and sea scallops. The larger sea scallops are best for grilling because, like shrimp, they have a meatier texture and can be easily skewered. They cook fast, though, so keep a close eye on them.

Shrimp: Large shrimp are best for grilling. They can be easily skewered, and they cook quickly.

Swordfish: This mild but distinctive-tasting fish has a firm, gray-white flesh and a meaty texture. Its natural oil content keeps it moist while grilling. You can usually find it sold as steaks.

Tuna: If you're new to grilling fish, fresh tuna is a good starter. It cooks like a beefsteak, and its deep red meat almost never sticks to the grill.

How to Grill Kebabs

You may call them shish kebabs or skewers: They're the same thing. Kebabs are accommodating and easy to customize; they're a natural for mixing ingredients, flavors, and cooking styles.

And kebabs are as easy to serve as they are to prepare—with everything already cut into bite-size pieces, your guests will be good to go with only a paper plate.

> "I like to grill kebabs instead of steaks for company because they cook so fast that I'm not busy slaving over a hot grill while my guests are left to amuse themselves." Mike Wilson, Test Kitchens Staffer

Skewer Savvy

Our "king of kebabs," Mike Wilson, shares his tips for successful skewering.

Soak wooden skewers in water for 15 to 30 minutes so they won't burn on the grill.

When grilling meat kebabs, be sure the pieces are all the same size to ensure even cooking. Pounding chicken to an even thickness helps it cook quickly and evenly.

Shrimp, scallops, and other wobbly bits benefit from the double-skewer technique: Thread the pieces on a skewer, then run another one through the pieces parallel to the first, about a half-inch away.

Expecting vegetarians? Cook the meat and vegetables on separate skewers, so guests who don't want meat can pick up a stick of vegetables. If your guests will assemble their own skewers, place meat and vegetables in separate bowls.

If you have to move the party inside, you can broil kebabs; it doesn't take any longer than grilling.

How to Grill Vegetables

Grilling adds a whole new taste sensation to veggies, especially when they take on a char-grilled flavor as well as look. Depending on the recipe, you can either grill the vegetable first, then slice them, or you can slice first. If the vegetables are large enough, you can place them directly on the grill. If not, you can use a grill basket (see below).

The best vegetables for grilling are the sturdy ones such as eggplant, yellow squash, zucchini, tomatoes, bell peppers, potatoes, and onions.

Grill Baskets

Test Kitchen SECRET

Grill baskets work fine for grilling pieces of vegetables and some types of tender fish. With a basket, you don't have to worry about small pieces of vegetables falling through the grill rack. However, if you don't have one, there's no real reason to go out and buy a special piece of equipment. You can grill vegetables whole, or you can cut them into large pieces, then cut into smaller pieces after you remove them from the grill.

How to Grill Pizza

Don't be afraid of putting raw dough on a hot grill. We have some suggestions to help turn your fears into fun. We have make-ahead instructions for pizza dough, and it takes only a few minutes to grill the thin crusts. You'll get a light, crusty pizza that tastes as if it were cooked in a smoky wood-fired oven.

> **"We think pizza is one of the most unique and fun things to grill."**
> **Tiffany Vickers, Test Kitchens Staffer**

Grilling a Great Pizza

- We prefer to make the crust with bread flour because it's higher in protein than all-purpose flour and makes a firmer, denser crust. You can, however, substitute all-purpose flour.
- To add a more pronounced smoky flavor, soak a couple of handfuls of aromatic wood chips in water for about 30 minutes. Sprinkle them over the hot coals, and close the lid to your grill. Wait a few minutes before you place the pizza crust on the grill rack.
- Before you cook, remove the grill rack, and coat it with cooking spray to prevent the pizza crust from sticking.
- Have all of your topping ingredients ready and nearby before you start to grill the pizza dough.

Quick-and-Easy Pizza Crust

Cook both crusts at the same time if your grill is large enough. (See page 68 for the entire grilled pizza recipe.)

- 2 cups bread flour
- ½ teaspoon salt
- ½ teaspoon sugar
- 1 package quick-rise yeast (about 2¼ teaspoons)
- ¾ cup warm water (100° to 110°)
- 1 tablespoon olive oil
- Cooking spray
- 2 tablespoons cornmeal

1. Combine first 4 ingredients in a large bowl; make a well in center of mixture. Combine water and oil; add to flour mixture. Stir until mixture forms a ball.
2. Turn dough out onto a lightly floured surface; knead until smooth and elastic (about 10 minutes). Place the dough in a large bowl coated with cooking spray, turning to coat top. Cover and let rise in a warm place (85°), free from drafts, 45 minutes or until doubled in bulk. Punch dough down; divide in half. Cover and let dough rest 10 minutes.
3. Working with 1 portion at a time (cover remaining dough to keep from drying), roll into a 10-inch circle on a lightly floured surface. Sprinkle each of 2 baking sheets with 1 tablespoon cornmeal. Place dough on prepared baking sheets. Yield: 2 (10-inch) pizza crusts (serving size: 1 crust).

CALORIES 603 (14% from fat); FAT 9.7g (sat 1.3g, mono 5.3g, poly 1.6g); PROTEIN 18.5g; CARB 108.5g; FIBER 1.4g; CHOL 0mg; IRON 7mg; SODIUM 589mg; CALC 24mg

To make ahead, chill the rolled, uncooked crusts for up to 4 hours, or freeze the dough for up to 2 weeks. Be sure the dough is brought to room temperature before rolling it out and grilling it.

Pizza Margherita

Don't fret if your crusts have irregular puffy circles and grill marks. That's part of their rustic attraction.

2	teaspoons olive oil
⅛	teaspoon salt
⅛	teaspoon pepper
¼	cup thinly sliced fresh basil
2	tablespoons chopped fresh oregano
2	(10-inch) Quick-and-Easy Pizza Crusts

Cooking spray

4	plum tomatoes, thinly sliced (about ½ pound)
1	cup (4 ounces) shredded part-skim mozzarella cheese

1. Combine first 3 ingredients in a small bowl; set aside.

2. Combine basil and oregano in a small bowl; set aside.

3. Prepare grill. Place 1 crust on grill rack coated with cooking spray; grill 3 minutes or until puffy and golden. Turn crust, grill-mark side up; brush with half of oil mixture. Top with half each of tomatoes, mozzarella, and herb mixture. Cook 4 to 5 minutes or until cheese melts and crust is lightly browned. Repeat with remaining crust and toppings. Yield: 6 servings (serving size: ⅓ pizza).

CALORIES 286 (26% from fat); FAT 8.3g (sat 2.6g, mono 3.8g, poly 1g); PROTEIN 11.7g; CARB 41.6g; FIBER 1.8g; CHOL 11mg; IRON 3.4mg; SODIUM 339mg; CALC 161mg

Making Pizza on the Grill

1. Roll each crust into a 10-inch circle.

2. Place each crust on a baking sheet sprinkled with cornmeal.

3. Gently lift crust from the baking sheet to the grill.

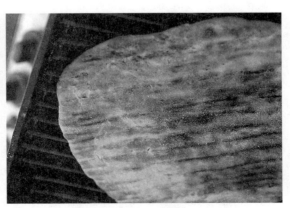

4. Turn crust, grill-mark side up, after about 3 minutes.

Marinades and Rubs

You can use two traditional methods to perk up the flavors of meat, poultry, or seafood before you grill—one wet, one dry.

Marinade The wet way—called marinating—relies on a seasoned liquid in which the food is soaked to absorb flavor. Generally speaking, the longer you marinate a food, the stronger it will taste. Remember, however, that some foods, such as delicate fish, should not marinate longer than 2 to 4 hours. As a rule, ⅔ to 1 cup of marinade will flavor 1 to 1½ pounds of food. Mix the marinade in a zip-top plastic bag, toss your food inside, seal the bag, and chill. **Marinated foods lend themselves well to grilling because you can baste the food with the remaining marinade.** (See page 196 for specific information on marinating beef.)

Rub The alternative to marinating—a dry rub—is a blend of dry herbs and spices. **Many rub recipes call for whole spices to be crushed; to do this, a mortar and pestle are the tools of choice.** Or you can place whole spices in a plastic bag, and pound with a rolling pin. Store dry rubs indefinitely in an airtight container in a cool, dry place.

When using rubs, apply them to a food that is completely dry. The most effective way to apply the rub is to place the mixture in a zip-top bag, put the food inside, and shake. Although the amount of rub you use is up to your taste buds, a general rule is 3 tablespoons per 1 pound of food.

Marinating Safety
Keep It SAFE

Always marinate in the refrigerator. If you're also using the marinade as a sauce, you must place the marinade in a small saucepan, bring it to a boil and boil for 1 minute to kill any germs that might have been transferred from the food.

Stovetop Grill Pan

A grill pan adds more than just pretty grill marks and smoky flavors. Its ridges elevate food so air can circulate underneath and fat can drip away, so your food doesn't sauté or steam as it does in a plain skillet; instead, flavor is seared into the food. Meat and fish turn out juicy, with no need for added fat.

> "Using a grill pan is a healthy way to cook because the fat drips away from the food, just like it does on the grill."
> **Susan Stone, Food Editor**

Vegetables stay crisp-tender, and their nutrients don't leach out into cooking water. You can buy them at your local discount or kitchen store from less than $20 to more than $100; nonstick pans are also available.

Buying a Stovetop Grill Pan
Cooking Light **Recommends**

If you are planning to purchase a grill pan, here are some things to look for.

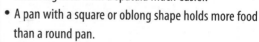

- High ridges produce results similar to those of an outdoor grill. If the ridges are too low, you might as well be using a regular skillet.
- Low sides make flipping burgers and removing food with a spatula much easier.
- A pan with a square or oblong shape holds more food than a round pan.
- A lidless pan is a good choice, since there's no reason to lock in moisture when grilling.
- Nonstick grill pans are easier to clean than cast-iron pans. If you buy a cast-iron grill pan, see page 23 for how to season a cast-iron skillet.
- There's no specific brand that we think is better, but we do prefer to use the larger-size pans.

Oven Frying

"When you 'fry' foods in the oven instead of the deep-fat fryer, you can often cut the fat by more than 75 percent."
Mary Creel, Food Editor

After much experimentation, we've found that creating crisp, crunchy faux-fried food in the oven is possible and comes down to three simple techniques involving (1) the breading, (2) the oil, and (3) the heat. Now, you can have the crispy, crunchy, chewy satisfaction of fried food—and guilt-free pleasure as well.

> "The popularity of fried food has much to do with its texture. The crisp exterior contrasted with the moist, tender interior is a large part of the appeal."
> Jan Smith, Photo Stylist

Low-Fat Frying

Breading, breading, breading: With the exception of french fries, most foods are well served by a double dip—sometimes even a triple dip—in flour or some other breading to create a substantial crunchy coating. For instance, our Oven-Fried Chicken (page 71) is marinated in buttermilk, dusted with flour, sprayed with cooking spray, and then dusted with flour again.

Oil up: Give the food a shot of cooking spray after breading it, just before it goes in the oven. This helps brown and crisp the surface.

Heat it up: The higher the heat, the browner and crispier the coating will get. All of these recipes bake in at least 400° ovens.

Garlic Fries

"My kids like these fries as much as the ones at the fast food restaurants." Jill Melton, Food Editor

- 3 pounds peeled baking potatoes, cut into ¼-inch-thick strips
- 4 teaspoons vegetable oil
- ¾ teaspoon salt
- Cooking spray
- 2 tablespoons butter
- 8 garlic cloves, minced (about 5 teaspoons)
- 2 tablespoons finely chopped fresh parsley
- 2 tablespoons freshly grated Parmesan cheese

1. Preheat oven to 400°.
2. Combine first 3 ingredients in a large zip-top plastic bag, tossing to coat.
3. Arrange potatoes in a single layer on a baking sheet coated with cooking spray. Bake at 400° for 50 minutes or until potatoes are tender and golden brown, turning after 20 minutes.
4. Place butter and garlic in a large nonstick skillet; cook over low heat 2 minutes, stirring constantly. Add potatoes, parsley, and cheese to pan; toss to coat. Serve immediately. Yield: 6 servings.

CALORIES 256 (27% from fat); FAT 7.7g (sat 3.3g, mono 2g, poly 2g); PROTEIN 5.9g; CARB 42.3g; FIBER 3.5g; CHOL 12mg; IRON 1.9mg; SODIUM 386mg; CALC 55mg

---

Tossing the fries in butter and garlic after cooking makes them unbelievably rich.

Beer-Battered Fish

The secret to getting the fish browned just right is to broil them for an additional minute after they're baked.

1½   tablespoons vegetable oil
1   cup all-purpose flour
½   teaspoon pepper
¼   teaspoon garlic salt
⅔   cup beer
2   large egg whites
2   cups dry breadcrumbs
½   cup chopped fresh parsley
1½   pounds grouper or other firm white fish
      fillets, such as catfish or tilapia, cut into
      4 x 1-inch strips
Cooking spray
Malt vinegar (optional)

1. Preheat oven to 450°.
2. Coat the bottom of a jelly-roll pan with oil.
3. Lightly spoon flour into a dry measuring cup; level with a knife. Combine flour, pepper, and garlic salt in a large bowl. Add beer; stir well. Beat egg whites with a mixer at high speed until stiff peaks form. Gently fold egg white mixture into flour mixture.
4. Combine breadcrumbs and parsley in a shallow dish. Working with 1 fish strip at a time, dip in flour mixture; dredge in breadcrumb mixture. Repeat procedure with remaining strips, flour mixture, and breadcrumb mixture. Place on prepared baking sheet. Lightly coat strips with cooking spray.
5. Bake at 450° for 15 minutes or until fish flakes easily when tested with a fork. Remove from oven.
6. Preheat broiler.
7. Broil the fish strips 1 minute or until tops are lightly browned. Serve fish with malt vinegar, if desired. Yield: 4 servings.

CALORIES 351 (13% from fat); FAT 5.1g (sat 1g, mono 1.4g, poly 1.9g); PROTEIN 39.1g; CARB 32.9g; FIBER 1.4g; CHOL 63mg; IRON 4.4mg; SODIUM 371mg; CALC 122mg

Oven-Fried Chicken

Marinating in buttermilk results in tender, juicy chicken, and double breading gives a crisp crust. For a smoky taste, use ground chipotle pepper in place of the ground red pepper.

¾   cup low-fat buttermilk
2   chicken breast halves (about 1 pound),
      skinned
2   chicken drumsticks (about ½ pound),
      skinned
2   chicken thighs (about ½ pound), skinned
½   cup all-purpose flour
1   teaspoon salt
½   teaspoon ground red pepper
¼   teaspoon white pepper
¼   teaspoon ground cumin
Cooking spray

1. Combine first 4 ingredients in a large heavy-duty zip-top plastic bag; seal. Marinate in refrigerator 1 hour, turning occasionally.
2. Preheat oven to 450°.
3. Combine flour, salt, peppers, and cumin in a second large zip-top plastic bag. Remove chicken from first bag, discarding marinade. Add chicken, 1 piece at a time, to flour mixture, shaking bag to coat chicken. Remove chicken from bag, shaking off excess flour; lightly coat each chicken piece with cooking spray. Return chicken, 1 piece at a time, to flour mixture, shaking bag to coat chicken. Remove chicken from bag, shaking off excess flour.
4. Place chicken on a baking sheet lined with parchment paper. Lightly coat chicken with cooking spray. Bake at 450° for 35 minutes or until done, turning after 20 minutes. Yield: 4 servings (serving size: 1 breast half or 1 thigh and 1 drumstick).

CALORIES 263 (15% from fat); FAT 4.4g (sat 1.2g, mono 1.1g, poly 0.9g); PROTEIN 38.4g; CARB 14.9g; FIBER 0.8g; CHOL 110mg; IRON 2.2mg; SODIUM 754mg; CALC 73mg

Poaching

Poaching is a classic method of cooking that yields flavor with virtually no fat.

At *Cooking Light*, we don't believe in gimmicks, so we often find ourselves going back to the basics. Poaching is a time-honored way to give foods great depths of flavor without adding fat.

It can be applied to all kinds of dishes beyond the predictable eggs, including fish, chicken, and fruit. And because poaching preserves the shape and texture of food, dishes prepared this way can be visually stunning, particularly those using fruit.

In poaching, the food is immersed in liquids, such as wine or stock, then simmered until done. Although poaching is usually done on the stovetop, we've also included an example that's done in the oven. All you really need is a skillet or Dutch oven, plus a slotted spoon or spatula.

Poaching Pointers
Test Kitchen SECRET

- Technically, poaching is different from simmering in that poaching is cooking food at a slightly lower temperature (160° to 180°) than a simmer (185°). But sometimes if you are poaching large pieces of food, you'll need to poach at a low simmer.
- Poaching is ideal for delicate foods that need to be treated with care so they won't break apart or overcook, such as eggs, fish, and fruit.
- Poach foods whole or in large pieces to keep the food moist.
- Cover the pan while the food is cooking to prevent excess evaporation.
- Remove cooked food from the liquid immediately, or it will continue to cook.

Oven-Poached Halibut Provençale
This recipe uses a moderate oven temperature to accomplish the same results as stovetop poaching.

 Cooking spray
1 cup dry white wine
6 (6-ounce) halibut steaks
6 cups diced tomato
2 cups finely chopped onion
¼ cup chopped fresh or 4 teaspoons dried basil
¼ cup chopped fresh parsley or 4 teaspoons dried parsley flakes
2 tablespoons minced kalamata olives
1 tablespoon olive oil
½ teaspoon salt
½ teaspoon anchovy paste
⅛ teaspoon pepper
2 garlic cloves, minced
¼ cup dry breadcrumbs
1 tablespoon grated fresh Parmesan cheese
1 teaspoon olive oil

1. Preheat oven to 350°.
2. Coat a 13 x 9-inch baking dish with cooking spray. Pour wine into dish, and arrange halibut steaks in dish. Combine tomato and next 9 ingredients in a bowl; stir well, and spoon over steaks. Bake at 350° for 35 minutes or until fish flakes easily when tested with a fork.
3. Combine breadcrumbs, cheese, and 1 teaspoon oil in a bowl; stir well. Sprinkle over tomato mixture, and broil until crumbs are golden. Serve immediately. Yield: 6 servings (serving size: 5 ounces fish and 1 cup tomato mixture).

CALORIES 305 (22% from fat); PROTEIN 38.9g; FAT 8.6g (sat 1.3g, mono 3.8g, poly 2.1g); CARB 17.9g; FIBER 3.8g; CHOL 81mg; IRON 3.1mg; SODIUM 446mg; CALC 139mg

Poaching Pears

1. Using a corer, core pears from bottom, cutting to but not through, stem end.

2. Cut a thin slice from bottom of each pear so fruit will stand upright.

3. Gently lower pears into saucepan for poaching in sugar mixture.

"Poaching is one of the best ways to cook fruit because it preserves the shape and the color of the fruit."
Kellie Kelley, Food Stylist

Poached Pears in Vanilla Sauce

You can refrigerate extra poaching liquid up to 3 months; serve it over ice cream or pancakes.

 4   cups water
 1   cup sugar
 1   vanilla bean, split lengthwise
 1   (3-inch) cinnamon stick
 4   small firm Bosc pears

1. Combine water and sugar in a medium saucepan; bring to a boil, stirring until sugar dissolves. Add vanilla bean and cinnamon. Cover, reduce heat, and simmer 15 minutes.
2. Peel and core pears, leaving stems intact. Cut about ¼ inch from base of each pear so they will sit flat. Add pears to sugar mixture. Cover and cook over medium heat 10 minutes or until tender. Remove pears with a slotted spoon; chill thoroughly. Discard cinnamon stick. Scrape seeds from vanilla bean, and stir seeds into sugar mixture. Discard bean. Set aside 2 cups of sugar mixture; reserve remaining mixture for another use.
3. Return 2 cups sugar mixture to pan; bring to a boil over high heat. Cook until slightly syrupy and reduced to ½ cup (about 12 minutes). Cover and chill thoroughly. Serve sauce with pears. Serve at room temperature or chilled. Yield: 4 servings (serving size: 1 pear and 2 tablespoons sauce).

CALORIES 227 (2% from fat); PROTEIN 0.5g; FAT 0.6g (sat 0g, mono 0.1g, poly 0.1g); CARB 58.5g; FIBER 3.3g; CHOL 0mg; IRON 0.4mg; SODIUM 0mg; CALC 16mg

Roasting

When you want to get a lot of flavor from food, roast at a high temperature.

Intense flavor. No added fat. It's what we're all about at *Cooking Light*. When you turn the oven dial up to the max, a scorching 475° to 500°, the natural flavors of foods are intensified. Thanks to caramelization, roasting concentrates flavors without adding fat, giving foods a crispy exterior, tender interior, and rich, dark color.

Roasting Meats and Poultry

As intense dry heat penetrates the chicken or meat inside the oven, the juices bubble to the surface. The liquid evaporates, leaving proteins and sugars that caramelize the meat to create the characteristic roasted color, aroma, and flavor.

Roasting generally requires tender cuts, which are usually higher in fat. We recommend using beef tenderloin, pork loin, leg of lamb, or whole chicken, which are all moderately lean. We don't recommend leaner cuts of beef and pork for roasting because they require moist cooking (such as braising or stewing) to make them tender. (See page 55 for more information on braising.)

A roast needs a brief rest when it comes out of the oven before you slice or carve. While the meat is resting on the counter, its internal temperature continues to rise. This finishes the cooking process and allows the juices to settle and redistribute. That means they'll stay in the meat rather than escape to your cutting board. Although a chicken needs to cook fully before you take it out of the oven, it too needs to stand briefly so that the juices can settle and redistribute. After you've taken the meat or chicken from the oven and put it on a plate, you can deglaze the pan, which involves pouring liquid into the roasting pan and scraping up all the browned bits in the bottom. This broth can be served as is or used as the base for a sauce. (See page 50 for more information about deglazing.)

Ask the *Cooking Light* Cooks

What's the ideal degree of doneness for roasts? Leaner roasts will be succulent if cooked medium-rare or medium.

Where do I put the meat thermometer to get an accurate reading? Place the thermometer in the thickest part of the roast, away from bone or gristle, for the most accurate reading.

What temperature do meats need to reach to be safe and still taste good? We recommend the following degrees of doneness:
• Beef and lamb: medium-rare (145° internal temperature after resting) to medium (160° internal temperature after resting)
• Pork: medium (160° internal temperature after resting)
• Chicken: fully cooked (180° internal temperature)

What do you mean by "resting"? You should pull the roast from the oven at 5° below the final recommended temperature—the roast will continue to cook slightly as it rests. Allow about 10 minutes for the roast to rest and fully reabsorb the juices. (The exception to this is roasted chicken, which should cook fully to 180°).

Equipment for Perfect Roasting

You need only a few essentials for roasting: an oven; a heavy, shallow roasting pan; and a thermometer to determine doneness. Here's how to make those essentials work optimally in the process.

Oven: Position the rack in the center—usually the second level from the bottom—so hot air can evenly surround the roast.

Pan: Most roasting pans are at least 13 x 9 inches or larger and are designed for cooking large cuts of meat or a turkey and for cooking vegetables at high temperatures. These heavy pans come in large rectangular or oval shapes with 2- to 4-inch vertical sides, which keep the pan juices from overflowing in the oven. **Ideally, the pan should extend 2 or 3 inches beyond the edges of the roast. If the pan is too large, meat juices will evaporate too quickly, and the drippings may burn instead of caramelizing.**

Some pans come with racks; others are sold separately. If your pan doesn't have a rack, you can elevate the meat with vegetables (such as whole carrots and ribs of celery) or on a wire rack that fits the pan, unless the roast has to cook for several hours (in which case the drippings help the meat stay moist).

You don't necessarily have to invest in an expensive pan; your oven's broiler pan can work just as well. This broiler pan sometimes comes with a rack that prevents the meat from cooking in its drippings and allows adequate circulation.

Thermometer: Three types can be used.
- A standard meat thermometer is inserted into the thickest part of the roast prior to cooking. It stays in the oven during the process. These are inexpensive and, for the most part, accurate.

- An instant-read thermometer is inserted into the roast, read, then taken out. It does not stay in the oven. It's more accurate than a basic meat thermometer, but you have to check the temperature early and more frequently. If you wait too long into the cooking time, there is a possibility of overcooking your roast.
- There is also a digital thermometer that sits outside of the oven (see below).

Mediterranean Roasted Leg of Lamb with Red Wine Sauce

The drippings from the roast are combined with red wine to make a flavorful sauce that complements the lamb perfectly. Use a full-bodied, dry red wine, such as Cabernet Sauvignon, Merlot, or Cabernet Franc. Increasing the oven temperature for the last 20 minutes browns the lamb.

1	(5½- to 6-pound) rolled boned leg of lamb
1	teaspoon minced fresh rosemary
¾	teaspoon kosher salt, divided
2	garlic cloves, minced
⅛	teaspoon pepper
1	tablespoon olive oil
6	rosemary sprigs
2	cups dry red wine, divided
1½	tablespoons cornstarch

1. Preheat oven to 400°.

2. Unroll roast; trim fat. Spread minced rosemary, ¼ teaspoon salt, and garlic into folds of the roast. Reroll roast; secure at 3-inch intervals with heavy string. Sprinkle with ¼ teaspoon salt and ⅛ teaspoon pepper. Drizzle with oil. Secure rosemary sprigs under strings on roast. Place roast on the rack of a broiler pan or roasting pan; insert a meat thermometer into thickest portion of roast. Bake at 400° for 1 hour. Increase oven temperature to 425° (do not remove roast from oven). Bake an additional 20 minutes or until thermometer registers 140° (medium-rare) to 155° (medium). Place roast on a platter; cover with foil. Let stand 10 minutes for roast to reabsorb juices (temperature of roast will increase 5° upon standing). Remove string and rosemary sprigs before slicing.

3. Remove rack from pan. Combine ½ cup wine and cornstarch; set aside. Add ½ cup wine to drippings in pan; scrape pan to loosen browned bits. Combine drippings mixture and 1 cup wine in a saucepan; bring to a boil. Cook 5 minutes. Add ¼ teaspoon salt and cornstarch mixture; return to a boil. Cook 1 minute or until thick, stirring constantly. Serve with lamb. Yield: 19 servings (serving size: 3 ounces lamb and about 1½ tablespoons sauce).

CALORIES 175 (38% from fat); FAT 7.4g (sat 2.5g, mono 3.4g, poly 0.5g); PROTEIN 24.4g; CARB 1.1g; FIBER 0g; CHOL 76mg; IRON 1.9mg; SODIUM 153mg; CALC 10mg

Because heat draws moisture to the surface of the roast, cover it and let it stand for 10 minutes before carving. This helps the roast reabsorb the juices.

Preparing the Roast

1. Unroll the roast, and trim the fat. To infuse the roast with flavor, spread with rosemary, salt, and minced garlic.

2. Reroll roast, and secure at 3-inch intervals with string. Tuck rosemary sprigs under string.

Pepper-Crusted Beef Tenderloin with Horseradish Sauce

Because roasting is a dry-heat cooking method, it's best to use a tender cut of beef such as a tenderloin.

1	(4-pound) beef tenderloin
1½	teaspoons olive oil
3	tablespoons dry breadcrumbs
3	tablespoons minced fresh flat-leaf parsley
1½	teaspoons coarsely ground black pepper
¾	teaspoon kosher salt, divided
	Cooking spray
1	cup fat-free sour cream
2	tablespoons prepared horseradish
1	teaspoon grated lemon rind
½	teaspoon Worcestershire sauce
¼	teaspoon hot pepper sauce

1. Preheat oven to 400°.

2. Trim fat from tenderloin; fold under 3 inches of small end. Rub the tenderloin with oil. Combine breadcrumbs, parsley, pepper, and ½ teaspoon salt. Rub tenderloin with crumb mixture; coat with cooking spray. Place tenderloin on the rack of a broiler pan or roasting pan; insert a meat thermometer into thickest portion of tenderloin. Bake at 400° for 30 minutes. Increase oven temperature to 425° (do not remove roast from oven). Bake an additional 10 minutes or until thermometer registers 140° (medium-rare) to 155° (medium). Place tenderloin on a platter, and cover with foil. Let stand 10 minutes for tenderloin to reabsorb juices (temperature of roast will increase 5° upon standing).

3. Combine ¼ teaspoon salt, sour cream, and remaining ingredients in a small bowl. Serve with beef. Yield: 16 servings (serving size: 3 ounces beef and 1 tablespoon horseradish sauce).

CALORIES 195 (39% from fat); FAT 8.4g (sat 3.2g, mono 3.4g, poly 0.4g); PROTEIN 25.3g; CARB 2.4g; FIBER 0.2g; CHOL 71mg; IRON 3.2mg; SODIUM 193mg; CALC 12mg

We suggest a cutting board with a built-in moat designed to catch juices. If you don't have this kind of board, you can improvise one by placing a heavy wooden cutting board in a baking sheet with sides or in a jelly-roll pan.

Preparing the Tenderloin

1. Trim excess fat from tenderloin. Notice that the end is tapered and thinner than the middle section; fold the thin end under, making the end about the same thickness as the middle. This encourages even cooking and prevents the end from overcooking.

2. Rub beef with a mixture of breadcrumbs, parsley, pepper, and salt. This creates a flavorful crust.

Roasting Chicken

- Use a roasting chicken. While you can roast a broiler/fryer with good results, chickens specifically for roasting are labeled "roasting broilers." These birds generally weigh more, are meatier, moister, and more succulent (due in part to an added salt solution, which increases our sodium figures only negligibly). However, if you are roasting a broiler/fryer (which normally weighs about 3 pounds), decrease the baking time by about 45 minutes.
- Always roast the chicken on a rack so the fat can drip off and away from the bird.
- Don't fret that all of the flavorings are lost when the skin is removed. The seasonings that are tucked under the skin will permeate not only the meat but the pan drippings as well, creating flavorful juices for the gravy and sauce.
- Roasting the chicken at a high temperature (450°) for a short time, then lowering it to a moderate temperature (350°) for the remaining cooking time seals in the juices, keeping the chicken moist and tender.
- Let the roasted chicken stand about 10 minutes after removing it from the oven. This standing time "sets" the juices and makes for a moister, more flavorful bird.

Garlic-Rosemary Roasted Chicken

The beauty of roasted chicken is its versatility. For a variation of this recipe, rub the chicken with paprika before cooking, and add fresh tomatoes 20 minutes before it's done.

1	(5- to 6-pound) roasting chicken
1	tablespoon chopped rosemary
8	garlic cloves, crushed
8	medium red onions
2	whole garlic heads
2	teaspoons olive oil

1. Preheat oven to 450°.

2. Remove the giblets and neck from chicken, and discard. Rinse chicken under cold water; pat dry. Trim excess fat. Starting at neck cavity, loosen skin from breast and drumsticks by inserting fingers and gently pushing between skin and meat. Place chopped rosemary and crushed garlic cloves beneath skin on breasts and drumsticks. Lift the wing tips up and over back, and tuck under chicken.

3. Place chicken, breast side up, on a broiler pan. Cut a thin slice from end of each onion. Remove white papery skins from garlic heads (do not peel or separate cloves). Cut tops off garlic, leaving root ends intact.

4. Brush onions and garlic with olive oil. Arrange onions and garlic around chicken. Insert meat thermometer into meaty part of thigh, making sure not to touch bone. Bake at 450° for 30 minutes. Reduce oven temperature to 350°, and bake an additional 1 hour and 15 minutes or until meat thermometer registers 180°. Discard skin. Yield: 8 servings (serving size: 3 ounces chicken, 1 onion).

CALORIES 231 (30% from fat); FAT 7.7g (sat 1.9g, mono 3.1g, poly 1.6g); PROTEIN 26.5g; CARB 13.5g; FIBER 2.7g; CHOL 76mg; IRON 1.4mg; SODIUM 133mg; CALC 50mg

"The best thing about roasting chicken is the simplicity. Nothing is easier." Alison Ashton, Food Editor

Roasting Chicken in a Clay Pot

Cooking in clay or terra-cotta is practically as old as civilization itself. This simple, basic cooking method can result in some of the most tender, tasty chicken you've ever eaten. Clay-pot cooking is just too simple not to try at home. Soak your terra-cotta pot and lid in water for 10 minutes, then pour out the water; pat pot dry. Put the chicken in the pot, cover, and slide it into the oven.

Even though the equipment is simple, the chemistry inside is quite sophisticated. The combination of high heat and moisture roasts and steams at the same time. The technique is perfect for cooking poultry as well as lean cuts of meat because the high heat forces moisture inward, cooking the interior of the meat. The moisture is then trapped as the clay lid reflects sufficient heat to cook the meat's surface. Basically, it's an oven within an oven.

Choose Your Pot
Cooking Light Recommends

Because clay-pot cookers come in a variety of sizes and types, labeling can vary greatly among brands. Look for cookers labeled "for 3 to 6 people" or "4- to 6-pound capacity." These are best suited for all-purpose applications and work perfectly with the *Cooking Light* clay-pot recipes. In testing, we used both Romertopf and Schlemmertopf bakers, as well as handmade specialty varieties. Clay pots are available in cookware shops or at Internet kitchen-supply sources.

Lemon-Herb Roasted Chicken

To get the chicken golden brown, remove the top of the pot, and broil 15 minutes.

    2   lemons
    2   tablespoons dried oregano
    1   tablespoon dried basil
    2   teaspoons cracked black pepper
    1   teaspoon salt
    1   teaspoon olive oil
    6   garlic cloves, minced
    1   (5-pound) roasting chicken

1. Peel and section lemons, reserving the peel. Combine lemon sections, oregano, and next 5 ingredients in a bowl, and mash with a fork.
2. Immerse the top and bottom of a 2-quart clay cooking pot in water for 10 minutes. Empty pot, drain well, and pat dry.
3. Remove and discard the giblets and neck from chicken. Rinse chicken with cold water; pat dry. Trim excess fat. Starting at neck cavity, loosen skin from breast and drumsticks by inserting fingers and gently pushing between skin and meat. Rub lemon mixture under and over loosened skin. Tie ends of legs together with cord. Place lemon peel in body cavity. Place chicken, breast side up, in bottom of clay pot, and cover with top of clay pot.
4. Place clay pot in cold oven, and set to 450°. Bake chicken for 50 minutes, and remove top (the chicken is done when a meat thermometer registers 180°).
5. Preheat broiler (do not move oven rack).
6. Broil chicken, uncovered, for 15 minutes or until golden brown.
7. Carefully remove clay pot from oven. Remove chicken from clay pot. Cover chicken loosely with foil; let stand for 10 minutes. Discard skin. Yield: 8 servings (serving size: 3 ounces chicken).

CALORIES 180 (36% from fat); FAT 7.1g (sat 1.9g, mono 2.7g, poly 1.6g); PROTEIN 25.1g; CARB 3.4g; FIBER 0.5g; CHOL 76mg; IRON 2mg; SODIUM 367mg; CALC 49mg

Roasting Fruits and Vegetables

Roasting food at very high temperatures isn't just for big hunks of meat. It also does wonders for vegetables and fruits, making them sweeter and meltingly soft.

The high heat—400° to 500°—locks in flavors while caramelizing outer layers. With little enhancement, a metamorphosis occurs: Unadorned vegetables become beautifully glazed side dishes, and plain fruits become full-blown desserts.

> "Roasting brings out the best in vegetables by making them golden and soft and concentrating their flavors." Ann Pittman, Food Editor

Roasted Spiced Plums

These are great over low-fat ice cream or pound cake.

    4   plums, halved
    Cooking spray
    ½   cup orange juice
    ¼   cup packed brown sugar
    ½   teaspoon ground cinnamon
    ⅛   teaspoon freshly grated nutmeg
    ⅛   teaspoon ground cumin
    ⅛   teaspoon ground cardamom
    1   tablespoon slivered almonds, toasted

1. Preheat oven to 450°.
2. Place plums, cut sides up, in an 11 x 7-inch baking dish coated with cooking spray. Combine orange juice, sugar, cinnamon, nutmeg, cumin, and cardamom; stir well. Drizzle orange juice mixture over plums. Bake at 450° for 20 minutes. Top with toasted almonds. Yield: 4 servings (serving size: 2 plum halves and ¾ teaspoon almonds).

CALORIES 96 (13% from fat); FAT 1.4g (sat 0.1g, mono 0.8g, poly 0.3g); PROTEIN 1.1g; CARB 21.4g; FIBER 1.7g; CHOL 0mg; IRON 0.5mg; SODIUM 4mg; CALC 22mg

Roasted Sweet Potato Wedges

Roasting sweet potatoes makes them taste even richer and sweeter.

    2   (8-ounce) peeled sweet potatoes
    1   teaspoon olive oil
    ½   teaspoon curry powder
    ¼   teaspoon salt
    ¼   teaspoon ground cumin
    ⅛   teaspoon ground cloves
    ⅛   teaspoon pepper

1. Preheat oven to 425°.
2. Cut sweet potatoes in half lengthwise; cut each half lengthwise into 6 wedges. Combine sweet potatoes and remaining ingredients in a bowl; toss gently to coat. Place wedges on a baking sheet (do not overlap); bake at 425° for 25 minutes or until very tender. Yield: 4 servings (serving size: 6 wedges).

CALORIES 101 (13% from fat); FAT 1.5g (sat 0.2g, mono 0.9g, poly 0.2g); PROTEIN 1.5g; CARB 20.9g; FIBER 2.7g; CHOL 0mg; IRON 0.7mg; SODIUM 158mg; CALC 22mg

Really Great Roasted Vegetables
Test Kitchen SECRET

To get the very best results when you roast vegetables, here are a few things to keep in mind.

- Cut vegetables into uniform-size pieces so they will cook evenly.
- Spread the pieces of food out in a single layer in the roasting pan. If they are piled up on the pan, not all of the pieces will get roasted.
- Stir several times while the vegetables are roasting so that all sides can get evenly browned.
- Use very high heat (no lower than 400°) to get the best flavor.

Roasted Bell Peppers

Red, yellow, and orange bell peppers are virtually identical in flavor and are interchangeable. Green peppers aren't as sweet, so keep this in mind when making substitutions.

4   large bell peppers (about 2 pounds)

1. Preheat broiler.

2. Cut bell peppers in half lengthwise; discard seeds and membranes. Place pepper halves, skin sides up, on a foil-lined baking sheet; flatten with hand. Broil 20 minutes or until thoroughly blackened.

3. Immediately place peppers in a large zip-top plastic bag; seal. Let stand 20 minutes. Peel peppers; discard skins. Yield: 4 servings (serving size: 1 pepper).

CALORIES 44 (6% from fat); FAT 0.3g (sat 0.1g, mono 0g, poly 0.2g); PROTEIN 1.5g; CARB 10.6g; FIBER 3.1g; CHOL 0mg; IRON 0.8mg; SODIUM 3.3mg; CALC 15mg

Pointers for Roasted Peppers

The key step in roasting bell peppers is to seal them in a bag immediately after taking them out of the oven. The steam produced in the bag makes the skins slide off easily.

If you are roasting 1 large or 2 small bell peppers, steam the peppers in the foil you used to line the baking sheet. Larger amounts need to be transferred to large zip-top plastic bags.

One large roasted bell pepper will yield about 1/2 cup when chopped. A typical baking sheet will hold 8 flattened large bell pepper halves.

Roasted peppers can be refrigerated in a covered bowl for up to 5 days. Before using, drain any liquid, and blot peppers with paper towels.

Roasting the Right Way

Whether you're roasting meats, poultry, or vegetables, here's what you need to get great results each time.

Be sure your oven is clean. Small bits of debris on oven walls or doors can begin to smoke at high temperatures. Even with modern ovens, you may need to use an exhaust fan or open a window. If your smoke detector is extremely sensitive, you may want to turn it off before roasting.

Use the correct pan. The pan should be large enough to hold food in a single layer. The sides of the pan should be no higher than 2 to 3 inches so that steam is not retained.

Position oven racks correctly. If the food is placed near the bottom of the oven, it's more like sautéing. If the food is placed very close to the top of the oven, it's more like broiling. For roasting, the food should be in the middle of the oven.

Roast at a high temperature. Not only does it reduce the overall cooking time, it also intensifies the flavors of the food without adding fat, giving food a crispy exterior but tender interior.

Steaming

The beauty of steaming foods is that it's so simple and so low in fat.

Whether you're steaming in a stainless-steel or bamboo steamer or in the microwave oven, steaming is an easy low-fat cooking method because you don't need to add any fat to prevent food from sticking and burning. To steam, you insert a steamer basket into a saucepan or stockpot containing steaming water, then you cover the pan with a lid. The food does not touch the water, but the steam is trapped in the pan and cooks the food.

Steaming Success

Make sure you don't overcook anything. The water has to be boiling before you set steamer racks over it. Think of it as preheating an oven.

If you don't have a wok—although they're so handy you might want to get one—you can use almost any kind of pot or pan that accommodates your steamer. It should keep food out of the water but not prevent the steam from rising up through the food. Inexpensive metal rings that fit in the bottoms of larger pots to keep steamers above the water are sold in cookware shops.

You should usually set something—aluminum foil, parchment paper, banana leaves (a traditional method), cabbage leaves, or a heatproof dish—in the bottom of the steamer rack to hold the food. Not only does this make cleanup easier, but it's also a good way to keep any juices released during cooking. You can use these juices to make a sauce.

Steaming Equipment
Cooking Light Recommends

- If you're using a steamer basket, there are many different kinds: Some pasta pots have a deep, perforated steamer basket that can steam almost anything. The basket holds a lot of food, but that doesn't leave much room for water, so this type of basket is best for foods that cook in less than 30 minutes.
- Shallow steamer baskets hold less food, but there's room for more water in the saucepan. Foldable stainless-steel baskets are inexpensive and can fit into any size saucepan. Other options include stacked oval metal steamers and bamboo steamers. (See next page for more information on bamboo steamers.)
- You can also steam food in a foil packet or *"en papillote,"* (in parchment paper). Cooking in a pressure cooker is also a way to cook with steam—in this case, pressurized steam, which speeds up the steaming process considerably. (See page 84 for more information on pressure cookers.)

Stainless-steel steamer basket

Bamboo Steamer

Bamboo steamers—two or three 10- to 12-inch thatched, stackable trays, plus a lid to hold in the steam—are sold in Asian markets and in many mainstream cookware shops. They're inexpensive and also simple to use. Just line each rack of the steamer with parchment paper, put ingredients on the paper, cover with lid, and place the trays over a container filled with boiling water. The steam rises up through the holes in the bottom of the trays, cooking the food. The lid holds in the steam.

Woks are the traditional basin, but you can use any pot big enough to hold the deep-bowled steamer above the water. The final bamboo bonus: You can serve the food directly from the baskets—no interim bowls required. For cleanup, just discard the parchment paper, and wipe the bamboo with a damp cloth.

The Health Benefits of Steaming

Test Kitchen SECRET

Because the food is not immersed in the liquid, steaming is one of the best ways to preserve vitamins B and C (water-soluble vitamins) in foods. Recent studies have also shown that steaming is the best way to preserve flavonoids (compounds that may help fight against disease) in foods.

Steamed Chicken with Black Bean Salsa

Using a bamboo steamer for chicken helps keep it tender and moist and infuses it with the flavor of the other ingredients.

- 4 (6-ounce) skinned, boned chicken breast halves
- 2 garlic cloves, minced
- 1 cup thinly sliced onion
- 1 cup chopped tomato
- 2 tablespoons red wine vinegar
- 1 tablespoon fresh lime juice
- 1 tablespoon olive oil
- 1 teaspoon chopped fresh cilantro
- ½ teaspoon freshly ground black pepper
- ¼ teaspoon salt
- 1 (15-ounce) can black beans, rinsed and drained
- 1 jalapeño pepper, seeded and minced

1. Cut 2 pieces of parchment paper to fit into each rack of a bamboo steamer. Rub chicken with garlic; arrange in steamer. Top chicken with onion, and cover with steamer lid. Add water to a wok to a depth of 1 inch, and bring to a boil. Place steamer basket in wok; steam chicken 20 minutes or until chicken is done. Cut chicken into slices.

2. While the chicken cooks, combine remaining ingredients in a bowl. Divide onion evenly among 4 plates; top with chicken. Serve with salsa. Yield: 4 servings (serving size: 1 chicken breast half, ¼ cup onion, and 1 cup salsa).

CALORIES 277 (19% from fat); FAT 5.8g (sat 1.1g, mono 3.2g, poly 0.9g); PROTEIN 42.5g; CARB 14.1g; FIBER 3.9g; CHOL 99mg; IRON 2.4mg; SODIUM 449mg; CALC 53mg

> "Use a bamboo steamer for the fastest, simplest, and best meal this side of Asia." Ann Pittman, Food Editor

Pressure Cookers

Pressure cookers save you time by cooking foods at above-boiling-point temperatures, usually from 212° to 250°. And the heat stays in the pot, not in your kitchen. Both types of cookers—the traditional jiggle-top from manufacturers such as Presto and the spring-valve from leaders such as Kuhn Rikon, Magefesa, and Fagor—are safe, but they vary in design, operation, and cost. (See the chart below for a comparison.)

The models with a spring-release valve are more expensive but are quieter and quicker to decompress. Both kinds of pressure cookers cook just the same inside where superheated steam seals in nutrients. Both types require very little fat and can put a meal on the table in a half hour.

"We use jiggle-top and spring-valve pressure cookers in our Test Kitchens and like both types equally well. It's really a matter of which one you get used to using."
Vanessa Johnson, Test Kitchens Director

Types of Pressure Cookers

	Jiggle-Top	Spring-Valve
Sound	Noisy	Little or no hissing
Material	Aluminum	Stainless steel with triple-ply bottom
Weight	Light	Heavy
Operation	Must be placed under cold running water for quick release of pressure	Quick pressure-release mechanism can be used on stovetop
Cost	About $50 to $70	About $140

Here are some tips from the *Cooking Light* Test Kitchens on using pressure cookers.

• We tested all of the recipes in a 6-quart pressure cooker, using a variety of brands—from expensive models to less costly ones. We found no significant difference in performance among brands.

• We prefer the cold-water method for releasing pressure: Run cold water over the lid of the pot until all pressure has been released. This method discharges less steam into your kitchen.

• Don't fill your pressure cooker more than half full with food or two-thirds full with liquid (as when making soup) because foods cooked under pressure have a tendency to increase in volume. Most pressure cookers have a two-thirds indicator inside the pot.

• Reduce the presoaking time for dried beans to 1 or 2 minutes when you use a pressure cooker. With traditional stovetop cooking, beans are soaked in cool water overnight or cooked in boiling water for a couple of minutes before soaking for an hour.

• Don't salt beans before cooking—doing so will keep the beans tough.

• Season with herbs just before serving because herbs don't hold up well under pressure cooking.

Lemon-Basil Risotto with Tomato

Cook risotto in just 15 minutes with minimal stirring.

1½ cups chopped seeded tomato
2   tablespoons chopped green onions
1½ teaspoons extra-virgin olive oil
1   teaspoon balsamic vinegar
¼   teaspoon crushed red pepper
Dash of sugar
Dash of salt
Dash of freshly ground black pepper
2   tablespoons butter
1   cup chopped onion
1½ cups Arborio rice
2   garlic cloves, minced
½   cup dry white wine
4   cups fat-free, less-sodium chicken broth
½   teaspoon salt
¼   teaspoon freshly ground black pepper
⅛   teaspoon ground nutmeg
1   cup (4 ounces) grated fresh Parmesan cheese
1   teaspoon grated lemon rind
3   tablespoons fresh lemon juice
⅓   cup finely chopped fresh basil

1. Combine first 8 ingredients. Cover and let stand at room temperature.

2. Melt butter in a 6-quart pressure cooker over medium heat. Add 1 cup onion; cook 2 minutes, stirring frequently. Add rice and garlic; cook 2 minutes, stirring constantly. Add wine; cook 1 minute or until liquid is absorbed, stirring frequently. Stir in broth and next 3 ingredients. Close lid securely, and bring to high pressure over high heat. Adjust heat to medium or level needed to maintain high pressure; cook 6 minutes. Remove from heat; place cooker under cold running water. Remove lid. Stir in cheese, rind, juice, and basil. Top with tomato topping. Yield: 6 servings (serving size: 1 cup risotto and ¼ cup topping).

CALORIES 368 (24% from fat); FAT 10g (sat 5.7g, mono 3.4g, poly 0.4g); PROTEIN 13.7g; CARB 52.6g; FIBER 2.3g; CHOL 23mg; IRON 1mg; SODIUM 869mg; CALC 262mg

White Bean, Basil, and Tomato Soup

When you cook dried beans in a pressure cooker, they're tender in less than half the time it takes with regular stovetop cooking.

2   cups dried Great Northern beans (about 1 pound)
Cooking spray
1   cup chopped onion
6   garlic cloves, chopped
1   cup diced peeled baking potato
2   teaspoons chopped fresh or ½ teaspoon dried thyme
3   (14-ounce) cans fat-free, less-sodium chicken broth
2   bay leaves
2   cups diced seeded tomato
¼   cup chopped fresh basil
1   tablespoon lemon juice
¾   teaspoon salt
¼   to ½ teaspoon crushed red pepper
¼   cup (1 ounce) grated fresh Parmesan cheese

1. Sort and wash beans; set aside. Place a 6-quart pressure cooker coated with cooking spray over medium heat until hot. Add onion, and sauté 2 minutes. Add garlic; sauté 1 minute. Add beans, potato, thyme, broth, and bay leaves. Close lid securely; bring to high pressure over high heat (about 7 minutes). Adjust heat to medium or level needed to maintain high pressure; cook 35 minutes. Remove from heat; place pressure cooker under cold running water. Remove lid. Discard bay leaves.

2. Partially mash bean mixture. Stir in tomato and next 4 ingredients. Cook, uncovered, over medium heat 5 minutes or until thoroughly heated, stirring frequently. Sprinkle with cheese. Yield: 10 servings (serving size: 1 cup).

CALORIES 183 (7% from fat); FAT 1.4g (sat 0.6g, mono 0.3g, poly 0.3g); PROTEIN 11.8g; CARB 30.5g; FIBER 15.7g; CHOL 4mg; IRON 2.4mg; SODIUM 327mg; CALC 119mg

Stir-frying

This low-fat technique works well with a variety of foods.

Asian Vegetable Stir-fry

This is a particularly light vegetarian stir-fry dish. To make it heartier, add tofu or chicken.

    2   tablespoons tomato paste
    1   tablespoon rice vinegar
    1   tablespoon low-sodium soy sauce
    1   teaspoon curry powder
    ½   teaspoon salt
    ⅛   teaspoon black pepper
    2   tablespoons vegetable oil
    1   sweet onion, cut into 8 wedges
    1   zucchini, quartered lengthwise and cut
            into 1-inch-thick slices
    1   yellow squash, quartered lengthwise
            and cut into 1-inch-thick slices
    1   cup chopped celery
    2   cups sliced green bell pepper
    ½   cup water
    ¼   cup drained, sliced water chestnuts
    2   cups thinly sliced napa (Chinese) cabbage
    1   tablespoon pine nuts

1. Combine first 6 ingredients in a small bowl.
2. Heat oil in a stir-fry pan or wok over medium heat. Add onion; stir-fry 1 minute. Increase heat to medium-high. Add zucchini, yellow squash, and celery; stir-fry 5 minutes. Add bell pepper, water, and water chestnuts; stir-fry 3 minutes.
3. Add tomato paste mixture; bring to a boil, and cook 1 minute. Stir in cabbage and pine nuts. Yield: 6 servings (serving size: 1 cup).

CALORIES 102 (57% from fat); FAT 6.5g (sat 1.1g, mono 2.7g, poly 2.3g); PROTEIN 2.5g; CARB 10.8g; FIBER 3.1g; CHOL 0mg; IRON 1.6mg; SODIUM 303mg; CALC 56mg

Shrimp and Broccoli in Chili Sauce

Chili sauce comes in a 12-ounce bottle, and is usually next to the ketchup in the supermarket.

1½	pounds medium shrimp, peeled and deveined
2	tablespoons minced seeded jalapeño pepper (about 2 peppers)
2	tablespoons dry sherry
1½	teaspoons paprika
½	teaspoon ground red pepper
4	garlic cloves, crushed
⅓	cup water
¼	cup chili sauce
2	teaspoons cornstarch
2	teaspoons sugar
½	teaspoon salt
1	tablespoon vegetable oil
3	cups broccoli florets
4	cups cooked soba (about 8 ounces uncooked buckwheat noodles) or vermicelli

1. Combine first 6 ingredients in a medium bowl; cover and chill 1 hour.

2. Combine water and next 4 ingredients in a small bowl; set aside.

3. Heat oil in a stir-fry pan or wok over medium-high heat. Add broccoli; stir-fry 2 minutes. Add shrimp mixture; stir-fry 5 minutes or until shrimp are done. Add cornstarch mixture, and bring to a boil. Cook 1 minute or until sauce thickens. Serve over soba noodles. Yield: 4 servings (serving size: about 1 cup stir-fry and 1 cup noodles).

CALORIES 441 (14% from fat); FAT 7g (sat 1.3g, mono 2g, poly 2.6g); PROTEIN 35.7g; CARB 54.2g; FIBER 5.6g; CHOL 194mg; IRON 5.1mg; SODIUM 1219mg; CALC 130mg

You can substitute rice for noodles. To avoid chopping, buy the prechopped broccoli florets in a bag.

Stir-fry Success

Food Editor Ann Pittman shares tips for stir-fry cooking.

Divvy it up: Gather several small bowls in which to organize your ingredients. Place the sauce in one and the diced vegetables in the others. Sure, you'll have to wash them later, but they are small.

Slice it right: Vegetables should be sliced, chopped, or diced in roughly the same size. This ensures they'll cook quickly and evenly. Slice vegetables on the diagonal so more of their surface area comes in contact with the pan. Slice lean cuts of meat thinly across the grain, or cut them into small cubes to marinate. A Chinese chef's knife or cleaver is the most efficient tool for this, but any high-quality chef's knife will do.

Scoop it: You'll need an efficient way to scoop the vegetables off of the cutting board. A flat metal scraper (also called a dough scraper) does a great job.

Stirred, not shaken: For actually stirring and tossing ingredients, a long-handled stir-fry spatula is perfect, but we've also used a long-handled wooden spoon and a heat-resistant rubber spatula. Stir-fry utensils are available in stainless steel and also in wood and heat-resistant nylon, which are safe to use on nonstick cooking surfaces.

Keep It Clean

Keep It SAFE

Take care maintaining your cutting board for food safety's sake. Chop vegetables before meats or seafoods to avoid contamination, and hand-wash your cutting board after each use with mild soap and warm water. Rinse and dry the board immediately, treating wooden ones with a food-safe oil. Periodically sponge the board with cold water and mild household bleach, rinsing and drying it thoroughly.

How to Stir-fry

1. Prepare all your ingredients in advance. This is helpful due to the frenzied pace of stir-frying. *Start with the sauce, even though it's added at the very end.* Combine the chicken broth, oyster sauce, cornstarch, honey, and other ingredients in a small bowl with a whisk. Set aside.

2. Chop all the vegetables, and arrange in separate bowls or small piles so that they're ready to be scooped up and tossed into the pan. *Chopping them ahead also allows them some time to dry out, which is good because lots of moisture will make the vegetables steam or braise rather than stir-fry.*

3. Heat the oil in a stir-fry pan or wok over medium-high heat for 2 minutes. *You want the oil very hot so the vegetables will cook quickly.* Add the onions, and stir-fry 1 minute. Add the remaining vegetables, stir-frying 2 minutes for each. Remove the vegetables from the skillet. Keep warm.

4. Add the sauce, vegetables, pineapple, cashews, and crushed red pepper to the pan after you've stir-fried the chicken. Then bring mixture to a boil. *Sauces thickened with cornstarch must be brought to a boil for the cornstarch to activate and not taste starchy.* Cook 1 minute or until thick.

Chicken-Cashew Stir-fry

This sweet-and-sour stir-fry is a basic recipe for which you can vary the ingredients as you like.

½ cup fat-free, less-sodium chicken broth
3 tablespoons oyster sauce (such as KA-ME)
1½ tablespoons cornstarch
1½ tablespoons honey
1 tablespoon low-sodium soy sauce
2 teaspoons rice or white wine vinegar
½ teaspoon salt
2 tablespoons vegetable oil, divided
1 cup chopped green onions, divided
1 small onion, cut into 8 wedges
1 cup julienne-cut red bell pepper
½ cup diagonally sliced carrot
1 cup sliced mushrooms
1 cup snow peas
1 pound skinned, boned chicken thighs, cut into bite-size pieces
¼ cup canned pineapple chunks in juice, drained
⅓ cup cashews
½ to 1 teaspoon crushed red pepper
6 cups hot cooked long-grain rice

1. Combine first 7 ingredients in a small bowl.
2. Heat 1 tablespoon oil in a stir-fry pan or wok over medium-high heat. Add ½ cup green onions and onion wedges; stir-fry 1 minute. Add bell pepper and carrot; stir-fry 2 minutes. Add mushrooms and peas; stir-fry 2 minutes. Remove vegetable mixture from pan. Keep warm.
3. Heat 1 tablespoon oil in pan over medium-high heat. Add chicken; stir-fry 5 minutes. Add broth mixture, vegetable mixture, pineapple, cashews, and crushed red pepper; bring to a boil, and cook 1 minute or until thick. Stir in ½ cup green onions. Serve with rice. Yield: 6 servings (serving size: 1⅓ cups stir-fry and 1 cup rice).

CALORIES 474 (22% from fat); FAT 11.8g (sat 2.4g, mono 4.5g, poly 3.8g); PROTEIN 22.5g; CARB 68.5g; FIBER 3.8g; CHOL 60mg; IRON 4.3mg; SODIUM 553mg; CALC 67mg

Pad Thai

This is Thailand's most well-known stir-fry noodle dish.

6¾ cups water, divided
½ pound uncooked rice sticks or vermicelli
2 tablespoons vegetable oil, divided
¼ cup low-sodium soy sauce
¼ cup Thai fish sauce
2 tablespoons brown sugar
2 large eggs, lightly beaten
¾ pound skinless, boneless chicken breasts, cut into 1-inch strips
2 garlic cloves, minced
½ pound medium shrimp, peeled and deveined
½ cup (1-inch) sliced green onions
2 teaspoons paprika
2 cups fresh bean sprouts
½ cup chopped fresh cilantro
2 tablespoons chopped peanuts
6 lime wedges

1. Place 6 cups water in a stir-fry pan or wok; bring to a boil. Add noodles; cook 4 minutes. Drain. Rinse with cold water; drain well. Place noodles in a bowl. Add 1 teaspoon oil; toss well.
2. Combine ¾ cup water, soy sauce, fish sauce, and brown sugar; set aside. Heat 1 teaspoon oil in a stir-fry pan over medium heat. Add eggs; stir-fry 1 minute. Add eggs to noodle mixture. Heat 1 teaspoon oil in pan over medium-high heat. Add chicken and garlic; stir-fry 5 minutes. Add to noodle mixture. Heat 1 tablespoon oil in pan. Add shrimp, onions, and paprika; stir-fry 3 minutes. Add soy sauce mixture and noodle mixture to pan; cook 3 minutes or until thoroughly heated. Remove from heat; toss with sprouts and cilantro. Sprinkle with peanuts. Serve with lime wedges. Yield: 6 servings (serving size: 1 cup noodle mixture and 1 lime wedge).

CALORIES 347 (24% from fat); FAT 9.3g (sat 1.4g, mono 4.3g, poly 2.5g); PROTEIN 24.5g; CARB 41.6g; FIBER 1.2g; CHOL 150mg; IRON 2.6mg; SODIUM 1,364mg; CALC 57mg

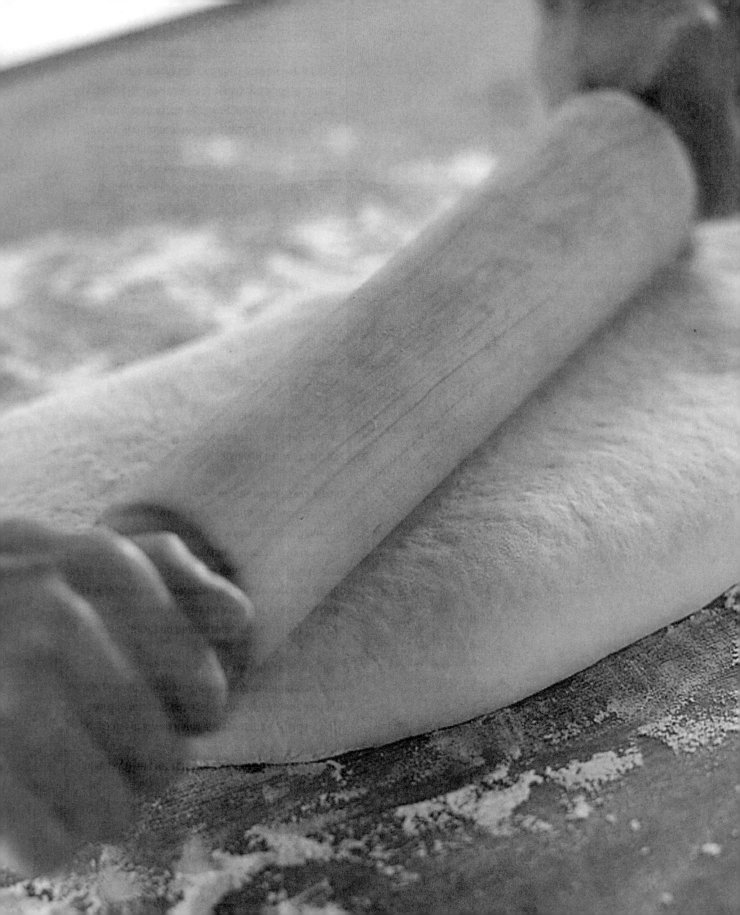

CHAPTER 3

Baking Basics

Whether you're making a loaf of bread, a batch of cookies, a pie, or a layer cake, the key to light baking success is decreasing the fat or sugar without compromising flavor or texture. Here are our basic techniques and key ingredient tips for baking the *Cooking Light* way.

What does sugar do in baked goods?

Sugar can replace some of the fat and act as a tenderizer in the recipe. When there is more than 2 tablespoons of sugar per cup of flour in a recipe, sugar offers a tenderizing effect by preventing all of the flour proteins from joining together to create a tough structure.

Sugar also caramelizes in baking, which enriches flavors. Some sugars, like honey and brown sugar, absorb moisture from the atmosphere, which means that products baked with them will stay soft and moist longer.

Why does *Cooking Light* use sugar instead of sugar substitutes?

Sugar is a key ingredient in baking, providing structure and mass. Consider a cake: If you substitute an artificial sweetener for sugar, you lose some of the volume that sugar contributes, and the cake batter might not have enough structure to become a cake. Also, the tastes and textures of some sugar substitutes can change when they're heated.

Sugar substitutes simply don't work as well as real sugar—they alter the taste and texture of baked goods. Also, sugar substitutes don't tenderize like sugar does.

How can you lighten a cookie?

Of all the desserts, cookies are the hardest for us to lighten. Because we use less butter, our cookies generally err on the chewy, fudgy side rather than the crisp side. **However, small amounts of yogurt, applesauce, or egg whites can help give lower-fat cookies the texture of high-fat ones.**

Why does butter make cookies crisp?

Cookies made with butter spread during baking, which means they're thinner. **Trimming the amount of fat just a little will limit the spreading.** If you want a puffy cookie that stays soft, use shortening to limit the spread in baking.

Crisp Cookies — Test Kitchen SECRET

If you want to reduce the amount of butter but preserve the crispness in cookies, add a little corn syrup to the dough. Substituting as little as a tablespoon of corn syrup for sugar can make cookies much browner because corn syrup browns at a lower temperature than sugar.

Why is butter necessary in cakes?

Butter makes cakes light and delicate by holding air bubbles produced by leaveners like baking powder or soda. It also makes cakes tender by coating the flour protein, and it carries the rich flavors of other ingredients.

You can substitute margarine and shortening for butter, but you'll lose a little of the rich butter flavor. Since shortening is already aerated before you buy it, it can produce a fine, tender cake. However, a whipped margarine spread or low-fat margarine is not a good substitute for butter in baking because the whipped products have added water, which does not contribute to tenderness. (For more information on butter, see pages 123 and 367.)

Low-Fat Margarine	Test Kitchen SECRET

In most cases, a low-fat margarine is not a good substitute for real butter. The baked good will not be as tender, and it will taste different.

Why doesn't *Cooking Light* use applesauce or fruit puree to replace fat?

We don't normally replace all of the fat in baked goods with applesauce or fruit purees because it generally doesn't work. In our opinion, baked products made with fruit purees have an inferior texture and taste. **We get far better results by simply reducing the fat.** However, there are a few recipes in which the use of applesauce to replace part of the fat works quite well—see the tips for using applesauce in baking on page 149.

Why are eggs necessary in cakes?

Eggs have two parts, whites and yolks, which do two different things. Whites are a drying and leavening agent; yolks contribute to a creamy texture. When yolks are added to the recipe, the yolk protein coats the droplets of whatever fat is in the recipe, thus keeping the fat dispersed throughout the liquid mixture (emulsification). Keeping the fat spread throughout a dough or a batter is crucial to the tenderness of a product. (See page 242 for more information on eggs.)

Why can't you replace all the eggs in baking with egg substitute?

Egg substitutes are usually composed of egg whites and oil, along with coloring agents and stabilizers. Because they don't have yolks, they can't serve as emulsifiers; it's the lecithin in the yolks that helps make an emulsion.

No Substitute?	Test Kitchen SECRET

Instead of substituting egg substitute for all of the eggs, we often opt for using fewer yolks and more whites rather than an equal amount of egg substitute simply because most people usually have eggs in the fridge, but not necessarily egg substitute.

What difference does the way you measure flour make?

The way you measure flour can make a terrific difference—as much as an ounce per cup of flour! When fat is reduced in baking, the precise measurement of flour becomes crucial. When a reader has a problem with one of our recipes, one of the first things we ask is how the flour was measured. If the flour was scooped out of the canister with the measuring cup, it's likely that too much flour was used.

Correct measuring of flour is so important to the success of the recipe that we include the method in every recipe that calls for cup measures of flour.

What's the most accurate way to measure liquid ingredients?

Always use liquid measuring cups for liquids because dry measures and liquid measures are not exactly the same. If you measure liquid ingredients in a dry measuring  cup, you might be adding too much liquid.

After you pour in the liquid, check the amount at eye level. Or use the new liquid measuring cups with an angled surface (such as the ones from OXO Good Grips) that allow you to look down into the cup and read the measurement correctly.

How to Measure Flour

1. Fluff the flour with fork, then spoon flour into a dry measuring cup without compacting it. (Don't scoop the flour out of the canister with the measuring cup because you can get up to 3$\frac{1}{2}$ tablespoons per cup [1 ounce] too much flour that way.)
2. Level the top of the flour with a straight edge to get an even cup.

What pans do I really need for light baking?

Here's a guide to the baking pans we use most often in our kitchens.

Baking Sheet Also called a cookie sheet, a baking sheet is a flat pan with a low rim on one or two ends, or rims on all four sides with open corners for air circulation. It's designed for sliding cookies onto a wire rack. You can buy baking sheets with nonstick surfaces or insulated sheets. Insulated sheets bake cookies a little slower than the nonstick pans.

Jelly-Roll Pan A jelly-roll pan is a 15 x 10-inch pan that's used to make thin cakes, such as sponge cakes and jelly-rolls. It's sometimes called a sheet pan, and has a rim on all four sides and closed corners. Jelly-roll pans come with both shiny and dark finishes and may have nonstick surfaces.

Bundt Pan This pan has a central tube, fluted sides, a fixed bottom, and no feet. It can be used for pound cakes instead of a tube pan. Be sure to coat the pan well with cooking spray and coat with flour, making sure that the crevices are coated, so the cake won't stick. If you are using a nonstick bundt pan with a dark interior (such as the one pictured at right), you need to reduce the baking temperature by 25°.

Tube Pan The 10-inch tube pan, also called an angel food cake pan, is a classic tall-sided, round cake pan with a tube in the center. Sometimes it has a removable center; sometimes it doesn't. Some types have small metal feet on the top rim so you can turn the pan upside down for cooling. If your pan doesn't have feet, and your recipe tells you to "hang" the cake upside down to cool, as many angel food cake recipes do, you can invert it on a bottle with a long neck.

Baking sheet

Jelly-roll pan

Bundt pan

Tube pan

> "One key ingredient in light baking is using the right pan." Kathryn Conrad, Test Kitchens Staffer

Springform Pan A springform pan is a round, deep pan with tall, removable sides; it's most often used for baking cheesecakes. Springform pans with glass bottoms conduct heat better and decrease baking time, and those with extended edges around the base keep the batter from leaking. **Nine-inch pans are the most popular—if your springform pan isn't the size called for in the recipe, you can use a smaller one, but your cake will be thicker and may need to bake longer.** Conversely, if you use a larger pan than the recipe calls for, your cake will be thinner and may require less baking time.

The Silpat Mat

Made of a flexible fiberglass and silicone weave, the Silpat was first introduced as a professional baker's tool. Now it's being used in home kitchens and is widely available at cookware shops and through specialty catalogs. It comes in several sizes; we tried the standard $11^5/8$ x $16^1/2$-inch version for a 13 x 18-inch baking sheet.

The Verdict: Food stylist Kellie Kelley recommends the Silpat for meringues. "There's no need for parchment. You pipe the meringues on, then pull them off once you're done."

"It's especially good for light baking because there's no need to grease it," adds Test Kitchens staffer Kathryn Conrad.

Just wipe it down and rinse. It requires almost no storage space—we like everything about it!

And when used as a pan liner, the Silpat puts pans that have lost their nonstick surfaces back to good use.

"I baked it up to 500°, put it in the dishwasher, froze it, and rolled it repeatedly," Conrad says. "It's perfect as both a work and baking surface, for candy making, and also great because candy will not stick. There's no scorching, no burning, no worry. The only thing you shouldn't do is cut or crease it."

Check www.demarleusa.com or call 888-353-9726 for pricing and availability information.

Quick Breads

Don't overmix. That's the key to tender and low-fat quick breads.

Muffins, soda breads, biscuits, scones, fruit and vegetable breads, and even some coffeecakes are leavened with baking powder, baking soda, or both. The leavening occurs in the oven while the bread bakes, rather than on your counter while the yeast rises for an hour or two. Most quick breads can be assembled in less than 20 minutes and baked in under an hour. They usually freeze nicely, too.

Quick breads also tend to have more varied flavors. Unlike yeast breads, which develop their wheaty and relatively complex flavors through fermentation, quick breads rely on their good ingredients—butter, nuts, spices, herbs, dried fruit, and sweeteners.

Measuring Ingredients

The ingredient mix in quick breads is carefully balanced—especially the proportion of liquid to dry ingredients. You can get away with adding an extra third-cup of nuts in a quick bread, but add an extra third-cup of milk, and it will alter the outcome dramatically. Likewise, if you decrease the fat in a bread, you will more than likely end up with a tough, dense loaf. So measure your ingredients carefully. It's especially important that you measure the flour correctly (see page 93). **Stirring the flour mixture with a wire whisk evenly distributes the leavening and spices.** Measure liquid ingredients in a liquid measuring cup, not dry measuring cups (see page 93).

Ask the *Cooking Light* Cooks

Is it really that important to spoon flour and not scoop it when you're making a quick bread? It sure is, particularly in lighter recipes. Bread tends to toughen or dry more easily when there's less fat, so it's especially important to ensure you don't add too much flour. And scooping packs flour more tightly.

"In most quick bread recipes, there's no need to sift the dry ingredients. We've found that as long as you stir them well with a fork or a whisk, sifting isn't necessary."

Kathryn Conrad, Test Kitchens Staffer

Cutting in the Fat

When you make biscuits, scones, and soda breads, you need to cut the butter into the dry ingredients. **It's important that the butter is chilled so that it doesn't melt.** Butter is best cut into dry ingre-  dients with a pastry blender, a stainless-steel device that consists of a series of curved rigid wires attached to a handle. Push the wires into the butter-flour mixture, using your fingers to push out clumps that accumulate. The purpose of this procedure is to coat the flour particles with butter until the mixture resembles coarse meal. As the butter melts during baking, the moisture contained in it produces steam, which gives these breads a flaky, tender crumb.

Blending Dry and Liquid Ingredients

For quick breads and muffins, the most common and efficient way to blend the ingredients is to  make a well in the dry ones (flours, spices, leavening, dried fruits, nuts) and add the liquid mixture (milk, oil, eggs, fruit juice, flavorings, extracts) all at once. It's like scooping out a hole in beach sand and filling it with water. The ingredients can all be stirred smoothly, with no more mixing than necessary to blend the batter. This is the best way to maintain tenderness. If you overmix, the flour's gluten will start to develop, which will toughen the final product.

The rule of thumb for quick bread batters is to stir ingredients about ten times.

Baking

Quick breads are usually baked in a preheated oven on the center rack. With experience, you'll learn to read the visual cues that let you know the quick bread is done.

In general, there should be even browning and some resistance to light finger pressure. If your bread feels squishy, it isn't done. **To check quick breads, pierce them in the center with a toothpick, a bamboo skewer, or a long and skinny knife; it should come out clean, with no batter attached.**

Picking the Right Pan
Test Kitchen SECRET

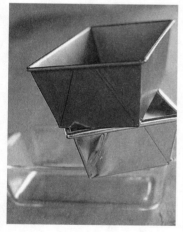

We routinely test quick-bread recipes in shiny metal pans, but glass or dark metal pans are OK, too. Glass conducts heat better, though, so you'd need to decrease your oven temperature by 25° and bake about 10 minutes less than our recipes indicate. When using a dark metal pan, decrease the cooking time by 10 minutes also.

Cooling

Cooling quick breads in the pan on a wire rack for 5 to 10 minutes will make them easier to remove. After removal, transfer the bread to a rack so the it can cool evenly on all sides. **If quick bread is left to cool in the pan completely, the heat from the pan can make the bread sweat and turn the bottom soggy.**

Biscuits

Fat is the main ingredient in biscuits and the thing that gives them flavor and tenderness. We've discovered how to keep the tenderness but get rid of much of the fat.

Types of Biscuits Dropped biscuits and rolled biscuits are the two most common types. To make dropped biscuits, you simply drop the dough by tablespoonfuls onto the baking sheet. They have a higher proportion of liquid to dry ingredients than rolled biscuits, so you have a thick batter instead of a soft dough. Rolled biscuits take a bit more practice because the dough must be lightly kneaded, rolled out, and cut with a biscuit cutter. It's easy to overdo it on the kneading and the rolling, and you end up with tough biscuits.

The Tenderness Factor The butter must be cut into the dry ingredients so the biscuits will be tender. The "cutting" action distributes little lumps of butter throughout the dough that melt during baking and give biscuits their trademark flakiness. When adding the liquid ingredients, stir just until the dry ingredients are moistened. Too much mixing makes the biscuits heavy.

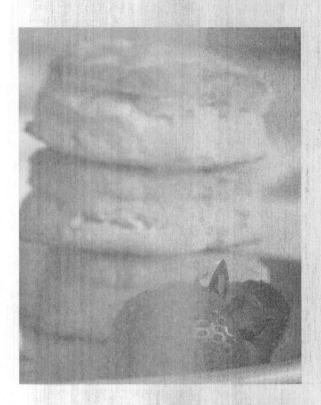

Reduce Fat with Buttermilk

Test Kitchen SECRET

To reduce the fat in biscuits, we've found that you can use less butter than you would use in a traditional biscuit. You can and add some flavor and tenderness by using low-fat buttermilk. The amount of butter in our light biscuit recipes usually ranges from 3 tablespoons to no more than 1/4 cup.

"The secret to getting tender, flaky biscuits and scones is handling the dough as little as possible. Overworking the dough will make them tough."

Krista Montgomery, Food Editor

Buttermilk Biscuits

A good biscuit dough will be slightly sticky to the touch and should be kneaded lightly just a few times.

2 cups all-purpose flour
2 teaspoons baking powder
¼ teaspoon baking soda
¼ teaspoon salt
3 tablespoons plus 1 teaspoon chilled butter, cut into small pieces
¾ cup low-fat or nonfat buttermilk

1. Preheat oven to 450°.
2. Lightly spoon flour into dry measuring cups; level with a knife.
3. Combine flour and next 3 ingredients in a bowl. Cut in butter with a pastry blender or 2 knives until mixture resembles coarse meal. Add buttermilk; stir just until dry ingredients are moist.
4. Turn dough out onto a lightly floured surface; knead lightly 4 or 5 times. Roll dough to a ½-inch thickness; cut with a 2½-inch biscuit cutter. Place on a baking sheet. Bake at 450° for 12 minutes or until golden. Yield: 1 dozen (serving size: 1 biscuit).

CALORIES 102 (23% from fat); FAT 2.6g (sat 1.2g, mono 1g, poly 0.2g); PROTEIN 2.7g; CARB 16.9g; FIBER 0.6g; CHOL 6mg; IRON 1.1mg; SODIUM 189mg; CALC 67mg

If your biscuits aren't rising properly, you might want to check the expiration dates on your baking powder and baking soda. These products start to weaken after 6 months. To check the strength of baking powder, stir 2 teaspoons powder into 1 cup hot water. If there's an immediate fizz, the powder if fine. To check baking soda, stir 1 teaspoon into ¼ cup of vinegar and check for the fizz.

Basic Techniques for Rolled Biscuits

1. Cut in chilled butter with a pastry blender until mixture resembles coarse meal. If you don't have a pastry blender, use 2 knives, pulling them through the butter until mixture resembles coarse meal.

2. Turn dough out onto a floured surface, and knead lightly 4 or 5 times.

3. Roll dough to a ½-inch thickness. Cut with a 2½-inch biscuit cutter.

Scones

Making the dough for scones is the same as in making biscuit dough. The difference is that, for scones, you pat the dough into a round and cut into wedges instead of cutting out individual rounds. **Traditional scone recipes often have both butter and cream; we use less butter, as in biscuits, and we replace the cream with low-fat milk.**

Basic Techniques for Scones

1. Cut in butter until it resembles coarse meal. If you don't have a pastry blender, use 2 knives, or you can pulse it in your food processor.

2. Once you add the milk mixture, turn the dough out onto a floured surface, and knead 4 or 5 times. The dough will be sticky, but don't add more flour.

3. Pat the dough into an 8-inch round. Cut the circle into 10 wedges; do not separate the pieces.

Coffee-Nut Scones

Cut through the circle of dough, but don't separate the wedges. When you bake them as one large scone, they are much moister than if you bake them separately.

⅔	cup 1% low-fat milk
2½	tablespoons instant coffee granules
1	teaspoon vanilla extract
1	large egg, lightly beaten
2¼	cups all-purpose flour
⅓	cup sugar
2½	teaspoons baking powder
¾	teaspoon salt
¼	teaspoon ground cinnamon
¼	cup chilled butter, cut into small pieces
3	tablespoons finely chopped walnuts
	Cooking spray
2	teaspoons 1% low-fat milk
2	teaspoons sugar

1. Combine milk and coffee granules in a microwave-safe bowl. Microwave at HIGH 1 minute; stir until coffee dissolves. Cover and chill completely. Stir in vanilla and egg.
2. Preheat oven to 425°.
3. Spoon flour into dry measuring cups; level with a knife. Combine flour and next 4 ingredients in a bowl; cut in butter with a pastry blender or 2 knives until mixture resembles coarse meal. Stir in walnuts. Add milk mixture, stirring just until moist (dough will be sticky).
4. Turn dough out onto a lightly floured surface; knead 4 times with floured hands. Pat dough into an 8-inch circle on a baking sheet coated with cooking spray. Cut into 10 wedges; do not separate. Brush dough with 2 teaspoons milk; sprinkle with 2 teaspoons sugar. Bake at 425° for 20 minutes or until browned. Serve warm. Yield: 10 servings (serving size: 1 wedge).

CALORIES 207 (30% from fat); FAT 7g (sat 3.3g, mono 1.9g, poly 1.3g); PROTEIN 4.9g; CARB 31g; FIBER 1g; CHOL 35mg; IRON 1.7mg; SODIUM 361mg; CALC 101mg

Loaves and Muffins

The basic method for loaves and muffins is the same—it's the shape of the pan that makes the difference. **Probably the most important thing is not to overstir the batter.**

Dried Plum and Port Bread

This quick bread won our Test Kitchens' highest rating. It's great for dessert, a snack, or for breakfast. Prunes are actually dried plums; we use the latter name in our title because more people find it appealing.

2	cups chopped pitted prunes
1¾	cups port or other sweet red wine
1½	cups all-purpose flour
½	cup whole wheat or all-purpose flour
¾	cup packed brown sugar
2½	teaspoons baking powder
½	teaspoon salt
½	teaspoon ground cinnamon
¼	cup vegetable oil
¼	cup plain low-fat yogurt
2	teaspoons grated lemon rind
1	teaspoon vanilla extract
2	large eggs, lightly beaten

Cooking spray

1	tablespoon turbinado or granulated sugar

1. Combine prunes and port in a small saucepan; bring to a boil. Cover and remove from heat; let stand 30 minutes.

2. Preheat oven to 350°.

3. Lightly spoon flours into dry measuring cups; level with a knife. Combine 1½ cups all-purpose flour and next 5 ingredients in a medium bowl; stir well with a whisk. Make a well in center of mixture. Drain prunes in a colander over a bowl, reserving liquid. Combine reserved liquid, oil, and next 4 ingredients; stir well with a whisk. Stir in prunes. Add to flour mixture, stirring just until moist.

Basic Techniques for Quick Bread Loaves

1. Combine dry ingredients, stirring with a whisk or fork. Make a well in the center, and pour the liquid ingredients into the well.

2. Stir the batter just until moistened. Overmixing at this point can make the bread tough.

3. Spoon mixture into baking pan coated with cooking spray. If desired, sprinkle additional sugar on top to create a crunchy topping.

4. Spoon batter into a 9 x 5-inch loaf pan coated with cooking spray; sprinkle with turbinado sugar. Bake at 350° for 1 hour and 15 minutes or until a wooden pick inserted in center comes out clean. Cool in pan for 10 minutes on a wire rack; remove from pan. Cool completely on a wire rack. Yield: 12 servings (serving size: 1 slice).

CALORIES 254 (21% from fat); FAT 5.9g (sat 1.2g, mono 1.8g, poly 2.5g); PROTEIN 4.5g; CARB 48g; FIBER 3.1g; CHOL 37mg; IRON 2.1mg; SODIUM 222mg; CALC 100mg

Muffin Magic

What is the secret ingredient to great muffins? Light ricotta cheese. Although it's certainly not new, ricotta isn't something typically added to muffins. A more popular way to make low-fat muffins is to replace most or all of the recipe's fat with fruit purees made from apples, apricots, prunes, and the like. But this strategy often makes muffins overly moist—to the point of being gummy and too dense.

When you work ricotta into the muffin mix, the creamy cheese acts as a tenderizer by adding just enough moisture. And because its rich taste is amazingly subtle, it doesn't overwhelm the other flavors.

"When you replace all of the fat in muffins with a fruit puree, the muffins end up being too moist and gummy. If we are adding a fruit puree, we usually just replace a portion of the fat with the puree." Jan Moon, Test Kitchens Staffer

Banana-Spice Muffins

This recipe features our secret muffin ingredient—light ricotta cheese—and is proof that this cheese really does make the muffins tender instead of gummy.

2½	cups all-purpose flour
⅓	cup granulated sugar
⅓	cup packed brown sugar
1	tablespoon baking powder
1	teaspoon baking soda
½	teaspoon salt
1	teaspoon ground allspice
1	teaspoon ground ginger
1	cup mashed ripe banana (about 2 small)
⅔	cup 2% low-fat milk
⅓	cup low-fat buttermilk
⅓	cup light ricotta cheese
2	tablespoons vegetable oil
1	tablespoon vanilla extract
1	large egg white
1	large egg

Cooking spray

1. Preheat oven to 400°.
2. Lightly spoon flour into dry measuring cups; level with a knife. Combine flour and next 7 ingredients in a large bowl, and make a well in center of mixture. Combine banana and next 7 ingredients in a bowl, and add to flour mixture. Stir just until moist. Spoon batter into 18 muffin cups coated with cooking spray.
3. Bake at 400° for 18 minutes or until done. Remove from pans immediately, and cool on a wire rack. Yield: 1½ dozen (serving size: 1 muffin).

CALORIES 125 (17% from fat); FAT 2.4g (sat 0.8g, mono 0.7g, poly 0.9g); PROTEIN 3.2g; CARB 22.6g; FIBER 0.8g; CHOL 13mg; IRON 1mg; SODIUM 194mg; CALC 59mg

Low-Fat Substitutions for Muffins

We tested some additional ingredient substitutions to see how they might affect the texture of the Banana-Spice Muffins (left). Here's what we found:

We tried this ingredient...	Instead of...	the result was...
Fat-free ricotta cheese	light ricotta	muffins were tough
Egg substitute	whole eggs	acceptable, but not nearly as tender as a recipe that uses a combination of whole eggs and egg whites
Applesauce	vegetable oil	not as tender; best when eaten hot
"Mock" buttermilk (lemon juice and milk)	"real" buttermilk	muffins were tough

Blueberry-Almond Streusel Muffins

The streusel topping has a mere 1 tablespoon of butter and is the crowing glory for these sweet and tender muffins.

2½   cups all-purpose flour
1   cup granulated sugar
1   tablespoon baking powder
1   teaspoon baking soda
½   teaspoon salt
¾   cup 2% low-fat milk
½   cup low-fat buttermilk
⅓   cup light ricotta cheese
2   tablespoons vegetable oil
1   tablespoon vanilla extract
1   teaspoon almond extract
3   large egg whites
1⅓   cups blueberries
  Cooking spray
¼   cup all-purpose flour
½   cup finely chopped almonds
1   tablespoon brown sugar
1   tablespoon butter, melted

1. Preheat oven to 400°.
2. Lightly spoon flour into dry measuring cups; level with a knife. Combine flour and next 4 ingredients in a large bowl; make a well in center of mixture. Combine milk and next 6 ingredients; stir well with a whisk. Add to flour mixture, stirring just until moist. Gently stir in blueberries. Spoon batter into 18 muffin cups coated with cooking spray.
3. Combine ¼ cup flour and remaining ingredients; sprinkle evenly over batter. Bake at 400° for 18 minutes or until done. Remove from pans immediately, and cool on a wire rack. Yield: 1½ dozen (serving size: 1 muffin).

CALORIES 173 (23% from fat); FAT 4.4g (sat 1g, mono 2.2g, poly 0.9g); PROTEIN 4.3g; CARB 29.6g; FIBER 1g; CHOL 4mg; IRON 1mg; SODIUM 249mg; CALC 90mg

More Muffin Flavor

Test Kitchen SECRET

Sprinkling with a streusel topping is one way we add additional flavor and texture to our low-fat muffins. Another trick we use to add flavor is to add a couple of teaspoons of vanilla.

Popovers

Although you can make them in muffin cups, popovers are not really quick breads because

they are leavened with steam and eggs instead of baking powder or soda. Popovers are the American cousin of Yorkshire pudding. These miniature "bread balloons" are crusty on the outside and almost hollow on the inside.

Because they are typically flavored with butter, 50 percent of the calories comes from fat in a traditional popover recipe. With a few simple substitutions, we reduced the fat by more than half.

Reducing the Fat We used a 1% low-fat milk instead of whole milk, which saved almost 50 calories and 5.5 grams of fat. We cut the number of eggs in half and decreased the fat by another 5.5 grams. But we got the most significant cut in fat—22.5 grams—from cutting out two-thirds of the butter. These changes more than halved the fat without changing the popovers' shape, golden crust, and flavor.

Processor Popovers

Test Kitchen SECRET

"I use my food processor to combine all of the ingredients for popovers—I think it helps achieve better volume."
Kathleen Kanen, Food Stylist

Perfect Popovers

Test Kitchen SECRET

- Baking popovers in popover pans produces taller, airier results, but you can use a muffin pan with some minor adjustments.
- Muffin pan cups are smaller than popover pan cups, so if you're using muffin pans, the popovers will need 5 minutes less baking time.

Popover pan

- If using a muffin pan instead of a popover pan, divide the batter evenly among 6 heated cups, filling each cup two-thirds full.
- Whichever pan you use, heat it for about 3 minutes before adding the batter—this ensures a higher volume because the batter crawls up the heated cups.
- Use a pastry brush to oil the popover cups or muffin cups before you pour in the batter.
- Popovers should be golden and crispy on the outside and soft on the inside; undercooked ones are pale on the outside and gummy on the inside. Popovers "deflate" quickly, so serve them immediately. When done, the interior of a popover should be somewhat hollow and moist.

> "If you don't have a popover pan, it's not a problem. They really come out just as good in muffin cups."

Vanessa Johnson, Test Kitchens Director

Popovers

These lightened popovers are lower in fat than a traditional popover because we used low-fat milk and decreased the amount of butter.

1   cup all-purpose flour
½   teaspoon salt
1   cup 1% low-fat milk
2   large eggs
1   tablespoon butter, melted
Cooking spray
1   teaspoon vegetable oil

1. Preheat oven to 375°.
2. Lightly spoon flour into a dry measuring cup; level with a knife. Combine flour and salt, stirring with a whisk. Combine milk and eggs in a bowl, stirring with a whisk until blended; let stand 30 minutes. Gradually add flour mixture, stirring well with a whisk. Stir in butter.
3. Coat 9 popover cups with cooking spray; brush oil evenly among cups to coat. Place popover cups in a 375° oven for 5 minutes. Divide the batter evenly among prepared popover cups. Bake at 375° for 40 minutes or until golden. Serve immediately. Yield: 9 servings (serving size: 1 popover).

CALORIES 141 (32% from fat); FAT 5g (sat 2.1g, mono 1.5g, poly 0.8g); PROTEIN 5.6g; CARB 18.1g; FIBER 0.6g; CHOL 78mg; IRON 1.2mg; SODIUM 257mg; CALC 62mg

The popovers puff more when you take some of the chill out of the eggs and milk.

Don't Peek!

Test Kitchen SECRET

Although it's tempting, don't open the oven door to peek at the popovers—use the oven light, and view through the glass to see when they're golden brown.

Popover Possibilities

Once you've mastered basic popovers, why not show your stuff and add some flavor variations? The technique is the same; you just stir a few extras into the batter.

Herbed Popovers

Stir 1 tablespoon of your choice of chopped fresh herbs into the batter. We like dill, basil, oregano, and rosemary. Rosemary is a bit stronger than the other herbs listed here, so you might want to cut back to 2 teaspoons.

Parmesan Popovers

Stir 2 tablespoons of shredded fresh Parmesan cheese into the batter for a bread that's great with soups.

Cinnamon-Sugar Popovers

Stir 2 teaspoons of sugar and ½ teaspoon cinnamon into the batter for a sweet breakfast treat.

Yeast Breads

"We tested recipes using quick-rise yeast and bread-machine yeast and found that they produce similar results to regular yeast." Vanessa Johnson, Test Kitchens Director

Yeast breads without a lot of added fat or sugar are naturally low in fat. To get the perfect light loaf, here are our tips.

Choosing Flour

There isn't much difference between bread made with bread flour or all-purpose flour. Bread flour is a little higher in protein and can, for the most part, be used with all-purpose. **Some of our recipes call for bread flour, but we also like using all-purpose simply because that's what most people have on hand.** Unbleached flour is really a matter of personal preference—it's simply not as white as bleached, but it works the same, and is not, as people often think, any more nutritious.

Proof the Yeast

The first step in making yeast bread is to proof, or activate, the yeast. To proof yeast, dissolve it in a warm liquid, then set it aside for 5 to 10 minutes until it swells and becomes bubbly. The temperature of the liquid is critical—it must be warm enough to activate the yeast, but not so hot that it kills it. **To test the temperature, put your finger in the liquid. If you can't keep it there, the liquid is too hot. Or use an instant-read thermometer; the temperature should be 100° to 110°.**

Yeast might not activate for several reasons: The liquid was too cold and didn't activate the yeast; the liquid was too hot and it killed the yeast; or the yeast was very old and therefore already dead. (There should be a "use by" date on the yeast.)

If the yeast doesn't proof, start over. It's better to waste one package of yeast and water than 4 cups of flour and a lot of time. Sugar is a food source for yeast and is often added to the liquid to jump-start activation.

Picking a Pan The type of pan you use to bake your bread does make a difference in the final product. **We tested all our recipes in shiny metal loaf pans. If you're using a dark metal loaf pan or a glass baking dish, lower the oven temperature by 25°.**

Homemade White Bread

If you are just learning to make homemade bread, start with this basic loaf.

1	package dry yeast (about 2¼ teaspoons)
1	tablespoon sugar
1⅔	cups warm fat-free milk (100° to 110°)
2	tablespoons butter, melted
4¾	cups all-purpose flour, divided
1½	teaspoons salt

Cooking spray

1. Dissolve yeast and sugar in warm milk in a large bowl; let stand 5 minutes. Stir in butter. Lightly spoon flour into dry measuring cups; level with a knife. Add 4¼ cups flour and salt to yeast mixture; stir until blended. Turn dough out onto a floured surface. Knead until smooth and elastic (about 10 minutes); add enough of remaining flour, 1 tablespoon at a time, to prevent dough from sticking to hands (dough will feel tacky).
2. Place dough in a large bowl coated with cooking spray, turning to coat top. Cover and let rise in a warm place (85°), free from drafts, 1 hour or until doubled in size. Punch dough down; let rest 5 minutes. Roll into a 14 x 7-inch rectangle on a floured surface. Roll up tightly, starting with short edge, pressing firmly to eliminate air pockets; pinch seam and ends to seal. Place roll, seam side down, in a 9 x 5-inch loaf pan coated with cooking spray. Cover and let rise 1 hour or until doubled in size.
3. Preheat oven to 350°.
4. Uncover dough. Bake at 350° for 45 minutes or until loaf is browned on the bottom and sounds hollow when tapped. Remove loaf from pan, and cool on a wire rack. Yield: 1 loaf, 16 servings (serving size: 1 slice).

CALORIES 162 (11% from fat); FAT 1.9g (sat 0.4g, mono 0.7g, poly 0.6g); PROTEIN 4.9g; CARB 30.5g; FIBER 1.1g; CHOL 1mg; IRON 1.8mg; SODIUM 219mg; CALC 38mg

---

Rising the Dough

Test Kitchen SECRET

A "warm place" (85°) is best to rise your dough. Basically, you can place the dough anywhere in the house that is warm and free of drafts. We've discovered that our ovens are the perfect place. To warm the oven up a bit, turn it on for about 10 seconds, and then turn it off. Or place a cup of hot water in the oven. That provides about all the warmth that the dough really requires.

If you set your dough in the oven to rise and it has a crust on it after the rising time, your oven was too warm. But proceed with the recipe; it will be fine. It's OK if your dough rises, then begins to fall during the first rising. Just proceed according to the recipe, and the bread still should turn out fine.

You can also rise your dough in a microwave oven. Just make sure that there is enough room above the bowl or pan for the dough to rise. To warm the inside of the microwave, bring 1 cup of water to a boil and remove it from the microwave before placing the dough inside to rise.

When cleaning a bowl that had a flour product in it (such as dough), wash the bowl with cold water, not hot. Hot water will bind the flour and make it harder to wash off.

From Yeast to Oven

1. Proofing the Yeast Making sure that your yeast is alive, a process known as proofing, is the most crucial step in baking bread. If the yeast is dead, it can't leaven your bread. Live yeast will swell and foam (or activate) a few minutes after it's stirred into the warm liquid.

2. Making the Dough To make the initial bread dough, add most of the flour to the liquid ingredients all at once, and stir just until the mixture is combined (be sure to save some of the flour for kneading). Then turn out the dough onto a floured surface, and you're ready to knead.

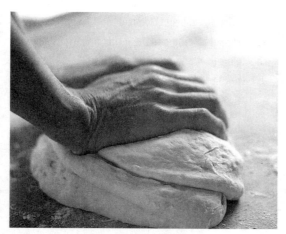

3. Kneading the Dough Here's where the process gets fun. Don't be afraid to knead your dough with authority— just push it out with the heels of your hands, fold the dough over, give it a quarter-turn, and repeat. Don't be alarmed if you don't use all of the remaining flour—in fact, you want to use as little of it as possible. After about 10 minutes of kneading, the dough should be noticeably smooth and elastic but still slightly tacky to the touch.

4. The First Rising Place the dough in a large bowl because the dough will double in size during this rising. For this step, cover the bowl with a slightly damp, light-weight dishtowel to keep the dough from drying and forming a thin crust.

5. The Touch Test To tell when the dough has risen enough, press a finger into it. If an impression remains, it is ready. If the dough springs back, it needs more rising time.

6. Punching Down Punch the dough down to deflate it. Then turn dough out onto a floured surface for rolling.

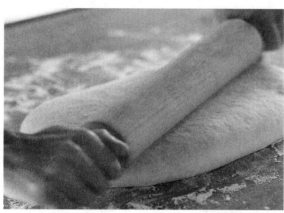

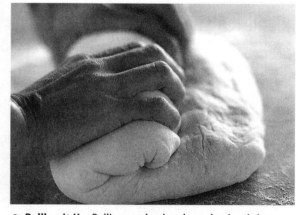

7. Rolling It Out To shape the bread, begin by rolling it out. Lift the rolling pin up slightly as you near each end of the rectangular shape.

8. Rolling It Up Rolling up the dough, or shaping, is just as important as rolling it out. The purpose is to eliminate air bubbles, giving a better crumb—or texture—to the bread. Roll the dough tightly, pressing firmly as you go.

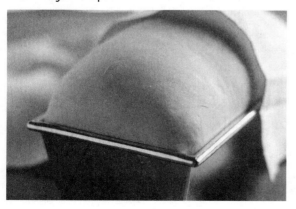

9. Second Rising Once you roll up the dough and place it in a loaf pan, it needs to rise a second time in the pan. Watch carefully. If the dough rises too much and starts to fall, your finished bread will be dense (though still edible). You can avoid this problem—irreversible once it begins—by checking the dough occasionally to make sure it has not begun to deflate. Once it's doubled in size (which will take about 1 hour), the dough is ready to put in the oven and bake.

Rustic Yeast Breads

Making Your Own Rustic Breads

With these easy-to-do recipes, you can make your own European breads at home for only a fraction of what they may cost in a bakery. **Although you can knead the dough for a rustic bread by hand, in these recipes, the doughs are kneaded in a food processor.** With this method, less flour is incorporated into the dough. A wetter dough gives these breads their characteristic texture and bigger holes. Don't worry if the dough is a little sticky—when you stop the food processor and touch the dough, the texture should be similar to that of hot chewing gum.

Making a Sponge

Some rustic bread recipes call for a sponge, also known as a dough starter. It's a small portion of the total bread dough that is made ahead. Our Basic Sponge recipe isn't as time-consuming to make as a full-fledged starter that can take days to ripen. You can go ahead and use the starter after 2 hours, but the longer it sits in the refrigerator, the more flavorful your bread will be. The sponge's appearance won't change all that dramatically—it will simply rise a little and look puffy. Be sure to let the sponge come to room temperature before starting the recipe that calls for it. And again, it's OK if the dough is a little sticky; resist the temptation to add more flour as you would with traditional yeast breads. You need a moist dough to get the characteristic rustic look.

Basic sponge

Basic Sponge

This is the foundation for the both the French Country Bread with Currants and Rosemary and Ciabatta recipes.

- 1 cup bread flour
- 2 teaspoons sugar
- 1 package dry yeast (about 2¼ teaspoons)
- ¾ cup very warm water (120° to 130°)

1. Lightly spoon flour into a dry measuring cup; level with a knife.
2. Place all ingredients in a food processor; process for 1 minute or until well blended. Spoon mixture into a medium bowl; cover and chill for 2 to 24 hours.

French Country Bread with Currants and Rosemary

Whole wheat dough is typical in many rustic breads, giving them their trademark hearty, nutty flavor.

- 1 cup bread flour
- 1 cup whole wheat flour
- Basic Sponge (at room temperature)
- ¾ cup water
- ½ cup rye flour
- ¼ cup regular oats
- 1½ teaspoons salt
- ¼ cup currants
- 2 tablespoons bread flour
- 2 tablespoons dried rosemary
- Cooking spray

1. Lightly spoon 1 cup bread flour and whole wheat flour into dry measuring cups; level with a knife.
2. Combine with sponge and next 4 ingredients in a food processor; process until dough forms a ball. Process 1 additional minute. Turn out onto a lightly floured surface, and knead in currants, 2 tablespoons bread flour, and rosemary. Shape

> "You can get a really nice crust if you use a pizza stone, but a baking sheet works fine, too."
>
> Ann Pittman, Food Editor

into a 9-inch round loaf, and place loaf on a baking sheet coated with cooking spray. Cover and let rise in a warm place (85°), free from drafts, 45 minutes or until doubled in size.

3. Preheat oven to 375°.

4. Uncover loaf, and make a ¼-inch-deep tic-tac-toe slash across top of loaf using a sharp knife. Bake at 375° for 40 minutes or until loaf sounds hollow when tapped. Remove from pan, and cool on a wire rack. Yield: 16 servings (serving size: 1 slice).

CALORIES 115 (5% from fat); FAT 0.7g (sat 0.1g, mono 0.1g, poly 0.2g); PROTEIN 4g; CARB 23.4g; FIBER 1.9g; CHOL 0mg; IRON 1.5mg; SODIUM 221mg; CALC 13mg

Ciabatta

Ciabatta is Italian for "slipper." This bread is so named because the ends of the dough are tapered into a slipperlike shape.

    4   cups bread flour
    Basic Sponge (at room temperature)
    1¼   cups warm water (100° to 110°)
    2   teaspoons nonfat dry milk
    1   package dry yeast (about 2¼ teaspoons)
    1   teaspoon salt
    2   tablespoons cornmeal
    2   tablespoons bread flour

1. Lightly spoon 4 cups flour into dry measuring cups; level with a knife. Combine with sponge and next 4 ingredients in a food processor; process until dough forms a ball. Process 1 minute.

2. Turn dough out onto a floured surface (dough will be sticky and soft); divide dough in half. Working with 1 portion at a time (cover the remaining dough to keep from drying), roll each portion into a 12 x 6-inch rectangle. Place dough on a parchment paper-lined baking sheet sprinkled with cornmeal. Taper ends of dough to form a "slipper" shape. Sprinkle 2 tablespoons flour over loaves. Cover and let rise 30 minutes or until doubled in size.

3. Preheat oven to 425°.

4. Uncover; bake at 425° for 25 minutes or until loaves sound hollow when tapped. Remove from pan; cool on a wire rack. Yield: 2 loaves, 24 servings (serving size: 1 slice).

CALORIES 112 (4% from fat); FAT 0.5g (sat 0.1g, mono 0.1g, poly 0.2g); PROTEIN 3.8g; CARB 22.4g; FIBER 0.2g; CHOL 0mg; IRON 1.4mg; SODIUM 99mg; CALC 7mg

Shaping Ciabatta

Test Kitchen SECRET

Place the dough on a baking sheet lined with parchment paper (below), taper the ends, and let it rise. Then slide the dough, still on the parchment paper, directly onto a pizza stone or leave it on the baking sheet to bake.

Classic French Bread

This rustic yeast bread does not start with a starter dough such as the Basic Sponge.

- 1 package dry yeast (about 2¼ teaspoons)
- 1 cup warm water (100° to 110°)
- 3 cups bread flour
- 1 teaspoon salt
- Cooking spray
- 1 tablespoon water
- 1 large egg white

1. Dissolve yeast in 1 cup warm water in a small bowl; let stand 5 minutes.

2. Lightly spoon flour into dry measuring cups; level with a knife. Place flour and salt in a food processor, and pulse 2 times or until blended. With food processor on, slowly add yeast mixture through food chute, and process until dough forms a ball. Process for 1 additional minute. Turn dough out onto a lightly floured surface, and knead lightly 4 or 5 times.

3. Place dough in a large bowl coated with cooking spray, turning to coat top. Cover and let rise in a warm place (85°), free from drafts, 45 minutes or until doubled in size.

4. Punch dough down, and shape into a 6-inch round loaf. Place loaf on a baking sheet coated with cooking spray. Cover dough and let rise 30 minutes or until doubled in size.

5. Preheat oven to 450°.

6. Uncover dough, and make 3 (¼-inch-deep) diagonal cuts across top of loaf using a sharp knife. Combine 1 tablespoon water and egg white, and brush mixture over top of loaf. Bake at 450° for 20 minutes or until loaf sounds hollow when tapped. Yield: 12 servings (serving size: 1 slice).

CALORIES 127 (5% from fat); FAT 0.7g (sat 0.1g, mono 0.1g, poly 0.3g); PROTEIN 4.6g; CARB 25.1g; FIBER 0.2g; CHOL 0mg; IRON 1.6mg; SODIUM 200mg; CALC 6mg

---

How to Get the Crustiest Crust

Test Kitchen SECRET

- The crunchiest crusts are formed by creating steam in the oven. Use an inexpensive plastic bottle such as a plant sprayer, and spritz inside the oven several times during baking. (Be careful not to spray water directly on the oven light.)
- A pizza stone placed on the lower shelf of the oven is about as close as you can get to baking thick-crusted loaves like bakers have been doing for centuries. Preheat the pizza stone on the lower shelf of the oven.

A baguette is a long, thin cylinder-shaped loaf of bread. To make a baguette, let the bread dough rise once. Punch dough down, and roll into an 18 x 9-inch rectangle on a lightly floured surface. Roll up the dough starting at the longer edge, pressing down firmly to eliminate any air pockets; then pinch seam and edges to seal. Cover the dough, let rise, and bake according to the recipe instructions above.

For slicing bread, an electric knife yields the best results. If you don't have one, a serrated knife will do. Or you can buy a bread-slicing stand, available at department and variety stores.

Potato Fougasse

A fougasse (FOO-gass) is a French bread shaped by slashing the dough and stretching it to resemble a ladder or tree-of-life design. This dough is made with a mixer instead of a food processor.

2	cups cubed peeled Yukon gold potato
1	package dry yeast (about 2¼ teaspoons)
1	teaspoon brown sugar
½	cup warm water (100° to 110°)
6	cups all-purpose flour, divided
2	tablespoons olive oil
2	tablespoons chopped fresh rosemary
2	teaspoons salt

Cooking spray

1. Place potato in a saucepan; cover with water. Bring to a boil. Reduce heat; simmer for 25 minutes or until tender. Drain in a colander over a bowl, reserving 1 cup cooking liquid. Return potato to pan; beat with a mixer at medium speed until smooth.

2. Dissolve yeast and sugar in warm water in a large bowl; let stand 5 minutes. Lightly spoon flour into dry measuring cups, and level with a knife. Add 2 cups flour, mashed potato, reserved cooking liquid, oil, rosemary, and salt to the yeast mixture; beat with a mixer at medium speed until smooth. Stir in 3½ cups flour. Turn dough out onto a lightly floured surface. Knead until smooth and elastic (about 10 minutes); add enough of remaining flour, 1 tablespoon at a time, to prevent dough from sticking to hands.

3. Place dough in a large bowl coated with cooking spray, turning to coat top. Cover and let rise in a warm place (85°), free from drafts, 45 minutes or until doubled in size. (Press two fingers into dough. If indentation remains, dough has risen enough.) Punch dough down; roll dough into a 14 x 10-inch rectangle. Place dough on a large baking sheet coated with cooking spray. Imagine a lengthwise line running through the center of the rectangle. Starting at imaginary line, cut 5 (4-inch-long) diagonal slits in dough on alternating sides of line (be careful not to cut through edge of dough). Gently pull slits open. Cover and let rise 30 minutes or until doubled in size.

4. Preheat oven to 425°.

5. Uncover dough, and bake at 425° for 25 minutes or until browned. Remove from pan. Cool on a wire rack. Cut loaf in half lengthwise; cut each half crosswise into 12 pieces. Yield: 1 loaf, 24 servings (serving size: 1 slice).

CALORIES 137 (10% from fat); FAT 1.5g (sat 0.2g, mono 0.9g, poly 0.2g); PROTEIN 3.6g; CARB 26.7g; FIBER 1.1g; CHOL 0mg; IRON 1.6mg; SODIUM 197mg; CALC 7mg

Making Potato Fougasse

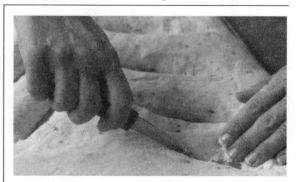

1. Cut 5 diagonal slashes in the dough; be sure not to cut to the outside border of the dough.

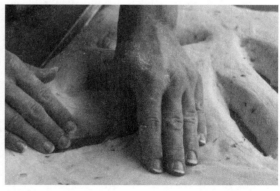

2. Using your hands, gently pull the slits apart so they remain open during baking.

Pizza Dough

"Homemade pizza crust is better than anything you can buy. And since you only need a few basic ingredients, it's simple to make." Jill Melton, Food Editor

All-Purpose Pizza Dough

This basic recipe, which can be used to make calzones and focaccia, can easily be doubled. (The nutrient analysis is for the entire recipe of dough.)

1	package dry yeast (about 2¼ teaspoons)
1¼	cups warm water (100° to 110°)
3¼	cups all-purpose flour, divided
½	teaspoon salt

Cooking spray

1. Dissolve yeast in warm water in a large bowl, and let stand 5 minutes. Lightly spoon flour into dry measuring cups; level with a knife. Add 1 cup flour and salt to yeast mixture; stir well. Stir in 2 cups flour, 1 cup at a time, stirring after each addition. Turn dough out onto a floured surface. Knead until smooth and elastic (about 10 minutes); add enough of the remaining flour, 1 tablespoon at a time, to prevent dough from sticking to hands (dough will feel tacky).
2. Place dough in a large bowl coated with cooking spray, turning to coat top. Cover and let rise in a warm place (85°), free from drafts, 1 hour or until doubled in size. (Press two fingers into dough. If an indentation remains, the dough has risen enough.) Punch dough down; cover and let rest 5 minutes. Shape dough according to the recipe directions. Yield: 1 pizza dough.

CALORIES 1,505 (3% from fat); FAT 5g (sat 0.8g, mono 0.7g, poly 2.1g); PROTEIN 44.6g; CARB 312.7g; FIBER 12.9g; CHOL 0mg; IRON 20mg; SODIUM 1,184mg; CALC 66mg

To freeze, let the dough rise once, punch down, and shape into a ball. Place in a heavy-duty zip-top plastic bag coated with cooking spray; squeeze out all air, and seal. Store in freezer for up to 1 month. To thaw, place dough in refrigerator 12 hours or overnight. With scissors, cut away the plastic bag. Place dough on a floured surface, and shape according to recipe directions. For pizza, instead of shaping into a ball to freeze, roll it out, wrap in foil, and freeze. To bake, remove from freezer; top and bake according to recipe instructions (no need to thaw).

Dough Tips From *Cooking Light* Food Editor Jill Melton

While kneading, massage the dough gently, as though it were a baby. If you overwork the dough, it will absorb too much flour, producing a dense, heavy bread or a dry, tough crust. If you're a novice, be sure to set your kitchen timer for 10 minutes so you won't be inclined to over- or underknead.

To produce a crunchy crust, you need to bake pizza in a very hot oven (from 450° to 550°). Make sure your oven is preheated.

Stretching the dough with your fists is a great way to shape the pizza because you get a more natural look, with bumps and blisters. The dough may tear slightly; just pinch it back together.

Making the Perfect All-Purpose Pizza Dough

1. Once the yeast is dissolved, gradually add about 2 cups flour, stirring with a wooden spoon. You may need to use less flour or add more. A slightly sticky dough, though messy to handle, will make a more tender crust or bread.

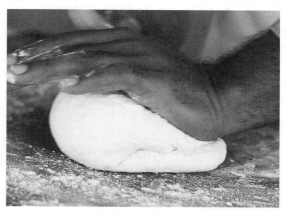

2. Turn dough out onto a floured surface, and knead until smooth and elastic (about 10 minutes). To knead, push out the mound of dough with the heels of your hands, fold it over, give it a quarter-turn, and repeat. The dough should become smooth. If necessary, add slightly more flour while kneading.

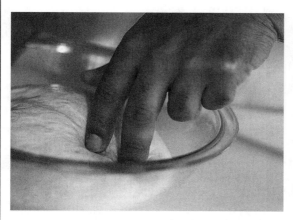

3. Place dough in a large bowl; let rise in a warm place (85°) about an hour, or until doubled in size. (See page 108-109 for more information about rising dough.) The dough is ready when you can press it with a few fingers and the indentations remain. Just prior to shaping, punch down the dough, and let it rest for five minutes. This important step gives the gluten time to relax, making the dough easier to roll and shape.

4. To shape the pizza, pat the dough with floured hands, or stretch it with a rolling pin, starting at the center of the dough and moving toward the edge. To get an even crust, roll the dough into a 15-inch circle. For a free-form shape, try stretching the dough with your fists, as they do in pizzerias.

Tomato and Basil Pizza

We love this pizza's flavor with Gruyère cheese, but you can use another Swiss cheese or mozzarella if you prefer. And if fresh tomatoes are in season, use them instead of canned.

All-Purpose Pizza Dough (page 114)
- 2   teaspoons yellow cornmeal
- 2   teaspoons olive oil
- 2   garlic cloves, minced
- 1   (14.5-ounce) can diced tomatoes, undrained

Cooking spray
- ¾   cup (3 ounces) shredded Gruyère or Swiss cheese
- ¼   cup thinly sliced fresh basil
- ¼   cup (1 ounce) grated fresh Parmesan cheese

1. Roll the prepared dough into a 15-inch circle on a floured surface. Place the dough on a 15-inch round pizza pan sprinkled with cornmeal. Cover the dough, and let rise in a warm place 20 minutes or until puffy.
2. Preheat oven to 450°.
3. Heat oil in a large nonstick skillet over medium-high heat. Add garlic; sauté 30 seconds. Add tomatoes; cook 5 minutes or until liquid almost evaporates.
4. Lightly coat dough with cooking spray. Spread tomato mixture over dough, leaving a 1-inch border, and top with Gruyère, basil, and Parmesan. Bake at 450° for 15 minutes or until golden. Yield: 4 servings (serving size: 2 slices).

CALORIES 547 (21% from fat); FAT 12.9g (sat 5.9g, mono 4.7g, poly 13g); PROTEIN 21.7g; CARB 84.6g; FIBER 4g; CHOL 29mg; IRON 5.8mg; SODIUM 668mg; CALC 363mg

Three-Cheese Pizza Bianca

Bianca, which means "white" in Italian, refers to a dish without tomato sauce. You won't miss it.

All-Purpose Pizza Dough (page 114)
- 2   teaspoons yellow cornmeal
- 2   teaspoons olive oil
- 3   garlic cloves, minced

Cooking spray
- ¾   cup fat-free ricotta cheese
- ¾   cup (3 ounces) finely shredded Gruyère cheese
- 2   tablespoons (½ ounce) grated fresh Parmesan cheese

1. Roll the prepared dough into a 15-inch circle on a floured surface. Place the dough on a 15-inch round pizza pan sprinkled with cornmeal. Cover the dough, and let rise in a warm place 20 minutes or until puffy.
2. Preheat oven to 450°.
3. Combine oil and garlic in a small bowl. Cover and microwave at MEDIUM-HIGH (70% power) for 1 minute or until bubbly. Cool 10 minutes.
4. Lightly coat dough with cooking spray. Combine garlic mixture and ricotta. Spread the ricotta mixture over dough, leaving a 1-inch border. Sprinkle with Gruyère and Parmesan. Bake at 450° for 15 minutes or until golden. Yield: 4 servings (serving size: 2 slices).

CALORIES 541 (19% from fat); FAT 11.5g (sat 5.1g, mono 4.3g, poly 1.2g); PROTEIN 25.6g; CARB 83.5g; FIBER 3.3g; CHOL 31mg; IRON 5.1mg; SODIUM 449mg; CALC 356mg

Crisp Crust	Test Kitchen SECRET
Sprinkling cornmeal on the pan before you place the dough on it keeps the crust from getting soggy.	

Herbed Focaccia

This is a basic focaccia recipe. Create your own variations with different herbs or sprinkling with a cheese such as fresh Parmesan.

All-Purpose Pizza Dough (page 114)
- 1   tablespoon chopped fresh flat-leaf parsley
- 1   teaspoon dried rubbed sage
- 1   teaspoon dried rosemary
- 1   teaspoon dried thyme

Cooking spray
- 1   tablespoon yellow cornmeal
- 1   tablespoon extra-virgin olive oil
- ½   teaspoon kosher salt

1. Roll prepared dough into a 12 x 8-inch rectangle on a floured surface. Sprinkle parsley, sage, rosemary, and thyme over dough. Fold dough into thirds. Knead lightly 1 minute, until herbs are blended into dough. Cover; let stand 10 minutes. Roll dough into a 14 x 12-inch rectangle. Place on a baking sheet coated with cooking spray and sprinkled with cornmeal. Cover and let rise in a warm place 35 minutes or until doubled in size.

2. Preheat oven to 450°.

3. Uncover the dough. Make indentations in top of dough using the handle of a wooden spoon or your fingertips. Gently brush the dough with olive oil. Sprinkle with kosher salt. Bake dough at 450° for 15 minutes or until browned. Yield: 8 servings (serving size: 1 slice).

CALORIES 209 (11% from fat); FAT 2.5g (sat 0.4g, mono 1.4g, poly 0.5g); PROTEIN 5.7g; CARB 40.2g; FIBER 1.8g; CHOL 0mg; IRON 2.9mg; SODIUM 295mg; CALC 16mg

---

The Best Focaccia
Test Kitchen SECRET

To make your focaccia the best it can be, use kosher salt. The coarse texture of kosher salt provides a wonderful crunch and salty burst on focaccia, reminiscent of a big, soft pretzel. Kosher salt comes in a large box found next to the salt and spices in your supermarket.

Making Focaccia

1. After rolling out dough, make indentations in top of dough with a wooden spoon or your fingers.

2. After baking, you end up with crusty, rustic focaccia.

Sausage, Fennel, and Provolone Calzones

If you can't find fennel, increase the bell pepper to 3 cups. Green bell peppers will also work.

4   ounces sweet Italian sausage
2   cups thinly sliced fennel bulb (about 1 medium bulb)
1½ cups sliced red bell pepper
1   cup vertically sliced onion
All-Purpose Pizza Dough (page 114)
1   large egg
1   tablespoon water
¾   cup (3 ounces) grated sharp provolone cheese
1   tablespoon yellow cornmeal

1. Remove casing from sausage. Cook sausage in a large nonstick skillet over medium-high heat until browned, stirring to crumble. Add fennel, bell pepper, and onion. Cover, reduce heat, and cook for 9 minutes, stirring frequently. Cool slightly.
2. Preheat oven to 450°.
3. Divide the prepared dough evenly into 6 equal portions on a lightly floured surface; shape each piece into a ball. Roll each ball into a 6-inch circle. Combine egg and water with a whisk in a small bowl. Brush edge of each circle with egg mixture; reserve remaining egg mixture.
4. Place ⅔ cup sausage mixture on half of each circle, leaving a 1-inch border, and sprinkle each with 2 tablespoons cheese. Fold dough over sausage mixture until edges almost meet. Bring bottom edge over top edge; crimp edges of dough with fingers to form a rim. Place calzones on a baking sheet sprinkled with cornmeal. Brush tops with reserved egg mixture. Bake at 450° for 12 minutes or until golden brown. Yield: 6 servings (serving size: 1 calzone).

CALORIES 409 (26% from fat); FAT 11.7g (sat 4.9g, mono 4.2g, poly 1.4g); PROTEIN 16.3g; CARB 58.9g; FIBER 3.3g; CHOL 61mg; IRON 5.1mg; SODIUM 474mg; CALC 162mg

To divide the dough into equal portions, roll it into a rectangle, making sure that the entire rectangle is the same thickness. Then cut into the number of portions called for in the recipe.

Making Calzones

1. Divide dough into 6 equal portions; shape each into a ball. Roll each portion out to a 6-inch circle. Place filling mixture on half of dough, leaving a 1-inch border.

2. Fold dough over until edges almost meet; then bring bottom edge of dough over top edge and crimp with your fingers to form a rim.

Shrimp and Prosciutto Calzones

Fontina cheese works well in this calzone, but you can also use Swiss, Monterey Jack, or mozzarella.

1 pound medium cooked shrimp, peeled
   and deveined
1 cup (4 ounces) shredded fontina cheese
1 ounce diced prosciutto or ham
2 tablespoons thinly sliced fresh basil
1 tablespoon minced fresh chives
All-Purpose Pizza Dough (page 114)
1 large egg
1 tablespoon water
1 tablespoon yellow cornmeal

1. Preheat oven to 450°.
2. Combine the first 5 ingredients in a bowl.
3. Divide the prepared dough evenly into 6 equal portions on a lightly floured surface; shape each piece into a ball. Roll each ball into a 6-inch circle. Combine egg and water with a whisk in a small bowl. Brush edge of each circle with egg mixture; reserve remaining egg mixture.
4. Place ⅙ of shrimp mixture on half of each circle. Fold the dough over shrimp mixture until edges almost meet. Bring the bottom edge over top edge; crimp edges of the dough with fingers to form a rim. Place calzones on a baking sheet sprinkled with cornmeal. Brush tops with reserved egg mixture. Bake calzones at 450° for 12 minutes or until golden brown. Yield: 6 servings (serving size: 1 calzone).

CALORIES 408 (19% from fat); FAT 8.6g (sat 4.3g, mono 2.4g, poly 1.1g); PROTEIN 26.4g; CARB 53.6g; FIBER 2.2g; CHOL 172mg; IRON 5.3mg; SODIUM 558mg; CALC 143mg

Be sure to finely chop the prosciutto so that it disperses well. We recommend using a chef's knife.

Two-Cheese Oregano Bread

With this recipe, you can use the basic Pizza Dough to make a loaf bread.

All-Purpose Pizza Dough (page 114)
½ cup (2 ounces) shredded provolone cheese
2 tablespoons (½ ounce) grated fresh
   Parmesan cheese
¼ teaspoon dried oregano
⅛ teaspoon crushed red pepper
1 tablespoon yellow cornmeal
1 teaspoon extra-virgin olive oil

1. Roll prepared dough into a 12 x 8-inch rectangle. Combine cheeses, oregano, and red pepper; sprinkle over dough, leaving a ½-inch border. Beginning with long side, roll up jelly-roll fashion, pressing firmly to eliminate air pockets; pinch seam and ends to seal. Place roll, seam side down, on a baking sheet sprinkled with cornmeal. Cut slits in top of dough. Cover and let rise in a warm place 40 minutes or until doubled in size.
2. Preheat oven to 450°.
3. Brush loaf with oil. Bake at 450° for 20 minutes or until loaf sounds hollow when tapped. Yield: 8 servings (serving size: 2 slices).

CALORIES 230 (14% from fat); FAT 3.6g (sat 1.7g, mono 1.2g, poly 0.4g); PROTEIN 8.2g; CARB 40.2g; FIBER 1.7g; CHOL 6mg; IRON 2.6mg; SODIUM 243mg; CALC 87mg

Beginning with long side, roll dough up jelly-roll fashion; press firmly to eliminate air pockets.

Bread Machines

Without kneading or shaping the dough, you can make a loaf that's similar in shape to what you'd make by hand and bake in a bread pan.

Before you start, read the instruction book that comes with your machine. Different machines require adding ingredients in varying orders, depending on whether the machine features a yeast dispenser. Also, various machines make different amounts of bread, ranging from 1- to 2-pound loaves. (The most common loaf sizes are 1½ to 2 pounds.) **We've specified the size we achieved in testing; if your machine is smaller, look at the amount of flour called for in your instruction book and decrease the amount of flour and other ingredients proportionally. Increase ingredient amounts for a larger machine.**

Finding the Right Bread Machine

We test recipes in a variety of bread machines in our Test Kitchens. The type you pick is largely a matter of personal choice in terms of the features that you'd like to have. Here are some things to keep in mind when looking for a bread machine.

- Make sure the machine will fit on your counter—with the lid open.
- Choose from machines that make 1-pound loaves—or for bigger families—machines that make 1½- or 2-pound loaves.
- Check out the time cycles of the many machines available. Some take 2 hours from start to finish; others have a 4-hour cycle.
- Decide just how fancy you want your machine to be. They come in different sizes, with a variety of settings and timers. A simple machine may be purchased for as little as $45, while deluxe models often cost upwards of $300.

Extra Features

Here are some of the extra features you can choose on a bread machine.

- *Delay timer:* Add the ingredients, choose the baking cycle, and set it to start anywhere from 3½ to 24 hours later.
- *Quick/rapid bake:* This cycle makes bread in as little as 1 hour. It produces a denser loaf, though, because it allows less time for rising.
- *Crust control:* Most models allow you to choose light, medium, or dark crusts.
- *Power-saver memory:* Some machines adjust and restart where they left off after a power outage (up to an hour).
- *Special cycles:* Many machines can handle wheat bread, French bread, pizza dough, and fruit-and-nut bread (it either automatically adds the extras at the correct time or signals you to do so).

"I actually prefer to use a machine without all of the extras. I've found that you get just a good a loaf with the simple models." Kathryn Conrad, Test Kitchens Staffer

Our Favorite Bread Machines

- TR2200C Breadman "Ultimate" Professional (866-372-5866 or www.esalton.com)

Lower-priced alternatives include:

- West Bend Automatic Bread and Dough Maker (262-334-6949 or www.westbend.com)
- Toastmaster's 1183N Corner Bakery Bread & Dessert Maker (866-372-5866 or www.esalton.com)

If you have limited counter space, consider:

- West Bend Automatic front-loading machine, which nestles under a cabinet
- Oster's Expressbake Breadmaker (Compact Modern Design, 800-438-0935 or www.oster.com), a smaller machine that makes full-size horizontal loaves

"One of the best things about a bread machine is that it allows you to have fresh bread when you get home from work." Jan Moon, Test Kitchens Staffer

Multigrain Bread

For this bread, you do all of the steps in the machine.

3½	cups bread flour
1	cup warm water (100° to 110°)
½	cup low-fat buttermilk
¼	cup yellow cornmeal
¼	cup regular oats
¼	cup wheat bran
¼	cup packed brown sugar
2	tablespoons honey
2½	teaspoons bread-machine yeast
2	teaspoons salt

1. Lightly spoon flour into dry measuring cups; level with a knife. Follow manufacturer's instructions for placing flour and the remaining ingredients into bread pan, and select the bake cycle; start the bread machine. Yield: 1 (2-pound) loaf, 16 servings (serving size: 1 slice).

CALORIES 150 (5% from fat); FAT 0.8g (sat 0.1g, mono 0.1g, poly 0.3g); PROTEIN 4.7g; CARB 31g; FIBER 0.8g; CHOL 0mg; IRON 1.8mg; SODIUM 299mg; CALC 19mg

Ingredients Primer

- Bread flour is a high-gluten, high-protein flour that produces a light, springy loaf. Gluten creates an elastic network in the dough that traps gas created by the yeast and makes the bread rise. (All-purpose flour has less gluten.)
- Bread-machine yeast is finely granulated to disperse well during mixing and kneading. It's not temperature-sensitive, so it can grow without first being proofed in warm water; just add it with the dry ingredients in your machine. It's convenient because you can measure it straight from the jar. You can substitute instant, rapid-rise, or quick-rise yeast. One packet of dry yeast is equal to 2¼ teaspoons of bread-machine yeast. Although you can use rapid-rise yeast, we found that bread machine or dry yeast works best. Occasionally, bread-machine yeast causes the bread to rise so much that it touches the top of the machine and burns. If this happens, next time reduce the amount of yeast by one-fourth, then by one-third, if needed.
- Sugar feeds the yeast, allowing it to grow. It also helps bread retain moisture, adds flavor and tenderness, and helps brown the crust.
- Salt is needed for flavor and to control yeast by delaying fermentation so the dough rises at a slower rate, allowing the gluten to strengthen.

Cookies

"Using the right kind of fat is crucial in a light cookie. Don't use diet margarine—it just never works in cookies."

Alison Ashton, Food Editor

We've got recipes for all types of cookies—bars, dropped, rolled, and sliced. We show you how to get great results every time and guide you all the way through the process—from measuring through mixing, shaping, baking, and cooling.

Equipment

Both handheld and stand mixers work fine for most cookie doughs. Newer handheld electric mixers are very powerful and can handle even the thickest doughs. A stand mixer, however, frees your hands. (For more information on mixers, see page 30.)

For even baking, use a heavy baking or cookie sheet (which has a lip on one or both ends). Baking sheets make it easier to add or remove silicon pan liners (see page 95) or parchment paper, both of which eliminate any need for greasing the pan and help maintain the cook-ies' shape during baking. A larger baking sheet (17 x 14 inches) allows you to bake more cookies at a time than a standard 15 x 12-inch pan.

For bar cookies, hav-ing a 13 x 9-inch pan and both 8- and 9-inch square pans are useful. You'll also need a sturdy spatula and one or two large wire cooling racks.

Air-cushioned pans work fine, but they're not necessarily better than a good-quality heavy cookie sheet. And you can't put the air-cushioned pans in the dishwasher.

**"Nonstick baking sheets tend to make the cookies too dark on the bottom. We prefer silver-colored aluminum pans such as Mirro, Wear Ever, or Chicago Metallic."
Krista Montgomery, Food Editor**

Let the baking sheet cool completely between batches. Placing dough on a hot cookie sheet will cause the dough to spread too quickly, and the cookies will bake flat.

Be sure to bake cookies in the size of pan indicated in the recipe; otherwise, the baking time and texture of the bar will vary.

Here's the equipment you need to make cookies:
- Mixer
- Baking sheet
- Large wire cooling racks
- Sturdy spatula
- Baking pan

The Right Fat

Not only do our cookie recipes minimize fat, but they're also specific about what type to use. Some call for vegetable oil or a combination of vegetable oil and butter; oil disperses better than butter and keeps the cookies moist and tender, while butter keeps the cookies from spreading too much.

Butter is Best	Test Kitchen SECRET

Don't replace butter with diet margarine or a tub-style spread. These have too much water and too little fat to produce the right results. We use Land O'Lakes butter because we've found that using store-brand butters often results in inferior cookies.

Storing and Freezing Cookies

You can use an airtight container to store soft, chewy cookies and bars. If you stack cookies, be sure that if the cookie has a glaze on top, you use wax paper between layers to keep the cookies from sticking together. Bar cookies will also keep in their baking pan—simply seal them tightly with aluminum foil. To store crisp cookies, place them in a jar with a loose-fitting lid.

You can freeze most cookie dough and baked cookies up to 6 months. Thaw baked cookies at room temperature an hour before serving. Thaw cookie dough in the refrigerator or at room temperature until it's the right consistency for shaping into cookies as the recipe directs. You can even slice some refrigerator cookies straight from the freezer without thawing them.

6 Tips for Great Low-Fat Cookies	Test Kitchen SECRET

Here are our Test Kitchens Staffers' tips for making cookies that melt in your mouth:

1. Measure flour correctly; too much flour will make the cookies tough (see page 93 for how to measure).

2. If the batter seems dry, don't give in to the temptation to add more liquid. This makes for a cakelike cookie that spreads too much.

3. Use the exact ingredients called for in the recipe. Baking cookies is like conducting a science experiment—the right balance and type of ingredients is crucial.

4. Bake cookies in an oven that has been preheated for 15 minutes. Check for doneness at the earliest suggested time. Opening and closing the oven too often can change baking times.

5. We bake cookies on the second rack from the bottom. Be sure there is room left for air to circulate on all sides after the baking sheet is placed on the rack.

6. Cookies bake more evenly when they're about the same size. And don't forget they need plenty of space between them to allow for spreading.

"When our recipes call for measuring the dough by level tablespoons, we are referring to a measuring spoon tablespoon, not a tablespoon from your flatware."

Vanessa Johnson, Test Kitchens Director

Bar Cookies

Bar cookies are a great option when you don't have the time for rolling, slicing, or dropping dough. Besides, who can resist a brownie or a lemon square, especially a light version that tastes like a full-fat treat?

Chocolate-Mint Brownies

Each layer needs to cool completely before the next step.

Brownies:

6	tablespoons butter
1	cup Dutch process cocoa
3	tablespoons evaporated fat-free milk
1	cup packed brown sugar
½	cup granulated sugar
2	teaspoons vanilla extract
4	large egg whites
1	cup all-purpose flour
½	teaspoon baking powder
¼	teaspoon salt

Cooking spray

Icing:

1	cup powdered sugar
1	tablespoon butter, softened
1	tablespoon crème de menthe or
	¼ teaspoon mint extract

Glaze:

1	ounce unsweetened chocolate
1	tablespoon butter

1. Preheat oven to 325°.

2. To prepare brownies, melt 6 tablespoons butter in a saucepan over medium heat. Stir in cocoa and milk; cook 1 minute, stirring constantly. Add brown sugar, granulated sugar, and vanilla; cook 1 minute, stirring constantly (mixture will be granular). Remove mixture from heat; cool 5 minutes. Add egg whites, 1 at a time, stirring well after each addition.

> ## Bar Cookie Basics
> **Test Kitchen SECRET**
>
> - Cool cookies in the pan completely before cutting them into bars. This will help ensure that you get a nice "clean" cut.
> - Set a timer for the least amount of bake time given in the recipe. Check at this point to prevent overbaking. Overbaked bar cookies are dry and crumbly.
> - Store bar cookies in the pan in which they were baked. Seal pan tightly with plastic wrap to keep cookies fresh.

3. Lightly spoon flour into a dry measuring cup; level with a knife. Combine flour, baking powder, and salt, stirring well with a whisk. Add flour mixture to cocoa mixture, stirring until well blended. Pour batter into a 9-inch square baking pan coated with cooking spray. Bake at 325° for 25 minutes or until brownie barely springs back when touched lightly in center; cool completely on a wire rack.

4. To prepare icing, combine powdered sugar, 1 tablespoon butter, and liqueur. Beat with a mixer at medium speed until smooth. Spread the icing evenly over brownie layer; refrigerate 30 minutes or until icing is set.

5. To prepare glaze, place chocolate in a small microwave-safe dish. Microwave at HIGH for 45 seconds; stir in 1 tablespoon butter. Microwave at HIGH for 20 seconds. Stir until smooth. Drizzle the glaze over icing; refrigerate for 30 minutes or until glaze is set. Yield: 25 servings (serving size: 1 brownie).

CALORIES 146 (30% from fat); FAT 4.9g (sat 2.9g, mono 1.4g, poly 0.2g); PROTEIN 2.3g; CARB 23.5g; FIBER 0.2g; CHOL 10mg; IRON 1.1mg; SODIUM 83mg; CALC 25mg

Two-Layer Caramel-Pecan Bars

These bars have a crunchy brown sugar base and a gooey caramel top. Try cutting the panful into four equal strips, using firm pressure with a pizza cutter. After removing the strips, cut each crosswise into five pieces.

⅓ cup packed brown sugar
¼ cup butter, softened
1 teaspoon vanilla extract
¼ teaspoon salt
¾ cup all-purpose flour
Cooking spray
2 tablespoons fat-free milk
40 small soft caramel candies
1 teaspoon vanilla extract
¼ cup finely chopped pecans

1. Preheat oven to 375°.
2. Beat first 4 ingredients with a mixer at medium speed until well blended. Lightly spoon flour into dry measuring cups, and level with a knife. Add flour to sugar mixture, stirring until well blended (mixture will be crumbly). Firmly press mixture into bottom of an 8-inch square baking pan coated with cooking spray. Bake at 375° for 15 minutes.
3. While crust is baking, combine milk and caramel candies in a medium saucepan. Place over low heat; cook until candies melt, stirring occasionally. Stir in 1 teaspoon vanilla; remove from heat.
4. Remove the crust from oven. Pour caramel mixture evenly over hot crust. Sprinkle with

pecans. Bake at 375° for 3 additional minutes. Cool completely on a wire rack. Yield: 20 bars (serving size: 1 bar).

CALORIES 123 (34% from fat); FAT 4.7g (sat 2.6g, mono 1.5g, poly 0.4g); PROTEIN 1.4g; CARB 19.6g; FIBER 0.4g; CHOL 7mg; IRON 0.3mg; SODIUM 94mg; CALC 29mg

Easy Lemon Squares

These taste just like the traditional version!

Crust:
¼ cup granulated sugar
3 tablespoons butter, softened
1 cup all-purpose flour
Topping:
3 large eggs
¾ cup granulated sugar
2 teaspoons grated lemon rind
⅓ cup fresh lemon juice
3 tablespoons all-purpose flour
½ teaspoon baking powder
⅛ teaspoon salt
2 teaspoons powdered sugar

1. Preheat oven to 350°.
2. To prepare crust, beat ¼ cup granulated sugar and butter with a mixer at medium speed until creamy. Spoon 1 cup flour into a dry measuring cup; level with a knife. Gradually add 1 cup flour to sugar mixture, beating at low speed until mixture resembles fine crumbs. Press into an 8-inch square baking pan. Bake at 350° for 15 minutes; cool on a wire rack.
3. To prepare topping, beat eggs at medium speed until foamy. Add ¾ cup granulated sugar and next 5 ingredients; beat until blended. Pour over crust. Bake at 350° for 20 minutes. Cool on rack. Sift powdered sugar over top. Yield: 16 servings (serving size: 1 square).

CALORIES 118 (24% from fat); FAT 3.2g (sat 1.7g, mono 1g, poly 0.3g); PROTEIN 2.2g; CARB 20.5g; FIBER 0.3g; CHOL 47mg; IRON 0.6mg; SODIUM 68mg; CALC 16mg

Finger Finesse

Test Kitchen SECRET

Use your fingers to press the flour mixture evenly and firmly into the bottom of the pan; a compact layer holds together when cut.

Biscotti

Biscotti are twice-baked Italian cookies that are made by baking the dough in a loaf first, then slicing the loaf and baking the slices.

Toffee Biscotti

The almond toffee bits add a sweet crunch to the cookie.

2¾	cups all-purpose flour
½	cup granulated sugar
½	cup packaged almond toffee bits
½	cup packed brown sugar
2	teaspoons baking powder
1	tablespoon vegetable oil
1	teaspoon vanilla extract
3	large eggs
	Cooking spray

1. Preheat oven to 350°.
2. Lightly spoon flour into dry measuring cups; level with a knife. Combine flour, granulated sugar, and next 3 ingredients. Combine oil, vanilla, and eggs; add to flour mixture, stirring until well blended (dough will be dry and crumbly). Turn dough out onto a lightly floured surface; knead 7 or 8 times. Divide dough in half. Shape each portion into an 8-inch-long roll. Place rolls 6 inches apart on a baking sheet coated with cooking spray, and flatten each roll to 1-inch thickness.
3. Bake at 350° for 35 minutes. Remove from baking sheet; cool 10 minutes on a wire rack. Cut each roll diagonally into 15 (½-inch) slices. Place slices, cut sides down, on baking sheet. Reduce temperature to 325°; bake 10 minutes. Turn cookies over; bake 10 minutes (cookies will be slightly soft in center but will harden as they cool). Remove from baking sheet; cool completely on a wire rack. Yield: 2½ dozen (serving size: 1 biscotto).

CALORIES 103 (22% from fat); FAT 2.5g (sat 0.8g, mono 0.7g, poly 0.9g); PROTEIN 1.8g; CARB 18.2g; FIBER 0.3g; CHOL 23mg; IRON 0.7mg; SODIUM 62mg; CALC 25mg

---

Biscotti Basics — Test Kitchen SECRET

- If you want a crispier, more dunkable version, bake them longer. We found that when baked an additional five minutes on each side, the cookies weren't soft in the middle.
- Instead of flipping the slices, you can stand slices up on their flat sides on the baking sheet instead of laying them cut sides down. This allows you to bake the sliced cookies without opening the oven to flip the cookies over. We've called for the more traditional flip technique, but try this and see if it works for you.

Making Biscotti

1. Use your hands to gently shape dough into 8-inch rolls.

2. Careful patting and forming allows you to flatten dough to 1-inch thickness.

3. Cut each roll diagonally into 15 slices of equal width. A sharp knife is a must.

Lemon Biscotti with Lemon Drizzle

Here's a real treat for lemon lovers. If you're making enough to freeze, store them without the drizzle, then make the drizzle and add before serving.

2¾   cups all-purpose flour
1   cup granulated sugar
2   teaspoons baking powder
1   tablespoon grated lemon rind
2   tablespoons fresh lemon juice, divided
1   tablespoon lemon extract
1   tablespoon vegetable oil
3   large eggs
Cooking spray
⅔   cup powdered sugar

1. Preheat oven to 350°.
2. Lightly spoon flour into dry measuring cups; level with a knife. Combine flour, granulated sugar, and baking powder in a bowl. Combine rind, 1 tablespoon lemon juice, extract, oil, and eggs, and add to flour mixture, stirring until well blended (dough will be dry and crumbly). Turn dough out onto a lightly floured surface, and knead lightly 7 or 8 times. Divide dough in half. Shape each portion into an 8-inch-long roll. Place rolls 6 inches apart on a baking sheet coated with cooking spray, and flatten each roll to 1-inch thickness.
3. Bake at 350° for 35 minutes. Remove rolls from baking sheet; cool 10 minutes on a wire rack. Cut each roll diagonally into 15 (½-inch) slices. Place slices, cut sides down, on baking sheet. Reduce oven temperature to 325°; bake 10 minutes. Turn cookies over; bake 10 minutes (cookies will be slightly soft in center but will harden as they cool). Remove from baking sheet; cool on wire rack.
4. Combine 1 tablespoon lemon juice and powdered sugar; drizzle over the biscotti. Yield: 2½ dozen (serving size: 1 biscotto).

CALORIES 91 (12% from fat); FAT 1.2g (sat 0.3g, mono 0.4g, poly 0.4g); PROTEIN 1.8g; CARB 18.4g; FIBER 0.3g; CHOL 22mg; IRON 0.6mg; SODIUM 39mg; CALC 23mg

Espresso-Chocolate Chip Biscotti

The coffee and chocolate make these perfect for dunking in milk or café au lait.

2¾   cups all-purpose flour
1   cup sugar
½   cup semisweet chocolate chips
2   teaspoons baking powder
1   teaspoon ground cinnamon
⅛   teaspoon salt
¼   cup instant espresso
2   teaspoons hot water
1   tablespoon vegetable oil
2   teaspoons vanilla extract
3   large eggs
Cooking spray

1. Preheat oven to 350°.
2. Lightly spoon flour into dry measuring cups; level with a knife. Combine flour and next 5 ingredients in a bowl. Combine espresso and water; stir well with a whisk. Stir in oil, vanilla, and eggs, and add to flour mixture, stirring until well blended (dough will be dry and crumbly). Turn the dough out onto a lightly floured surface; knead lightly 7 or 8 times. Divide dough in half. Shape each portion into an 8-inch-long roll. Place rolls 6 inches apart on a baking sheet coated with cooking spray, and flatten each roll to 1-inch thickness.
3. Bake at 350° for 35 minutes. Remove rolls from baking sheet; cool for 10 minutes on a wire rack. Cut each roll diagonally into 15 (½-inch) slices. Place slices, cut sides down, on baking sheet. Reduce oven temperature to 325°; bake 10 minutes. Turn cookies over; bake 10 minutes (cookies will be slightly soft in center but will harden as they cool). Remove from baking sheet; cool completely on wire rack. Yield: 2½ dozen (serving size: 1 biscotto).

CALORIES 97 (20% from fat); FAT 2.2g (sat 0.8g, mono 0.7g, poly 0.4g); PROTEIN 2g; CARB 17.6g; FIBER 0.4g; CHOL 22mg; IRON 0.8mg; SODIUM 50mg; CALC 25mg

Drop Cookies

The key to making drop cookies is to make sure that you spoon out the same amount of dough for each cookie so that the cookies will be a uniform size.

Easy Measuring

Test Kitchen SECRET

Measure your first few spoonfuls with a teaspoon or tablespoon from your measuring spoon set so you can gauge the correct amount of dough, then increase your speed with this two-spoon technique:

1. With one spoon (from your flatware), pick up the same amount of dough.

2. With the other spoon, push the dough off onto the baking sheet.

"If you prefer soft and chewy cookies, take them out of the oven at the lower time specified. Leave them in the oven a minute or two longer if you prefer your cookies crispier." Jan Smith, Photo Stylist

Butter is soft enough when it gently yields to the pressure of a finger. If you can push your finger deeply into the butter, it is too soft.

Lemon-Honey Drop Cookies

You can make these easy drop cookies with orange juice and orange rind instead of lemon.

½	cup granulated sugar
7	tablespoons butter, softened
2	teaspoons grated lemon rind
⅓	cup honey
½	teaspoon lemon extract
1	large egg
1¾	cups all-purpose flour
1	teaspoon baking powder
½	teaspoon salt
¼	cup plain fat-free yogurt
	Cooking spray
1	cup powdered sugar
2	tablespoons fresh lemon juice
2	teaspoons grated lemon rind

1. Preheat oven to 350°.

2. Beat first 3 ingredients with a mixer at medium speed until light and fluffy. Add honey, extract, and egg; beat until well blended. Lightly spoon flour into dry measuring cups; level with a knife. Combine flour, baking powder, and salt; stir well with a whisk. Add flour mixture to sugar mixture alternately with yogurt, beginning and ending with flour. Drop by tablespoons 2 inches apart onto baking sheets coated with cooking spray. Bake at 350° for 12 minutes or until lightly browned.

3. Combine powdered sugar and juice in a bowl; stir with a whisk. Brush evenly over hot cookies. Sprinkle with 2 teaspoons rind. Remove cookies from pan; cool on wire racks. Yield: 32 cookies (serving size: 1 cookie).

CALORIES 89 (28% from fat); FAT 2.8g (sat 1.6g, mono 0.8g, poly 0.2g); PROTEIN 1.1g; CARB 15.3g; FIBER 0.2g; CHOL 14mg; IRON 0.4mg; SODIUM 81mg; CALC 15mg

"Let cookies cool completely before storing. Don't stack them or let the sides touch while they're warm, or they'll stick together." Susan Stone, Food Editor

Spicy Oatmeal Crisps

Pepper may sound like an odd ingredient for a cookie, but it complements the other spices well.

¾ cup all-purpose flour
1 teaspoon ground cinnamon
½ teaspoon baking soda
½ teaspoon ground allspice
½ teaspoon grated whole nutmeg
¼ teaspoon salt
¼ teaspoon ground cloves
¼ teaspoon freshly ground black pepper
1 cup packed brown sugar
5 tablespoons butter, softened
1 teaspoon vanilla extract
1 large egg
½ cup regular oats
Cooking spray

1. Preheat oven to 350°.
2. Lightly spoon flour into dry measuring cups; level with a knife. Combine flour and next 7 ingredients. Beat sugar, butter, and vanilla with a mixer at medium speed until light and fluffy. Add egg; beat well. Stir in flour mixture and oats.
3. Drop by level tablespoons 2 inches apart onto baking sheets coated with cooking spray. Bake at 350° for 12 minutes or until crisp. Cool on pan 2 minutes. Remove from pan; cool on wire racks. Yield: 2 dozen (serving size: 1 cookie).

CALORIES 81 (34% from fat); FAT 3.1g (sat 1.7g, mono 0.9g, poly 0.3g); PROTEIN 1.5g; CARB 12.2g; FIBER 0.7g; CHOL 15mg; IRON 0.6mg; SODIUM 71mg; CALC 12mg

Chewy Coconut Macaroons

A classic macaroon is made with almond paste or ground almonds; this version substitutes coconut for the almonds. The result is a cookie that's crisp on the outside and chewy on the inside.

¾ cup all-purpose flour
2½ cups flaked sweetened coconut
1½ teaspoons vanilla extract
⅛ teaspoon salt
1 (14-ounce) can fat-free sweetened condensed milk

1. Preheat oven to 250°.
2. Lightly spoon flour into dry measuring cups; level with a knife. Combine flour and coconut in a medium bowl; toss well. Add vanilla, salt, and milk; stir until well blended (mixture will be very thick).
3. Drop batter by scant tablespoons (about 2 teaspoons) 2 inches apart onto a baking sheet lined with parchment paper. Bake at 250° for 50 minutes or until golden brown. Remove from pan; cool on wire racks. Yield: 32 cookies (serving size: 1 cookie).

CALORIES 82 (29% from fat); FAT 2.6g (sat 2.3g, mono 0.1g, poly 0g); PROTEIN 1.5g; CARB 13.3g; FIBER 0.5g; CHOL 2mg; IRON 0.3mg; SODIUM 41mg; CALC 33mg

Rolled Cookies

Rolled cookies are prepared from dough that has been rolled to a designated thickness and cut with cookie cutters. They are especially popular around the holidays, but with an assortment of cookie cutter shapes, you'll have festive cookies year-round. Another great thing about these cookies is that the dough can be frozen for up to a month, but if you freeze it, be sure to double wrap the dough.

To be rolled and shaped properly, the dough typically needs to be firmer than dough for most other cookies. Many recipes call for chilling the dough to firm it before rolling. Large amounts of dough can be divided so you can work with one portion while the rest remains chilled. If your dough still seems too soft to roll after chilling, roll it directly on a baking sheet, cut with cutters, and peel away the scraps. This eliminates transferring cut dough to baking sheets, a task that can be virtually impossible when the dough is soft. **Some of our Test Kitchens staffers prefer to roll the dough between two sheets of wax paper. If you do this, the dough will need to be closer to room temperature.**

Unless otherwise directed, remove warm cookies from baking sheets immediately to wire racks to cool.

> **"Always roll or pat the dough to the recommended thickness because baking times and the finished texture (crisp or soft) are directly related to thickness."**
> **Kellie Kelley, Food Stylist**

Instead of wax paper, you can roll your dough between two sheets of parchment paper. Then you can bake on it, too.

Sugar Cookies

You may want to start this recipe early in the day because the dough requires about 4 hours to chill. This cookie dough is cut into squares, so you don't have to use cookie cutters unless you want to make other shapes.

1	cup granulated sugar
½	cup butter, softened
1	large egg
1	large egg white
1	tablespoon fat-free milk
1	teaspoon grated lemon rind
1	teaspoon vanilla extract
2	cups all-purpose flour
¼	cup toasted wheat germ
1	teaspoon baking powder
½	teaspoon baking soda
⅛	teaspoon salt

1. Beat sugar and butter in a large bowl with a mixer at medium speed until well blended (about 4 minutes). Add egg, egg white, 1 tablespoon milk, lemon rind, and 1 teaspoon vanilla, beating well. Lightly spoon flour into dry measuring cups; level with a knife. Combine flour, wheat germ, baking powder, baking soda, and salt in a bowl. Add flour mixture to sugar mixture, stirring well. Spoon dough onto plastic wrap; flatten to 1½-inch thickness. Cover tightly with plastic wrap; chill 4 hours or overnight.
2. Preheat oven to 400°.
3. Roll dough to a 15 x 12-inch rectangle on a heavily floured surface. Cut dough into 20 (3-inch) squares using a sharp knife. Place cookies 2 inches apart on ungreased baking sheets. Bake at 400° for 8 minutes or until golden. Immediately remove cookies from pans using a wide spatula; cool on wire racks. Yield: 20 cookies (serving size: 1 cookie).

CALORIES 135 (34% from fat); FAT 5.1g (sat 2.4g, mono 2g, poly 0.3g); PROTEIN 2.3g; CARB 20.4g; FIBER 0.6g; CHOL 23mg; IRON 0.8mg; SODIUM 110mg; CALC 20mg

Gingerbread Little Cakes

Many years ago, cookies were sometimes called "little cakes." This updated version is soft and spicy, with an extra flavor boost from crystallized ginger and cardamom. If you don't have cardamom on hand, you can substitute either ½ teaspoon ground allspice or ½ teaspoon nutmeg. You can also use the rim of a 2½-inch glass to cut the cookies.

- ⅓   cup finely chopped crystallized ginger
- 1   tablespoon all-purpose flour
- ½   cup packed brown sugar
- ½   cup molasses
- 1   tablespoon ground cinnamon
- 2   teaspoons ground ginger
- 1   teaspoon ground cardamom
- 1½   teaspoons baking soda
- ½   cup butter
- 1   large egg
- 2⅔   cups all-purpose flour
  Cooking spray

1. Preheat oven to 325°.
2. Combine crystallized ginger and 1 tablespoon flour, tossing to coat; set mixture aside.
3. Combine sugar, molasses, cinnamon, ground ginger, and cardamom in a medium saucepan. Bring mixture to a boil over medium heat, stirring occasionally. Stir in baking soda (mixture will become thick and foamy). Remove mixture from heat. Add butter, stirring until butter melts. Add egg, and stir well with a whisk. Lightly spoon 2⅔ cups flour into dry measuring cups, and level with a knife. Gradually stir 2⅔ cups flour and crystallized ginger mixture into sugar mixture.
4. Turn dough out onto a flat surface, and knead lightly 4 or 5 times. Cool slightly. Divide dough in half. Roll each portion into a ¼-inch thickness on a lightly floured surface; cut dough with a 2½-inch cutter. Place on baking sheets coated with cooking spray. Bake at 325° for 12 minutes. Cool the cookies on pans for 2 minutes or until firm. Remove cookies from pans; cool on wire racks. Repeat the procedure with remaining dough. Yield: 3 dozen (serving size: 1 cookie).

CALORIES 87 (30% from fat); FAT 2.9g (sat 1.7g, mono 0.8g, poly 0.2g); PROTEIN 1.1g; CARB 14g; FIBER 0.3g; CHOL 13mg; IRON 1mg; SODIUM 66mg; CALC 18mg

Making Rolled Cookies

1. Working with half of the dough at a time, roll it to a ¼-inch thickness. Try not to use too much additional flour on the countertop, since it can make the cookies dry.

2. Cut the dough into little "cakes" with a 2½-inch cutter.

3. Transfer each cut-out cookie to a baking sheet with a flat spatula.

Slice-and-Bake Cookies

Slice-and-bake cookies, or refrigerator cookies, are great because you can make the dough ahead. Store the roll of dough in the refrigerator for up to a week, or freeze for up to 1 month. Then, at a moment's notice, you can have warm cookies.

"The logs of dough are similar to a commercial brand at the supermarket, but our recipes are lower in fat and calories." Krista Montgomery, Food Editor

Basic Icebox Sugar Cookies

This basic recipe is made from ingredients you probably have on hand. Just mix up the dough, form the log, and keep it handy in your refrigerator or freezer.

1	cup all-purpose flour
¼	teaspoon baking soda
⅛	teaspoon salt
¼	cup butter, softened
⅔	cup sugar
1	teaspoon vanilla extract
1	large egg white

Cooking spray

1. Combine first 3 ingredients in a bowl; set aside. Beat butter with a mixer at medium speed until light and fluffy. Gradually add sugar, beating at medium speed until well blended. Add vanilla and egg white; beat well. Add flour mixture; stir until well blended. Turn dough out onto wax paper, and shape into a 6-inch log. Wrap in wax paper; freeze 3 hours or until firm.
2. Preheat oven to 350°.
3. Cut log into 24 (¼-inch) slices, and place slices 1 inch apart on a baking sheet coated with cooking spray. Bake at 350° for 8 to 10 minutes. Remove from pan; cool on wire racks. Yield: 2 dozen (serving size: 1 cookie).

CALORIES 58 (31% from fat); FAT 2g (sat 1g, mono 0.8g, poly 0.1g); PROTEIN 0.7g; CARB 9.6g; FIBER 0.1g; CHOL 5mg; IRON 0.2mg; SODIUM 41mg; CALC 2mg

To slice cookie dough, wrap dough in wax paper; twist ends of wax paper securely. Freeze for 3 hours or until very firm. Cut log into ¼-inch slices using a very sharp knife or dental floss.

Chocolate Icebox Cookies

Rolling dough in turbinado sugar gives cookies a sugary edge. Turbinado sugar is a coarse, blond-colored sugar with a delicate molasses flavor.

¾	cup all-purpose flour
¼	cup unsweetened cocoa
¼	teaspoon baking soda
⅛	teaspoon salt
¼	cup butter, softened
⅔	cup granulated sugar
1	teaspoon vanilla extract
1	large egg white
2	tablespoons turbinado sugar

Cooking spray

1. Combine first 4 ingredients in a bowl; set aside. Beat butter with a mixer at medium speed until light and fluffy. Gradually add granulated sugar, beating at medium speed until well blended. Add vanilla and egg white; beat well. Add flour mixture; stir until well blended. Turn dough onto wax paper; shape into a 6-inch log. Wrap log in wax paper; freeze 3 hours or until dough is firm.

> "The great thing about refrigerator cookies is that you can make the dough ahead, then slice and bake whenever you crave fresh, warm cookies." Ann Pittman, Food Editor

2. Preheat oven to 350°.

3. Roll log in turbinado sugar. Cut log into 24 (¼-inch) slices; place 1 inch apart on a baking sheet coated with cooking spray. Bake at 350° for 8 to 10 minutes. Remove from pan; cool on wire racks. Yield: 2 dozen (serving size: 1 cookie).

CALORIES 59 (32% from fat); FAT 2.1g (sat 1g, mono 0.8g, poly 0.1g); PROTEIN 0.8g; CARB 10.1g; FIBER 0.4g; CHOL 5mg; IRON 0.3mg; SODIUM 42mg; CALC 3mg

Sugar Cookie Basics

Test Kitchen SECRET

Test Kitchens Staffer Tiffany Vickers shares her tips for making sugar cookies.

- Too much flour will make these cookies bake up dry and crumbly (for more on measuring flour, see page 93).
- Each time you slice off a cookie from the log, turn log one quarter to prevent flattening on one side.
- If the dough is too soft to shape into designs (such as pinwheels), simply chill until slightly firm.
- Dough logs may be frozen up to 1 month, but be sure to double wrap for extra protection.

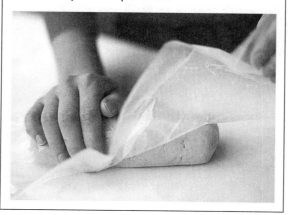

Peanut Butter Icebox Cookies

Transform basic sugar cookies into peanut butter treats with the addition of a few simple ingredients.

1   cup all-purpose flour
¼   teaspoon baking soda
⅛   teaspoon salt
3   tablespoons butter, softened
2   tablespoons chunky peanut butter
½   cup packed brown sugar
¼   cup granulated sugar
1   teaspoon vanilla extract
1   large egg white
Cooking spray

1. Combine first 3 ingredients; set aside. Beat butter and peanut butter with a mixer at medium speed until light and fluffy. Gradually add sugars, beating at medium speed until well blended. Add vanilla and egg white; beat well. Add flour mixture; stir well. Turn dough onto wax paper; shape into a 6-inch log. Wrap log in wax paper; freeze 3 hours or until firm.

2. Preheat oven to 350°.

3. Cut log into 24 (¼-inch) slices, and place slices 1 inch apart on a baking sheet coated with cooking spray. Bake at 350° for 8 to 10 minutes. Remove from pan; cool on wire racks. Yield: 2 dozen (serving size: 1 cookie).

CALORIES 66 (29% from fat); FAT 2.1g (sat 0.9g, mono 0.9g, poly 0.3g); PROTEIN 1g; CARB 10.8g; FIBER 0.2g; CHOL 4mg; IRON 0.4mg; SODIUM 46mg; CALC 6mg

Cakes

There are no fat substitutes or replacers here. These are the real deal, only lighter.

Layer Cakes

Layer cakes from scratch are not only tastier than cakes from a box, they're also surprisingly easy. A heavy-duty mixer (a handheld mixer also will work), a rubber spatula, cake pans, and wax paper are the only pieces of equipment you need. Beat the shortening or butter with the sugar and flavorings for a few minutes, then beat in the eggs, and finally mix in the dry ingredients alternately with the liquid for a smooth batter. Why use a cake mix when you can make your own this easily?

There's even better news. Layer cakes don't have to be full of fat. So while you're loving every bite, you can also love the fact that **our cakes bear only half the fat of the more conventional versions, with no sacrifice of taste or texture.**

How is this possible? Doesn't fat make a cake moist and tender? Yes, but you don't need huge amounts of it to achieve that melt-in-your-mouth texture. As for flavor—you get the full strength by sticking with natural ingredients, such as whole eggs and real chocolate, although in more judicious measures.

If you're in a high altitude (above 3,500 feet), you may want to try the following adjustments when baking layer cakes:
- Increase oven temperature to 375°.
- Decrease each cup of sugar by 2 tablespoons.
- Decrease each teaspoon of baking powder by $1/8$ teaspoon.
- Increase liquid by 2 tablespoons for each cup used.
- Decrease baking time by 5 minutes.

Making Perfect Cakes

We use either all-purpose flour or cake flour in our cake recipes. Although cake flour generally produces a tender cake, sometimes using cake flour in a lower-fat cake makes the results crumbly and dry.

We use a stand mixer in these recipes, but a handheld mixer will work fine.

Tap the cake pans on the counter after the batter is added to help remove air bubbles and make the cakes rise more evenly.

The correct oven temperature is critical for baking. Be sure to use an oven thermometer. Inexpensive metal ones are available at your grocery store. Tip: Buy the kind you can leave in your oven permanently, and you'll always know the temperature.

Overbaking is more of a problem with low-fat cakes than with traditional ones. Check for doneness 5 to 10 minutes before the stated time in the recipe. Lightly press it in the center. If it springs back, it's done. Or you can insert a toothpick in the center. If it comes out clean, it's done.

Avoid fallen cakes by waiting until 5 to 10 minutes before the end of the baking time to open the oven door. Open the door gently because sudden movements or temperature changes can cause a cake to fall.

Making Layer Cakes

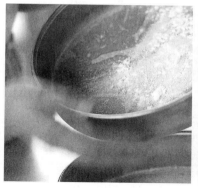

1. Since the pans are not heavily-greased in low-fat baking, for some cake recipes we line the pan to make sure the cake doesn't stick. Coat the bottoms of the pans with cooking spray; line with wax paper. Coat the wax paper with cooking spray; dust with flour.

2. Although sifting flour isn't necessary these days, it's still a good idea to stir your flour to make sure there aren't any lumps. And measure flour accurately. Lightly spoon it into a dry measuring cup, and level it with a knife. Don't scoop—you'll likely get too much, and the cake will be dry.

3. Remember that when you beat the shortening and sugar together (traditionally called creaming) for a low-fat cake, the mixture will not look creamy and fluffy as in a traditional cake recipe. Instead, the consistency will be more like damp sand—fine-textured, but not cohesive. Don't worry. It's supposed to be that way.

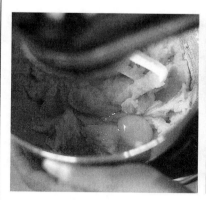

4. We've opted for whole eggs (as opposed to whites or substitutes) because they make a low-fat cake moist and tender. Add them one at a time to the batter, beating each one thoroughly before adding the next.

5. Add the flour mixture alternately with the liquid, as you would with any cake. Beat just until each component is incorporated. Overbeating at this stage can produce a tough cake.

6. When icing the cake, first brush away any loose crumbs. Tear off four strips of wax paper, each 3 inches wide; place them in a square on the cake plate. Place the cake layers on top of the strips. Ice the cake. As soon as the cake is iced, remove the wax paper strips—you'll be left with a clean cake plate.

The Cake Sleuths

Since cake baking requires precise measuring as well as mixing and baking procedures, it's only natural that any number of things can go wrong. Here are the problems that can occur with light cakes and reasons for them. These are the things we discuss when we're trying to figure out what to do with a cake recipe that doesn't work.

If the batter overflows:
- Overmixing
- Too much batter in pan

If the cake falls:
- Oven not hot enough
- Undermixing
- Insufficient baking
- Opening oven door during baking
- Too much baking powder, soda, liquid, or sugar

If cake cracks and falls apart:
- Removing cake from pan too soon
- Too much fat, baking powder, soda, or sugar

If texture is heavy:
- Overmixing when adding flour and liquid
- Oven temperature too low
- Too much fat, sugar, or liquid

If texture is coarse:
- Inadequate mixing
- Oven temperature too low
- Too much baking powder or soda

If texture is dry:
- Overbaking
- Overbeating egg whites
- Too much flour, baking powder, or soda
- Not enough fat or sugar

Red Velvet Cake

This cake has half the fat of the traditional version because we reduced the amount of shortening, used fewer eggs, replaced the whole buttermilk with low-fat, and used our revolutionary reduced-fat buttercream frosting instead of a cream cheese frosting.

Cooking spray
1   tablespoon all-purpose flour
1⅔   cups sugar
5   tablespoons vegetable shortening
1   large egg white
1   large egg
3   tablespoons unsweetened cocoa
1   (1-ounce) bottle red food coloring
2¼   cups all-purpose flour
1   teaspoon salt
1   cup low-fat buttermilk
1¼   teaspoons vanilla extract
1   tablespoon white vinegar
1   teaspoon baking soda
Cooked Buttercream Frosting

1. Preheat oven to 350°.
2. Coat 2 (9-inch) round cake pans with cooking spray, and dust with 1 tablespoon flour.
3. Beat sugar and shortening with a mixer at medium speed 5 minutes or until well blended. Add egg white and egg; beat well. Combine cocoa and food coloring in a small bowl; stir well with a whisk. Add to sugar mixture; mix well.
4. Lightly spoon 2¼ cups flour into dry measuring cups; level with a knife. Combine with salt. Add flour mixture to sugar mixture alternately with buttermilk, beginning and ending with flour mixture. Add vanilla; mix well. Combine vinegar and baking soda in a small bowl; add to batter, mixing well.
5. Pour batter into prepared pans. Sharply tap pans once on counter to remove air bubbles. Bake at 350° for 28 minutes or until a wooden

pick inserted in center comes out clean. Cool in pans 10 minutes; remove from pans. Cool completely on wire racks.

6. Place 1 cake layer on a plate; spread with ⅓ cup Cooked Buttercream Frosting, and top with another cake layer. Spread the remaining frosting over the top and sides of the cake. Store cake loosely covered in refrigerator. Yield: 16 servings (serving size: 1 slice).

CALORIES 322 (24% from fat); FAT 8.7g (sat 3.3g, mono 1.4g, poly 0.3g); PROTEIN 4.9g; CARB 57.9g; FIBER 0.6g; CHOL 30mg; IRON 1.3mg; SODIUM 310mg; CALC 44mg

Cooked Buttercream Frosting

Don't substitute margarine for the light butter in this recipe. The texture and taste will not be the same.

> 1 cup fat-free milk
> 7 tablespoons all-purpose flour
> ¾ cup light butter, chilled
> 2½ cups powdered sugar
> 1 teaspoon vanilla extract

1. Cook milk and flour in a small heavy saucepan over medium heat 2½ minutes or until very thick, stirring constantly with a whisk. Spoon into a bowl; cover and chill thoroughly.

2. Beat butter and chilled flour mixture with a mixer at medium speed until smooth. Gradually add sugar, and beat just until blended (do not overbeat). Stir in vanilla; cover and chill. Yield: 2⅓ cups.

> **Although we don't usually call for light butter in our recipes,** we've used it for the Cooked Buttercream Frosting because ¾ cup of regular butter would make the recipe too high in fat. The flavor of light butter, while not as good as the real thing, is better than that of margarine.

Making Cooked Buttercream Frosting

1. Cook the milk and flour in a small heavy saucepan over medium heat for 2½ minutes or until very thick, stirring constantly with a whisk.

2. Beat butter and chilled flour mixture with a mixer at medium speed until smooth.

3. While beating the mixture, gradually add sugar, beating just until blended (be careful not to overbeat the mixture).

Coconut Triple-Layer Cake

We started with the traditional version, and cut the fat by more than 50 percent in this cake.

Cooking spray
1   tablespoon cake flour
3½ cups cake flour
2   teaspoons baking powder
¾   teaspoon salt
½   teaspoon baking soda
1¾ cups sugar
¼   cup butter, softened
1½ tablespoons vegetable oil
2   large egg whites
1⅔ cups fat-free milk
½   cup plain fat-free yogurt
2½ teaspoons vanilla extract
¼   teaspoon butter extract
Fluffy Coconut Frosting (page 139)
⅔   cup flaked sweetened coconut

1. Preheat oven to 350°.
2. Coat 3 (8-inch) round cake pans with cooking spray; dust with 1 tablespoon flour.
3. Lightly spoon 3½ cups flour into dry measuring cups; level with a knife. Combine sifted flour, baking powder, salt, and baking soda. Combine sugar, butter, and oil in a large bowl, and beat with a mixer at medium speed until well blended (about 5 minutes). Add egg whites, 1 at a time, beating well after each addition. Combine the milk and yogurt. Add the flour mixture to the creamed mixture alternately with the milk mixture, beginning and ending with flour mixture. Stir in extracts.
4. Pour cake batter into prepared pans. Sharply tap pans once on counter to remove air bubbles. Bake at 350° for 25 minutes or until a wooden pick inserted in center comes out clean. Cool in pans 10 minutes on wire racks; remove from pans. Cool completely on wire racks.
5. Place 1 cake layer on a plate; spread with ⅔ cup Fluffy Coconut Frosting, and top with another cake layer. Spread with ⅔ cup frosting, and top with the remaining cake layer. Spread the remaining frosting over the top and sides of the cake. Sprinkle top of cake with coconut. Store cake loosely covered in refrigerator. Yield: 16 servings (serving size: 1 slice).

CALORIES 298 (18% from fat); FAT 5.8g (sat 3.3g, mono 1.3g, poly 0.8g); PROTEIN 4.4g; CARB 57.3g; FIBER 0.2g; CHOL 8mg; IRON 2mg; SODIUM 195mg; CALC 83mg

Softening Butter

Test Kitchen SECRET

Instead of waiting for cold butter to soften so you can start baking, speed up the process. Cut ½-inch slices of butter from the stick, and heat them in the microwave at MEDIUM-LOW for about 30 seconds. Or cut the cold butter into small, mixable pieces with a handheld grater or vegetable peeler.

Ask the *Cooking Light* Cooks

What is cake flour? Cake flour is a fine-textured soft wheat flour that usually makes cakes more tender. Cake flours (such as Softasilk, Swan's Down, or White Lily) typically come in a box rather than a bag. Look for them with the cake mixes in the supermarket (make sure you purchase plain cake flour, not self-rising).

What if I don't have any cake flour? You can substitute the all-purpose variety. Substitute ¾ cup plus 2 tablespoons all-purpose flour for 1 cup cake flour.

Do I need to sift the flour? No. Most flours, including cake flours, are pre-sifted many times. As long as you are measuring flour correctly (see page 93), there's no need to sift.

How We Lightened the Coconut Cake · Test Kitchen SECRET

We cut the fat in half from the traditional version by doing the following:

- Decreasing butter and replacing some of the butter with vegetable oil
- Using egg whites instead of whole eggs
- Using fat-free milk and yogurt instead of whole milk
- Decreasing the sugar by $1/4$ cup
- Decreasing the coconut
- Coating cake pans with cooking spray instead of shortening
- Making the frosting with sugar and egg whites instead of whipping cream and powdered sugar

Fluffy Coconut Frosting

    1   cup sugar
    1/4 cup water
    1/4 teaspoon cream of tartar
Dash of salt
    3   large egg whites
    1   teaspoon vanilla extract
    1/4 teaspoon coconut extract

1. Combine first 5 ingredients in top of a double boiler; place mixture over barely simmering water in bottom of double boiler on cooktop. Beat with a handheld mixer at high speed until stiff peaks form and candy thermometer registers 160°. Add extracts; beat until blended. Yield: 4 cups.

Making Fluffy White Frosting

1. Attach candy thermometer to side of pan, making sure the end is in the unbeaten egg white mixture but not touching the bottom of the pan (candy thermometers usually have adjustable hooks or clips so they can be attached to the pan).

2. Beat at high speed with a handheld mixer until stiff peaks form and candy thermometer registers 160°. The temperature ensures that the egg whites have cooked to a safe temperature.

"It's important to use a double boiler for the coconut frosting. Otherwise, the egg mixture might get too hot and clump, or the sugar might burn."

Jan Moon, Test Kitchens Staffer

Classic Yellow Layer Cake with Caramel-Pecan Frosting

We've reduced the fat in this basic cake by halving the amount of butter, omitting one egg, and adding fat-free milk instead of whole. We've reduced the fat in the frosting by replacing a portion of the butter with fat-free evaporated milk.

Cooking spray
  1   tablespoon all-purpose flour
1⅔   cups sugar
  ½   cup butter, softened
  1   tablespoon vanilla extract
  3   large eggs
2¼   cups all-purpose flour
2¼   teaspoons baking powder
  ½   teaspoon salt
1¼   cups fat-free milk
Caramel-Pecan Frosting

1. Preheat oven to 350°.
2. Coat bottoms of 2 (9-inch) round cake pans with cooking spray (do not coat sides of pan); line bottoms with wax paper. Coat wax paper with cooking spray; dust with 1 table-spoon flour.
3. Beat sugar, butter, and vanilla with a mixer at medium speed until well blended (about 5 minutes). Add eggs, 1 at a time; beat well after each. Spoon 2¼ cups flour into dry measuring cups; level with a knife. Combine with baking powder and salt; stir well with a whisk. Add flour mixture to sugar mixture alternately with milk, beginning and ending with flour mixture.
4. Pour batter into prepared pans. Sharply tap pans once on counter to remove air bubbles. Bake at 350° for 30 minutes or until a wooden pick inserted in center comes out clean. Cool in pans 10 minutes on wire racks; remove from pans. Remove wax paper. Cool completely on wire racks.
5. Place 1 cake layer on a plate; spread with ½ cup Caramel-Pecan Frosting, and top with remaining layer. Spread remaining frosting over top and sides of cake. Store cake loosely covered in refrigerator. Yield: 18 servings (serving size: 1 slice).

CALORIES 326 (27% from fat); FAT 9.9g (sat 5.1g, mono 3.2g, poly 0.7g); PROTEIN 3.8g; CARB 56g; FIBER 0.5g; CHOL 57mg; IRON 1.1mg; SODIUM 234mg; CALC 83mg

Caramel-Pecan Frosting
  ¼   cup butter
  ½   cup packed dark brown sugar
  6   tablespoons evaporated fat-free milk
  2   teaspoons vanilla extract
  3   cups powdered sugar
  ¼   cup chopped pecans

1. Melt butter in a medium saucepan over medium heat. Add brown sugar. Cook 3 minutes; stir constantly with a whisk. Add milk, 1 tablespoon at a time; cook 3 minutes, stirring constantly. Cool. Stir in vanilla. Combine butter mixture and powdered sugar in a bowl; beat with a mixer at high speed until smooth. Frost cake as directed; sprinkle with pecans. Yield: 2 cups.

CALORIES: 130 (26% from fat); FAT 3.7g (sat 1.7g, mono 1.4g, poly 0.4g); PROTEIN 0.5g; CARB 24.2g; FIBER 0.1g; CHOL 7mg; IRON 0.2mg; SODIUM 35mg; CALC 20mg

If frosting is too thick, add 1 tablespoon evaporated fat-free milk.

"To get the neatest, cleanest slices of cake, I use a serrated knife." Kathleen Kanen, Food Stylist

Upside-Down Cakes

Basically an upside-down cake is made by covering the bottom of a cake pan with butter and sugar topped with fruit. Then the cake batter is added. During the baking process, the sugar, butter, and fruit juices combine to create a gooey caramelized glaze. Compared to a traditional recipe, our cakes on average contain more than 100 fewer calories per serving, with one-third less fat. Without compromising tenderness, we cut the butter back by half, added yogurt to the batter, decreased the eggs, and reduced both the brown sugar and the granulated sugar.

Plus, we topped our upside-down cakes with apricots, cherries, pears, mangoes, and apples, instead of limiting ourselves to pineapple.

The Best Time to Serve

Test Kitchen SECRET

Upside-down cakes are best served within 2 hours or so after baking. To serve later than that, let the cake cool in the pan; then, just before serving, heat it in a 375° oven for about 4 minutes or until the bottom of the pan is hot. Run a spatula around the sides of the cake to loosen it, then invert.

From a *Cooking Light* Cook

"When you're making an upside-down cake, remove the cake from the pan while it's warm—if it cools in the pan, the sugar-fruit mixture will harden and stick. When you first take the cake out of the oven, let it cool for 5 minutes. Then run a small spatula around the sides to loosen it. Next, put a serving plate on top and firmly hold the cake pan with an oven mitt. Invert the pan and the plate, and remove the pan. It'll be perfect every time!" Jan Moon, Test Kitchens Staffer

Mango Upside-Down Orange Cake

Mom's pineapple upside-down cake lives on in this healthy, full-flavored cake that features a different tropical fruit.

1	tablespoon butter, melted
¼	cup packed brown sugar
1½	cups thinly sliced peeled mango (about 2 medium)
1	cup all-purpose flour
¾	teaspoon baking soda
⅛	teaspoon salt
¼	cup butter, softened
⅔	cup granulated sugar
2	teaspoons grated orange rind
1	teaspoon vanilla extract
1	large egg
½	cup plain fat-free yogurt

1. Preheat oven to 350°.

2. Coat bottom of a 9-inch round cake pan with melted butter. Sprinkle brown sugar over butter. Arrange mango slices spoke-like over brown sugar, working from center of pan to edge; set aside.

3. Combine flour, baking soda, and salt in a bowl; stir well. Set aside. Beat ¼ cup butter and granulated sugar with a mixer at medium speed until well blended. Add orange rind, vanilla, and egg; beat well. Add flour mixture to creamed mixture alternately with yogurt, beginning and ending with flour mixture; beat well after each addition. Pour batter over mango slices.

4. Bake at 350° for 30 minutes or until a wooden pick inserted in center comes out clean. Let cake cool in pan 5 minutes on a wire rack. Loosen cake from sides of pan, using a narrow metal spatula. Invert onto a cake plate, and cut into wedges. Serve cake warm. Yield: 8 servings (serving size: 1 wedge).

CALORIES 246 (29% from fat); FAT 8g (sat 3.8g, mono 3.2g, poly 0.4g); PROTEIN 3.3g; CARB 42g; FIBER 1g; CHOL 46mg; IRON 1mg; SODIUM 226mg; CALC 36mg

Crumb Cakes

Traditional crumb cakes call for a stick or more of butter, plus whole milk. We drastically reduce the amount of butter and use 1% low-fat milk, low-fat cream cheese, buttermilk, and in a few recipes, add ricotta cheese to the batter.

Crumb Cake Pointers

If you live at a high altitude (above 3,500 feet), decrease the amount of baking powder and baking soda by half and increase the oven temperature to 375°.

Use regular butter instead of margarine or reduced-calorie spreads. Reduced-calorie products will make the finished product dry and tough.

Use a pastry blender or two table knives to cut the butter into the flour-sugar mixture. If you use your fingers, the heat from your hands can warm the butter and interfere with crumb formation.

To test for doneness, gently press the top of the cake with your fingers; if it springs back fully when touched lightly in the center, the cake is ready to remove from the oven.

Mocha Crumb Cake

The cocoa and the coffee add richness to this mild-flavored, tender cake.

1¼   cups all-purpose flour
⅔   cup sugar
3   tablespoons unsweetened cocoa
1   tablespoon instant coffee granules
⅛   teaspoon salt
¼   cup chilled butter, cut into small pieces
½   teaspoon baking powder
¼   teaspoon baking soda
⅓   cup 1% low-fat milk
1   teaspoon vanilla extract
1   large egg
Cooking spray
1½   teaspoons water

1. Preheat oven to 350°.
2. Lightly spoon flour into dry measuring cups; level with a knife. Combine flour and next 4 ingredients; cut in butter with a pastry blender or 2 knives until mixture resembles coarse meal. Reserve ½ cup flour mixture for topping and set aside.
3. Combine remaining flour mixture, baking powder, and baking soda; add milk, vanilla, and egg. Beat with a mixer at medium speed until blended. Spoon batter into an 8-inch round cake pan coated with cooking spray. Combine reserved ½ cup flour mixture and water; stir with a fork. Sprinkle crumb mixture over batter. Bake at 350° for 30 minutes or until cake springs back when touched lightly in center. Cool on a wire rack. Yield: 8 servings (serving size: 1 wedge).

CALORIES 206 (30% from fat); FAT 9g (sat 3.3g, mono 2.7g, poly 0.4g); PROTEIN 3.6g; CARB 33.5g; FIBER 1.2g; CHOL 42mg; IRON 1.4mg; SODIUM 162mg; CALC 41mg

Apricot-Orange Crumb Cake

This fruit-flavored version can be served for breakfast, brunch, or as a late-night snack.

1¼ cups all-purpose flour
½ cup sugar
⅛ teaspoon salt
¼ cup chilled butter, cut into small pieces
3 tablespoons tub-style light cream cheese
½ teaspoon baking powder
¼ teaspoon baking soda
⅓ cup 1% low-fat milk
3 tablespoons part-skim ricotta cheese
1 teaspoon vanilla extract
1 teaspoon grated orange rind
1 large egg
¼ cup chopped dried apricots
Cooking spray
¼ cup apricot preserves

1. Preheat oven to 350°.
2. Spoon flour into dry measuring cups; level with a knife. Combine flour, sugar, and salt in a mixing bowl, and cut in butter and cream cheese with a pastry blender or 2 knives until mixture resembles coarse meal. Reserve ½ cup flour mixture for topping; set aside.
3. Combine remaining flour mixture, baking powder, and baking soda; add milk, ricotta cheese, vanilla extract, orange rind, and egg. Beat with a mixer at medium speed until blended (batter will be lumpy), and fold in chopped apricots. Spoon batter into an 8-inch round cake pan coated with cooking spray. Dot batter with apricot preserves, and swirl preserves into batter using a knife. Sprinkle reserved ½ cup flour mixture over batter. Bake at 350° for 30 minutes or until cake springs back when touched lightly in center. Cool on a wire rack. Yield: 8 servings (serving size: 1 wedge).

CALORIES 195 (34% from fat); FAT 7.4g (sat 3.9g, mono 2.5g, poly 0.3g); PROTEIN 3.6g; CARB 28.7g; FIBER 0.5g; CHOL 20mg; IRON 1mg; SODIUM 188mg; CALC 57mg

Making a Crumb Cake

1. Using a large spoon, stir flour gently before measuring, and spoon into a dry measuring cup.

2. Level flour with a knife or small metal spatula. Don't shake the cup—it packs the flour.

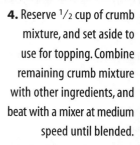

3. After combining flour, sugar, and salt, cut in chilled butter and cream cheese with a pastry blender or two knives until the mixture resembles coarse meal.

4. Reserve ¹/₂ cup of crumb mixture, and set aside to use for topping. Combine remaining crumb mixture with other ingredients, and beat with a mixer at medium speed until blended.

5. Spoon batter into an 8-inch round cake pan coated with cooking spray. Sprinkle with reserved ¹/₂ cup crumb mixture.

Angel Food Cakes

A traditional angel food cake is naturally light because it's made with stiffly beaten egg whites, but not yolks or other fats. The key to making a light and airy angel food cake is beating the egg whites properly.

Angel Food Cake

How many cake recipes do you know of that have less than 1 gram of fat? Here's one.

1	cup cake flour
1¼	cups sugar, divided
10	egg whites
1¼	teaspoon cream of tartar
⅛	teaspoon salt
⅛	teaspoon vanilla extract

1. Preheat oven to 350°.
2. Lightly spoon flour into a dry measuring cup; level with a knife. Sift together flour and ¼ cup sugar; set aside. Beat egg whites until foamy. Add cream of tartar and salt; beat until soft peaks form. Add remaining sugar, 2 tablespoons at a time, beating until stiff peaks form. Sift flour mixture over egg white mixture, ¼ cup at a time; fold in flour mixture. Fold in vanilla.
3. Spoon batter into an ungreased 10-inch tube pan, spreading evenly. Break air pockets by cutting through batter with a knife. Bake at 350° for 40 minutes or until cake springs back when lightly touched. Invert pan; cool completely. Loosen cake from sides of pan using a narrow metal spatula; invert cake onto a serving plate. Yield: 12 servings (serving size: 1 slice).

CALORIES 126 (0% from fat); FAT 0.1g (sat 0g, mono 0g, poly 0g); PROTEIN 3.5g; CARB 27.6g; FIBER 0.3g; CHOL 0mg; IRON 0.6mg; SODIUM 70mg; CALC 3mg

Break air pockets by cutting through batter with a knife.

From the *Cooking Light* Cooks

Here are some words of wisdom on egg whites from our experts in the kitchen.

Eggs are easier to separate when cold, but beat up to a greater volume at room temperature. For best results, separate eggs as soon as you take them out of the refrigerator. But because of food safety concerns, we don't recommend that you let the eggs sit out until they reach room temperature.

When the humidity is high, add 1 teaspoon of cornstarch along with the sugar when making a meringue. This will help stabilize the egg whites (for more information on meringues, see pages 159 and 161).

Cream of tartar increases volume and stabilizes the egg whites, especially during baking.

Always use a clean bowl and beaters to beat egg whites. Even the smallest speck of food or grease will prevent the whites from achieving full volume.

Devilish Angel Food Cake

Add chocolate flavor with cocoa, which is very low in fat.

⅔ cup cake flour
⅓ cup unsweetened cocoa
¼ cup sugar
½ teaspoon ground cinnamon
12 large egg whites
1 teaspoon cream of tartar
2 teaspoons warm water (100° to 110°)
1 teaspoon vanilla extract
½ teaspoon salt
1 cup sugar

1. Preheat oven to 350°.
2. Lightly spoon flour into dry measuring cups; level with a knife. Sift together flour and next 3 ingredients; set aside. Beat egg whites, cream of tartar, warm water, vanilla extract, and salt in a large bowl with a mixer at high speed until foamy. Gradually add 1 cup sugar, 2 tablespoons at a time, beating until stiff peaks form. Sift flour mixture over egg white mixture, ¼ cup at a time, and fold flour mixture in gently.
3. Spoon batter into an ungreased 10-inch tube pan, spreading evenly. Break air pockets by cutting through batter with a knife. Bake at 350° for 45 minutes or until cake springs back when lightly touched. Invert pan; let cool completely. Loosen cake from sides of pan using a narrow spatula; invert cake onto plate. Yield: 8 servings (serving size: 1 slice).

CALORIES 196 (3% from fat); FAT 0.6g (sat 0.3g, mono 0g, poly 0.1g); PROTEIN 6.9g; CARB 41g; FIBER 0g; CHOL 0mg; IRON 1.4g; SODIUM 227mg; CALC 12mg

The best way to remove a bit of yolk from egg whites is to dab it with a small piece of bread; the speck will usually cling to the bread. Egg whites that contain even a speck of yolk will not whip up to maximum volume.

Beating Egg Whites for Angel Food Cake

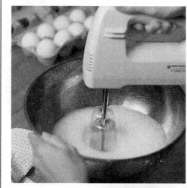

1. Beat egg whites and cream of tartar with a mixer at high speed until foamy.

2. Gradually add sugar, 2 tablespoons at at time, beating with mixer at high speed.

3. At soft-peak stage, the egg whites will gently fold over when beaters are pulled away.

4. When glossy peaks form, the egg whites are stiff. At this stage, they will stand up when the beaters are pulled away.

Pound Cakes

Lightening up a pound cake is simply a matter of decreasing and replacing. We reduced the butter by more than half, used only three eggs instead of five or six, replaced whole milk with fat-free, and reduced the amount of sugar slightly. Instead of greasing the pan, we coated it with cooking spray and sprinkled it with breadcrumbs so that the cake wouldn't stick.

Sour Cream-Lemon Pound Cake

The sour cream adds extra richness to this tangy lemon-flavored cake.

Cooking spray
- 3 tablespoons dry breadcrumbs
- 3¼ cups all-purpose flour
- ½ teaspoon baking soda
- ¼ teaspoon salt
- ¾ cup butter, softened
- 2½ cups granulated sugar
- 2 teaspoons lemon extract
- 3 large eggs
- 1½ tablespoons grated lemon rind (about 2 lemons)
- ¼ cup fresh lemon juice, divided
- 1 (8-ounce) carton low-fat sour cream
- 1 cup powdered sugar

1. Preheat oven to 350°.
2. Coat a 10-inch tube pan with cooking spray, and dust with breadcrumbs.
3. Lightly spoon flour into dry measuring cups; level with a knife. Combine flour, baking soda, and salt in a bowl; stir well with a whisk. Beat butter in a large bowl with a mixer at medium speed until light and fluffy. Gradually add granulated sugar and lemon extract, beating until well blended. Add eggs, 1 at a time, beating well after each addition. Add grated lemon rind and 2 tablespoons lemon juice; beat 30 seconds. Add flour mixture to sugar mixture alternately with sour cream, beating at low speed, beginning and ending with flour mixture.
4. Spoon batter into prepared pan. Bake at 350° for 1 hour and 10 minutes or until a wooden pick inserted in center comes out clean. Cool in pan 10 minutes on wire rack; remove from pan. Cool completely on a wire rack. Combine 2 tablespoons lemon juice and powdered sugar. Drizzle glaze over top of cake. Yield: 18 servings (serving size: 1 slice).

CALORIES 323 (29% from fat); FAT 10.4g (sat 6g, mono 3g, poly 0.6g); PROTEIN 4g; CARB 53.4g; FIBER 0.7g; CHOL 62mg; IRON 1.3mg; SODIUM 172mg; CALC 27mg

Pound Cake Pointers

Jan Moon, Test Kitchens Staffer, offers these tips for baking and storing pound cakes.

Be precise about measuring your flour. If you use too much, you'll end up with a cake that is dry and heavy. (See page 93 for how to measure.)

We prefer to bake pound cakes in 10-inch tube pans, but you can use a 12-cup Bundt pan. Just reduce the oven temperature to 325°.

To freeze pound cake, let it cool completely on a wire rack, then cut it into individual slices. Place unglazed slices in a heavy-duty zip-top plastic bag. Remove excess air from the bag, then seal and place it in your freezer for up to 4 months. To thaw, let it stand at room temperature.

Spice Pound Cake

While you're baking this cake, the rich blend of spices will fill your kitchen with holiday aroma.

Cooking spray
- 3 tablespoons dry breadcrumbs
- 3 cups all-purpose flour
- 2 teaspoons ground cinnamon
- 1 teaspoon baking powder
- 1 teaspoon ground ginger
- ½ teaspoon grated whole nutmeg
- ½ teaspoon ground allspice
- ¼ teaspoon salt
- 10 tablespoons butter, softened
- 1⅓ cups granulated sugar
- 1 cup packed brown sugar
- 2 teaspoons vanilla extract
- 3 large eggs
- 1 cup fat-free milk
- 1 tablespoon powdered sugar

1. Preheat oven to 350°.

2. Coat a 10-inch tube pan with cooking spray, and dust with breadcrumbs.

3. Lightly spoon flour into dry measuring cups; level with a knife. Combine flour and next 6 ingredients; stir well with a whisk. Beat butter in a large bowl with a mixer at medium speed until light and fluffy. Gradually add granulated and brown sugars and vanilla, beating until well blended. Add eggs, 1 at a time, beating well after each addition. Add flour mixture to sugar mixture alternately with milk, beating at low speed, beginning and ending with flour mixture.

4. Spoon batter into prepared pan. Bake at 350° for 1 hour and 5 minutes or until a wooden pick inserted in center comes out clean. Cool in pan 10 minutes on a wire rack; remove from pan. Cool completely on wire rack. Sift powdered sugar over top of cake. Yield: 18 servings (serving size: 1 slice).

CALORIES 263 (26% from fat); FAT 7.6g (sat 4.3g, mono 2.2g, poly 0.5g); PROTEIN 3.9g; CARB 45g; FIBER 0.7g; CHOL 54mg; IRON 1.6mg; SODIUM 158mg; CALC 58mg

Brown Sugar Pound Cake

When we were fine-tuning our methods for making pound cakes by preparing lots of them, this basic pound cake was our staff's favorite. The brown sugar gives the cake a rich caramel-like flavor.

Cooking spray
- 3 tablespoons dry breadcrumbs
- 3 cups all-purpose flour
- 1 teaspoon baking powder
- ¼ teaspoon salt
- ¾ cup butter, softened
- 2 cups packed light brown sugar
- 1 tablespoon vanilla extract
- 3 large eggs
- 1 cup fat-free milk
- 1 tablespoon powdered sugar

1. Preheat oven to 350°.

2. Coat a 10-inch tube pan with cooking spray, and dust with breadcrumbs.

3. Lightly spoon flour into dry measuring cups; level with a knife. Combine flour, baking powder and salt in a bowl; stir well with a whisk. Beat butter in a large bowl with a mixer at medium speed until light and fluffy. Gradually add brown sugar and vanilla, beating until well blended. Add eggs, 1 at a time, beating well after each addition. Add flour mixture to sugar mixture alternately with milk, beating at low speed, beginning and ending with flour mixture.

4. Spoon batter into prepared pan. Bake at 350° for 1 hour and 5 minutes or until a wooden pick inserted in center comes out clean. Cool in pan 10 minutes on a wire rack; remove from pan. Cool completely on wire rack. Sift powdered sugar over top of cake. Yield: 18 servings (serving size: 1 slice).

CALORIES 265 (30% from fat); FAT 8.9g (sat 5.1g, mono 2.6g, poly 0.5g); PROTEIN 3.9g; CARB 42.6g; FIBER 0.6g; CHOL 58mg; IRON 1.7mg; SODIUM 176mg; CALC 65mg

Sheet Cakes

Why do we love sheet cakes? Well, for starters, they're easy and quick because you don't have to worry about baking cake layers or spreading frosting over layers. They're also easy to transport and to cut into squares. What's not to love? We've lightened two popular sheet cakes, and we don't think you'll be able to tell the difference.

Texas Sheet Cake

We reduced the fat and calories by more than half in this reader recipe by decreasing the butter in the cake, taking some butter and sugar out of the icing, and decreasing the pecans.

"When you are making sheet cakes, always use a baking pan (or jelly-roll pan) instead of a glass dish. Cakes brown better in metal pans." Jan Moon, Test Kitchens Staffer

Cake:
Cooking spray
2   teaspoons all-purpose flour
2   cups all-purpose flour
2   cups granulated sugar
1   teaspoon baking soda
1   teaspoon ground cinnamon
¼   teaspoon salt
¾   cup water
½   cup butter
¼   cup unsweetened cocoa
½   cup low-fat buttermilk
1   teaspoon vanilla extract
2   large eggs
Icing:
6   tablespoons butter
⅓   cup fat-free milk
¼   cup unsweetened cocoa
3   cups powdered sugar
¼   cup chopped pecans, toasted
2   teaspoons vanilla extract

1. Preheat oven to 375°.

2. To prepare cake, coat a 15 x 10-inch jelly-roll pan with cooking spray, and dust with 2 teaspoons flour.

3. Lightly spoon 2 cups flour into dry measuring cups; level with a knife. Combine 2 cups flour and next 4 ingredients in a large bowl; stir well with a whisk. Combine water, ½ cup butter, and ¼ cup cocoa in a small saucepan; bring to a boil, stirring frequently. Remove from heat; pour into flour mixture. Beat with a mixer at medium speed until well blended. Add buttermilk, 1 teaspoon vanilla, and eggs; beat well. Pour batter into prepared pan; bake at 375° for 17 minutes or until a wooden pick inserted in center comes out clean. Place on a wire rack.

4. To prepare icing, combine 6 tablespoons butter, milk, and ¼ cup cocoa in a medium saucepan; bring to a boil, stirring constantly. Remove from heat, and gradually stir in powdered sugar, pecans, and 2 teaspoons vanilla. Spread over hot cake. Cool completely on wire rack. Yield: 20 servings (serving size: 1 slice).

CALORIES 298 (30% from fat); FAT 10g (sat 5.5g, mono 3.2g, poly 0.7g); PROTEIN 3.1g; CARB 49.8g; FIBER 0.5g; CHOL 44mg; IRON 1.1mg; SODIUM 188mg; CALC 25mg

You can also make this recipe in a 13 x 9-inch baking pan. Bake at 375° for 22 minutes.

Half-the-Fat Carrot Cake with Cream Cheese Frosting

Traditional carrot cakes can have as much as 1 1/2 cups of oil; this one has far less fat but is still moist and tender. Drain the carrots in a colander to help maintain the cake's texture and keep it from becoming too heavy.

Cake:

¾	cup applesauce
5	cups shredded carrot (about 1 pound)
¾	cup granulated sugar
¾	cup packed dark brown sugar
½	cup butter, softened
1	teaspoon vanilla extract
1	teaspoon coconut extract
2	large eggs
2	large egg whites
2	cups all-purpose flour
2	teaspoons baking powder
1	teaspoon baking soda
½	teaspoon ground nutmeg
½	teaspoon ground cinnamon
¼	teaspoon salt
1	cup golden raisins

Cooking spray

Frosting:

4	cups sifted powdered sugar
2	teaspoons vanilla extract
1	(8-ounce) block fat-free cream cheese, chilled
1	(8-ounce) block ⅓-less-fat cream cheese, chilled

1. Preheat oven to 350°.

2. To prepare cake, spoon applesauce into a fine sieve over a bowl; let stand 15 minutes. Discard liquid. Scrape drained applesauce into a bowl; cover and refrigerate.

3. Combine carrot and granulated sugar in a colander. Drain 20 minutes.

4. Beat brown sugar and butter with a mixer at medium speed until well blended (about 2 minutes). Add applesauce, 1 teaspoon vanilla, and coconut extract; beat until well blended (about 2 minutes). Add eggs and egg whites, 1 at a time, beating well after each addition (batter will have a slightly curdled look).

5. Lightly spoon flour into dry measuring cups; level with a knife. Combine flour and next 5 ingredients; stir well with a whisk. Add brown sugar mixture to flour mixture, stirring just until moist. Fold in carrot mixture and raisins (batter will be very thick). Spoon batter into a 13 x 9-inch baking pan coated with cooking spray.

6. Bake at 350° for 40 minutes or until a wooden pick inserted in center comes out clean. Cool completely on a wire rack.

7. To prepare frosting, beat powdered sugar, 2 teaspoons vanilla, and cheeses with a mixer at low speed just until well blended (do not over-beat). Spread frosting over cake; cover and chill 1 hour. Yield: 20 servings (serving size: 1 slice).

CALORIES 322 (23% from fat); FAT 8.1g (sat 4.8g, mono 2.3g, poly 0.5g); PROTEIN 5.6g; CARB 57.7g; FIBER 1.7g; CHOL 45mg; IRON 1.2mg; SODIUM 327mg; CALC 91mg

Applesauce for Fat?

Test Kitchen SECRET

We've rarely replaced fat with applesauce in our recipes because the results have seldom met our standards. So we were skeptical when we learned about this trick: draining the applesauce, either by paper towel or by strainer. It makes all the difference, and we're sold. Here's how to do it.

The Paper-Towel Approach

1. Spoon applesauce onto several layers of heavy-duty paper towels; spread to a 1/2-inch thickness.

2. Cover with additional paper towels; let stand 5 minutes.

3. Scrape applesauce into a bowl using a rubber spatula; cover and refrigerate.

The Strainer Approach

1. Place a fine sieve into a bowl large enough so that the sieve doesn't touch the bottom of the bowl.

2. Spoon applesauce into sieve. Let stand 15 minutes.

Génoise (Zhehn-wahz)

You could call this classic cake the original low-fat confection. Génoise is a chameleon of a cake—a basis for layer cakes, tortes, ice cream cakes, and jelly-rolls. Unlike typical layer cakes, it is based on eggs, with flour, sugar, and only a bit of butter mixed in. You can brush generous amounts of tasty liquids over the dense, golden body, and it won't disintegrate. It also holds up to rolling and slicing. Traditional adaptations include baked Alaska, ladyfingers, and petits fours.

A Perfect Génoise

Our cake expert, Jan Moon, shares her tips for making a perfect génoise.

Read the recipe completely before beginning, and have equipment and ingredients organized. Work quickly to get the cake in the oven before the eggs begin to deflate.

Make sure the oven temperature is correctly set at 375°. Check temperature with an oven thermometer.

Eggs at room temperature will beat up to a higher volume. If you've just taken your eggs out of the refrigerator, place them in a bowl of warm, but not steaming, water for 5 minutes.

Stand mixers have stronger motors than the handheld kind, so they beat quicker and more thoroughly. We found both worked successfully, but the hand mixer took more time to beat the eggs.

Use cake flour for a génoise because, in this case, it makes a lighter, more delicate cake.

Classic Génoise

To bake this cake a day ahead, let it cool completely, wrap it in plastic wrap, and store at room temperature.

Cooking spray
1   tablespoon cake flour
2   tablespoons butter
1   cup unsifted cake flour (about 3¾ ounces)
⅛   teaspoon salt
½   cup sugar
1   teaspoon vanilla extract
4   large eggs

1. Preheat oven to 375°.
2. Coat a 15 x 10-inch jelly-roll pan or a 9-inch springform pan with cooking spray; line with wax paper. Coat paper with cooking spray; dust with 1 tablespoon flour. Set aside.
3. Cook butter in a small saucepan over medium heat until lightly browned (about 4 minutes). Pour into a small bowl; cool and set aside.
4. Lightly spoon 1 cup flour into a dry measuring cup; level with a knife. Combine 1 cup flour and salt in a sifter. Sift the flour and salt once; set aside.
5. Beat sugar, vanilla, and eggs with a mixer at high speed until ribbons fall from beaters (about 10 to 15 minutes or until the egg mixture holds its shape). Lightly spoon one-third of flour mixture onto egg mixture; quickly fold. Repeat procedure twice with remaining flour mixture.
6. Stir 1 cup batter into cooled browned butter. Fold butter mixture into remaining batter. Spoon batter into pan; spread evenly. Bake in jelly-roll pan at 375° for 12 minutes or in springform pan for 20 minutes, or until a wooden pick inserted in center comes out clean or cake springs back when touched lightly in center. Loosen from sides of pan; turn out onto a wire rack. Peel off wax paper. Cool completely. Yield: 12 servings.

CALORIES 109 (31% from fat); FAT 3.8g (sat 1.7g, mono 1.2g, poly 0.3g); PROTEIN 2.9g; CARB 15.5g; FIBER 0g; CHOL 79mg; IRON 0.9mg; SODIUM 66mg; CALC 10mg

Making a Génoise

1. Coat the pan with cooking spray; line bottom with wax paper. Then coat the paper with cooking spray, and dust with flour. Because génoise is a delicate yet sturdy cake, it's important to prepare the pan well so the cake doesn't stick.

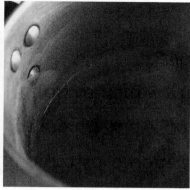

2. "Cook" the butter over medium heat until lightly browned to give the génoise a marvelous, nutty flavor. Be forewarned that margarine will not brown, so it's important to use butter. Watch the butter carefully because it can burn quickly.

3. Sift flour and salt together. This "lightens" the flour, making it easier to incorporate into the beaten eggs, thereby minimizing lumps. A few lumps of flour, though, are typical.

4. Combine sugar, vanilla, and eggs; beat until mixture falls in ribbons from beaters, about 10 to 15 minutes. If ribbons don't form after beating for 15 minutes, continue to beat the mixture until they do.

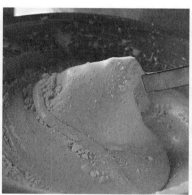

5. Sprinkle one-third of flour mixture over the egg mixture, and fold into the egg mixture. Folding gently combines the flour with the egg mixture without deflating the eggs. To do this, use a rubber spatula to cut through the batter in the center of the bowl until you reach the bottom; then draw the spatula up the side of the bowl. Give the bowl a quarter turn and repeat the process. Work quickly, but don't stir.

6. Stir about one cup batter into the cooled browned butter, then fold back into remaining batter. This helps disperse the butter.

Cheesecakes

A cheesecake is not exactly the picture of light baking with pounds of cream cheese, almost a half-dozen egg yolks, and heavy cream. But we've created breakthrough recipes that match traditional cheesecakes in richness and texture while cutting the fat by at least half.

Ask the *Cooking Light* Cooks

How can you lighten a cheesecake? We do it by reducing the fat in the crusts, using combinations of fat-free and light cream cheeses, replacing some of the egg yolks with egg whites, and using low-fat milk instead of heavy cream.

What's the best way to know it's done? The center will jiggle slightly and should be about 3 inches in diameter. Place the pan on a wire rack, and run a knife around the outside edge; cool completely to room temperature.

What's wrong if my cheesecake cracks? Some cracking on the top is normal and can even make it look prettier. The most common cause of cracking is a drastic change in temperature when cooking or cooling. Generally, the slower the cheesecake is cooked, the less chance of cracking. To bake slowly and evenly, use an oven thermometer to see if your oven is staying at the correct temperature. *You can also prevent cracking if you run a knife or small metal spatula around the edge of the cheesecake immediately after removing it from the oven. This allows the loosened sides to contract freely.*

What type of springform pan should I use? Our cheesecakes were prepared in two types of springform pans: shiny aluminum and those with a dark, almost black surface. If you use a dark pan, decrease the baking time by 10 minutes.

Chocolate Cheesecake

This cheesecake has a chocolate cookie-crumb crust, plus cocoa and semisweet chocolate in the filling.

Crust:
 1 cup packaged chocolate cookie crumbs
 2 tablespoons sugar
 1 tablespoon butter, melted
 Cooking spray
Filling:
 ½ cup Dutch process cocoa
 ¼ cup 1% low-fat milk
 3 ounces semisweet chocolate, melted
 4 (8-ounce) blocks fat-free cream cheese, softened
 1 (8-ounce) block ⅓-less-fat cream cheese, softened
 1½ cups sugar
 3 tablespoons all-purpose flour
 2 teaspoons vanilla extract
 4 large eggs
 2 tablespoons sliced almonds, toasted

1. Preheat oven to 325°.
2. Combine first 3 ingredients; toss with a fork until moist. Press into bottom of a 9-inch springform pan coated with cooking spray.
3. Combine cocoa, milk, and chocolate; stir well. Beat cheeses with a mixer at high speed until smooth. Add 1½ cups sugar, flour, and vanilla; beat well. Add chocolate mixture; beat well. Add eggs, 1 at a time, beating well after each addition.
4. Pour cheese mixture into pan; bake at 325° for 1 hour and 10 minutes or until almost set (cheesecake is done when center barely moves when pan is touched). Remove from oven; run a knife around outside edge. Cool to room temperature. Cover and chill at least 8 hours. Sprinkle with almonds. Yield: 16 servings (serving size: 1 wedge).

CALORIES 284 (31% from fat); FAT 9.9g (sat 4.7g, mono 3.3g, poly 1.2g); PROTEIN 13.1g; CARB 35.3g; FIBER 0.4g; CHOL 78mg; IRON 1.5mg; SODIUM 471mg; CALC 191mg

"We combined pureed fat-free cottage cheese and reduced-fat cream cheese to get a creamy New York-style cheesecake. The results were perfect." Kellie Kelley, Food Stylist

New York Cheesecake

The crust in a New York-style cheesecake is a flour-butter mixture that is sprinkled on the bottom of the pan and does not come up the sides.

Crust:

⅔	cup all-purpose flour
3	tablespoons sugar
2	tablespoons chilled butter, cut into pieces
1	tablespoon ice water

Cooking spray

Filling:

4	cups fat-free cottage cheese
2	cups sugar
2	(8-ounce) blocks ⅓-less-fat cream cheese, softened
¼	cup all-purpose flour
½	cup fat-free sour cream
1	tablespoon grated lemon rind
1	tablespoon vanilla extract
¼	teaspoon salt
5	large eggs

1. Preheat oven to 400°.

2. To prepare crust, lightly spoon ⅔ cup flour into dry measuring cups; level with a knife. Place ⅔ cup flour and 3 tablespoons sugar in a food processor; pulse 2 times or until combined. Add butter; pulse 6 times or until mixture resembles coarse meal. With processor on, slowly pour ice water through food chute, processing just until blended (do not allow dough to form a ball).

3. Firmly press mixture into bottom of a 9 x 3-inch springform pan coated with cooking spray. Bake at 400° for 10 minutes or until lightly browned; cool on a wire rack.

4. Reduce oven temperature to 325°.

5. To prepare filling, strain cottage cheese through a cheesecloth-lined sieve for 10 minutes; discard liquid. Place cottage cheese in food processor; process until smooth.

6. Place 2 cups sugar and cream cheese in a large bowl; beat with a mixer at medium speed until smooth. Lightly spoon ¼ cup flour into a dry measuring cup; level with a knife. Add ¼ cup flour, sour cream, and remaining 4 ingredients to cream cheese mixture; beat well. Add cottage cheese, stirring until well blended. Pour mixture into prepared crust.

7. Bake at 325° for 1 hour and 30 minutes or until almost set. Turn oven off. Cool cheesecake in closed oven 1 hour. Remove cheesecake from oven; run a knife around outside edge. Cool to room temperature. Cover and chill at least 8 hours. Yield: 16 servings (serving size: 1 wedge).

CALORIES 291 (30% from fat); FAT 9.8g (sat 5.7g, mono 3g, poly 0.5g); PROTEIN 12.9g; CARB 37.7g; FIBER 0.2g; CHOL 98mg; IRON 0.7mg; SODIUM 410mg; CALC 93mg

We wanted the height of a traditional New York-style cheesecake, so we baked this in a springform pan with 3-inch sides. If you're not sure about the dimensions of your pan, use a ruler to measure the inside of the pan. You can also use a 10 x 2½-inch springform pan: Bake at 300° for 1 hour and 30 minutes or until almost set. Turn oven off. Cool cheesecake in closed oven 30 minutes.

Sweet Potato Cheesecake

Canned sweet potatoes and packaged graham cracker crumbs are great time-savers. For the smoothest, most velvety texture, puree the potatoes completely so there are no lumps.

Crust:

2 cups graham cracker crumbs (about 12 sheets)
3 tablespoons sugar
2 tablespoons butter, melted
1 tablespoon water
   Cooking spray

Filling:

½ cup vanilla fat-free yogurt
2 (8-ounce) blocks ⅓-less-fat cream cheese, softened
2 (8-ounce) blocks fat-free cream cheese, softened
⅓ cup all-purpose flour
1¼ cups sugar
1 tablespoon vanilla extract
1 tablespoon light molasses
¾ teaspoon ground cinnamon
½ teaspoon ground ginger
¼ teaspoon salt
¼ teaspoon ground nutmeg
3 large eggs
2 (15-ounce) cans sweet potatoes, drained

1. Preheat oven to 350°.

2. To prepare crust, combine first 4 ingredients, tossing with a fork until well blended. Press into bottom of a 9-inch springform pan coated with cooking spray. Bake at 350° for 10 minutes; cool on a wire rack. Reduce oven temperature to 325°.

3. To prepare filling, place yogurt and cheeses in a large bowl; beat with a mixer at high speed until smooth. Lightly spoon flour into a dry measuring cup; level with a knife. Add flour and next 7 ingredients to cheese mixture; beat well. Add eggs, 1 at a time, beating well after each addition.

4. Place sweet potatoes in a food processor; process until smooth. Add sweet potatoes to cheese mixture, stirring until well blended.

5. Pour cheese mixture into prepared crust. Bake at 325° for 1 hour and 20 minutes or until cheesecake center barely moves when pan is touched. Turn oven off. Cool cheesecake in closed oven 1 hour.

6. Remove cheesecake from oven; run a knife around outside edge. Cool to room temperature. Cover and chill at least 8 hours. Yield: 16 servings (serving size: 1 wedge).

CALORIES 310 (29% from fat); FAT 10.1g (sat 5.5g, mono 3.2g, poly 1g); PROTEIN 10.3g; CARB 44g; FIBER 1.6g; CHOL 67mg; IRON 1.2mg; SODIUM 434mg; CALC 134mg

---

Freezing Cheesecake
Test Kitchen SECRET

You can freeze cheesecake for up to 1 month. Remove pan; place cheesecake on a cardboard circle, if desired, and wrap tightly in heavy-duty foil. Thaw in the refrigerator the day before serving.

"Some cheesecakes should be removed from the cooling oven just as they set, while others require more time in the oven. We specify which to do in each recipe."

Kathleen Kanen, Food Stylist

Zebra-Stripe Cheesecake
The stripes are impressive but easy to make!

1   cup graham cracker crumbs (about 6 sheets)
2   tablespoons butter, melted
Cooking spray
3   (8-ounce) blocks fat-free cream cheese, softened
1   (8-ounce) block ⅓-less-fat cream cheese, softened
1   cup sugar
½   cup 1% low-fat milk
2   teaspoons vanilla extract
2   large eggs
2   large egg whites
4   ounces semisweet chocolate, melted

1. Preheat oven to 325°.
2. Combine crumbs and butter; toss until moist. Press into the bottom of a 9-inch springform pan coated with cooking spray.
3. Beat cheeses with a mixer at high speed. Add sugar, milk, and vanilla; beat well. Add eggs and egg whites, 1 at a time, beating after each addition. Pour half into another bowl. Add chocolate to remaining batter. Pour one-third of white batter into pan. Pour one-half of chocolate batter in center of white batter in pan; spread to within 1 inch of edge of white. Pour one-third of white batter in center of chocolate; spread to within 1 inch of edge of chocolate. Pour remaining chocolate batter in center of white; spread to within 1 inch of edge of white. Pour remaining white batter in center of chocolate; spread to within 1 inch of chocolate.
4. Bake at 325° for 1 hour and 10 minutes or until almost set (cheesecake is done when center barely moves when pan is touched). Remove from oven; run a knife around outside edge. Cool to room temperature. Cover and chill at least 8 hours. Yield: 16 servings (serving size: 1 wedge).

CALORIES 210 (36% from fat); FAT 8.4g (sat 4.7g, mono 2.7g, poly 0.5g); PROTEIN 9.7g; CARB 23.8g; FIBER 0.1g; CHOL 50mg; IRON 0.6mg; SODIUM 385mg; CALC 147mg

Making the Zebra Stripes

1. Pour one-third of the white batter into prepared pan.

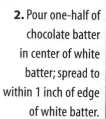

2. Pour one-half of chocolate batter in center of white batter; spread to within 1 inch of edge of white batter.

3. Pour one-third of white batter in center of chocolate batter; spread to within 1 inch of edge of chocolate batter.

4. Pour remaining chocolate batter in center of white batter; spread to within 1 inch of edge of white batter.

5. Pour remaining white batter in center of chocolate batter; spread to within 1 inch of edge of chocolate batter.

Pies

A classic piecrust requires the right combination of butter and shortening and the best proportion of flour to ice water.

A Crust You Can Trust

Typically, the piecrust is responsible for more fat and calories than the filling. In an average apple pie, for example, the crust contributes 70 percent of the fat and more than half the calories of each slice.

If you're committed to making a pie from scratch, start with the crust. Most of the pies featured here use pastry crust (see our Piecrust recipe on facing page). Great pastry relies on fat to deliver tender texture and delicate flavor; specifically, vegetable shortening creates flakiness, and butter lends richness. We've added just enough of each to yield a peerless crust with minimal fat. Even though the actual difference in fat and calories between our pastry and the store-bought variety may be small, the difference in flavor is great.

We've come up with a a crust that's a snap to make and adaptable enough for our best fillings. It stands up to a side-by-side blind taste test against the full-fat version, and it's so easy that even an inexperienced baker can pull it off with panache.

Getting a Great Crust	Test Kitchen SECRET

Measure your flour correctly to ensure a tender crust. (See page 93.) Scooping the measuring cup into the flour will give you too much flour.

Chill the butter before you add it to the flour mixture. If it's too soft, it will melt and toughen the crust.

Be patient when cutting the butter or shortening in with a pastry blender or knife; it may take as long as 5 minutes for it to look like coarse meal. This is how the fat gets distributed in the flour, creating pockets that, when heated, makes the pastry flaky.

Chill the flour to make a piecrust flakier. Chill it in the freezer for 1 hour prior to making the pastry dough. This helps prevent the fat being cut into the flour from melting—which makes for tough crusts.

Freeze the dough to make it easier to handle. You want to handle the dough as little as possible—overhandling will make the crust tough. Place the rolled-out pastry in the freezer for 10 minutes. Fit the dough into a 9-inch pie plate by inverting the dough over the plate. Then peel off the plastic wrap. If the dough tears or cracks, just press it back together.

Piecrust

This recipe makes a 9- or 10-inch crust that's much tastier than commercial pie dough. This dough can be rolled out and frozen in between sheets of plastic wrap for up to a week, or rolled out, placed in a pie plate, covered tightly, and refrigerated for 2 days.

1½ cups all-purpose flour
2   tablespoons sugar
¼   teaspoon salt
3   tablespoons butter
2   tablespoons vegetable shortening
4   tablespoons ice water
Cooking spray

1. Preheat oven to 400°.
2. Lightly spoon flour into dry measuring cups; level with a knife. Combine flour, sugar, and salt in a bowl; cut in butter and shortening with a pastry blender or 2 knives until mixture resembles coarse meal. Sprinkle surface with ice water, 1 tablespoon at a time; toss with a fork until moist and crumbly (do not form a ball).
3. Press mixture into a 4-inch circle on plastic wrap; cover and chill 15 minutes. Slightly overlap sheets of plastic wrap on a damp surface. Unwrap and place chilled dough on plastic wrap. Cover with 2 additional sheets of overlapping plastic wrap. Roll dough, still covered, into a 13-inch circle. Place dough in freezer 5 minutes or until plastic wrap can easily be removed.
4. Remove top sheets of plastic wrap; fit dough, plastic wrap side up, into a pie plate coated with cooking spray. Remove remaining plastic wrap. Fold edges under and flute. Pierce bottom and sides of dough with fork; bake at 400° for 15 minutes. Cool on a wire rack. Yield: 1 piecrust (10 servings).

CALORIES 113 (48% from fat); FAT 6g (sat 2.7g, mono 2.1g, poly 0.8g); PROTEIN 1.8g; CARB 13g; FIBER 0.5g; CHOL 9mg; IRON 0.8mg; SODIUM 65mg; CALC 1mg

Making the Perfect Pastry

1. Cutting in the fat means combining flour, butter, and shortening until pebble-size crumbs form.

2. Press mixture into a 4-inch circle on plastic wrap; cover and chill 15 minutes. Slightly overlap sheets of plastic wrap on a damp surface. Unwrap and place chilled dough on plastic wrap. Cover with 2 additional sheets of overlapping plastic wrap. Roll dough, still covered, into a 13-inch circle. Place dough in freezer 5 minutes or until plastic wrap can easily be removed.

3. Roll dough into a 13-inch circle. If you don't have a rolling pin, use a straight-sided jar or glass. To get an even thickness, think of rolling north, south, east, and west. Lift up the rolling pin as you near the edges so they won't get too thin.

Crust Swapping

Here's an approximate comparison of the crusts with no filling, based on a serving slice of one-tenth the total.

Crust	Calories	Fat	Notes
Cooking Light basic piecrust	113	6g (48% calories from fat)	You can use a commercial crust (such as Pillsbury refrigerated dough) to save time. The calories and fat are actually a little lower with a Pillsbury crust than with our crust, but we think commercial crusts are too salty. (Pillsbury refrigerated pie dough is the lowest in fat and calories of all the commercial brands we have checked.)
Commercial piecrust	95	5.5g (52% calories from fat)	
Cooking Light graham cracker crust	114	4.6g (36% calories from fat)	Our Graham Cracker Crust (below), is lower in fat than conventional homemade recipes that typically use more butter. It's also lower in fat than most commercial crusts, although some, such as Keebler and Ready Crust, are similar in fat to ours. The difference in flavor, though, still tips the scale to making our recipe.
Traditional homemade graham cracker crust	148	7.5g (46% calories from fat)	

Note: The nutritional analysis at the end of each of our pie recipes is for one serving and includes crust and filling.

Graham Cracker Crust

This crust is lower in fat than many commercial graham cracker crusts. You can use this in the Double-Chocolate Cream Pie (page 163) and the Peanut Butter-Banana Pie (page 162) instead of a pastry crust or a vanilla wafer crust.

    40   graham crackers (10 sheets)
     2   tablespoons sugar
     2   tablespoons butter, melted
     1   large egg white
    Cooking spray

1. Place crackers in a food processor; process until crumbly. Add sugar, butter, and egg white; pulse 6 times or just until moist. Press crumb mixture into a 9-inch pie plate coated with cooking spray. Bake at 350° for 8 minutes; cool on a wire rack 15 minutes. Yield: 1 piecrust (8 servings).

CALORIES 114 (36% from fat); FAT 4.6g (sat 1.7g, mono 1.8g, poly 0.2g); PROTEIN 1.7g; CARB 16.5g; FIBER 0.6g; CHOL 8mg; IRON 0.7mg; SODIUM 194mg; CALC 142mg

Making a Graham Cracker Crust
Test Kitchen SECRET

Pulsing cookies in a food processor will give you the best cookie crumbs, but if you don't have a food processor to make the graham cracker crumbs, you can do one of three things:
- Buy boxed graham cracker crumbs; the work is already done for you, and the calories and fat are the same as if you'd made your own crumbs.
- Use a blender instead of a food processor, but make crumbs in smaller batches and pulse; don't pulverize.
- Place the graham crackers in a zip-top plastic bag, and roll with a heavy rolling pin or bottle to make crumbs.

Cream Pies

We gave a few of our favorite cream pies a nutritional makeover. Here's what we learned.

The Filling The filling, which requires the most attention, should hold its shape when sliced but shouldn't be too firm. Whether thickened with flour or cornstarch (we've used both), the best custards are made with 1% or 2% milk. Using fat-free milk or juice alone will yield a thin custard. Just a dab of butter adds richness and flavor. Some egg yolks are necessary for consistency; using egg substitute or egg whites by themselves won't work.

The Topping For food safety reasons, we use Italian meringues rather than the traditional (uncooked) variation. Italian meringues are made by whipping egg whites with cooked sugar syrup. This procedure heats the whites to 238°, which renders them safe to eat (see page 161 for meringue techniques). Meringues are delicate and will disintegrate or "weep" over time, so add them just before serving. If you choose to use whipped topping instead, it can be added before chilling.

Using a sauce whisk is a must for stirring custards. It's the best way to get all the ingredients blended without excess air, and to get rid of the lumps.

Pie Custard Basics — Test Kitchen SECRET

When making a custard for a cream pie, you should gradually add the hot custard to the eggs—this is called tempering. Then you return the mixture to the pan and cook until thick. If the eggs are added directly to the hot custard, they might curdle.

For cornstarch to thicken properly, cook the custard until thick and bubbly, even if you exceed the time stated in the recipe. Cornstarch must come to a full boil and boil for 1 minute. Stir constantly with a whisk so the custard will be smooth. Undercooked custard is thin and tastes starchy.

Place a bowl of hot custard in a bowl of ice to cool quickly. The filling sets better if cooled completely when spooned into the crust.

Coconut Cream Pie

This pie takes a brief turn under the broiler to brown the peaks of the Italian meringue.

Crust:
1   (10-inch) Piecrust (page 157) or ½ (15-ounce) package refrigerated pie dough

Filling:
¼   cup all-purpose flour
½   cup sugar
⅛   teaspoon salt
2   large eggs
¾   cup 2% reduced-fat milk
¾   cup light coconut milk
¼   teaspoon coconut extract
¼   teaspoon vanilla extract

Meringue:
3   large egg whites
⅔   cup sugar
¼   cup water
1   tablespoon flaked sweetened coconut, toasted

1. Prepare and bake piecrust in a 10-inch deep-dish pie plate. Cool completely on a wire rack.
2. To prepare filling, lightly spoon flour into a dry measuring cup; level. Combine flour, ½ cup sugar, salt, and eggs in a large bowl; stir well with a whisk.

3. Heat milk and coconut milk over medium-high heat in a small, heavy saucepan to 180° or until tiny bubbles form around edge (do not boil). Gradually add hot milk mixture to sugar mixture, stirring constantly with a whisk. Place mixture in pan; cook over medium heat until thick and bubbly (about 10 minutes), stirring constantly.
4. Remove from heat. Spoon custard into a bowl; place bowl in a large ice-filled bowl for 10 minutes or until custard comes to room temperature, stirring occasionally. Remove bowl from ice. Stir in extracts; spoon mixture into prepared crust. Cover and chill 8 hours until firm.
5. Preheat broiler.
6. To prepare meringue, place egg whites in a large bowl; beat with a mixer at high speed until soft peaks form. Combine ⅔ cup sugar and water in a saucepan; bring to a boil. Cook, without stirring, until a candy thermometer registers 238°. Pour hot sugar syrup in a thin stream over egg whites, beating at high speed until stiff peaks form.
7. Spread meringue over chilled pie; sprinkle with coconut. Broil for 1 minute or until meringue is lightly browned; cool 5 minutes on a wire rack. Serve immediately. Yield: 10 servings (serving size: 1 wedge).

CALORIES 281 (30% from fat); FAT 9.3g (sat 5.6g, mono 2.6g, poly 0.4g); PROTEIN 5.3g; CARB 45.6g; FIBER 0.6g; CHOL 63mg; IRON 1.4mg; SODIUM 208mg; CALC 28mg

---

Baking Crusts for Refrigerated Pies

For refrigerated pies, the pastry is baked without the filling; this is also called blind baking. To do it, line the pastry with foil or wax paper, and fill it with pie weights or uncooked dried beans, which work just as well (save the beans for this purpose only, as they can't be cooked afterward). This weighs down the pastry and prevents it from bubbling up as it bakes in the oven.

To avoid the smell that beans can cause, bake with a glass pie dish instead. Line dough in a pie pan, prick it with a fork, cover with parchment paper, and place a glass dish on top. The glass is heavy enough to keep the crust weighted while it's baking. To brown the crust, uncover it a few minutes before it's done baking.

Mango-Lime Icebox Pie

Look for mango nectar in the Latin foods section of your supermarket.

Crust:

1   (9-inch) Piecrust (page 157) or ½ (15-ounce) package refrigerated pie dough

Filling:

1   cup mango nectar
¾   cup sugar
½   cup fresh lime juice (about 4 limes)
¼   cup cornstarch
¼   cup fresh orange juice
2   large eggs
2½ tablespoons butter
2   teaspoons grated lime rind

Meringue:

3   large egg whites
⅛   teaspoon salt
½   cup sugar
¼   cup water

1. Prepare and bake piecrust in a 9-inch pie plate. Cool completely on a wire rack.

2. To prepare filling, combine nectar and next 5 ingredients in a large saucepan, stirring with a whisk. Bring to a boil over medium heat, stirring constantly. Cook 1 minute, stirring constantly. Remove from heat; stir in butter and 2 teaspoons rind. Spoon mango mixture into a bowl; place bowl in a large ice-filled bowl for 10 minutes or until mixture comes to room temperature, stirring occasionally. Remove bowl from ice; spoon mixture into crust. Cover and chill 8 hours or until firm.

3. To prepare meringue, place egg whites and salt in a large bowl; beat with a mixer at high speed until soft peaks form. Combine ½ cup sugar and water in a saucepan; bring to a boil. Cook, without stirring, until candy thermometer registers 238°. Pour hot sugar syrup in a thin stream over egg whites, beating at high speed until stiff peaks

form. Spread meringue over filling. Yield: 9 servings (serving size: 1 wedge).

CALORIES 267 (30% from fat); FAT 9g (sat 3g, mono 3.3g, poly 2g); PROTEIN 3.4g; CARB 44.4g; FIBER 0.5g; CHOL 56mg; IRON 0.3mg; SODIUM 190mg; CALC 14mg

How to Make an Italian Meringue

1. Beat egg whites until soft peaks form (above). Overbeating—incorporating too much air—will cause them to separate (right). See page 145 for more information on beating egg whites.

2. Combine sugar and water in a saucepan. Bring to a boil. Using a candy thermometer, cook until 238° (or soft ball stage). Do not stir.

3. Slowly pour the sugar syrup into the egg whites, beating with a mixer at high speed until the syrup is thoroughly incorporated. The meringue should look smooth and glossy.

Peanut Butter-Banana Pie

Use bananas that are firm rather than extraripe so that the banana slices will hold their shape. The filling needs the creaminess of regular creamy peanut butter, so don't substitute with natural peanut butter.

Crust:
- 1 cup reduced-calorie vanilla wafer crumbs (about 30 cookies)
- 2 tablespoons butter, melted and cooled
- 1 large egg white, lightly beaten

Cooking spray

Filling:
- ⅔ cup sugar
- 3½ tablespoons cornstarch
- ¼ teaspoon salt
- 1⅓ cups 1% low-fat milk
- 2 large eggs, lightly beaten
- 2 tablespoons creamy peanut butter
- 1 teaspoon vanilla extract
- 2½ cups sliced banana
- 1½ cups frozen reduced-calorie whipped topping, thawed

1. Preheat oven to 350°.

2. To prepare crust, combine first 3 ingredients; toss with a fork until moist. Press into bottom and up sides of a 9-inch pie plate coated with cooking spray. Bake at 350° for 12 minutes; cool crust on a wire rack.

3. To prepare filling, combine sugar, cornstarch, and salt in a saucepan. Gradually add milk, stirring with a whisk until well blended. Cook over medium heat until mixture comes to a boil; cook 1 minute, stirring with a whisk. Gradually add about ⅓ cup hot custard to beaten eggs, stirring constantly with a whisk. Return egg mixture to pan. Cook over medium heat until thick (about 1 minute); stir constantly. Remove from heat; stir in peanut butter and vanilla. Cool slightly.

4. Arrange banana in crust; spoon filling over bananas. Cover surface of filling with plastic wrap; chill 4 hours. Remove wrap. Spread whipped topping evenly over filling. Chill. Yield: 8 servings (serving size: 1 wedge).

CALORIES 294 (29% from fat); FAT 9.5g (sat 4.7g, mono 2.8g, poly 1.4g); PROTEIN 5.9g; CARB 47.8g; FIBER 1.4g; CHOL 65mg; IRON 0.8mg; SODIUM 225mg; CALC 80mg

Sticky Crumbs

Test Kitchen SECRET

Use wax paper coated with cooking spray to press the cookie-crumb mixture into pie plate. This keeps the crumbs from sticking to your hands.

Instead of the vanilla wafer crust, you can make this pie with the Graham Cracker Crust on page 158.

> "To reduce fat in a cream pie, you can use 1% low-fat milk in place of the whole milk. For a richer pie that's just slightly higher in fat, use 2% reduced-fat milk."
>
> Vanessa Johnson, Test Kitchens Director

Double-Chocolate Cream Pie

You can use our Graham Cracker Crust (page 158) instead of a pastry crust.

Crust:

1	(9-inch) Piecrust (page 157) or ½ (15-ounce) package refrigerated pie dough (such as Pillsbury)

Filling:

¾	cup sugar
¼	cup unsweetened cocoa
3	tablespoons cornstarch
⅛	teaspoon salt
2	cups 1% low-fat milk
1	large egg, lightly beaten
1½	ounces semisweet chocolate, grated
1	teaspoon vanilla extract
1½	cups frozen fat-free whipped topping, thawed

1. Prepare and bake piecrust in a 9-inch pie plate. Cool completely on a wire rack.

2. To prepare filling, combine sugar, cocoa, cornstarch, salt, and milk in a medium saucepan; stir well with a whisk. Cook, stirring constantly, for 1 minute until mixture comes to a full boil. Gradually add ⅓ cup hot milk mixture to beaten egg; stir well. Return egg mixture to pan. Cook 2 minutes or until mixture thickens, stirring constantly. Remove from heat; add grated chocolate, stirring until the chocolate melts and mixture is smooth. Stir in vanilla. Spoon mixture into pastry crust. Cover surface of filling with plastic wrap. Chill until set (about 2 hours). Remove plastic wrap; spread whipped topping evenly over filling. Yield: 8 servings (serving size: 1 wedge).

CALORIES 345 (31% from fat); FAT 12.1g (sat 6.7g, mono 2.8g, poly 1.1g); PROTEIN 6.1g; CARB 53.4g; FIBER 1.8g; CHOL 41mg; IRON 1.6mg; SODIUM 194mg; CALC 87mg

Grating Chocolate
Test Kitchen SECRET

Grate the chocolate with a handheld grater or zester, or use the smallest holes on your box grater. Grating the chocolate helps it melt faster, but you can chop it into small pieces, too.

Fruit Pies

We cut back slightly on the amount of sugar in our fruit pie fillings and allow the pies to brim with natural sweetness of the fruit. To get the peak flavor of the fruit, we recommend using fresh fruits whenever you can.

Brown Sugar-Peach Pie with Coconut Streusel

We tested this pie with a refrigerated pie dough for convenience, but you can use the homemade crust on page 157. See page 346 for tips on peeling peaches.

½	(15-ounce) package refrigerated pie dough
⅔	cup packed brown sugar, divided
3	tablespoons all-purpose flour
½	teaspoon ground cinnamon
8	cups sliced peeled ripe peaches (about 3½ pounds or 12 peaches)
⅓	cup regular oats
¼	cup flaked sweetened coconut
1½	tablespoons butter, melted

1. Preheat oven to 425°.

2. Fit dough into a 9-inch pie plate. Fold edges under; flute. Line dough with a piece of foil; arrange pie weights or dried beans on foil. Bake at 425° for 10 minutes. Reduce oven temperature to 350°. Remove pie weights and foil. Bake at 350° for 5 minutes. Cool crust on a wire rack.

3. Combine ⅓ cup sugar, flour, and cinnamon; sprinkle over peaches. Toss. Spoon into crust. Bake at 350° for 30 minutes. Combine ⅓ cup sugar, oats, coconut, and butter; sprinkle over peach mixture. Shield edges of crust with foil. Bake 30 minutes or until golden. Cool on a wire rack. Yield: 8 servings (serving size: 1 wedge).

CALORIES 320 (30% from fat); FAT 10.6g (sat 5.1g, mono 4g, poly 1g); PROTEIN 2.1g; CARB 55.8g; FIBER 3.1g; CHOL 11mg; IRON 0.9mg; SODIUM 137mg; CALC 29mg

> **If your peaches are very ripe and juicy,** you may need to use an additional 1 to 2 tablespoons flour to thicken the filling. If you see that there's a good bit of liquid after you peel the peaches (before they're tossed with sugar), then you'll probably need to add more flour.

Making Brown Sugar-Peach Pie with Coconut Streusel

1. Peel the peaches, then toss them gently with the sugar, flour, and cinnamon. The sugar will draw the natural sugars out of the peaches, so you'll notice at once that the mixture will be very juicy.

2. To make the streusel, combine sugar, oats, coconut, and butter with a fork until crumbly and all the dry ingredients are moist. This may take 2 to 3 minutes.

Lattice-Topped Blueberry Pie

The crust in this recipe is the same as our basic Piecrust (page 157), but in this recipe, you divide the dough so you can make a lattice, and you don't prebake the crust.

Crust:

1½	cups all-purpose flour
2	tablespoons sugar
¼	teaspoon salt
3	tablespoons butter
2	tablespoons vegetable shortening
4	tablespoons ice water
	Cooking spray

Filling:

1	cup sugar, divided
3½	tablespoons cornstarch
⅛	teaspoon salt
6	cups fresh blueberries
1½	tablespoons butter, melted
¾	teaspoon vanilla extract

1. Lightly spoon flour into dry measuring cups; level with a knife. Combine flour, 2 tablespoons sugar, and salt in a bowl; cut in butter and shortening with a pastry blender or 2 knives until mixture resembles coarse meal. Sprinkle surface with ice water, 1 tablespoon at a time; toss with a fork until moist and crumbly (do not form a ball).
2. Gently press two-thirds of dough into a 4-inch circle on heavy-duty plastic wrap; cover with additional plastic wrap. Roll dough into a 12-inch circle. Press remaining dough into a 4-inch circle on plastic wrap; cover with additional plastic wrap. Roll dough into a 9-inch circle. Freeze both portions of dough 10 minutes.
3. Working with large portion of dough, remove 1 sheet of plastic wrap; fit dough into a 9-inch pie plate coated with cooking spray. Remove top sheet of plastic wrap.
4. To prepare filling, combine ¾ cup plus 3 tablespoons sugar, cornstarch, and ⅛ teaspoon salt in a bowl, and sprinkle over blueberries. Toss gently. Stir in butter and vanilla. Spoon blueberry mixture into crust.
5. Preheat oven to 375°.
6. Remove top sheet of plastic wrap from remaining dough. Cut dough into 6 (1½-inch) strips. Gently remove dough strips from bottom sheet of plastic wrap; arrange in a lattice design over blueberry mixture. Seal dough strips to edge of crust. Place pie on a baking sheet covered with foil. Sprinkle lattice with 1 tablespoon sugar.
7. Bake at 375° for 1 hour and 15 minutes or until crust is browned and filling is bubbly. Cool on a wire rack. Yield: 8 servings (serving size: 1 wedge).

CALORIES 354 (25% from fat); FAT 10g (sat 4.8g, mono 2.9g, poly 1.2g); PROTEIN 3.2g; CARB 64.6g; FIBER 3.6g; CHOL 17mg; IRON 1.3mg; SODIUM 183mg; CALC 12mg

Making a Lattice
Test Kitchen SECRET

We've cut the dough into six large strips (12 thinner strips are more typical). Large strips are easier to work with because you can hold the whole strip with two fingers without it tearing. To form the lattice top, alternate the horizontal and vertical strips of dough.

Frozen Pies

Frozen pies can be a little tricky in terms of their texture—you don't want your pies as hard as a rock, nor do you want "pie soup." Because low-fat ice creams and frozen yogurts have less butter-fat and a higher water content, they melt quickly. Our Test Kitchens staff did numerous retests of ways to achieve the best consistency. We found that the techniques below will help you make a pie that's creamy and soft (but not too soft).

Frozen Assets

As we've tested recipes for frozen pie stories, we've figured out how to save ourselves a lot of hassles.

While the piecrust is cooling, take frozen yogurt or ice cream out of the freezer, and let it soften. This makes it easier to fold in the other ingredients for the filling.

Freeze the piecrust 30 minutes. The ice cream or yogurt mixture won't melt as it would if you put it into a piecrust at room temperature.

It's best to partially refreeze the filling before spooning it into the pie shell. To do this, combine the slightly softened frozen yogurt or ice cream and other ingredients specified in the recipe in a chilled extralarge bowl. Put the bowl back in the freezer for about 30 to 45 minutes to let it set again. Don't let the mixture freeze solid, or the consistency will be too hard to spoon into the piecrust.

Place the filled piecrust back in the freezer until set, then cover with plastic wrap.

Take the pie out of the freezer, and let it stand in the refrigerator about 30 minutes before serving. It will be easier to cut the pie into wedges.

Tropical Sundae Pie

If you're making this for kids, replace the white rum with 3 tablespoons of pineapple juice.

1½	cups diced fresh pineapple
¼	cup sugar
3	tablespoons white rum
24	gingersnaps
1	tablespoon butter, melted
1	large egg white
	Cooking spray
4	cups vanilla low-fat frozen yogurt
2	tablespoons sliced almonds, toasted
2	tablespoons flaked sweetened coconut, toasted

1. Combine diced pineapple and sugar in a small saucepan; bring to a boil. Cook over medium heat 10 minutes or until reduced to 1 cup. Remove from heat, and stir in rum. Cool completely; set aside.

2. Preheat oven to 350°.

3. Place gingersnaps in a food processor; process until crumbly. Add butter and egg white; pulse 5 times or just until moist. Press crumb mixture evenly into a 9-inch pie plate coated with cooking spray. Bake at 350° for 7 minutes; cool on a wire rack 15 minutes. Freeze piecrust 30 minutes.

4. Place an extralarge bowl in freezer. Remove yogurt from freezer, and let stand at room temperature while the crust is cooling.

5. Spoon yogurt into chilled bowl; fold in pineapple mixture. Freeze 30 minutes or just until set but not solid. Spoon yogurt mixture into prepared crust. Sprinkle mixture with almonds and coconut; freeze until set. Cover with plastic wrap, and freeze 6 hours or until firm.

6. Place pie in refrigerator 30 minutes before serving to soften. Yield: 8 servings (serving size: 1 wedge).

CALORIES 268 (20% from fat); FAT 5.9g (sat 2.5g, mono 2.6g, poly 0.6g); PROTEIN 6.6g; CARB 45.4g; FIBER 1.1g; CHOL 9mg; IRON 1.5mg; SODIUM 217mg; CALC 178mg

Plum-Berry Swirl Ice Cream Pie

This is a great summertime pie to serve to guests because you can make it a day or two ahead.

1½ cups coarsely chopped plums
3   tablespoons sugar
1   tablespoon water
40 low-fat honey graham crackers (10 sheets)
2   tablespoons sugar
2   tablespoons butter, melted
1   large egg white
Cooking spray
4   cups vanilla low-fat ice cream
1   cup wild berry sorbet
1   cup frozen reduced-calorie whipped
    topping, thawed

1. Combine first 3 ingredients in a saucepan; stir well. Cover and cook over low heat 15 minutes or until plums are tender, stirring occasionally. Spoon into a blender; pulse 3 times. Cool to room temperature.

2. Preheat oven to 350°.

3. Place crackers in a food processor; process until crumbly. Add 2 tablespoons sugar, butter, and egg white; pulse 5 times or just until moist. Press crumb mixture evenly into a 9-inch pie plate coated with cooking spray. Bake at 350° for 8 minutes; cool on a wire rack 15 minutes. Freeze piecrust 30 minutes.

4. Place an extralarge bowl in freezer. Remove ice cream from freezer; let stand at room temperature while piecrust is cooling.

5. Spoon ice cream into chilled bowl. Fold plum mixture and sorbet into ice cream to create a marbled effect; freeze 45 minutes or just until set but not solid.

6. Spoon mixture into prepared crust; freeze until set. Cover with plastic wrap; freeze 6 hours or until firm.

7. Place pie in refrigerator 30 minutes before serving to soften. Serve with whipped topping.

Yield: 8 servings (serving size: 1 wedge and 2 tablespoons topping).

CALORIES 273 (20% from fat); FAT 6.2g (sat 3.1g, mono 1.6g, poly 0.2g); PROTEIN 6.6g; CARB 50.3g; FIBER 1g; CHOL 18mg; IRON 0.8mg; SODIUM 203mg; CALC 157mg

Chocolate Chip-Cherry Pie

We like to use the minichips because it looks like you have more chocolate in the pie!

40 chocolate wafers
2   tablespoons sugar
2   tablespoons butter, melted
1   large egg white
Cooking spray
4   cups vanilla fat-free frozen yogurt
1   cup chopped pitted sweet cherries
½   cup semisweet chocolate minichips
½   cup black cherry preserves, melted

1. Preheat oven to 350°.

2. Place wafers in a food processor; process until crumbly. Add sugar, butter, and egg white; pulse 5 times or just until moist. Press mixture evenly into a 9-inch pie plate coated with cooking spray. Bake at 350° for 8 minutes; cool on a wire rack 15 minutes. Freeze crust 30 minutes.

3. Place an extralarge bowl in freezer. Remove yogurt from freezer; let stand at room temperature while crust is cooling.

4. Spoon yogurt into chilled bowl. Stir cherries and minichips into yogurt; freeze 30 minutes or just until set but not solid.

5. Spread preserves over bottom of prepared crust. Spoon yogurt mixture evenly over preserves; freeze until set. Cover with plastic wrap; freeze 6 hours or until firm. Place pie in refrigerator 30 minutes before serving to soften. Yield: 9 servings (serving size: 1 wedge).

CALORIES 316 (24% from fat); FAT 8.3g (sat 3.9g, mono 3.1g, poly 0.7g); PROTEIN 7g; CARB 55.4g; FIBER 1.6g; CHOL 12mg; IRON 1.3mg; SODIUM 286mg; CALC 154mg

Traditional Holiday Pies

What would the holidays be without pecan or pumpkin pies? Here's how to make them with less fat without cutting flavor.

Classic Pecan Pie

This crust is different from our other homemade pastry crusts. It contains baking powder and is not as flaky, but it goes great with the rich, gooey pecan filling. It's lower in fat and calories, but we don't recommend it for other pies, which need flakier crusts.

Crust:

1	cup all-purpose flour
2	tablespoons granulated sugar
½	teaspoon baking powder
¼	teaspoon salt
¼	cup fat-free milk
1	tablespoon butter, melted

Cooking spray

Filling:

1	large egg
4	large egg whites
1	cup light or dark-colored corn syrup
⅔	cup packed dark brown sugar
¼	teaspoon salt
1	cup pecan halves or chopped pecans
1	teaspoon vanilla extract

1. To prepare crust, lightly spoon flour into a dry measuring cup; level with a knife. Combine flour, granulated sugar, baking powder, and ¼ teaspoon salt in a bowl. Add milk and butter; toss with a fork until moist.

2. Press mixture gently into a 4-inch circle on heavy-duty plastic wrap; cover with additional plastic wrap. Roll dough, still covered, to an 11-inch circle. Freeze 10 minutes or until plastic wrap can be easily removed.

3. Remove 1 sheet of plastic wrap; fit dough into a 9-inch pie plate coated with cooking spray.

Remove top sheet of plastic wrap. Fold edges under; flute.

4. Preheat oven to 350°.

5. To prepare filling, beat egg and next 4 ingredients with a mixer at medium speed until well blended. Stir in pecan halves and vanilla extract. Pour into prepared crust. Bake at 350° for 20 minutes, then cover with foil. Bake 20 additional minutes or until a knife inserted 1 inch from the edge comes out clean (do not overbake). Cool pie on a wire rack. Yield: 10 servings (serving size: 1 wedge).

CALORIES 288 (29% from fat); FAT 9.2g (sat 1.5g, mono 5.1g, poly 2g); PROTEIN 4.3g; CARB 48.1g; FIBER 1g; CHOL 25mg; IRON 1.1mg; SODIUM 253mg; CALC 52mg

Storing and Freezing

If you buy nuts already shelled, store them in airtight containers in the freezer or in a cool, dry place. Most nuts will keep in the freezer for 6 months to a year or in the refrigerator for about 3 months.

You can freeze balls or flat discs of pastry dough up to 6 months if wrapped tightly in wax paper or plastic wrap and then placed in an airtight container. When ready to use, allow time to thaw the dough overnight in the refrigerator.

If you freeze a baked pie, the texture of the pastry may lose a bit of crispness in the freezing and defrosting.

Use frozen pies within 2 months. Thaw baked pies at room temperature 30 minutes, then reheat at 350° until warm.

A pecan pie keeps well and is just as good the day after baking, so it's an ideal make-ahead holiday dessert.

Classic Pumpkin Pie

Bake the pie in the lower third of the oven so the crust won't get too brown before the filling is done.

Filling:

¾	cup packed brown sugar
1¾	teaspoons pumpkin pie spice
¼	teaspoon salt
1	(12-ounce) can evaporated low-fat milk
2	large egg whites
1	large egg
1	(15-ounce) can unsweetened pumpkin

Crust:

½	(15-ounce) package refrigerated pie dough (such as Pillsbury)
	Cooking spray

Topping:

¼	cup whipping cream
1	tablespoon amaretto (almond-flavored liqueur)
2	teaspoons powdered sugar

1. Position oven rack to lowest position.
2. Preheat oven to 425°.
3. To prepare filling, combine first 6 ingredients in a bowl; stir with a whisk. Add pumpkin; stir with a whisk until smooth.
4. To prepare crust, roll dough into an 11-inch circle; fit into a 9-inch pie plate coated with cooking spray. Fold edges under; flute.
5. Pour pumpkin mixture into crust. Place pie plate on a baking sheet. Place baking sheet on lowest oven rack. Bake at 425° for 10 minutes. Reduce oven temperature to 350° (do not remove pie from oven); bake an additional 50 minutes or until almost set. Cool on a wire rack.
6. To prepare topping, beat cream with a mixer at high speed until stiff peaks form. Add amaretto and powdered sugar, and beat until blended. Serve with pie. Yield: 12 servings (serving size: 1 wedge pie and about 1 tablespoon topping).

CALORIES 222 (30% from fat); FAT 7.4g (sat 3.7g, mono 0.7g, poly 0.1g); PROTEIN 4.1g; CARB 35.3g; FIBER 3g; CHOL 32mg; IRON 0.8mg; SODIUM 241mg; CALC 104m

A Note on Using Fresh Pumpkin — Test Kitchen SECRET

If you want to use fresh pumpkin instead of canned, buy a small cooking pumpkin that weights about 2 to 3 pounds. Wash it, and cut it in half crosswise. Place the halves, cut sides down, in a roasting pan or on a jelly-roll pan. Bake at 325° for 40 to 45 minutes or until fork-tender. Cool 10 minutes. Peel pumpkin, and discard or roast the seeds. Place pumpkin pulp in a food processor, and process until pureed, or mash thoroughly. Yield: about 1½ to 2 cups.

"If you want to do something healthy during the holidays, eat pumpkin pie. Pumpkin is packed with vitamin A, a powerful antioxidant that may help prevent heart disease." Krista Montgomery, Food Editor

Strudels

Phyllo dough has less than half the fat of a butter-rich dough, but it has the delicate texture necessary for crisp, flaky strudels.

Traditional strudels are high in fat because of the buttery layers of dough. We reduced the fat by using frozen phyllo dough and coating each layer of dough with butter-flavored cooking spray instead of brushing with butter.

Apple Strudel

McIntosh apples are highly aromatic and cook down to a sauce-like mixture inside the strudel.

- 4   ounces day-old French bread or other firm white bread, coarsely chopped
- 3   tablespoons butter, divided
- 5   cups finely chopped peeled McIntosh apples (about 1¼ pounds)
- 1   cup sugar
- ½   cup golden raisins
- 1   teaspoon ground cinnamon
- 8   sheets frozen phyllo dough, thawed

Cooking spray

1. Preheat oven to 375°.
2. Place bread in a food processor, and pulse 10 times or until coarse crumbs measure 1¼ cups.
3. Melt 1 tablespoon butter in a skillet over medium-high heat; add breadcrumbs. Cook 4 minutes, stirring frequently. Combine breadcrumbs, apple, sugar, raisins, and cinnamon; toss.
4. Lightly coat each of 4 phyllo sheets with cooking spray, placing one on top of the other. Cover with plastic wrap, pressing gently to seal sheets together; discard wrap. Spoon 3 cups apple mix-

ture along 1 long edge of stacked phyllo, leaving a 2-inch border. Fold short edges of phyllo to cover 2 inches of mixture on each end. Starting at long edge with 2-inch border, roll up jelly-roll fashion (do not roll tightly, or strudel may split). Cut several diagonal slits in top of strudel. Place, seam side down, on a jelly-roll pan coated with cooking spray. Repeat with remaining phyllo, cooking spray, and apple mixture.
5. Melt 2 tablespoons butter; brush over strudels. Bake at 375° for 25 minutes or until golden. Cool on a wire rack 20 minutes. Yield: 8 servings (serving size: 1 [3-inch] slice).

CALORIES 302 (18% from fat); FAT 6.1g (sat 3.1g, mono 2g, poly 0.5g); PROTEIN 3.1g; CARB 61g; FIBER 2.7g; CHOL 11mg; IRON 1.2mg; SODIUM 223mg; CALC 25mg

---

Successful Strudel
Test Kitchen SECRET

- Look for phyllo dough with the frozen foods in the grocery store, though a specialty market may carry it unfrozen.
- Check the size of phyllo sheets called for in the recipe. (A new, smaller size is now available and will not be enough if the recipe calls for the larger size.)
- Thaw frozen phyllo in the refrigerator for 2 days.
- Set up an assembly line to coat, layer, fill, and fold the strudel. A little organization goes a long way.
- Handle phyllo sheets slowly and gently. Phyllo is thin and delicate; rough handling will cause breaks or tears.
- Keep phyllo covered with a damp cloth and plastic wrap when you're not working with it—it dries out easily.

Making Strudel

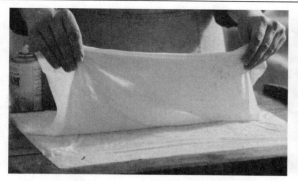

1. Working with one phyllo sheet at a time, coat each sheet with cooking spray, and place one on top of the other.

2. Place a sheet of plastic wrap over phyllo, pressing gently to seal sheets together. The plastic wrap covering will allow you to press more evenly without the risk of tearing the phyllo, and you won't get cooking spray all over your hands. Discard plastic wrap.

3. Spoon filling mixture along one long edge of phyllo sheet, leaving a 2-inch border. Fold over short edges of phyllo to cover 2 inches of filling on each end.

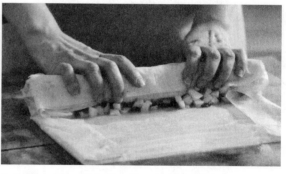

4. Roll in a jelly-roll fashion. Do not roll too tightly, or the strudel may split.

We use serrated knives to cut baked phyllo dough. The blade gently saws through the delicate pastry so it crumbles less.

5. Using a knife, cut several diagonal slits into top.

Baked Custards

Custards require slow, even heat for the best results.

Custards rely on eggs for their texture and richness. Because of the way egg protein cooks, custards require slow, even heat for the best results. Baked custards are usually cooked in a water bath to ensure gradual, even hands-off cooking and creamy results that more than justify the effort. Here are the standard *Cooking Light* recipes and techniques for our favorite baked custards.

We cut the fat in baked custards by using fewer egg yolks than a traditional version and replacing whole milk or cream with reduced-fat milk.

Crème Caramel

Crème caramel is too good not to have in your repertoire. Correctly cooking the custard and caramelizing the sugar are not difficult to master with attention to detail and timing. With a few simple things—eggs, milk, sugar, vanilla, and salt—you can get cooking with our step-by-step photos and no-fail recipes as your guide.

Classic Crème Caramel

Making the caramel syrup and baking the custard on top of the syrup are the two crucial steps here.

⅓ cup sugar
3 tablespoons water
Cooking spray
3 large eggs
1 large egg white
2 cups 2% reduced-fat milk
1 tablespoon vanilla extract
⅔ cup sugar
⅛ teaspoon salt

1. Preheat oven to 325°.
2. Combine ⅓ cup sugar and 3 tablespoons water in a small, heavy saucepan over medium-high heat; cook until sugar dissolves, stirring frequently. Continue cooking 4 minutes or until golden. Immediately pour into 6 (6-ounce) ramekins or custard cups coated with cooking spray, tilting each cup quickly until caramelized sugar coats bottom of cup. Set aside.
3. Beat eggs and egg white in a bowl with a whisk. Stir in milk, vanilla, ⅔ cup sugar, and salt. Divide mixture evenly among custard cups. Place cups in a 13 x 9-inch baking pan; add hot water to pan to a depth of 1 inch. Bake at 325° for 45 minutes or until a knife inserted in center comes out clean. Remove cups from pan. Cover and chill at least 4 hours.
4. Loosen edges of custards with a thin, sharp knife. Place a dessert plate, upside down, on top of each cup; invert onto plates. Drizzle remaining syrup over custards. Yield: 6 servings.

CALORIES 212 (18% from fat); FAT 4.3g (sat 1.8g, mono 1.5g, poly 0.4g); PROTEIN 6.5g; CARB 37.6g; FIBER 0g; CHOL 117mg; IRON 0.4mg; SODIUM 131mg; CALC 113mg

Cooking Crème Caramel

1. Combine sugar and water in a heavy saucepan over medium-high heat; stir until sugar dissolves. Continue to heat without stirring. In about 2 minutes, it will start to caramelize and turn light brown. Heat 1 to 2 more minutes until mixture is golden.

2. Immediately pour just enough caramel into a ramekin or custard cup to cover the bottom of the cup.

3. Tilt the cup so that its bottom is completely covered with caramel. Repeat for remaining cups.

4. Divide the custard mixture (eggs, milk, and flavorings) evenly among prepared cups.

5. Place cups in a 13 x 9-inch baking pan. Carefully add hot tap water to the pan to a depth of 1 inch. Bake at 325° for recommended cooking time.

6. After custards have cooled and chilled, run a thin knife along the edge of each to loosen it from its cup.

7. Place a dessert plate, upside down, on top of each cup. Invert the cup and plate. Lift the cup; the custard should slip out easily with the caramel syrup on top.

The custard in a crème caramel can be flavored many ways, but how to make the dessert doesn't change. For exact ingredients, quantities, and cooking times, see the individual recipes.

Pumpkin-Maple Crème Caramel

Freshly grated nutmeg gives this crème caramel its distinctive spiciness. You can use regular ground nutmeg, but the flavor won't be as intense.

½ cup granulated sugar
¼ cup water
Cooking spray
⅓ cup packed dark brown sugar
2 tablespoons maple syrup
3 large eggs
½ cup canned pumpkin
½ cup 2% reduced-fat milk
¼ teaspoon ground nutmeg
½ teaspoon vanilla extract
⅛ teaspoon salt
1 (12-ounce) can evaporated fat-free milk
Freshly grated nutmeg (optional)

1. Preheat oven to 325°.
2. Combine ½ cup granulated sugar and ¼ cup water in a small, heavy saucepan over medium heat; cook until sugar dissolves, stirring frequently. Continue cooking until golden (about 4 minutes). Immediately pour into 6 (6-ounce) ramekins or custard cups coated with cooking spray, tilting each cup quickly until caramelized sugar coats bottom of cup. Set aside.
3. Beat brown sugar, syrup, and eggs in a medium bowl with a whisk. Add pumpkin and next 5 ingredients, stirring until well blended. Divide mixture evenly among prepared custard cups. Place cups in a 13 x 9-inch baking pan; add hot water to pan to a depth of 1 inch. Bake at 325° for 1 hour and 10 minutes or until a knife inserted in center comes out clean. Remove cups from pan. Cover and chill at least 4 hours.
4. Loosen edges of custards with a knife or rubber spatula. Place a dessert plate, upside down, on top of each cup; invert onto plates. Drizzle any remaining syrup over custards.

Garnish with freshly grated nutmeg, if desired. Yield: 6 servings.

CALORIES 230 (13% from fat); FAT 3.3g (sat 1.2g, mono 1.2g, poly 0.4g); PROTEIN 8.4g; CARB 42.2g; FIBER 0.8g; CHOL 114mg; IRON 1.1mg; SODIUM 164mg; CALC 222mg

Egg Substitute

Test Kitchen SECRET

You can't use egg substitutes to make custards because the substitutes don't have yolks. Without yolks, custards wouldn't be smooth and creamy.

Crème Caramel Troubleshooting

To keep the sugar from crystallizing, stir as little as possible after it has melted. If some caramel crystallizes on the side of the pan, wash the crystals down with a wet pastry brush. Never touch or taste hot caramel.

If the caramel has a blackish-brown color, it's probably burned. To start over, allow the caramel to cool, add some water to the pan, and heat over low heat until the caramel dissolves. Discard the liquid, rinse the pan out, and add more sugar and water.

For neater pouring, mix the custard ingredients in a bowl with a spout, or mix them in a regular bowl and transfer the mixture to a 4-cup glass measuring cup before pouring into the custard cups.

Check the custards for doneness 5 minutes before the end of the recommended cooking time because oven temperatures can vary. Remember, custard continues to cook as it cools.

Chill the crème caramel thoroughly (we recommend at least 4 hours), so that none of the caramel sticks to the bottom of the cup. If it does, just scrape out the remaining syrup with a rubber spatula.

Flan

Flan is the Spanish version of a crème caramel, but it's usually made in one round pan (a flan pan) rather than individual custard cups. Cooling flan in a water bath helps it reach room temperature gradually, which reduces the chances of shrinking and cracking. Instead of a flan pan, we used a 9-inch round cake pan.

Dulce de Leche Flan

Dulce de leche is sweetened milk that's cooked down to a thick paste. This step takes about 45 minutes.

    1   (14-ounce) can fat-free sweetened
            condensed milk
    ½   cup sugar
    ¼   cup water
    Cooking spray
    2   cups 2% reduced-fat milk
    3   large eggs
    2   large egg whites
    ½   teaspoon vanilla extract

1. Preheat oven to 425°.
2. Pour condensed milk into a 1-quart baking dish; cover and place in bottom of a broiler pan. Add hot water to pan to a depth of 1 inch. Bake at 425° for 45 minutes or until milk is thick and caramel-colored. Remove dish from pan; uncover and cool to room temperature.
3. Reduce oven temperature to 325°.
4. Combine sugar and ¼ cup water in a small, heavy saucepan, and cook over medium-high heat until sugar dissolves, stirring frequently. Continue cooking 5 minutes or until golden, stirring constantly. Immediately pour into a 9-inch round cake pan coated with cooking spray, tilting quickly until caramelized sugar coats bottom of pan.
5. Spoon condensed milk into a large bowl. Add 2% milk, eggs, egg whites, and vanilla; stir with a whisk until well blended. Strain milk mixture through a fine sieve into prepared pan, and discard solids.
6. Place cake pan in bottom of broiler pan; add hot water to pan to a depth of 1 inch. Bake at 325° for 40 minutes or until a knife inserted in the center comes out clean. Remove from oven, and cool flan to room temperature in water bath. Remove cake pan from water bath; cover and chill at least 3 hours or overnight. Loosen edges of flan with a knife or rubber spatula. Place a plate, upside down, on top of cake pan; invert flan onto plate. Drizzle any remaining caramelized syrup over flan. Yield: 8 servings (serving size: 1 wedge).

CALORIES 250 (12% from fat); FAT 3.2g (sat 1.3g, mono 1.1g, poly 0.3g); PROTEIN 9.6g; CARB 45.7g; FIBER 0g; CHOL 88mg; IRON 0.3mg; SODIUM 120mg; CALC 223mg

A water bath (a shallow pan of warm water in which containers of food are cooked) insulates and protects custards from the heat of the oven so they cook slowly and evenly. The depth of the water should be half the height of the custard container (ramekin, cake pan, etc.). If you're baking multiple custards, the pan must be large enough so that the containers don't touch.

Testing for Doneness   Test Kitchen SECRET

While various factors—including the individual recipe and application—determine a custard's doneness, there is a time-honored guidepost. When you (carefully) tap the side of the ramekin or pan, the custard should jiggle. If it ripples like water, it's not done. If it doesn't jiggle at all, has shrunk, or is beginning to crack, the custard is overcooked.

Crème Brûlée

Literally, the name means "burnt cream." This dessert is a baked and chilled custard that is sprinkled with sugar just before serving. The sugar topping is quickly caramelized, forming a brittle topping that is a delicious contrast to the creamy custard. A brûlée is different from a crème caramel because the sugar is sprinkled on top after the custard is baked; in a crème caramel, the sugar mixture is poured into the custard cups and is caramelized while the custard bakes.

Great Brûlée

The brûlée lovers on our staff got together to offer their best tips for making their favorite indulgence.

You can make the custards in almost any small ovenproof dishes. Just make sure that they are shallow, to provide ample surface area for the sugar shell.

We tested both a small kitchen torch and a propane torch for melting the sugar. The large propane torch is more powerful and melts the sugar faster, but the kitchen torch works equally well. You can buy a kitchen torch at most cookware stores. Propane torches are available at most hardware stores.

Serve the crème brûlée within an hour of melting the sugar, or the hard sugar shells will become soft as they start to dissolve into the custards.

Espresso Crème Brûlée

We recommend using a small kitchen torch to caramelize the sugar. (See "Two Ways to Brûlée," page 178, for using the alternate stovetop method.)

    2   cups 2% reduced-fat milk
    1   cup whole espresso coffee beans
    ¾   cup nonfat dry milk
    3   tablespoons sugar, divided
    1   teaspoon vanilla extract
Dash of salt
    4   large egg yolks
    ¼   cup sugar

1. Combine 2% milk, espresso beans, dry milk, and 2 tablespoons sugar in a medium saucepan. Heat mixture over medium heat to 180° or until tiny bubbles form around the edge (do not boil), stirring occasionally. Remove from heat. Cover and steep 30 minutes.
2. Preheat oven to 300°.
3. Strain mixture through a sieve into a bowl; discard solids. Stir in vanilla.
4. Combine 1 tablespoon sugar, salt, and egg yolks in a medium bowl, stirring well with a whisk. Gradually add milk mixture to egg mixture, stirring constantly with a whisk.
5. Divide the mixture evenly among 4 (4-ounce) ramekins, custard cups, or shallow baking

---

Espresso Tips

- For the most intense coffee flavor, use strong coffee beans. If you don't have espresso beans, French roast or dark roast coffee beans will work. The darker the bean, the more intense the flavor.
- For the best flavor, steep the beans in the milk for 30 minutes. For a more subtle coffee flavor, steep them 15 minutes.

dishes. Place ramekins in a 13 x 9-inch baking pan, and add hot water to a depth of 1 inch. Bake at 300° for 25 minutes or until center barely moves when ramekin is touched. Remove ramekins from pan; cool completely on a wire rack. Cover and chill at least 4 hours or overnight.

6. Sift 1 tablespoon sugar evenly over each custard. Holding a kitchen blowtorch about 2 inches from the top of each custard, heat the sugar, moving the torch back and forth, until sugar is completely melted and caramelized (about 1 minute). Serve immediately or within 1 hour. Yield: 4 servings (serving size: 1 creme brûlée).

CALORIES 262 (26% from fat); FAT 7.7g (sat 3.2g, mono 2.7g, poly 0.7g); PROTEIN 11.3g; CARB 36g; FIBER 0g; CHOL 225mg; IRON 0.6mg; SODIUM 215mg; CALC 315mg

Cold custards stand up well to the heat when melting the sugar, so it's best to make them 1 to 2 days ahead.

Fire It Up

Some recipes are worth investing in special equipment. For caramelizing the sugar crusts in brûlées, a torch is an indispensable tool. There are two types—industrial propane torches and smaller butane-powered torches—and both come with simple, safe, single-click lighting mechanisms. "If you already have a propane torch, there's no need to consider a kitchen torch," says Test Kitchens Staffer Kathryn Conrad. But if you don't, she recommends the kitchen variety (like a model by Bonjour at www.cooking.com). "It's lighter and has a smaller flame." *In addition to crème brûlée, use your torch to brown meringues, toast marshmallows, and blister peppers.*

Rum Crème Brûlée

For the crunchy brittle topping, white granulated sugar works best. When melted and caramelized, it hardens to a thin sheet that's fun to break into.

1	cup evaporated fat-free milk
1	cup 2% reduced-fat milk
⅔	cup nonfat dry milk
¼	cup sugar
1	teaspoon sugar
⅛	teaspoon salt
5	large egg yolks
1½	tablespoons dark rum
3	tablespoons sugar

1. Preheat oven to 300°.
2. Combine first 4 ingredients in a medium, heavy saucepan. Heat mixture over medium heat to 180° or until tiny bubbles form around edge (do not boil), stirring occasionally. Remove from heat.
3. Combine 1 teaspoon sugar, salt, and egg yolks in a medium bowl, stirring well with a whisk. Gradually add hot milk mixture to egg mixture, stirring constantly with a whisk. Stir in rum.
4. Divide milk mixture evenly among 6 (4-ounce) ramekins or custard cups. Place ramekins in a 13 x 9-inch baking pan; add hot water to pan to a depth of 1 inch. Bake at 300° for 50 minutes or until center barely moves when ramekin is touched. Remove ramekins from pan; cool completely on a wire rack. Cover and chill 4 hours or overnight.
5. Sift 1½ teaspoons sugar evenly over each custard. Holding a kitchen blowtorch about 2 inches from the top of each custard, heat the sugar, moving the torch back and forth, until sugar is completely melted and caramelized (about 1 minute). Serve immediately or within 1 hour. Yield: 6 servings (serving size: 1 crème brûlée).

CALORIES 197 (24% from fat); FAT 5.2g (sat 1.9g, mono 1.9g, poly 0.6g); PROTEIN 9.6g; CARB 26.3g; FIBER 0g; CHOL 183mg; IRON 0.7mg; SODIUM 166mg; CALC 285mg

Two Ways to Brulée

Using a Torch

1. Carefully sift the sugar, using a small sieve, over each custard. This disperses the sugar evenly.

2. Torch the sugar immediately after it is sifted onto the custards, or it will start to dissolve into the custards. Hold the torch about 2 inches away and work from side to side until all the sugar is melted and caramelized.

On the Stovetop

1. In a small saucepan or skillet, cook the sugar over medium heat until golden (about 5 to 8 minutes). Resist the urge to stir because doing so will allow the sugar to crystallize.

2. Working quickly, evenly drizzle sugar topping over cold custards. Using a rubber spatula coated with cooking spray, spread caramel evenly to form a thin layer. Work quickly because the caramel hardens quickly.

Sweet Soufflés

"When you really want to impress guests, serve soufflés for dessert. But you've got to be prepared to serve them right away." Ann Pittman, Food Editor

What may look as if it takes an act of culinary genius to prepare actually couldn't be easier, but it's important to keep some key instructions in mind. Soufflés are delicate things that rise and deflate quickly, and they must be eaten immediately. One of the most important components of a soufflé is the egg whites—see pages 144 and 145 for details on beating egg whites and page 159 for adding a hot liquid mixture to egg yolks (tempering).

Hot Maple Soufflés

We heat the small amount of bourbon mixture in the microwave for speed and convenience. You can heat it up in a small saucepan over medium heat if you prefer.

1	tablespoon butter, softened
2	tablespoons granulated sugar
3	tablespoons bourbon
3	tablespoons maple syrup
1	cup maple syrup
4	large egg whites
1/8	teaspoon salt
1	teaspoon baking powder
1	tablespoon sifted powdered sugar

1. Preheat oven to 425°.
2. Coat 6 (10-ounce) ramekins with butter; sprinkle evenly with granulated sugar. Combine bourbon and 3 tablespoons syrup in a small microwave-safe bowl; microwave at HIGH 1½ minutes or until mixture boils. Pour about 1 tablespoon bourbon mixture into each prepared ramekin.
3. Cook 1 cup syrup in a medium, heavy saucepan over medium-high heat 8 minutes or until a candy thermometer registers 250°.
4. Beat egg whites and salt with a mixer at medium speed until foamy. Pour hot maple syrup in a thin stream over egg whites, beating at high speed, until stiff peaks form. Add baking powder; beat well.
5. Spoon evenly into ramekins; place on a jelly-roll pan. Bake at 425° for 13 minutes or until puffy and set. Sprinkle with powdered sugar. Serve immediately. Yield: 6 servings (serving size: 1 soufflé).

CALORIES 222 (9% from fat); FAT 2.1g (sat 1g, mono 0.8g, poly 0.1g); PROTEIN 2.5g; CARB 48.1g; FIBER 0g; CHOL 5mg; IRON 0.9mg; SODIUM 187mg; CALC 90mg

Is it Done Yet?

Test Kitchen SECRET

Here's how to know: Leave the soufflé undisturbed during baking. Even if you're tempted to open the oven door and watch it rise, DON'T! You may be watching it fall instead. First, look through your oven window. When the top appears browned, crusty, and dry, it's time to test the soufflé for doneness. Do so by inserting a knife blade into the center. If it comes out moist and clean, the soufflé should be ready. Otherwise, slide it back into the oven, and bake it 10 additional minutes.

Hot Chocolate Soufflé

An egg yolk adds richness to the base of this soufflé.

Cooking spray
1 tablespoon granulated sugar
¾ cup 1% low-fat milk
¼ cup granulated sugar
4 teaspoons cornstarch
1 teaspoon instant coffee granules
⅛ teaspoon salt
1 large egg yolk
1 teaspoon vanilla extract
4 ounces bittersweet chocolate, chopped
4 large egg whites
3 tablespoons light brown sugar
¾ cup low-fat coffee ice cream, softened

1. Preheat oven to 375°.
2. Coat a 1½-quart soufflé dish with cooking spray; sprinkle with 1 tablespoon sugar.
3. Combine milk, ¼ cup granulated sugar, cornstarch, coffee granules, and salt in a saucepan, stirring constantly with a whisk until blended. Bring to a boil over medium heat; cook 1 minute or until thick, stirring constantly. Remove from heat.
4. Gradually add hot milk mixture to egg yolk, stirring constantly with a whisk. Return milk mixture to pan. Cook over medium heat until thick (about 2 minutes), stirring constantly. Remove from heat. Add vanilla and chocolate, stirring until chocolate melts.
5. Place egg whites in a large bowl; beat with a mixer at high speed until soft peaks form. Gradually add 3 tablespoons brown sugar, 1 tablespoon at a time, beating until stiff peaks form.
6. Gently stir one-fourth of egg white mixture into chocolate mixture; fold in remaining egg white mixture. Spoon into soufflé dish. Bake at 375° for 25 minutes until puffy and set. Serve immediately topped with ice cream. Yield: 6 servings (serving size: about ⅔ cup soufflé and 2 tablespoons ice cream).

CALORIES 253 (29% from fat); FAT 8.2g (sat 4.6g, mono 2.7g, poly 0.4g); PROTEIN 6g; CARB 41.4g; FIBER 1.3g; CHOL 39mg; IRON 0.9mg; SODIUM 122mg; CALC 81mg

Folding in Egg White Mixture for a Soufflé

To gently fold in egg white mixture, cut through the egg whites using a large rubber spatula. Then cut through the base until the spatula reaches the bottom of the bowl. Lift spatula along the inside of bowl, bringing the contents at the bottom to the top. As soon as the mixture is blended, stop folding.

PART TWO

The Guide to Essential Ingredients

High-quality, wholesome ingredients are the building blocks for healthy cooking and eating. In this section, we highlight the wide variety of foods that we think are vital for the *Cooking Light* lifestyle. You'll get the real scoop on how to pick the best ingredients, tips and tidbits on how to use them in recipes, and our Test Kitchens staff's picks for the best of the best.

CHAPTER 4

Stocking Up

What ingredients are really essential for healthy cooking? Here's how *Cooking Light* stocks up for eating smart and living well.

There's an art to building a healthy working pantry. Why not take your first lessons today? If you stock your pantry with the ingredients in our pantry list, you'll almost always be able to cook some of your favorite *Cooking Light* recipes. You'll figure out what you need to keep on hand so you can be ready in a flash to get a tasty, healthy meal on the table without stopping at the store on the way home from work.

On the next page, you'll find a list to help you build a healthy pantry. We call it the "Ultimate Pantry" list. Use it when you initially stock up and as you go to the grocery store to replenish your pantry. We've organized the list in the following categories:

- *Pantry Basics:* items that can be the building blocks for a variety of meals
- *Condiments:* ingredients that give your recipes extra flavor and character
- *Refrigerator/Freezer:* meats, poultry, seafood, dairy products, fresh produce, and other flavoring ingredients that must be kept refrigerated
- *Sweets:* sugar and other sweeteners

You might want to reorder your list based on your supermarket's layout so that you can efficiently shop for items in the order that you move throughout the store. Most of these ingredients can be found at your local supermarket, but for some of the more unusual items, you may need to find an Asian market or a gourmet grocery store.

Storage Savvy
Test Kitchen SECRET

- Store foods in an airtight container, such as heavy-duty plastic containers or zip-top plastic bags. For dishes that go from freezer to oven, cover containers with heavy-duty aluminum foil.
- Freeze food in small portions and in shallow containers to prevent the formation of big ice crystals. Big crystals can rupture food cells and worsen the food's texture and flavor upon thawing.

For more storage tips, see page 185 and pages 190-191.

"I keep certain products on hand to avoid dashing around the kitchen in a panic. I can usually pull together a great meal at the last minute." Alison Ashton, Food Editor

Ultimate Pantry *Checklist*

Here's a list of items we'd include in our perfect well-stocked pantry.

Pantry Basics
- ❑ Broth, chicken
- ❑ Broth, vegetable
- ❑ Canned beans
  - ❑ black
  - ❑ cannellini
  - ❑ garbanzo
  - ❑ great Northern
  - ❑ pinto
- ❑ Canned salmon
- ❑ Canned tuna
- ❑ Cornmeal
- ❑ Grains
  - ❑ barley
  - ❑ bulgar
  - ❑ millet
  - ❑ quinoa
- ❑ Grits
- ❑ Pastas
  - ❑ couscous
  - ❑ penne
  - ❑ spaghetti
- ❑ Pasta sauce
- ❑ Rice
  - ❑ Arborio
  - ❑ basmati
  - ❑ jasmine
  - ❑ sticky
  - ❑ sweet
  - ❑ white
  - ❑ wild
- ❑ Semolina flour
- ❑ Tomato products, canned

Condiments
- ❑ Anchovy paste
- ❑ Bottled roasted red bell peppers
- ❑ Capers
- ❑ Chili paste
- ❑ Chipotle chiles in adobo sauce
- ❑ Chutneys
- ❑ Curry paste
- ❑ Dried herbs and spices
- ❑ Fresh garlic
- ❑ Mustards
  - ❑ Dijon
  - ❑ honey
  - ❑ stone-ground
- ❑ Oil, dark sesame
- ❑ Oil, extra-virgin olive
- ❑ Peanut butter
- ❑ Raisins
- ❑ Salsa
- ❑ Sauces
  - ❑ fish sauce
  - ❑ hoisin sauce
  - ❑ low-sodium soy sauce
  - ❑ oyster sauce
- ❑ Sun-dried tomatoes
- ❑ Vinegars
  - ❑ balsamic
  - ❑ red wine
  - ❑ rice
  - ❑ sherry
- ❑ Wines
  - ❑ red
  - ❑ sherry
  - ❑ white

Refrigerator/ Freezer
- ❑ Butter
- ❑ Cheeses
  - ❑ blue
  - ❑ feta
  - ❑ mozzarella
  - ❑ Parmesan
  - ❑ Romano
- ❑ Eggs
- ❑ Egg substitute
- ❑ Fresh chiles
  - ❑ jalapeño
  - ❑ serrano
- ❑ Fresh fish
  - ❑ catfish
  - ❑ salmon
  - ❑ shrimp
- ❑ Fresh herbs
- ❑ Frozen spinach
- ❑ Jellies
- ❑ Lemons
- ❑ Limes
- ❑ Nuts
  - ❑ almonds
  - ❑ hazelnuts
  - ❑ pecans
  - ❑ pine nuts
  - ❑ walnuts
- ❑ Olives
  - ❑ kalamata
  - ❑ niçoise
- ❑ Pork Tenderloin
- ❑ Preserves

- ❑ Reduced-fat salad dressings
- ❑ Skinless, boneless chicken breast halves
- ❑ Tofu
  - ❑ firm
  - ❑ soft
- ❑ Tubes of polenta

Sweets
- ❑ Cocoa
- ❑ Honey
- ❑ Maple syrup
- ❑ Molasses
- ❑ Semisweet chocolate
- ❑ Sugars
  - ❑ brown
  - ❑ granulated
  - ❑ powdered

Finding the Goods

If you live in an urban area, your local supermarket may carry an abundant selection of imported cheeses, quality extra-virgin olive oils, flavored vinegars, and ethnic ingredients. Many organic markets and specialty-food shops also carry these ingredients. If you live in a more remote area—or are pressed for time—consider ordering foods over the Internet. Here are some of the sites we use when we can't find an ingredient locally.

www.chefshop.com While other sites may offer hundreds of olive oils and vinegars, ChefShop narrows the selection to the cream of the crop. Product descriptions are succinct and insightful.

www.yndella.com Check out this site for Italian ingredients.

www.gourmetunderground.com Find inexpensively priced oils and vinegars on this easy-to-navigate site.

www.indiangrocerynet.com Go here for hard-to-find Indian ingredients.

www.levillage.com Check out this site for French ingredients.

www.mexgrocer.com Go here if you're looking for truly authentic Mexican ingredients.

www.nextdaygourmet.com You can order fresh herbs from this site by going to the Cross Valley Farms mini-store link on the home page. Herbs will be delivered in 1 day.

www.oakvillegrocery.com You can find most of our favorite oils and vinegars at this "little country store" that's now on the Internet.

www.tavolo.com If it's variety you want, this site has specialty food products as well as kitchen gadgets.

www.zingermans.com This highly regarded Michigan specialty-foods store offers a notable selection of choice oils and vinegars from around the world, all hand-picked favorites of its staff. It's also one of the few places from which you can order Parmigiano-Reggiano cheese by mail.

Cooking Light Storage Tips

Maintaining an organized and well-stocked pantry is the key to creating quick weeknight meals and entertaining with ease. Here are some storage suggestions from one of *Cooking Light's* contributors, a professional organizer.

Let usage be your guide. Keep frequently used items, such as pasta, rice, and broth, where you can get to them easily. Reserve high shelves and out-of-the-way nooks for items you don't use as often, such as bread machines and stockpots.

Like goes with like. Organize staples according to function. Group flour and sugar with sweet spices; put savory spices, bottled sauces, and marinades in another space.

Rise to the occasion. Use risers on pantry shelves so you can see the back row of items as easily as the front row.

Shop for the right fit. Buy more baskets, boxes, and other organizers than you'll need because some containers might prove more functional than others. Once you've organized everything the way you want it, return any unused items.

If you end up with a collection of bottled and jarred sauces (plum, hoisin, chili, chutney, and soy) in your refrigerator, they will keep for up to a year before you need to throw them out. Be sure to keep the lids on tight.

Ingredient Spotlight

These are some groups of ingredients that we like to promote because of their health benefits or because they make cooking easier without compromising flavor and style.

Type	Description
Super Foods That Are Super to Eat	
Edamame (eh-dah-MAH-meh)	Edamame (the Japanese name for fresh whole soybeans) is a trendy snack with major nutritional credentials. Look for them, either fresh or frozen, in supermarkets, Asian markets, and health-food stores.
Dried mango	This sweet treat is loaded with beta carotene and vitamin C.
Flaxseed	This nutrient-packed seed adds a tasty, crunchy spin to breads, cookies, and muffins; it's high in phytoestrogens and omega-3 fatty acids.
Fruit juice with calcium	Two are better than one, and you need both calcium and vitamin C in a balanced diet. This is an excellent alternative calcium source for those who don't drink milk.
Tofu	The emperor of soy superfoods, tofu has hundreds of applications, often as a substitute—in place of sour cream in your favorite dip, for example.
Throw-Together Meal Musts	
Dried pasta	You can always make a meal if you have some pasta on hand.
Garlic	You could cook without it, but why bother? Purchase firm, plump garlic bulbs; store in a cool, dry place, and they will stay fresh for 4 months.
Green onions	Onion flavor with a taste of "green," these can fill in for leeks, onions, garlic, or chives.
Low-sodium soy sauce	You'll never find a kitchen in China without soy sauce. Few sauces go as well with so many foods.
Parmesan cheese	A little sprinkle makes almost anything taste good.
Spices to Keep in Stock	
Cinnamon	It may seem common, but don't limit it to sweets. It's great with savory dishes, too, especially when used with other allies like chili powder, coriander, and cumin.
Cumin	This is a must-have spice for many international-style dishes.
Coriander	It's an up-and-coming flavor that's particularly crucial to Middle Eastern dishes.
Curry powder	It adds ethnic flavor to ordinary dishes. Try sprinkling some into your favorite chicken salad recipe.

Type	Description
Light Products That Sacrifice No Taste	
50% light white Cheddar cheese	Less fat—not no fat—means better flavor and texture. We like Cabot the best. This sweet treat is loaded with beta carotene and vitamin C.
Fat-free caramel sauce	It's virtually indistinguishable from its high-fat cousin. Our favorite is Smucker's caramel topping in a jar.
Flavored chicken sausages	These precooked links add a lower-fat gourmet touch to any recipe (who wants to clean the stove after frying up pork sausage?). We like the Aidells and Gerhard's brands.
Light coconut milk	This is Thai and other Asian-influenced cuisines' new best friend.
Low-fat mayonnaise	It can stand in for regular in most uses and is just as creamy. We like Hellmann's.
Convenience Products Almost Like the Real Thing	
Frozen bread dough	It saves you the trouble of measuring and kneading. Use in place of higher-fat doughs in tarts, rolls, and breads, or as a base for flavored breads.
Ready-to-eat polenta	Its handy tube shape makes it easy to slice and layer into lasagna and casseroles.
Pizza crusts (prebaked and refrigerated)	Making your own pizza couldn't be easier; just get creative with the toppings (which is half the fun anyway). We like Pillsbury and Boboli brands.
Pesto in a jar	If you don't have time to make it using fresh basil, Alessi's or Crespi & Figli's pesto will do nicely.
Spice blends	Blends can be such time-savers. We especially like Spice Islands' new blends—try the Louisiana Style Cajun, Jamaican Jerk, and Thai seasonings.
Bottled roasted red bell peppers	Save yourself the fuss of roasting and peeling bell peppers. Another plus: You can find this year-round.
Snacks Too Good Not to Keep On Hand	
Mini candy bars	Need a chocolate fix? Keep these pint-size versions on hand and not just for Halloween.
Edy's Whole Fruit Sorbet	The creamy, rich flavor comes from real fruit, not a juice concentrate as in some other brands.
Terra Chips	With up to 50 percent less fat than regular potato chips and exotic varieties like Jalapeño Sweet Potato, Yukon Gold, and Yogurt & Green Onion, these chips are irresistible.
Pretzels	The old-fashioned snack still rules. We like Snyder's of Hanover and Rold Gold.
Soy nuts	These nutritious nuggets are gaining in popularity. Look for them near gourmet produce or with nuts and snacks in your supermarket or local health-food store.

Start with the Best

Quality specialty ingredients deliver big, bold flavors that elevate a dish from simply good to truly extraordinary.

Used sparingly as accents or finishing touches, premium ingredients act as catalysts to bring out the flavors of the whole dish. They don't overwhelm food, yet by some bit of culinary magic, they set it apart. Here are a few of the superior ingredients that we think no kitchen should be without.

Balsamic Vinegar: A few drops of this rich, sweet, intense vinegar is all you need to dramatically change the flavors of a finished dish. (See page 373 for more information.)

Sherry Vinegar: This is a great everyday vinegar for salad dressing and marinades or for drizzling over cooked vegetables.

Fresh Herbs: There really isn't any comparison between dried and fresh herbs. Once you start using fresh, you won't go back. (See pages 376-379 for more information on herbs.)

Good Bread: Thick, dense, chewy bread can make a sandwich or strata go from good to great. Check out the varieties at either your local bakery or the bakery at the supermarket.

Parmesan Cheese: Real Parmesan is a world apart in flavor from the canned version, particularly when it's the top-of-the-line Parmigiano-Reggiano. (See page 239 for more information on Parmesan cheese.)

Prosciutto: This speciality Italian ham isn't smoked like American ham. Instead, it's air-cured with salt and seasonings, a process that gives it a distinct flavor.

Premium Oils: High-quality oils are like good wines: No two are alike, and each has a distinct character. The use of premium oils is often one of the features that makes the food you eat in fine restaurants memorable. (See page 361-362 for more information on oils.)

Balsamic Vinegar

Fresh Herbs

Parmesan Cheese

Premium Oils

10 Easy Ingredient Substitutions

When you're in a pinch, try any of these quick switches from the *Cooking Light* Food Editors and Test Kitchens staff.

Ingredient	Substitution
1 tablespoon **capers**	1 tablespoon chopped **dill pickles**
1 stalk chopped **lemongrass**	1 teaspoon grated **lemon zest**
1 teaspoon **chili paste**	1/4 teaspoon **hot red pepper flakes**
1/2 cup **honey**	1/2 cup **molasses** or **maple syrup**
1 cup **tahini**	3/4 cup **creamy peanut butter** and 1/4 cup **sesame oil**
1 teaspoon **cider vinegar**	2 teaspoons **lemon juice** mixed with a pinch of **sugar**
1 teaspoon **wasabi**	1 teaspoon **horseradish** or **hot dry mustard**
1 cup **low-fat buttermilk**	1 cup **fat-free milk** and 1 tablespoon **lemon juice**, stirred well
1 teaspoon **baking powder**	1/4 teaspoon **baking soda** mixed with 1/2 teaspoon **cream of tartar**
1 tablespoon **cornstarch**	2 tablespoons **all-purpose flour** or 4 tablespoons **quick-cooking tapioca**

For more ingredient substitution charts, turn to pages 466-469 at the end of the book.
- **Common Ingredient Substitutions: page 466**
- **Low-Fat Substitutions: page 468**
- **Alcohol Substitutions: page 469**

"When time is short, I pull out a bottle of roasted red bell peppers; I either puree the peppers for an easy sauce or simply toss them with pasta."

Jan Moon, Test Kitchens Staffer

Freezer Guide

Use your freezer as your ultimate make-ahead strategy and to stock up on seasonal or sale-priced products.

When you have the time, cook several meals, and freeze the results for the hurried pace of the rest of the week. Or when certain seasonal items are available, stock up, and store in the freezer so you'll have them when you need them.

Freezer Tips

Don't overcook food items that are intended for the freezer, and be particularly careful to slightly undercook pasta, rice, and vegetables.

Cool foods completely by setting meals in the refrigerator for at least an hour before freezing.

Allow time for your frozen foods to thaw before reheating. About 24 to 48 hours in the refrigerator will completely thaw most freezer items.

Label (we use a permanent ink marker) with reheating instructions before freezing. This will streamline your preparation. Include the name of the meal, date frozen, number of servings, temperature and length of time it bakes, and any other necessary information.

Thaw casseroles (unless directed otherwise in the recipe) before baking. We find that in most cases, going straight from freezer to oven with frozen unbaked dishes causes uneven baking. The outer edges tend to overcook, while the middle is uncooked.

Freezer No-No's

Test Kitchen SECRET

The two biggest enemies of frozen food are air and moisture because they can cause freezer burn. That's why moistureproof, airtight containers and packaging are a must. Just say no to the temptation to use any of the following items for freezer storage—you'll be glad you did.

- Milk or juice cartons, or plastic jugs
- Ricotta, cottage cheese, or yogurt containers
- Butter/margarine tubs
- Glass jars that don't have "Ball" or "Kerr" on them
- Glass jars with narrow mouths (even if they're Ball or Kerr jars)
- Plastic zip-top storage bags (as opposed to plastic zip-top freezer bags)
- Plastic sandwich bags
- Plastic produce or bread bags

To freeze fresh berries such as blackberries, blueberries, cranberries and raspberries, spread them out in a single layer on a baking sheet, and freeze until firm. Then you can transfer them to smaller containers and use them for smoothies, sauces, or desserts that call for frozen berries. Measure the amount of berries by the cupful as you transfer to containers, and record this information on a label.

Quality Checklist

Here's how to judge the potential quality of all your make-ahead frozen food. Before you put prepared food in the freezer, check off as many boxes as applicable. The more checks, the better your frozen dish will be.

❏ Food is slightly undercooked (except baked goods)

❏ The container or packaging is moisture-proof, air-tight, and odorless

❏ Food is packaged in small portions

❏ Food is packaged in shallow containers

❏ Container or packaging fits the shape and size of the food to be frozen

❏ Food is packed tightly to eliminate as much air space as possible

❏ Container or packaging is almost full, leaving only a little space for the food to expand as it freezes

❏ Excess air is pressed from freezer bags

❏ Container or bag is tightly sealed

❏ Contents of freezer are organized so wrappings don't become loose or pierced

❏ Packages are labeled with a freezer marker indicating the contents, number of servings, and date of storage

❏ Food is placed in a single layer on freezer shelves until frozen

❏ Freezer is set to and maintains 0° or below

❏ Freezer is not freezing too much food at a time

❏ An inventory identifying each food in the freezer and its "use by" date is posted on the outside of the freezer and is updated each time an item is removed

" In our Test Kitchens, we stock up on cranberries and pecans in the fall when they're at the peak of their season and freeze them so we'll have them when we're testing our holiday recipes in the middle of the summer."
Vanessa Johnson, Test Kitchens Director

Freezer Storage

Here are some guidelines for the length of time you can keep foods in the freezer without a compromise in quality.

Eggs and Cheeses	
cheese	4 months
egg whites or egg substitute	6 months
egg yolks	8 months
Fruits and Vegetables	
commercial frozen fruits	1 year
commercial frozen veggies	8 months
Meats and Poultry	
ground meat	3 to 4 months
beef	6 months to 1 year
veal, lamb	6 to 9 months
pork	3 to 6 months
cooked meats	3 months
turkey	6 months
chicken pieces	3 months
whole chicken	3 to 6 months
cooked chicken	1 month
Breads and Desserts	
muffins, baked	1 month
quick breads, baked	1 month
yeast bread, baked	1 month
layer cakes, baked	1 month
pound cakes, baked	1 month
cookies, baked	1 month
Nuts	6 to 12 months
Soups and Stews (without potatoes)	1 month

CHAPTER 5

Meats, Poultry, Fish & Shellfish

Here's all you need to know to buy, prepare, and cook the tastiest and healthiest selections of beef, pork, lamb, chicken, turkey, fish, and shellfish.

Beef

Beef can be part of a healthy diet, especially when you select lean cuts and use low-fat cooking methods. We'll guide you through those low-fat methods and tell you about the leanest cuts.

Ask the *Cooking Light Cooks*

What are *Cooking Light's* favorite beef cuts?
Two cuts show up repeatedly in our recipes: tenderloin and flank steak. Tenderloin is the most tender, luxurious cut you can buy, and it's very lean. We like it roasted whole, cut into steaks and pan-seared, or cut into cubes and grilled on skewers. Flank steak is a tough cut, but it's especially flavorful. Sear it quickly and slice thinly, or braise it slowly and shred. Its flat shape and coarse grain absorb flavors quickly, making it good for marinades.

What about the fat and calories in these two cuts? Flank steak and tenderloin have similar amounts of calories, protein, and fat. And though you might think of tenderloin as an expensive meat for special occasions, the price—on a per-serving basis—is just a few dollars higher than flank steak. And that velvety, melt-in-your-mouth taste is well worth a little splurge.

The Skinny on Beef

Here's how cuts of beef stack up against one another. Figures are for 3 ounces of Choice-grade cooked meat, trimmed of all visible fat.

Cut	Calories	Fat
Bottom round	164	6.6g
Brisket	207	11.7g
Chuck arm pot roast	186	7.4g
Eye of round	149	4.8g
Flank steak	176	8.6g
Ground beef (regular)	248	16.5g
Ground beef (80% lean)	228	15.0g
Ground beef (85% lean)	204	12.0g
Ground beef (90% lean)	169	9.0g
Porterhouse steak	190	10.9g
Prime rib	215	12.8g
Short ribs	196	11.6g
Sirloin tip roast	170	7.6g
T-bone steak	217	14.4g
Tenderloin	180	8.6g
Top round	176	4.9g
Top sirloin	170	6.6g

In *Cooking Light* recipes, one serving is a 4-ounce portion of uncooked beef (about 3 ounces cooked).

How to Buy Beef

Beef should have a cherry red or—if it's vacuum-packed—a dark, purplish red color; avoid meat with gray or brown blotches. The visible fat should be very white. Seek a moist surface and a fresh smell. Avoid packaged meat with a lot of liquid in the tray—that's usually a sign the meat has been frozen and thawed.

Grades of Beef The two most important factors in U.S. Department of Agriculture (USDA) grading are the age of the animal and the marbling in the meat. Beef can be one of eight grades, but only the top three—Prime, Choice, and Select—are sold in supermarkets and butcher shops. Most of the Prime meat is bought by restaurants; supermarkets sell mostly Choice and Select. Look for Choice when tenderness and juiciness matter most, such as for oven roasts or steaks for grilling. For pot roast or stew meat, Select is fine.

USDA grading has nothing to do with food safety; it's a measure of taste.

Keeping it Fresh Tightly wrapped and refrigerated, raw beef will last 3 to 4 days (ground beef, 1 to 2 days). At that point, it should be cooked or frozen. Cooked, it will keep in the refrigerator 3 to 4 days longer; frozen, it's best used within 2 months.

Ground Beef Ground beef is beef muscle (not organ meat) that's ground or very finely chopped. Its flavor, texture, and, to some degree, its fat percentage are determined by which part that muscle comes from. Ground beef labels can be quite confusing. Some ground beef is labeled by cut (chuck, sirloin, or round), while some is labeled by percent fat to percent lean.

The cut listed on the label is not necessarily an indication of leanness. By law, all packaged ground beef may have fat added to it, as long as the label says how much. A package labeled "80 percent lean ground sirloin" is 20 percent fat—5 percent more fat than a piece of ground sirloin naturally contains.

Of the three cuts most commonly used for ground beef, here's how the fat percentages stack up:
- Ground chuck: 20 percent fat
- Ground sirloin: 15 percent fat
- Ground round: 11 percent fat

Lean and Tender Cuts
Test Kitchen SECRET

The leanest, most tender, and most expensive cuts of beef come from the loin (the part of the animal that is exercised the least): beef tenderloin roast, Porterhouse, T-bone, filet mignon, and New York strip steaks.

Lean Ground Beef
Test Kitchen SECRET

The maximum fat content in any ground beef is 30 percent (70 percent lean). Look for labels that tell the amount of percent fat to percent lean—then there will be no guessing about which has the least fat.

Or choose a whole piece of chuck, sirloin, or round, and ask the person behind the meat counter to trim and grind it for you.

Although extralean ground beef (4 percent to 8 percent fat) is available, we prefer using ground round, which is usually between 11 percent and 15 percent fat. For burgers, where the meat is truly in the spotlight, that bit of extra fat yields a more tender patty with a better texture.

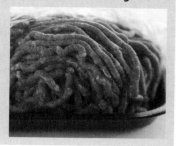

"We prefer using ground round for burgers because it is usually between 11 percent and 15 percent fat which makes a more tender patty." Tiffany Vickers, Test Kitchens Staffer

How to Cook Beef

Cooking beef is a matter of using the right cooking method for the particular cut of beef. Generally, it's best to cook tender cuts with dry heat, and tough cuts with moist heat.

Dry-Heat Methods

- *Roast* large tender cuts of beef. Roasting refers to cooking meat without added liquid. It's the gentlest dry-heat method, perfect for roasts from the rib and loin (and a few cuts from the chuck and round, too).
- *Sauté* small tender cuts. Sauté quickly on the stove over direct, intense heat. Sautéing best suits small pieces of any tender cut like sirloin, tenderloin, or top blade steak.

- *Grill or broil* small tender cuts. Grill on a rack with the heat source below the food; broil on a rack with the heat source above the food. These methods are best for relatively small tender cuts like rib, loin, or flank steak.

Moist-Heat Methods

- *Braise* large tough cuts of beef. Sear the meat to crusty dark brown, then add a small amount of liquid. Cover the pan, and cook it low and slow on the stove or in the oven until the meat is fork-tender.

"Generally, it's best to cook tender cuts with dry heat, and tough cuts with moist heat." Sam Brannock, Test Kitchens Staffer

Because boiling water can't rise above 212°, braising ensures steady, gentle heat. Pot roast and short ribs are classic examples of braised meats. (See page 55 for more information on braising.)

- *Stew* small tough cuts of beef. Stewing is similar to braising, but with more liquid and smaller pieces of meat. Chunks of beef are browned very well, a few at a time, and then covered completely with seasoned liquid in a pot. The liquid regulates the cooking temperature of the meat and forms the sauce.

Doneness: A Matter of Taste Doneness is an issue of personal preference. One person's medium-rare may seem very rare to someone else, and those who prefer their meat well done should be allowed to enjoy it that way.

Beef steaks and roasts should be cooked to a minimum of 145° (medium-rare). For ground beef, the minimum is 160°. A temperature of 160° is considered medium and 170° is well done.

It's important to know when the meat has reached the desired degree of doneness. For larger cuts of meat, use a thermometer (preferably an instant-read one), and remove the meat from the oven when it's slightly more rare than you like it. (See page 75 for more information on meat thermometers.) After a roast comes out of the oven, its internal temperature will continue to rise by 5° to 20°. The higher the cooking temperature, the greater the carry over.

Nick, Peek, and Cheat	Test Kitchen SECRET

Though using a thermometer is the only way to truly know how done meat is, the "nick, peek, and cheat" method works well for steaks: Nick the meat with a sharp knife, and take a peek inside to check its doneness. Don't worry about juices escaping when you cut into the meat; the small amount you'll lose is preferable to under- or overcooking your steak.

Ask the *Cooking Light Cooks*

Why do recipes tell you to let meat rest before you cut it? As a roast cooks, external heat drives its juices toward the center. Once the meat comes out of the oven and cools slightly, the juices are reabsorbed and redistributed, so they won't run out as freely when you carve.

If loin cuts are the leanest and most tender, why use other cuts? For flavor. The parts of the animal that are exercised the most produce the most flavorful meat, even it it's not the most tender. If you're willing to accept a little chewiness in the name of flavor, try a chuck roast or rump roast; it offers taste you just can't get from tenderloin.

Marinating Beef	Test Kitchen SECRET

Don't count on marinades to make chewy steaks tender. Marinating is great for adding flavor, but high-acid mixtures will only soften the surface, turning it mushy before the liquid can penetrate the meat.

The length of time marinating beef varies. A few hours will transfer flavor without making the surface of the meat mushy. Low-acid mixtures like teriyaki sauce can remain on for up to 48 hours, but don't let beef sit in a high-acid liquid, like lime juice, for more than 1 or 2 hours. See page 69 for more information on marinades.

Roasted Beef Tenderloin with Merlot-Shallot Sauce

The tenderloin is the least used muscle of the animal and is meltingly tender (though expensive). The center cut used here, also called Châteaubriand, is the most tender part of the tenderloin.

Tenderloin:

Cooking spray
- ⅓ cup finely chopped fresh sage
- 1 tablespoon cracked black pepper
- 3 tablespoons minced garlic
- 2 teaspoons kosher salt
- 1 (2½-pound) center-cut beef tenderloin

Sauce:
- ⅓ cup finely chopped shallots
- 1½ cups Merlot or other dry red wine
- 1½ cups low-salt beef broth
- 1 teaspoon butter
- 3 tablespoons chopped fresh parsley
- ¼ teaspoon kosher salt

1. Preheat oven to 350°.

2. To prepare tenderloin, heat a large nonstick skillet coated with cooking spray over medium-high heat. Combine sage, pepper, garlic, and salt; rub over tenderloin. Add tenderloin to pan; cook 6 minutes, lightly browning on all sides.

3. Insert a meat thermometer into thickest portion of tenderloin. Cover handle of pan with foil. Bake at 350° for 25 minutes or until thermometer registers 140° (medium-rare) or until desired degree of doneness. Place tenderloin on a cutting board; cover loosely with foil. Let stand 15 minutes (temperature of tenderloin will increase 5° upon standing).

4. To prepare sauce, heat same pan over medium-high heat. Add shallots; sauté 3 minutes or until tender. Stir in wine. Bring to a boil; cook until reduced to ¾ cup (about 4 minutes), scraping pan to loosen browned bits. Stir in broth; cook until reduced to 1¼ cups (about 6 minutes). Add butter, stirring until melted. Stir in parsley and ¼ teaspoon salt. Serve with tenderloin. Yield: 10 servings (serving size: 3 ounces tenderloin and 2 tablespoons sauce).

CALORIES 216 (34% from fat); FAT 8.2g (sat 3.1g, mono 3.1g, poly 0.4g); PROTEIN 25.3g; CARB 3.1g; FIBER 0.3g; CHOL 72mg; IRON 3.6mg; SODIUM 495mg; CALC 28mg

Tenderloin is best cooked using a dry-heat method such as roasting.

The Best Burgers

Test Kitchen SECRET

- Be careful not to overmix ground meat—doing so will make the patties dense.
- Likewise, use a light hand when shaping the burgers so they don't become too compacted.
- To keep meat from sticking to your skin as you form the patties, work with damp hands.
- Resist the urge to press the burgers with a spatula as they cook—you'll press away flavorful juices.
- Freeze uncooked burgers in a heavy-duty zip-top plastic bag for up to 3 months; place between sheets of wax paper or plastic wrap so they'll be easy to pry apart.

Asian Flank Steak

Because this is a high acid, high-flavor marinade with lime juice, soy sauce, and ginger, the flank steak only needs to marinate about 2 hours.

- 1 (1½-pound) lean flank steak
- ⅓ cup fresh lime juice
- ¼ cup minced fresh mint
- ¼ cup low-sodium soy sauce
- 2 tablespoons minced peeled fresh ginger
- 2 tablespoons minced seeded jalapeño pepper
- 3 garlic cloves, minced
- Cooking spray
- 1½ pounds green beans, trimmed
- 1 cup halved cherry tomatoes

1. Trim fat from steak. Combine steak and next 6 ingredients in a large heavy-duty zip-top plastic bag. Seal bag, and marinate in refrigerator 2 hours, turning bag occasionally. Remove steak from bag, reserving marinade.

2. Prepare grill or broiler.

3. Place steak on grill rack or broiler pan coated with cooking spray; cook 8 minutes on each side or until desired degree of doneness. Cut steak diagonally across the grain into thin slices; thread steak on skewers, if desired. Set aside; keep warm.

4. Pour reserved marinade through a sieve into a large microwave-safe bowl. Microwave at HIGH 1 minute or until marinade boils. Steam green beans, covered, 3 minutes. Add beans and tomatoes to hot marinade; toss gently. Serve with steak. Yield: 6 servings (serving size: 3 ounces steak and 1 cup green bean mixture).

CALORIES 252 (45% from fat); PROTEIN 23.3g; FAT 12.6g (sat 5.3g, mono 5.2g, poly 0.5g); CARB 11.5g; FIBER 2.8g; CHOL 57mg; IRON 3.4mg; SODIUM 338mg; CALC 53mg

---

Promoting Pot Roast?
Test Kitchen SECRET

A great pot roast is the best way to convince people that inexpensive, tough cuts can be just as delicious as more expensive tender ones.

Choosing the right roast is easy: Pick top blade roast (also called 7-bone roast because the blade bone resembles the number "7"), boneless shoulder roast, arm pot roasts, or chuck eye roast. Bottom round and rump roasts are also recommended for pot roast. Besides choosing the right cut, these few steps ensure a juicy, flavorful pot roast.

- Searing browns the meat well; a good crusty exterior creates flavors that spread throughout the dish.
- Use a covered pot that will hold the meat snugly, so that the liquid will come halfway up the sides, and the top half of the roast will be bathed in steam as it cooks.
- Cook the roast a day ahead. All braises and stews taste better the second day, and chilling allows you to skim off excess fat before reheating.

When serving flank steak, use a very sharp knife, and cut diagonally (at an angle) across the grain. Flank steak tends to toughen as it stands, so you'll want to slice the entire steak immediately after cooking.

Veal

Veal is the meat of a calf up to 3 months of age.

- *Milk-fed veal* is the most tender and flavorful. It has a creamy pink color and fine-grained texture.
- *Formula-fed veal* is also tender and pale, but it does not have as much flavor as milk-fed veal.
- *Free-range veal* is from a calf that has been weaned and fed on grass and grains. This veal has a redder color and meatier flavor.

> **Good veal is pale pink;** the redder the color, the older the veal. Any visible fat should be very pale.

How to Cook Veal

The lack of fat can cause veal to become tough and dry if not cooked properly. Veal roasts and shanks are best cooked by moist-heat methods such as braising and stewing. (See page 195.) Cutlets and scallops are best when quickly pan-fried or sautéed; chops are good when pan-fried, broiled, or grilled.

Veal Shanks   **Test Kitchen**
                                   SECRET

To create a succulent meal from inexpensive veal shanks, cook them using a moist-heat method such as braising, either in a Dutch oven or an electric slow cooker.

A great example of a braised veal dish is osso buco, a traditional Italian dish made with veal shanks that are braised in olive oil, white wine, stock, tomatoes, anchovies, garlic, and usually celery or carrots. Osso buco is traditionally served with gremolata—a topping of minced parsley, lemon peel, and garlic.

Veal Marsala

Veal scaloppine is a superthin veal cutlet.

- 1 pound veal scaloppine
- ¼ cup all-purpose flour, divided
- ⅔ cup beef consommé
- 1 tablespoon butter
- ½ cup dry Marsala wine
- 1 cup sliced mushrooms
- ¼ teaspoon salt
- 1 tablespoon chopped fresh parsley

1. Dredge veal in 3 tablespoons flour. Combine 1 tablespoon flour and consommé, stirring with a whisk; set aside.

2. Melt butter in a large nonstick skillet over medium-high heat. Add veal; cook 1½ minutes. Turn veal over; cook 1 minute. Remove veal from pan.

3. Add wine to pan, scraping pan to loosen browned bits. Add consommé mixture, mushrooms, and salt; bring to a boil. Reduce heat; simmer 3 minutes or until thick. Return veal to pan; sprinkle with parsley. Yield: 4 servings (serving size: 3 ounces veal and about 2 tablespoons sauce).

CALORIES 193 (28% from fat); FAT 6.1g (sat 3g, mono 1.1g, poly 0.4g); PROTEIN 26g; CARB 7.5g; FIBER 0.4g; CHOL 102mg; IRON 1.9mg; SODIUM 481mg; CALC 24mg

> "Veal requires careful cooking because it's so lean."
>
> Sam Brannock, Test Kitchens Staffer

Lamb

Today, lamb is leaner than ever. And because lamb cuts are leaner, it's very important that you watch the cooking time and temperature carefully, or your meat will be overcooked and tough. For the best flavor and tenderness, cook lamb only until it's pink: medium-rare (145°) or medium (160°). Most of the fat on lamb is on the outside, not inside the meat, so if you cook the lamb to 180° or 185° (well done), the meat will be tough and dry.

Lean Lamb For the leanest cuts of lamb, look for those with the words "loin" or "leg" on the label. Some lean cuts of lamb include the leg, loin chops, arm chops, and foreshanks. Ground lamb is also fairly lean and can be used in the same way that you use ground beef. If you're not a lamb fan, you can use ground round in place of the lamb in almost any recipe that calls for ground lamb. A 3-ounce cooked portion of ground lamb has 241 calories, 16.7 grams of fat, and 83 grams of cholesterol; the same amount of cooked ground round beef has 191 calories, 9 grams of fat, and 72 grams of cholesterol.

Roast Lamb with Rosemary and Garlic

This roast cooks with just a simple rub of rosemary and garlic; coarse salt goes on the second the lamb is taken from the oven.

    1 (3-pound) rolled boneless leg of lamb, trimmed
    1 tablespoon chopped fresh rosemary
    3 garlic cloves, minced
    1 teaspoon kosher or sea salt

1. Preheat oven to 450°.
2. Secure roast at 1-inch intervals with heavy string. Rub surface of roast with rosemary and garlic. Place roast on rack of a broiler pan or roasting pan; insert a meat thermometer into the thickest portion of roast. Bake at 450° for 1 hour and 15 minutes or until thermometer registers 140° (medium-rare) to 155° (medium).
3. Sprinkle roast with salt. Place roast on a cutting board; cover loosely with foil. Let stand 10 minutes (temperature of roast will increase 5° upon standing). Remove string before slicing. Yield: 8 servings (serving size: 3 ounces).

CALORIES 165 (36% from fat); FAT 6.6g (sat 2.4g, mono 2.9g, poly 0.4g); PROTEIN 24.2g; CARB 0.5g; FIBER 0g; CHOL 76mg; IRON 1.9mg; SODIUM 293mg; CALC 12mg

> **It's easy to overcook lean lamb,** so watch your cooking time and temperature carefully. If you cook it too long, the meat will be tough.

Greek Lamb Chops

Try this with couscous tossed with chopped tomato, cucumber, and feta cheese.

    2 tablespoons lemon juice
    1 tablespoon bottled minced garlic
    1 tablespoon dried oregano
    ½ teaspoon salt
    ¼ teaspoon pepper
    8 (4-ounce) lamb loin chops, trimmed
    Cooking spray

1. Preheat broiler.
2. Combine first 5 ingredients; rub over both sides of chops. Place chops on a broiler pan coated with cooking spray; broil 4 minutes on each side or until desired degree of doneness. Yield: 4 servings (serving size: 2 chops).

CALORIES 192 (39% from fat); FAT 8.4g (sat 3g, mono 3.6g, poly 0.6g); PROTEIN 25.8g; CARB 1.7g; FIBER 0.1g; CHOL 81mg; IRON 1.8mg; SODIUM 367mg; CALC 36mg

Pork

From pork chops to prosciutto, using the right cooking method for each cut guarantees flavorful, tender results.

Ask the *Cooking Light Cooks*

What are the best cuts of fresh pork to use for healthy recipes? The fresh cuts of pork that we use the most in our recipes are pork tenderloin, chops, loin, and shoulder roast.

What about cured pork? Is it off-limits? No. We use small amounts of bacon, prosciutto, pancetta, and ham hocks to add intense flavor to a variety of dishes.

How to Buy Pork

Here are the cuts of fresh pork that we use and what we look for at the grocery store.

Pork Tenderloin Pork tenderloin comes from the sirloin (the back part of the loin). It is a narrow cylinder about 1 foot in length and about 3 inches in diameter. Usually, you'll see 1-pound packages or 2 (¾-pound) tenderloins packaged together. **The tenderloin is the leanest and most tender cut of pork.**

Pork Loin Pork loin is sold both on the bone and boneless, usually in 2- to 4-pound roasts, and it is also cut into chops. The meat is tender but lean, especially the short loin (in the lower back). **The rib area, which has a little more fat, is more flavorful and is the pork equivalent of the standing rib roast of beef or a rack of lamb; this cut is often labeled "center-cut pork loin."** When pork loin is sold boneless, it's hard to tell where the piece has come from, but a skilled butcher should be able to guide you.

Pork Chops Chops come from the loin. They may be bone-in or boneless, and they are usually named for the section of the loin from which they're cut. **Buy chops at least 1 to 1¼ inches thick; they tend to brown nicely without overcooking.**
- *Rib chops* are from the rib area and include some back-rib bone.
- *Loin chops* are from the lower back and have a characteristic T-shaped bone; they include a lot of loin meat and a bit of tenderloin meat.
- *Sirloin chops* are from the area around the hip and often include a big chunk of hipbone.

Pork Shoulder Roast (Boston Butt) Often labeled "pork shoulder butt," this large, inexpensive chunk of meat is a well-marbled square cut from the upper part of the shoulder. The arm part of the shoulder, called "picnic shoulder," is quite fatty and gristly, and thus best avoided. Sometimes the pork shoulder is sliced into steaks, which are sold as blade chops.

Though it seems like it describes opposite parts of the body, the phrase pork shoulder butt is not an oxymoron. "Butt" describes the barrels used to pack the meat in Colonial New England.

Blade chops come from the beginning of the shoulder area and may contain some blade bone as well as back-rib bone. They are too tough and gristly to cook like other chops, and are best cooked by moist heat to tenderize them. They are often butterflied and sold as country-style spareribs.

Ham Ham refers both to the fresh hind leg of the pig and to the hind leg cured in salt. The salt-cured version is produced by injecting the leg with water, salt, sugar, and other flavorings, then curing it for a few days. The ham is usually smoked after the brine has penetrated the meat, and then cooked in smokehouses.

Country ham, found mostly in the South, is dry-cured, smoked, and aged from a few weeks to more than a year.

Regular hams can contain added water, and phosphates are added to keep that water in the hams during cooking. Although hams without any added water are available (and expensive), in most grocery stores, you are more likely to find hams labeled "ham with natural juices." These hams have been pumped with brine before smoking and cooking. Cheaper hams are labeled "ham—water added," so you're buying some water weight along with your ham. The cheapest hams of all say "ham and water product." These hams can include as much water as the manufacturer wishes, but the label must state the percentage of extra water in the ham.

The best (and the most expensive) hams have not been pumped with brine nor do they have any added water. They are simply labeled "ham."

Selecting a Ham
Cooking Light **Recommends**

Avoid cheaper hams, which are soft and spongy and have a manufactured taste. Bone-in hams are the most flavorful but are harder to carve. Since a whole bone-in ham can easily weigh 15 to 20 pounds, you may wish to purchase a half ham. Choose halves that are labeled "butt end"—they have more meat and less connective tissue than shank ends.

Ham Hocks Ham hocks, from the meaty portion of the lower leg bone, typically come cured and smoked. Hocks have a rich smoky flavor, which is great for flavoring beans, split peas, and rustic vegetables like cabbage and kale. Usually sold with the skin attached, ham hocks provide flavor; the gelatin released when the skin cooks gives body and richness to whatever you cook with the hocks.

Using Ham Hocks
Test Kitchen SECRET

Because they're tough, ham hocks take up to 3 hours to cook completely; they're best when the meat is almost falling off the bone. We usually cook them a day or so ahead, then refrigerate. When we're ready to use them in a dish, we remove skin, fat, and bone, and chop the remaining meat to add at the end of the cooking.

Bacon Bacon comes from the belly of the animal and is usually cured and smoked. It's generally about 50 percent fat, although reduced-fat versions are available. As bacon cooks, the fat separates from the meat and can be poured off and discarded or used for sautéing.

Because bacon has such an intense smoky flavor, a little goes a long way. Look for thick center-cut bacon; applewood-smoked bacon is particularly flavorful.

"When you are using bacon to flavor a dish, choose the best bacon you can find so that a little will go a long way." Jan Moon, Test Kitchens Staffer

"Instead of using reduced-fat bacon, we usually opt for the real thing and just use a small amount." Kathleen Kanen, Food Stylist

Pancetta Pancetta is cured but unsmoked pork belly (the same cut from which bacon is made). Think of it as unsmoked bacon. Most pancetta sold in the United States is produced domestically. Manufacturers rub pork belly with salt or immerse it in brine until the salt completely penetrates the meat. Then they rub the cured belly with aromatic spices and/or herbs. Italians often eat pancetta thinly sliced as a cold cut, but we use it most often chopped or pan-fried to flavor pastas, soups, and salads.

Prosciutto Prosciutto is a pork leg rubbed with salt and refrigerated for several weeks. When it penetrates to the bone, the salt is then washed away, and the pork ages in a cool place from 14 to 24 months. The aging gives this special kind of ham a distinctly unique flavor and silky texture when cut into very thin slices. Because prosciutto is lean, it adds little fat to a dish.

When you're buying prosciutto, buy only what you need, since flavor is best when the cut is fresh. Ask for paper-thin slices. Keep it tightly wrapped in the refrigerator, and use within 3 to 5 days.

How to Cook Lean Pork

Today's pork has a fat content so low that it favorably compares to chicken. The leanest cuts, such as loin chops, loin roasts, and tenderloins, have less overall fat, saturated fat, and cholesterol than equal amounts of skinless chicken thighs.

Except for fattier cuts like the Boston butt, spare ribs, and blade shoulder chops, pork has little or no marbling; it must be cooked carefully so it won't dry out. In Grandma's day, pork was cooked beyond well done to temperatures of 170° to 180°. Cooking today's lean cuts to these temperatures will yield dry, hard results. Instead, cook to 150° to 155°. (See "Keep It Safe," below.)

"Lean pork has little or no marbling. You need to cook it carefully it won't dry out."
Mike Wilson, Test Kitchens Staffer

Pork Tenderloin Like beef tenderloin, pork tenderloin has a mild flavor; thus, it's best to add a spice rub, marinade, stuffing, or flavorful sauce. Pork tenderloin is small, so it cooks fast and is an ideal quick supper. Pork tenderloin is also great grilled whole, butterflied and stuffed, or cut into cross sections (called medallions) and cooked in a skillet. Just don't overcook it—because tenderloin is so lean, it can dry out easily.

Pork Loin Loin on the bone usually stays juicier and more flavorful than boneless loin, but the bone makes it more difficult to carve. Pork loin is best roasted, and it's easy to butterfly and stuff. Cooking for a long time over indirect heat in a covered gas or charcoal grill is also a great way to cook pork loin. Fresh herbs such as rosemary, sage, and thyme make ideal rubs for the surface of a pork loin, especially when combined with fennel seed and garlic. **Pork loin is a more forgiving cut; its slightly higher fat content makes it harder to overcook than the tenderloin.**

> **Don't cook pork loin for long periods** in moist heat (braising or stewing); doing so toughens the meat and eventually makes it fall apart into stringy fibers.

Pork Chops Chops are great cooked by dry heat—whether pan-seared, grilled, broiled, or baked. For these cooking methods, bone-in chops cut from the rib section are best; they stay moister. Treat boneless chops the same as bone-in chops, or pound them thin to make scallops. If you have wafer-thin chops, coat them first in breadcrumbs, nuts, or even egg and flour to slow down the cooking of the interior.

Cutting Pork Loin for Stuffing

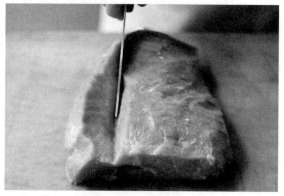

1. Starting at the right of the center of the roast, slice the pork lengthwise, cutting to, but not through, the other side. (This is called "butterflying.")

2. Open butterflied portions, laying pork flat. Turn the knife blade parallel to surface of cutting board.

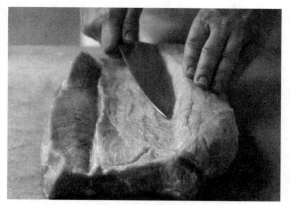

3. Slice the larger portion of pork in half horizontally, cutting to, but not through, other side; open flat.

Apple and Corn Bread-Stuffed Pork Loin

This tender pork loin is stuffed with and baked atop apples. The apple wedges that the pork cooks over are discarded, but they contribute lots of flavor. The double-butterfly method used to flatten the pork for stuffing creates an attractive pinwheel pattern that's evident when the pork is sliced.

```
    Cooking spray
 ½  cup finely chopped onion
 ¼  cup finely chopped celery
1¼  teaspoons freshly ground black pepper,
       divided
 ½  cup diced peeled Granny Smith apple
1½  cups corn bread stuffing mix (such as
       Pepperidge Farm)
1⅓  cups apple juice or cider, divided
1½  teaspoons dried rubbed sage, divided
 1  large egg, lightly beaten
 1  (4-pound) boneless center-cut pork loin
       roast, trimmed
1½  teaspoons salt, divided
 3  Granny Smith apples, peeled, cored, and
       cut into 1-inch wedges
 2  teaspoons cornstarch
 1  (14-ounce) can fat-free, less-sodium
       chicken broth
```

1. Preheat oven to 450°.

2. Heat a nonstick skillet coated with cooking spray over medium heat. Add onion, celery, and ⅛ teaspoon pepper; cover and cook 10 minutes or until tender, stirring occasionally. Add diced apple; cook 1 minute, stirring constantly. Place apple mixture in a large bowl, and cool slightly. Stir in the stuffing mix, ⅓ cup juice, ½ teaspoon sage, and egg; set aside.

3. Starting off-center, slice pork lengthwise, cutting to, but not through, other side. Open butterflied portions, laying pork flat. Turning knife blade parallel to surface of cutting board, slice larger portion of pork in half horizontally, cutting to, but not through, other side; open flat. Place plastic wrap over pork; pound to 1-inch thickness using a meat mallet or rolling pin. Sprinkle with ½ teaspoon salt.

4. Spread stuffing over pork, leaving a ½-inch margin around outside edges. Roll up pork, jelly-roll fashion, starting with a long side. Secure at 2-inch intervals with twine. Combine 1 teaspoon pepper, 1 teaspoon sage, and 1 teaspoon salt; rub over pork.

5. Arrange apple wedges in a single layer in bottom of a broiler pan coated with cooking spray; place pork on apples. Bake at 450° for 20 minutes. Reduce oven temperature to 325° (do not remove the pork from oven). Bake an additional 1 hour and 15 minutes or until a thermometer registers 155°. Remove pork from pan; cover and let stand 10 minutes. Discard apple wedges.

6. Combine 1 cup juice, cornstarch, and broth in a small saucepan; stir with a whisk. Bring broth mixture to boil. Reduce heat, and simmer 5 minutes. Stir in ⅛ teaspoon pepper. Cut pork into ½-inch-thick slices, and serve with sauce. Yield: 12 servings (serving size: about 5 ounces stuffed pork and about 2½ tablespoons sauce).

CALORIES 249 (30% from fat); FAT 8.3g (sat 2.9g, mono 3.6g, poly 0.8g); PROTEIN 24.3g; CARB 18.2g; FIBER 2.6g; CHOL 81mg; IRON 1.5mg; SODIUM 567mg; CALC 40mg

Barbecued Pork Chops

Make sure each chop is no thicker than ¹/₂ inch. If they're thicker, they won't get done in the time specified in this recipe; if thinner, they'll be overcooked.

Sauce:

¼ cup packed brown sugar
¼ cup ketchup
1 tablespoon Worcestershire sauce
1 tablespoon low-sodium soy sauce

Pork Chops:

6 (6-ounce) bone-in center-cut pork chops (about ½ inch thick)
1 teaspoon dried thyme
1 teaspoon garlic salt
¼ teaspoon ground red pepper
   Cooking spray

1. Prepare grill or broiler.
2. To prepare sauce, combine first 4 ingredients in a small bowl. Place ¼ cup sauce in a small bowl, and set aside.
3. To prepare pork chops, trim fat from pork. Combine thyme, garlic salt, and pepper; sprinkle over pork. Place pork on a grill rack or broiler pan coated with cooking spray; cook 6 minutes on each side, basting with remaining sauce. Serve pork chops with reserved ¼ cup sauce. Yield: 6 servings (serving size: 1 pork chop and 2 teaspoons sauce).

CALORIES 244 (42% from fat); FAT 11.3g (sat 3.9g, mono 5g, poly 1.4g); PROTEIN 24.6g; CARB 9.9g; FIBER 0.2g; CHOL 77mg; IRON 1.5mg; SODIUM 649mg; CALC 22mg

Pork Tenderloin with Maple Pan Juices

Searing the pork in a skillet before putting it in the oven browns the outside of the pork and helps seal in the juices before you put it in the oven.

⅓ cup diced onion
¼ cup fresh orange juice, divided
¼ cup maple syrup, divided
2 tablespoons sake (rice wine)
2 tablespoons low-sodium soy sauce
⅛ teaspoon pepper
2 garlic cloves, minced
1 (1-pound) pork tenderloin
   Cooking spray
⅓ cup fat-free, less-sodium chicken broth

1. Combine onion, 2 tablespoons juice, 2 tablespoons syrup, sake, soy sauce, pepper, and garlic in a large heavy-duty zip-top plastic bag. Trim fat from pork. Add pork to bag; seal and marinate in refrigerator 2 hours.
2. Preheat oven to 400°.
3. Heat a 9-inch heavy ovenproof skillet coated with cooking spray over medium-high heat. Remove pork from bag, reserving marinade. Add pork to pan; cook 5 minutes, browning on all sides. Insert a meat thermometer into thickest portion of pork. Place pan in oven; bake at 400° for 30 minutes or until meat thermometer registers 155°. Remove pork from pan; cover and let stand 10 minutes. Keep warm.
4. Combine 2 tablespoons juice, 2 tablespoons syrup, reserved marinade, and broth in a small bowl. Add syrup mixture to pan, and place over medium-high heat, scraping pan to loosen browned bits. Bring to a boil; reduce heat, and simmer 5 minutes or until slightly thick. Serve sauce with pork. Yield: 4 servings (serving size: 3 ounces pork and 2 tablespoons sauce).

CALORIES 204 (13% from fat); FAT 3g (sat 1g, mono 1.3g, (poly 0.4g); PROTEIN 24.4g; CARB 16.9g; FIBER 0.3g; CHOL 74mg; IRON 1.8mg; SODIUM 293mg; CALC 29mg

Poultry

Chicken, along with other types of poultry, is one of the most versatile foods we know.

Chicken

We're always surprised if we hear someone who is trying to eat healthfully complain that "they're so tired of eating chicken!" We use a lot of chicken in our Test Kitchens: whole, breast halves, tenders, thighs, and rotisserie chickens.

How to Buy Chicken

Here's what you need to know about different types of chicken when you're making decisions about what to buy.

Whole Chickens Whole chickens are marketed by different names, depending on their weight.

- *Broiler-fryers* are about 7 weeks old, and weigh 3 to 4 pounds. They're good for making stock (they're not as meaty as roasters) and will work in any recipe that calls for a cut-up fryer.
- *Roasters* are 3 to 5 months old, and weigh 4 to 7 pounds. If you want to bake a whole chicken, look for a roaster—they have the highest meat-to-bone ratio. Stewing hens, at 10 months to 1½ years old, are literally tough old birds, best used for chicken and dumplings or soup; when roasted, they're almost jaw-exhausting.

If you're buying chicken tenders, buy an amount that equals 6 ounces per serving; the number of tenders will vary.

Rotisserie Chicken Roasted chicken from the supermarket is one of our favorite things. We like to use it to jump-start creative homemade recipes such as pizzas, pasta dishes, sandwiches, and salads. A rotisserie chicken keeps for 3 or 4 days in the refrigerator, so it's a great item to keep on hand for a quick meal. If you're adding rotisserie chicken to a hot recipe, just stir it in at the end to warm it up.

Another advantage of using a store-cooked chicken is that it's easy to slice and remove the meat from the bone.

You can choose from a variety of flavors—from plain to barbecue and herb-roasted. **Most of the seasoning (and the salt) is in the skin, so once the skin is removed, these chickens are comparable to fresh-cooked chicken in terms of fat, and they are only slightly higher in sodium.**

Rotisserie Tips	Test Kitchen SECRET

- When you're buying rotisserie chicken at the grocery store, pick it up at the end of your shopping trip so it stays hot until you get home.
- Serve or refrigerate it within 2 hours (sooner in hot weather).
- Cut, shred, or chop the chicken, and store it, uncovered, in a shallow container in the refrigerator to help it cool quickly. Cover container when the chicken has cooled.

"To trim the fat from chicken before you cook it, use your kitchen shears. It gets a little tricky with a knife." Kellie Kelley, Food Stylist

Take It Off	Test Kitchen SECRET

If you remove the skin from a whole bird before cooking, you reduce its fat grams by about half. However, the skin adds moisture and protects lean meat from drying out. You'll get the best results by cooking the poultry with the skin on, then removing it before serving—the fat savings are still substantial. Rub flavorings under the skin. When it's removed, some seasoning will cling to the meat.

Organic and Free-Range Chicken

You've likely seen these birds in your supermarket and noticed that they're more expensive than conventionally produced chicken.

Organic poultry is fed a diet of pesticide-free grain with no hormones or antibiotics. (Actually, hormones have been banned in the poultry business for decades.)

Free-range poultry has more growing space than conventionally produced chicken along with access to open spaces, though that doesn't necessarily mean that the birds walk around outside. More movement means these birds develop more muscle, which can contribute to more full-flavored meat.

We tried both kinds side by side with conventionally farmed chicken to see if we could tell a difference. What we found was that both organic and free-range chickens have a "cleaner" chicken flavor and better texture than conventionally farmed varieties. But are these birds worth the extra trouble or expense? Unless you're cooking simple roasted chicken, probably not.

Precooked Chicken

If you're using precooked chicken in a recipe, here are some substitution amounts that will be useful:

Type	Cup Measures
1 pound uncooked boneless, skinless chicken	3 cups chopped cooked chicken
1 (5.5-ounce) boneless skinless chicken breast half	1 cup chopped cooked chicken
1 (2-pound) uncooked chicken	2¼ cups chopped cooked chicken
1 (2-pound) rotisserie chicken	3 to 3½ cups chopped chicken
1 (6-ounce) package grilled chicken strips	1⅓ cups chopped cooked chicken
1 (9-ounce) package frozen chopped cooked chicken	1⅔ cups chopped cooked chicken

Chicken Breasts We use boneless, skinless chicken breasts a great deal because they're versatile, convenient, low in fat, and readily available.

Some brands of chicken breasts now on the market are injected with a sodium broth for added juiciness. (Butterball brand is one example.) If the chicken has been injected, a statement will be on the label. Some injected brands of chicken taste a little salty, but they do seem to be more moist. However, because of the salty flavor of the injected brands, we tend to use the non-injected chicken breasts most often.

To save prep and cooking time, there are plenty of chicken breast options. We often use chicken tenders in recipes that use small pieces of chicken. Or you can buy packages of frozen chicken breasts in which individual pieces are marinated to enhance juiciness and tenderness and then frozen and packed loosely in resealable bags. Skinless breasts, tenders, breast halves, and drumsticks are available this way.

Some options for chicken that is already cooked include frozen chopped cooked chicken, grilled chicken strips, single servings of roasted chicken breasts or drumsticks, and deli-roasted or rotisserie chicken (see tips on page 208).

Thighs The *Cooking Light* food staff is crazy about chicken thighs. Now don't get us wrong—we think chicken breasts definitely have their place. But when it comes to flavor, thighs rule.

Thighs have a slightly higher fat content than the oh-so-lean breast. But dark meat with the skin removed has less total fat than the same amount of beef sirloin or tenderloin, a pork chop, or a portion of salmon. Another plus: Thighs are now widely available in a boneless, skinless model. (If your fresh-meat counter doesn't carry them, check the freezer case for bargain-size bags of individually frozen portions.) Or you can bone your own—with a bit of practice, boning a thigh becomes a matter of a minute's effort. (See "Boning a Chicken Thigh" on page 212.) Boneless, skinless thighs can be as versatile as chicken breasts, but they're significantly less expensive.

> **For long simmering in dishes that feature hearty flavors, use thighs—either bone-in or skinless, boneless thighs.**

> In *Cooking Light* **recipes,** one serving of chicken thighs is about 6 ounces of uncooked meat. The size of thighs can vary, but usually one serving is 2 (4-ounce) bone-in thighs, skinned, or 2 (3-ounce) skinless, boneless thighs.

The Top 10 Ways to Use Chicken Breasts

Here's how our Test Kitchens staffers use boneless, skinless chicken breast halves at home.

1. Chicken sauté: Pound breasts thin, cut into long strips, toss with commercial peanut sauce, skewer, and grill.

Pounding boneless chicken breast halves

helps to make them more tender. Plus, when they are thinner, they cook more quickly than thicker breasts. We also pound chicken in recipes for stuffed chicken breasts—the pounding gives you more surface area to work with and makes the chicken easier to fold or roll.

Pound the chicken using a meat mallet or rolling pin. Place the chicken between two sheets of plastic wrap to keep your work surface clean.

2. BBQ pizza: Shred cooked chicken breasts, toss with barbecue sauce, and arrange on pizza dough with smoked Cheddar cheese and chopped green onions.

3. Blackened chicken sandwiches: Season chicken breasts with blackening seasoning, grill, and arrange on hoagie rolls with coleslaw.

4. Fried rice: Cut chicken into bite-sized pieces, sauté with garlic and green onions, then stir in cold leftover rice.

5. Pesto focaccia sandwiches: Grill chicken breasts; serve with roasted red bell peppers on focaccia spread with pesto.

6. Quesadillas: Shred cooked chicken breasts, and place between flour tortillas with cheese and black or refried beans. Cook a few minutes per side in a nonstick skillet.

7. Salad: Grill chicken breasts, slice thinly, and fan atop a Greek salad of romaine lettuce, kalamata olives, pepperoncini peppers, and feta cheese.

8. Skewers: Dip chicken in low-fat Italian dressing, cut into bite-sized pieces, skewer with olives and artichoke hearts, and grill.

9. Stuffed breasts: Cut a horizontal slit into chicken breasts to form a pocket, stuff with ham and reduced-fat Swiss cheese, and sauté. Other combinations to try: goat cheese and chutney, or spinach and feta cheese. (See "How to Make a Pocket," page 211.)

10. Stuffed potatoes: Cut chicken into bite-sized pieces, season with cumin and chili powder, and sauté; toss with thawed frozen corn, chopped green onions, lime juice, and chopped cilantro. Spoon over baked potatoes.

We call for 6-ounce portions of uncooked chicken per serving in our recipes: a 6-ounce skinless, boneless breast half or an 8-ounce skinless bone-in breast half.

Artichoke and Goat Cheese-Stuffed Chicken Breasts

Stuffed chicken breasts never fail to impress. With our step-by-step instructions, we show you how to master this not-so-tricky technique.

    1   (14-ounce) can artichoke bottoms
    ½   cup (2 ounces) crumbled goat cheese or feta cheese
    ¼   cup chopped fresh chives, divided
    1½   teaspoons chopped fresh thyme, divided
    1½   teaspoons grated lemon rind, divided
    8   (6-ounce) skinless, boneless chicken breast halves
    ¼   teaspoon pepper
    2   teaspoons olive oil, divided
    1   teaspoon cornstarch
    2   tablespoons lemon juice

1. Drain artichokes, reserving liquid. Coarsely chop artichoke bottoms. Combine artichokes, cheese, 2 tablespoons chives, 1 teaspoon thyme, and 1 teaspoon lemon rind in a medium bowl; stir.
2. Cut a horizontal slit through thickest portion of each chicken breast half. Stuff ¼ cup artichoke mixture into each pocket. Sprinkle with pepper.
3. Heat 1 teaspoon oil in a skillet over medium-high heat. Add 4 chicken breasts, and sauté 6 minutes on each side or until chicken is done. Remove chicken from skillet. Set aside; keep warm. Repeat procedure with 1 teaspoon oil and remaining chicken breasts. Add reserved artichoke liquid, ½ teaspoon thyme, and ½ teaspoon lemon rind to skillet. Combine cornstarch and lemon juice; stir well. Add to skillet. Bring to a boil; cook 1 minute, stirring constantly. Return chicken to skillet. Cover and simmer 2 minutes or until thoroughly heated. Spoon sauce over chicken. Top with 2 tablespoons chives. Yield: 8 servings (serving size: 1 chicken breast half and 1 tablespoon sauce).

CALORIES 251 (21% from fat); FAT 5.8g (sat 2.5g, mono 2g, poly 0.7g); PROTEIN 42.7g; CARB 4.6g; FIBER 0.7g; CHOL 106mg; IRON 2.1mg; SODIUM 280mg; CALC 85mg

How to Make a Pocket

1. Place chicken breast half on a cutting board and trim all visible fat from chicken. Then insert tip of a thin, sharp knife (such as a boning knife) into thickest side of the chicken breast. Make a 2-inch slit. Cut to, but not through, the opposite side of the breast.

2. Holding the knife blade parallel to the cutting board, guide the blade around the inside of the breast, creating a pocket. Be careful not to cut through the sides of the breast.

3. Using your fingers, stuff the breast, getting as much filling as you can into the pocket.

Chicken Thighs with Garlic and Lime

After the chicken is baked, it's removed from the pan, and the drippings are reduced on the stovetop to a slightly syrupy sauce that is spooned over the thighs.

- 1 tablespoon minced garlic
- 1½ teaspoons ground cumin
- ½ teaspoon dried oregano
- ¼ teaspoon salt
- ⅛ teaspoon pepper
- 2 tablespoons fresh lime juice, divided
- 4 (4-ounce) bone-in chicken thighs, skinned
- 3 tablespoons fat-free, less-sodium chicken broth
- 1 tablespoon white vinegar
- 2 teaspoons chopped fresh cilantro
- 2 lime wedges

1. Preheat oven to 350°.

2. Combine first 5 ingredients in a small bowl; stir in 1 tablespoon juice. Rub garlic mixture over chicken. Place chicken in a medium skillet.

3. Combine 1 tablespoon juice, chicken broth, and vinegar; pour over the chicken. Place over medium-high heat; bring to a boil. Remove from heat. Wrap handle of pan with foil. Cover and bake at 350° for 30 minutes or until a meat thermometer registers 180°.

4. Remove chicken from pan; keep warm. Place pan over medium-high heat. Bring to a boil, and cook until liquid is reduced to ¼ cup (about 3 minutes). Spoon over chicken. Sprinkle with cilantro, and serve with lime wedges. Yield: 2 servings (serving size: 2 thighs and 2 tablespoons sauce).

CALORIES 200 (25% from fat); FAT 5.5g (sat 1.3g, mono 1.6g, poly 1.3g); PROTEIN 26.4g; CARB 10.4g; FIBER 1g; CHOL 107mg; IRON 2.2mg; SODIUM 475mg; CALC 44mg

Boning a Chicken Thigh

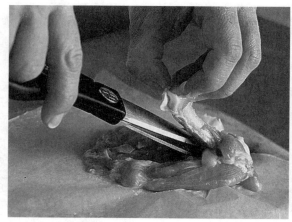

1. Work from the inside of the thigh, and cut along both sides of the thigh bone, separating it from the meat.

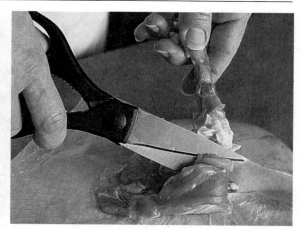

2. Cut around the cartilage at the joint, and remove the thigh bone and cartilage.

Duck

For a sophisticated meal, it's hard to surpass duck's rich flavor. Whole duck at supermarkets is usually of the Peking variety. And like turkey, the bird is now frequently sold in parts. Your gourmet market, for example, may carry boned duck breast and leg quarters. Boneless duck breast (often sold by its French name, *magret*) usually comes from the Moulard duck, a cross of the Peking and Muscovy varieties.

Duck is the only poultry we recommend serving medium-rare. If you cook it past that, it will lack flavor and be slightly tough. The quarters are great for ragoûts (remove the skin before cooking, and skim the fat from the broth). Duck skin is thick and fatty, but duck meat has little marbling and is only about 2 percent fat.

If your supermarket doesn't carry fresh duck breast, look for duck breast in the freezer section.

> "In preparing duck breast, think of it as the steak of the poultry world: Cook it past medium-rare, and you'll lose flavor and compromise its texture."

Sam Brannock, Test Kitchens Staffer

Duck Breast with Pineapple-Cherry Chutney

When you're looking for an elegant and quick recipe, consider this entrée with Asian flavors. Serve with stir-fried bok choy and steamed jasmine rice.

Chutney:
- 2 cups (¾-inch) cubed fresh pineapple
- ¾ cup pineapple juice
- ⅓ cup dried tart cherries
- 2 tablespoons brown sugar
- 2 tablespoons balsamic vinegar
- 1 tablespoon minced peeled fresh ginger
- 1 tablespoon minced shallots
- ⅛ teaspoon crushed red pepper
- 1 garlic clove, minced

Duck:
- Cooking spray
- 1 pound boneless duck breast halves, skinned
- ¾ teaspoon salt
- ¾ teaspoon five-spice powder

Remaining ingredient:
- 2 tablespoons chopped fresh cilantro

1. To prepare chutney, combine first 9 ingredients in a saucepan; bring to a boil over medium-high heat. Cook 10 minutes or until syrupy, stirring frequently; remove from heat.

2. To prepare duck, heat a large, heavy skillet coated with cooking spray over high heat. Sprinkle duck with salt and five-spice powder. Add duck to skillet; cook 4 minutes. Turn duck over. Reduce heat to medium, and cook 6 minutes or until desired degree of doneness. Place duck on a cutting board; cover loosely with foil. Let stand 5 minutes. Cut duck into ¼-inch-thick diagonal slices.

3. Add chutney and cilantro to skillet; cook over medium heat 1 minute; scrape pan to loosen browned bits. Yield: 4 servings (serving size: 3 ounces duck and 3 tablespoons chutney).

CALORIES 278 (17% from fat); FAT 5.2g (sat 1.5g, mono 1.4g, poly 0.8g); PROTEIN 23.7g; CARB 33g; FIBER 2.3g; CHOL 87mg; IRON 5.9mg; SODIUM 514mg; CALC 32mg

Turkey

Turkey is not just for Thanksgiving anymore. Because it's lean, versatile, and has great flavor, we use it all year long.

How to Buy Turkey

Whole turkeys These birds are often sold by the sex of the bird. Hens weigh up to 16 pounds, while toms weigh more. There is no flavor difference; **buy the size that suits your needs, figuring about 1 pound (including skin and bones) per person to allow for seconds and leftovers.**

Breasts and Tenderloins Turkey cuts have come a long way. Newer ones include skinless, boneless turkey breast halves (sometimes labeled "turkey London broil"); turkey cutlets (often labeled "turkey breast filets"), and turkey tenderloins. Turkey breast is very lean, so keep a close eye on these cuts to avoid overcooking.

> **For smaller parties** or white-meat-only crowds, a whole turkey breast is a smart alternative to a whole bird. A 5-pound breast can be substituted for a 12-pound bird with a few minor adjustments.
> - Insert a meat thermometer into the meaty part of the turkey breast; make sure it doesn't touch the breastbone.
> - Bake the breast at 350° for 1 hour and 45 minutes or until the thermometer registers 170°. Cover the breast loosely with aluminum foil if it gets too brown.
> - Slice the breast directly off the bone. Discard skin.

Ground turkey You'll see several types of ground turkey in the supermarket, so read the label to be sure you get what you want. The leanest (about 3 percent fat) is white meat only, with no skin. It's labeled "ground turkey breast." Regular "ground turkey" is made from white and dark meat with some skin, and is about 10 percent fat (similar to ground round). Frozen ground turkey is usually all dark meat with skin, and is 15 percent fat, similar to ground sirloin.

Turkey Handling — Keep It SAFE

You can defrost a turkey safely a number of ways.
- The best method is to set the bird in a shallow pan in the refrigerator for 24 hours per 5 pounds of turkey. This process will take several days, so plan accordingly and make room in the refrigerator.
- If you lack refrigerator space, submerge the unwrapped turkey in a sink filled with cold water for about an hour per pound, changing the water every 30 minutes.
- In any case, the turkey is fully thawed when a meat thermometer inserted into a thick part of the turkey registers 40°. Store thawed turkey in the refrigerator until ready to cook.

When you're roasting a turkey, we do not recommend stuffing the bird because of food safety reasons.
- The stuffing may prevent the inside part of the turkey from reaching the safe temperature, then the bacteria from the uncooked turkey might cross-contaminate the stuffing. Besides, you'll save calories and fat without the stuffing anyway.
- If you want stuffing or dressing, we recommend baking it in a separate dish and serving it with the turkey. You can season inside the cavity with spices, herbs, or fruit.
- Or season it from the outside in by marinating or coating it with a spice rub. You can also insert fresh herbs such as sage, parsley, or thyme under the skin before baking the bird.

Ultimate Roasted Turkey

This recipe won our Test Kitchens' highest rating.

¾ cup apple cider
5 tablespoons dark corn syrup, divided
1 (12-pound) fresh or frozen turkey, thawed
1 tablespoon poultry seasoning
1 tablespoon dried rubbed sage
1 teaspoon salt
¼ teaspoon pepper
4 garlic cloves, sliced
2 onions, quartered
2 Golden Delicious apples, cored and quartered
   Cooking spray
1 teaspoon butter
1 (14-ounce) can fat-free, less-sodium chicken broth
1 tablespoon cornstarch

1. Preheat oven to 375°.
2. Combine cider and 4 tablespoons corn syrup in a small saucepan; bring to a boil. Remove from heat; set aside.
3. Remove and reserve giblets and neck from turkey. Rinse turkey with cold water; pat dry. Trim excess fat. Lift wing tips up and over back; tuck under turkey. Combine poultry seasoning, sage, salt, and pepper. Rub seasoning mixture into skin and body cavity. Place half each of garlic, onion quarters, and apple quarters into body cavity. Place turkey, breast side up, in a shallow roasting pan coated with cooking spray. Arrange remaining garlic, onion, and apple around turkey in pan. Insert a meat thermometer into meaty part of thigh, making sure not to touch bone. Bake at 375° for 45 minutes. Baste turkey with cider syrup; cover with foil. Bake at 375° an additional 2 hours and 15 minutes or until meat thermometer registers 180°, basting with cider syrup 4 times at regular intervals. Let stand 10 minutes. Discard skin. Remove turkey from pan, reserving drippings for sauce. Place turkey on a platter; keep warm.
4. Strain drippings through a colander into a bowl; discard solids. Place a zip-top plastic bag inside a 2-cup glass measure. Pour drippings into bag; let stand 10 minutes (fat will rise to top). Seal bag; carefully snip off 1 bottom corner of bag. Drain drippings into a bowl, stopping before fat layer reaches opening; discard fat.
5. While turkey bakes, melt butter in a medium saucepan over medium-high heat. Add reserved giblets and neck; sauté 2 minutes on each side or until browned. Add broth, and bring to a boil. Cover, reduce heat, and simmer 45 minutes. Strain mixture through a colander into a bowl, discarding solids. Reserve ¼ cup broth mixture. Combine remaining broth mixture with drippings in roasting pan on stovetop over medium heat, scraping pan to loosen browned bits. Combine ¼ cup reserved broth mixture and cornstarch; add to roasting pan. Add 1 tablespoon corn syrup, stirring with a whisk. Bring to a boil; cook 1 minute. Serve gravy with turkey (gravy will be dark and thin). Yield: 12 servings (serving size: 6 ounces turkey and about 3 tablespoons gravy).

CALORIES 331 (24% from fat); FAT 8.8g (sat 3g, mono 1.9g, poly 2.5g); PROTEIN 50.4g; CARB 9.4g; FIBER 0.1g; CHOL 130mg; IRON 3.2mg; SODIUM 396mg; CALC 52mg

"A 12-pound bird will feed a dozen people easily, and you'll still have a little for leftovers—but not enough to dine on turkey for the next month." Jan Smith, Photo Stylist

Fish & Shellfish

Eating fish and shellfish is one of the tastiest ways to stay healthy.

Fish

Aside from being a source of vitamins, protein, and minerals, several varieties of fish have high levels of omega-3, the fatty acid that lowers blood pressure, lessens the risk of heart disease, and helps prevent cancers.

> In most *Cooking Light* recipes, we call for 6-ounce raw fillets or steaks, which yield 4$\frac{1}{2}$- to 5-ounce portions when cooked.

The Fat in Fish

The amount of fat in fish varies, but the fat is a heart-healthy type of fat that helps prevent heart disease.

Fish	Serving Size	Calories	Fat (g)
Amberjack	4$\frac{1}{2}$ ounces	135	2.3
Arctic char	4$\frac{1}{2}$ ounces	234	10.1
Catfish	4$\frac{1}{2}$ ounces	194	10.2
Cod	4$\frac{1}{2}$ ounces	134	1.1
Halibut	4$\frac{1}{2}$ ounces	179	3.8
Mahimahi	4$\frac{1}{2}$ ounces	139	1.2
Pompano	4$\frac{1}{2}$ ounces	269	15.5
Red snapper	4$\frac{1}{2}$ ounces	163	2.2
Salmon	4$\frac{1}{2}$ ounces	224	10.5
Sole/Flounder	4$\frac{1}{2}$ ounces	149	2.0
Swordfish	4$\frac{1}{2}$ ounces	198	6.6
Tilapia	4$\frac{1}{2}$ ounces	106	1.0
Trout	4$\frac{1}{2}$ ounces	243	10.8
Tuna	4$\frac{1}{2}$ ounces	178	1.6

How to Buy and Store Fresh Fish

What should I look for when buying fresh fish? Look for fish that is free of blemishes, neither slick nor soggy, and springs back when touched. If it smells "fishy," it's not fresh. Avoid fish displayed directly on ice—the contact can cause quality to deteriorate. Buying fish that has been frozen at sea is your next-best alternative.

Is it OK to buy frozen fish? Yes. When possible, purchase vacuum-packed frozen fish, and look for "once frozen" on the label. Avoid any fish that has symptoms of freezer burn, such as brown or dry edges. Defrost frozen fish in the refrigerator overnight.

Is is better to buy fillets or the whole fish? Buying fillets or steaks is the easiest and best way to buy fish, but buying it whole is the most economical way. If the fish market has whole fish, ask the fishmonger to fillet and portion it for you. Cook what you need, and freeze the rest. Keep the bones so you can make fish stock for soups and stews—the bones will freeze, and the stock will, too.

What should I look for when buying a whole fresh fish? Look for clear, glossy eyes; shiny, red gills; and a firm body, free of any dark blemishes. The tail should not be dried out or curled.

How should I store fresh fish? Buy fish on your way out of the store, take it directly home, and cook (or freeze) it within 24 hours. Keep the fish as cold as possible until you are ready to cook it.

Our Favorite Fish

The variety of fish at the market is so broad, there is a fish to suit anyone's palate. Still, it can be daunting to stand in front of the fish case and see so many kinds. Of the many varieties, we chose 14 fish based on their flavor, availability, ease of cooking, and popularity. Seasons affect availability, but you should be able to get most of these fish at some point during the year.

Amberjack Full flavor and firm flesh make amberjack, which stands up to more assertive flavors, ideal to grill, pan-fry, or broil. Amberjack is available in fillets or steaks year-round, especially in the South, since it comes primarily from the Gulf of Mexico.

Arctic char (farmed freshwater) Arctic char, most often sold in fillets, has a distinctive pink flesh with a rich flavor similar to salmon and steelhead trout. You can substitute arctic char for salmon in almost any recipe, and vice versa. Like salmon, this fish lends itself to almost any cooking method.

Catfish (farmed freshwater) Farmed catfish is available fresh year-round and accounts for close to 99 percent of the catfish sold in the United States. Catfish's sweet flavor and firm texture make it ideal for grilling, roasting, pan-frying, and braising. It can also substitute for other firm-flesh fish, such as pompano.

Cod The darling of New England, cod is a flaky white fish with a mild, sweet flavor. Those who are wary of seafood tend to gravitate to it because of the mild flavor. Cod is often used to make fish cakes and fish sticks and is often used in chowders and stews. Cod is generally plentiful year-round.

Halibut Popular because of its mild flavor, this flaky white fish should be prepared with subtle

Mercury in Fish — Keep It SAFE

Certain fish contain high levels of a form of mercury that can cause chronic fatigue and memory loss in adults and harm an unborn child's developing nervous system. Eating them occasionally poses no real health risk. However, if you're pregnant, considering pregnancy, or nursing, it's best NOT to eat the following fish:

- Halibut
- King mackerel
- Largemouth bass
- Marlin
- Oysters (from the Gulf of Mexico)
- Sea bass
- Shark
- Swordfish
- Tilefish
- Tuna
- Walleye
- White croaker

flavors that won't overwhelm its delicacy. Atlantic halibut fishery is virtually extinct, but Pacific halibut is plentiful and is available fresh from March to November. It's sold frozen the rest of the year.

Mahimahi Originally called dolphinfish, the Hawaiian name mahimahi was adopted to alleviate confusion that this fish is related to the aquatic mammal. Popular because of its versatility, mahimahi pairs well with fruits and spicy sauces. It grills, broils, pan-fries, and braises beautifully.

Pompano Pompano has a delicate, sweet flavor. While there is no season for pompano, catch limitations affect its availability; catfish makes a suitable substitute when pompano is scarce. Grill, broil, or pan-fry pompano.

Red snapper The most prized member of the large snapper family is American red snapper, which has a sweet flavor, similar to shrimp. Many varieties of snapper are available year-round. Although they may not be as sweet as American red snapper, they are excellent substitutions.

Salmon Most of what we get at the market is farmed Atlantic salmon. The peak season for wild salmon is April to October; farmed salmon, which is harvested upon demand, is available fresh year-round.

Salmon is not only versatile; it's also naturally tender and cooks quickly. **It even provides a hedge for beginning cooks—its high fat content keeps it moist even when overdone.** In fact, salmon stays moist when cooked by almost any method—you can pan-fry, grill, roast, steam, poach, or smoke it.

Wild or Farmed?

As far as salmon fillets go, it's difficult to distinguish wild from farmed. Some farmed salmon, however, are fed carotene pigments to deepen their color, creating an orange hue. Wild-salmon flesh ranges from a light pink (pinks) to a deep red (sockeyes). A whole Atlantic salmon (the farmed choice) is easy to spot because of its sloping head and spots on its back resembling little "X"s. By contrast, wild king salmon has round spots on its skin, a somewhat squat head, and a black mouth. When sold whole, wild salmon is usually labeled as such.

Taste is also a good indicator of whether a salmon is wild or farmed. Wild salmon has a greater range of flavors, from rich, distinctive king salmon to delicately flavored pink. The flavor of farmed salmon will vary depending on the feed mixture each farm uses, but the end result is usually a midrange mild taste—a big improvement over the fish-oil aftertaste farmed salmon once had.

Sole/Flounder Although sole are actually members of the flounder family, sole and flounder are terms that are used interchangeably. (You're likely to see flounder at the fish market and sole on restaurant menus.) Sauté this flaky white fish with lemon and a little butter to enhance its delicate flavor. It's harvested year-round, but turbot, plaice, or fluke (sometimes called summer flounder) substitute well.

Swordfish Popular for its mild flavor and meaty texture, swordfish became endangered in the early '90s, and in 1997, conservation groups called on chefs and consumers to boycott it. The swordfish population is slowly recovering with careful management of its fishery. Fresh swordfish appears in markets year-round, usually as steak, and is generally best when it's pan-fried or grilled.

Tilapia (farmed freshwater) Tilapia, which has a very mild flavor, is a great fish for people who say they don't like fish. This fish has a firm texture and mild flavor that make it a great canvas on which to paint layers of flavor. Readily available year-round, tilapia can be pan-fried, broiled, baked, or braised in a flavorful broth or sauce.

Trout (farmed freshwater) Trout's flavor ranges from subtle and mild to sweet. Most of the trout sold at markets is rainbow trout, although you'll also see other varieties such as brook trout. At its best, trout is subtle; prepare it simply to avoid masking its flavor.

Tuna The many species of tuna vary in flavor and texture. The type most widely available in grocery stores tends to be meaty with an assertive flavor. Tuna is ideal for grilling or searing, which caramelizes the outside and leaves the interior moist. Many chefs think tuna is best seared on the outside and left almost raw inside. It is less forgiving than other fish, and when overcooked, it can be dry and tough.

Fish Substitutions

Fish divide easily into three categories: delicate, medium, and firm fleshed. These categories reflect how fish respond to cooking methods and which substitutions work.

Category of fish	If a recipe calls for:	You can substitute:
Delicate Treat delicate fish with care when you cook them; they flake easily and have a soft texture when cooked. These fish are traditionally sold as fillets, and they are best prepared by poaching, braising, pan-frying, or baking.	sole/flounder	turbot, plaice, fluke, all varieties of sole/flounder
	cod	orange roughy (mild)
Medium These fish flake easily, but they have more resistance than delicate fish and are firmer when cooked. They are the most versatile fish to cook and can be used when your recipe specifies "or other flaky white fish." They are best prepared by baking, broiling, braising, pan-frying, or grilling.	arctic char	steelhead trout, salmon
	mahimahi	grouper, monkfish
	red snapper	halibut, walleye (sweet, delicate), all varieties of snapper
	tilapia	bass (fresh water), pike, tilefish
Firm These fish don't flake easily when cooked and have a meaty texture. They are best prepared over high heat—by grilling or sautéing, for example.	pompano	amberjack, catfish
	tuna	swordfish, trigger fish (mildly sweet)

West Indies Mahimahi

A bit sweet, tangy, and spicy, this marinade is reminiscent of Jamaican jerk seasoning.

- ¼ cup fresh lime juice
- ¼ cup fresh orange juice
- 3 tablespoons chopped fresh cilantro
- 3 tablespoons low-sodium soy sauce
- 2 tablespoons honey
- 2 teaspoons vegetable oil
- ¾ teaspoon ground allspice
- ¾ teaspoon ground cumin
- 2 finely chopped seeded jalapeño peppers
- 2 garlic cloves, peeled
- 2 green onions, chopped
- 4 (6-ounce) mahimahi fillets
- Cooking spray

1. Combine first 11 ingredients in a blender or food processor; process until smooth. Place fish in a shallow dish; pour marinade over fish. Cover and marinate in refrigerator 30 minutes, turning once.

2. Prepare grill or broiler.

3. Remove fish from dish, reserving marinade. Place fish on grill rack or broiler pan coated with cooking spray. Cook 5 minutes on each side or until fish flakes easily when tested with a fork, basting frequently with reserved marinade. Yield: 4 servings.

CALORIES 218 (15% from fat); FAT 3.6g (sat 0.7g, mono 0.7g, poly 1.6g); PROTEIN 31.4g; CARB 14.6g; FIBER 0.8g; CHOL 120mg; IRON 2.4mg; SODIUM 548mg; CALC 40mg

"Don't be afraid to ask when the fish came in, and don't buy anything more than 1 day old—especially if you don't plan to cook it that night." Kathleen Kanen, Food Stylist

Pan-Fried Sole with Cucumber-Tomato Salsa

When you pan-fry in a nonstick skillet, you need only a small amount of oil.

2	cups quartered cherry tomatoes
¾	cup finely chopped cucumber
⅓	cup finely chopped yellow bell pepper
3	tablespoons chopped fresh basil
2	tablespoons capers
1½	tablespoons finely chopped shallots
1	tablespoon balsamic vinegar
2	teaspoons grated lemon rind
1	teaspoon salt, divided
¼	teaspoon freshly ground black pepper, divided
1	tablespoon olive oil
4	(6-ounce) sole fillets, skinned

1. Combine first 8 ingredients in a bowl; stir in ½ teaspoon salt and ⅛ teaspoon black pepper.
2. Heat oil in a large nonstick skillet over medium-high heat. Sprinkle fish with ½ teaspoon salt and ⅛ teaspoon black pepper. Add fish to pan; cook 1½ minutes on each side or until fish flakes easily when tested with a fork. Serve with salsa. Yield: 4 servings (serving size: 1 fillet and ½ cup salsa).

CALORIES 175 (27% from fat); FAT 5.3g (sat 0.9g, mono 2.8g, poly 0.9g); PROTEIN 25.2g; CARB 6.5g; FIBER 1.6g; CHOL 61mg; IRON 1.1mg; SODIUM 826mg; CALC 40mg

Chili-Seared Salmon with Sweet Pepper Salsa

Because salmon can stand up to bold flavors, it's great topped with this lively salsa.

1	cup diced yellow bell pepper
¾	cup diced red onion
½	cup diced plum tomato
2	tablespoons chopped fresh cilantro
1	tablespoon minced seeded jalapeño pepper
1	tablespoon fresh lemon juice
2	teaspoons cider vinegar
¼	teaspoon ground cumin
⅛	teaspoon sugar
⅛	teaspoon salt
⅛	teaspoon ground coriander
⅛	teaspoon ground red pepper
2	tablespoons chili powder
¼	teaspoon salt
⅛	teaspoon black pepper
4	(6-ounce) salmon fillets (about 1 inch thick)
2	teaspoons olive oil

1. Combine first 12 ingredients in a bowl; stir well. Let stand at least 30 minutes, stirring occasionally.
2. Combine chili powder, ¼ teaspoon salt, and black pepper; rub over fillets. Heat oil in a skillet over medium-high heat. Add fillets; cook 4 minutes on each side or until fish flakes easily when tested with a fork. Serve with salsa. Yield: 4 servings (serving size: 1 fillet and ⅔ cup salsa).

CALORIES 348 (46% from fat); FAT 17.8g (sat 3g, mono 8.8g, poly 3.8g); PROTEIN 37.7g; CARB 8.9g; FIBER 2.9g; CHOL 115mg; IRON 2.2mg; SODIUM 351mg; CALC 35mg

Shellfish

There are two main categories of shellfish: crustaceans and mollusks. *Crustaceans* have elongated bodies and jointed, soft, crustlike shells and include crabs, crawfish, lobster, and shrimp. *Mollusks* are invertebrates with soft bodies covered by a shell of one or more pieces. Mollusks with two shells hinged together are called bivalves and include clams, mussels, and oysters. **The best time of year to cook with bivalves is January, when clams, oysters, and mussels are at their most plentiful.** Many of our recipes call for cooking shellfish in their shells, which makes for a dramatic presentation. Here's our guide to selecting and cooking these different types of shellfish.

Buying, Storing, and Cleaning Clams, Oysters, and Mussels

Here are some things to keep in mind when you buy fresh oysters, clams, or mussels.

Bivalves must be alive when you buy them, so it's important that shells are not chipped, cracked, or open. To determine if bivalves that gape are still alive, tap them a few times on a counter. If they close, they're alive. Ask for the shipper's tag that must accompany all molluscan shellfish.

Most fish markets will shuck oysters and clams if you call a few hours ahead.

Ask for bivalves to be packed on ice on warm days; they prefer cool, damp conditions. Store them between 32° and 40° F (keep mussels at the low end and clams at the high end). Put them in net bags, on trays, or in large bowls draped with wet cloths—this keeps them moist and allows them to breathe. If kept in closed containers, bivalves suffocate.

It's no longer necessary to place clams in a sink or bowl full of water with cornmeal to get rid of sand and grit before cooking. Most bivalves now are farm-raised and aren't as sandy.

Mussels contain beards, or wisps of fibrous material that protrude from the shell; snip or pull these just prior to cooking.

Shellfish Safety

Keep It SAFE

Bivalves live in coastal waters, which are monitored by individual states under the guidelines established by the National Shellfish Sanitation Program (with technical oversight by the Food and Drug Administration). If shellfish waters do not meet purity standards, they are closed to harvests. Aqua farming has helped minimize contamination because the closed environments where mussels, clams, and oysters grow are easy to monitor. If you're concerned about seafood safety you can call the FDA's Automated Information Line at 888-723-3366 (888-SAFEFOOD) for 24-hour recorded information; to reach an FDA representative, call between 10 a.m. and 4 p.m. Eastern time, Monday through Friday.

"Many of our recipes call for cooking shellfish in their shells, which makes for a dramatic table presentation."

Kellie Kelley, Food Stylist

Clams

There are two main types of clams: soft shells and hard shells. Both types vary in size from those that are no bigger than a thumbnail to large ones that weigh hundreds of pounds. Generally, the smaller the clam, the more tender the meat.

Clams are among the leanest of bivalves, with only 1 gram of fat and 60 calories per 3 ounces of edible meat.

While oysters can be eaten whole regardless of size, the larger the clam, the more likely it is to be chopped up or tenderized before eaten. Tiny imported Manila clams, for example, are simply steamed, whereas the giant, leathery geoduck (pronounced "gooey duck") clams have to be pounded for sautéing.

The surf clam is the most common variety; it generally winds up minced for chowders or cut into strips for breading. Soft-shell clams, so named because they have a thin, brittle exterior, are usually fried or steamed in the shell. The soft-shelled steamer is the pride of New England; the razor clam (the shell resembles a straight razor) is its West Coast counterpart. **The clams most often sold in markets are the hard-shells. Littlenecks, the smallest, are ideal for steaming. The larger cherrystones and topneck clams can be steamed or baked.** Then there are chowder clams, which are chopped up for soups and stews because their meat is rather chewy.

> "Generally, the smaller the clam, the more tender the meat." Kathryn Conrad, Test Kitchens Staffer

How to Buy Clams Buy clams in the shell alive. Dead clams smell bad and are unsafe to eat. You can tell if a soft-shell clam is alive because it will retract further into its shell if it's poked. The shell of a live hard-shell clam will be clamped tight so that it's very difficult to pry it apart. If you can move the shell easily, the clam is probably dead. Store clams in an open bowl in the refrigerator, and use them as soon as possible. **Do not store clams in a sealed plastic bag or on ice because they will die.**

Cleaning Clams

Scrub clams under cold running water with a stiff brush to remove sand and dirt. Shuck clams; release meat from bottom shells.

Canned Clams

Test Kitchen SECRET

While we love the visual presentation of clams in their shells, for chowders and other dishes that use only the meat of the clams, we often call for canned clams. You can buy them whole or chopped. As with most canned seafood, the canned versions are higher in sodium than the fresh. (See the recipe for Clam Sauce on page 45.)

Mussels

There are two varieties of mussels generally available in the United States: the blue (or common) mussel and the New Zealand mussel. The blue mussel has a shiny black exterior and an iridescent blue interior shell. The New Zealand mussel is also called the green-shelled mussel because of its color. The classic way to eat mussels is steamed with wine, garlic, and herbs. Italians love them in tomato sauce, with or without pasta. A 3-ounce serving of mussels contains 73 calories and 2 grams of fat.

Mussels Marinara

A traditional way to serve mussels is in a rich tomato broth over pasta.

    1   tablespoon olive oil
    1   cup finely chopped onion
    3   garlic cloves, minced
    2   cups chopped tomato
    ½   cup dry white wine
    ⅓   cup chopped fresh flat-leaf parsley
    2   tablespoons chopped fresh basil
    ½   teaspoon salt
    ½   teaspoon black pepper
    ¼   teaspoon crushed red pepper
    2   bay leaves
    5   pounds fresh mussels, scrubbed and
         debearded (about 100 mussels)
    5   cups hot cooked linguine (about 10 ounces
         uncooked pasta)

1. Heat oil in a large stockpot over medium-high heat. Add onion and garlic; sauté 3 minutes. Add tomato and next 7 ingredients; cook over medium heat 5 minutes. Add mussels; cover and cook 10 minutes or until mussels open.
2. Discard bay leaves and any unopened shells. Remove mussels with a slotted spoon, and divide into 5 individual shallow bowls. Spoon tomato mixture over mussels. Serve over linguine. Yield: 5 servings (serving size: about 20 mussels, ½ cup sauce, and 1 cup pasta).

CALORIES 305 (17% from fat); PROTEIN 16g; FAT 5.6g (sat 0.9g, mono 2.5g, poly 1.2g); CARB 47.6g; FIBER 4.1g; CHOL 20mg; IRON 5.8mg; SODIUM 451mg; CALC 56mg

Scrubbing and Debearding Mussels

1. Scrubbing mussels: Use a stiff brush to scrub mussels; rinse them well.

2. Debearding mussels: The "beard" is the name given to the strands of tissue attached to the shell. To "debeard," simply snip or pull the strands off. (Some mussels do not have beards when they are harvested.) Mussels spoil quickly after debearding, so prepare them immediately. Fresh mussels are usually cooked in the shell.

Oysters

Not only are oysters remarkably versatile in how they can be prepared, they're also packed with minerals such as zinc and iron, as well as heart-healthy omega-3 fatty acids. There are

A 3-ounce portion of raw oysters adds up to only 69 calories and contains less than half a gram of saturated fat. They're also packed with minerals as well as heart-healthy omega-3 fatty acids.

many kinds of oysters, and they usually take the name of the place where they grow. There are three main species of oysters sold in the United States: Pacific or Japanese, Atlantic or Eastern, and Olympia. Pacific oysters are mild and sweet and can reach up to a foot long. They're found along the Pacific seaboard. Atlantic oysters come in various sizes, have a briny flavor, and are known for their place of origin, such as Apalachicola or Chesapeake Bay. Olympia oysters are usually very small and are harvested from Washington's Puget Sound.

Grading Oysters Shucked oysters come in numerous grades, depending on the origin of the oysters, the size, and the region where they're sold. Our recipes using shucked oysters are based on the standard size.

- *West Coast grades* are large (less than 8 per pint); medium (8 to 12 per pint); small (12 to 18 per pint); and extrasmall (more than 18 per pint).
- *East Coast grades* are extralarge counts (less than 20 per pint); large or extraselect (20 to 26 per pint); medium or select (26 to 38 per pint); small or standard (38 to 63 per pint); and very small (more than 63 per pint).

Oyster Months?   Keep It SAFE

You may have heard the old saying that you should only eat oysters during months with an "R" in them, which leaves out May through August. Today, thanks to regular safety monitoring for microbes and rapid refrigeration that prevents spoilage, this proscription no longer applies to most of us—especially if oysters are cooked.

As with any raw shellfish, there is a small risk of contracting hepatitis A from eating raw oysters harvested from polluted waters. That's why all our recipes call for cooked oysters.

Cooking Oysters When cooking with oysters, keep the fatter ones for frying and baking and the smaller ones for soups, stews, and stuffings. Add oysters toward the end of cooking. This allows just enough time for heating them thoroughly but not enough time to overcook. Overcooked oysters are tough and rubbery.

Ask the *Cooking Light* Cooks

Do you always shuck your own oysters? No, not unless it's a recipe where the oysters are served on their shells. If you're going to shuck your own, you'll need an oyster knife. OXO Good Grips offers an inexpensive model with an easy-to-hold soft handle. Visit www.oxo.com to order.

What is oyster sauce? It's a thick, dark brown sauce that is made from oyster extracts and some seasonings. It has a smoky, sweet flavor and is often used in Chinese dishes to add both color and flavor.

Due to the risk of eating raw oysters from polluted waters, the oysters in all of our recipes are cooked.

Crabs

There are hundreds of varieties of crabs, and the type you'll see most often in the market depends on where you live. Some of the common varieties include blue crabs, stone crabs, Dungeness, king crabs, snow crabs, and soft-shell crabs. The only part of stone crabs that is eaten is the claws. Soft-shell crabs are meant to be eaten whole, shell and all. (See additional information at right.)

How to Buy Crabs When selecting hard-shelled crabs, look for those that move their claws when poked. They should look moist and soft, and the shell should not look like it is hardening. When you lift a crab, if its claws drop, don't buy it. Ideally, you should buy them just before you plan to cook them because, like lobsters, they must be kept alive until they're cooked. **Even though the meat that you pull from the shell has the best flavor, you can also buy delicious crabmeat that is freshly cooked, unpasteurized, and packed in plastic tubs.** Lump crabmeat (also called backfin or jumbo) is the most desirable. It's taken from the center of the body and is in large pieces. Flake crabmeat is light and dark meat from the center and the legs, and it comes in smaller pieces.

Storage While it's best to use fresh crabs on the day you buy them, you can store them in the refrigerator for up to 2 days if they are properly packed. Lay them in a shallow bowl, and place that bowl in a larger bowl filled with ice. Cover the crabs with a damp towel, and replace the ice as needed. **Before you cook them, discard any crabs that are no longer alive.** You can store freshly cooked crabmeat in the refrigerator for 2 days.

Soft-Shell Crabs In their natural environment, blue crabs begin shedding their outgrown shells on the first full moon of May to become the highly prized soft-shell crab. Once molting is complete, most of the crab is edible. They are so succulent and juicy that they seem to be a tiny piece of the ocean itself. Although technically "shell-less," the soft-shell crab's outer coating provides a crispy-chewy barrier to the soft interiors. Luckily, soft-shell crabs are easy to prepare and cook at home. Cleaning them is as simple as a couple of snips and a rinse. (See "Cleaning Soft-Shell Crabs" on page 226.) Put live crabs on ice until almost immobilized before you clean them.

When buying soft-shell crabs, live ones are the best, but they're not always easy to find. If you find them frozen, they've been frozen in the molting stage. To select the tastiest, use your nose. When fresh, they smell clean and astringent, like sea mist. **Soft-shell crabs are only available from spring until early autumn.**

Cooking Soft-Shell Crabs | Test Kitchen SECRET

Because soft-shell crabs need direct heat to give them their characteristic outer crispness, they should not be boiled or steamed like hard-shell crabs (they'd end up a soggy mess). Soft-shell crabs take only minutes to cook, so they're traditionally simply fried or sautéed. But they do lend themselves nicely to the broiler or grill, as well. From there, they can be taken in any direction, from sushi to a salad. They're most commonly served sandwiched between two slices of bread.

"In recipes that call for fresh crabmeat, we prefer to use lump crabmeat." Tiffany Vickers, Test Kitchens Staffer

Cleaning Soft-Shell Crabs

1. Hold the crab in one hand, and, using a pair of kitchen shears, cut off the front of the crab, about ½ inch behind the eyes and mouth. Squeeze out the contents of the sack located directly behind the cut you just made.

2. Lift one pointed end of the crab's outer shell; remove and discard the gills. Repeat on the other side.

3. Turn the crab over and snip off the small flap known as the apron. Rinse the entire crab well and pat dry. Once cleaned, crabs should be cooked or stored immediately.

Grilled Soft-Shell Crab and Pineapple Salad with Watercress

Because they have soft shells, these crabs are ideal for cooking on the grill.

  2 cups pineapple juice
  ¼ cup maple syrup
  ¼ cup spiced rum (such as Captain Morgan)
  ½ cup plain low-fat yogurt
  2 tablespoons white wine vinegar
  ¼ teaspoon salt
  ¼ teaspoon freshly ground black pepper
  1 small pineapple, peeled, cored, halved lengthwise, and cut into 12 slices
Cooking spray
  6 (5 to 6-ounce) soft-shell crabs, cleaned
  6 cups baby spinach
  4 cups trimmed watercress (about 2 bunches)
  2 cups thinly sliced red onion, separated into rings
  2 cups diced peeled avocado

1. Prepare grill.
2. Combine first 3 ingredients in a saucepan. Bring to a boil, and cook until reduced to ½ cup (about 20 minutes). Cool. Combine one-fourth pineapple juice mixture, yogurt, vinegar, salt, and pepper in a small bowl. Cover and chill.
3. Place pineapple on grill rack coated with cooking spray; grill 2 minutes on each side. Place crab on grill rack. Grill 5 minutes, turning and basting frequently with yogurt mixture.
4. Divide spinach and watercress evenly among 6 plates. Top each serving with pineapple pieces, onion, avocado, and crab; drizzle each with dressing. Yield: 6 servings (serving size: 1 cup spinach, ⅔ cup watercress, 2 pineapple pieces, ⅓ cup onion, ⅓ cup avocado, 1 crab, and 2 tablespoons dressing).

CALORIES 385 (25% from fat); FAT 10.7g (sat 1.8g, mono 5.3g, poly 2.1g); PROTEIN 30.2g; CARB 38.9g; FIBER 5.3g; CHOL 1mg; IRON 5.4mg; SODIUM 156mg; CALC 122mg

Crawfish

Crawfish season begins each December and peaks in April or May, when the crawfish are the fattest and most lively. If live crawfish aren't available in your area, order them by telephone or online for next-day delivery. (See the ordering information below.)

Most sources sell live crawfish by the 30- or 40-pound sack. Some also sell fresh boiled crawfish, crawfish tail meat, and parboiled crawfish. (Most sources also sell shrimp, which you can substitute, if you prefer.) You can find frozen crawfish tail meat in some supermarkets.

Sizing Crawfish

Like shrimp, crawfish come in grades based on their size.

Type	Size
Peelers	21 to 30 crawfish per pound
Medium or restaurant grade	16 to 20 crawfish per pound; these offer the highest percentage of meat
Jumbos	10 to 15 crawfish per pound; the most prized, although they're sometimes hard to peel

Ordering Crawfish   *Cooking Light* Recommends

Good sources we've found for ordering crawfish are:
- Simply Seafood, 877-706-4022 or www.simplyseafood.com
- B & T Seafood, 866-243-6092 or www.crawfish.cc
- Louisiana Crawfish Company, 888-522-7292 or www.lacrawfish.com

The Shell Game

1. Before you peel the shell, you need to separate the tail from the head. Begin by holding the head in one hand and the tail in the other.

2. Gently twist your hands in opposite directions until the crawfish splits in half. Gently squeeze the tail until you hear the shell crack.

3. Beginning at the top, peel away a few segments of the shell until there is enough exposed meat for you to grasp securely.

4. Holding the fan of the tail in one hand, pull the meat away from the shell. If the meat breaks apart, peel away the remaining shell segments.

5. Now you're ready to eat. For a more authentic Cajun experience, after you remove the head, suck the seasoned cooking liquid before discarding.

Lobster

The best locale to eat a lobster dinner is on the Maine coast. The second best? Your place. Use our tips for buying and cooking fresh lobster.

How to Buy Lobster Buy only live lobsters. The more active they are—legs, claws, and tails moving—the better. Once you get the lobsters home, it's best to cook them immediately. **If you can't cook them immediately, you can refrigerate lobsters with hard shells, covered with a damp cloth or seaweed, for up to 24 hours.**

Cooking Lobster The two best methods for cooking fresh lobster are boiling and steaming.
• *Boiling* is probably the most familiar way to cook lobster, but it presents the risk of over-cooking, so you'll need to pay attention to time. Boiling makes removing the meat easier, since the intense, immediate heat causes it to shrink from the shell as the boiling water cooks the lobster from the outside in.

> "If you're boiling lobster to use in another recipe, boil the lobster for about 10 minutes instead of 12." Jan Moon, Test Kitchens Staffer

Boiled Lobster

We think boiling is the best way to cook lobster, but be careful not to overcook.

    3   gallons water
    ¾   cup salt
    4   (1½-pound) live Maine lobsters

1. Bring water and salt to a boil in a 5-gallon stockpot; add lobsters. Cover; cook 12 minutes or until shells are bright orange-red and tails are curled. Yield: 4 servings (serving size: 1 lobster).

CALORIES 111 (6% from fat); FAT 0.7g (sat 0.1g, mono 0.2g, poly 0.1g); PROTEIN 23.2g; CARB 1.5g; FIBER 0g; CHOL 82mg; IRON 0.5mg; SODIUM 2,189mg; CALC 70mg

• *Steaming* cooks lobsters slower than boiling, so it reduces the chance of overcooking. Place a vegetable steamer in the bottom of a pot, or use a metal colander turned upside down. If you don't have anything in your kitchen that will work as a steamer, you can do without. Pour in enough water so that it reaches a depth of 2 inches, and add 2 tablespoons of salt. Place the live lobsters, head first, into the steamer rack or directly into the water in the bottom of the pot.

Steamed Lobster

Steaming decreases the chance of overcooking lobster.

    4   cups water
    2   tablespoons salt
    4   (1½-pound) live Maine lobsters

1. Bring the water and salt to a boil in a 5-gallon stockpot. Place a vegetable steamer or rack in the bottom of the pot. Add lobsters; steam, covered, for 14 minutes or until done. Yield: 4 servings (serving size: 1 lobster).

CALORIES 111 (5% from fat); FAT 0.7g (sat 0.1g, mono 0.2g, poly 0.1g); PROTEIN 23.2g; CARB 1.5g; FIBER 0g; CHOL 82mg; IRON 0.4mg; SODIUM 504mg; CALC 69mg

---

Lobster Meat — Test Kitchen SECRET

To get meat from a cooked lobster:
• Twist the tail from the body, then cut the tail lengthwise on top with scissors to split it open; remove the meat.
• Twist off the claws. Pull the pincers apart, and remove the lower pincer. Use a lobster cracker to break the claw shell. Break the legs in half with your hands, and push the meat out with a cocktail or shellfish fork.

If you're sensitive about dropping live lobsters into boiling water, consider that they're invertebrates. With a simple nervous system and no brain, they cannot feel pain. If you're still concerned, the University of Maine's Lobster Institute has determined that 10 minutes in the freezer before cooking helps minimize movement after the lobster is dropped into the water—a reflex commonly mistaken for an indication of pain.

Frozen Lobster

For recipes where you need only the meat of the lobster (such as lobster Newburg or a lobster salad), it's fine to use frozen lobster tails. To get 1 cup of chopped lobster meat, use 3 (6-ounce) tails, and steam them for about 8 minutes.

How to Prepare Lobster Tails for Broiling or Baking

1. Using your index finger, gently loosen lobster meat from top inside of shell.

2. Cut lengthwise through top of lobster shell using kitchen shears.

3. Pull back sides of shell to expose lobster meat.

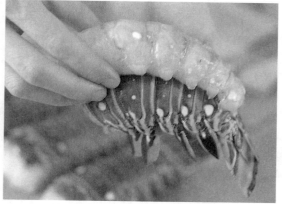

4. Starting at cut end of tail, carefully loosen lobster meat from bottom of shell.

Shrimp

We use a lot of shrimp in our Test Kitchens because of their succulent flavor, versatility, and largely year-round availability. And despite the fact that shrimp contain more cholesterol than some other types of seafood, the total fat and saturated fat (the real culprit in heart disease) content is very low. So we think that it's fine to include shrimp in a heart-healthy diet.

How Much to Buy?

To save prep time, instead of peeling and deveining your own shrimp, you can buy peeled and deveined raw shrimp at the seafood counter of most supermarkets. The chart below shows how much peeled and deveined shrimp to buy when the recipe calls for unpeeled shrimp.

Unpeeled Raw Shrimp		Peeled and Deveined Raw Shrimp
2/3 pound	=	1/2 pound
1 pound	=	3/4 pound
1 1/3 pound	=	1 pound
2 pounds	=	1 1/2 pounds
2 2/3 pounds	=	2 pounds
4 pounds	=	3 pounds

Storing and Using Fresh Shrimp

Because most shrimp are quick-frozen at sea and then defrosted for sale, we often get asked if it's OK to refreeze them. We've done it for years without any problem so that we could store unused shrimp for later use. When you want to use your refrozen shrimp, just thaw them out in a bowl or sink filled with tap water.

The only bad way to cook shrimp is to cook them too long. An overcooked shrimp is either rubbery or mushy. Either way, it's a waste of taste.

Barbecue Shrimp

The peels are left on the shrimp so they can add flavor to the lush butter-pepper sauce.

1/2	cup fat-free Caesar dressing
1/3	cup Worcestershire sauce
2	tablespoons butter
1	tablespoon dried oregano
1	tablespoon paprika
1	tablespoon dried rosemary
1	tablespoon dried thyme
1 1/2	teaspoons pepper
1	teaspoon hot pepper sauce
5	bay leaves
3	garlic cloves, minced
2	pounds large shrimp
1/3	cup dry white wine
10	(1-ounce) slices French bread baguette
10	lemon wedges

1. Combine first 11 ingredients in a large nonstick skillet; bring to a boil. Add shrimp, and cook 7 minutes, stirring occasionally. Add wine, and cook 1 minute or until shrimp are done. Serve with bread and lemon wedges. Yield: 5 servings (serving size: 5 ounces shrimp with sauce and 2 bread slices).

CALORIES 403 (20% from fat); FAT 9.1g (sat 3.8g, mono 2.4g, poly 1.7g); PROTEIN 34.4g; CARB 41.7g; FIBER 2.8g; CHOL 219mg; IRON 7mg; SODIUM 1,021mg; CALC 211mg

Recipes often call for shrimp to be peeled and deveined. However, except for the largest shrimp, there's neither danger nor distaste in leaving the thin black line (vein) right where it is. (If you're butterflying your shrimp, deveining occurs anyway.)

To butterfly shrimp, split the shrimp down the center of the back of the shrimp using a sharp knife, cutting almost through the shrimp. Open the halves flat, making a butterfly shape.

"Boiled, steamed, sautéed, baked, grilled, stewed—all are great ways to serve shrimp. Just make sure you don't overcook it." Jan Moon, Test Kitchens Staffer

Preparing Shrimp

Deveining

1. Using a deveining tool or a sharp knife, remove the dark vein.

2. Peel back the shell.

Peeling

1. Grasp the tail in one hand and the legs in the other. In one motion, pull the legs off.

2. Peel back the shell and remove.

CHAPTER 6

Dairy, Eggs & Soy

Let *Cooking Light* show you the best ways to use dairy products, eggs, and soy products in your recipes. These ingredients add flavor as well as high-protein nutrition to a variety of dishes.

Milk

Current research leaves us no room to doubt calcium has a number of health benefits and may play a role in weight loss. As the best source of calcium, milk provides these benefits whether you're using it for drinking or cooking. You'll notice in our recipes that we use a variety of milk products, as we've found that some milks work better in certain recipes that others. Here's a guide to the milks we use most often.

Fat-Free Milk Also known as "skim milk," fat-free milk has less than 0.5 percent milk fat. It's also labeled as nonfat milk. We usually use fat-free milk in recipes for beverages, milk shakes, baked goods, sauces, and desserts in which the milk's primary role is to provide liquid, not contribute creaminess. For custards and sauces, we think that 1% or 2% milk gives a better result than fat-free.

Low-Fat Milk Low-fat milk has 3 grams or less fat per 1-cup serving. Milk labeled "1% milk" (1 percent milk fat) is low-fat milk. We use this milk in soups, sauces, and pie fillings.

Reduced-Fat Milk This milk contains 25 percent less fat that whole milk and is usually labeled "2% milk," since it contains 2 percent milk fat.

We often use 2% milk instead of fat-free in cream pie fillings to help achieve a creamier texture and flavor.

Evaporated Fat-Free Milk This milk has been concentrated and is sold in cans. Once it's opened, it needs to be refrigerated. We like to use evaporated milk in recipes such as soups because it adds a little more body and creaminess than regular fat-free milk.

Fat-Free Condensed Milk Similar to evaporated fat-free milk, fat-free condensed milk has added sweeteners. The primary use for condensed milk is in desserts.

Nonfat Dry Milk Powder Nonfat dry milk powder is milk with the fat and water removed. It has the same nutrients as fat-free milk and can be rehydrated by adding water according to the package directions. **If you don't drink much milk, but want to keep some on hand for recipes, keep milk powder on hand to use in recipes that call for fat-free milk.** Then you can simply mix enough of the powder and water for the amount of milk you need. Store the powder in the refrigerator in an airtight glass container. Once the powder is reconstituted, it will keep for up to 1 week in the refrigerator.

Nonfat and Low-Fat Buttermilk Buttermilk does not have butter added. Today, most buttermilk isn't churned from heavy cream but is "cultured," meaning it's created by fermenting pasteurized fat-free or low-fat milk with a friendly bacteria culture in the same way that yogurt and sour cream are made. The bacteria culture produces buttermilk's unique flavor.

> **"Buttermilk adds moisture, richness, and a bit of tang to baked products."**
> **Kathryn Conrad, Test Kitchens Staffer**

Buttermilk is the secret ingredient for making exceptionally tender and delicious baked goods—from biscuits and pancakes to crumb cakes and layer cakes. (See page 98 for information on baking with buttermilk.)

Buttermilk Basics	Test Kitchen SECRET

Although buttermilk has a refrigerator shelf life of up to 3 weeks, it tends to separate, so shaking is important.

To make a quick stand-in for buttermilk, stir 1 tablespoon of fresh lemon juice or white vinegar into 1 cup of milk, and let it stand for about 10 minutes or until the milk thickens and begins to curdle.

Sour Cream

Commercial sour cream is cream that has been treated with a lactic acid culture to give it a characteristic tangy flavor. Regular sour cream contains from 18 to 20 percent fat, and often has additional ingredients such as gelatin and enzymes, which act as stabilizers.

Light sour cream contains about 40 percent less fat than regular; fat-free sour cream contains no fat at all.

Store sour cream in its carton in the refrigerator for up to 1 week after the date stamped on the bottom of the container. Discard any carton that has mold forming on the surface of the sour cream.

We typically use sour cream in dips and spreads and sometimes in baked goods such as pound cakes. It's also good as a topping for soups and chilis, or on Tex-Mex dishes such as enchiladas or quesadillas. In addition to low-fat or fat-free sour cream, we also use yogurt in some of these same ways.

Which Sour Cream?	Test Kitchen SECRET

We prefer to use reduced-fat sour cream instead of fat-free whenever we can because the texture and taste is better. Occasionally we might use fat-free sour cream in a recipe that has a number of high-fat ingredients that are contributing to a high percentage of calories from fat.

> **"If you don't have any sour cream, you can substitute the same amount of plain fat-free yogurt."**
>
> Jan Moon, Test Kitchens Staffer

Yogurt

It's easy to transform yogurt into a velvety substitute for high-fat dairy products in recipes. Draining yogurt overnight makes a low-fat, high-calcium alternative to cream cheese and sour cream and can be used in dips and sauces. Yogurt cheese made from plain low-fat or fat-free yogurt is mildly tart. **For a slightly sweet yogurt cheese that is delicious in fruit dips or desserts, use vanilla low-fat or fat-free yogurt.**

How to Drain Yogurt

Quick-Drain Method One 8-ounce carton of plain low-fat yogurt yields ¼ cup quick-drained yogurt cheese. Use this method when you just need a small amount of soft yogurt cheese.

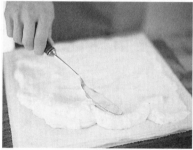

1. Spoon yogurt onto several layers of heavy-duty paper towels; spread to ½-inch thickness.

2. Cover with additional paper towels; let stand 5 minutes.

3. Scrape into a bowl using a rubber spatula; cover and refrigerate.

Overnight-Drain Method One 16-ounce carton of plain low-fat yogurt yields 1 cup overnight-drained yogurt cheese. You get a slightly firmer cheese when you use the overnight method.

1. Place colander in a medium bowl or 2-quart glass measure. Line with four layers of cheesecloth, allowing cheesecloth to extend over outside edges.

2. Spoon yogurt into colander. Cover loosely with plastic wrap; refrigerate 12 hours.

3. Spoon yogurt cheese into a bowl; discard liquid. Cover and refrigerate.

Cream

We sometimes call for whipping cream in the same flavor-enhancing ways we call for other high-fat ingredients such as chocolate, nuts, and oils: in small amounts that are designed to enhance flavor, not add unnecessary fat and calories. Cream is best used in moderation as an enhancement instead of the base of a recipe—in tablespoons instead of cups.

> "The bottom line with cooking has always been that how you use ingredients is just as important as which ones you use, and that's even more true with light cooking. No ingredient should be forbidden." Jill Melton, Food Editor

Choose Your Cream Cream generally comes in two forms: whipping cream (also known as heavy cream) and half-and-half. (You also may see "ultrapasteurized whipping cream," which has been briefly heated so the product won't sour so quickly. Although it has a longer shelf life than regular heavy cream, it does not whip as well and has a slight "cooked" flavor.)

The U.S. Department of Agriculture says whipping or heavy cream must contain at least 35 percent milk fat; typical amounts range from 36 percent to 40 percent. It's the fat that allows heavy cream to be whipped or added to hot liquid without curdling. If you've ever made something with milk that curdled or "broke," it's because milk doesn't have enough fat to coat the proteins. **Don't forget, though, that even cream can break if overheated—which is why it's usually added at the end of a recipe and heated gently.**

Half-and-half, also called light cream, is a mixture of equal parts milk and cream and must contain at least 10½ percent milk fat. Half-and-half is more delicate than whipping cream and will break easier. **It's best used to finish a soup or thicken a pasta sauce where other ingredients are present to temper the heat. Half-and-half can't be whipped.**

Cream is Back!
Test Kitchen SECRET

Here are a couple of our favorite ways to use cream:
Classic reduction sauce: Chicken broth, wine, or juice is stirred along with other seasonings into skillet drippings, then reduced. The addition of cream produces a silky-smooth sauce. *Anything lower in fat, such as regular milk or evaporated skimmed milk, would only create a curdled mess.*
Cream soups: Use cream to finish a soup, where just a dash creates a velvety texture while uniting a variety of flavors. *(In this particular application, either whipping cream or half-and-half will do the trick.)*

Is Fat-Free Half-and-Half Worth It?
Cooking Light Recommends

You may have seen fat-free half-and-half in your dairy case. Could it really stand in for regular half-and-half? Imagining the possibilities, we tested it in a side-by-side tasting and cooking comparison in our Test Kitchens.

The fat-free version mimics the real thing in appearance—nice body and a rich, white appearance. The fat-free version does not have the underlying buttery flavor of regular half-and-half, but you can cook with it and get acceptable results. It does contain corn syrup, so it has a tiny bit of sweetness.
Bottom line: For the best flavor results, we prefer to use real half-and-half and just use less of it.

Creamy Lentil Soup

This is no ordinary lentil soup—half-and-half creates a satiny finish and creamy body, making typically watery lentils truly sublime.

3	bacon slices
2	cups chopped leek
1	cup chopped onion
3	cups water
2	cups chopped peeled baking potato
1	cup dried lentils
¾	cup chopped carrot
½	teaspoon salt
1	(14-ounce) can fat-free, less-sodium chicken broth
½	cup half-and-half
2	tablespoons dry sherry

1. Cook bacon in a Dutch oven over medium heat until crisp. Remove bacon from pan, reserving drippings in pan. Crumble bacon; set aside. Add leek and onion to pan; sauté 4 minutes. Add water, potato, lentils, carrot, salt, and broth; bring to a boil. Cover, reduce heat, and simmer 1 hour or until vegetables are tender.
2. Place vegetable mixture in a blender or food processor; process until smooth. Return pureed mixture to pan; stir in half-and-half and sherry. Cook until thoroughly heated. Sprinkle with bacon. Yield: 6 servings (serving size: 1⅓ cups).

CALORIES 287 (29% from fat); FAT 9.4g (sat 4g, mono 3.7g, poly 1.1g); PROTEIN 13.6g; CARB 37.4g; FIBER 5.8g; CHOL 15mg; IRON 4.2mg; SODIUM 465mg; CALC 72mg

Chicken Fricassee with Orzo

Cream is added to the vegetable mixture at the end to create a rich-tasting sauce that is soaked up by the orzo.

4	(6-ounce) skinless, boneless chicken breast halves
½	teaspoon salt
¼	teaspoon pepper
2	teaspoons butter
¾	cup chopped green onions
½	cup diced carrot
½	cup diced ham
2	garlic cloves, minced
1	cup fat-free, less-sodium chicken broth
½	cup dry white wine
⅓	cup whipping cream
3	cups hot cooked orzo (about 1½ cups uncooked rice-shaped pasta)
¼	cup chopped fresh parsley

1. Sprinkle chicken with salt and pepper. Melt butter in a large nonstick skillet over medium-high heat. Add chicken; cook 3 minutes on each side or until browned. Remove chicken from pan.
2. Add onions, carrot, ham, and garlic to pan; sauté 4 minutes or until lightly browned. Stir in broth and wine, scraping pan to loosen browned bits. Return chicken to pan; bring to a boil. Cover, reduce heat, and simmer 10 minutes or until chicken is done. Remove chicken from pan with a slotted spoon; keep warm. Add whipping cream; cook, uncovered, over medium heat 8 minutes. Spoon orzo onto plates. Top with chicken breast half, sauce, and parsley. Yield: 4 servings (serving size: ¾ cup orzo, 1 chicken breast half, ⅓ cup sauce, and 1 tablespoon parsley).

CALORIES 597 (23% from fat); FAT 15.2g (sat 7.9g, mono 4.5g, poly 0.9g); PROTEIN 54.9g; CARB 58.7g; FIBER 3.4g; CHOL 142mg; IRON 4.4mg; SODIUM 805mg; CALC 83mg

Cheese

The secret to using cheese, especially a high-fat cheese, in a healthy diet lies in its concentrated flavor—a little goes a long way. Cheese provides big payback in taste from a small investment.

Here is a rundown of some of the cheeses we use most often in our Test Kitchens.

Blue Cheese The distinctive flavor of blue cheese drives people to love it or hate it. Whether its source is goat's, cow's, or sheep's milk, a little blue packs a potent punch.

Brie Traditionally a French cheese, Brie is earthy and slightly musty or mushroomy. Brie's buttery flavor is great paired with sharp, tangy foods.

Cheddar This has always been America's favorite cheese. Look for the many wonderful white Cheddars made domestically. **The sharper the Cheddar, the better, because you can use less of it for the same amount of flavor.**

Cream Cheese This soft, unripened cheese made from cow's milk has a smooth, creamy texture with a tangy flavor. One of the most common uses for this cheese is as a key ingredient in cheesecakes.

We use both light and fat-free cream cheese in our recipes, depending on the method and the role of the cheese in the recipe. **Fat-free cream cheese has a slightly waxy texture and tends to become watery when it's beaten or whipped.** The type of cream cheese we use most often is ⅓-less-fat cream cheese, which has slightly less fat than regular, but is still creamy and full of flavor.

Feta Greek feta is popular and is best known for its salty, tangy flavor and versatility, but we also like French feta packed in brine for its smooth texture and flavor.

Making the Grate

When a recipe calls for cheese to be grated, shredded, or shaved, there is a reason. The success of your dish depends on which method you use.

Grated: Rub the cheese against the small starlike holes on a box-style cheese grater. This gives it a powdery texture like that of canned, processed Parmesan cheese. For the best taste, grate just before using.

Finely shredded: Use the next-larger holes on your cheese grater. You can also drop a hunk of cheese into a food processor fitted with a fine-shredding disk. Or you can use a handheld cheese mill made especially for grating Parmesan; grind it as you would a pepper mill.

Shredded: Use the largest hole on a box-style grater.

Shaved: Pull a cheese plane or a swivel-blade peeler across a flat side of the cheese.

Fontina One of Italy's great cheeses, fontina has a mildly nutty flavor and a creamy texture; it melts easily.

Goat With a characteristic acidic flavor, goat cheese ranges from soft and spreadable to dry and crumbly. Soft goat cheese comes in cones, discs, or logs—sometimes rolled in herbs. There are other goat cheeses that are similar in flavor and texture to some cow's milk cheeses such as hard Cheddar and Parmesan; there is a ricotta-like fromage blanc, and a surface-ripened goat cheese that is comparable to Brie.

Goat cheese's appeal is not only based on flavor; it's also popular for its nutrition. Soft, fresh chèvre (SHEHV-ruh) has 20 percent fewer calories than cream cheese (76 per ounce compared to 99) and 30 percent fewer than Cheddar (76 per ounce to 114). Its 6 grams of fat per ounce weighs in well below cream cheese's 10 grams and Cheddar's 9.4.

> "We rarely use the grated Parmesan cheese in the can. If we need to use a convenience product, we use a bag of preshredded fresh Parmesan." Sam Brannock, Test Kitchens Staffer

Use unflavored dental floss or a cheese cutter with a wire to cut delicate soft cheeses such as blue cheese, cream cheese, or soft goat cheese.

Parmigiano-Reggiano Knowledge — Test Kitchen SECRET

Why It's Worth the Cost: In our taste tests, we preferred the complex, sharp flavor of the imported variety to the domestic. (The latter tasted saltier.) If you're not inclined to pay the premium price ($6 to $7 a half pound), domestic Parmesan will work fine.

Buying Tips: Look for the name "Parmigiano-Reggiano" spelled out repeatedly in red around the rind. Without this rind, it isn't Parmigiano-Reggiano.

Storage Tips: For the best flavor, grate only the cheese you need at one time. The rest, lightly wrapped in plastic, should last for 6 months in the refrigerator—but change the plastic wrap frequently so it doesn't collect moisture.

Gruyère An assertive, nutty Swiss cheese, Gruyère pairs well with both sweet and savory dishes alike.

Mascarpone A traditional dessert cheese, mascarpone has a silky texture and a rich, creamy flavor.

Monterey Jack This delicate, buttery cheese is a good medium to carry or enhance flavors. It's a natural complement to spicy foods and therefore a good choice for Mexican dishes.

Parmesan This hard, dry, granular cheese from Italy is so flavorful that a little goes a long way, making it an excellent cheese for healthy cooking. Its sharp taste gives dishes a big flavor boost, and the aroma becomes even more inviting as it melts. **For unrivaled flavor, Italy's preeminent and most versatile cheese is our favorite.**

For the best flavor, seek out the real thing—look for the words "Parmigiano-Reggiano" imprinted on the rind. The flavor is sharper and the texture crumblier than that of domestic Parmesan.

Parmigiano-Reggiano is higher in sodium than some other cheeses and has a saltier taste, so if you're using it, you probably won't need to add additional salt.

Parmigiano-Reggiano is surprisingly high in calcium (336 milligrams of calcium is in 1 ounce of cheese, which is about ¼ cup shredded or crumbled). It will also keep for 6 months in the refrigerator if tightly wrapped.

Although we prefer the distinctive flavor and texture of Parmigiano-Reggiano, it is pricey. Domestic Parmesans work just as well in recipes; the cheese flavor just won't be as sharp.

Milk Makes the Cheese

The type of milk used to make cheese provides a clue to the flavor. Taste cheeses made from different types of milk side by side to familiarize yourself with the subtle flavor differences.

Cow's milk cheeses: Cow's milk cheeses range in flavor from mild and milky (such as mozzarella, fontina, and Monterey Jack) to strong and pungent (such as Limburger, Gruyère, and Gorgonzola). The textures of these cheeses run from soft to hard, depending on the cheese and its age. Parmesan is a popular example of a hard, aged cow's milk cheese.

Goat's milk cheeses: These tangy, acidic cheeses can taste a little bit strong, depending on how they are made and how long they are aged. Young goat cheeses are refreshing and earthy, while aged goat cheeses range from buttery and nutty to strong and pungent.

Sheep's milk cheeses: Sheep's milk has more protein and calcium than cow's milk. Younger cheeses sometimes have a gamy character, while the aged ones, such as Pecorino Romano and Manchego, take on a rich, buttery quality.

In addition to the type of milk, pay attention to the cheese's texture, which also provides a window into the flavor: Soft cheeses tend to be fresh and mild, and hard cheeses tend toward salty, nutty, pungent flavors.

Storing Cheese Cheese's longevity is part of its charm. Storing cheese is just as important as knowing how to buy it.

- Store cheese in a refrigerator drawer—not in the door, where it is vulnerable to temperature swings.
- Wrap hard cheeses in waxed paper, then store them in zip-top plastic bags.
- If your semihard or hard cheeses have grown blue or green mold, trim ¼ to ½ inch beneath the mold; the rest is fine to use. Even cheese that has become dry and hard is still good to use—just grate it.
- Most cheeses can be frozen for up to 6 weeks; hard cheeses freeze better than soft. Freezing will slightly change the texture, but the flavor will remain the same. It's better to use thawed cheese in a cooked recipe rather than for slicing and serving.

"For easier grating, place softer cheeses (such as fontina and Monterey Jack) in the freezer for 10 to 15 minutes beforehand." Mike Wilson, Test Kitchens Staffer

> "Look at cheese as a flavorful accent in a recipe; if it's the focus of the dish, use it in a quantity that provides satisfaction—not excess." Kathryn Conrad, Test Kitchens Staffer

Cheese Substitutions

Cheese is one of the most interchangeable ingredients. The most important guideline is to substitute similar textures. Use personal flavor preferences and this chart as your guide.

Type of cheese:	When a recipe calls for:	You can substitute:
Fresh cheeses (not aged or ripened)	Queso blanco fresco	Feta or goat cheese
	Ricotta	Cottage cheese
	Mascarpone	Fromage blanc or Quark (yogurt cheese)
	Scamorza	Mozzarella or Oaxaca cheese
Soft-ripened cheeses are good eating cheeses because of their creamy texture. They are also well suited for cooking, and they melt smoothly.	Brie	Camembert
	Saint André	Explorateur
Semisoft cheeses are also good eating cheeses. They make suitable accents for bread, salad, and salad dressings.	Roquefort	Gorgonzola, Stilton, or Saga blue
	Reblochon	Teleme or Taleggio
	Livarot	Muenster, Epoisses, or Havarti
	Brick	Limburger
Semihard cheeses are excellent cooking cheeses that melt easily. Shred to top pizzas or casseroles.	Cantal	Colby or Cheddar
	Emmenthaler	Jarlsberg, Swiss, or Gruyère
	Edam	Gouda or Tilsit
	Kasseri	Provolone
	Manchego	Monterey Jack
Hard cheeses are often used as grating cheeses and are good for baked dishes such as gratins, pasta toppings, or for shaving over salads. Generally, with these full-flavored cheeses, only a little bit is needed.	Pecorino Romano	Parmigiano-Reggiano
	Dry Jack	Aged Cheddar
	Asiago	Romano

Eggs

Not only are eggs prime sources of protein, they're essential ingredients for many *Cooking Light* recipes.

In addition to egg dishes such as omelets and frittatas, eggs are an essential ingredient for cakes and cookies, meat loaves, casseroles, puddings, custards, and mousses. It's not their flavor that makes eggs so hard to do without. It's the cooking chemistry. The strong binding power of the proteins, as well as the ability to cause either expansion or thickening, is critical in recipes.

Egg Yolks Refrigerate unbroken raw egg yolks, covered with water, for up to 2 days in an airtight container. If you can't use the yolks in 2 days, hard cook them just as you would cook whole eggs in the shell, drain, and store in the refrigerator in an airtight container for up to 4 to 5 days.

When you freeze raw egg yolks, they tend to thicken or gel, eventually becoming gelatinous and unusable. To help slow down the thickening process, beat in either ⅛ teaspoon of salt or 1½ teaspoons of sugar per 4 yolks.

Egg Whites To reduce the fat in a recipe, you can replace some of the egg yolks with additional egg whites. For example, if a recipe calls for two whole eggs, you can replace one of those whole eggs with two egg whites. (We don't recommend this substitution in recipes such as custards or sauces where the yolk is essential for thickening.)

Egg Substitutes Egg substitutes are egg whites combined with corn oil, water, flavorings, and preservatives. Because of these additives, they can't be beaten to peak stage. One-fourth cup of egg substitute is equal to one whole egg. Egg whites work the same, if not better, in most applications. (See page 92 for more information.)

Handling Eggs — Keep It SAFE

Food safety is crucial when you're handling eggs. Here are some things to keep in mind:

Don't eat raw eggs or use them in recipes. Although the risk of salmonella contamination is small, cook eggs to a temperature of 160°. If you have recipes that call for raw eggs, either cook the eggs, or use pasteurized egg products such as egg substitutes. If you bring food containing eggs to a temperature of 160°, you will kill any bacteria that may be there.

Use clean eggs with unbroken shells, and discard any that are unclean, cracked, broken, or leaking. Eggshells are washed and sanitized before packing, so there is no need to wash eggshells before you use the eggs.

Remove blood spots with the tip of a knife if you wish. Chemically and nutritionally, an egg with a blood spot is fine to eat. Blood spots in an egg do not mean that the egg has been contaminated with bacteria.

Use eggs straight from the refrigerator for most recipes. Although egg whites reach their fullest volume if allowed to stand at room temperature, for creamed cakes and separately beaten egg whites, it's really only necessary to take the chill off the eggs. They don't actually have to reach room temperature.

Store raw eggs in their cartons to guard against breakage and odor absorption and to help prevent the loss of carbon dioxide (which lowers egg quality). Place egg cartons on a middle or lower shelf where the temperature will fluctuate less than it does in the refrigerator door. Refrigerated raw eggs in the shells will keep for about 3 weeks after you bring them home.

Ask the *Cooking Light* Cooks

What are the the white ropelike strands in egg whites?
They are chalazae (kuh-LAY-zee), and they hold the yolk in place. They are not, contrary to popular belief, the beginnings of an embryo. In fact, the more prominent the chalazae are, the fresher the egg.

Is there any difference between white and brown eggs?
No, other than the color. They're the same on the inside.

What's the easiest way to separate an egg?
First, eggs are easier to separate when they're cold.

If you're like most people, you separate an egg by pouring the yolk back and forth from one half of the eggshell to the other so that the white slides off into a bowl. But neither we nor the American Egg Board recommends this: It can introduce bacteria from the eggshell pores into the egg, and there's a greater chance of the shell breaking the yolk.

It's fine to use your hands. Your fingers are softer and don't bring in bacteria. Just crack the egg, and let the the white run through your fingers into a bowl. Of course, wash your hands before and after. If you prefer to use an egg separator, that's fine, too.

Scrambling Eggs
Test Kitchen SECRET

When you're making scrambled eggs, fluffy and light are the goals, so don't stir the eggs too much. The key to large, fluffy curds is to allow the eggs to set in the pan for about 30 seconds. Don't touch them. Then, with a rubber spatula, gently pull the cooked edges away from the pan, creating an almost folded effect. Remove the eggs from the heat before they look completely done because they will continue to cook. Use a nonstick skillet and medium-low heat.

The Perfect Hard-Boiled Egg
Test Kitchen SECRET

Cooking eggs for too long at too high a temperature results in two common problems: greenish yolks and cracked shells. Here's an easy way to avoid that: Place eggs in a single layer in a saucepan with enough cool water to cover the eggs by at least 1 inch. Cover the pan, and bring just to a boil; immediately turn off the heat. Let the eggs stand, covered, for 15 minutes. Run the eggs under cold water until completely cooled. Gently crack each shell, and peel under running water, starting with the large end. Use older eggs because eggs older than 7 days are easier to peel.

Egg-and-Tuna Salad Sandwiches
What better use for hard-cooked eggs than in an egg salad sandwich? The tuna is the bonus.

4	hard-cooked large eggs, chopped
1	(6-ounce) can chunk light tuna in water, drained
2	tablespoons minced red onion
3	tablespoons light mayonnaise
2	tablespoons Dijon mustard
½	teaspoon freshly ground black pepper
10	(1-ounce) slices whole wheat bread
5	large red leaf lettuce leaves
5	(¼-inch-thick) slices tomato
1¼	cups alfalfa sprouts

1. Combine first 6 ingredients in a bowl. Spread ½ cup egg mixture over each of 5 bread slices. Top each with 1 lettuce leaf, 1 tomato slice, ¼ cup alfalfa sprouts, and 1 bread slice. Yield: 5 sandwiches (serving size: 1 sandwich).

CALORIES 294 (30% from fat); FAT 9.8g (sat 2.3g, mono 2.5g, poly 3.4g); PROTEIN 19.5g; CARB 34.8g; FIBER 4.8g; CHOL 184mg; IRON 4mg; SODIUM 697mg; CALC 176mg

Even though egg whites beat up to a higher volume when they're at room temperature, we don't recommend letting them sit out on the counter before beating because of food safety concerns.

Beating Egg Whites

The condition and type of bowl in which you beat egg whites really does matter. Keep it dry and clean; if it's wet or harbors any residual oil, the whites won't whip properly. Glass, ceramic, or metal bowls are best. (See pages 144 and 145 for information on beating egg whites for angel food cakes.)

Soft: For most soufflés, you will want soft peaks—the stage just before stiff peaks form. To know if you have soft peaks, lift the beaters out of the egg mixture; the peaks should curve over gently, like waves. You create a puffed soufflé by beating egg whites separately and then folding them into the base that has been thickened with the yolks.

Stiff: Beat room-temperature egg whites with cream of tartar (which helps stabilize them) and salt until foamy. Then add the sugar, beating until stiff peaks form. You can tell if you have stiff peaks versus soft peaks by lifting the beaters from the mixture. Stiff peaks will stand up.

Overbeaten: You don't ever want overbeaten egg whites, particularly not in a mousse, as they won't fold in smoothly. Watch carefully for the above indicators because egg whites can go from stiff to dry and overbeaten in as little as 30 seconds. If you do overbeat them, it's best to throw them away and start over.

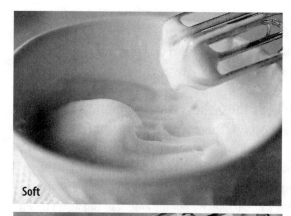
Soft

Stiff

Overbeaten

Soy

The joy of soy products is that they're easy to cook with, taste great, and have significant health benefits.

Soy products—such as soybeans, flour, milk, miso, tempeh, and tofu—have been linked to decreased risk of heart disease, breast cancer, and prostate cancer; lowered blood cholesterol; fewer menopause symptoms; and better bone health. But what we like about soy products is their flavor.

Sources of Soy Protein

Consuming 25 grams of soy protein per day, as part of a diet low in saturated fat and cholesterol, might reduce the risk of heart disease, according to the Food and Drug Administration. These are some of the most concentrated sources of soy protein:

Food	Serving Size	Protein
Tempeh	1 cup	32 grams
Tofu	1 cup	20 grams
Yellow soybeans	1/2 cup	14 grams
Soy nuts	1/3 cup	13 grams
Edamame	1/2 cup	11 grams
Soy milk (plain, calcium-fortified)	1 cup	10 grams

Edamame Served in Japanese restaurants and now offered in many supermarkets, these sweet, bright green soybeans are delicious served in the pod or shelled like baby limas. Edamame are not a variety of soybean—they are immature soybeans that are picked green and served fresh. In season, usually from late July to September, you might find fresh edamame at local farmers' markets. Frozen, they are available year-round, both in the pod and shelled. They're also available shelled, fully cooked, and packaged in a moisture-proof bag that you can store in the refrigerator for up to 3 weeks.

> "I've started adding edamame to green salads for a little extra crunch and nutty flavor. Or I just eat them for a snack." Krista Montgomery, Food Editor

Not least among their merits is a buttery, nutty flavor and wonderfully crisp texture that makes edamame a fun snack food. You simply use your teeth to squeeze the beans out of the cooked, salted pods, which are picked while young and look like large, fuzzy sugar snap peas. Or just buy the ones that are already shelled. The beans themselves are similar in color to fresh fava or lima beans.

> "We find most of our soy products in the supermarket, except for tempeh and miso, which we purchase at a local Asian market." Mike Wilson, Test Kitchens Staffer

Roasted Chile–Spiced Edamame

A slight crunch on the outside gives way to a meaty texture inside.

    1   (14-ounce) package frozen blanched
         shelled edamame (green soybeans),
         thawed
    Cooking spray
    1   tablespoon New Mexico red chile powder
    1   teaspoon onion powder
    3/4 teaspoon sea salt
    1/2 teaspoon ground ginger
    1/2 teaspoon ground red pepper

1. Preheat oven to 300°.
2. Arrange edamame in a single layer on a baking sheet, and coat with cooking spray. Combine chile powder and remaining ingredients. Sprinkle over edamame; toss to coat.
3. Bake edamame at 300° for 2 hours, stirring beans every 30 minutes. Store in an airtight container. Yield: 5 servings (serving size: about $1/4$ cup).

CALORIES 113 (28% from fat); FAT 3.5g (sat 0.4g, mono 0.7g, poly 1.7g); PROTEIN 8.7g; CARB 10.9g; FIBER 4.8g; CHOL 0mg; IRON 2mg; SODIUM 393mg; CALC 59mg

Yellow and Black Soybeans As soybeans mature, they ripen into hard, dry beans. Though most mature soybeans are yellow, there are also black varieties. These dried beans require an overnight soak and about 3 hours of cooking time to make them tender. They have a slippery texture and firm bite. Yellow soybeans require assertive seasoning to enhance their bland taste; black soybeans, however, can stand alone in salads and side dishes. Both are good in chilis, stews, and soups, and pureed for dips.

Canned Soybeans

Test Kitchen
SECRET

- Canned soybeans, usually found on the organic food aisle, are a fast alternative to soaking and cooking dried soybeans. Use them as you would other canned beans, rinsing and draining before using.
- As with regular canned beans, canned soybeans have more sodium than dried. A $1/2$-cup serving has 140 milligrams of sodium, compared to 0.9 milligrams for the same amount of cooked dried beans. But like regular canned beans, you can reduce the sodium when you drain and rinse. Or you can buy no-salt-added canned soy beans.

Soy Flour Made of finely ground dried soybeans, this high-protein soy food can replace some of the all-purpose flour in many recipes. Commercial bakeries often use soy flour in breads and pastries because it retains moisture and gives baked goods longer shelf life. Soy flour also creates a large, fluffy crumb. You can add a small amount to your favorite bread recipes to boost protein. **Soy flour does not contain gluten, so you can't use all soy flour: We use 20 to 30 percent soy flour along with all-purpose.** Higher amounts can produce a heavy, grainy result. Full-fat soy flour works better than defatted in baking. Store soy flour in a glass jar in the refrigerator or freezer for up to 6 months.

Soy Milk Soy milk is squeezed from dried soybeans that have been soaked, ground, and cooked. Asian markets sell it just as it comes from the bean, thin and strong-tasting, perhaps

sweetened. The soy milk sold in supermarkets and natural-foods stores tastes mild by comparison and is thickened to resemble dairy milk. Besides chocolate and vanilla, it comes in flavors such as chai and latte. It varies significantly by brand in taste, protein, and fat content. (To reduce fat, water is added.) Most soy milk is calcium-fortified to equal dairy milk.

Soy Milk Substitution	Test Kitchen
	SECRET

To use soy milk as a replacement for dairy milk in recipes, use unsweetened soy milk. Substitutions usually work better in dessert recipes and some savory dishes.

Miso Made from a blend of soy and grain or with soy alone, miso instantly adds rich flavor to all kinds of dishes.

Miso not only adds flavor, it also adds creaminess to sauces and soups, and thickens them slightly.

Resembling peanut butter, miso ranges in color from light to dark and in taste from mildly sweet to very salty. It contains less sodium per serving than salt and regular soy sauce. Miso keeps indefinitely, refrigerated in a glass jar. Varieties of miso include:

Light: Use with fish, poultry, dressings, creamy soups, and vegetables. Light miso contains the least salt. Examples include Sweet and Mellow White (*Shiro*) and Mellow Beige (*Tanshoku*). **Dark:** All dark misos are good with grains and legumes, and in stews, tomato sauces, and gravies. Examples include All-Soy (*Hatcho*), Barley (*Mugi*), and Red (*Aka*).

Soy Protein Products From crumbles that resemble ground beef to soy sausage and bacon, these refrigerated and frozen products can replace meat in most recipes. Made with soy protein, they are cholesterol-free and cook quickly.

If you're substituting veggie burgers, burger crumbles, or sausage made from textured soy protein for ground beef or pork, use the soy product in the same amount as the meat called for in the recipe, but decrease the cooking time. Refer to the cooking times on the packages.

Tempeh Tempeh is made from partly cooked soybeans inoculated with spores of a friendly mold in a process that is very similar to cheese-making. The mold creates threads that bind the soybeans into a flat cake. Tempeh is blanched or frozen to slow fermentation and preserve active enzymes. It has a yeasty flavor and firm texture.

Tempeh can be made with soybeans alone, but you'll often find it composed of soy and a grain such as rice or barley. **All-soy tempeh is highest in protein, has the most pronounced flavor, and is highest in fat.** Good grilled, sautéed, pan-crisped, or braised, tempeh is sold in Asian markets, natural-foods stores, and in some large supermarkets.

Tofu's subtle flavor and tender texture merge so well with a multitude of Western and Asian seasonings that there's no need to think of this Japanese classic as merely a substitute for something else.

Tofu Tofu (soybean curd) is low in calories—3 ounces of tofu carry only 35 to 55 calories. It's also a storehouse of vitamins and minerals, including folic acid and iron. As much as half of tofu's calories can come from fat—about 3 grams in 3 ounces—but in light versions, the ratio plummets to 1 gram in 3 ounces. None of the fat is saturated, which is the type of fat that increases the risk of heart disease.

Tofu varies in texture from creamy and smooth to firm enough to slice. It also is sold marinated and smoked, or flavored with such seasonings as teriyaki or garlic and herbs. At some supermarkets and Asian-food stores, you can find it smoked, marinated, spiced, fermented, freeze-dried, or deep-fried.

Before preparing tofu, rinse it in cold water. To store it, keep it in water in the refrigerator, and change the water every 2 days. Tofu will last this way for a week. It may also be kept frozen for up to 3 months, but freezing makes the texture chewier.

Ask the *Cooking Light* Cooks

Does tofu just absorb the flavors of the ingredients that are in the recipe instead of contributing its own flavor? The common notion that tofu absorbs flavors that somehow turn it into something else isn't really true. If you marinate tofu, you've probably noticed that the marinade mostly remains on the surface, penetrating only slightly. But marinades can lend some flavor and color to tofu, and they are usually used as part of the sauce for the recipe later, and that's their main virtue. *If you heat your firm tofu first, then marinate it, you will find that it is more receptive than if you simply go from the box to a marinade.*

What do the different names on tofu labels mean? The labels soft, firm, and extra-firm have to do with the texture and density of tofu. Softer tofu is best used where it's handled as little as possible—when it's added to a soup or a gently simmering stew. It's also the tofu to puree and add to ricotta cheese, hummus, mayonnaise, muffin batters, and the like. *The more firm the tofu is, the more you can handle it—marinate it, sauté it, fry it. But do note that the tofu in aseptic packages tends to be pretty delicate, regardless of whether it's called firm or extra-firm, while the water-packed tofu tends to be sturdier.*

How do I keep tofu from falling apart or crumbling? You can make tofu stronger by heating it, either in simmering water or by "frying" it in a nonstick skillet. This toughens the proteins and, in the case of the skillet method, pulls out the excess water while browning it a little. (This is best when done with the water-packed tofu.) *Another way to get rid of excess moisture is to press the water-packed tofu, once removed from its liquid, with a heavy weight for a half hour or so to force out the excess liquid. It's not necessary to do this with tofu such as the Mori-Nu brand that comes packaged in a small, aseptic juice container-style box.*

Creamy Lemon-Lime Tofu Cheesecake

We've used a fat-free lemon curd rather than a traditional one made with egg yolks and butter. Look for lemon curd on the jelly aisle of the supermarket.

Crust:

1⅓	cups graham cracker crumbs (about 8 cookie sheets)
2	tablespoons brown sugar
1	tablespoon butter, melted
	Cooking spray

Filling:

1	cup 2% low-fat cottage cheese
⅔	cup tub-style light cream cheese (about 5 ounces)
1	(12.3-ounce) package reduced-fat firm silken tofu, drained
1	cup granulated sugar
⅓	cup all-purpose flour
½	cup bottled lemon curd (such as Crosse & Blackwell)
2	teaspoons grated lime rind
6	tablespoons fresh lime juice
2	large eggs
1	large egg white

Topping:

1¼	cups reduced-fat sour cream
½	cup granulated sugar
1	teaspoon grated lemon rind
½	teaspoon vanilla extract

1. Preheat oven to 325°.
2. To prepare crust, combine first 3 ingredients in a small bowl; toss well with a fork. Sprinkle into bottom of a 9-inch springform pan coated with cooking spray.
3. To prepare filling, place cheeses and tofu in a food processor, and process until smooth. Add 1 cup granulated sugar, flour, and next 5 ingredients; process until smooth, scraping sides of bowl occasionally. Pour filling into prepared pan. Bake at 325° for 1 hour and 20 minutes or until almost set. Remove from oven.
4. To prepare topping, place sour cream, ½ cup granulated sugar, lemon rind, and vanilla in a small bowl; stir well. Spread sour cream mixture over cheesecake, and bake 8 additional minutes. Turn oven off, and partially open oven door; leave cheesecake in oven 30 minutes. Remove from oven. Cool 20 minutes on a wire rack; cover and chill 8 hours. Yield: 12 servings.

CALORIES 320 (26% from fat); FAT 9.3g (sat 5g, mono 1.2g, poly 0.5g); PROTEIN 9.2g; CARB 50.6g; FIBER 1.8g; CHOL 69mg; IRON 1mg; SODIUM 271mg; CALC 90mg

The Right Kind of Tofu
Cooking Light Recommends

Selecting the right kind of tofu is the key to the success of tofu recipes. Here are the best uses for each variety.

Silken (Kinugoshi, or Japanese-style): Sold in aseptic boxes and available in soft, firm, and extra-firm textures, silken tofu is custardlike and ideal to puree for dressings, dips, soups, milk shakes, cheesecakes, and smoothies. It's much too delicate to grill, sauté, or stir-fry.

Regular (Momen, or Chinese-style): Also found in soft, firm, and extra-firm textures, this tofu is packed in water in plastic tubs and pouches. Its dense texture makes it ideal to sauté, grill, or broil. Choose soft, water-packed tofu for scrambling and to use in spreads, thick dips, and some desserts; it's also good for mashing and pureeing. Select firm for grilling, sautéing, and stir-frying. Firm and extra-firm are also good for crumbling into lasagna, chili, or spaghetti sauce, or for slicing in sautés and stir-fries.

Reduced-fat tofu: *We found reduced-fat tofu to be just as delicious and versatile in recipes as regular tofu.* (We've used both in *Cooking Light* recipes.) To lower the fat content even further in the recipes that call for the regular, substitute the reduced-fat variety. Regular tofu gets 57 percent of its calories from fat, while reduced-fat tofu gets 26 percent of its calories from fat.

CHAPTER 7

Grains & Pasta

Grains, including pastas, are an important part of a healthy, low-fat diet. Let *Cooking Light* be your guide through the field of grains—barley through wheat—as we show you how to select and prepare the most nutritious grain products.

All About Grains

Although we typically use the term "grains," it might be more clear to call them "cereal grains." Cereal includes any plant from the grass family that produces an edible seed, or grain. The grains that we use most often in our recipes include barley, corn, oats, rice, rye, and wheat. (Pastas and flours made from these grains are also included in this group.)

Not only are grains easily grown and prepared, they're also highly nutritious—rich in complex carbohydrates, vitamins, minerals, and fiber. They fill you up—yet they're almost free of fat. Versatility is another bonus, as they provide a neutral background against which to highlight other ingredients.

Whole Grains

Whole grains and groats are interchangeable terms for unrefined grains. These are grains in their most natural form—chewy, hearty, and high in fiber and nutrients. **Because the bran, endosperm, and germ are intact, they are higher in fiber and minerals and take longer to cook than refined forms.** Examples of whole grains include barley,

buckwheat groats, oats, wheat berries, and whole-grain rye.

Refined or Processed Grains

Processed grains are whole grains that have been changed in some way, usually through grinding, cutting, rolling, or steaming. They are refined to change their form and, in many cases, to make them easier to cook and digest. The following are some examples of familiar processed grains.

Cracked grains, such as bulgur and steel-cut oats, result when grains are ground into smaller pieces. Some cracked grains are derived from whole grains, others from refined grains.

Flakes are sliced whole grains or cracked grains that have been steamed and rolled. Rolled oats are probably the most familiar, but you'll also find rolled barley, wheat, and rye.

Instant and quick-cooking grains are grains such as rice or oats that have been processed or precooked and packaged for convenience. These convenience products don't necessarily have fewer nutrients than their regular counterparts (although sometimes, that is the case), but they often have less flavor or texture.

Flour is grain that has been milled to a powder. Whole wheat flour is the product of processing whole wheat berries.

Polished grains include pearl barley (right) and brown rice (see page 259). These grains have been refined to remove the tough exterior husk and most (or all) of the bran. This makes them less chewy and quicker to cook than whole grains.

Buying Grains	Test Kitchen SECRET

In the past, you would have had to go to a health- or natural-foods store to buy out-of the-ordinary grains, but now you can find many of them at the supermarket. Arrowhead Mills and Bob's Red Mill are two commonly available brands. Grains—especially whole ones—have oils that eventually turn rancid. Shop at stores where the turnover seems high, and buy only what you plan to use within a few months. If you have space, it's best to refrigerate grains, but you still can't keep them forever. You can tell if they've lost their freshness by their smell—old grains, including flours, will have a stale odor.

Barley

Barley has been a staple food for man and beast since the Stone Age, and it may be best known as an ingredient in beer. This hardy grain is a good source of fiber and potassium and is used frequently in cereals, breads, and soups. Two varieties of barley are most often found at markets. **The most nutritious form is whole-grain (hulled) barley, which has only the outer husk removed.** It's most commonly used to make a thick, oatmeal-like cereal. Pearl barley is less nutritious because the bran has been removed. This type of barley is steamed and polished and is good in soups and stews. Quick-cooking barley, which takes only 20 minutes to prepare, is the most popular form of pearl barley.

Pearl barley

Quick-cooking barley

Barley flour has a strong nutty flavor when toasted; try adding it to breads. Pearl barley is a great source of fiber; $1/2$ cup provides more than 12 grams.

Cornmeal

Wonderfully versatile and the foundation of many products, corn is a vegetable in which the whole plant is used: husks, kernels, silks, and stalks. When thinking of corn in the context of grains and cereals, we'll focus on the kernels that are ground into meal. (See pages 276-277 for more information on corn.)

Dried corn kernels are ground into one of three textures—fine, medium, or coarse—to produce cornmeal. There are two basic methods of grinding. **The oldest method is called stone-ground, and this method retains some of the hull and the germ of the corn, so it's more nutritious than cornmeal that is ground using the modern milling method.** The modern method uses steel rollers that remove the husk and germ completely. Stone-ground cornmeal, because it has part of the germ of the corn, contains fat and won't keep as long as cornmeal with the germ removed. Store it in an airtight container in the refrigerator for up to 4 months.

Cornmeal is either yellow, white, or blue, depending on the type of corn that is used. Yellow and white cornmeal are the most common. Both grits and polenta are made from dried corn kernels; the difference lies in how those kernels are milled. When the corn is ground, the coarser particles become grits, while the finer granules are used for polenta.

Grits Stone-ground grits, our choice for most recipes, have a chunkier texture and a more "corny" flavor than quick grits. They do take longer to cook than their counterpart, and they also need more stirring to release the starch and soften the grains, but stone-ground grits are certainly worth the effort.

Getting the Grits

Frank Stitt, an award-winning chef and restaurateur in Birmingham, Alabama, shared with us some of his thoughts on grits—an ingredient that is featured in some of his restaurant's signature dishes.

"When I opened Highlands Bar and Grill in 1982, I wanted to focus on Southern ingredients and traditions, but I also wanted to use a little bit more finesse and more refined techniques. Grits were a natural addition to the menu. We wanted to do an appetizer like a grits soufflé, a grits pudding, or a grits cake, into which we would incorporate Parmigiano-Reggiano cheese, country ham, and wild mushrooms. We chose to use coarse-ground grits, which offer much more flavor. We experimented, cooking the grits a long time, letting them cool a bit, adding eggs, Parmesan, and some butter, then putting them into a mold and baking them. When we took them out, we had a very nice grits timbale.

I'm not Italian, nor Italian-American. I'm Southern. So I don't think of polenta; I think of grits. It's a historical way, a romantic way, of remembering experiences from my youth at my granddaddy's farm, and it's nice to bring that into our kitchens today."

Cornmeal and Grits
Cooking Light Recommends

To make polenta, we like the whole-grain cornmeal from both Hodgson Mill (www.hodgsonmill.com) and Arrowhead Mills (www.arrowheadmills.com). Look for both brands in the grocery store near the flour.

Coarse stone-ground grits aren't always available in supermarkets, but you can find them in specialty food markets or by contacting mills directly.

Our favorite grits come from Nora Mill Granary (www.noramill.com or 800-927-2375) and War Eagle Mill (www.wareaglemill.com).

Grilled Grits with Chicken-Apple Sausages

Chilling the grits makes them firm enough to grill.

Grits:

5	cups water
¾	teaspoon kosher salt
1	cup stone-ground yellow grits
½	cup (2 ounces) grated fresh Parmesan cheese
¼	teaspoon white pepper
¼	teaspoon hot pepper sauce
	Cooking spray

Tomato sauce:

2	teaspoons olive oil
2	cups finely chopped onion
1	cup thinly sliced celery
6	fennel seeds
2	garlic cloves, minced
1	(28-ounce) can whole tomatoes, undrained
¼	teaspoon dried marjoram
6	basil leaves
2	bay leaves
2	dried chile peppers, lightly crushed

Remaining ingredient:

12	(½-ounce) chicken-apple sausages (such as Aidell's)

1. To prepare grits, bring water and salt to a boil in a large saucepan; gradually stir in grits. Reduce heat; simmer 30 minutes or until thick, stirring frequently. Remove from heat; stir in cheese, white pepper, and pepper sauce.

2. Spread into a 15 x 10-inch jelly-roll pan coated with cooking spray; cool completely on a wire rack. Cover with plastic wrap; chill 30 minutes.

3. To prepare tomato sauce, heat oil in a large non-stick skillet over medium-high heat. Add onion and celery; sauté 5 minutes or until onion is tender. Add fennel seeds and garlic; sauté 2 minutes. Reduce heat to medium-low. Add tomatoes, marjoram, basil, bay leaves, and chiles; cook 20 minutes, stirring frequently. Discard bay leaves.

4. Prepare grill pan.

5. Invert grits onto a cutting board; cut into 12 squares. Place the squares on grill pan coated with cooking spray, and grill 3 minutes on each side or until lightly browned and thoroughly heated. Remove from pan; keep warm.

6. Place sausages in pan; grill 8 minutes, turning occasionally. Arrange 3 grits squares in each of 4 bowls. Top each serving with 3 sausages and ¼ cup sauce. Yield: 4 servings.

CALORIES 368 (30% from fat); FAT 12.4g (sat 4.5g, mono 5g, poly 1.9g); PROTEIN 17.3g; CARB 47.7g; FIBER 4.6g; CHOL 49mg; IRON 2.4mg; SODIUM 939mg; CALC 254mg

Polenta In *Cooking Light* recipes, we use whole-grain yellow cornmeal—which yields a richly flavored and textured polenta.

You can eat soft polenta alone or with browned butter. Or use it as a bed for a quick sauté of pancetta and broccoli rabe. Firm polenta is good served sliced as a side dish. This is also the polenta to cut into diamonds, rectangles, or small croutons, which can then be sprinkled with cheese and roasted, or brushed with oil and grilled, fried, or sautéed.

Precooked Polenta   **Test Kitchen SECRET**

As a shortcut to making polenta in a saucepan, we often use tubes of precooked polenta. The precooked polenta works well in recipes in which the polenta is cut into slices or cubes and sautéed or grilled.

Look for plain and flavored 16-ounce tubes of polenta in the produce section of the supermarket. This polenta has 200 milligrams of sodium per 4-ounce slice, which is not really much different than what you'd get if you made your own and added about ¼ teaspoon of salt.

Soft Polenta

For variations on this recipe, use stock or broth in place of water for a richer dish, or use a different cheese for a whole new flavor.

4	cups boiling water
1	tablespoon butter
¼	teaspoon sea salt
1	cup whole-grain yellow cornmeal (such as Arrowhead Mills)
¼	cup (1 ounce) grated fresh Parmesan cheese

1. Combine first 3 ingredients in a medium saucepan. Gradually add cornmeal, stirring with a whisk. Bring cornmeal mixture to a boil, stirring constantly. Reduce heat to low; cook 25 minutes, stirring frequently.

2. Remove from heat; stir in cheese. Serve immediately. Yield: 4 servings (serving size: ¾ cup).

CALORIES 184 (27% from fat); FAT 5.6g (sat 3.2g, mono 1.6g, poly 0.4g); PROTEIN 5.9g; CARB 27.1g; FIBER 2.6g; CHOL 13mg; IRON 0.5mg; SODIUM 306mg; CALC 100mg

"When it comes to side dishes, creamy, soft polenta is a great alternative to rice and mashed potatoes."

Jan Smith, Photo Stylist

Flaxseed

Its nutty flavor is temptation enough, but flaxseed is also a health powerhouse. Although it has the

distinction of being one of the oldest cultivated grains on the planet, flaxseed is a relative stranger to the American kitchen. It shouldn't be, though. Not only does flaxseed's flavor transform cooking, but the tiny, reddish-brown seed is also a mini-bastion of nutrition and other healthy properties. Among its bragging rights:

Fiber Because flaxseed contains both soluble and insoluble fiber, it packs a dual healthy punch. The soluble fiber helps lower cholesterol levels and keep blood sugar steady, while the insoluble fiber helps ward off constipation.

Lignans These estrogens found in plants (phytoestrogens) are compounds that are similar to isoflavones, the potent disease-fighters in soybeans. And like isoflavones, they may play a role in warding off hormone-dependent cancers, such as those found in breasts and prostates. Long-term studies are testing the impact of flaxseed on the medical treatment of women with breast cancer.

Omega-3 fats More than 70 percent of the fat in flaxseed comes from alpha-linolenic acid, a member of the omega-3 family and cousin to the heart-healthy fats found in fish such as salmon and mackerel. Researchers suspect that the benefits of the fat in flaxseed may even exceed those of the fat in fish. In fact, flaxseed's fat may someday be useful in treating diseases in which the body's immune system goes awry, such as rheumatoid arthritis, psoriasis, and multiple sclerosis.

Lemon-Flaxseed Loaf Cake

Adding flaxseed to this sweet cake transforms it into a nutrient-packed treat.

Cooking spray
- 1 tablespoon granulated sugar
- ¼ cup flaxseed
- 1 cup granulated sugar
- 2 large eggs
- 2 cups all-purpose flour
- 1½ teaspoons baking powder
- ½ teaspoon baking soda
- ½ teaspoon salt
- ¾ cup low-fat buttermilk
- ¼ cup vegetable oil
- 2 teaspoons grated lemon rind
- 1 teaspoon vanilla extract
- ½ cup powdered sugar
- 1 tablespoon fresh lemon juice

1. Preheat oven to 350°.
2. Coat an 8 x 4-inch loaf pan with cooking spray; sprinkle with 1 tablespoon granulated sugar. Place flaxseed in a blender; process until ground to measure 6 tablespoons flaxseed meal; set aside.
3. Combine 1 cup granulated sugar and eggs; beat with a mixer at high speed 3 minutes. Lightly spoon flour into dry measuring cups; level with a knife. Combine flaxseed meal, flour, and next 3 ingredients; stir with a whisk. Combine buttermilk, oil, rind, and vanilla. Add flour mixture to egg mixture alternately with buttermilk mixture, beginning and ending with flour mixture.
4. Spoon batter into prepared pan. Bake at 350° for 55 minutes or until a wooden pick inserted in center comes out clean. Cool in pan 5 minutes on a wire rack; remove from pan. Cool completely on wire rack. Combine powdered sugar and lemon juice; drizzle over top of loaf. Yield: 12 servings (serving size: 1 slice).

CALORIES 242 (28% from fat); FAT 7.4g (sat 1.4g, mono 2.1g, poly 3.5g); PROTEIN 4.5g; CARB 40.7g; FIBER 1.4g; CHOL 37mg; IRON 4.6mg; SODIUM 232mg; CALC 70mg

---

Flaxseed Flour
Test Kitchen SECRET

- To glean the most flaxseed benefits, you'll need to grind the seeds. That breaks through the tough outer hull (which might otherwise pass through your body undigested) and unleashes all the heart- and health-beneficial compounds. Either a blender or a clean coffee grinder does the job neatly. Just pulse until the seeds form a flourlike powder. Keep in mind that once you grind flaxseed, the delicate oil in the seed is exposed to air and light and can therefore spoil and produce rancid flavors.
- To prolong their shelf life, store ground seeds (or flaxseed meal) in the refrigerator in an airtight opaque container. Stored carefully, ground seeds will stay fresh for up to 90 days. Left whole, flaxseed can be stored at room temperature for up to a year.

"I hadn't used flaxseed much until I did some recipe testing for a story. Now it's a staple in my kitchen because of the health benefits and the flavor."

Maureen Callahan, *Cooking Light* Contributor

Oats

The soluble fiber that's so plentiful in oatmeal and oat bran appears to help lower cholesterol and reduce the risk of heart disease. Oats also have plenty of vitamins B1, B2, and E and are low in calories—only 150 in a half-cup of dry oats, which also carries 4 grams of dietary fiber.

Know Your Oats Although oats are most widely available in rolled form, you can also find steel-cut oats. These oats are cracked whole-grain oats; when cooked, they are chewy. Steel-cut oats are also called Irish oatmeal. A good source of fiber, ½ cup of steel-cut oats has 7.5 grams. You may also see oat groats or whole-grain oats in supermarkets or health-food stores.

Regular rolled oats usually come in three forms: regular (or "old-fashioned"), quick-cooking, and instant. The first two can be used interchangeably in recipes, although we specify in our recipes the kind that works best.

Instant oats, to which you only add hot water, aren't recommended in our recipes because they are preprocessed and too finely cut to provide enough substance and texture.

Getting Your Oats

Test Kitchen
SECRET

Here are some of our favorite ways to use oats in our recipes.
- Plump up a meat loaf with nutty richness
- Add texture to a piecrust
- Contribute crunchiness to the topping of an upside-down cake
- Add heartiness and texture to chocolate chip cookie dough
- Sprinkle on top of yeast bread dough
- Stir into quick bread batter
- Add to coating mixture for oven-fried chicken or fish

Spiced Fruity Oatmeal

Cooking the oatmeal in a mixture of juice and water adds extra sweetness to the cereal.

1½	cups apple juice
½	cup water
⅛	teaspoon salt
1⅓	cups regular oats
¼	cup sweetened dried cranberries (such as Craisins) or raisins
¼	cup 1% low-fat milk
1	tablespoon brown sugar
¾	teaspoon ground cinnamon
⅛	teaspoon ground nutmeg
2	tablespoons chopped walnuts

1. Combine first 3 ingredients in a medium saucepan; bring to a boil. Stir in oats and cranberries; reduce heat, and simmer 4 minutes, stirring occasionally. Stir in milk, sugar, cinnamon, and nutmeg; cook 1 minute. Spoon into bowls; sprinkle with walnuts. Yield: 4 servings (serving size: ¾ cup oatmeal and 1½ teaspoons walnuts).

CALORIES 212 (18% from fat); FAT 4.2g (sat 0.6g, mono 1.1g, poly 2.1g); PROTEIN 5.8g; CARB 38.9g; FIBER 3.7g; CHOL 1mg; IRON 1.8mg; SODIUM 86mg; CALC 49mg

Microwave variation: Combine first 5 ingredients in a 2-quart glass measure or medium bowl, and microwave at HIGH 4 minutes or until slightly thick, stirring after 2 minutes. Stir in milk, sugar, cinnamon, and nutmeg; let stand, covered, 1 minute. Spoon into bowls; sprinkle with walnuts.

Rice

A pot of perfect, fluffy rice is a commendable kitchen achievement. Yet even experienced cooks sometimes have trouble cooking rice. We'll teach you how to get it right every time.

You will also learn some great rice secrets and how best to use and cook any variety of rice you choose. And when you're finished, you'll be able to cook your way around the world.

> Most people in America don't rinse their rice before cooking, but it's routine in China. Rinsing removes the white powder caused by polishing and allows the grains to separate during cooking, creating a fluffier effect.

The Long and Short of It

More than 40,000 varieties of rice generally fall into one of three categories: short-, medium-, and long-grain. The most important differences are in cooking properties and taste. All rice is composed of two types of starch—dry and sticky. The dry starch, amylose, is higher in long-grain (indica) rice and, when cooked, produces drier rice with separate grains. The sticky starch, amylopectin, is higher in short-grain (japonica) rice and, when cooked, produces soft rice with clinging grains.

Long-grain varieties are four to five times longer than wide. This includes the white rice that most Americans grew up eating.

Medium-grain varieties are two to three times longer than wide. Medium-grain rice absorbs flavors readily, which is why it's popular for paella and risotto.

Short-grain rice is plump—almost round—and cooks into soft grains that cling together. It is popular in Asian countries but is less familiar in the United States.

How to Cook Basic White Rice

1. Select a broad, shallow saucepan; deep skillet; or sauté pan with a snug-fitting lid.

2. Heat water to boiling. To get soft, tender rice, use 2 cups water per 1 cup rice. To get dry, separate grains, use 1³/4 cups water per 1 cup rice.

3. Add salt and rice; stir once.

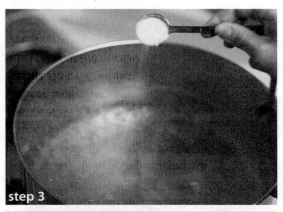

step 3

step 4

4. Return to boiling; stir once.

5. Cover and reduce heat to low.

6. Cook for 15 minutes or until all the water is absorbed. Do not lift the lid or stir.

7. Remove lid carefully. (Try not to let the condensation on the underside of the lid drip into the rice.)

8. Fluff with a fork, stir, and remove from pan.

> **One cup uncooked** rice will yield about 3 cups cooked rice. A general rule of thumb is to use 2 cups of water per 1 cup of uncooked rice.

Do not lift the lid or stir while the rice is cooking. Think: "Rice is cooking. Do not disturb." Lifting the lid allows steam to escape, and stirring the rice will release more starch, causing the grains to stick together in lumps.

Arborio This popular Italian rice is used to make risotto. Each medium-length grain has a white "eye" that remains firm to the bite, while the rest of the grain softens and lends creaminess. Once grown exclusively in Italy, Arborio is now grown in California and Texas. Other Italian rices used to make risotto are *carnaroli* and *vialone nano*.

Basmati Sometimes called "popcorn rice," this long-grain variety is highly regarded for its fragrance, taste, and slender shape. True basmati is grown in India and Pakistan, but many hybrids are grown elsewhere, including the United States. Texmati, for example, is grown in Texas.

Black Both medium- and short-grain, this rice is grown mostly in Southeast Asia and in limited quantities in California. It gets its color from the black bran that surrounds the endosperm, or kernel. When cooked, the rice might turn purple or lavender—the bran dyes the white kernel inside. Look for Black Japonica or Forbidden Rice.

Brown This is rice that has been hulled with the bran intact. The bran lends chewy texture and nutty flavor and contains vitamins, minerals, and fiber. It requires a longer cooking time because the bran is a barrier to water.

Glutinous This word describes sticky rice. The term is confusing, however, because rice does not contain gluten, a protein found in wheat.

Instant Rice Also called precooked, this rice has been partially or completely cooked and dried; it takes only a few minutes to prepare.

Jasmine Thailand's favorite, this aromatic rice has more amylopectin, or sticky starch, than other long-grain rice, so it's moist and tender. It's grown in Asia and the United States.

Parboiled Steam-pressure treatment before milling produces this firm tan grain that stays separate when cooked. Do not confuse it with instant rice—parboiled rice takes longer to cook. Look for Uncle Ben's version, called Converted Rice. (Boil-in-bag rice is another example of parboiled rice.)

Red This aromatic rice with reddish-brown bran has a nutty flavor and a chewy consistency. Look for Wehani (American grown), Bhutanese Red Rice (imported), and Camargue (imported from France's Provence region) in specialty markets. Red rice is great with hearty foods like pork or butternut squash.

Sushi This short-grain sticky rice is glassy and smooth. It grows throughout Asia and in California.

Wild The only grain native to North America, this is actually an aquatic grass. It's often sold mixed with long-grain white rice.

Risotto with Asparagus

Risotto is traditionally made with Arborio rice because of its high starch content and firm texture.

3 (14-ounce) cans fat-free, less-sodium chicken broth
1 tablespoon olive oil
½ cup finely chopped onion
1½ cups uncooked Arborio rice
2 teaspoons grated lemon rind
½ cup dry white wine
3 cups (1-inch) diagonally cut asparagus
2 ounces grated fresh Parmesan cheese
2 tablespoons fresh lemon juice
2 teaspoons fresh thyme leaves

1. Bring broth to a simmer in a large saucepan (do not boil). Keep warm over low heat.
2. Heat oil in a large skillet over medium heat. Add onion; cook 5 minutes, stirring frequently. Add rice and rind; cook 2 minutes, stirring constantly. Stir in wine; cook 3 minutes until liquid is nearly absorbed, stirring constantly. Add 3½ cups broth, ½ cup at a time, stirring until each portion of broth is absorbed before adding the next (about 20 minutes). Stir in asparagus. Add remaining broth, ½ cup at a time, stirring until each portion of broth is absorbed before adding the next (about 10 minutes). Remove from heat; stir in cheese and lemon juice. Sprinkle with thyme. Yield: 6 servings (serving size: about 1¼ cups).

CALORIES 307 (14% from fat); FAT 4.9g (sat 1.9g, mono 2.4g, poly 0.3g); PROTEIN 11.7g; CARB 51.2g; FIBER 2.7g; CHOL 6mg; IRON 1.2mg; SODIUM 532mg; CALC 154mg

---

Perk Up Rice Sides
Test Kitchen SECRET

1. When rice is done, stir in grated Parmesan cheese and dried basil.
2. Sauté garlic, add rice, and cook in chicken broth.
3. Stir chopped dried fruit into cooked rice.
4. Cook in a mixture of chicken broth and white wine.
5. Stir in toasted nuts.

Using Leftover Rice

Store cooked rice, tightly covered and refrigerated, for up to 6 days. To use leftovers, consider these simple ideas:

Rice salad: Add bottled vinaigrette to room-temperature rice. Stir in feta cheese, chopped red onion, carrot, celery, and bell pepper.

Frittata: Sauté bell pepper, onion, and garlic in olive oil until tender. Stir in cold rice, and cook until heated. Add 4 beaten eggs; cover, reduce heat, and cook until set. Sprinkle with Parmesan cheese.

Soup: Add rice and your favorite vegetables to any kind of stock.

Marinara: Reheat rice in microwave (1 cup takes about 1 minute); serve with hot marinara sauce and grated cheese.

Quinoa [KEEN-wah] is an ancient grain that is

a good alternative to rice because of its lightness. Try it for breakfast by serving it with maple syrup and milk, adding it to pancake and muffin batter, or mixing it with potatoes for croquettes. It's also good in soups and stews. The tiny beige-colored seeds, about the size of pellets of couscous, cook in about 20 minutes. The only special handling required with quinoa is to give it a good rinse before cooking; otherwise, the grains can be bitter. A good source of protein and fiber, ½ cup of quinoa has 14 grams of protein and 6 grams of fiber.

Wild Rice

Wild rice isn't rice at all—it's the seed of an annual water grass, *Zizania aquatica*, which is natural to the cold waters
of Minnesota and Canada. Wild rice serves as a perfect accent to both savory and sweet ingredients. It can mingle in a meat dish, adding an undercurrent of gaminess, or cozy up well with fruit. Paired with vegetables, it adds resonance in much the way that nuts do. Cooked, its grains retain a slight springiness (to the point of chewiness) which adds texture.

Savvy cooks know that rice and wild rice are not the same thing, and while the former is perfect as the base of many a dish, wild rice is more wisely used as a flavoring mixed with other ingredients. It's a matchless complement to brown or white rice and can turn a simple pilaf or ordinary stuffing into a gourmet treat. However you use it, remember its untamed origins—a little wild rice goes a long way, and even a modest presence can make a dramatic difference in a meal.

Wild, Wild Rice
Test Kitchen SECRET

- Wild rice certainly can live up to its free-spirited image. For a start, it sometimes takes over an hour to cook fully. The best way to tell when it's done is to notice when the grains start to split. And although sometimes you have to drain off excess water, sometimes you don't.

- Results depend on the variety you use. In most of our recipes, we call for 100 percent wild rice. The brand is not as important as the fact that it's 100 percent wild rice and not a blend. We test with a variety of brands that come in 6-ounce boxes and are available nationally. If you have wild rice blends, don't substitute them for wild rice.

Minnesota Wild Rice Pilaf

The wild rice and mushrooms give this pilaf an earthy flavor that pairs well with duck or pork.

1¼   cups water
2   (16-ounce) cans fat-free, less-sodium chicken broth
1½   cups uncooked wild rice
1   tablespoon butter
3   cups sliced mushrooms
1   cup chopped onion
½   cup finely chopped fresh parsley
⅓   cup chopped pecans, toasted
¾   teaspoon poultry seasoning
½   teaspoon salt
¼   teaspoon pepper
Cooking spray

1. Bring water and broth to a boil in a medium saucepan. Add wild rice; cover, reduce heat, and simmer 1 hour or until tender. Drain.

2. Preheat oven to 325°.

3. Melt butter in a large nonstick skillet over medium-high heat. Add mushrooms and onion; sauté 6 minutes. Remove from heat; stir in parsley and next 4 ingredients. Combine rice and mushroom mixture in a 2-quart casserole coated with cooking spray. Cover and bake at 325° for 25 minutes. Yield: 8 servings (serving size: 1 cup).

CALORIES 177 (27% from fat); FAT 5.4g (sat 1.2g, mono 2.6g, poly 1.1g); PROTEIN 6.9g; CARB 27.2g; FIBER 2.8g; CHOL 4mg; IRON 1.4mg; SODIUM 347mg; CALC 21mg

---

"Sometimes I don't have an hour to cook wild rice, so I use one of the quick-cooking wild rices."

Sam Brannock, Test Kitchens Staffer

Rye

Rolled rye

Rye is most commonly seen as flour, both light and dark. Pumpernickel bread is made from dark rye flour. Also available are whole rye berries, which are green and work nicely in salads. Rye berries are a lot like wheat berries, kamut berries, and other whole grains—chewy and neutral in flavor, they hold their shape when cooked. Like wheat berries, they can be added to breads. Rye is now often available rolled as well. Look for it in supermarkets or health-food stores. **Rolled rye cooks quickly and makes tasty breakfast cereals.**

Wheat

Wheat grain is the world's largest cereal grass crop, with thousands of varieties. The three major types of wheat are soft, hard, and durum wheat. Hard wheat is high in protein and yields a flour that is rich in gluten, so it's good for making bread. Soft wheat produces a flour that is lower in gluten, and durum wheat, although high in gluten, is usually ground into semolina, the base of pasta.

Whole wheat flour

Wheat bran

Wheat berries

Wheat Berries These berries are big, chewy, unprocessed kernels of wheat. **High in protein and fiber, they must be soaked for 8 hours, then cooked for 1 hour (they're chewy when cooked).** Once cooked, they can go into salads, soups, and mixed-grain dishes. They are best in pilafs and casseroles, and they make an excellent crouton alternative for salad toppings. They can also be kneaded into bread, providing welcome texture.

> "If you're not much of a meat eater, wheat berries provide protein as well as fiber. I like to add them to soups for a hearty, nutty flavor."
> **Krista Montgomery, Food Editor**

Wheat Bran The bran is the exterior layer of the wheat berry and is rich in fiber. It does not have much nutritional value other than the fiber. During milling, the bran can be removed from the kernel. It's often sold separately and used to add fiber to baked goods.

Cracked Wheat This is the whole wheat berry, broken into coarse, medium, and fine pieces. It's sometimes sold in health-food stores and may be cooked as a cereal, in a pilaf, or in bread.

Wheat Germ The germ of the wheat berry is a concentrated source of vitamins and minerals. A quarter-cup of wheat germ carries 130 calories, 12 grams of protein, 4 grams of fiber, and no sodium or cholesterol. It offers about a third of the daily requirement for vitamin E, one of the antioxidant nutrients. Add to this a little folic acid and a lot of trace minerals—zinc, iron, magnesium, manganese, and chromium—and you've got a powerhouse in each bite. And as for fat—it's mostly unsaturated and at the low end of the scale at 4 grams of total fat per quarter-cup.

This vitamin-rich "heart" of the wheat berry is milled out of white flour because it contains small amounts of fat that would limit shelf life.

Wheat Flour

Flour is the finely ground and sifted meal of any type of grain, with wheat being the most common source for flour. In addition to wheat flours, there are potato, rice, and soy flours, to name a few.

Some commonly used wheat flours include all-purpose, whole wheat, self-rising, cake and pastry flours, and unbleached.

See Chapter 3, Baking Basics, page 93 for more information on using flour in recipes.

Bulgur This grain is familiar to many of us through the Middle Eastern dishes tabbouleh and kibbeh. Bulgur is wheat berries that have been steamed, dried, and then cracked. Because bulgur is essentially precooked, it is quick to prepare. It comes in three types of grinds—coarse, medium, and fine. Fine and medium bulgurs are used for dishes like tabbouleh, and coarse bulgur is good in pilafs. **Bulgur, especially fine bulgur, needs only to be soaked to become tender, but it can also be cooked pilaf-style.** You can find bulgur at most supermarkets or in Middle Eastern markets and natural-foods stores.

Best Uses for Bulgur

Test Kitchen
SECRET

Here are our suggestions for using the different grinds of bulgur in a variety of recipes.

Coarse-grind is good for low-fat stuffings, casseroles, and vegetarian tacos, and it can also be used in pilafs, soups, salads, and artisan breads.

Medium-grind is an all-purpose size used in salads, stews, soups, multi-grain bakery goods, and especially in meatless burgers and chili.

Fine-grind makes a nutritious breakfast cereal and is perfect for breads and even desserts. Fine and medium grinds are both used in tabbouleh salads, pilafs, and in any recipe as a substitute for rice.

Coarse-grind bulgur   Medium-grind bulgur   Fine-grind bulgur

Ancient Grains

Some of the trendiest grains are actually some of the oldest. The more we learn about these ancient grains, the more reasons we can think of to eat them.

Amaranth [AM-ah-ranth] was a principle food of the Aztecs. This high-protein grain has a slightly peppery, molasses-like flavor with a faint nuttiness. The grains (or seeds) are tiny, shiny, and can be yellow and black. They're so small that they seem almost lost when served alone as a side dish. *But amaranth is good as a thickener in soups because, when cooked, it has a slightly gummy texture, like okra.*

Amaranth grains

Amaranth flour

Grano [gra-NO] is unfamiliar to most Americans, since it's a new product in the United States. Grano (Italian for "grain") is essentially polished durum wheat (a variety of wheat used to make pasta) and is reminiscent of barley. It has a golden hue and an appealing chewiness when cooked. Because the bran has been removed, the starch is more accessible, which means you can cook grano as you would Arborio rice for risotto. Or you can simmer it without stirring, which leaves the grains intact. It provides a nice combination of texture and neutral flavor. *Use grano in soups, stews, salads, and other dishes in which you might use a small pasta such as orzo.* Grano has yet to appear on supermarket shelves, but it is available at www.sunnylandmills.com

Grano

Kamut berries   Kamut flour   Whole-grain spelt

Kamut [kah-MOOT] is a primitive high-protein variety of wheat and takes its name from the ancient Egyptian word for wheat. Kamut berries are similar in flavor and texture to wheat berries, although kamut is twice as big. *Substitute kamut for wheat berries; buy kamut flour to use in place of or alongside wheat flour.*

Spelt is another primitive form of wheat that is similar to kamut. It has become quite fashionable among restaurant chefs. *Both kamut and spelt contain a more digestible form of gluten than that found in wheat, so people with an intolerance to wheat are often able to eat these grains.*

All About Pasta

Pasta is one of the most versatile and popular types of grain products, and it's one we use frequently in our Test Kitchens in all types of dishes.

The term "pasta" is used as a general term to describe a wide variety of noodles made from a dough of durum wheat flour and liquid. There are many types of pasta; most are made from wheat flour, but there are also pastas made from rice or soy flours.

Choosing Pasta We think there's actually very little practical cooking difference among the brands of pasta available at the supermarket. Once they're incorporated into a recipe, they all taste about the same, so **we don't recommend paying more for a fancy name, domestic or imported. In fact, some independent studies have shown that many people find American-made pasta just as good as Italian.**

What about dried versus fresh? It's pretty much up to you. **In our recipes, we use mostly dried, which is basically a mixture of semolina flour—ground from durum wheat—and water.** In commercial factories, the mix is made into a paste that is turned into different shapes by passing through dies, or large metal discs filled with holes. The pasta is then dried and packaged.

Fresh pasta, which can be substituted in any of the recipes, is perishable, so it's generally pricier than dried. It also takes almost no time to cook—2 to 3 minutes on average.

Pastas are interchangeable if you use a variety that is similar to the shape and size specified in the recipe.

Long thin noodles: fettuccine, linguine, spaghetti, spaghettini, vermicelli

Twisted and curve-shaped pasta: cavatappi, elbow macaroni, farfalle, fusilli, orecchiette, radiatore, rotelle, seashell macaroni

Tubular-shaped pasta: mostaccioli, penne, rigatoni, ziti

Small tubular or rice-shaped pasta: orzo, tubetti

Putting Pasta in the Pot

Cooking pasta itself is fairly simple, and most packages give directions. Here are some additional recommendations from our staff.

- Use a large pot that's as full of water as possible. For 8 ounces of dried pasta, you'll want to fill a 4-quart pot.
- Cover pot, and bring water to a full rolling boil over high heat before adding pasta. (There's no need to add oil to prevent the pasta from sticking—just keep the water at a rolling boil.)
- Add pasta, and stir with a pasta fork. Start timing cooking when water returns to a rolling boil. If you use fresh pasta, remember that it cooks more quickly than dried.
- Always cook uncovered over high heat.
- Start testing for doneness a few minutes before indicated cooking time. Pasta that offers resistance to the bite but has no trace of brittleness is *al dente,* and this is how you want it. If an undercooked piece of pasta is cut in half, a white dot or line is clearly visible in the center. Al dente pasta has only a speck of white remaining, meaning the pasta has absorbed just enough water to hydrate it.
- Set a large colander in the sink so water drains quickly. Do not rinse.
- Return pasta to the warm cooking pot or add to the skillet with sauce; toss immediately with large tongs or a pasta fork.

How to Sauce Pasta Long strands are most compatible with smoother sauces that coat them all over. Short shapes work well with chunky sauces that can be caught in the nooks and crannies. It's important to balance the amount of sauce and the way it's combined with the pasta. **Think of sauce as a seasoning or dressing that is tossed with the pasta, much like a salad and dressing, until each piece of pasta is moistened.** Plain pasta is bland. The idea is to impart well-flavored seasoning to each bite of the finished dish.

Salting Pasta

We agree with most cooks that adding salt to the cooking water helps bring out the flavor of the pasta. While we didn't find that salted water changed the pasta's consistency (as some folks assert), it certainly makes the pasta taste better on its own. But when tossing the pasta with flavorful sauces, salting the water is far less critical. So to avoid adding unnecessary sodium, we choose not to salt the water in our recipes, and our nutritional analyses reflect that.

For more information on pasta sauces, see "Cooking Basics," pages 44-49.

Pasta can be tricky to serve because it has a

tendency to slip and slide. The best serving utensil, especially for longer pasta, is a metal or wooden pasta fork or tongs. For short pasta, a large spoon works fine.

Amounts of Dry and Cooked Pasta

Use this guide to help you determine either how much pasta you'll need or how much you'll get. Approximate cooking times are also included.

Type	Dry Weight (8 ounces)	Cooked Volume	Cooking Time
Acini de pepe	1¼ cups	3 cups	5 minutes
Alphabets	2 cups	4 cups	5 minutes
Capellini or angel hair		3½ cups	5 minutes
Cavatappi	3 cups	5 cups	8 minutes
Conchiglie rigate	3 cups	4 cups	14 minutes
Egg noodles, medium	4 cups	5 cups	5 minutes
Egg noodles, wide	4½ cups	5 cups	5 minutes
Elbow macaroni	2 cups	4 cups	5 minutes
Farfalle (bow tie pasta)	3 cups	4 cups	11 minutes
Fettuccine		4 cups	10 minutes
Fusilli (short twisted spaghetti)	3 cups	4 cups	10 minutes
Gemelli	2 cups	4 cups	10 minutes
Linguine		4 cups	10 minutes
Orecchiette ("little ears" pasta)	2½ cups	4 cups	11 minutes
Orzo (rice-shaped pasta)	1¼ cups	2½ cups	6 minutes
Penne or mostaccioli (tube-shaped pasta)	2 cups	4 cups	10 minutes
Penne rigate	2 cups	4 cups	10 minutes
Perciatelli		4 cups	11 minutes
Radiatore (short coiled pasta)	3 cups	4½ cups	10 minutes
Rigatoni	2½ cups	4 cups	10 minutes
Rotini (corkscrew pasta)	4 cups	4 cups	10 minutes
Small seashell pasta	2 cups	4 cups	8 minutes
Spaghetti		3½ cups	10 minutes
Vermicelli		4 cups	5 minutes
Ziti (short tube-shaped pasta)	3 cups	4 cups	10 minutes

"We don't recommend paying more for pasta with a fancy name, domestic or imported."

Mike Wilson, Test Kitchens Staffer

Farfalle Carbonara

This dish needs to go straight from the stove to the table—after sitting for just a few minutes, it loses its creaminess. If it's a little thick when it's done, add some low-fat milk to thin it out.

     2   tablespoons water
     2   garlic cloves, minced
     4   quarts water
     3   cups uncooked farfalle (about 8 ounces bow tie pasta) or other short pasta
     2   large eggs, lightly beaten
     ½   cup (2 ounces) grated fresh pecorino Romano cheese or Parmesan cheese
     4   bacon slices, cooked and crumbled

1. Heat a large nonstick skillet over medium heat. Add 2 tablespoons water and garlic; remove from heat.

2. Bring 4 quarts water to a boil in a large stockpot. Add farfalle; return to a boil. Cook, uncovered, 10 minutes or until al dente, stirring occasionally. Remove ½ cup pasta cooking water, and whisk into the eggs, stirring vigorously. Drain farfalle; add to garlic mixture in skillet. Stir well. Add egg mixture to farfalle.

Cook mixture over medium-low heat until thick (about 4 minutes), stirring constantly. Remove from heat; stir in cheese and bacon. Serve immediately. Yield: 4 servings (serving size: 1 cup).

CALORIES 348 (28% from fat); FAT 10.8g (sat 4.3g, mono 3.8g, poly 1.2g); PROTEIN 17g; CARB 43.6g; FIBER 1.4g; CHOL 123mg; IRON 2.8mg; SODIUM 333mg; CALC 167mg

Spaghetti Aglio e Olio

In Italian, *aglio e olio* (AH-lyoh ay OH-lyoh) means "garlic and oil." Typically, the garlic is fried in olive oil on the stovetop, but we've cooked it with olive oil in the microwave, which is easier and omits the risk of burning the garlic. You can add some crushed red pepper flakes for a spicier version.

     2   tablespoons extra-virgin olive oil
     ¼   teaspoon dried oregano
     4   large garlic cloves, minced
     4   quarts water
     8   ounces uncooked spaghetti
     ½   cup fat-free, less-sodium chicken broth
     2   tablespoons minced fresh parsley

1. Combine olive oil, oregano, and minced garlic in a small microwave-safe bowl. Cover bowl with wax paper, and microwave at HIGH 1 minute.

2. Bring water to a boil in a large stockpot. Add spaghetti; return to a boil. Cook, uncovered, 10 minutes or until al dente, stirring occasionally. Drain. Return to pot. Stir in the garlic mixture and broth. Cook over medium heat 4 minutes or until broth is absorbed, stirring constantly. Stir in parsley. Yield: 4 servings (serving size: 1 cup).

CALORIES 278 (25% from fat); FAT 7.7g (sat 1.0g, mono 5.1g, poly 1.0g); PROTEIN 7.9g; CARB 43.7g; FIBER 1.5g; CHOL 0mg; IRON 2.4mg; SODIUM 66mg; CALC 20mg

---

Pasta Carbonara

Test Kitchen SECRET

In classic carbonara, the heat of the pasta actually cooks the eggs. But for safety's sake, we cook the eggs on top of the stove. Once the egg mixture is added to the pasta and cooked over low heat, it's important to stir the mixture constantly. This ensures that the eggs get creamy instead of scrambled.

The garlic procedure here may strike you as unorthodox, but we think it works very well. When you combine the water and garlic in a hot skillet, it softens the garlic and infuses the garlic flavor in the pan.

Couscous

Regarded by many as a grain, couscous is actually a pasta made from semolina (durum wheat) flour and salted water. In Tunisia, Algeria, and Morocco, where it is a national favorite, couscous ranges in size from fine- to medium-grained; Israeli couscous, recently discovered by American gourmands, is larger. Whatever the configuration, its earthy flavor is famously friendly to seasonings and other ingredients. We've discovered that not only is couscous a terrific side dish, but it also makes a fabulous entrée—and a great salad.

The couscous we use most often in the Test Kitchens is the Near East brand, which is available nationwide. It comes in a 10-ounce box and is on the grocery shelves near the rice and pasta. One 10-ounce box will yield about 4½ cups of cooked couscous.

No-Cook Couscous
Test Kitchen SECRET

Instead of leaving the couscous to stand in boiling water, you can simply add that same amount of water to the couscous, then cover and chill overnight until all of the water is absorbed.

When you prepare the couscous this way, it's fluffier and doesn't stick together, so it's great to use in a salad.

Picnic Couscous Salad

This piquant, lemony salad is good for a side dish or a light one-dish meal.

1¼	cups fat-free, less-sodium chicken broth or water
1	cup uncooked couscous
1	teaspoon grated lemon rind
2	tablespoons fresh lemon juice
1	tablespoon olive oil
¾	teaspoon Dijon mustard
1	cup quartered cherry tomatoes
½	cup chopped pimento-stuffed olives
¼	cup chopped red onion
¼	cup chopped fresh parsley
¼	teaspoon salt
¼	teaspoon freshly ground black pepper
1	(15.8-ounce) can Great Northern beans, rinsed and drained

1. Bring broth to a boil in a medium saucepan; gradually stir in couscous. Remove pan from heat; cover and let stand 5 minutes. Fluff with a fork; cool.

2. Combine lemon rind, juice, oil, and mustard in a large bowl; stir well with a whisk. Add couscous, tomatoes, and remaining ingredients; toss well. Yield: 5 servings (serving size: 1 cup).

CALORIES 236 (19% from fat); FAT 4.9g (sat 0.7g, mono 2.8g, poly 0.5g); PROTEIN 10.4g; CARB 40.7g; FIBER 5.4g; CHOL 1mg; IRON 4.1mg; SODIUM 449mg; CALC 85mg

---

"Couscous is low in fat and simple to make. The directions simply read: Pour the amount desired into a pot of boiling water; turn off the heat, cover, and let stand 5 minutes." Kathryn Conrad, Test Kitchens Staffer

Asian Noodles

The range of Asian noodles is extraordinary. But don't worry—it's not necessary to be familiar with every type on the market, just the main varieties. Although most supermarkets stock several kinds of these noodles, a wider selection is available at Asian markets.

> **Because they're made with substantial ingredients** such as buckwheat flour and rice, Asian noodles can handle strong flavors such as soy sauce, cilantro, and ginger. Available in varying textures, shapes, and sizes, they can, like any noodle, be served hot, at room temperature, or cold.

Cellophane noodles Also called bean threads, these translucent dried noodles are made from the starch of mung beans, potatoes, or green peas. **When softened in warm water, cellophane noodles absorb the flavors of the foods they are cooked with and become slippery.** Serve them in soups, stews, stir-fries, and salads. These noodles are commonly deep-fried in hot oil to create crisp noodle nests.

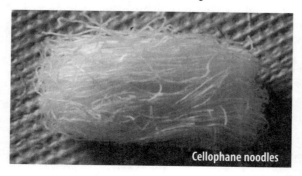

Cellophane noodles

"Asian noodles are a fast, healthy, economical, and tasty alternative to pasta."

Kellie Kelley, Food Stylist

Chinese egg noodles Chinese egg noodles are usually made from a dough of wheat flour, eggs, and salt. If they don't contain eggs, they may be labeled "imitation" or "egg-flavored." Egg noodles are primarily used in stir-fried and pan-fried dishes and soups. **In most recipes, you can substitute angel hair pasta or vermicelli for Chinese noodles.**

Chinese egg noodles

Chinese egg noodles

Chinese wheat-flour noodles These noodles are made with flour and water. Many stores offer a wide variety of "flavored" noodles (shrimp, crab, and chicken), and they may be round or flat. Generally, wheat-flour noodles are used in soups and in some stir-fry dishes. **As with egg noodles, any Italian pasta that has a similar thickness and shape can be substituted.**

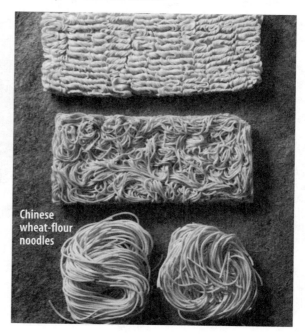

Chinese wheat-flour noodles

"Asian noodles are an extremely versatile component of soups, salads, and stir-fries. Because they're made with substantial ingredients, they can handle strong flavors." Kathleen Kanen, Food Stylist

Moo Shu Wrappers These are also called lumpia wrappers or spring roll skins. Lumpia wrappers are often deep-fried. In our recipes, we microwave them. They are usually sold frozen. **In some recipes calling for steamed wrappers, tortilla wrappers may be substituted.**

Moo shu wrappers

Rice Sticks The most popular of all Asian noodles, rice sticks are made from rice flour and water. **Although any type of rice-flour noodle may be called rice sticks, we use this term for flat rice noodles,** which are sold mainly in three forms. Thin flat rice noodles are used mainly in soups and in some stir-fried dishes.

Rice sticks

Medium-thick rice sticks (called *pho* in Vietnamese) are all-purpose and may be used in soups, stir-fries, and salads (a slightly wider Thai version is called *jantaboon*). The widest rice sticks (*sha he fen* in Chinese) are used in meat, seafood, and vegetable stir-fries. **Vermicelli can be substituted for rice sticks.**

Soba Soba noodles from Japan are made with a combination of buckwheat flour, wheat flour, and water. **This is one of the few Asian noodles for which there is no suitable substitute.**

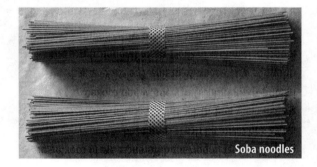
Soba noodles

Somen The most delicate of noodles, these are made with wheat flour, a dash of oil, and water. Somen are served cold with a dipping sauce or hot in soups. **The closest substitution would be a very fine pasta, such as capellini or vermicelli.**

Somen noodles

CHAPTER 8

Vegetables

Here's our guide to the "go-to vegetables"—the ones we use over and over because of their great taste as well as their health benefits.

We're partial to fresh, in-season veggies, since that's when they're at their best in terms of flavor, texture, and appearance. And because just knowing about vegetables is not as much fun as eating them, we've provided a few recipes so that you can share the pleasure of the harvest.

To make our guide more useful, we've listed the vegetables alphabetically, grouping similar vegetables together in their families. The recipes appear along with the information about that particular vegetable.

Keeping the Nutrients	Test Kitchen SECRET

To keep vitamins and minerals as intact as possible, cut vegetables just before cooking, and keep the pieces reasonably large (small pieces expose more surface area and therefore increase nutrient loss). Boiling saps nutrients the most, followed by steaming and microwaving. If you use the liquid that vegetables are cooked in and don't overcook, you retain the nutrients.

Ask the *Cooking Light* Cooks

Do I need to buy organic produce?

It's largely a matter of personal choice. For produce, there's no scientific evidence to show that organic farming is better than conventional in terms of what it does to the food itself. Organic produce is currently more expensive due to extra care and handling, so if you can afford it and think organic is a better choice, then that's what you should buy.

But it's not always possible to make that choice, since only a small percentage of the farming in this country is organic. And conventional farming is not all about pesticide-packing bad guys who are out to destroy the environment. In fact, on many farms today, conventional practices are growing closer in style to organic methods.

For us, selecting foods comes down to freshness, flavor, and, to a lesser degree, cost. With those factors to guide us, we feel comfortable selecting both conventional and organic products.

"We can't think of anything healthier than eating fresh-from-the-garden veggies. Ten minutes from garden to table? It just doesn't get any better than that." *Cooking Light* Food Editors

Asparagus

When selecting asparagus, reach for green instead of white: The green variety is higher in vitamins A and C and in folate. **Choose asparagus spears with tight, compact tips and a similar diameter so they'll all cook at the same rate.**

As for cooking asparagus, the secret is simple: Don't overcook it. The slender shoots should turn out crisp and bright in color. And while you might want to snip the woody ends of the shoots before cooking, there's no reason to toss them away. You can make a fantastic asparagus soup out of those ends.

Sesame-Roasted Asparagus

Roasting is one of the simplest (and one of the best) ways to cook asparagus. Because the flavor of fresh asparagus is so good, all you need to add is a little oil and pepper.

36	asparagus spears (about 1 pound)
1½	teaspoons dark sesame oil
1	teaspoon low-sodium soy sauce
⅛	teaspoon pepper

1. Preheat oven to 450°.
2. Snap off tough ends of asparagus spears. Combine asparagus and remaining ingredients in a jelly-roll pan, turning asparagus to coat.
3. Bake at 450° for 10 minutes or until the asparagus is crisp-tender, turning once. Yield: 4 servings (serving size: 9 asparagus spears).

CALORIES 43 (44% from fat); FAT 2.1g (sat 0.3g, mono 0.7g, poly 0.9g); PROTEIN 3g; CARB 4.9g; FIBER 1.2g; CHOL 0mg; IRON 0.9mg; SODIUM 53mg; CALC 23mg

Broccoli

It's available year-round, but the peak season for buying broccoli is October through April. Look for broccoli with a deep green color, or green with purple. The buds should be tightly closed and the leaves crisp. The florets have more vitamin C than the stalks; florets that are bluish green or purplish green have more vitamin C than their paler counterparts.

Roasted Lemon-Garlic Broccoli

If you've bought a stalk of broccoli to cut up for florets, don't throw away the leaves or the stalks. Chop them up to use in salads or stir-fries.

6	cups broccoli florets
1	teaspoon grated lemon rind
2	teaspoons olive oil
¼	teaspoon salt
⅛	teaspoon pepper
2	garlic cloves, thinly sliced

Cooking spray

1. Preheat oven to 425°.
2. Combine broccoli and next 5 ingredients on a jelly-roll pan coated with cooking spray. Bake at 425° for 15 minutes or until crisp-tender and lightly browned, stirring occasionally. Yield: 4 servings (serving size: 1½ cups).

CALORIES 53 (46% from fat); FAT 2.7g (sat 0.4g, mono 1.8g, poly 0.4g); PROTEIN 3.3g; CARB 6.2g; FIBER 3.2g; CHOL 0mg; IRON 1mg; SODIUM 177mg; CALC 55mg

---

Limp Broccoli

Test Kitchen SECRET

To revive limp broccoli, trim ½ inch from the base of the stalk, and set the head in a glass of cold water in the refrigerator overnight.

Brussels Sprouts

Brussels sprouts look like tiny cabbages and are, in fact, members of the cabbage family. They're at their peak in the late fall and early winter. In the fall, you're more likely to find Brussels sprouts  on the stalk, which is usually a sign of freshness and better flavor. And there's really no flavor difference between the small and large sprouts. Store them in the refrigerator in a paper bag for up to 3 days; if they're refrigerated longer, they'll develop a strong flavor.

Before you cook Brussels sprouts, remove any brown parts on the bottom of the sprouts. If you have small sprouts, you can cook them whole; **if they're much larger than a half-inch wide, it's best to cut them in half or into quarters so they'll cook more quickly.**

Getting the Best Flavor   Test Kitchen SECRET

Brussels sprouts' reputation of tasting too strong may be undeserved. They might taste too strong because they've been overcooked. When they're overcooked, they end up soggy and quite odoriferous. Although they'll still have a distinct flavor, they're at their best when they are either lightly cooked (5 to 10 minutes) or cooked with a savory or smoky ingredient such as bacon, which balances their flavor. Another way to enhance the flavor of Brussels sprouts is roasting, which brings out their natural sugars.

Cabbage

One cup of cooked cabbage contains half the recommended daily amount of vitamin C, less than a gram of fat, and 3.4 grams of fiber. It packs calcium, iron, and folic acid as well. And cabbage is in a family of vegetables (along with broccoli, Brussels sprouts, and cauliflower) containing phytochemicals that have been shown to reduce the risk of certain types of cancer. Cabbage is budget friendly and can be stored in the refrigerator for up to 3 months because of its tightly wrapped leaves that lock out oxygen.

Preparing Cabbage   Start by removing and discarding the tough outer leaves. Unlike its loose-leafed cousins mustard and kale, cabbage is very compact, so it doesn't pick up grit from the garden. A quick rinse is sufficient.

Cooking Cabbage   Boiled, cabbage disintegrates and releases smelly chemicals called sulfides. **Steam, stir-fry, or braise cabbage briefly—just long enough to release its sweet flavor yet leave some bite.**

Leafy Distinctions

Green: This is the most common form of cabbage. The waxy outer leaves are dark green, and the inner leaves vary from white to pale green.

Napa: Sometimes you'll see rounded shapes, but napa cabbage is usually elongated and similar in appearance to romaine lettuce. It is thin, delicate, and has a mild flavor.

Red: Other than its ruby red to purple color, this cabbage is very similar to green cabbage.

Savoy: The crinkled leaves of this cabbage are mild. It's a good choice for salads and one of the best cabbages for cooking.

Corn

Although we generally think of corn as a vegetable, it's actually a grain. (See page 253 for  information on cornmeal.) Sweet corn is available fresh, frozen, and canned, and there's a significant difference between freshly picked sweet corn and corn that has been stored, even for a few days. Fortunately, farmers' markets and roadside stands provide garden-fresh corn that's only hours old and is at its peak.

Sweet corns are classified by the percentage of sugar in their kernels. "Sweet" has 5 to 10 percent and "Supersweet" has 25 to 30 percent. The sugar in an ear of corn normally begins to convert to starch the moment it's picked. That accounts for the "rule" to have your water boiling on the stove before the corn is picked in the field. But today, many supersweet varieties are being bred to delay conversion of sugar to starch for 2 weeks or longer.

Kernels of Truth

Selection: For the freshest corn possible, look for ears tightly wrapped in bright green husks that have pale silks with dry brown tips. The cut end should be moist. If the ears feel warm, they are probably no longer fresh: The conversion of sugar to starch generates heat. Peel back the tops of the husks, and use your thumbnail to pierce a kernel; a fresh ear of corn will squirt slightly clouded juice.

Storage: Keep fresh corn as cool as possible. Buy it in the morning, before the sun can damage it. Make the trip home quickly, and store it in the refrigerator.

Cooking Corn
Test Kitchen SECRET

In addition to grilling, here are some tips on getting great flavor from fresh corn in a variety of ways.

Roasting If you don't want to grill corn, you can get that same caramelized taste by roasting an ear, husks removed, directly over the flame of a gas stove. Hold the ear with a pair of tongs, and turn it so that it scorches slightly on all sides, about 3 to 4 minutes. Roasting corn in a hot oven (450° to 500°) works better than most oven broilers. If you roast the ears in their husks, it takes about 6 to 8 minutes to get the corn thoroughly hot.

Boiling Salt toughens the skins of the kernels, so don't salt the water you boil for corn. With supersweets, the briefer the dip into boiling water, the better. Fresh corn needs minimal cooking; the corn experts don't dip a corn ear for more than 30 seconds. Place husked ears in a pot of cold water, then bring the water to a boil over high heat. Once the water boils, remove from heat, and let stand 1 minute before serving.

Steaming If you prefer to use a steamer to avoid immersing the ears in water, don't steam too long. The length of time depends on how many ears and the size of the steamer, but it may take as much as 5 to 10 minutes for the ears to heat through.

Microwaving Microwave ovens do well with corn if you are cooking only one or two ears. Cook them with the husks on and at the highest setting.

Cooking with the Husks The husks not only increase the flavor, they steam the corn. They also retain heat so that your ears will stay warmer once they've cooked. Remove all but the inner layer of husks, snip off the silk tassel with scissors, and cook until you can see the silhouette of the kernels through the husk and the husk begins to pull away from the lip of the ear.

Creamed Corn with Bacon and Leeks

Scraping cut ears of corn releases the remaining starchy milk, giving the creamed corn its thick consistency.

6	ears fresh corn
2	cups 1% low-fat milk
1	tablespoon cornstarch
1	teaspoon sugar
½	teaspoon salt
¼	teaspoon freshly ground black pepper
4	slices bacon
1	cup chopped leek

1. Cut kernels from ears to measure 3 cups. Using the dull side of a knife blade, scrape milk and pulp from cobs into a bowl. Place 1½ cups kernels, low-fat milk, cornstarch, sugar, salt, and pepper in a food processor; process until smooth.
2. Cook bacon in a large skillet over medium heat until crisp. Remove bacon from pan, reserving 1 teaspoon drippings in pan; crumble bacon. Add leek to pan; cook 2 minutes, stirring constantly. Add pureed corn mixture, 1½ cups corn kernels, and corn milk mixture to pan. Bring to a boil, reduce heat, and simmer 3 minutes or until slightly thick. Stir in crumbled bacon just before serving. Yield: 6 servings (serving size: ⅔ cup).

CALORIES 151 (27% from fat); FAT 4.6g (sat 1.7g, mono 1.9g, poly 0.8g); PROTEIN 7g; CARB 23.1g; FIBER 2.4g; CHOL 9mg; IRON 0.8mg; SODIUM 325mg; CALC 111mg

How to Cut Corn Off the Cob

Peel and discard silks and husks. Stand corn cob on end, and cut kernels off the cob using a sawing motion.

Best Way to Grill Corn

Test Kitchen SECRET

We've experimented a lot to find the best and easiest ways to get a grilled taste without overcooking the corn. We don't like to soak the husks first in cold water as many do because that steams the corn on the grill. We prefer to either grill the corn in the husks without soaking so that the husks char a bit on the outside and transmit some of that flavor to the kernels, or to husk it and grill the nude ears directly over the heat.

Cajun-Grilled Corn on the Cob

Remove the husks, and place the ears directly on the grill rack. This caramelizes the sugar in the corn and gives it a wonderful color and flavor.

1	teaspoon dried oregano
1	teaspoon paprika
¾	teaspoon garlic powder
¾	teaspoon onion powder
½	teaspoon salt
¼	teaspoon dried thyme
¼	teaspoon black pepper
⅛	teaspoon ground red pepper
4	ears corn with husks
2	teaspoons butter, melted

1. Prepare grill.
2. Combine first 8 ingredients in a small bowl; set aside.
3. Pull husks back from corn, and scrub silks. Brush butter over corn; sprinkle with spice mixture. Place corn on grill rack; grill 12 minutes or until done, turning occasionally. Yield: 4 servings (serving size: 1 ear of corn).

CALORIES 105 (26% from fat); FAT 3g (sat 1.4g, mono 0.9g, poly 0.6g); PROTEIN 2.7g; CARB 20.3g; FIBER 3.1g; CHOL 5mg; IRON 0.9mg; SODIUM 326mg; CALC 13mg

Cucumbers

Generally, the smaller the cucumber, the smaller the seeds and the better the flavor. Because they have a thin skin, cucumbers don't require peeling unless

they're waxed or if peeling is specified in the recipe. The smaller varieties are usually used for making pickles. English cucumbers may be as large as 2 feet long and are seedless.

Storing Keep cucumbers away from apples and citrus fruits because these produce ethylene gas that can decay cucumbers. **Store unwashed cucumbers unwrapped in the crisper bin of the refrigerator.**

Seedless Cucumbers
Test Kitchen SECRET

- English, or seedless, cucumbers are usually twice the size of regular cucumbers and contain not only fewer seeds but also less water. They're also usually more expensive and milder than regular cucumbers.
- For most of our recipes, we use regular cucumbers, seeding them if necessary.
- It's not really that much trouble to seed cucumbers. Cut the cucumber in half lengthwise, and scrape the seeds out with a spoon.

Eggplant

This vegetable is actually a member of the nightshade family of fruits, which also includes peppers, potatoes, and tomatoes. Eggplants come in

an assortment of colors, sizes, and shapes, and they have virtually no fat. An eggplant is mostly water, with only 13 calories per ½ cup.

With its colorful, tough skin and meaty, spongy flesh, it's more versatile than it seems—it can be sliced, grilled, mashed, pureed, or sautéed. It stands up well to garlic and complements sesame and soy; it mixes well with meats, cheese, and all sorts of vegetables.

Look for eggplants that have smooth, shiny skin and are firm but slightly springy. Store them in a cool place, and use them within 2 days.

The eggplant season ranges from summer to early fall; it can be bitter out of season. **A fresh eggplant has a sparkling jewel-like complexion with shiny, smooth, tight skin, and a bright green stem.** No matter the size, it should feel heavy in your hand (this indicates fully developed flesh and small, undeveloped seeds). Spongy, dull-skinned eggplants are old and can be riddled with large acrid seeds.

Extremely versatile, eggplants respond to a variety of cooking methods. Braise or stew the garden variety, since, like tofu, it's bland and easily takes on other more assertive flavors. Dry heat, such as grilling and broiling, concentrates flavor and transforms the texture to a creamy consistency. Long, thin Japanese eggplants are best suited for broiling or pan-frying because their dry, firm flesh is excellent for high-heat cooking. Baby eggplants are suited for roasting and make a charming presentation for individual portions.

Caponata with Garlic Crostini

The skin of an eggplant is edible, so you don't need to peel it unless specified in the recipe.

Caponata:

1	tablespoon olive oil
4	cups diced eggplant (about 1 pound)
1	cup coarsely chopped Vidalia or other sweet onion
½	cup diced red bell pepper
½	cup diced yellow bell pepper
1	garlic clove, minced
1	tablespoon brown sugar
2	tablespoons fresh lemon juice
½	teaspoon salt
¼	cup golden raisins
2	tablespoons capers, drained
1	tablespoon pine nuts, toasted
2	tablespoons chopped fresh basil

Crostini:

24	(½-inch-thick) slices diagonally cut French bread baguette (about 10 ounces)
1	garlic clove, halved

Olive oil-flavored cooking spray

1. To prepare caponata, heat oil in a large non-stick skillet over medium-high heat. Add eggplant and next 4 ingredients; sauté 5 minutes. Stir in sugar, lemon juice, and salt; cook 1 minute. Stir in raisins, capers, and pine nuts. Place mixture in a large bowl; stir in basil.
2. Preheat oven to 375°.
3. To prepare crostini, place bread slices on a baking sheet. Bake at 375° for 7 minutes. Rub cut sides of garlic clove over 1 side of each bread slice. Coat bread slices with cooking spray; bake 2 minutes. Yield: 8 servings (serving size: ⅓ cup caponata and 3 crostini).

CALORIES 174 (20% from fat); FAT 3.8g (sat 0.6g, mono 2g, poly 0.8g); PROTEIN 4.9g; CARB 31.4g; FIBER 3.2g; CHOL 0mg; IRON 1.6mg; SODIUM 552mg; CALC 44mg

---

To Salt or Not?

Test Kitchen SECRET

Salting draws excess water from eggplant, which, in turn, helps collapse the internal cell structure. This firms the flesh and prevents it from absorbing too much oil. (If you've cooked with eggplant before, you know that it acts like a sponge and can soak up large amounts of oil.) By drawing out liquid, salting decreases bitterness, since the liquid contains the bitter substances. If your eggplant is fresh and in season, there's no need to salt. If it's out of season, salting certainly can't hurt. Follow these steps for salting eggplant:

- Slice eggplant into desired shape; toss with coarse salt.
- Leave in colander to drain for 30 minutes to 1 hour.
- Squeeze out or pat off the liquid; rinse well. Pat dry.

Colorful Choices

The most common eggplant is the large, dark-purple American eggplant found in supermarkets throughout the year.

Other types include the long, thin, pale purple Chinese eggplant, which has a mild flavor. The Japanese version carries the same deep color as the American but is about one-quarter the size.

A wide array is available at farmers' markets during late summer, when the season is at its peak. Whether white, purple, orange, black, or striped, the flavors do not vary greatly. White eggplant is a bit milder than other varieties; as a rule, the lighter the color, the milder the flavor.

Greens

Dark, leafy greens are often interchangeable in recipes, which adds to their appeal.

Dark green leafy vegetables are nutritional powerhouses. But it's their captivating flavors and wonderful versatility that makes greens such a joy. Some of the mild, tender greens are usually eaten raw in salads, while some of the more assertive greens need to be cooked with care to mellow their slight bitterness. Greens' nutritional performance is legendary: They're dense with vitamins A and C and contribute calcium, iron, and fiber.

Winter Greens Greens such as collards, turnip greens, and mustard greens are often called winter greens, even though they're available almost year-round. **But in deep winter, they become sweeter.** Winter greens do their serious root-building work in the fall and spend less energy cranking out natural pesticides during the cooler months that follow. Some of the unused sugars are thought to end up in the leaves, sweetening and tenderizing them.

Spring Greens In addition to having a pleasant range of flavors, from mellow to pungent, spring greens are the first shoots to come up in the garden when little else is ready to grow. Greens tolerate the cool temperatures of early spring, and they grow very fast; this means you can harvest the leaves well before planting most other vegetables. Some examples of spring greens include spinach, romaine lettuce, and Swiss chard.

Cleaning Greens Leafy greens harbor sand and other debris, so you'll need to wash them thoroughly. **Avoid using a colander for the job because just running water over the leaves isn't enough to clean them.** Instead, dunk greens in a large bowl, pot, or sink filled with cold water. The dirt will sink to the bottom while the greens float to the top. Remove leaves by hand, and place them in another bowl. Pour out the water, and repeat the procedure until the water is free of debris. Dunking and soaking greens is the only method that removes all the grit. Next, spin the greens in a salad spinner if they need to be dry for a salad or recipe. Unless your recipe specifies that the greens be dry, forgo the spinner, and cook the greens with the water that clings to them.

> Store leafy greens unwashed in plastic bags in the refrigerator; any added moisture will cause them to spoil more rapidly. When you're ready to use them, remove unwanted stems, and tear the leaves into smaller pieces.

Cooking Greens
Test Kitchen SECRET

Whether leafy greens are part of a main course or are served as a side dish, the key to bringing out their flavor lies in cooking them properly. All that's really needed is a few minutes of simmering so that the leaves become tender yet retain their bright green color.

Arugula

Also known as rocket, roquette, rugula, and rucola, this peppery, pungent leafy green is a staple of Italian fare and is often found in mesclun salad mixes, where it behaves like a cross between lettuce and herb. Spring is arugula prime time. Leaves that grow in cool weather are more tender and mellow than those suffering the heat of summer. **When you're using arugula, don't overdo it: Its flavor is bold in any season.**

Preparing Arugula	Test Kitchen
	SECRET

Most arugula from grocery stores has short, tender stems. If you buy yours in bulk or from a farmers' market, however, it may have longer, thicker stems. Trim these away by cutting them off at the base of the leaf. To measure arugula, lightly pack clean stem-free leaves in your measuring cup.

Collards

Full-bodied in flavor, collards have white-veined, wide green leaves with a leathery texture. Choose bunches with small leaves and stems that aren't too thick.

Curly Endive

This lettucelike salad green has an off-white, compact center and loose, lacy, green-rimmed outer leaves that curl at the tips. It has a prickly texture and a slightly bitter taste. Use it in salads, or stir into soups and bean dishes.

Dandelion Greens

The slender, saw-toothed leaves have a slightly bitter taste. You may find these greens more often as part of a mix of greens called mesclun (see below).

Escarole

Escarole has broad bright green leaves that grow in loose heads. It's a variety of endive but is not as bitter as Belgian endive or chicory.

Kale

The curly-edged leaves are greenish blue or grayish green, and they hold their texture well when cooked.

Mesclun

This term applies to a mixture of salad greens such as arugula, dandelion, frisée, oak leaf, radicchio, and sorrel. **It's often packaged as "gourmet salad greens" and is best eaten raw.**

Mustard Greens

These greens have a light color that's almost lime green and a pungent, mustard-like flavor. The leaves are softer and more delicately ruffled than kale. **Turnip greens can be substituted for mustard greens or collards.**

Radicchio

This bitter-flavored member of the chicory family has burgundy-red leaves with white ribs. Most often used in salads, radicchio can also be grilled or roasted. **Escarole, another member of the chicory family, is a good substitute.**

Sorrel

The sharp, sour flavor of this green is almost too strong when raw but works well in small amounts in soups and sauces. The leaves are tender and smooth, and they range from light to dark green. **Spinach is a good substitute for sorrel.**

Spinach

Spinach has dark green leaves that may be curled or smooth, depending on the variety. Choose leaves that are crisp and dark green with a fresh fragrance. **Spinach is usually very gritty and must be thoroughly washed.** Like other dark, leafy greens, spinach is abundant in beta carotene, vitamin A, potassium, and folic acid. And while we know from Popeye that spinach is high in iron, the form of iron is not as well absorbed as that found in meats.

Swiss Chard

This earthy-flavored green has crinkly green leaves and either silvery celery-like stalks or bright scarlet stalks. It's sold in bunches, with each bunch being about half stems and half leaves. **If you buy a bunch with large leaves, it will be easier to clean.** Spinach is a good substitute for Swiss chard leaves. Most recipes just call for the leaves, but you can cook the stalks as you would cook asparagus.

Watercress

This member of the mustard family has small, crisp dark green leaves with a sharp, peppery flavor. It's best eaten raw. Choose leaves with a deep green color. **A good substitute for watercress is another pungent-flavored green, such as arugula.** Or if you don't care for the sharp flavor, you can use spinach.

Legumes

We sometimes prefer lentils to beans because there is no need for presoaking; they cook in less than a half-hour, and they taste great.

Legumes are plants that have seed pods that split along both sides when ripe. Some members of the legume family that you may be familiar with are beans, lentils, peanuts, peas, and soybeans. Beans come in two broad categories: fresh and dried, although some beans, such as lima beans, can be found in both fresh and dried forms. Legumes are generally high in protein and are good sources of B-vitamins and minerals. (See pages 245-246 for information on soybeans; see page 364 for information on peanuts.)

Fresh Beans

Fresh beans are generally sold in their pods. A few of the most common types of beans are green beans (which are eaten with their pod), lima beans, and broad beans (or fava beans), which are not eaten with their pods. Store fresh beans in a tightly covered container in the refrigerator up to 5 days. Both flavor and color begin to decrease after that period.

Dried Beans

Beans are versatile, adaptable, and a great source of nonmeat protein. You can do almost anything with beans: bake, puree, sauté, simmer in a slow cooker, stew, or stir-fry. They're also incredibly cheap and in season all year long. In many recipes, dried beans are interchangeable, so you can use any bean you choose: black, kidney, navy, Northern, or pinto, just to name a few. We like the convenience of canned beans, but you can use dried if you prefer. (See below for more tips on soaking beans and substituting dried for canned.) If you are limiting the sodium in your diet, there are no-salt and low-sodium canned beans available.

Dried or Canned Beans?
Test Kitchen SECRET

If you're using dried beans, you'll have to soak them before using them so they'll get tender.

For quick-soaking, add 6 to 8 cups of water to 1 pound of dried beans, and bring to a boil in a Dutch oven. Cover and cook 2 minutes; remove from heat, and let stand 1 hour. Rinse and drain, and then cook by package directions, or add to the recipe as directed.

For overnight soaking, add 6 cups of water to 1 pound of dried beans. Let stand 8 hours at room temperature. Cook according to package directions, or add to the recipe as directed.

To substitute canned beans for dried beans:
- 1 (15-ounce) can of beans = 1 3/4 cup drained beans
- 1 pound (about 2 cups) dried beans = 5 1/2 to 6 1/2 cups cooked beans

For the best results, rinse thoroughly with tap water before using, and drain in a colander. Rinsing canned beans gets rid of the thick liquid in the can and reduces the sodium by 40 percent.

Curried Kidney Bean Burritos

We like these burritos with black beans, too.

    1   tablespoon olive oil
  1½   cups finely chopped onion
    1   tablespoon chopped jalapeño pepper
    1   teaspoon sugar
    ½   teaspoon curry powder
    2   (14.5-ounce) cans diced tomatoes, drained
    2   (15-ounce) cans kidney beans, drained
    1   tablespoon minced fresh cilantro
    4   (8-inch) flour tortillas

1. Heat oil in a nonstick skillet over medium-high heat. Add onion; sauté 6 minutes. Add jalapeño, sugar, curry, and tomatoes; cover, reduce heat, and simmer 10 minutes. Add beans; cover and cook 3 minutes or until thoroughly heated. Remove from heat; stir in cilantro.
2. Warm tortillas according to package directions. Spoon 1¼ cups bean mixture in center of each tortilla; roll up. Yield: 4 servings (serving size: 1 burrito).

CALORIES 414 (17% from fat); FAT 8g (sat 1.6g, mono 3.1g, poly 2.7g); PROTEIN 18.4g; CARB 70.3g; FIBER 9.2g; CHOL 0mg; IRON 6.4mg; SODIUM 710mg; CALC 182mg

Lentils

Lentils are legumes you can learn to love, and for good reason. They can be fashioned into all kinds of dishes, and they cook quickly—in 30 minutes or less—and don't require the planning of beans cooked from scratch. You can eat lentils in salads year-round, and they also do wonders for hearty winter dishes and can meld with a wide variety of other ingredients.

Because lentils can overcook quickly, especially the smaller ones, you should always start checking for doneness before the specified time.

Pairings for Lentils

Test Kitchen SECRET

Greens such as spinach, chard, kale, and beet greens work very well with lentils and are often found in traditional lentil recipes.

Similarly, yogurt is often used to finish lentil dishes, especially those from the Middle East. Vinegar, lemon, and mustard raise the flavor profile of the lentil, so if you find yourself thinking that your dish needs a little something, you might reach for some red wine vinegar or a spoonful of prepared mustard. As a side dish, lentils are often simmered with a mixture of diced carrots, celery, and onions.

Take Your Pick

Most grocery stores stock brown lentils, but there are many other kinds. Try any of these.

U.S. Regular or Brewer (brown lentils): This is the most common variety sold at American supermarkets. They're a bit larger than the Pardina and Red Chief.

De Puy: Sometimes called French green lentils, this tasty variety is mostly grown in Canada.

Red Chief: These colorful lentils are split in two, making them smaller and also quicker to cook. Because they are more likely than other types to turn mushy, they're best mixed in burgers, meat loaves, or soups.

Pardina: This smallest of lentils holds its shape during cooking and has an earthy, nutty flavor. They're terrific for pilafs and salads.

You can find lentils in most supermarkets and specialty food stores. For more sources, call the USA Dry Pea & Lentil Council at 208-882-3023, or visit its Web site: www.pea-lentil.com

Lentil-Vegetable Soup

This is a soup that tastes even better the next day. We think French dark green lentils make the most attractive and delicious soup, but any type of lentil will work.

1½	tablespoons olive oil
1⅓	cups finely diced onion
⅓	cup finely diced celery
⅓	cup finely diced carrot
2	bay leaves
2	tablespoons tomato paste
1	teaspoon salt
2	garlic cloves, minced
6	cups water
1	cup dried French dark green or other lentils
6	cups chopped spinach
⅓	cup chopped fresh parsley
2	teaspoons red wine vinegar
2	teaspoons Dijon mustard
¼	teaspoon pepper
¾	cup (3 ounces) shaved fresh Parmesan cheese

1. Heat olive oil in a large Dutch oven over medium-high heat. Add onion, celery, carrot, and bay leaves; sauté 10 minutes. Add tomato paste, salt, and garlic; sauté 1 minute. Add 6 cups water and lentils; bring mixture to a boil. Partially cover, reduce heat, and simmer mixture for 25 minutes. Stir in spinach and next 4 ingredients; cook 15 minutes. Discard bay leaves. Ladle soup into bowls; top with cheese. Yield: 6 servings (serving size: 1 cup soup and 2 tablespoons cheese).

CALORIES 234 (30% from fat); FAT 7.8g (sat 2.9g, mono 3.7g, poly 0.7g); PROTEIN 16.6g; CARB 26.6g; FIBER 7.3g; CHOL 10mg; IRON 5.1mg; SODIUM 729mg; CALC 260mg

Peas

Although most of the peas in this country are sold frozen, fresh ones are worth the search and the fingerwork.

- Choose young pods that are well filled and velvety soft to the touch. Peas that seem about to explode are too mature and will taste tough and mealy when cooked.
- To prevent the sugar in peas from converting to starch, store them in their pods, uncovered, in the refrigerator. The sooner they go from bowl to stove, the better. Use them within 2 to 3 days of when you purchase them.

Fresh Peas with Lettuce

Mild herbs such as thyme and parsley don't overpower the sweetness of fresh peas.

1½	teaspoons butter, divided
1	cup chopped Vidalia or other sweet onion
½	cup coarsely chopped celery
1	teaspoon chopped fresh thyme
2	cups shelled green peas (about 2 pounds unshelled green peas)
1	cup fat-free, less-sodium chicken broth
1	teaspoon sugar
¼	teaspoon salt
1	cup shredded romaine lettuce
2	tablespoons chopped fresh parsley
¼	teaspoon coarsely ground black pepper

1. Melt 1 teaspoon butter in a nonstick skillet over medium-high heat. Add onion, celery, and thyme; sauté 5 minutes or until tender. Add peas, broth, sugar, and salt; bring to a boil. Reduce heat; simmer 15 minutes or until peas are tender.
2. Stir in ½ teaspoon butter, lettuce, and parsley. Remove from heat, and sprinkle with pepper. Yield: 6 servings (serving size: ½ cup).

CALORIES 69 (16% from fat); FAT 1.2g (sat 0.7g, mono 0.3g, poly 0.2g); PROTEIN 3.8g; CARB 11.1g; FIBER 2.6g; CHOL 3mg; IRON 1.1mg; SODIUM 201mg; CALC 29mg

Mushrooms

More than 2,500 varieties of mushrooms grow around the world. Just take a glance at any upscale market's produce aisle—you'll find mushrooms in all sizes, shapes, colors, textures, and flavors.

The most readily available varieties are cultivated. Some cultivated mushrooms are so flavorful and unique that consumers tend to think of them as wild. **These farm-grown mushrooms have been termed "exotics" by the United States Department of Agriculture (USDA) to distinguish them from the true wild ones that pop up in forests, fields, and even deserts.** Portobello, shiitake, cremini, and oyster mushrooms account for most of the exotic mushroom sales in the United States. In metropolitan areas, you may also find such cultivated varieties as hen-of-the-woods (*maitake*), beech (*honshimeji*), yellow oyster, and bluefoot.

Storing Our time-tested method for storing fresh mushrooms is easy. Place them in a wicker basket lined with a paper towel, cover with a slightly dampened paper towel, and store in the fridge. Avoid the vegetable bin as well as plastic—high humidity is death for mushrooms. Most mushrooms will hold well for 3 to 7 days, but it really depends on when they were harvested and how well they were transported.

Mushroom Know-How

Choosing: Mushrooms should, above all, have a mushroomy aroma. If they don't smell good, chances are they won't taste much better. Avoid wet spots; dry, cracking edges; flattened gills (under the cap); splayed-out caps; wrinkled flesh; telltale insect holes; and white mold.

Cleaning: Some mushrooms carry little sand or dirt and only need a quick wipe with a damp paper towel to clean; others—especially wild varieties—attract ferns, pine needles, dirt, and other cling-ons. Figure in extra time to clean wild mushrooms. Remove the stems, discarding or saving for later use. Use a damp paper towel or a soft brush to wipe both sides of the cap. If there are little holes, check to make sure insects have not embedded themselves in the cap. If so, discard those mushrooms.

Dried Mushrooms

- The best varieties to use in dried form are porcini, shiitake, and morel, although many other kinds also pack a flavorful punch. When mushrooms are dried, they shrivel, and their flavor concentrates. Look inside a package of dried mushrooms to see how big the pieces are; if they've crumbled to dust, don't buy them.
- Check the package for Latin names. The choicest morels are *Morchella esculaenta, Morchella conica,* and *Morchella deliciosa,* which are all wonderful when cooked. The porcini/cèpe is called *Boletus edulis;* others in the same family are *Boletus luteus* and *Boletus barrosii,* which are still fine to eat but may have a bitter aftertaste. Also, look for countries of origin, if any. Morels from the United States are often shipped to Europe, dried, packaged, and reshipped here to capitalize on a French or Swiss name, which means you pay more for the cachet but not necessarily for better quality.
- Soak dried mushrooms in hot liquid, such as water or heated chicken broth. They should reconstitute in about 30 minutes. Drain mushrooms into a fine sieve lined with paper towels or cheesecloth and placed over a bowl, reserving the liquid (which makes a flavorful sauce). To get rid of any remaining sand, rinse and drain the mushrooms again. Then proceed with the recipe.

"Substitute buttons for half the wild mushrooms called for in any recipe—they'll adopt the flavor of the wild variety and add crunch." Tiffany Vickers, Test Kitchens Staffer

Button For practicality, this mushroom can't be beat. Its subtle scent is distinctive in simple  preparations such as sautéed mushrooms, but the button also stands up to spices—think curry, cumin, and chipotle. Onions lend a sweet note, while lemon brings out its assertiveness. The button's comparatively low price makes it a good budget stretcher, too.

Chanterelle The pumpkin-colored, flower-shaped chanterelle is a head turner. Its intoxicating, fruity aroma is well matched with herbs such as chives, tarragon, and chervil, and is great  in combinations with ham, corn, and poached salmon. Moderately expensive, this mushroom comes from eastern Canada, the Pacific Northwest, and Europe. It ranges in size from fingernail-tiny to a sprawling 4 inches. Pine needles and sand often hitch a ride in the cap's hollow and under its gills, so clean well before cooking. **Sautéing coaxes the best flavor from chanterelles, but they're also great roasted. The chanterelle dries well, although it renders a crunchy texture.**

Cremini When you want the juiciness and crunchy bite of the button but also want rich  flavor, cremini mushrooms are the way to go. They're shaped like buttons, with beige to brown caps. Whether speedily sautéed or slowly roasted, cremini stay plump and juicy. Garlic, thyme, and balsamic vinegar bring out cremini's flavor. **This is one mushroom that is as good eaten raw as cooked, and it marinates well.**

Enoki Shaped like a cotton swab, the enoki sits on a slender, edible stem. These mushrooms  usually come in clumps, attached by roots at the bottom. Trim off the root end of the cluster, separate the mushrooms, and get ready to snack. The enoki adds crunch, mild flavor, and bulk to any dish—from aromatic Asian soups to quick stir-fries and salads.

Morels More than any other, this expensive mushroom variety holds people in thrall and

opens the doors to their culinary imaginations. A morel's deep-woods flavor, springy texture, and little cream-catching pits invite us to sauté, stuff, and simmer it. Morels are hollow, shaped like a cone, and covered with ridges. They come in shades from light beige to gray to black. Smoky, earthy morels hold their own paired with hearty red meats and rich wine sauces. They transform eggs and pasta into elegant meals and become heavenly with a little cream. Fresh morels are available in spring and summer; dried varieties can be found year-round and perform admirably. **The morel's cavity is a natural sand collector, so slice the mushroom lengthwise to wipe out the interior before cooking.**

Oyster The fan-shaped oyster mushroom, with its namesake's mild flavor, is fabulous with fish,

seafood, red meat, and poultry. The creamy white, beige, or gray caps grow in a cluster, which is stunning when roasted whole. Mushroom farmers have had a lot of success growing yellow, pink, and blue oysters, which can be substituted for white ones in most recipes (the colors fade when cooked, however).

Wild Mushrooms **Keep It SAFE**

It's vitally important to know which species of wild mushrooms are edible and which are poisonous. Never pick or eat wild mushrooms unless they've been identified by an expert. Most supermarkets now carry wild mushrooms that have been professionally farmed and are safe.

Porcini Pricey porcini (known in France as cèpes) are some of the most sought-after wild

mushrooms, and for good reason. Their essence-of-forest flavor, combined with a juicy, slippery-soft texture, is superb. Porcini come from the woods, so you need to clean them thoroughly by wiping them with a damp paper towel. The stems can be sautéed and are delicious tucked into highly seasoned omelets. The caps can go a number of directions—sauté, roast, and grill them, for starters. Serve over pasta, or use them to garnish strongly flavored meats and game.

"There's nothing like sinking your teeth into roasted oyster mushrooms, especially when they're mingled with more assertive varieties, such as shiitakes or chanterelles." Kathryn Conrad, Test Kitchens Staffer

Mushrooms and water don't mix—after a light touch with a damp paper towel, they're ready to go.

If you can find them, frozen porcini are a terrific substitute for fresh, as they retain nearly the same texture and are actually juicier. Don't defrost before using; roast them whole in a moderate oven for an hour, or slice and toss them right into the skillet. With the juices they produce, frozen porcini make a great pasta sauce.

Porcini Pointers

Test Kitchen SECRET

The most easily obtained form of porcini is dried. But be careful when purchasing them: Less flavorful varieties are sometimes substituted for the real thing, so buy from a trusted source, and check that the mushroom's botanical name is listed as *Boletus edulis*. Once reconstituted, dried porcini yield a strong, earthy, smoky flavor. Use them to flavor soups, stews, sauces, and stuffings. To get around dried mushrooms' chewy texture, chop them finely after reconstituting and rinsing them.

Portobello Let a cremini grow a few days longer, and you end up with a portobello. This

flying saucer–like disk, which often measures from 3 to 6 inches across, is firm, meaty, and intensely flavorful. The portobello stands up to such gutsy flavors as acidic marinades, fresh rosemary and basil, and chile peppers. Grilling or roasting best preserves the mushroom's steaklike texture, but other cooking methods work just as well.

When sautéing, remove the black gills on the underside of the cap to prevent the mushrooms from blackening. Sautéed portobellos are delicious in ragoûts, as a topping for polenta or pizza, or as a filling for fajitas, quesadillas, or tacos.

Shiitake This Asian import came to America years ago, and we have embraced it as our own.

The soft, brown, open cap lends itself to several cooking styles. Sautéing brings out the shiitake's strong smoky flavor, softens the texture to velvety smoothness, and allows the mushroom to easily mingle with other ingredients. Combined with crunchy vegetables, the shiitake takes naturally to the wok; with leeks and cream, it goes French and fancy.

Dried Shiitakes

Test Kitchen SECRET

For maximum flavor, use dried shiitakes, which are chewier and more intense than fresh. Discard the thin, tough stalks, or use them to flavor stock.

Onions & Other Alliums

Freshly harvested onions of any variety have a much stronger taste than stored onions.

Alliums—onions, garlic, chives, leeks, shallots, and green onions—make up one of the most important culinary plant families. There are more than 300 species of alliums, and many of these have, at one time or other, been used in cooking. Here's a look at the six alliums we use most often in our Test Kitchens.

Onions *(allium cepa)*

This allium's bulb keeps it alive during dormancy. As onions age, they become sweeter and milder.

Red onions and sweet onions, including Vidalia, Walla Walla, Oso, and Yellow Bermuda, contain more sugars than brown- or white-skinned Spanish varieties.

Onions are the workhorses of the allium family, yet some varieties are more suitable for specific uses than others. Sweet onions are great raw in salads and for making quick pickles. Hotter brown- and white-skinned onions are best for soups and stews and for baking or roasting whole or in wedges. Red onions cook to an unappetizing grayish brown, so use them only in salads or quick-cooking dishes that allow them to maintain their glorious color. Small onions are useful for cooking whole in stews and ragoûts and for pickling. Cipollini

onions are small and pale yellow, and their flatness allows them to cook quickly and evenly.

Vidalias They only grow in a small corner of Georgia, but Vidalia onions are famous around the country for their subtle sweetness. Vidalias are juicy, mild, and very sweet due to the area's unique combination of soils and climate. Sweet onions from other states share with Vidalias the high sugar and water content that is their delicious signature. But to onion connoisseurs, the pale yellow bulbs are the cream of the crop.

Always use Vidalias to play to their strength. Typical onion applications, such as pickling, stewing, and stir-frying, are better suited to stronger, no-name yellows. **Vidalias shine in recipes that let them steal the show—mixed into a tangy relish for fish, baked whole with rosemary, or caramelized to the fullest extent of their generous sugar.**

> **Purchasing and Preparing Onions** | **Test Kitchen SECRET**
>
> - When purchasing onions, look for ones with dry, clean, paper-thin skin, and be sure the onions are firm. A pound of onions equals about 3 cups sliced or 4 servings of cooked onions.
> - For a shortcut to peeling small onions and shallots, place them in a large bowl, cover with boiling water for 3 minutes, then drain. The skins should come off easily.
> - You can freeze chopped raw onion in a heavy-duty zip-top plastic bag for handy use at a moment's notice.

Cooked Onions

Onions are among the world's most pungent foods when eaten raw. But when they're cooked a bit, they start losing some of that sharp flavor.

When cooked to the point that their natural sugars caramelize, onions darken to a deep golden brown color and take on an interesting sweetness.

Sometimes an onion browns quickly or exudes lots of juice when sautéed. This is due to its high sugar content—the sweeter the onion, the quicker it will brown and caramelize.

No More Tears

Test Kitchen
SECRET

When an onion is cut, it releases gases that can mix with the moisture in your eyes to form a mild sulfuric acid and cause tears (although similar  gases are released when garlic, leeks, chives, and other alliums are sliced, those gases don't irritate your eyes). To avoid weeping while chopping an onion, peel and chill the onion in the refrigerator before slicing.

Sweet-and-Hot Onion Salsa

This salsa highlights the sweetness of onions such as Vidalias. Serve it with baked tortilla chips, grilled chicken, fish, or pork.

1	cup chopped Vidalia or other sweet onion
¼	cup orange juice
2	tablespoons water
1	teaspoon sugar
1¼	cups diced red plum
1	cup diced Granny Smith apple
1	tablespoon chopped seeded jalapeño pepper
1	tablespoon white wine vinegar
2	teaspoons lime juice
⅛	teaspoon salt
⅛	teaspoon black pepper
1	garlic clove, minced

1. Combine first 4 ingredients in a small saucepan. Bring to a boil; cover, reduce heat, and simmer 10 minutes. Uncover and cook 3 minutes or until liquid almost evaporates, stirring frequently.
2. Place onion mixture in a bowl, and cool to room temperature. Stir in plum and remaining ingredients. Cover and chill. Yield: 2½ cups (serving size: ¼ cup).

CALORIES 30 (6% from fat); FAT 0.2g (sat 0g, mono 0.1g, poly 0.1g); PROTEIN 0.5g; CARB 7.3g; FIBER 1.1g; CHOL 0mg; IRON 0.1mg; SODIUM 30mg; CALC 7mg

---

Onions, shallots, and garlic will keep for months in a cool, dry, dark place.

Ask the *Cooking Light* Cooks

What's the best onion to use when you're caramelizing onions? We prefer to use yellow onions because they aren't too sweet or too pungent. But really, any type of onion—yellow, white, red, or sweet—works just fine.

Caramelized Onions

To caramelize a larger quantity of onions (4 to 8 cups), use a large Dutch oven. You won't need additional olive oil. Another great option is to caramelize onions in a slow cooker. See page 59 for the recipe.

1½ teaspoons olive oil
    Cooking spray
  3 cups vertically sliced onion (sweet, yellow, white, or red onion)

1. Heat oil in a 12-inch nonstick skillet coated with cooking spray over medium-high heat. Add sliced onion, and cook 5 minutes, stirring frequently. Continue cooking 15 to 20 minutes or until deep golden brown, stirring frequently. Yield: 1 cup.

CALORIES 260 (28% from fat); FAT 8.2g (sat 1.1g, mono 5.1g, poly 0.9g); PROTEIN 5.9g; CARB 44g; FIBER 9.4g; CHOL 0mg; IRON 1.1mg; SODIUM 16mg; CALC 102mg

How to Caramelize Onions

1. Slice the onion in half vertically. Place halves, cut sides down, on cutting board, and slice into thin slivers.

2. Cook over medium-high heat, stirring often. After about 10 minutes, the onions begin to soften and release their liquid.

3. At 15 minutes of cooking, keep stirring frequently. The onions begin to take on a golden color, but they're not quite done yet.

4. At 20 minutes, the onions are a deep golden brown and are done.

"Caramelizing isn't difficult, but it does require a little time, a watchful eye, and frequent stirring."
Jan Smith, Photo Stylist

Beer-Battered Onion Rings

To get ⅓ flat beer, measure ½ cup beer into a bowl, and stir with a fork. Without the foam, the volume is less.

2	large onions, peeled (about 1½ pounds)
⅔	cup all-purpose flour
½	teaspoon salt
¼	teaspoon paprika
¼	teaspoon freshly ground black pepper
⅓	cup flat beer
1	large egg white, lightly beaten
1½	tablespoons vegetable oil, divided
Cooking spray	
¼	cup ketchup

1. Preheat oven to 400°.
2. Cut onions crosswise into ¾-inch-thick slices, and separate into rings. Use 16 of the largest rings; reserve remaining onion for another use.
3. Lightly spoon flour into dry measuring cups; level with a knife. Combine flour, salt, paprika, and pepper in a medium bowl. Stir in beer and egg white (batter will be thick).
4. Heat 1½ teaspoons oil in a large nonstick skillet over medium-high heat. Dip 5 onion rings in batter, letting excess drip off. Add onion rings to pan; cook 2 minutes on each side or until golden. Place onion rings on a jelly-roll pan. Repeat procedure of dipping onion rings in batter and cooking in remaining oil, ending with 6 rings. Coat rings with cooking spray. Bake at 400° for 10 minutes or until crisp. Serve with ketchup. Yield: 4 servings (serving size: 4 onions rings and 1 tablespoon ketchup).

CALORIES 209 (25% from fat); FAT 5.8g (sat 1g, mono 1.5g, poly 2.7g); PROTEIN 5.1g; CARB 34.1g; FIBER 3.7g; CHOL 0mg; IRON 1.5mg; SODIUM 490mg; CALC 39mg

How to Make Low-Fat Onion Rings

1. Dip onion rings in batter, letting excess batter drip off.

2. Add onion rings to hot oil in pan; cook 2 minutes on each side or until golden.

3. Place onion rings on a jelly-roll pan; coat onion rings with cooking spray, and bake according to recipe.

Shallots (allium cepa varieties)

Shallots differ from onions because many varieties produce a cluster of several bulbs to a plant. Shallots also have finer layers and less water. Because of the low water content, their flavor is more concentrated than that of onions, but they can also burn and toughen easily, so use caution when sautéing.

> **"Shallots are small onions that have a cross in flavor between an onion and garlic. You can substitute small white onions, although you will miss the unique flavor of the shallot."**
> **Tiffany Vickers, Test Kitchens Staffer**

Use shallots when you want full onion flavor without the bulk of a full-sized onion. Traditionally, shallots are used to flavor the reductions in some French sauces, including béarnaise, bordelaise, and duxelles. Shallots are also delicious cooked whole—try them caramelized with sugar and a few tablespoons of cognac, port, or sherry, or oven-roasted with rosemary or thyme. Finely chopped shallots are good in salad dressings and as a classic accompaniment to fresh oysters or beef dishes.

When peeling a shallot, remove a couple of the outer layers along with the peel. You might need an extra shallot to make up for the discarded layers, but this method is a lot faster than removing only the thin peel.

Green onions (allium cepa varieties and allium fistulosum)

These are also known as scallions, spring onions, or salad onions. They derive from several different types of wild alliums, and they can vary in thickness and length. Look for red spring onions in farmers' markets—they add flavor and color to salads. Served raw, green onions have a sweet, delicate flavor that is excellent in potato or rice salads and in salsas with chiles. Cooked green onions are great for fast recipes such as pasta, omelets, pancakes, and stir-fries.

Choose slender green onions for stir-fries or for chopping into salsas and salads; cook the thicker ones whole, or add them sliced to dishes that cook quickly.

Removing the Smell   Test Kitchen SECRET

To remove the smell of onion from your hands, rub your hands with a little lemon juice. Or try rubbing your fingertips on the bowl of a stainless-steel spoon under warm running water or rubbing your hands over the stainless-steel kitchen faucet. Apparently, there is something about the ions in stainless steel that can break down the odor-causing compounds in the onions.

If a recipe calls for ¼ cup chopped green onions, you'll need one large green onion.

Leeks (*allium ampeloprasum* or *allium porrum*) Although leeks resemble large green onions, they're milder and sweeter, and they don't cause any tears when they're chopped. **Unlike other alliums, leeks are almost always enjoyed cooked, since they're very fibrous when raw.** The tougher green part usually has a coarser flavor than the white part. Use the green part to flavor soups and stocks; add the white part (which is tender and needs only brief cooking) to soups and stews toward the end of cooking.

Leek soups rank among the world's favorites: from vichyssoise to the more provincial *potage bonne femme,* a creamy vegetable soup. Leeks are also delicious in potato, rice, and pasta dishes. In some markets, you may find finger-slim "baby" or "miniature" leeks. These are great for cooking whole; try them grilled with an herb salsa or vegetable dip, or in a tomato sauce or red-wine reduction that includes Greek flavors such as coriander, bay, and oregano.

Dirt is sometimes trapped between the layers of leeks. To clean, cut the root end, then slit the leek lengthwise. Fan the layers out, and rinse under cold water.

Leeks, scallions, and chives all need to be refrigerated. Keep them tightly wrapped so their flavors don't permeate milk, cheese, eggs, and butter.

Braised Leeks and Mushrooms

Braising tenderizes leeks and brings out their mild sweetness.

6	leeks (about 3 pounds)
1	cup fat-free beef broth
1	tablespoon tomato paste
¼	teaspoon salt
¼	teaspoon dried thyme
⅛	teaspoon pepper
1½	teaspoons butter
2	cups quartered mushrooms

1. Remove roots, outer leaves, and tops from leeks, leaving 6 inches of each leek. Cut each diagonally into thirds, then diagonally in half to form 6 triangular pieces. Rinse under cold water; drain.
2. Combine beef broth, tomato paste, salt, thyme, and pepper in a bowl, and stir with a whisk.
3. Melt butter in a large nonstick skillet over medium-high heat. Add leeks and mushrooms, and sauté 6 minutes or until vegetables are lightly browned. Add broth mixture. Cover, reduce heat, and simmer 15 minutes or until leeks are tender. Uncover and simmer 7 minutes or until liquid almost evaporates, stirring occasionally. Yield: 4 servings (serving size: ½ cup).

CALORIES 144 (14% from fat); FAT 2.2g (sat 1g, mono 0.4g, poly 0.5g); PROTEIN 3.8g; CARB 29.3g; FIBER 2.9g; CHOL 4mg; IRON 4.6mg; SODIUM 204mg; CALC 115mg

Chives *(allium schoenoprasum)*

Chives are among the mildest culinary alliums. We use them primarily as an herb or garnish, but  their subtle onion flavor can add just the right note of freshness to an otherwise lackluster dish. Chives are especially delicious with potatoes, eggs, rice, and smoked or pickled fish. The edible lilac-pink flowers of homegrown chives are attractive scattered over salads or omelettes.

Chives	Test Kitchen SECRET

- Chives are perhaps the easiest allium to grow yourself. They do well in a pot on the windowsill.
- Use scissors to snip chives; chopping with a knife can tear them.
- If you cook with chives, keep cook times brief to preserve their flavor.
- Chives vary from grass-fine to pencil-thick. The thicker the chive, the more flavor it packs.
- Always use chives fresh. Dried chives lack the bright flavor that is the key to their charm.

If you cook chives too long, they not only lose flavor and crispness, but also their bright green color.

Garlic *(allium sativum)*

Garlic is the most pungent of all alliums, and the more it is chopped, the stronger it tastes. **For**  **subtle garlic flavor, add whole unpeeled cloves to pot roasts and roasted vegetable dishes.** Asian stir-fries use sliced garlic, which adds warm, toasty flavor. Both finely chopped and crushed garlic add strong, "hot" flavor, especially when uncooked.

There are many types of garlic, some purple-skinned, others pearly white. Some produce huge, fat cloves with more subtle flavor than smaller-cloved garlics. So-called "elephant" garlics, with huge, mild-tasting bulbs as long as 3 inches, are related to the wild leek (*allium ampeloprasum*). Young, or green, garlic is a mild seasonal treat that usually arrives in markets in early summer. Both young garlic and elephant garlic can be baked whole in foil, then squeezed out of their skins to yield a deeply flavored puree that's good in pasta sauces and dips, with goat cheeses, or spread on toasted sourdough. Garlic stores well— you can keep it hung on a rope or braid in a cool place for several months.

Pungent Garlic	Test Kitchen SECRET

- Stored garlic cloves can develop green shoots in the center; remove them before cooking, since they can taste bitter and burn easily.
- Be careful when you sauté garlic; burnt garlic will add an acrid, bitter flavor to the finished dish.
- When cooking garlic and onions together, add the garlic after the onions have begun to soften.

Peppers

From sweet bells to hot jalapeños, peppers are packed with flavor and nutrients, and they add an unbeatable color and texture to many types of dishes.

Bell Peppers

Sweet peppers, also called "bells," should have brightly colored, glossy skins. They should be free of soft spots and wrinkles, which are signs of  aging, and their stems should be firm and green. "Weigh" a pepper in your hand; it should feel heavy for its size—a sign of thick, juicy flesh.

Sweet peppers come in an assortment of colors: green, red, yellow, orange, brown, and purple. Color depends on variety and ripeness. Like tomatoes, when peppers are picked before they reach maturity, they are green. But when left on the vine a little longer, a pepper ripens and changes color, depending on its variety. Green peppers with red or yellow streaks are sweeter than solid green peppers, and once harvested, they will turn completely red or yellow. (See page 81 for tips on roasting bell peppers.)

Braising Bell Peppers — Test Kitchen SECRET

Braising bell peppers draws out their strength over time. You can keep them in the refrigerator for a few days, and they'll yield thick, syrupy juices that can be used to moisten strands of pasta or provide a sauce for polenta.

Braised Bell Peppers

Serve these peppers as a side dish, or use them in other recipes. Although the aniseed is optional, it adds a subtle sweetness to the peppers. For a more robust flavor, try using 2¹⁄₂ teaspoons of finely chopped fresh rosemary in place of the aniseed, and omit the basil.

Olive oil-flavored cooking spray
- 4 cups red bell pepper strips (about 1¹⁄₄ pounds)
- 4 cups yellow bell pepper strips (about 1¹⁄₄ pounds)
- 2¹⁄₂ cups vertically sliced onion
- ¹⁄₂ teaspoon salt
- ¹⁄₄ teaspoon aniseed, crushed (optional)
- 2 garlic cloves, minced
- 2 cups water
- 2 tablespoons tomato paste
- 1 tablespoon chopped fresh basil
- 1 tablespoon red wine vinegar
- ¹⁄₄ teaspoon black pepper

1. Place a large nonstick skillet coated with cooking spray over medium-high heat. Add bell peppers; onion; salt; aniseed, if desired; and garlic. Sauté 15 minutes, stirring occasionally. Stir in water and tomato paste. Bring mixture to a boil; reduce heat, and simmer 30 minutes or until bell peppers are soft. Stir in basil, vinegar, and black pepper. Yield: 4 cups (serving size: ¹⁄₂ cup).

CALORIES 45 (12% from fat); FAT 0.6g (sat 0.1g, mono 0.1g, poly 0.3g); PROTEIN 1.5g; CARB 9.6g; FIBER 2.5g; CHOL 0mg; IRON 1.5mg; SODIUM 153mg; CALC 17mg

Pepper Storage

Store unwashed, uncut fresh peppers in a plastic bag in the refrigerator. They will keep for about a week, depending on how fresh they were when purchased.

Because red peppers remain on the plant longer and are more perishable than green, they cost more. Also, since red peppers are typically softer and more mature than green peppers, they do not keep as well.

Romesco Sauce

This sauce is thick and smooth. You can thin the consistency by stirring in some hot water.

1	large red bell pepper
⅓	cup blanched almonds (about 1½ ounces)
1	teaspoon paprika
½	teaspoon salt
¼	teaspoon ground red pepper
4	plum tomatoes, quartered and seeded
2	(1-inch-thick) slices Italian bread, toasted
3	garlic cloves, peeled
¼	cup extra-virgin olive oil
2	tablespoons sherry vinegar

1. Preheat broiler.
2. Cut bell pepper in half lengthwise; discard seeds and membranes. Place halves, skin sides up, on a foil-lined baking sheet; flatten with hand. Broil 10 to 15 minutes or until blackened. Place in a zip-top plastic bag; seal. Let stand 15 minutes; peel.
3. Combine bell pepper, almonds, and next 6 ingredients in a food processor; process until minced. Add oil and vinegar; process until smooth. Yield: 2 cups (serving size: 1 tablespoon).

CALORIES 35 (67% from fat); FAT 2.6g (sat 0.3g, mono 1.8g, poly 0.4g); PROTEIN 0.7g; CARB 2.4g; FIBER 0.5g; CHOL 0mg; IRON 0.3mg; SODIUM 54mg; CALC 6mg

Chile Peppers

Chile peppers come in four forms: fresh, dried, canned, and powdered. The fresh peppers vary in length as well as in degree of heat.

While many chiles are indeed hot, there are a variety of methods to tame them so that the chile contributes its unique flavor, not just its bite.

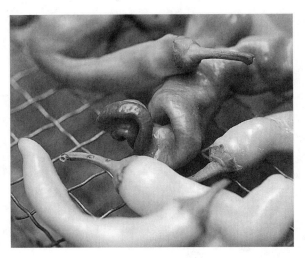

Taming the Heat
Test Kitchen SECRET

One of the best ways to tame a chile pepper's heat is to remove the chile's seeds and membranes, which hold most of the heat-inducing capsaicin. Wear rubber gloves, or wash your hands immediately; otherwise, skin that isn't accustomed to the oils in chiles will begin to burn.

If your mouth is on fire from eating a hot chile pepper, drink some milk or eat a slice of bread to neutralize the burning sensation.

As a general rule, the larger the chile, the milder the flavor because the smaller peppers proportionally contain more seeds and membranes, and that's where most of the heat is found.

Ancho Anchos are dried poblano chiles with a maroon luster. They have a rich, almost mochalike flavor, with a slow heat. They are the sweetest of the dried chiles.

Chipotle This hot chile is really just a dried, smoked jalapeño. It has a wrinkled, dark skin and a smoky, sweet flavor. Chipotles (chih-POHT-lays) are often pickled and canned in adobo sauce.

Habanero A tiny, superhot, bright orange chile shaped like a Chinese lantern, the habanero is one to be reckoned with.

Jalapeño These smooth, dark green chiles, which are bright red when ripe, can be very hot. They have a rounded tip and are about 2 inches long.

Poblano A dark green chile used in classic chiles rellenos, the poblano is usually fairly mild. It is about 3 inches wide and 4 to 5 inches long, tapering from top to bottom in a triangular shape.

Serrano A small, pointed chile (about 1½ inches long), this chile may be smaller than the similar jalapeño, but it's about twice as fierce. As it matures, it turns from bright green to scarlet red, then yellow. Serrano chiles have crisp heat, which mellows beautifully when roasted, lending a high note to salsas and sauces.

Three-Pepper Salsa

This spicy salsa is not for those who can't take the heat.

1½	cups boiling water
3	dried ancho chiles or ½ teaspoon crushed red pepper
2	large poblano chiles
1	large yellow bell pepper
1	cup diced tomato
½	cup diced red onion
¼	cup chopped fresh cilantro
3	tablespoons orange juice
2	tablespoons lime juice
2	tablespoons minced seeded serrano chile
¼	teaspoon salt

1. Combine water and ancho chiles in a small bowl; cover anchos, and let stand for 30 minutes or until soft. Drain well; seed and chop.

2. Preheat broiler. Cut poblanos and bell pepper in half lengthwise; discard seeds and membranes. Place poblanos and bell pepper halves, skin sides up, on a foil-lined baking sheet; flatten with hand. Broil 10 to 15 minutes or until blackened. Place in a zip-top plastic bag; seal. Let stand 10 minutes. Peel and dice poblanos and bell pepper.

3. Combine anchos, roasted poblanos and bell pepper, tomato, and remaining ingredients in a medium bowl; cover salsa and chill. Yield: 9 servings (serving size: ¼ cup).

CALORIES 26 (14% from fat); FAT 0.4g (sat 0.1g, mono 0g, poly 0.2g); PROTEIN 1g; CARB 5.6g; FIBER 1.5g; CHOL 0mg; IRON 0.6mg; SODIUM 79mg; CALC 12mg

Potatoes

Potatoes boast a tapestry of tints, tastes, and textures—red, blue, white, and purple; nutty and earthy; starchy, waxy, firm, and creamy.

Although most people stick to the basics (red-skinned, white, baking, and sometimes Yukon gold), there are now a number of other varieties available.

Types of Potatoes

If the only type of potato that you know of is a baking potato, here's a guide to some varieties that we use in our recipes and the best uses for each.

Type	Varieties	Uses
Baking Potatoes These long, dusky brown tubers with numerous eyes are the gold standard for potatoes: starchy, floury, large, and slightly nutty. Some call them "Idaho" potatoes because that state traditionally grows more than any other; today, Idaho produces almost a third of the country's potato crop.	Generic, hybridized baking potatoes have begun showing up in markets, but the preferred choice is the ashen-skinned russet, with its unique balance of starch and moisture. Certain dishes, like gnocchi, call specifically for russets. There are different strains—including the Russet Burbank, which is the best baking potato—but stores rarely label potatoes so exactly.	Despite the name, baking potatoes are also great for making gratins, mashed potatoes, and gnocchi.
Purple Potatoes These ancient potatoes are related to those the Incas were cultivating when the Spanish landed in the New World. Today, most purple potatoes still grow in South America. They have a strong, distinct flavor: nutty, earthy, and a little bitter. They run the gamut from medium-starchy to quite waxy and from deep purple to bright blue. *Many varieties turn gray when cooked. Most will stain your hands, so wear rubber gloves while peeling.*	Blues and purple Peruvians have the nuttiest taste, but because they are dry, you'll need to add fat to enhance their flavor and texture. Caribes have purple skin and white flesh; their skins are quite bitter, almost metallic, while the flesh is creamy and delicate.	Purple potatoes are good to roast or mash, depending on their starch content, and they are delicious in salads.
Red-Skinned Potatoes Once called "new" potatoes, red-skinned potatoes are waxy, meaning they have very little starch. *They are the workhorses of potatoes: great most ways, with less fuss than high-starch potatoes, which can scorch and burn.* Red-skinned potatoes have the thinnest skins of any type, so they're usually cooked unpeeled.	Red-skinned potatoes encompass far more than Red Bliss, the variety most commonly thought of as a new potato. Nutty and drier exotics, like Desirees, French fingerlings, and Red La Sodas, are often available at local farmers' markets.	Red potatoes shine when boiled, roasted, steamed, or tossed in salads or soups.

Look for firm potatoes without green bits, sprouted eyes, or mushy spots. The skin should adhere evenly and firmly to the flesh.

Type	Varieties	Uses
White-Fleshed Potatoes Characterized by pale beige skin and white flesh, these medium- to low-starch potatoes are oblong (usually grown in California or Arizona) or spherical (most often from Maine). *Some old-fashioned cookbooks refer to them as "boiling" potatoes, but because they are moist yet firm, they are also good braised and stewed.*	Irish Cobblers and California long whites, excellent all-around potatoes, are the most common type—they are slightly dry, very firm, and mildly earthy in taste. Sweeter Katahdins and Kennebecs from Maine also serve many purposes, although they may have too much starch for successful roasting. They become crisp on the outside but stay very creamy inside. If you enjoy this textural contrast—irresistible to some, cloying to others—try white creamers: tiny, velvety spheres with a woody taste that take on an unbelievable creaminess when roasted in their skins.	Try white-fleshed potatoes boiled, roasted, or steamed in gratins, salads, and scalloped dishes. They're also excellent wrapped in foil and placed in the embers of a charcoal fire.
Yellow-Fleshed Potatoes These buttery, creamy potatoes have a good balance of starchiness and waxiness, so they work well in complicated dishes. They are also quite good prepared simply—steamed or boiled, for example. *Their flesh has too much moisture and starch, however, for baking or roasting; the skins rarely get crisp, and the insides turn mushy.* Yellow-fleshed potatoes store exceptionally well.	By far, the most common is the Yukon gold. A wonderful addition to stews or braised dishes, it also pairs with greens like spinach and dandelion. Other varieties such as Ozettes, Rattes, and Charlottes are waxier and even drier; they do best with butter or olive oil.	These work well in gratins and stews, and they make mashed potatoes that look already buttered.

Fingerlings are actually immature potatoes with a long, thin shape rather than a variety of potato. They can be white potatoes, red-skinned, yellow-fleshed, or purple, and they vary in texture from waxy to starchy. They are most often cultivated in small batches and tend to have a pronounced flavor.

Potato Storage

Store potatoes in a cool, dark place, preferably hanging in a net bag to allow air to circulate. Try this method: Fill the legs of old panty hose with potatoes, then pin the hose to the wall of your pantry or basement. At 70°, potatoes will keep about 10 days; at 50°, up to 6 weeks. **Never put potatoes in the refrigerator, since temperatures below 45° cause the starch to change into sugar. Also, never store them alongside onions and shallots, since the fumes from the onions encourage sprouting.**

Potatoes don't freeze well because they get mushy. It's better to cut the recipe in half if it yields more than you need in a day or two.

Cleaning Potatoes

Don't clean potatoes until you're ready to use them. After you make sure the skin isn't withered or loose, scrub potatoes under cool running water with a stiff brush, removing any dirt from pockets or dimples. But be careful not to scrub so hard that you break the skin.

"When we call for a medium-size baking potato, we are referring to a potato that is 8 to 10 ounces."
Krista Montgomery, Food Editor

Potatoes with Sprouts
Keep It SAFE

If the potato has sprouted, cut out each eye by digging a deep well into the flesh. Also, cut out any green spots, which come from chlorophyll-induced alkaloids blooming in the flesh. You'd have to eat about 2 1/2 pounds of green potato flesh to become seriously ill, but you can get a stomachache on less. The alkaloids are concentrated in the skin, so peel greenish potatoes to a 1/8-inch depth.

Potato Salad Preferences
Test Kitchen SECRET

- Use low- to medium-starch potatoes for salads; high-starch potatoes absorb water readily and do not hold their shape. Low- to medium-starch potatoes include Red Bliss, Yukon Gold, all-purpose white, and White Rose.
- Select potatoes of the same size so they cook uniformly. Cover the potatoes with cold water, bring to a boil, and cook until done. Test for doneness with a knife, which lets in less water than a fork. When they're ready, the knife will go in easily.
- Cooking the potatoes with their skins on will preserve their shape and add flavor.

To Peel or Not to Peel?

There's a popular misconception that peeling potatoes robs them of their vitamins. Actually, most of the vitamins—B6, C, niacin, potassium, thiamin, and zinc—cluster in a vein about half an inch below the skin. Thus, peeling is strictly a culinary matter.

- **Leave potatoes unpeeled when baking or frying (for a crunchier exterior)** and when adding to stews or braised dishes (for a little more flavor and for preventing the starch from leaching out and thickening the broths of lighter dishes).
- **Peel potatoes when you want a creamy dish** that takes full advantage of the starch as a thickener. Peeled potatoes yield softer texture, so they're good for casseroles and gratins. Or peel potatoes strictly for aesthetics—to keep a gratin creamy white, for example.
- **If you peel potatoes ahead of time,** place the potatoes in cold water to prevent them from turning brown. Remove them from the water when you're ready to use them, and pat dry.

> "When I cook potatoes, I like to cook them in chicken broth and water to add flavor. I also stir a little chicken broth into my mashed potatoes."

Vanessa Johnson, Test Kitchens Director

The Best Baked Potato

Test Kitchen SECRET

Nothing inspires culinary rivalries like the simple task of baking a potato. Follow our Test Kitchens' tips for success:

- Use only baking potatoes, preferably Russet Burbanks that weigh 8 to 10 ounces each.
- Don't wrap the potato in aluminum foil: The skin will steam instead of becoming crunchy.
- Position the rack in the bottom third of the oven; preheat oven to 400°.
- Prick the potato in a few places with a fork before baking. Doing so lets excess moisture escape, rendering a fluffier inside and preventing the skin from cracking.
- Don't insert an aluminum potato nail into the flesh. It lets too much moisture escape and creates a rift of tough, fibrous flesh in the potato's center.
- Sprinkle with kosher or sea salt, if desired.
- Bake at 400° for 1 hour or until tender when pierced with a knife.
- For faster results, prick the potato in several places, and microwave at HIGH 3 minutes (cook 1 minute extra for each additional spud). Transfer to a 400° oven and bake 30 minutes or until the potato is crunchy outside and soft inside.

Potato, Fontina, and Cremini au Gratin

Use baking potatoes in this au gratin dish because they hold their shape during baking.

3   pounds peeled baking potatoes, cut into ¼-inch-thick slices
Cooking spray
1   tablespoon butter
1   cup chopped onion
4   cups sliced cremini mushrooms
½   teaspoon salt
½   teaspoon dried thyme
⅛   teaspoon pepper
¼   cup all-purpose flour
2¼ cups fat-free milk
2   cups (8 ounces) shredded fontina cheese

1. Preheat oven to 350°.
2. Place peeled potatoes in a large saucepan. Cover with water; bring to a boil. Reduce heat; simmer 15 minutes or until potatoes are tender. Drain. Arrange in a 13 x 9-inch baking dish coated with cooking spray.
3. Melt butter in pan over medium heat. Add onion, and cook 3 minutes or until tender. Add mushrooms, salt, thyme, and pepper; cook 5 minutes, stirring occasionally. Lightly spoon flour into a dry measuring cup, and level with a knife. Sprinkle mushroom mixture with flour, and cook 1 minute, stirring constantly. Gradually add milk, stirring with a whisk until blended. Bring to a boil, and cook 3 minutes or until thick, stirring constantly. Remove from heat, and add cheese, stirring until cheese melts. Pour sauce over potatoes, tossing gently to coat. Bake at 350° for 40 minutes or until bubbly. Yield: 8 servings (serving size: 1 cup).

CALORIES 343 (29% from fat); FAT 11g (sat 6.5g, mono 3g, poly 0.8g); PROTEIN 14.3g; CARB 46.7g; FIBER 3.5g; CHOL 38mg; IRON 1.4mg; SODIUM 208mg; CALC 258mg

Test Kitchen Tips for Marvelous Mashed Potatoes

Cube potatoes before cooking. Although you can cook them whole, it takes longer.

Russet and thin-skinned white potatoes have a fluffy, dry texture and require more liquid for creamy results. If you have a potato ricer, use it with these potatoes.

Waxy red potatoes and Yukon golds make good chunky smashed potatoes. Peel before or after cooking, or leave the skins on for rustic appeal (and increased fiber).

After you drain the potatoes, place the pan over low heat, then shake the potatoes in the pan to dry them before mashing. If your pan is stainless, mash the potatoes right in the pan over low heat to keep them warm.

Warm the milk or broth before you mash it with the potatoes to reduce the potential for lumps.

If your menu includes gravy or jus, keep your mashed potatoes simple.

Which Tool to Use?

Cooking Light Recommends

Potato masher: Whether you prefer your potatoes chunky or silky, potato mashers give you a multitude of options. They're your best bet if you like the texture of the skin in your potatoes.

Potato ricers: Loved by food purists, potato ricers and food mills make smooth mashed potatoes. These do double duty, peeling and mashing at the same time. Look for ricers and food mills at specialty cookware stores.

Electric mixer: An electric mixer whips potatoes in an instant, but a food processor is so powerful it will overmix potatoes and make them gummy.

Creamy Herbed Mashed Potatoes

Yukon golds make brilliant mashed potatoes, thanks to their balance of waxiness and starch. Because yellow potatoes are more flavorful than others, they don't need a lot of fat to taste rich. Mash them by hand just until creamy—overworking the potatoes will make them gummy.

     4 cups cubed peeled Yukon gold potato
          (about 2 pounds)
    ½ cup 2% reduced-fat milk
    ¼ cup low-fat sour cream
     3 tablespoons butter
     3 tablespoons chopped fresh chives
     2 tablespoons chopped fresh parsley
    ½ teaspoon salt
    ¼ teaspoon freshly ground black pepper

1. Place potato in a saucepan; cover with water. Bring to a boil; cover, reduce heat, and simmer 10 minutes or until tender. Drain. Return to pan. Add milk and remaining ingredients; mash with a potato masher to desired consistency. Yield: 6 servings (serving size: ¾ cup).

CALORIES 215 (30% from fat); FAT 7.1g (sat 4.5g, mono 1.8g, poly.3g); PROTEIN 4.5g; CARB 34.5g; FIBER 2.4g; CHOL 20mg; IRON 0.7mg; SODIUM 280mg; CALC 51mg

Root Vegetables

Roots are the cornerstone of good health.

Root vegetables (plants whose underground parts are edible) are at their peak during the winter months. And now they're taking center stage not just at Thanksgiving but throughout the cooler months. We are relearning what previous generations knew instinctively: Roots are the cornerstone of good health. Sweet potatoes are a powerful anticancer food. Parsnips provide potassium and folic acid (although their carbohydrates make them somewhat higher in calories than the carrots they so closely resemble). Turnips act as a starchy vegetable in your cooking, yet they are very low in calories. These and other gifts of the soil are powerful food, and science is discovering more about their benefits daily.

Touching Up Your Roots

Test Kitchen SECRET

Root vegetables are unpretentious, but handling them well can be a challenge. Here's a guide to preparing a few common types.

Celeriac: The gnarled, irregular shape and rough surface make a chef's knife a must. You'll lose almost 35 percent of the vegetable once it's peeled. To shred, use the largest holes on a box grater or the shredder attachment of your food processor.

Parsnips: Peel these with a vegetable peeler the same way you would a carrot.

Turnips: The waxy skin is fairly thin, and the texture is smooth, so all you'll need is a good vegetable peeler.

Rutabagas: Their skin is thick and tough, and their size makes them awkward to handle. Use a chef's knife to cut off the root ends first, and then peel around the sides.

Choosing Select Roots

Roots are available year-round in many supermarkets, but you should certainly seek them out during the cooler months, when their robust flavors peak.

Select roots by weight, looking for ones that are not too large but are heavy for their size, avoiding those with hairy rootlets that indicate age.

Choose regular shapes, which will make peeling easier. There's no trick to purchasing the roots of your choice.

Store them in a cool, dry place with good ventilation. Parsnips, celeriac, turnips, and rutabagas prefer the cool of a refrigerator, but they will outlast almost anything you have in there. Do not store potatoes in the refrigerator; they'll keep without refrigeration for several weeks.

Typically, root vegetables are more robust than spring and summer vegetables, and because of their various textures, they lend themselves to a variety of cooking methods.

Beets

Fresh beets have lately become as common on fine-restaurant menus as they once were in sensible root cellars. With hues ranging from yellow to purple, they lend themselves to dramatic presentations as few other vegetables do. Because of their texture, beets hold up well when baked, boiled, roasted, or julienned raw. And because of their sweetness, beets pair equally well with butter or vinegar and citrus. Their greens make flavorful additions to savory dishes, while the roots can be added to salads, sauced lightly or lavishly, and turned into hearty soups. You can even use them to make a deliciously moist cake (see page 307).

Picking the Best More beet varieties are becoming available, with golden-hued roots appearing in farmers' markets recently. When selecting fresh beets, buy small to medium globes with stems and leaves attached; firm, smooth skin; and no soft spots.

Storing Beets To store beets, immediately trim stems to about 1 inch. Beets will keep in plastic bags in the refrigerator for up to 2 weeks.

Handling Beets
Test Kitchen SECRET

One smart tip for handling beets is to wear disposable latex gloves from the drugstore. They're thin enough to allow dexterity while protecting hands from stains.

If you don't use gloves, you can get rid of beet juice stains on your hands by rubbing your hands with the cut side of a raw potato half. You may want to wear an apron if you're grating beets because they tend to splatter.

Roasting Beets

1. Trim stems to about 1 inch to minimize bleeding, and wash the beets whole. Place beets on a foil-lined baking sheet.

2. Bake at 425° for 45 minutes or until tender. After cooking, trim off about ¼ inch of the beet roots.

3. Rub off the skins. They should slip off easily after cooking.

"Because of their sweetness, using beets in desserts works great. We discovered that they're a perfect ingredient for a tender, sweet cake." Kathleen Kanen, Food Stylist

Beet Cake with Cream Cheese Frosting

This cake is similar to a carrot cake. The batter is bright red but bakes to a golden brown.

Cake:

1	pound beets (about 2 medium)
	Cooking spray
⅔	cup granulated sugar
⅔	cup packed dark brown sugar
½	cup vegetable oil
2	large eggs
2½	cups all-purpose flour
2	teaspoons baking powder
1	teaspoon ground ginger
1	teaspoon ground cinnamon
½	teaspoon baking soda
¼	teaspoon salt
½	cup 1% low-fat milk

Frosting:

2	teaspoons grated orange rind
1	teaspoon vanilla extract
1	(8-ounce) block ⅓-less-fat cream cheese, chilled
3	cups sifted powdered sugar
2	tablespoons finely chopped walnuts, toasted

1. Preheat oven to 350°.

2. To prepare cake, peel beets using a vegetable peeler. Grate beets, using the large holes of a grater, to measure 2 cups.

3. Coat 2 (9-inch) round cake pans with cooking spray; line bottoms with wax paper. Coat wax paper with cooking spray.

4. Combine granulated sugar, brown sugar, oil, and eggs in a large bowl; beat with a mixer at medium speed until well blended. Add beets; beat well. Lightly spoon flour into dry measuring cups; level with a knife. Combine flour and next 5 ingredients in a large bowl, stirring well with a whisk. Add flour mixture to sugar mixture alternately with milk, beginning and ending with flour mixture. Pour batter into prepared pans; sharply tap pans once on counter to remove air bubbles.

5. Bake at 350° for 30 minutes or until a wooden pick inserted in center comes out clean. Cool in pans 10 minutes on wire racks; remove from pans. Carefully peel off wax paper, and cool cakes completely on wire racks.

6. To prepare frosting, beat orange rind, vanilla, and cream cheese with a mixer at high speed until fluffy. Add the powdered sugar; beat at low speed just until blended (do not overbeat).

7. Place 1 cake layer on a plate; spread with ½ cup frosting; top with remaining cake layer. Spread remaining frosting over top and sides of cake. Sprinkle nuts over top of cake. Store cake loosely covered in refrigerator. Yield: 18 servings (serving size: 1 slice).

CALORIES 312 (30% from fat); FAT 10.5g (sat 3.3g, mono 3g, poly 3.6g); PROTEIN 4.5g; CARB 51.2g; FIBER 0.7g; CHOL 34mg; IRON 1.4mg; SODIUM 198mg; CALC 65mg

Carrots

Carrots are the Fort Knox of beta carotene, and the deeper the orange, the more beta carotene there is. (Beta carotene is a form of vitamin A and appears to help reduce the risk of cancer.) **Cooked carrots are better than raw ones because cooking unleashes more beta carotene.**

Storing Carrots If you buy carrots that still have their green tops, remove the greenery as soon as possible because it robs the roots of moisture and vitamins. Store carrots for up to 2 weeks in a plastic bag in the vegetable bin of the refrigerator. Don't store carrots near apples because the apples will give off ethylene gas that can give carrots a bitter taste.

Reviving Carrots — Test Kitchen SECRET

If your carrots have gone limp, soak them in ice water for 20 to 30 minutes until they are crisp again.

"Although bagged shredded carrots are a great convenience, they often seem a little too dry. When you're making a recipe where the moisture matters (such as carrot cake), it's best to shred your own." Jan Moon, Test Kitchens Staffer

Celeriac

Also known as "celery root," this rather unattractive vegetable is knobby, hairy, and brown. When you trim off the ends and peel away the rough exterior, you'll find a creamy, white flesh with a mild flavor. Its texture combines the crunch of celery with the smoothness of potatoes.

Fennel

Fennel has culinary versatility worth exploring. Native to the Mediterranean region, this licorice-flavored member of the parsley family is one of Italy's most popular vegetables.

Most fennel available in American markets is grown in California. The type you'll likely find—Florence, or bulb, fennel (sometimes labeled "fresh anise")—has a bulbous base, stalks like celery, and feathery leaves that resemble Queen Anne's lace. Like celery, the entire plant is edible. The crisp and slightly sweet bulb is especially delicious served raw in salads. Whether braised, sautéed, roasted, or grilled, the fennel bulb mellows and softens with cooking.

Look for small, heavy, white bulbs that are firm and free of cracks, browning, or moist areas. The stalks should be crisp, with feathery, bright green fronds. **Store fennel bulbs in a perforated plastic bag in the refrigerator for up to 5 days. After 5 days, the bulbs begin to toughen and lose flavor.**

Fennel, Leek, and Potato Soup

The mellow flavor of the fennel is a good complement to the leek and potato.

1	tablespoon butter
2	cups chopped fennel bulb (about 2 small bulbs)
2	cups thinly sliced leek (about 2 large)
1¾	cups (1-inch) cubed peeled baking potato
1¼	cups water
½	teaspoon salt
¼	teaspoon fennel seeds
⅛	teaspoon pepper
2	(14-ounce) cans fat-free, less-sodium chicken broth

Fennel fronds (optional)

1. Melt butter in a Dutch oven over medium-high heat. Add fennel bulb and leek; sauté

4 minutes. Add potato, water, salt, fennel seeds, pepper, and broth, and bring to a boil. Cover, reduce heat, and simmer 20 minutes or until potato is tender. Place half of soup in a blender; process until smooth. Pour pureed soup into a bowl. Repeat procedure with remaining soup. Return pureed soup to pan; simmer 5 minutes or until slightly thick. Garnish with fennel fronds, if desired. Yield: 7 servings (serving size: 1 cup).

CALORIES 85 (31% from fat); FAT 2.9g (sat 1.6g, mono 0.5g, poly 0.1g); PROTEIN 3.4g; CARB 12.7g; FIBER 1.7g; CHOL 7mg; IRON 0.8mg; SODIUM 193mg; CALC 39mg

Garlic-Roasted Potatoes and Fennel
You can chop the fronds to use as a garnish.

2   large fennel bulbs with stalks
2   pounds small red potatoes, halved
Cooking spray
1   tablespoon olive oil
1   whole garlic head, unpeeled
2   large green bell peppers, cut into strips
1   teaspoon fennel seeds, lightly crushed
1   teaspoon coriander seeds, crushed
½   teaspoon sweet paprika
½   teaspoon salt
⅛   teaspoon freshly ground black pepper
1½ cups vegetable broth
⅛   teaspoon saffron threads
1   tablespoon sherry vinegar

1. Preheat oven to 375°.
2. Trim tough outer leaves from fennel; reserve fronds for another use. Remove and discard stalks. Cut bulbs in half lengthwise; discard core. Cut bulb halves in half lengthwise.
3. Arrange potatoes in a single layer in a roasting pan coated with cooking spray; drizzle with oil. Remove white papery skin from garlic head. Separate and peel cloves. Chop 1 garlic clove; sprinkle over potatoes. Add peeled garlic cloves,

Using Fennel in Recipes
Test Kitchen SECRET

- Trim the stalks about an inch above the bulb. If you want pieces to stay together for grilling, keep the root end intact. Otherwise, trim about a half inch off the root end before cooking. To slice fennel, stand it on the root end, and cut vertically.
- Fennel stalks can take the place of celery in soups and stews, and can be used as a "bed" for roasted chicken and meats.
- Use fronds as a garnish, or chop them and use as you would other herbs, like dill or parsley. Chopped fennel works especially well in Italian tomato sauces, but add it late in the cooking process so the flavor isn't diluted.
- Fennel seeds don't come from bulb fennel but from common, or wild, fennel. The seeds are slightly nutty, with the expected licorice flavor, and are widely used in sausages, stews, soups, and curries.

"I think the best way to prepare fennel bulb is either roasting or braising because it develops a sweet, mellow flavor." Kellie Kelley, Food Stylist

pepper strips, and next 5 ingredients to potatoes; toss well.
4. Heat broth in a saucepan over medium heat until warm. Remove from heat; stir in saffron. Let stand 10 minutes. Stir in vinegar; drizzle broth over potatoes. Bake at 375° for 30 minutes. Remove from oven; arrange fennel over potatoes. Return to oven; bake 50 minutes or until broth almost evaporates and potatoes begin to brown; stir once. Yield: 6 servings (serving size: 1½ cups).

CALORIES 177 (15% from fat); FAT 2.9g (sat 0.3g, mono 1.7g, poly 0.3g); PROTEIN 6.5g; CARB 38.9g; FIBER 6.8g; CHOL 0mg; IRON 2.2mg; SODIUM 489mg; CALC 80mg

Parsnips

Available year-round, parsnips are at their peak in fall and winter. Purchase firm parsnips with no spots. Store them loosely covered in plastic wrap or in a zip-top plastic bag in the refrigerator crisper drawer for several weeks.

Parsnips are shaped like carrots, but they tend to taper more. To ensure parsnips cook evenly, cut the thicker ends into pieces about the same size as the narrow ends. Out-of-season parsnips can sometimes be woody. To remedy that, trim out the core, and proceed with your recipe. Another option is parboiling the chopped pieces for a few minutes to soften the core.

Roasted Parsnips

The natural sweetness of parsnips comes alive when they're roasted and caramelized.

    3   tablespoons balsamic vinegar
    1   tablespoon brown sugar
    2   teaspoons chopped fresh rosemary
    2   pounds (2-inch-thick) sliced peeled parsnip
    1   large red onion, peeled and quartered
Cooking spray
    1   tablespoon olive oil
    ½   teaspoon salt
    ¼   teaspoon freshly ground black pepper

1. Combine first 5 ingredients in a large zip-top plastic bag; seal and marinate in refrigerator 1 hour, turning twice. Remove parsnip and onion from bag, discarding marinade.
2. Preheat oven to 500°.
3. Place parsnip and onion in a shallow roasting pan coated with cooking spray. Drizzle with oil, and toss to coat. Sprinkle with salt and pepper. Bake at 500° for 30 minutes or until tender, stirring often. Yield: 4 servings (serving size: 1 cup).

CALORIES 235 (16% from fat); FAT 4.2g (sat 0.6g, mono 2.8g, poly 0.4g); PROTEIN 3.2g; CARB 49.3g; FIBER 11.9g; CHOL 0mg; IRON 1.7mg; SODIUM 319mg; CALC 97mg

Sweet Potatoes

Sweet potatoes are actually members of the morning glory family—they're warm-weather plants, happy in the Caribbean and other hot, humid climates. (Potatoes, by contrast, grow best at high altitudes and cold climates.)

Potatoes and sweet potatoes are not in the same family, despite the notion that two things that look alike must be related. During the years, no one has managed to extricate the truth from that old misunderstanding. Several years ago, Southern marketers tried to paste the name "yam" onto their sweet potatoes as a way to distinguish them from the Irish potato—but that seems to have only added more confusion. A true yam is native to West Africa and Asia and is entirely different botanically.

Varieties Sweet potatoes range from red to orange. The most familiar are Red Garnets, a favorite at Thanksgiving. There are also white sweet potatoes—most are quite dry and are better in stews or gratins with lots of added moisture.

Nutrients Sweet potatoes are rich in beta carotene, vitamin C, and vitamin E. One cup has more than six times the recommended amount of beta carotene and 50 percent of the Recommended Dietary Allowance (RDA) for vitamin C. Cook with the skin on to retain the vitamins.

Uses Their high moisture content means sweet potatoes are best for mashing or tossing into soups and stews, though many people also enjoy them baked or roasted.

Sweet Potato, Carrot, and Apple Gratin

Flavored with orange juice and ginger, this gratin makes a perfect accompaniment for a main dish of pork or ham. Because it has both sweet potatoes and carrots, this vegetable dish is an excellent source of beta carotene.

    4   cups water
    4   cups (½-inch) cubed peeled sweet potato
    2   cups thinly sliced carrot
 1½   cups diced peeled Granny Smith apple
    ⅓   cup orange juice
    ¼   cup dried cranberries
    2   tablespoons brown sugar
    1   teaspoon grated peeled fresh ginger
    ¼   teaspoon salt
    ¼   teaspoon pepper
        Cooking spray
    ¾   cup (3 ounces) shredded fontina or
          Cheddar cheese

1. Preheat oven to 375°.
2. Combine first 3 ingredients in a large saucepan; bring to a boil. Cover, reduce heat, and simmer 4 minutes or until vegetables are tender. Drain well.
3. Combine sweet potato mixture, apple, and next 6 ingredients in a large bowl; toss gently. Spoon into a 6-cup gratin dish coated with cooking spray; bake at 375° for 25 minutes. Sprinkle with cheese; bake an additional 10 minutes or until cheese is golden brown. Yield: 6 servings (serving size: 1 cup).

CALORIES 217 (21% from fat); FAT 5g (sat 2.8g, mono 1.3g, poly 0.4g); PROTEIN 5.8g; CARB 39g; FIBER 5.1g; CHOL 16mg; IRON 1mg; SODIUM 124mg; CALC 117mg

Turnips

Fresh turnips are usually available year-round, but their peak season is October through February. Choose turnips that feel heavy for their size—these are the young ones and will be more delicately flavored and textured than older ones. The roots should be firm, and the greens should be bright and fresh-looking. (Cook the greens as you would cook any other winter greens such as collards or mustard greens. See page 280-281.)

Glazed Turnips with Chestnuts

Wash, peel, and trim the turnips before cooking them.

    6   cups (¾-inch) cubed peeled turnips
          (about 2½ pounds)
 1½   tablespoons butter
    ¼   cup dark brown sugar
    2   tablespoons water
    ¼   teaspoon salt
    1   (7.4-ounce) bottle shelled whole chestnuts,
          halved

1. Cook turnips in boiling water 3 minutes; drain. Melt butter in a large, heavy skillet over medium-high heat. Add turnips and sugar; cook 10 minutes or until golden brown. Stir in water, salt, and chestnuts; cook until liquid evaporates, stirring occasionally. Yield: 6 servings (serving size: ¾ cup).

CALORIES 142 (19% from fat); FAT 3g (sat 1.8g, mono 0.8g, poly 0.2g); PROTEIN 2.2g; CARB 30g; FIBER 4.7g; CHOL 8mg; IRON 0.5mg; SODIUM 216mg; CALC 45mg

---

Terrific Turnips
Test Kitchen SECRET

Turnips are at their best when they're cooked with an ingredient that gives them a note of sweetness, either sugar or a sweet wine. Or enhance their flavor by serving turnips with meat or by cooking them in meat juices.

Squash

Squash are members of the gourd family, which is native to the Western Hemisphere. Generally, they're divided into two categories: winter squash and summer squash.

Winter Squash

Winter squash have thick skins and large seeds. These squash are picked in the fall and stored

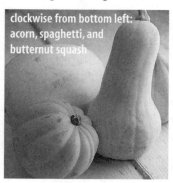

clockwise from bottom left: acorn, spaghetti, and butternut squash

until spring, so they're available in peak form throughout the winter. Winter squash varieties include acorn, butternut, hubbard, spaghetti, turban, and pumpkins.

Butternut Squash

Butternut may be one of the easiest winter squashes to cook because its smooth skin just pares away with a potato peeler, and its pulp cooks relatively fast. It seems to have fewer seeds than the rest of the winter squash family, and there's no mistaking it at the supermarket. Butternut squash is always the same; all you have to decide is whether you want a big one or a small one. **Look for a squash that has no cracks or soft spots and is heavy for its size. Butternut squash will keep for months in a cool, dry place.**

How to Peel Butternut Squash

1. Cut the squash in half, and remove its seeds and fibers with a spoon.

2. Peel the squash with a vegetable peeler, cut it in cubes, and proceed.

Mashing Squash
Test Kitchen SECRET

When a recipe calls for mashed squash, the easiest way to prepare it is to cut the squash in half vertically, then remove the seeds and fibers with a spoon. Place the halves, cut sides down, in a 13 x 9-inch baking dish. Add water to a depth of 1 inch, and bake at 375° for about 30 minutes or until tender—when you can pierce the squash easily with a small knife. (You can also microwave the squash at HIGH 10 to 15 minutes.) Let the squash cool, then scoop the pulp out with a spoon, and mash the pulp with a potato masher. One pound uncooked squash will yield about 1 cup mashed.

Spaghetti Squash

This squash is called "spaghetti" because when you cut it open and cook it, the insides separate into long, thin wisps that look amazingly like strands of spaghetti noodles. The spaghetti squash's slightly sweet, slightly nutty flavor adds wonderful nuances to a range of dishes. Strong flavors and robust salsas complement it perfectly.

Also known as "vegetable spaghetti," it is available year-round, though peak season is early fall through midwinter. **Look for smooth, hard squash, that are pale yellow in color. Store raw, cut spaghetti squash in the refrigerator for up to 2 days; cover with plastic wrap.**

Simple Baked Spaghetti Squash

Here's a basic spaghetti squash recipe. You can simply season the squash with a little butter and Parmesan cheese, or top with a fresh tomato sauce.

    1   (3-pound) spaghetti squash

1. Preheat oven to 350°.
2. Cut squash in half lengthwise, discarding seeds. Place squash halves, cut sides down, in a 13 x 9-inch baking dish; add water to dish to a depth of ½ inch. Bake at 350° for 45 minutes or until squash is tender when pierced with a fork.
3. Remove squash from dish, and cool. Scrape inside of squash with a fork to remove spaghetti-like strands. Yield: 5 cups (serving size: 1 cup).

CALORIES 45 (8% from fat); FAT 0.4g (sat 0.1g, mono 0g, poly 0.2g); PROTEIN 1g; CARB 10g; FIBER 2g; CHOL 0mg; IRON 0.5mg; SODIUM 28mg; CALC 33mg

Microwave variation: Be sure that your baking dish will fit into the microwave before adding the squash and water. Cover squash with heavy-duty plastic wrap; vent. Microwave at HIGH 15 minutes (or about 5 minutes per pound) until squash is tender when pierced with a fork.

The Scoop on Squash

1. Cut squash in half with a heavy knife, and scrape out seeds.

2. Place halves in a baking dish, and add water before cooking.

3. Bake until tender when pierced with a fork.

4. Scrape out strands of squash using a fork.

Pumpkins

Pumpkin is a most versatile squash, and clever cooks can turn plump fresh pumpkins into soups,

ragoûts, casseroles, entrées, and sides. Fresh pumpkin has a more delicate, nuanced flavor than canned, and it renders any dish the golden orange of autumn. In addition to tantalizing taste and inviting color, pumpkin brings a host of nutrients to the table, particularly beta-carotene, vitamin C, and potassium.

Pumpkins come in many sizes. For example, one record-setting field pumpkin weighed in at 1,140 pounds. But smaller types, called pie pumpkins, differ from their gargantuan kin: They contain less water and are prized for their more concentrated flavor and sweetness.

Though the season is short, pumpkins are plentiful at the supermarket. You can take home several and store them in the refrigerator for up to 3 months or in a cool, dry place for up to 1 month. (Root cellars are too damp, but an attic or spare room kept at 45° to 60° is ideal.)

Sugar-Roasted Pumpkin

When the pumpkin comes out of the oven, there will be a small pool of syrup in each wedge, but it's absorbed by the pumpkin almost immediately.

1   small pumpkin (about 2½ pounds)
Cooking spray
2   teaspoons butter, divided
2   tablespoons dark brown sugar, divided

1. Preheat oven to 425°.
2. Cut pumpkin into 4 wedges, discarding seeds and membrane. Place pumpkin wedges, cut sides up, in an 11 x 7-inch baking dish coated with cooking spray. Place ½ teaspoon butter on each wedge, and sprinkle each wedge with 1½ teaspoons sugar. Bake at 425° for 35 minutes or until tender. Yield: 4 servings (serving size: 1 wedge).

CALORIES 94 (20% from fat); FAT 2.1g (sat 1.3g, mono 0.6g, poly 0.1g); PROTEIN 2g; CARB 19.6g; FIBER 1g; CHOL 5mg; IRON 1.7mg; SODIUM 24mg; CALC 48mg

Pumpkin Know-how

When a recipe calls for baking pumpkin, cut the pieces large, and bake them with the skin on, scraping the softened flesh away from the rind with a spoon.

If a recipe calls for boiling pumpkin, cut the pieces smaller, and use a sharp, sturdy knife to peel the rind before putting it in the pot.

Use your hand or a spoon to remove the seeds and stringy flesh. Rinse and clean the seeds, and spread them out in a single layer to dry. Whether you decide to remove the hull or not, toss the seeds with a little oil, and bake at 350° for about 30 minutes.

Although the season is short, pumpkins can be stored in the refrigerator for up to 3 months or in a cool, dry place for up to 1 month.

Pork Stew with Pumpkin

You may also use butternut or acorn squash when pumpkin is out of season.

1	tablespoon olive oil
1½	pounds boneless pork loin, trimmed and cut into ½-inch pieces
1	cup finely chopped onion
1	cup finely chopped red bell pepper
¾	cup finely chopped celery
2	teaspoons dried rubbed sage
1	teaspoon salt
½	teaspoon freshly ground black pepper
1	(28-ounce) can diced tomatoes, undrained
1	(14-ounce) can fat-free, less-sodium chicken broth
4	cups (½-inch) cubed peeled fresh pumpkin
1	(10-ounce) package frozen whole-kernel corn
2	teaspoons grated orange rind
4½	cups cooked egg noodles (about 3 cups uncooked)
6	tablespoons chopped fresh flat-leaf parsley

1. Heat oil in a large Dutch oven over high heat. Add pork; cook 4 minutes or until browned, stirring occasionally. Add onion, bell pepper, and celery; cook for 2 minutes, stirring occasionally. Stir in sage, salt, black pepper, tomatoes, and broth; bring to a boil. Cover, reduce heat, and simmer 30 minutes. Stir in pumpkin and corn; bring to a boil. Cover, reduce heat, and simmer 1 hour or until pumpkin is tender. Stir in grated rind. Serve over noodles; sprinkle with parsley. Yield: 6 servings (serving size: 2 cups stew, ¾ cup noodles, and 1 tablespoon parsley).

CALORIES 463 (23% from fat); FAT 11.8g (sat 3.4g, mono 5.3g, poly 1.7g); PROTEIN 35.4g; CARB 56.2g; FIBER 5.7g; CHOL 108mg; IRON 5mg; SODIUM 715mg; CALC 122mg

Warm Pumpkin-Cheese Dip

The unusual combination of goat cheese and pumpkin was a surprise hit in our Test Kitchens. Serve the dip with crisp breadsticks, bagel chips, or toasted French or sourdough baguette slices.

1¼	cups plain low-fat yogurt
½	teaspoon butter
1	cup thinly sliced leek
2	teaspoons chopped fresh or ½ teaspoon dried thyme
1	teaspoon salt
¾	cup (3 ounces) goat cheese
⅓	cup evaporated fat-free milk
1	(15-ounce) can pumpkin
3	large egg whites

1. Preheat oven to 375°.
2. Spoon yogurt onto several layers of heavy-duty paper towels; spread to ½-inch thickness. Cover with additional paper towels; let stand 5 minutes. Scrape into a large bowl using a rubber spatula.
3. Melt butter in a skillet over medium-high heat. Add leek; sauté 5 minutes or until tender. Remove from heat, and stir in thyme and salt. Place strained yogurt, goat cheese, and remaining ingredients in a large bowl, and beat with a mixer at medium speed just until smooth. Stir in leek mixture. Spoon pumpkin mixture into a 1-quart baking dish. Bake at 375° for 25 minutes or until dip is bubbly and lightly browned. Serve warm. Yield: 3½ cups (serving size: ¼ cup).

CALORIES 57 (36% from fat); FAT 2.3g (sat 1.6g, mono 0.5g, poly 0.1g); PROTEIN 3.9g; CARB 5.5g; FIBER 1g; CHOL 7mg; IRON 0.7mg; SODIUM 306mg; CALC 81mg

Pumpkin Biscuits with Orange-Honey Butter

Serve these treats at breakfast or dinner with baked ham or pork chops. The analysis includes 1 teaspoon of Orange-Honey Butter per serving.

2 cups all-purpose flour
3 tablespoons sugar
2 teaspoons baking powder
1 teaspoon ground cinnamon
½ teaspoon baking soda
½ teaspoon salt
¼ teaspoon ground nutmeg
¼ cup chilled butter, cut into small pieces
¾ cup low-fat buttermilk
½ cup canned pumpkin
Cooking spray
¼ cup Orange-Honey Butter

1. Preheat oven to 450°.
2. Lightly spoon flour into dry measuring cups, and level with a knife. Combine flour and next 6 ingredients; cut in chilled butter with a pastry blender or 2 knives until mixture resembles coarse meal.
3. Combine buttermilk and pumpkin; add to flour mixture, stirring just until moist. Turn the dough out onto a lightly floured surface; knead lightly 5 times. Roll dough to about ½-inch thickness. Cut into 12 biscuits with a 2½-inch biscuit cutter. Place biscuits on a baking sheet coated with cooking spray. Bake at 450° for 11 minutes or until golden. Serve warm with ¼ cup Orange-Honey Butter. Yield: 12 servings (serving size: 1 biscuit and 1 teaspoon butter).

CALORIES 153 (33% from fat); FAT 5.6g (sat 3.4g, mono 1.6g, poly 0.3g); PROTEIN 2.9g; CARB 23.1g; FIBER 1g; CHOL 15mg; IRON 1.2mg; SODIUM 311mg; CALC 68mg

Orange-Honey Butter:

Store in the refrigerator for up to 2 weeks.

½ cup butter, softened
½ cup honey
½ teaspoon grated orange rind

1. Combine all ingredients in a medium bowl, and beat with a mixer at medium speed until well blended. Yield: 1¼ cups (serving size: 1 teaspoon).

CALORIES 22 (61% from fat); FAT 1.5g (sat 0.9g, mono 0.5g, poly 0.1g); PROTEIN 0g; CARB 2.3g; FIBER 0g; CHOL 4mg; IRON 0mg; SODIUM 16mg; CALC 1mg

---

Canned Pumpkin
Test Kitchen SECRET

While fresh pumpkin is available only in the fall and winter, canned pumpkin is a mainstay at most supermarkets. It's easy to prepare—a couple of twists of the can opener, and you're ready to go. Use it to lend wholesome flavor and color to biscuits and dessert soufflés while boosting the nutrition of every dish. Pumpkin offers fiber, potassium, and beta-carotene, an antioxidant that may help prevent heart disease and certain types of cancer.

Canned pumpkin is just as nutritious as its fresh counterpart (both are good sources of beta-carotene). Canned pumpkin is consistent in texture and flavor, making it an ideal ingredient in baking.

Place the unused portion of a can of pumpkin in an airtight container, and refrigerate for up to a week, or freeze for up to 3 months.

Summer Squash

Summer squash such as crookneck, pattypan, and zucchini have thin, edible skins and soft seeds. The flesh is tender, has a mild flavor, and doesn't require a long cooking time. Delicate crookneck squash, with its swanlike neck and pale yellow flesh, is perfect in chilled soups. Zucchini is used in almost everything, including salads, breads, and gratins.

Summer squash's mild taste and cool flavor make it perfect for blending with other ingredients or for using in simple preparations highlighting the taste of fresh herbs. Summer squash and zucchini are at their peak from June through late August.

Chilled Summer-Squash Soup with Curry

Because yellow squash has such a mild flavor, it's a perfect background for this soup with distinct notes of curry and mint.

```
2      teaspoons curry powder
1¼    pounds yellow squash, cubed
½      cup chopped onion
1      (14-ounce) can vegetable broth
1¾    cups low-fat buttermilk
1      tablespoon chopped fresh mint
½      teaspoon salt
```

1. Cook curry powder in a large saucepan over medium heat 1 minute or until toasted. Add squash, onion, and broth. Bring to a boil; cover, reduce heat, and simmer 25 minutes or until tender. Place squash mixture in a blender; process until smooth. Pour mixture into a bowl; cover and chill. Stir in the buttermilk, mint, and salt. Yield: 5 servings (serving size: 1 cup).

CALORIES 82 (24% from fat); FAT 2.2g (sat 1g, mono 0.6g, poly 0.4g); PROTEIN 4.8g; CARB 12.3g; FIBER 2.5g; CHOL 0mg; IRON 0.8mg; SODIUM 681mg; CALC 136mg

Lemon-Glazed Zucchini Quick Bread

Zucchini have the best flavor when they're very young and small. They also have a lot of water, so zucchini bread tends to be quite moist and tender.

```
2⅓    cups all-purpose flour
¾      cup granulated sugar
2      teaspoons baking powder
1      teaspoon ground cinnamon
½      teaspoon baking soda
½      teaspoon salt
¼      teaspoon ground nutmeg
1      cup finely shredded zucchini
½      cup 1% low-fat milk
¼      cup vegetable oil
2      tablespoons grated lemon rind
1      large egg
Cooking spray
1      cup sifted powdered sugar
2      tablespoons fresh lemon juice
```

1. Preheat oven to 350°.
2. Lightly spoon flour into dry measuring cups; level with a knife. Combine flour and next 6 ingredients in a large bowl; make a well in center of mixture. Combine zucchini, milk, oil, rind, and egg in a bowl; add to flour mixture. Stir just until moist.
3. Spoon batter into an 8 x 4-inch loaf pan coated with cooking spray. Bake at 350° for 1 hour or until a wooden pick inserted in center comes out clean. Cool 10 minutes in pan on a wire rack; remove from pan. Cool completely on wire rack.
4. Combine powdered sugar and lemon juice; stir with a whisk. Drizzle glaze over loaf. Yield: 12 servings (serving size: 1 slice).

CALORIES 230 (21% from fat); FAT 5.4g (sat 1.1g, mono 1.6g, poly 2.4g); PROTEIN 3.5g; CARB 42.6g; FIBER 0.8g; CHOL 19mg; IRON 1.4mg; SODIUM 243mg; CALC 69mg

Store summer squash in plastic bags in the refrigerator for no more than 5 days.

Tomatoes

There are few greater pleasures than a just-picked ripe red tomato still warm from the summer sun, or a basket of juicy heirloom tomatoes from your farmers' market. But even the reddest, plumpest specimens can disappoint when it comes to flavor and juiciness. Finding the best choice, knowing its flavor secrets, and understanding the best way to preserve that flavor will deepen your enthusiasm for one of summer's great tastes.

One pound of whole tomatoes yields about 2 cups chopped and seeded.

Ask the *Cooking Light* Cooks

How do you pick a good tomato? Not by looks. Some of the best-tasting tomatoes happen to be some of the homeliest. And picture-perfect tomatoes can be flavorless. Picking a good tomato starts at home or in your neighborhood. Home-grown tomatoes can't be beat. But when you buy tomatoes, smell them—a good tomato should smell like a tomato, especially at the stem end.

My grocer sells little net bags of tomatoes still attached to a vine. Are these really worth their high price? Those tomatoes were not necessarily ripe when picked, so they often lack flavor. They're generally not worth the extra expense unless you know for sure that they were ripened on the vine. (See "Best Winter Picks" (page 323) for tips on vine-ripened tomatoes.)

What is the best way to ripen and store tomatoes? Place them at room temperature in a single layer, shoulder-side up, out of direct sunlight. To store ripe tomatoes for any extended period of time, keep them between 55° and 65°.

What makes a tomato mealy? Tomatoes are greatly affected by temperature, even during the growing process. They originally came from the warm western coast of South America and don't respond well to temperatures below 50°. Cool temperatures can change a tomato's composition, converting its natural sugar to starch and resulting in a tasteless, mealy tomato. For this reason, never refrigerate a tomato. The cold environment causes the water in the tomato to expand, ruining the texture.

How can you tell if a tomato is mealy before slicing into it? If a tomato feels soft, there's a chance it will be mealy, but, unfortunately, it isn't always possible to tell before slicing.

When should you use canned tomatoes? Opt for canned tomatoes when you want their juice. Otherwise, let the season be your guide and use fresh tomatoes whenever possible.

> "For the best-tasting tomatoes, store them at room temperature, not in the refrigerator."
>
> Sam Brannock, Test Kitchens Staffer

Tomato Varieties

Here are some of our favorite tomatoes and our suggestions for the best ways to use them.

Beefsteak: Known as a slicing tomato, this large, ribbed, pumpkin-shaped type is common at farmers' markets. **Because its characteristic flavor balances sweetness and acidity, it's great for eating raw. It also maintains its shape and flavor when cooked.**

Cherry: This term refers to a family of tomatoes, which includes several types and colors, all of which are about an inch in diameter and similar in flavor. **The defining difference among the members of this family is their shape.** They include the following three varieties:

- *Cherry* also refers specifically to a small round type. Available in red, orange, green, or yellow, they taste similar to beefsteak and globe tomatoes but have a more pronounced sweetness. They're often good during winter months. Try them in salads or quick sautés. Use as a garnish, or eat them out of hand. Cut them in half so they'll be easier to eat.
- *Grape* tomatoes have a more elliptical shape, similar to a grape, and are almost always red. They have a more intense sweetness than the cherry kind, balanced by a subtle acidity. **For the best flavor, look for grape tomatoes that are no larger than an inch in diameter. If they're larger, they'll have a higher water content and a diluted taste.**
- *Pear tomatoes* are shaped liked small pears or teardrops. They are best eaten raw, but you can cook them briefly to finish a sauce or toss with pasta. Pear tomatoes are a bit smaller than the cherry variety and have a flavor similar to grape tomatoes. They're available in yellow, red, and orange.

Globe: This is the kind you usually find in grocery stores. A medium-sized, firm, juicy tomato similar to the beefsteak, it also has a good balance of sweetness and acidity. **It's best raw, so reserve globe tomatoes for salads, cold sandwiches, or eating over the kitchen sink.**

Green tomatoes: Picked before ripe, they have a sharp, tart taste and firm flesh, which makes them excellent for frying, broiling, and stewing. **You don't want to eat them raw, but cooking green tomatoes softens the flesh and tempers the acidity.**

Heirloom: These tomatoes are old or original tomato varieties that fell out of production and have been reintroduced in recent years. They are open-pollinated and are not genetically altered to suit modern commercial production. **Look for heirloom tomatoes at farmers' markets, or grow your own.** Flavors vary widely among the hundreds of types, and there is a huge assortment of colors, shapes, and sizes. Among the best-loved varieties: mortgage lifter, brandywine, Arkansas traveler, Cherokee, and zebra.

Plum: Also called Roma or Italian, this egg-shaped red or yellow tomato is not as sweet or acidic as the beefsteak and globe varieties. **Plum tomatoes have lower water content and fewer seeds, so they are especially good for cooking and canning.** Plum are the best year-round supermarket tomatoes.

Open-Faced Bacon, Lettuce, and Fried Green Tomato Sandwiches

Double-breading the tomato slices gives them a crunchy coating. Soaking the tomatoes in hot water draws out their moisture, which helps keep them crisp when cooked. On their own, the fried green tomatoes in this recipe are a classic Southern side dish.

2	medium green tomatoes, cut into 12 (¼-inch-thick) slices (about 1 pound)
2	tablespoons fat-free milk
4	large egg whites, lightly beaten
1½	cups yellow cornmeal
¾	teaspoon salt
¼	teaspoon freshly ground black pepper
2	tablespoons olive oil, divided
5	tablespoons light mayonnaise
1	teaspoon fresh lemon juice
¼	teaspoon hot sauce
6	(1½-ounce) slices white bread, toasted
6	Bibb lettuce leaves
9	bacon slices, cooked and cut in half
2	tablespoons chopped fresh chives

1. Place tomato slices in a large bowl; cover with hot water. Let stand 15 minutes. Drain and pat dry with paper towels. Combine milk and egg whites, stirring with a whisk. Combine cornmeal, salt, and pepper in a shallow dish, stirring with a whisk. Dip each tomato slice in milk mixture; dredge in cornmeal mixture. Return tomato slices, 1 at a time, to milk mixture; dredge in cornmeal mixture.

2. Heat 1 tablespoon oil in a large nonstick skillet over medium-high heat. Add half of tomato slices; cook 4 minutes on each side or until crisp and golden. Repeat procedure with remaining oil and tomato slices.

3. Combine mayonnaise, juice, and hot sauce, stirring with a whisk. Spread about 1 tablespoon mayonnaise mixture onto each bread slice; top with 1 lettuce leaf, 3 bacon pieces, and 2 tomato

slices. Sprinkle each sandwich with 1 teaspoon chives. Serve immediately. Yield: 6 servings (serving size: 1 sandwich).

CALORIES 386 (30% from fat); FAT 12.8g (sat 2.8g, mono 4.5g, poly 2.6g); PROTEIN 12.2g; CARB 56.2g; FIBER 3.9g; CHOL 16mg; IRON 2.2mg; SODIUM 834mg; CALC 44mg

Tomato-Basil Salsa

Serve with grilled vegetables, beef, or poultry. Or try it as a condiment on a grilled chicken sandwich or toasted bagel with cheese.

2	cups chopped seeded peeled tomato
¼	cup chopped fresh basil
2	tablespoons chopped red onion
2	tablespoons red wine vinegar
¼	teaspoon salt
⅛	teaspoon freshly ground black pepper

1. Combine all ingredients in a bowl. Yield: 2 cups (serving size: ¼ cup).

CALORIES 11 (16% from fat); FAT 0.2g (sat 0g, mono 0g, poly 0.1g); PROTEIN 0.5g; CARB 2.5g; FIBER 0.6g; CHOL 0mg; IRON 0.2mg; SODIUM 77mg; CALC 5mg

Seeding a Tomato
Test Kitchen SECRET

To remove seeds, cut tomatoes in half horizontally. Cup each tomato half in the palm of your hand, cut side down; gently squeeze out seeds. You can also scoop out seeds using your fingers, or push them out with a spoon.

It's not always necessary to seed a tomato, but you might want to in recipes such as sauces where seeds may not be desirable, or in salads or salsas where the seeds may cling to other vegetables and create a less-than-desirable appearance.

Coring and Peeling Tomatoes

Coring

To core a tomato, use a small knife and cut a small circle around the stem end. With the tip of the paring knife, remove the core of the tomato.

Peeling

1. Using a sharp knife, cut a shallow "X" in the bottom of each tomato.

2. Drop tomatoes into boiling water for 30 seconds; remove with a slotted spoon or tongs.

3. Plunge into ice water; remove and discard skins. Or if appropriate to your recipe, cut the tomato in half, and use the largest side of a box grater to grate the tomato. The skin will stay behind.

Tomato-Garlic Soup

The tomato skins can become tough and chewy, so it's best to peel them for this soup.

4	large tomatoes, cored
2	quarts water
2	quarts ice water
1¼	cups uncooked seashell pasta
4	teaspoons olive oil, divided
¾	cup finely chopped red onion
8	garlic cloves, thinly sliced
1	cup water
1	tablespoon chopped fresh parsley
1	tablespoon minced fresh chives
1	teaspoon minced fresh oregano
1	teaspoon minced fresh thyme
2	(14-ounce) cans fat-free, less-sodium chicken broth
1	tablespoon red wine vinegar
½	teaspoon freshly ground black pepper

1. Score bottom of each tomato with an "X." Bring 2 quarts water to a boil in a Dutch oven. Add tomatoes; cook 30 seconds, and remove with a slotted spoon. Plunge tomatoes into ice water. Drain and peel. Cut each tomato in half crosswise. Push seeds out; discard seeds. Chop tomatoes.
2. Cook pasta according to package directions, omitting salt and fat; drain. Toss pasta with 1 teaspoon oil. Cool completely.
3. Heat 1 tablespoon oil in a Dutch oven over medium-low heat. Add onion; cook 7 minutes, stirring occasionally. Add garlic; cook 3 minutes, stirring frequently. Stir in tomatoes, 1 cup water, and next 5 ingredients; bring to a boil. Reduce heat; simmer 20 minutes, stirring occasionally. Add pasta, vinegar, and pepper; cook 1 minute. Yield: 4 servings (serving size: 1½ cups).

CALORIES 258 (22% from fat); FAT 6.4g (sat 1g, mono 3.9g, poly 1.3g); PROTEIN 10.2g; CARB 43.8g; FIBER 4.8g; CHOL 0mg; IRON 2.6mg; SODIUM 552mg; CALC 43mg

5 Ways to Make Winter Tomatoes Taste Like Summer

Even in the dead of winter, you can use these tricks on a store-bought winter tomato to satisfy your tomato craving. Here are our five simple techniques for bringing an off-season vegetable to life.

1 **Roasting** briefly at high heat leaves tomatoes juicy while condensing their flavors.

Roasted Tomatoes with Shallots and Herbs

Serve with roasted chicken or grilled fish.

    4   medium tomatoes, cut in half horizontally
            (about 2 pounds)
    ½   teaspoon salt, divided
    Cooking spray
    ¼   cup minced shallot
    1   tablespoon chopped fresh flat-leaf parsley
    1   teaspoon chopped fresh oregano
    1   teaspoon chopped fresh thyme
    ½   teaspoon chopped fresh rosemary
    ¼   teaspoon freshly ground black pepper
    2   teaspoons olive oil

1. Preheat oven to 350°.
2. Core and seed tomato halves. Sprinkle cut sides of tomato halves with ¼ teaspoon salt. Place halves, cut sides down, on paper towels. Let stand 20 minutes.
3. Place tomato halves, cut sides up, in a 13 x 9-inch baking dish coated with cooking spray. Sprinkle with ¼ teaspoon salt, shallot, and next 5 ingredients. Drizzle with oil. Bake at 350° for 1 hour and 15 minutes or until tomatoes soften. Yield: 8 servings (serving size: 1 tomato half).

CALORIES 38 (36% from fat); FAT 1.5g (sat 0.2g, mono 0.9g, poly 0.3g); PROTEIN 1.1g; CARB 6.2g; FIBER 1.3g; CHOL 0mg; IRON 0.6mg; SODIUM 121mg; CALC 10mg

2 **Grilling** caramelizes the natural sugars, producing slightly charred, juicy tomatoes with rich flavor. To grill tomatoes, core and cut large tomatoes in half horizontally, then seed them. Heat a grill pan coated with cooking spray over medium-high heat. Place tomato halves, cut sides down, in pan; grill about 5 minutes. Turn, grill 1 minute or until the tomato skin is blackened. Remove from pan and cool.

3 **Marinating** tomatoes in an acid such as lemon juice or balsamic vinegar (or a sweet ingredient such as honey) and sprinkling with salt and pepper enhances the natural flavors of the raw tomatoes. To marinate, slice the tomatoes, drizzle marinade over the slices, and let stand for 15 minutes. There's no need to refrigerate while marinating.

4 **Braising** (slow cooking in liquid over low heat) causes tomatoes to break down and absorb other flavors in the dish.

Better Flavor for Lackluster Tomatoes

Test Kitchen
SECRET

Even the very best tomatoes taste a little better with a sprinkle of salt, which accentuates the balance of sweetness and acidity.

If you have a tomato that's flavorless beyond a restorative touch of salt, drizzle a few drops of balsamic vinegar or honey over it to bring out both the sweetness and acidity.

Grilled Steak with Charred Tomato Salsa

The high heat used in grilling quickly caramelizes the natural sugars, producing slightly charred tomatoes with rich flavor.

- 1 pound large tomatoes, cored, cut in half horizontally, and seeded (about 2)
- Cooking spray
- ½ cup thinly sliced red onion
- 1 tablespoon red wine vinegar
- 1 teaspoon basil-flavored olive oil
- ¼ teaspoon salt, divided
- ¼ teaspoon freshly ground black pepper, divided
- 6 basil leaves, thinly sliced
- 1 (1-pound) boneless sirloin steak

1. Place tomato halves, cut sides down, on paper towels. Let stand 30 minutes.

2. Heat a grill pan coated with cooking spray over medium-high heat. Place tomato halves, cut sides down, in pan; grill 5 minutes. Turn tomato halves; grill 1 minute or until skin is blackened. Remove from pan; cool 5 minutes. Cut tomato halves into 1-inch pieces. Combine tomato, onion, vinegar, oil, ⅛ teaspoon salt, ⅛ teaspoon pepper, and basil.

3. Sprinkle steak with ⅛ teaspoon salt and ⅛ teaspoon pepper. Place steak in pan coated with cooking spray; grill 6 minutes on each side or until desired degree of doneness. Let stand 5 minutes. Cut steak diagonally across the grain into thin slices. Serve with tomato salsa. Yield: 4 servings (serving size: 3 ounces steak and about ¼ cup tomato salsa).

CALORIES 206 (35% from fat); FAT 8g (sat 2.8g, mono 3.7g, poly 0.5g); PROTEIN 26.4g; CARB 6.6g; FIBER 1.6g; CHOL 76mg; IRON 3.4mg; SODIUM 213mg; CALC 20mg

---

Best Winter Picks

Test Kitchen SECRET

Some tomatoes are better than others in winter. Best bets are vine-ripened, Roma and cherry tomatoes. Vine-ripened tomatoes are small to medium in size and are often sold in clusters still attached to a vine. Oval Roma, or plum, tomatoes have firmer pulp and fewer seeds than other varieties, so they hold their shape well. Cherry and grape tomatoes are always flavorful because their size, shape, and packaging protects them; they have less need to be hybridized to stand up to the rigors of mechanical harvesting and shipping.

5 **Oven Drying** is cooking tomatoes for a long time at a low temperature to dehydrate them and concentrate their flavor. Oven-dried tomatoes are plumper and softer than commercial sun-dried tomatoes and have a more delicate, rich flavor.

Oven-Dried Tomatoes

You can use these dried tomatoes in any recipe that calls for sun-dried tomatoes.

- 1½ pounds plum tomatoes, cored, and cut in half lengthwise (about 10)
- 1 teaspoon kosher salt

1. Sprinkle cut sides of tomato halves with salt. Place tomato halves, cut sides down, on paper towels. Let stand 1 hour.

2. Preheat oven to 300°.

3. Arrange tomato halves, cut sides up, in a single layer on a baking sheet. Bake at 300° for 3½ to 4 hours or until edges of tomatoes curl (tomatoes will feel dry to the touch). Yield: 1 cup (serving size: ¼ cup).

CALORIES 36 (15% from fat); FAT 0.6g (sat 0.1g, mono 0.1g, poly 0.2g); PROTEIN 1.5g; CARB 7.9g; FIBER 1.9g; CHOL 0mg; IRON 0.8mg; SODIUM 251mg; CALC 9mg

CHAPTER 9

Fruits

Fruits play a leading role in the kitchens at *Cooking Light*.
Not only are they packed with nutrients, they add superb
sweetness to desserts and savory dishes alike.

In this guide to our favorite fruits, we've grouped similar ones and listed those groups alphabetically. Our staff shares with you what we've learned about selecting and using fresh fruits.

Apples

Red Delicious, Golden Delicious, and Granny Smiths used to be the apple standards. But in supermarkets today, newer varieties like Pink Lady, Braeburn, and Cameo share space with the old standbys. How to know which one is best to use? That will depend on how you're planning to use the apples.

Picking Apples Look for firm, vibrantly colored apples with no bruises. They should smell fresh, not musty. Skins should be tight and smooth. We recommend that you extend your search for apples beyond the aisles of the grocery store. Check out roadside stands and farmers' markets for exceptional local apple varieties.

Though you may like to display apples in a fruit bowl, don't. Storing at room temperature can make them mealy. Store them in a plastic bag in the refrigerator for up to 6 weeks. Apples emit ethylene, a gas that hastens ripening; the plastic bag will prevent them from accelerating the ripening of other produce in your refrigerator.

Ask the *Cooking Light* Cooks

Which apples do you prefer? We picked 12 common supermarket varieties and evaluated them to come up with our staff's favorites.

Most Outstanding for Cooking and Eating: The prize goes to Braeburn. Great both raw and cooked, this rich, juicy apple deserves first place. The first runner-up was the Pink Lady; the second runner-up, Granny Smith. Cameo came in fourth.

Best looking: We loved the Gala's hefty size and its pink-orange striping. Pink Lady, with its soft blush and yellow undertones, came in a close second.

Best raw: Pink Lady's firm, crisp texture and complex tart-perfumy flavor make it best for eating out of hand. Because it doesn't discolor quickly after being sliced, it's terrific on a fruit tray or alongside a fondue. We also liked the sweet-spicy Braeburn; the hearty, juicy Cameo; and the complex Fuji.

Best cooked: Granny Smith was the hands-down favorite in this category. It remained tart, juicy, and crisp after baking. It's simply a natural for cooking. Braeburn fared well in this category, too, holding its texture, juiciness, and sweetness after cooking.

Apple Applications

Here are descriptions of some of our favorite apple varieties and their best uses.

Variety	Flavor/Texture (raw)	Flavor/Texture (cooked)	Best Applications
Braeburn	sweet, spicy, tart/crisp	slightly muted/juicy, crisp	raw and cooked
Cameo	complex, deep/juicy, hearty	not as good as raw/juicy, holds texture well	raw and cooked
Empire	aromatic but slightly bland/crisp	flat/does not hold texture well	raw
Fuji	sweet, ciderlike/crisp	flat/dry	raw
Gala	very sweet/crisp	lemony/crunchy-chewy	raw
Golden Delicious	wildflower, honey, grassy/juicy	cloying/soft	raw
Granny Smith	very tart, lemony/very crisp	mellowed tartness/juicy, firm	raw and cooked
Jonagold	tangy, sweet, gingery/pearlike	flat/squishy	raw
McIntosh	wine-cherry, old-fashioned apple flavor/a bit mealy	honey/falls apart	raw
Pink Lady	complex, perfumy, tangy/very firm	tangy/dry, crunchy	raw and cooked
Red Delicious	sugary with thick, bitter skin/semifirm	sweet, flat/mushy	raw
Rome	slightly sweet/a bit dry	very sweet/soft, cooks down a lot	cooked

Apple Cobbler

This cobbler comes together quickly with the help of packaged pie dough. Tart Granny Smith apples—our favorite for baking—remain firm and pleasantly sharp after cooking. You could also experiment with Rome or Braeburn apples.

8	cups sliced peeled Granny Smith apple (about 2⅔ pounds)
⅓	cup apple cider
¼	cup all-purpose flour
½	cup packed brown sugar
½	teaspoon ground cinnamon
1	tablespoon chilled butter, cut into small pieces
½	(15-ounce) package refrigerated pie dough (such as Pillsbury)
1	teaspoon water
1	large egg white, lightly beaten
1	tablespoon turbinado sugar or granulated sugar

1. Preheat oven to 350°.

2. Arrange apple in an 11 x 7-inch baking dish. Drizzle cider over apple.

3. Lightly spoon flour into a dry measuring cup; level with a knife. Combine flour, brown sugar, and cinnamon; cut in butter with a pastry blender or 2 knives until mixture resembles coarse meal. Sprinkle flour mixture over apple mixture.

4. Roll dough into a 12 x 8-inch rectangle. Place dough over apple mixture; fold edges under, and flute. Cut 3 slits in top of dough to allow steam to escape.

5. Combine water and egg white, stirring well with a whisk. Brush dough with egg white mixture; sprinkle evenly with turbinado sugar. Bake at 350° for 40 minutes or until crust is golden brown. Yield: 8 servings.

CALORIES 275 (29% from fat); FAT 8.8g (sat 3.8g, mono 3.6g, poly 0.9g); PROTEIN 1.5g; CARB 48.5g; FIBER 2.3g; CHOL 9mg; IRON 0.6mg; SODIUM 129mg; CALC 21mg

> "Granny Smith has the flavor of every apple pie I remember my grandmother making."
>
> Krista Montgomery, Food Editor

Candied Apples

These apples make great Halloween treats. Green Granny Smiths go well with both the sweet white and bittersweet chocolates, but feel free to use any apple you like. Look for wooden sticks at craft supply stores, or use forks instead.

- 6   Granny Smith apples
- 3   ounces bittersweet chocolate, coarsely chopped
- 2½ ounces premium white baking chocolate (such as Baker's), coarsely chopped

1. Wash and dry apples; remove stems. Insert a wooden stick into the stem end of each apple.
2. Place bittersweet chocolate in a glass bowl; microwave at HIGH 1 minute or until melted, stirring every 20 seconds until smooth. Working with 1 apple at a time, hold apple over bowl. Using a spoon, drizzle apple with about 2 teaspoons bittersweet chocolate. Place apple, stick side up, on a baking sheet covered with wax paper. Repeat procedure with remaining apples.
3. Place white chocolate in a glass bowl, and microwave at HIGH 1 minute or until melted, stirring every 15 seconds until smooth. Working with 1 apple at a time, hold apple over bowl. Using a spoon, drizzle apple with about 1½ teaspoons white chocolate. Place apple, stick side up, on baking sheet covered with wax paper. Repeat procedure with remaining apples. Chill apples until ready to serve. Yield: 6 servings (serving size: 1 apple).

CALORIES 260 (30% from fat); FAT 8.7g (sat 5g, mono 2.5g, poly 0.4g); PROTEIN 1.9g; CARB 48.4g; FIBER 7.8g; CHOL 2mg; IRON 0.8mg; SODIUM 11mg; CALC 38mg

Rustic Applesauce

Mashing the apples creates a chunky sauce; for a smoother version, process part or all of the apple mixture in a food processor or blender.

- 4   cups cubed peeled Braeburn or Pink Lady apple
- 4   cups cubed peeled Granny Smith apple
- ½   cup packed brown sugar
- 2   teaspoons grated lemon rind
- 3   tablespoons fresh lemon juice
- 1   teaspoon ground cinnamon
- 1   teaspoon vanilla extract
- Dash of salt
- 2   tablespoons crème fraîche (or full-fat sour cream)

1. Combine first 8 ingredients in a Dutch oven over medium heat. Cook 25 minutes or until apples are tender, stirring occasionally.
2. Remove from heat; mash to desired consistency with a fork or potato masher. Stir in crème fraîche. Serve warm or chilled. Yield: 7 servings (serving size: about ½ cup).

CALORIES 140 (12% from fat); FAT 1.8g (sat 1g, mono 0.5g, poly 0.2g); PROTEIN 0.3g; CARB 32.5g; FIBER 2.3g; CHOL 3mg; IRON 0.5mg; SODIUM 30mg; CALC 31mg

Applesauce Flavor	Test Kitchen SECRET

To get the best flavor balance for applesauce, use a combination of sweet Braeburns and tart Granny Smiths.

Pears

Pears are sweet and spicy, with a subtle, intoxicating perfume. And although a pear is usually thought of as a fruit to be eaten in its natural state, it's actually as versatile as the apple, especially during its peak season. Unlike some fruits, pears come to ripeness on a long continuum that extends throughout much of the year. The colder months of winter are traditionally considered the peak of pear season, but some varieties begin to appear in the fall, and others last until early spring. The best pears for cooking are varieties such as Bosc, Comice, Seckel, and red and green Anjous.

<table>
<tr><td>**Is it Ripe Yet?**</td><td>**Test Kitchen**
SECRET</td></tr>
</table>

If your pears aren't quite ripe, place them on the kitchen counter in a brown paper bag, and check them daily. It may take 3 to 5 days for them to fully ripen. If the neck area yields to gentle thumb pressure, the pear is ready to eat or cook in desserts, pancakes, and even meat dishes.

Pepper-Pear Relish

The spicy sweetness of the pear is a good match for the hot peppers and acidic vinegar.

- ¾ cup rice vinegar
- ½ cup firmly packed brown sugar
- ½ cup chopped red bell pepper
- ¼ cup minced fresh onion
- 1 teaspoon minced seeded jalapeño pepper
- ⅛ teaspoon black pepper
- ⅛ teaspoon crushed red pepper
- 3 cups chopped peeled pear (about 3 medium)

1. Combine first 7 ingredients in a large saucepan; bring to a boil. Reduce heat to medium; cook vinegar mixture 10 minutes, stirring occasionally. Stir in pear. Partially cover; reduce heat to low, and simmer 45 minutes or until most of liquid evaporates. Serve relish warm with chicken or pork. Yield: 6 servings (serving size: ¼ cup).

CALORIES 128 (3% from fat); FAT 0.4g (sat 0g, mono 0.1g, poly 0.1g); PROTEIN 0.5g; CARB 31.7g; FIBER 2.5g; CHOL 0mg; IRON 0.8mg; SODIUM 11mg; CALC 27mg

Pear Comparison

These are the five varieties of pears that we use most often in *Cooking Light* recipes, when they're usually available, and some suggested uses for each.

Type	Availability	Description
Anjou	October through June	one of the best pears for eating out of hand when ripe; cooks well, and works in most recipes
Bartlett	almost year-round; peaks July through January	the classic pear—from its shape and aroma to its freckled yellow skin
Bosc	September through May	dramatic appearance makes them perfect for a bowl on the kitchen table; firmer texture is best for cooking
Comice	September through April	the Cadillac of pears, and the one you usually find in gift boxes; best eaten out of hand or sliced and served with fruit and cheese
Seckel	August through February	miniature pears that are particularly sweet

Quince

The quince, long considered an emblem of love, has a heady scent. In fact, leaving a few quinces out on the table will infuse your home with a wonderful aroma. But don't let that keep you from cooking with them. **Slow cooking yields a pale apricot-colored, firm-textured fruit that tastes like a cross between an apple and a pear, with slight pineapple flavors.** Quinces are often used in the United States to make jams and jellies because of their high pectin content, but in much of the Middle East and northern Africa, quinces are more commonly cooked in stews and with roasts. They stay firm through long, slow cooking and develop beautiful color.

Available from September through December, quinces bruise very easily, but they can be kept in the refrigerator for as long as 2 to 3 months. A noticeable perfume is the best indicator of ripeness. Peel and core them as you would an apple or a pear.

Quinces take longer to cook than apples, so the filling for tarts and pies is usually simmered on the stovetop before baking.

For More Information
Cooking Light Recommends

- Frieda's, a specialty produce importer, has a large selection of exotic fruits and vegetables for sale. (www.friedas.com)
- One of the most comprehensive books on the subject is *Uncommon Fruits and Vegetables* by Elizabeth Schneider. Schneider details flavors, then guides you through selecting, storing, and preparing each item.

Quince Upside-Down Tart

This dessert is similar to *tarte Tatin,* the classic upside-down apple tart from France. Quince works well here because its high pectin content helps the tart hold its shape when inverted and sliced.

1½	tablespoons butter
¼	cup sugar, divided
2½	pounds quince, cored, peeled, and thinly sliced (about 5 quinces)
¼	cup honey
3	tablespoons fresh lemon juice
½	(15-ounce) package refrigerated pie dough (such as Pillsbury)

1. Melt butter in a 10-inch cast-iron or large, heavy skillet over medium heat. Stir in 3 tablespoons sugar; remove from heat. Arrange quince slices spokelike on top of butter mixture, working from center of pan to edge.
2. Combine 1 tablespoon sugar, honey, and juice, stirring well with a whisk. Drizzle mixture evenly over quince slices. Cover pan with foil; cook over medium heat 30 minutes.
3. Remove pan from heat; carefully remove foil. Cool 10 minutes.
4. Preheat oven to 400°.
5. Roll dough into an 11-inch circle; place over quince mixture. Tuck edges of crust into sides of pan. Cut 2 small slits in top of dough to allow steam to escape. Bake at 400° for 20 minutes or until lightly browned. Let stand 5 minutes. Place a plate upside down on top of pan, and invert onto plate. Serve warm. Yield: 9 servings (serving size: 1 wedge).

CALORIES 246 (30% from fat); FAT 8.2g (sat 3.8g, mono 2.5g, poly 1.5g); PROTEIN 1g; CARB 44.6g; FIBER 21.9g; CHOL 10mg; IRON 0.9mg; SODIUM 121mg; CALC 16mg

Berries

Blueberries, blackberries, raspberries, and strawberries—they're gorgeous, bursting with flavor, and able to turn desserts into shameless bites of pleasure.

Beneath berries' beauty and flavor lurk legions of antioxidants—damage-control warriors that attack the free radicals that contribute to cancer, heart disease, and aging. **Other plants have those disease-fighters, too, but researchers worldwide are learning that berries—blueberries, especially—are stellar sources.**

Blueberries

Blueberries' antioxidants may help keep your mind sharp and prevent some of middle age's memory loss. Blueberries may also play a role in the treatment of Alzheimer's and Parkinson's disease. Plus, they're high in fiber, low in calories, and virtually fat-free.

Look for firm berries with a silvery frost, and discard any that are shriveled and moldy. Don't wash blueberries until you're ready to use them. Store them in the refrigerator (in a single layer if possible) in a moisture-proof container for up to 5 days. Or you can freeze them (see below).

Buy blueberries when they're in season and less expensive. Then freeze them to enjoy months later. It's best to freeze the berries, unwashed, in a single layer on a baking sheet, then transfer to a heavy-duty zip-top plastic bag.

Baking with Blueberries	Test Kitchen SECRET

When making a cake or bread with blueberries, toss them in the flour mixture before adding the liquid ingredients. This helps keep the berries from turning the batter blue and keeps them from sinking to the bottom.

Cool Summer-Berry Soup

We used raspberries and strawberries in this chilled soup, but you can use any summer berries you prefer.

Soup:

- 2 cups fresh raspberries
- 2 cups halved fresh strawberries
- ½ cup cranberry-raspberry juice drink
- ½ cup dry white wine
- ¼ cup sugar
- ⅛ teaspoon ground cinnamon
- 1 (8-ounce) carton strawberry low-fat yogurt

Garnish:

- 1 cup fresh blueberries
- 2 teaspoons sugar
- 2 teaspoons cranberry-raspberry juice drink

1. To prepare soup, place first 3 ingredients in a blender, and process until smooth. Strain raspberry mixture through a sieve into a medium saucepan. Stir in wine, ¼ cup sugar, and cinnamon. Bring to a boil over medium heat; cook 2 minutes. Remove from heat. Place in a large bowl; cover and chill 3 hours. Stir in yogurt.

2. To prepare garnish, place blueberries and remaining ingredients in a blender; process until smooth. Strain blueberry mixture through a sieve.
3. Spoon 1 cup soup into each of 4 bowls. Drizzle each serving with 1 tablespoon garnish. Yield: 4 servings (serving size: 1 cup).

CALORIES 208 (6% from fat); FAT 1.4g (sat 0.5g, mono 0.3g, poly 0.4g); PROTEIN 3.6g; CARB 48.4g; FIBER 7g; CHOL 2mg; IRON 0.9mg; SODIUM 37mg; CALC 109mg

Blackberries

Blackberries, the largest type of wild berries, grow on thornbushes. The berries are purplish black and range in size from ½ inch to 1 inch long. They're usually available from May through August. Buy plump berries with deep color and no hull. **If the hulls are still attached, the berries are not mature and will be tart.**

Although fresh from the bush is the best way to enjoy blackberries, you can refrigerate them (in a single layer if possible), lightly covered, for 1 to 2 days.

Cranberries

Cranberries are in season only from October to December, a small window of opportunity to get them fresh (which is why most of us probably think of cranberries only at Thanksgiving or Christmas). **But fresh cranberries freeze beautifully, so get enough while they're available to tide you over until next season.**

Unlike other fruits, cranberries need to be cooked to release their full flavor and to absorb that of other ingredients—one of which is usually sugar.

Health Benefits Cranberries have tannins, which are compounds that keep bacteria from binding to cells, preventing them from multiplying and causing infections. Tannins are also

antioxidants—compounds that appear to help prevent certain cancers and contribute to cardiovascular health. **On a per-serving basis, cranberry juice, sweetened dried cranberries, cranberry sauce, and cooked cranberries have comparable amounts of tannins.** With anti-adhesion and antioxidant capabilities, cranberries have a dual-action health formula.

Good Cranberries — Test Kitchen SECRET

How can you tell if a cranberry is good? Before machines took over the job of checking for quality, people used to roll cranberries down stairs. The soft, undesirable berries didn't have the oomph to make it down, so they'd languish on the steps; the fresh ones made it to the bottom. Try dropping one onto the kitchen floor or countertop. It should bounce like a rubber ball. Not feeling so playful? Top-quality cranberries float.

Cranberry Sauce with Apple Cider

Apple cider stands in for water to add dimension to this cranberry sauce. It's great with pork or turkey. Try some as a relish on a sandwich made with leftovers.

1 cup sugar
1 cup apple cider or apple juice
1 (12-ounce) package fresh cranberries

1. Combine all ingredients in a medium saucepan; bring to a boil over medium-high heat. Reduce heat; simmer 10 minutes or until cranberries pop, stirring occasionally. Chill. Yield: 8 servings (serving size: ¼ cup).

CALORIES 135 (0% from fat); FAT 0g; PROTEIN 0.3g; CARB 35g; FIBER 1.8g; CHOL 0mg; IRON 0.1mg; SODIUM 1mg; CALC 3mg

Cranberry Scones

As the scones bake, the cranberries absorb the sugar in the dough and become sweet and juicy.

1¾	cups all-purpose flour
½	cup granulated sugar
¼	cup yellow cornmeal
2	teaspoons baking powder
¼	teaspoon baking soda
¼	teaspoon salt
2	tablespoons chilled butter, cut into small pieces
½	cup halved fresh cranberries
½	cup low-fat buttermilk
½	teaspoon grated orange rind
1	large egg, lightly beaten
	Cooking spray
1	teaspoon powdered sugar

1. Preheat oven to 375°.

2. Lightly spoon flour into dry measuring cups; level with a knife. Combine flour and the next 5 ingredients in a bowl; cut in butter with a pastry blender or 2 knives until mixture resembles coarse meal. Add cranberries, tossing to coat.

3. Combine buttermilk, rind, and egg; add to flour mixture, stirring just until moist (dough will be sticky).

4. Turn dough out onto a lightly floured surface, and knead lightly 5 times with floured hands. Pat dough into a 7-inch circle on a baking sheet coated with cooking spray. Cut dough into 10 wedges, cutting into, but not completely through, dough. Bake at 375° for 30 minutes or until golden. Sift powdered sugar over scones; serve warm. Yield: 10 servings (serving size: 1 scone).

CALORIES 168 (17% from fat); FAT 3.2g (sat 1.7g, mono 0.9g, poly 0.3g); PROTEIN 3.7g; CARB 31.2g; FIBER 1.1g; CHOL 28mg; IRON 1.4mg; SODIUM 231mg; CALC 75mg

Raspberries

These intensely flavored berries are composed of many connecting sections of fruit, each with its own seed, surrounding a central core. There are three main varieties of raspberries: black, golden, and red, with red being the most common. These berries are usually available from May through November. Choose brightly colored, plump berries without hulls. **Like blackberries, if the hulls are still attached, the berries are not mature and will be tart.** Store raspberries in the refrigerator in a moisture-proof container for 2 to 3 days. **Because they are fragile, store them in a single layer if possible.**

Strawberries

You know spring is here when you take that first bite into a plump, juicy strawberry. Enjoy them while you can because the season peaks in May. Choose brightly colored berries that still have their green cap attached. They should have a potent strawberry fragrance; if they don't, they aren't fully ripe, and they won't ripen after they're picked. Do not wash strawberries until you're ready to use them. Store (in a single layer if possible) in a moisture-proof container in the refrigerator for 2 to 3 days.

It's best not to overwhelm the fresh flavor with too many ingredients. Try a mousse or a simple sweet soup—or toss the berries with fresh salad greens.

Strawberries-and-Feta Salad

The sweet strawberries are a nice contrast to the sharp feta cheese in this springtime salad.

- 2 tablespoons orange juice
- 1 tablespoon white wine vinegar
- 2 teaspoons extra-virgin olive oil
- ¾ teaspoon sugar
- 6 cups gourmet salad greens
- 1 cup sliced strawberries
- ¼ cup (1 ounce) crumbled feta cheese

1. Combine first 4 ingredients in a small bowl; stir with a whisk. Combine greens, strawberries, and cheese in a large bowl; add orange juice mixture, tossing to coat. Serve immediately. Yield: 4 servings (serving size: 1½ cups).

CALORIES 70 (53% from fat); FAT 4.1g (sat 1.4g, mono 2g, poly 0.4g); PROTEIN 2.7g; CARB 6.6g; FIBER 2.3g; CHOL 6mg; IRON 1.1mg; SODIUM 87mg; CALC 71mg

Strawberry Soup

Strawberries in soup? Absolutely—they make for a unique, refreshing dessert.

- 3⅓ cups quartered strawberries
- ½ cup orange juice
- ½ cup Riesling or other slightly sweet white wine
- 2½ tablespoons sugar
- 1⅓ cups plain fat-free yogurt
- 2 teaspoons finely chopped fresh mint

1. Place first 4 ingredients in a blender; process until smooth. Pour strawberry puree into a bowl; add yogurt, stirring with a whisk. Cover and chill. Spoon 1 cup soup into each of 5 bowls; sprinkle with mint. Yield: 5 servings.

CALORIES 116 (4% from fat); FAT 0.5g (sat 0.1g, mono 0.1g, poly 0.2g); PROTEIN 4.3g; CARB 21.2g; FIBER 2.4g; CHOL 1mg; IRON 0.7mg; SODIUM 48mg; CALC 139mg

---

Strawberry Size

Test Kitchen SECRET

There's just no substitute for a good vine-ripened strawberry. Because strawberries are highly perishable, any intended for the supermarket are usually picked early—before they're fully ripe. Taste also suffers because commercial growers opt for large and hardy—if less flavorful—varieties. So don't let the smaller size of fresh, locally grown strawberries fool you: Ounce for ounce, those precious red gems carry more flavor than their commercial counterparts. If you need convincing, pop one in your mouth.

To slice strawberries for a recipe or for garnishing, use an egg slicer.

Citrus Fruits

They are high in vitamin C, but the reason we really like them is because of their range of flavors from tart to sweet.

Here's the lowdown on a few of our favorite members of the citrus family: grapefruit, kumquats, lemons, limes, and oranges.

Grapefruit

Grapefruit is the second largest citrus fruit (after the pomelo) and has a tart flavor and abundant juice. The pulp ranges in color from white to pale pink to ruby red. The peel is usually yellow, although sometimes you'll see a pink blush. Choose grapefruit that are heavy for their size, and avoid those with soft spots. Don't worry about small blemishes on the skin because those usually don't indicate poor quality. Store grapefruit at room temperature for up to 1 week or in the refrigerator for up to 3 weeks.

Great Grapefruit
Test Kitchen
SECRET

Use a serrated knife to slice whole grapefruit. Because the skin is tough and slick, the serrated blade is best for this task. Use a paring knife for peeling grapefruit. (See "How to Section Citrus Fruit" on page 338.)

If you've stored your grapefruit in the refrigerator, bring them back to room temperature before serving, and they will be juicier and sweeter.

Kumquats

One of the most striking aspects of the kumquat is that the skin is sweet and the flesh very tart. These beautiful 2-inch oblong fruits are golden orange and can be served whole or chopped. The juicy fruit has an intense sour orange flavor, which is why you'll often see them candied, pickled, or preserved. Kumquats can thicken sauces while adding a bittersweet note, and are often prepared to accompany roast meats and game.

The piquant flavor is a nice addition to chutneys and marmalades paired with beef, pork, or chicken. Use them whole and uncooked to garnish holiday platters and grace ornamental fruit bowls.

Kumquat Care

Kumquats are in season as early as October and as late as June, but they're most plentiful from December through April.

Because of their thin skin, kumquats don't keep particularly well. Store them at room temperature if you'll eat them within a few days; keep them for up to 2 weeks when refrigerated.

Test with a gentle squeeze, and buy only firm fruit. You can eat kumquats whole, seeds included.

Lemons

It might be fair to say that we use lemons in our Test Kitchens more than any other fruit, not only as a fruit, but as a flavoring ingredient. Whether we're using juice, lemon zest (rind), or slices, the acidity of lemon adds to the final balance of flavor in all types of food, from savory to sweet.

When using lemons in desserts, the key to transforming the lemon is to give it some sweetness. Lemons, compared to other fruits, have a very low percentage of sugar—not nearly enough to counter the fruit's wallop of citric acid. As anyone who's enjoyed a good glass of lemonade knows, lemon and sugar taste heavenly when combined in the right proportion.

Lemons are bright yellow and oval in shape, with a pronounced bulge at the blossom end. They can range in size from a large egg to a small grapefruit. Look for smooth, brightly colored skin (green signals underripeness), and lemons that are heavy for their size. Store for 2 to 3 weeks in plastic in the refrigerator. **Once the juice is squeezed, there is a quick loss of vitamin C.**

A Zest for Lemons

Get double-duty from lemons by removing the zest before squeezing the juice. To remove the zest, use a special zester, handheld grater, or our favorite—the Microplane Food Grater, which peels several strips at a time. Or you can peel the lemon, being careful to remove as little of the white pith as possible (it's very bitter), place in a food processor, and pulse until you have a fine zest. Once you've removed the zest or peel from a lemon (or any other citrus fruit), you can refrigerate the fruit for up to 1 week.

It's important not to use too much zest, which can add bitterness rather than tartness.

In general, fresh lemons convert to these standard measurements:

1 medium lemon	=	2 to 3 tablespoons juice
1 medium lemon	=	1 teaspoon grated rind (zest)
5 to 6 lemons	=	1 cup juice

Sectioning Lemons

1. Grate lemon rind before sectioning the fruit. Use a handheld grater or a box grater. Grate only the colored peel, not the white pith, which is bitter.

2. To get sections, cut off both ends of lemon. Then cut off peel (white pith and all) to expose the fruit.

3. Cut between membranes to obtain the sections, removing seeds as you go. Squeeze juice from remaining membrane into a bowl, and reserve for another use.

"We generally use fresh lemon juice, not bottled. It makes a world of difference in the flavor, and the bottled lemon juice just doesn't compare." Tiffany Vickers, Test Kitchens Staffer

"If you will microwave the lemons for about 30 seconds before squeezing, you'll get more juice. I like to use a handheld juice squeezer and put the lemon half upside down in the press. This will extract the most juice and trap the seeds better." Kellie Kelley, Food Stylist

Loving Those Lemons

Anytime we need to add flavor to a recipe, the first thing that is often said in our Test Kitchens is, "Let's add some lemon juice." Here are some of our staff's favorite ways to use lemons (juice, zest, wedges, slices) in recipes:

Flavoring Agent: Sprinkle lemon juice over fresh green vegetables such as broccoli and asparagus, or squeeze a lemon wedge over fresh fish.

Salt Replacer: Sometimes if you drizzle a bit of lemon juice over vegetables, fish, or poultry, it tastes like you've added a bit of salt. Perhaps it's because the acid in the lemon can bring out the other flavors in a dish.

Balancing Agent: If a salad dressing, marinades or sauce is too sweet or spicy, a dash of lemon juice will balance the flavors.

Fat Replacer: Instead of drowning a salad in dressing, if you squeeze a bit of lemon juice over the greens, you'll have plenty of flavor without using so much dressing.

Lemon Ice with Crystallized Ginger
The sweetness of the crystallized ginger and the sugar balances the tartness of the lemon juice in this frozen treat.

1¼	cups sugar
2¼	cups water
1	cup fresh lemon juice (about 5 large lemons)
½	teaspoon unflavored gelatin
2	tablespoons water
2	tablespoons finely chopped crystallized ginger

1. Combine sugar and 2¼ cups water in a saucepan; bring to a boil. Cook 5 minutes without stirring. Remove from heat; stir in juice.
2. Sprinkle gelatin over 2 tablespoons water in a small saucepan; let stand for 1 minute. Cook over low heat, stirring until gelatin dissolves. Remove from heat; cool slightly. Stir gelatin mixture and ginger into sugar syrup.
3. Pour mixture into the freezer can of an ice-cream freezer, and freeze according to the manufacturer's instructions. Spoon into a freezer-safe container; cover and freeze at least 8 hours. Yield: 8 servings (serving size: ½ cup).

CALORIES 134 (0% from fat); FAT 0g; PROTEIN 0.3g; CARB 35g; FIBER 0.1g; CHOL 0mg; IRON 0.3mg; SODIUM 2mg; CALC 6mg

Seriously Lemon Tart

Fresh lemons are a must in this tart, which uses lemon sections and packs an intense lemon pucker.

Cooking spray
½ (15-ounce) package refrigerated pie dough
1½ cups granulated sugar
2 teaspoons grated lemon rind
1 cup lemon sections (about 4 large lemons), seeds removed
½ teaspoon salt
3 large egg whites, lightly beaten
2 large eggs, lightly beaten
12 very thin lemon slices
2 tablespoons brown sugar

1. Preheat oven to 450°.
2. Coat the bottom of a 9-inch round removable-bottom tart pan with cooking spray. Press dough into bottom and up sides of pan. Line bottom of dough with a piece of aluminum foil; arrange pie weights or dried beans on foil. Bake at 450° for 5 minutes. Remove pie weights and foil. Bake 5 additional minutes. Cool on a wire rack.
3. Reduce oven temperature to 350°.
4. Combine granulated sugar, lemon rind, lemon sections, and salt in a medium nonaluminum saucepan; cook 4 minutes over medium heat or until sugar dissolves. Combine egg whites and eggs in a large bowl, stirring well with a whisk. Gradually add hot lemon mixture to egg white mixture, stirring constantly with a whisk; pour into prepared piecrust. Arrange lemon slices on custard; bake at 350° for 10 minutes. Sprinkle with brown sugar. Bake an additional 10 minutes. Remove from oven.
5. Preheat broiler.
6. Broil about 1 minute or until lightly browned. Cool on wire rack 1 hour. Chill 4 hours or until set. Yield: 8 servings (serving size: 1 wedge).

CALORIES 309 (24% from fat); FAT 8.4g (sat 3.4g, mono 2.3g, poly 2.2g); PROTEIN 4g; CARB 56.4g; FIBER 0.1g; CHOL 60mg; IRON 0.5mg; SODIUM 285mg; CALC 22mg

---

The Right Pan
Test Kitchen SECRET

Be sure to use a nonaluminum saucepan when cooking the lemon filling because the acid in the lemon juice will react with aluminum and can cause discoloration to the mixture.

Limes

Limes are smaller and slightly more delicate than lemons. The variety that you'll see most often at the supermarket is Persian limes, which have a dark green skin. Key limes grow in south Florida and are very tart with thin, leathery yellow skins and green flesh. You can find them fresh occasionally in specialty produce markets, and you can buy quality Key lime juice in gourmet stores. Kaffir limes are large and slightly pear-shaped with a thick, bumpy yellow-green peel. The juice of this lime is not usually used in the kitchen, but its aromatic peel and leaves are traditionally used in Indonesian and Thai cuisines.

Buy limes that are plump and heavy for their size. They are more perishable than lemons, so the best way to store them is in a plastic bag in the refrigerator for up to 1½ weeks. **Exposure to light and air decreases some of the tartness of the juice.**

Zesting and Juicing
Test Kitchen SECRET

- One medium lime will give you 1½ teaspoons of rind and 1½ tablespoons of juice.
- Wash limes before zesting. Use a citrus zester or a cheese grater (fine grate). Remove only the colored part of the peel; the white part is bitter.
- You'll get more juice out of a lime if you bring it to room temperature before squeezing the juice.

Oranges

Whether sectioned, sliced, juiced, or zested, we find that sweet, juicy oranges are one of the staple fruits in our Test Kitchens.

There are three basic types of oranges, each with different benefits for eating and cooking.

Sweet oranges are great for eating and for juicing. They are generally large, and the skins cling closely to the fruit. Some popular sweet oranges are navel, Valencia, and blood oranges.

Loose-skinned oranges have skins that slip easily off the fruit. The sections are also loose and can be easily separated. Examples are members of the mandarin orange family: clementines, satsuma oranges, and tangerines. The best thing to do with these oranges is to peel and eat, although they can also be used in cooking. (See "Cooking with Clementines" on the next page.)

Bitter oranges are too sour to eat raw but are usually cooked for marmalades. The peel is often candied, and the essential oil is used to flavor foods and liqueurs.

Oranges are available all year, but different varieties have different peak seasons. Choose oranges that are heavy for their size and have smooth skins. Color is not an indicator of quality in oranges because they are sometimes dyed. Don't worry if you see brown patches on the skin because that does not indicate poor quality. Do avoid fruits that are soft or have mold. Store oranges at room temperature for up to 1 week or in the refrigerator up to 3 weeks.

For the best flavor, use oranges raw. If they are cooked, cook them only briefly.

Blood Oranges

The thin orange and often reddish skin of this fruit doesn't prepare you for the brilliant color within— solid or streaked crimson to deep violet. Somewhat expensive, the blood orange is prized for its bright citrus flavor as much as for its color. Moro, a variety usually available from December through March, is sweeter than common oranges.

A red blush (if any) on the skin does not predict internal color or flavor. The fruit's skin may be pitted or smooth, and blood oranges are usually smaller than traditional oranges. They keep refrigerated for 2 to 4 weeks. When cooking with the blood orange, consider different ways to highlight its beautiful color. Squeeze the fresh juice, or use the peeled sections as a garnish, for example.

How to Section Citrus Fruit

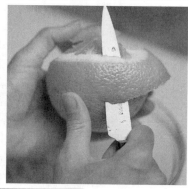

1. Peel the orange with a paring knife, and be sure to remove the white pith.

2. Holding the orange over a bowl to catch juices, slice between membranes and one side of one segment of orange. Lift the segment out with the knife blade.

Simple Citrus Tips

Making citrus rind strips: Use a channel knife or a vegetable peeler to remove strips before sectioning or juicing. Peel gently, being careful not to include the bitter white pith layer attached to the underside of the rind.

Grating citrus rind (zest): Always grate rind before sectioning or juicing. Hold the fruit firmly. Push down on a handheld grater or Microplane Food Grater, but don't push too hard. Just take off the color, not the white pith. One medium orange will give you 1 to 2 tablespoons of orange zest.

Juicing an orange: We prefer to use a handheld juicer that resembles a shallow bowl with a fluted, inverted cone in the center. Cut the fruit in half, and place the cut half over the cone, pressing down and turning to extract the juice. *One medium orange will give you about 1/2 cup juice.*

Extracting more juice: After you've sectioned the fruit (see the techniques on the previous page), take the left-over membranes, and squeeze over a bowl to collect the juice.

"After peeling an orange, store the peel in a zip-top plastic bag in the freezer. Later, add it to your tea, or grate it for use in recipes." Jan Moon, Test Kitchens Staffer

Clementines with Vanilla Sauce

You can make this dessert with tangerines or any other loose-skinned orange. Orange juice is an acceptable substitute for Grand Marnier, but the liqueur is what makes this an elegant dessert.

3	tablespoons sugar
¼	cup white wine vinegar
½	cup Grand Marnier (orange-flavored liqueur)
4	cups clementine sections (about 12 clementines)
1	tablespoon fat-free milk
1	(8-ounce) carton vanilla low-fat yogurt

1. Combine sugar and vinegar in a small, heavy saucepan. Bring to a boil; cook 6 minutes or until amber brown. Remove from heat; stir in liqueur.
2. Place clementine sections in a large bowl; pour sugar mixture over sections. Cover and chill 2 hours, stirring occasionally. Combine milk and yogurt, stirring with a whisk. Spoon clementine mixture into individual bowls or stemmed glasses, and top with yogurt mixture. Yield: 6 servings (serving size: about ½ cup clementine mixture and about 3 tablespoons sauce).

CALORIES 197 (4% from fat); FAT 0.9g (sat 0.4g, mono 0.2g, poly 0.1g); PROTEIN 3g; CARB 36.2g; FIBER 3.9g; CHOL 2mg; IRON 0.2mg; SODIUM 29mg; CALC 91mg

Cooking with Clementines

Even though clementines are great for snacking, the smart cook will insist on reserving as many as possible for cooking. With sugary as well as tart notes, clementines lend themselves to both savory and sweet dishes, and are especially good in sauces.

Clementines have a zippier flavor than most sweet oranges, but we sometimes use them in recipes that call for orange sections because they're so much easier to section.

"To taste figs fresh and cook with them seasonally—well, not much can compare."

Mike Wilson, Test Kitchens Staffer

Figs

The dense texture and subtle, sweet flavor of fresh figs is hard to beat. We use fresh figs in all types of recipes—from chutneys and sauces to salads and desserts. They're also a nice companion for braised meats and poultry. **Although dried figs are acceptable if fresh aren't available, they are entirely different from the fresh version and are not always interchangeable in recipes.** Dried compare to fresh

as raisins do to grapes, or prunes to plums.

There are hundreds of varieties of figs, ranging in color from dark purple to almost white. Some varieties have a round shape, while others are oval. Dark purple, intensely flavored Mission (or Black Mission) figs are one popular variety. Adriatic figs have red flesh and pale skins. Calimyrna figs have a nutlike flavor and tender, golden skin, and Kadota figs, which are small and thick-skinned, feature yellow-green fruit.

Fresh figs are available twice a year: The first crop is available from June through July; the second crop begins early in September and lasts through mid-October. The figs from the first crop are larger and more flavorful than those from the second. **Figs are extremely perishable, so you should use them soon after they're purchased, or store them in the refrigerator for no more than 2 to 3 days.**

Grapes

One cup of grapes has almost as much fiber as a slice of whole wheat toast, a good amount of potassium, just a trace of fat, and little more than 100 calories. **But their most potent benefits lie in their phytonutrients, particularly in the compound resveratrol—found within grape skins of all colors—that may help prevent several kinds of cancer and heart disease.** Resveratrol may fight breast, skin, and colon cancers. Although scientists don't totally understand its protective effects, part of its magic lies in its anti-inflammatory properties. Resveratrol protects the grape from fungal infections, so similar mechanisms may be what protect us from cancer. Grapes are also packed with other flavonoids that may help prevent cancer and heart disease.

Grape Varieties There are thousands of grape varieties, but they fall into some general categories, such as seedless or with seeds and "slip-skin" grapes in which the skins slip off easily or those with skins that cling to the flesh. There are also color categories. White grapes are pale yellow-green or light green; black grapes (also called "red") range from light red to blackish purple.

Resveratrol Revealed

In wine, the amount of resveratrol varies depending on the way the wine is processed. Red wine is usually higher in resveratrol because the grape juice ferments with the skins, which contain the resveratrol. White wine is made from juices strained of the skins after pressing, so it's usually not as high in resveratrol.

Grapes for juice undergo a quick press, so grape juice also has less resveratrol than wine.

The best sources of resveratrol, besides unpeeled grapes themselves, are red wine and raisins—dried whole grapes.

Melons

Melons don't ripen off the vine, but they do get juicier at room temperature. So leave them out on the counter a few days, then refrigerate whole to preserve vitamin C. Rinse the exterior prior to cutting.

Melons can be divided into two main categories, muskmelons and watermelons. Muskmelons include cantaloupes, honeydews, casaba, and Crenshaw melons. The two most commonly used muskmelons are cantaloupe and honeydew.

Cantaloupes

Cantaloupes are the most nutritious of melons:

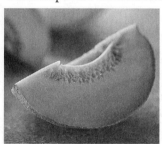

One cup contains 74 times the vitamin A of honeydew melon, more beta carotene than a small spinach salad, almost as much vitamin C as an orange, and roughly the same amount of fiber as a slice of whole wheat bread.

Skip the thumping and shaking; look for sweet-smelling melons that have a thick netting and a golden (not green) undertone. The stem end should have a small indentation; a small crack is a sign of sweetness, but avoid fruit with mold. The blossom end (opposite the stem end) should be slightly soft.

Honeydew

These melons have smooth skins that are pale green and ripen to a creamy yellow. The flesh is pale green, sweet, and juicy. Honeydews have less aroma and a more delicate flavor than cantaloupes, and a they also have a longer storage life. The peak season for honeydews is June to October, but they are at their best during the cool months of autumn.

Sweet Melons
Test Kitchen SECRET

Most unripe muskmelons will sweeten slightly (but not really ripen further) if you leave them in a paper bag at room temperature for a few days. But these melons will never be as sweet as those that have ripened on the vine. An exception is honeydew melon, which will stay only as sweet as it was when picked. Once they are ripe, you can store melons in the refrigerator for up to 5 days.

Wrap whole or cut melons in plastic wrap, or place in an airtight container because they absorb the flavors and odors of other foods as well as transfer their flavor and odor to other foods.

Watermelon

Watermelons are—with little debate—the quintessential food of summer. And in midsummer, watermelons are at their sweetest, juiciest best.

"Anytime you can, buy your watermelons at a roadside stand—they're always better than the ones at the grocery store." Jan Moon, Test Kitchens Staffer

They range in shape from small and round to heavy and oval, and although some varieties can grow up to 100 pounds, most average 10 to 15 pounds. Their color ranges from pale to deep green, and even the flesh varies from traditional red to pink and yellow. Watermelons labeled as "seedless" still have a few scattered seeds, but they are small soft, and edible. And although watermelons are best known as a picnic headliner, they can play other roles—in salads, desserts, and beverages.

Watermelon Wisdom

Test Kitchen
SECRET

- Look for a melon that is firm, symmetrically shaped, and free of dents and cuts. It should feel heavy for its shape and have a nice sheen.
- The underside of the melon (the side that grows against the ground) should be pale yellow.
- Slap the side of the melon. A resounding, hollow thump is a good indicator that it's ripe, but not a guarantee.
- Cut watermelon pieces should have a deep red color and a firm, unbroken flesh.
- Store whole watermelons in the refrigerator; cut pieces should be tightly wrapped.

Watermelon Margaritas

This is one of our favorites for summertime sipping.

2	teaspoons sugar
1	lime wedge
3½	cups cubed seeded watermelon
½	cup tequila
3	tablespoons sugar
3	tablespoons fresh lime juice
1	tablespoon triple sec (orange-flavored liqueur)
3	cups crushed ice

Lime wedges (optional)

1. Place 2 teaspoons sugar in a saucer. Rub rims of 6 glasses with 1 lime wedge; spin rim of each glass in sugar to coat. Set prepared glasses aside.
2. Combine watermelon and next 4 ingredients in a blender; process until smooth. Fill each prepared glass with ½ cup crushed ice. Add ½ cup margarita to each glass. Garnish each glass with a lime wedge, if desired. Serve immediately. Yield: 6 servings.

CALORIES 115 (3% from fat); PROTEIN 0.6g; FAT 0.4g (sat 0.2g, mono 0.1g, poly 0g); CARB 15.8g; FIBER 0.5g; CHOL 0mg; IRON 0.2mg; SODIUM 2mg; CALC 8mg

Add 2 to 3 drops of red food coloring to mixture in blender for a deeper red coloring, if desired.

Stone Fruits

Apricots, cherries, nectarines, peaches, and plums are called stone fruits because of their hard, rocklike center seeds.

Cherries, apricots, peaches, nectarines, and plums all have thin skins that protect delicate flesh and hard seeds in their centers. Step into the orchards with us, and become more familiar with the delights of the stone fruit family.

Apricots

Of all the stone fruits, the apricot is the first to appear in markets and the first to leave. Their fruit-bearing season is so short—from late May through July—that you can't put an apricot off until tomorrow unless it's been canned or dried. **Highly perishable, a ripe one can become mushy after even a single day.**

The apricot's unique flavor bears little, if any, taste resemblance to its nearest relative, the peach. As delicious as apricots are when eaten out of hand (at room temperature, never cold), they're even better when cooked. Despite their sensitive nature, cooking brings about an unexpected graciousness: They become meltingly tender, and their flavor intensifies, as do their perfume and color. Yet such boldness doesn't overpower other ingredients. Best of all, cooking allows you to preserve the apricot's freshness.

> **"As delicious as apricots are when eaten out of hand, they're even better when cooked." Alison Ashton, Food Editor**

Slightly oval, apricots always contain a pit that is "free," meaning it's not fused to the flesh of the fruit and can be removed easily. When ripe, a gentle scent and slight yield in the flesh herald an apricot's sweetness. Its skin is pale yellow, and newer varieties have strong rouge blushes. The rosy tint indicates which side of the fruit faced the sun as it hung on the tree.

> **All apricot varieties are interchangeable;** their sugar levels are about the same. In these recipes, any ripe variety will work. Store apricots at room temperature to avoid mealiness.

Fresh Apricot Jam

If you don't make your own jams and jellies because you're intimidated by canning, this easy recipe is for you.

- 6 cups coarsely chopped apricots (about 2 pounds)
- 3 cups sugar
- 2 tablespoons fresh lemon juice

1. Combine all ingredients in a large bowl; stir well. Cover and let stand at room temperature 24 hours.

2. Spoon apricot mixture into a large saucepan; bring to a boil over medium heat, stirring frequently. Reduce heat to low, and cook 25 minutes or until a candy thermometer registers 205°.

3. Pour jam into decorative jars or airtight containers. Store in refrigerator up to 3 weeks.
Yield: 4 cups (serving size: 1 tablespoon).

CALORIES 43 (2% from fat); PROTEIN 0.2g; FAT 0.1g (sat 0g, mono 0g, poly 0g); CARB 11g; FIBER 0.3g; CHOL 0mg; IRON 0.1mg; SODIUM 0mg; CALC 2mg

Pit Stop

Apricots seldom need peeling. But if you desire to do so, score the base with a small "X," and drop the entire fruit into boiling water for 30 seconds. Remove; quickly transfer to ice water for 2 minutes. The skin will peel away easily, without bruising the delicate flesh.

Although you don't have to peel apricots, you will need to remove the pits. Slice around the "seam," and gently twist the fruit in half. The pit should lift out easily. Place each half, flesh side up, on a cutting board, and chop or slice as directed in the recipe.

Apricot and Cherry Salad

Sweet fruits contrast with peppery green watercress in this refreshing side salad.

⅓	cup sugar
3	tablespoons water
3	tablespoons fresh lime juice
1	teaspoon salt
1	teaspoon dry mustard
2	tablespoons vegetable oil
1	tablespoon poppy seeds
6	cups trimmed watercress
4	cups sliced apricots (about 12)
3	cups halved pitted cherries

1. Place first 5 ingredients in a blender; process until blended. Add oil and poppy seeds; process until blended.
2. Place 1 cup watercress on each of 6 plates. Top each serving with ⅔ cup apricot slices and ½ cup cherries. Drizzle 2 tablespoons vinaigrette over each salad. Yield: 6 servings.

CALORIES 184 (30% from fat); FAT 6.2g (sat 1.1g, mono 1.7g, poly 2.9g); PROTEIN 3g; CARB 32.4g; FIBER 4.2g; CHOL 0mg; IRON 0.9mg; SODIUM 406mg; CALC 85mg

Cherries

Cherries open the stone fruit season in late May. Dark red Bing cherries are the popular American standard, but yellow Queen Annes, white and red Rainiers, and sour Montmorencys are widely available. Smaller and more rounded in shape, sour (or tart) cherries are usually used for pies. Most sour cherries are canned, frozen, dried, or used to make juice.

> "A good rule of thumb among sweet, dark cherries: The darker the fruit, the sweeter it is."
> **Kathleen Kanen,**
> **Food Stylist**

Cherries do not ripen after harvest, so once picked, their sweetness is set. Store fresh cherries for up to a week in the refrigerator in a bowl lined with paper towels.

Cherry pits have an almond flavor, so you'll often see cherry recipes flavored with almond extract. We've found that just a drop of almond extract in a cherry pie or cobbler will enhance the cherry flavor.

Pit a Cherry

Cherry pitters are seasonally available from a number of sources, but the one we prefer is by Leifheit, headquartered in Germany. Made of chromed steel and fashioned after an office stapler, it's easy on your hands and fingers. Just place a cherry in the rounded depression, and squeeze; the pit and stem fall away. It's available at Pickles, Peppers, Pots & Pans (www.picklespeppers.com) 815-842-3200, and at Williams-Sonoma, 800-541-2233.

You can also try one of those vintage pitters that resemble eyelash curlers, but we find them too hard on the hands.

Better still is the no-tech method: Cut around the cherry to extract the pit. Wear disposable plastic gloves because the juice can stain your fingers.

Nectarines

The peach has a fraternal twin—the nectarine, a natural mutation with fuzz-free skin. Otherwise, the two fruits are indistinguishable, with each

having red, yellow, or white flesh. White-fleshed varieties are sweeter because they are less acidic, though acid levels in all peaches or nectarines decrease as they ripen.

Both peaches and nectarines start the season as clingstones, meaning their meat adheres to their pits. Freestone varieties—where the pit easily pulls from the fruit—begin to ripen mid-season (late June to early July).

Nectarine and Raspberry Sorbet

Normally, you don't need to peel nectarines, but in this recipe, the skins interfere with the smooth texture of the sorbet. Any type of nectarines will work.

2	cups chopped peeled white nectarines (about 1½ pounds)
1⅓	cups raspberries (about 6 ounces)
2½	cups apricot nectar
½	cup honey
1	tablespoon fresh lemon juice

1. Combine nectarines and raspberries in a food processor; process until smooth. Stir in apricot nectar, honey, and lemon juice. Strain mixture through a sieve into a large bowl; discard solids.
2. Pour mixture into the freezer can of an ice-cream freezer; freeze according to manufacturer's instructions. Spoon sorbet into a freezer-safe container; cover and freeze 1 hour or until firm. Yield: 5 servings (serving size: 1 cup).

CALORIES 218 (2% from fat); FAT 0.6g (sat 0.1g, mono 0.2g, poly 0.3g); PROTEIN 1.4g; CARB 56.7g; FIBER 3.4g; CHOL 0mg; IRON 0.9mg; SODIUM 5mg; CALC 21mg

White-Fleshed Stone Fruit

Peaches, nectarines, and cherries are also available in delicate white-fleshed varieties. These taste sweeter because they have lower acidity than the yellow-fleshed fruit.

Sweet whites, like all stone fruits, are available during the summer months. Rainier and Queen Anne are common varieties of white-fleshed cherries. The donut peach is a throwback to its Chinese forebearers and is a naturally occurring variety. The stone is always free, and its flesh is white. This delicious peach is best eaten out of hand.

Hybrid Stone Fruits
Test Kitchen SECRET

Selective breeding and natural mutations have created new "interspecific" varieties of stone fruits. Interspecific refers to marrying two species to produce progeny with a desired taste, better texture, unique look, or longer storage life. Here's a description of some of the hybrids you may see:

Aprium: Cross a slightly fuzzy apricot with a plum, and you'll have an aprium, with the best of both parents.

Mango Nectarine: Although a hybrid of mango and nectarine, this fruit more closely resembles a nectarine. It is yellow and has a subtle perfumy sweetness when fully ripe.

Pluot: This union of the plum and apricot is sweeter than either of its parents, with a firm flesh and a mottled plumlike skin. It's also known as a plumeot or by its more familiar name, Dinosaur Egg.

Peaches

Peach season starts in late May in the warmer sections of the United States and runs through late September. There are hundreds of peach varieties, but one thing holds true for all peaches: An enticing aroma alerts us to their ripeness. Unlike many other fruits, which are best plucked and eaten on the spot, a just-picked peach is actually best if left uneaten for at least a couple of days. **Leave unripe peaches at room temperature for a few days to allow them to develop their full, sweet potential. Refrigeration retards ripening, resulting in flat-tasting, mealy fruit.**

Of all the pleasurable ways to enjoy fresh peaches, peeling and eating them fresh out of hand tops the list. And it isn't even necessary to peel them. **But if a recipe calls for peeled chopped peaches, use a vegetable peeler or paring knife for firm fruit, and blanch soft, ripe peaches like apricots.**

Peach Pointers	Test Kitchen
	SECRET

- To get the best peaches, scout local orchards and farmers' markets, where you can get to know the grower. Look for golden peaches without traces of green near the stem.

- If your peaches are firm, let them stand on the kitchen counter for a few days or until they're soft to the touch and display a deep, golden background color.

How to Skin a Peach

1. First, cut an "X" in the bottom of each peach, carefully cutting just through the skin. Heat a large pot of water to boiling, and drop in the peaches. Cook for 20 seconds to 1 minute—the riper they are, the less time they need.

2. Remove the peaches from the water with a slotted spoon, and place them in a sink filled with ice water.

3. Pick them out of the water, and use a paring knife or your fingers to remove the skins, which should slip right off, leaving picture-perfect peaches.

French Toast-Peach Cobbler

The sturdier the bread, the better for this simple dessert. Turbinado sugar crystals have a coarse texture and add a nice crunch to the topping, but granulated sugar can be used instead.

    12   large ripe peaches
     1   cup granulated sugar, divided
    1/3 cup all-purpose flour
    Cooking spray
     1   teaspoon grated orange rind
    1/3 cup fresh orange juice
    1/4 cup butter, melted
    1/4 teaspoon ground cinnamon
     3   large egg whites
     8   (1.5-ounce) slices hearty white bread
         (such as Pepperidge Farm)
     2   tablespoons turbinado sugar or granulated
         sugar

1. Cut an "X" on the bottoms of peaches, carefully cutting just through the skin. Fill a large Dutch oven with water, and bring to a boil. Immerse the peaches for 20 seconds; remove with a slotted spoon, and plunge into ice water. Slip skins off peaches using a paring knife (skin will be very loose). Cut peaches in half; remove pits. Slice peaches to yield 12 cups.
2. Preheat oven to 350°.
3. Combine peaches, 3/4 cup granulated sugar, and flour in a 13 x 9-inch baking dish coated with cooking spray, and let stand 30 minutes, stirring occasionally.
4. Combine 1/4 cup granulated sugar, orange rind, orange juice, butter, cinnamon, and egg whites in a shallow bowl, stirring with a whisk. Trim

> **"Fresh peaches are actually best if eaten a day or two after picking. Store them at room temperature—refrigerating them dulls the flavor." Jan Smith, Photo Stylist**

crusts from bread; cut each slice into 2 triangles. Dip bread triangles in the orange juice mixture; arrange on top of peach mixture. Sprinkle turbinado sugar over bread. Bake at 350° for 45 minutes or until golden. Yield: 10 servings.

CALORIES 289 (17% from fat); FAT 5.6g (sat 3g, mono 1.7g, poly 0.4g); PROTEIN 4.5g; CARB 58.5g; FIBER 4.6g; CHOL 13mg; IRON 1mg; SODIUM 162mg; CALC 35mg

Grilled Peach Halves with Savory Ginger Glaze

This is a great side dish served with pork or roasted chicken.

     6   peaches
     3   tablespoons brown sugar
     2   tablespoons minced shallots
     2   tablespoons low-sodium soy sauce
     2   tablespoons orange juice
     1   tablespoon minced peeled fresh ginger
     1   tablespoon hoisin sauce
     1   teaspoon grated orange rind
    Cooking spray

1. Cut an "X" on bottoms of peaches, carefully cutting just through the skin. Fill a large Dutch oven with water, and bring to a boil. Immerse peaches for 20 seconds; remove with a slotted spoon, and plunge into ice water. Slip skins off peaches using a paring knife (skin will be very loose). Cut peaches in half; remove pits.
2. Prepare grill.
3. Combine sugar and next 6 ingredients. Brush cut sides of peaches with marinade. Place peaches, cut sides down, on a grill rack coated with cooking spray; cook 10 minutes or until tender, turning and basting once with marinade. Yield: 6 servings (serving size: 2 peach halves).

CALORIES 80 (3% from fat); FAT 0.3g (sat 0g, mono 0g, poly 0.1g); PROTEIN 1g; CARB 19.5g; FIBER 2.4g; CHOL 0mg; IRON 0.3mg; SODIUM 176mg; CALC 13mg

Plums

Their skin is tart and a little rough, yet their flesh is sweet, soft, and juicy. When you cook plums, something magical happens. The sweetness of the flesh, tartness of the skin, and spectrum of colors come together in harmony.

"All plums taste pretty much the same. The difference is generally about seasonal availability and appearance."
Ann Pittman, Food Editor

Deciding which plum to buy, however, can be daunting. You never know which of the more than 250 varieties might turn up in the produce section on any given summer day. Relax. Fact is, all plums taste about the same: sweet flesh inside tart skins. The choices are not so much about flavor as appearance or seasonal availability. A green or black plum may be best for presentation, and a red Santa Rosa may be ready for market before a green Kelsey, but other than that, a plum's pretty much a plum.

It may seem odd, but most plums wind up as prunes. These "prune plums," also called blue or European plums, are very small—about twice the size of a grape—and very grainy to the taste. Almost all the ones we eat fresh or cook, however, are part of a general type known as Japanese plums. Japanese plums fall into three major categories: red, black, and green. The black Angeleno and Friar and red Santa Rosa are the top sellers. Each of the three types is suitable for everything from tarts to entrées. **And although some plums will change color as they ripen—green to yellow, yellow to red, and so on—the sugar content remains the same once picked.**

Some of the the most common plum varieties are listed in the chart on the following page.

All can be eaten fresh or cooked. In general, late-season plums are sweeter; early-season varieties tend to make better jams because of the higher tartness of the skins.

How to Buy Plums
Test Kitchen **SECRET**

Ripe plums yield slightly to the touch, but don't squeeze them. Let the fruit sit in your palm. It should give a little. If you buy firmer fruit, though, don't put it in the refrigerator or the kitchen window—put it in a paper bag in a dark place for a day or two. The paper bag traps ethylene, the gas that naturally ripens fruit, but the bag also lets the fruit breathe. And if you really want to see a huge difference in ripening, put a fruit that produces lots of natural ethylene, like an apple or a pear, in the bag with the plums. That really speeds up the process.

Although the plums might taste sweeter, it's actually a trick on your palate. The sugar level remains the same after picking, but the acidity falls, so it only seems sweeter.

Always leave the skin on when cooking plums, not only for the tartness but also for the color.

The Pick of the Plums

Here's our guide to some of the most common varieties of plums and their peak seasons.

Season	Type of Plum	Description
Early May	Red Beaut	bright red skin, yellow flesh; small to medium size; the first major variety of the year to produce
Mid-May	Black Beaut	black skin, yellow to reddish flesh
June	Santa Rosa	red skin, yellow flesh with gold streaks; an old variety
Mid-June	Blackamber	purplish black skin, yellow flesh; the first large plum of the season
July	Fortune	red skin, yellow flesh; another large-sized plum
	Friar	purplish black skin, yellow flesh; very large (8-ounce average); dramatic color
Mid-July	Frontier	purple skin, deep red flesh; one of Elephant Heart's replacements
Late July	Simka	red skin, yellow flesh; similar to the Santa Rosa
	Elephant Heart	green to brownish-purple skin, beet red flesh; a beautiful variety for tarts
	Mariposa	purple skin, pink to light purple flesh
August	Kelsey	green skin, yellow flesh; don't be fooled by the color—they're green when ripe
	Royal Diamond	red skin, yellow flesh; small in the late season
Late August	Casselman	red skin, yellow flesh; another smaller-sized plum
Late August to September	Moyer and French Prune	green skin, yellow flesh; very small plums with high sugar content; excellent for baking; dried to make prunes
	Angeleno	red skin, yellow flesh

Grilled Stone Fruit Antipasto Plate

Black pepper and vanilla heighten the sweetness of the fruit. Serve this as an appetizer or salad course.

1 tablespoon brown sugar
3 tablespoons white balsamic vinegar
2 tablespoons extra-virgin olive oil
2 tablespoons fresh lime juice
2 teaspoons vanilla extract
¼ teaspoon freshly ground black pepper
⅛ teaspoon salt
⅛ teaspoon hot sauce
1 pound firm black plums, halved and pitted
1 pound firm peaches, halved and pitted
½ pound firm nectarines, halved and pitted
½ pound firm pluots, halved and pitted
Cooking spray

1. Prepare grill.

2. Combine first 8 ingredients in a small bowl, stirring well with a whisk.

3. Place fruit on grill rack coated with cooking spray; grill 3 minutes on each side. Remove from grill. Drizzle fruit with dressing. Yield: 8 servings.

CALORIES 129 (29% from fat); FAT 4.1g (sat 0.5g, mono 2.9g, poly 0.4g); PROTEIN 1.4g; CARB 23.8g; FIBER 2.9g; CHOL 0mg; IRON 0.3mg; SODIUM 39mg; CALC 12mg

If you can't find pluots, double up on the peaches or plums. Firm fruit holds up best on the grill.

Tropical Fruits

Don't limit tropical fruits to desserts. Their sweetness is perfect for a wide variety of dishes.

Tropical fruits—banana, mango, papaya, pineapple, and pomegranates—are great for light entrées, salads, and breads, providing a sweet contrast with island-style flair. We've got advice on how to pick the best from the produce bin, as well as step-by-step instructions on what to do with it after you get home.

Bananas

When they look as if they've had it, bananas are at their sweetest and are perfect for desserts. Left

out for a few days, their peels develop brown spots, and their firm pulp goes soft, even squishy. It's at this point that people often think bananas are over the hill, which is hardly the case.

Overripe bananas may not be the best for eating out of hand, but when it comes to cooking, they couldn't be better: They're easier to mash, sweeter (as the fruit ripens, its starch turns to sugar), and more intense in flavor. Brown sugar, caramel, cinnamon, rum, nutmeg, orange, and pecans give overripe bananas an even richer, more complex flavor.

Dark Secrets

A small banana has more than 2 grams of fiber; that's more fiber than a bowl of cornflakes or a dish of fresh blueberries. And some of that fiber is the soluble kind that scientists find helps to lower blood cholesterol levels, which is even better news.

Let bananas ripen at room temperature until the skin is covered with brown speckles. Once they've reached this point of ripeness, they are ready to be used in these recipes or stored in the refrigerator. Refrigeration will continue to darken the outside of the bananas, but it will not affect the fruit inside.

If you can't wait for your bananas to brown, you can speed up the ripening process: Wrap bananas in a wet paper towel, then place them in a brown paper bag. Or leave them overnight in a brown paper bag with an apple or tomato.

One medium-size ripe banana yields about $1/2$ cup of mashed banana.

Jamaican Banana Bread

If you don't have dark rum, light rum will work fine. Or use ¼ teaspoon imitation rum extract.

Cooking spray
- 2 tablespoons butter, softened
- 2 tablespoons tub light cream cheese
- 1 cup granulated sugar
- 1 large egg
- 2 cups all-purpose flour
- 2 teaspoons baking powder
- ½ teaspoon baking soda
- ⅛ teaspoon salt
- 1 cup mashed ripe banana (about 2 bananas)
- ½ cup fat-free milk
- 2 tablespoons dark rum
- ½ teaspoon grated lime rind (about ½ lime)
- 2 teaspoons lime juice
- 1 teaspoon vanilla extract
- ¼ cup chopped pecans, toasted
- ¼ cup flaked sweetened coconut
- ¼ cup packed brown sugar
- 2 teaspoons butter
- 2 teaspoons lime juice
- 2 teaspoons dark rum
- 2 tablespoons chopped pecans, toasted
- 2 tablespoons flaked sweetened coconut

1. Preheat oven to 375°.
2. Coat an 8 x 4-inch loaf pan with cooking spray.
3. Beat 2 tablespoons butter and cheese with a mixer at medium speed; add 1 cup granulated sugar, beating well. Add egg; beat well.
4. Combine flour, baking powder, baking soda, and salt; stir. Combine banana and next 5 ingredients; stir. Add flour mixture to creamed mixture alternately with banana mixture, beginning and ending with flour mixture; mix after each addition. Stir in ¼ cup pecans and ¼ cup coconut.
5. Pour batter into prepared pan; bake at 375° for 60 minutes. Let cool in pan 10 minutes; remove from pan. Let cool slightly on a wire rack.
6. Combine brown sugar and 2 teaspoons each butter, lime juice, and rum in a saucepan; bring to a simmer. Cook 1 minute; stir constantly. Remove from heat. Stir in 2 tablespoons each pecans and coconut; spoon over loaf. Yield: 16 servings (serving size: 1 slice).

CALORIES 191 (25% from fat); FAT 5.3g (sat 2g, mono 2.1g, poly 0.8g); PROTEIN 3g; CARB 33.1g; FIBER 1.1g; CHOL 19mg; IRON 1.1mg; SODIUM 157mg; CALC 58mg

Great Banana Bread

Test Kitchen SECRET

The key to great banana bread is using very ripe bananas. If they're not very ripe, you'll have chunks of banana in the bread, rather than an almost liquid mixture that is better distributed in the batter.

Banana-Citrus Sorbet

Soft, ripe bananas are easier to blend to a smooth consistency than firm ones.

- 3 ripe bananas
- 1½ cups sugar
- ½ cup fresh lemon juice
- 2 cups water
- 1½ cups fresh orange juice

1. Place bananas in food processor; process until smooth. Add sugar and lemon juice; process until well blended. Pour mixture into the freezer can of an ice-cream freezer; add water and orange juice, stirring well.
2. Freeze according to manufacturer's instructions. Spoon into freezer-safe container; cover and freeze. Yield: 8 servings (serving size: 1 cup).

CALORIES 213 (1% from fat); FAT 0.2g (sat 0.1g, mono 0g, poly 0.1g); PROTEIN 0.8g; CARB 54.8g; FIBER 1.5g; CHOL 0mg; IRON 0.2mg; SODIUM 1mg; CALC 8mg

Coconut

Coconut is high in saturated fat, so we use it selectively in *Cooking Light* recipes. But you don't need to use much for it to contribute its distinctive sweetness and texture.

Fresh coconuts have hard green outer shells which are removed before they get to the market. What you'll see is a smaller, round brown shell that is covered with hairy fibers. Choose a coconut that is heavy and filled with liquid—shake it near your ear to listen for the liquid inside. The more liquid you hear, the fresher the coconut. They are available all year, but are more plentiful in the fall and winter months.

> "We can hardly tell the difference between fresh and canned coconut milk in recipes, so for convenience, we generally use canned." Sam Brannock, Test Kitchens Staffer

Here's how to crack a coconut:

- Drive an ice pick or a long nail through one of the three smooth eyes at the end of the coconut.
- Drain the liquid, and either use it immediately or cover and refrigerate for up to a few hours. (This is not coconut milk—coconut milk is made by soaking grated fresh coconut in water.)
- Put the coconut on a hard surface (the floor or porch), and crack it open with a hammer.
- Break the shell apart using your hands or a hammer.
- Cut the white meat away from the shell with a knife, and peel the brown skin from the meat.

Fresh or Bagged?

Although we think the flavor of fresh coconut is superior to that of processed coconut, sometimes convenience wins and we use packaged flaked coconut.

Processed coconut is almost always sweetened, although you can find it unsweetened in some health-food stores. The bags contain dry coconut shreds or flakes; the canned flakes are more moist than the bagged flakes.

Kiwifruit

A kiwifruit is small and egg-shaped with fuzzy  brown skin. The flesh is bright green and has a pattern of tiny black seeds. It has a sweet-tart flavor that perks up a fruit plate or salad, and it's also perfect for sauces and desserts.

Choose kiwifruit that are heavy for their size and have no bruises. They do bruise easily, so handle kiwifruit with care. Leave them at room temperature until they soften. Once they are soft and ripe, keep kiwifruit in a plastic bag in the refrigerator for up to 1 week.

To peel kiwifruit, removed the fuzzy skin with a vegetable peeler using a gentle sawing motion. If the fruit is soft and ripe, you can cut it in half and scoop out the flesh with a spoon. To show off the pattern of the seeds, slice a kiwifruit in half crosswise.

Speedy Ripening

You can speed up the ripening of kiwifruit by placing them in a paper bag with an apple or banana. The ethylene gas that is omitted by the apple or banana is what will help the fruit to ripen.

Mango

The mango is originally from India but is now grown in temperate climates around the world, including California and Florida.

This versatile fruit can shine on its own as a snack or appear on the table in every course from soups to desserts. Green mangoes are perfect for condiments, while nothing beats the aroma of a ripe beauty diced in a salad or sliced in a curry sauce.

Look for fruit with unblemished yellow skin that is blushed with red. Very fragrant when ripe, mangoes are ready to eat when they become soft to the touch.

Mango Tango Chicken Salad

The tropical fruits in this salad—mango, papaya, and pineapple—complement the chutney and ginger in this island-style chicken salad.

3¼	cups chopped ready-to-eat roasted skinned, boned chicken breasts (such as Tyson; about 4 breast halves)
½	cup diced peeled mango
½	cup diced fresh pineapple
½	cup drained, sliced water chestnuts
½	cup sliced celery
¼	cup sliced green onions
1	tablespoon mango chutney
1	tablespoon light mayonnaise
1	tablespoon low-fat sour cream
2	teaspoons lemon juice
1	teaspoon minced peeled fresh ginger
½	teaspoon salt
¼	teaspoon pepper
10	slices peeled papaya (about 1 large)

1. Combine first 6 ingredients in a large bowl. Combine chutney and next 6 ingredients in a small bowl, and stir chutney mixture into chicken mixture. Arrange papaya slices on each of 5 plates, and top with chicken salad. Yield: 5 servings (serving size: 1 cup salad and 2 papaya slices).

CALORIES 163 (15% from fat); FAT 2.8g (sat 1.1g, mono 0.8g, poly 0.8g); PROTEIN 8.7g; CARB 16.2g; FIBER 1.9g; CHOL 51mg; IRON 0.4mg; SODIUM 685mg; CALC 30mg

The mango can be tricky to cut because it has a rather large seed that grows horizontally inside the fruit. So, you must cut around it on both sides.

Cutting a Mango

1. Hold the mango vertically on the cutting board. With a sharp knife, slice the fruit lengthwise on each side of the flat pit.

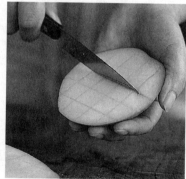

2. Holding the mango half in the palm of your hand, score the pulp in square cross-sections. Be sure that you slice to, but not through, the skin.

3. Turn the mango inside out, and cut the chunks from the skin.

Papaya

A papaya resembles a large pear that has pale green skin that gets yellow or orange blotches as it ripens. It has a hollow center with a mass of shiny black seeds. These seeds are edible and have a slightly peppery flavor.

Look for a papaya that gives slightly when pressed. The skin should be smooth and already starting to turn yellow. Leave papayas at room temperature until they are ripe. Once they are ripe, peel, slice, and store in a airtight container in the refrigerator for up to 2 days.

Ripening a Papaya	Test Kitchen SECRET

To reduce the bitterness of an underripe papaya, cut a few shallow score lines through the skin along the length of the fruit. Let the flesh show, but don't cut into it. Prop the papaya, stem down, in a glass jar. Leave it at room temperature overnight to activate the enzyme in the fruit that will make it taste sweeter. (This method will not make an already ripe papaya taste sweeter.)

Spicy Tropical Gazpacho

This chilled soup combines the sweetness of the tropical fruits with tangy tomato juice and hot sauce.

1	cup tomato juice
1	cup pineapple juice
½	cup chopped peeled mango
½	cup chopped peeled papaya
½	cup chopped fresh pineapple
½	cup chopped seeded peeled cucumber
¼	cup chopped green bell pepper
¼	cup chopped red bell pepper
2	tablespoons minced fresh cilantro
½	to 1 teaspoon hot sauce
¼	teaspoon salt

1. Combine all ingredients in a food processor or in a blender; pulse 4 times or until combined. Cover and chill. Yield: 4 servings (serving size: 1 cup).

CALORIES 83 (4% from fat); FAT 0.4g (sat 0.1g, mono 0.1g, poly 0.1g); PROTEIN 1.3g; CARB 20.5g; FIBER 1.7g; CHOL 0mg; IRON 1mg; SODIUM 375mg; CALC 31mg

Cutting a Papaya

1. Cut about 1 inch from each end.

2. With a paring knife or vegetable peeler, remove the skin in ¹/₂-inch slices.

3. Cut in half lengthwise, and remove the seeds with a spoon. The fruit can now be cut as needed for the recipe.

Pineapple

A ripe pineapple should be deep golden brown in color and have a slightly sweet smell; it should also be a bit soft to the touch. The leaves should pull out from the top without much effort. Avoid fruit that has dark, mushy spots or a woody-looking or whitish appearance. Soft or dark areas on the skin tell you that the pineapple may be overripe.

To store, refrigerate fresh pineapple, tightly wrapped, for 2 to 3 days. If it's slightly underripe, you can keep it at room temperature for a couple of days—it will become less acidic, but not necessarily sweeter.

Cutting a Pineapple

1. Cut about 1 inch from each end.

2. Stand the pineapple vertically on the cutting board. Using a sharp knife, slice down about ¹/₂ inch into the skin. This should remove the eyes from the pineapple flesh.

3. Keep turning the pineapple with one hand and slicing 1-inch-wide bands down in a straight line until the pineapple is peeled.

4. Cut the fruit into quarters. While holding each pineapple quarter firmly, remove the core.

5. Cut the pineapple wedges in half lengthwise, then cut as needed for the recipe.

Pomegranates

This ancient fruit changed the course of the Greek goddess Persephone's life when she ate its seeds. It symbolizes fertility in China, as well as in some Middle Eastern cultures. Cut one open, and you'll understand why pomegranates have intrigued people for millennia.

> "The flesh that surrounds the seeds is encased in an inedible, bitter membrane. To remove the seeds intact, cut the fruit in half and turn the skin inside out."
> Kellie Kelley, Food Stylist

You'll find hundreds of seeds that are surrounded by glistening, luminescent ruby-red pulp, which has an intense sweet-tart flavor. Pomegranates were originally the basis for grenadine syrup and are still used to make pomegranate molasses, a Middle Eastern staple (now available in specialty food stores in the United States).

Throughout the Middle East, pomegranates are often used to season foods. The juice makes a wonderfully vibrant syrup when reduced. The seeds provide a tart, crisp addition to salads and creamy desserts.

> "For a colorful bolt of sweet-tart flavor, sprinkle a few pomegranate seeds on salads, roasts, ice cream, or pies."
> Tiffany Vickers, Test Kitchens Staffer

Buying a Fresh Pomegranate

Pomegranates are available from late August through December.

Choose a pomegranate that seems heavy for its size and has a bright color. If the seeds are opaque and white, then the pomegranate is not ripe. You can still use it, but the juice will be less sweet. The skin should be uniform, free of blemishes, thin, and tough.

Refrigerate whole pomegranates for up to 3 months, and freeze the seeds in an airtight container for up to 3 months.

Seeding Pomegranates — Test Kitchen SECRET

- Take care when seeding and juicing pomegranates. You may want to wear gloves and an old shirt during this procedure because the fruit produces a red juice that will stain. (The Persians used pomegranates as a dye.)
- Cut pomegranate in half crosswise (like you cut an orange). With the cut sides away from you and your thumbs on the crown end, break each half in half.
- The pomegranate is now in quarters with the seeds protruding. Remove seeds from the base with thumbs; be careful not to break them. Remove white membrane.

"One good-size pomegranate will yield about ¾ cup seeds or ½ cup juice." Kellie Kelley, Food Stylist

Pomegranate Pound Cake

Pomegranate seeds add sweet-tart flavor to a basic buttermilk pound cake.

 ¾ cup sugar
 6 tablespoons butter
 2 large eggs
 1 large egg white
 ¾ cup low-fat buttermilk
 2 teaspoons grated lime rind
 2 teaspoons vanilla extract
 ½ teaspoon baking soda
 2½ cups all-purpose flour
 ¼ teaspoon salt
 ¾ cup pomegranate seeds (about 1 large)
 Cooking spray

1. Preheat oven to 350°.
2. Beat sugar and butter with a mixer at medium-high speed until well blended (about 7 minutes). Add eggs and egg white, 1 at a time, beating well after each addition. Combine buttermilk, rind, vanilla, and baking soda. Lightly spoon flour into dry measuring cups; level with a knife. Combine flour and salt, stirring well with a whisk. Add flour mixture to sugar mixture alternately with buttermilk mixture, beginning and ending with flour mixture. Fold in pomegranate seeds.
3. Spoon batter into an 8 x 4-inch loaf pan coated with cooking spray. Bake at 350° for 1 hour or until a wooden pick inserted in center comes out clean. Cool in pan 10 minutes on a wire rack; remove from pan. Cool completely on wire rack. Yield: 12 servings (serving size: 1 slice).

CALORIES 223 (29% from fat); FAT 7.2g (sat 4g, mono 2.1g, poly 0.5g); PROTEIN 4.7g; CARB 34.5g; FIBER 0.7g; CHOL 52mg; IRON 1.4mg; SODIUM 184mg; CALC 30mg

Juicing the Pomegranate Seeds

Test Kitchen SECRET

The best way to juice the seeds is to place them in a plastic bag, and crush them with a rolling pin. Then place the seeds, juice, and water in a nonaluminum saucepan, and bring to a boil. Cook 10 minutes; strain, and refrigerate. Three cups of seeds and 2 cups of water will yield about 2 cups of juice.

Pomegranate Syrup

This syrup is similar in consistency to maple syrup. It's delicious brushed on chicken, lamb, or pork. It can also be drizzled over pancakes or ice cream.

 2 cups pomegranate juice (see above)
 1¼ cups sugar
 1 (2 x 1-inch) strip orange rind

1. Combine all ingredients in a medium nonreactive saucepan. Bring to a boil; reduce heat to medium, and cook until reduced to 1½ cups (about 15 minutes). Discard rind. Yield: 1½ cups (serving size: 2 tablespoons).

CALORIES 98 (1% from fat); FAT 0.1g (sat 0g, mono 0g, poly 0g); PROTEIN 0.2g; CARB 25.2g; FIBER 0.1g; CHOL 0mg; IRON 0.1mg; SODIUM 1mg; CALC 1mg

Pomegranate Syrup can be kept in the refrigerator for up to 2 weeks. You can find bottles of commercial pomegranate syrup in Middle Eastern markets—labeled "pomegranate concentrated juice"—but it isn't as sweet or as good as this homemade version.

CHAPTER 10

Fats, Oils & Nuts

Learn which fats, oils, and nuts are important in light cooking
and how to use them in the proper amounts for maximum flavor.

Good Fats

Not all fats are created equal. **For a healthy heart, it's important to limit foods high in saturated fats and trans fats and to include a moderate amount of monoun-saturated and polyunsaturated fats.** It appears that monounsaturated fats and some polyunsaturated fats actually have the potential to boost your health. But total fat still counts because all fats—polys, monos, and otherwise—are concentrated sources of calories. And in a country such as ours, where more than half of the population is overweight, concentrated sources of calories are often a concern.

Saturated fat is found in animal products, such as meats, poultry, and dairy products, so it's a good idea to limit high-fat meats and full-fat dairy products.

Trans fats are found in margarines, fast-food items cooked in hydrogenated shortening, fried foods, and many commercial snack foods, such as crackers, cookies, pastries, candy bars, boxed cakes, and TV dinners. Any packaged food that has the words "hydrogenated oil" or "partially

hydrogenated oil" on the ingredients list is a source of trans fat.

Monounsaturated and polyunsaturated fats (particularly omega-3 fats) are the ones that appear to have health benefits. See the list of food sources of these fats on page 360.

Use our guide to oils, nuts, and other healthy fats to see how to use these ingredients in the proper amounts for maximum flavor. Plus, we'll share our strategy for using butter instead of margarine.

> **Best of Both Worlds** — Test Kitchen SECRET
>
> So how does *Cooking Light* cut down on saturated fat while incorporating "good" fats—and still keep from adding too many calories? *We include the good fats judiciously, using just enough to enliven flavor without piling on the pounds.* For instance, in our salmon dishes, most of the fat comes from the salmon itself. The rest of the flavoring comes primarily from herbs, spices and other low-fat flavoring ingredients. We think it's the perfect solution.

"By using the 'good' fats in just-enough amounts, we help you satisfy your taste buds without wreaking havoc on the rest of your body." Krista Montgomery, Food Editor

359

To incorporate fat into your diet in a healthy way, the *Cooking Light* food editors suggest that you:
- Eat a small handful of nuts instead of chips.
- Eat a sandwich made with natural peanut butter instead of one with deli meat and cheese.
- Have salmon for dinner instead of steak.
- Top salads with toasted almonds instead of croutons.
- Use "good fats" as ingredients in great-tasting recipes.
- Make your own nut butters. (See pages 365-366.)

The two types of fat you want to emphasize in your diet are monounsaturated fats and omega-3 fatty acids (which are a type of polyunsaturated fat).

Avocado

An avocado is actually a fruit, but because of its buttery, rich flavor and high fat content, it makes sense to group it with other sources of fat. More than half of its fat is monounsaturated.

Avocados are available year-round. To select a ripe one, press lightly on the skin, and feel the flesh yield to the pressure. It if feels mushy or is moldy, don't buy it.

The flesh will quickly turn brown when exposed to air, so don't cut an avocado until just before serving or using in a recipe. The buttery texture and rich flavor of an avocado go a long way. Thinly slice one for a sandwich, or chop one up to top your favorite Mexican dish.

Peeling and Seeding Avocado

1. Cut into the avocado all the way around using a sharp knife. You'll hit the large seed in the center, so don't expect to be able to cut all the way through the fruit. Once you've cut around it, twist both sides, and pull the halves apart. Take the knife and whack the seed; pull up to remove the seed, which will be stuck on the knife blade.

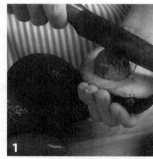

2. Using a spoon, gently scoop the flesh of the avocado from the shell.

Oils

Small amounts of oil are essential in light and healthy cooking.

The proportion of fatty acids in an oil—saturated, monounsaturated, and polyunsaturated—is what makes the difference in health benefits. The source of the oil is what makes the difference in the flavor. **The oils that have the most health benefits are the ones that are highest in monounsaturated fat;** the ones with a high saturated fat content (coconut and palm kernel oils) can contribute to the risk of heart disease.

Vegetable Oils

The vegetable oils that contain mostly unsaturated fats are canola, corn, safflower, sunflower, and soybean oils. Next to olive oil, canola oil is the one with the most monounsaturated fat. Safflower oil and sunflower oil contain mostly polyunsaturated fat. **If you're using oil in a recipe where the flavor of olive oil is not desirable, any of the unsaturated oils will work, but canola will be the best choice in terms of health benefits.** As with butter, the idea is to use small amounts of any type of oil.

Sesame Oil

Sesame oil is not as high in monounsaturated fat as olive oil, but it is high in polyunsaturated fat, ranking fourth behind safflower, soybean, and corn oil. Light sesame oil (light in color, not in fat) has a deliciously light, nutty flavor and is good for everything from sautéing to salad dressings. **Dark sesame oil has a much stronger flavor and fragrance and is often used for a distinct flavor accent.**

Olive Oil

Olive oil is not only better for you than most other oils, it also has a fresh taste, an aromatic smell, and is very versatile. It has 126 calories per tablespoon, which is about the same as the calorie content of other oils. And because good olive oil is intensely flavored, a little goes a long way. A good way to cut down on fat is to use good-tasting olive oil and just use less.

Choosing Olive Oil | Test Kitchen SECRET

There are a lot of choices in the market, and sometimes it's hard to know whether to opt for the 3-liter tin or the boutique bottle. Perhaps you often choose something in between: You don't buy the cheapest or the most expensive. Instead, you settle for a mid-priced oil and then use it for everything. But that strategy may actually be giving you the least taste for your money.

Olive oil is used for two very different purposes: as a fat for cooking and as a condiment to add flavor to a dish. If you use the same mid-range oil for both purposes, you're paying too much for cooking oil and aren't getting enough flavor as a condiment. **When you heat olive oil, it loses much of its taste, so it's a waste to use extra-virgin olive oil that way.** Besides, "pure" oil, a less expensive grade, is actually better to cook with because it's refined, with no olive particles at the bottom of the bottle that can burn at high heat.

But when you're using olive oil for its flavor—when tossing it with roasted vegetables or adding it to pasta, for example—a higher-priced extra-virgin oil will usually produce a much better result than a mid-priced one.

What's the Difference in Olive Oils?

Europeans have strict standards for labeling olive oil. In the United States, these standards are not as explicit but are generally observed. Below are some of the terms you'll see on olive oil labels.

Type	Description
Cold Pressed	All good condiment olive oils are cold pressed, meaning the oils are extracted using methods in which the temperature isn't raised. The oil may be filtered, but not refined, in any heat process.
Extra-virgin	This oil comes from whole unblemished olives pressed within a day after harvest. Less than 1 percent of the oil can be made up of free oleic acid, which can make the oil taste sharp. Most extra-virgin olive oils in the U.S. are blends of different grades of oils with a predictable flavor profile. Like wine, extra-virgin olive oils that come from a single location have a characteristic fragrance, taste, and color, depending on the variety of olive, growing conditions, and soil. Extra-virgin olive oil is what we use in our Test Kitchens. See "Oil Picks" below for some of the specific brands we like.
Virgin	Virgin olive oil is rarely sold in the U.S. Its standards are the same as for extra-virgin oil, except that its free oleic acid can be up to 3 percent, which means that the quality is good, but not equal to extra-virgin.
Pure	Pure olive oil is a blend of refined and extra-virgin olive oils. Usually the extra-virgin oil is added at the end of the process—from 5 percent to 30 percent of the total—to provide a color and taste profile that will be acceptable to the consumer.
Light	Light oils actually have no fewer calories than regular ones—the term applies to color and taste. These are mostly refined oils that have little or no extra-virgin oil added for taste. As a result, they are bland.

Premium Oils High-quality olive oils are like good wines: No two are alike, and each has a distinct character. Tastes run the gamut from buttery to fruity to peppery, depending on what type of olive was used and where it was grown. **While color isn't always a guide to quality or flavor, the greener oils, made from olives that aren't fully ripe, are generally the most prized.** Extra-virgin oils come from the first cold pressing of the olive. Since neither heat nor chemicals are used, the result is a rich, deep olive flavor. Use extra-virgin olive oils to make an outstanding vinaigrette, drizzle over bread, or add a finishing touch to just about any dish. Taste a variety to find one you like.

Buying Imported extra-virgin olive oils once were the most highly prized, but many California olive oils—such as DaVero—are winning international awards. Stores such as Williams-Sonoma and Whole Foods Market often let you sample oils before purchasing.

Storage Heat, light, and air are the enemies of extra-virgin olive oils. Store in a cool cabinet away from the stove, and use within 6 months.

Oil Picks
Cooking Light Recommends

Here are a few premium oils that we use. We think they're well worth the extra expense in terms of flavor.

- DaVero (California)
- Nuñez de Prado (Spain)
- Hain (Italy)
- Capoleuca Labbate (Italy)
- Morea (Greece)
- DaVinci (Italy)

You can find Hain and DaVinci brands in most supermarkets.

Nuts

Eating a handful of nuts or a nutty muffin is like eating a multivitamin—only much tastier.

Nutrition Benefits of Nuts

A healthy diet that includes regular nut-noshing and cooking with nuts can help improve cholesterol levels. And despite the high fat content, you can probably still lose weight while eating a few nuts, an effect some researchers suggest can be explained by the satiety-inducing effect of nuts, which results in less eating overall.

Strive to be a nut gourmand, not a nut glutton. Using them in cooking might be an even better way to enjoy their flavor and health benefits without getting seduced into overdoing it. Here are some healthy reasons to "go nuts."

Despite the high fat content, you can probably still lose weight while eating a few nuts.

Good-fat content Nuts have different amounts of fat, of course, but a quarter-cup of any nut contains about 20 grams of fat, roughly speaking. The fat in nuts, however, is highly monounsaturated—the same form found in abundance in heart-healthy olive and canola oils. Nuts are also rich in polyunsaturated fat, the other form known to lower cholesterol levels. They contain relatively modest amounts of artery-clogging saturated fat. So the fat you're getting is quite different than the kind found in red meat.

Omega-3 fatty acids Like mackerel, salmon, and other cold-water fish, nuts tend to be high in omega-3 fatty acids. This complex bio-molecule may help reduce the risk of strokes and heart attacks.

Nutrient density Nuts are jam-packed with micronutrients such as vitamin E, folic acid, niacin, copper, magnesium, and potassium. They're also rich in arginine, which the human body uses to make a potent natural vasodilator. And don't forget the abundant flavonoids and isoflavones—the most recently discovered "guardian angel" compounds now thought to help ward off cancer and cardiovascular disease.

A Toast to Nuts
Test Kitchen SECRET

One of the best ways to bring out the flavor in nuts is to toast them. Heating helps release flavor compounds that make for a richer, more intense nutty taste.

To toast, just place any kind of whole or chopped nuts in a shallow pan or on a baking sheet, and bake at 350° for 6 to 8 minutes. Be sure to watch them carefully; they can go from toasted to burned very quickly.

You can also toast nuts in a skillet or in the microwave oven. Place the nuts in a dry skillet, and cook them over medium heat, stirring frequently, for 1 to 2 minutes or until they're toasted. To toast in the microwave, place the nuts in a shallow microwave-safe dish, and microwave at HIGH 1 to 3 minutes, stirring every 30 seconds. The nuts won't turn golden, but they'll have a toasted flavor.

"Heart-healthy and full of nutrients, nuts are back from banishment." Mary Creel, Food Editor

Our Favorite Nuts

Although all nuts have nutrition benefits and taste great, here are some nuts we use most often.

Almonds Almonds have more vitamin E (a powerful disease-fighting nutrient) than any other nut. And about two-thirds of the fat is monounsaturated. These delicate, slightly sweet nuts come in a variety of forms. These are some of the forms we use, depending on the use in the recipe:
- *Whole natural:* whole almonds with skins
- *Blanched whole:* almonds without skins
- *Sliced natural:* whole almonds, thinly sliced lengthwise
- *Blanched slivered:* matchstick lengthwise slices
- *Blanched sliced:* without skins, thinly sliced lengthwise

Chestnuts Unlike other nuts, chestnuts have a large amount of starch and only a little oil. They're often treated more like a vegetable in recipes instead of a nut and are almost always cooked.

> We recommend that you always buy a few more chestnuts than the recipe calls for because there are usually a few bad ones in the batch.

You need to either boil them briefly or roast them in order to loosen their tough outer shells and thin, bitter skins.

To cook chestnuts, soak them in a bowl of water for about 30 minutes; drain well. Cut a slit in the shell in the rounded side of the chestnut. To roast in your oven, arrange chestnuts on a baking sheet. Bake at 400° for 25 minutes.

Or use your microwave; just arrange chestnuts in a single layer on a microwave-safe dish. Microwave at HIGH 2 minutes (do only 12 chestnuts at a time so they cook evenly). After either method, allow chestnuts to cool, then peel.

Peanuts Peanuts are actually legumes and are in the same family as beans, peas, and lentils, but they have a much higher fat content than other members of the legume family.

Peanuts are sold in a variety of ways: shelled and unshelled, with and without skins, roasted and unroasted, salted and unsalted. Although they're usually sold dried, you can find them fresh at farmers' markets during the late summer harvest.

Because they have a high fat content, peanuts can turn rancid fairly quickly if you leave them at room temperature. Wrap unshelled peanuts in a plastic bag and store in the refrigerator for up to 6 months. Store unopened jars or cans at room temperature for up to 1 year. Once you open them, store them in the refrigerator for up to 3 months.

Pecans Pecans have two crinkled lobes of nutmeat. There are many varieties, but they all have smooth, brown oval shells that break easily. The flavor is slightly sweeter and more delicate than walnuts.

> Generally, you get about 1/2 pound of nutmeats (around 2 cups) from 1 pound of unshelled nuts.

Pine Nuts Pine nuts, which are not nuts at all but are the pearly seeds borne on the cones of certain pine trees, are harvested throughout the Mediterranean and across much of Asia. Like other nuts, pine nuts are high in the "good" fats. They're also rather expensive—so we suggest toasting them in recipes to make the most of their flavor. That way, a little goes a lot further.

Versatile Pine Nuts
Test Kitchen SECRET

Certainly, pine nuts are essential to a good pesto, providing the resinous foundation upon which a pyramid of flavors is built. But pine nuts can also be a snack food that tastes great roasted and lightly salted, or a sweet and welcome crunch tucked into a rice dish or sprinkled in a salad.

Walnuts Like pecans, walnuts have dark shells that are hard to break, and their meat is double lobed. Black walnuts are usually sold whole, are hard to find, and have a stronger, more bitter flavor. Walnuts are the only nuts that contain both monounsaturated fats and omega-3s.

Chicken with Pecan Cream and Mushrooms

A simple chicken sauté gets an elegant makeover. This sauce is also great made with roasted almond butter.

¾	cup coarsely chopped pecans, toasted
1	cup water
1¼	teaspoons salt, divided
6	(6-ounce) skinless, boneless chicken breast halves
1	teaspoon freshly ground black pepper

Cooking spray

¼	cup finely chopped shallots
1	(8-ounce) package sliced mushrooms
4	cups cooked egg noodles

Chopped parsley (optional)

1. Place pecans in a food processor; process until smooth (about 1 minute), scraping sides of bowl once. Add water and ¾ teaspoon salt; process until smooth, scraping sides of bowl once.
2. Sprinkle chicken with ½ teaspoon salt and pepper. Heat a large nonstick skillet coated with cooking spray over medium-high heat. Add chicken; sauté 4 minutes on each side or until done. Remove chicken from pan; keep warm.
3. Add shallots and mushrooms to pan; sauté 3 minutes or until mushrooms are tender. Stir in pecan cream; bring to a boil. Cook 1½ minutes. Place ⅔ cup noodles on each of 6 plates. Top with 1 chicken breast half and ⅓ cup sauce. Garnish with parsley, if desired. Yield: 6 servings.

CALORIES 446 (30% from fat); FAT 14.4g (sat 1.8g, mono 7g, poly 4.1g); PROTEIN 47.3g; CARB 31.3g; FIBER 3.2g; CHOL 134mg; IRON 3.6mg; SODIUM 611mg; CALC 46mg

Nut Butters

In addition to topping dishes with nuts, you can process nuts into butters to use in a variety of recipes. Here's how to make butters from a variety of nuts and some suggested uses.

Almond Butter Roasted whole almonds have skins that fleck the butter. When the almonds start to come away from the sides of the food processor, the butter is ready. Slivered toasted almonds take 3½ minutes to form a butter; roasted whole almonds have more oil and will be ready in 2½ minutes. This mild, sweet butter is adaptable in sweet and savory dishes. Try almond butter on a sandwich with apples and Brie or Gouda cheese.

Cashew Butter The smooth butter forms after about 2 minutes of processing. It's ideal for sandwiches. Try it with vegetables in a pita, or substitute it for tahini when you make hummus.

Nut Butters and Creams

Test Kitchen
SECRET

Homemade nut butters are more perishable than commercial varieties, so make them in small batches. Store homemade butters covered in the refrigerator for up to a month. To make spreading easier, let nut butters return to room temperature. As a general rule, there is a 2 to 1 ratio of nuts used to the nut butter yield (1 cup nuts will make ½ cup nut butter, for example). To toast nuts, spread them on a baking sheet, and bake at 350° for 6 to 8 minutes.
To make a nut butter, grind nuts in a food processor until pasty. Some nut butters will be creamy; others will be a bit grainy. The higher the fat, the smoother the butter will be.
To make nut creams, whisk 1 cup water into ¼ cup nut butter; nut creams are a good substitute for heavy cream in pasta sauces and desserts. Start with neutral-flavored cashew or almond butter and then branch out to more flavorful nuts.

Sometimes you can use nut butters and creams to flavor, thicken, and replace dairy cream in traditional recipes.

Hazelnut Butter This grainy, thick butter with brown specks is fruity and naturally sweet. Processing it takes about 2½ minutes. Bags of chopped nuts have few skins, so don't worry about removing them. If the nuts are whole, toast them in a 400° oven for 5 minutes or until they start to look shiny and the skins begin to loosen. Rub them in a dishtowel to remove skins. Mix a 1 to 1 ratio of chocolate syrup and hazelnut butter for a delicious spread that's great on toasted honey wheat bread with bananas, or on apple wedges.

Macadamia Butter Hands down, this is our favorite nut butter. Because of macadamias' high fat content, in just 2 minutes, the nuts grind into a butter too thin for spreading on bread. Chill to thicken it. Its buttery flavor is great for desserts.

Peanut Butter Use plain roasted peanuts, rather than dry-roasted peanuts, which are often seasoned with paprika, garlic, and onion powder. This smooth butter has distinctive fresh peanut flavor, and the nuts take about 2 minutes to process. It is lighter in color than commercial peanut butters and is grainier than commercial hydrogenated brands.

As an alternative to making your own natural peanut butter, you can use one of the many brands of natural peanut butter on the market. See the Test Kitchen Secret on the right.

Pecan Butter With a rich, hearty flavor that stands up well, pecan butter is great over meats. Pecans process into butter in about a minute. It spreads easily, but skins give it a slightly bitter aftertaste, so it's best in recipes rather than for spreading.

Pistachio Butter A very dry, crumbly butter, it's best combined with something else, like softened cream cheese. Cream cheese–pistachio spread is nice on French or egg bread. It takes about 3½ to 4 minutes to grind into butter. It tends to clump during processing.

Walnut Butter This soft, oily butter is ready in about a minute. It has a bitter aftertaste from the skins, making it good for recipes but not on sandwiches. Walnut halves are expensive, so look for packages of walnut pieces.

Natural Peanut Butter — Test Kitchen SECRET

Natural peanut butter is the kind with the layer of oil on top. If you want to avoid trans fats in your diet, be sure to buy peanut butter labeled "natural" instead of the regular kind. Since natural peanut butter is not hydrogenated, it won't be as creamy as regular peanut butter, but it also will not have the trans fatty acids. Instead, it's high in monounsaturated fat.

We've found that natural peanut butter works better in cookies and sauces than the hydrogenated stuff because it has more peanut flavor. Brands not labeled natural—basically what we all grew up on, like Jif, Skippy, and Peter Pan—contain trans fatty acids.

In recipes where the creaminess is crucial to the recipe, we do call for regular peanut butter. But like other high-fat, high-flavor ingredients, we use only a small amount.

Butter & Margarine

We explain why we now use butter instead of margarine in *Cooking Light* recipes.

Best Uses

We prefer the taste of butter over margarine and call for it in small amounts in our recipes. While reduced-calorie margarines and spreads do not usually work well for cooking and baking because of their high water content, they are fine for spreading on toast and breads, stirring into hot cereals, and topping hot vegetables. If you choose to cook with something other than butter, it's a good idea to note the percentage of oil on the label of these products, as that percentage will be a good guide for the best use of that product. **Don't use a product with anything less than 80 percent milk fat or oil for baking. In other words, use either butter or regular stick margarine.**

Softened Butter
Test Kitchen SECRET

When a recipe calls for "butter, softened," it's the correct softness when it gently yields to the pressure of a finger. If you can push your finger deeply into the butter, it's too soft. To soften butter, leave it sitting out at room temperature 45 minutes to 1 hour, or place it in a microwave-safe dish and microwave on LOW about 30 seconds.

Butter or Margarine?
Cooking Light Recommends

From time to time, we get questions about why we call for butter in some of our recipes instead of margarine. It used to be that margarine was the clear choice for heart-healthy eating because it does not have any saturated fat. But recent research shows that the fat in stick margarine—trans fat—can actually be more harmful than saturated fat. Not only do trans fats raise the harmful type of cholesterol (LDL), they also lower the good kind (HDL).

There are trans-free margarines on the market, but they are not good substitutes in recipes because they, like other reduced-calorie spreads, have a higher water content than butter or regular stick margarine.

Healthwise, there's no real advantage to using margarine over butter; both have the same amount of total fat and the same number of calories. It's wise to use both of them with restraint. But we think butter tastes better, so sometimes you get more "bang" with butter in terms of flavor.

However, if you prefer to use margarine, most of our recipes that call for butter will work fine with margarine.

"Because there are no real health benefits to using margarine, I prefer to use small amounts of butter instead. The flavor of butter is beyond compare."

Jill Melton, Food Editor

CHAPTER 11

Condiments & Seasonings

Flavoring ingredients such as chutneys, mustards, vinegars, herbs, spices, and salt are essential to light cooking because they all enhance the flavor of foods and bring recipes to life without adding extra fat and calories.

Condiments

Webster defines a condiment as "something used to enhance the flavor of food." Since flavor is what we're all about, we put a lot of emphasis on high-flavor condiments, knowing that great things often come in little packages.

We recommend keeping a wide variety of condiments in your refrigerator or pantry so that you'll never be at a loss for adding just the right touch of flavor to your recipes. See the "Ultimate Pantry Checklist" on page 184 for a complete list of the items we always have on hand. We'll highlight a few of our favorites in this chapter.

Capers

Capers add their distinctively briny, bold flavor to food, so it's best to use them as accents instead of themes. The caper plant, whose immature buds are harvested and pickled to become a piquant flavoring, is thought to have originated in the hot, dry terrain of North Africa. Even today, most capers come from well-baked fields around the Mediterranean. It's a good thing that a little of

their tart astringency goes a long way because capers are pricey and become even more so when supplies of the annual hand-picked crop run low.

Choosing Capers
Test Kitchen SECRET

You'll find capers in the condiment section of your supermarket. The smaller immature buds are more expensive, but they're also the most intensely flavored. Larger capers (from raisin-size to the size of a small olive) are fine to use, too. We choose small capers when testing our recipes. At any size, capers have an assertive flavor, and you will find that even a somewhat pricey bottle will last up to a year in the refrigerator.

Chutney

Fruits, vegetables, spices, and vinegars combine in chutneys to produce a range of flavors as varied and complex as the Indian subcontinent that inspired them. Today, you can find these sweet, tangy condiments, in strengths from mild to hot, in almost any supermarket.

Chutneys of any strength are piquant and flavorful, so a little of this condiment goes a long way.

369

Amenable to almost any food, chutneys can be used to glaze meat and poultry or to add zing to a salad dressing. And whether they are based on mangoes, bananas, raisins, or any other fruit, the bottled brands are usually low in fat, so you can easily adjust to taste.

Homemade chutneys are delicious and easy to make—you just combine all the ingredients, then let the mixture simmer for 20 to 30 minutes. **However, for convenience, commercial chutneys are excellent, and we use them frequently in our recipes.**

Horseradish

Horseradish is a knobby white root with a pungent, spicy flavor that's been used as an aphrodisiac, a home remedy for hay fever and headaches, and a bitter herb for the feast of Passover. It's available fresh in most grocery stores and can be ground to create a piquant paste. Always grind or grate fresh horseradish in a well-ventilated room because the same oils that give horseradish its zing can create strong, stinging fumes.

> **You may buy prepared horseradish,** which is preground and jarred with vinegar or beet juice to temper the heat. Use this tongue-tingling condiment to wake up a roast beef sandwich or make a shrimp cocktail snappy.

Mustards

Beyond serving it as a condiment, straight-up on sandwiches, or as a pretzel dip, we like to use prepared mustard to add flavor as well as to bind sauces and vinaigrettes. As mustard inventories swell—as many as 80 new mustard blends enter the market each year, creative cooks will keep scraping the jar for new recipes. If American mustard (the classic yellow "ballpark" mustard) is the only one you have in your refrigerator, you can add some zip to your recipes just by adding a few more mustards to your collection.

Some of our favorite mustards to use in the Test Kitchens are coarse-grain or stone-ground mustard, Dijon, and honey mustard. We occasionally call for Chinese mustard—the hot, pale yellow mustard served in Chinese restaurants. Experiment with different types to see which flavors you prefer. **Naturally occurring compounds in prepared mustards inhibit the growth of bacteria, so it will keep indefinitely in the refrigerator in a tightly lidded glass jar.**

> **To start your own mustard collection** or to order a jar of mustard that your local grocer doesn't stock, call the Mount Horeb Mustard Museum at 800-438-6878. Or go to www.mustardmuseum.com for more information.

Olives

One of the world's greatest delicacies makes even the very simplest fare exquisite. Cured olives—steeped in oil, salted, or brined—are the vegetarian cousins of the cured pork and preserved anchovies of the Mediterranean. Generations of cooks have discovered ways to preserve and transform the olive—an acrid and bitter fruit—into salty, sour, pungent condiments that turn humble fare into cuisine ripe with vivid flavors. The olive's rich flesh can contribute a meaty sensation to a vegetarian dish, making it hearty and satisfying.

The color of olives depends on when they are picked. Green olives are picked before they ripen, while black olives are left on the tree until they are completely ripe. Both types are cured in a mixture of oil, salt, or water, or in the sun.

Selection Olives are available either pitted or unpitted and may be packed in brine or oil, dried in salt, or stuffed. Look for them in cans, jars, and plastic containers in the refrigerated section of the supermarket. **Olives that are packed in water, brine, or oil will keep for up to 1 year in the refrigerator.**

Know Your Olives

Here are four distinct types of olives, along with a guide to their considerable charms.

Kalamata: One of the more popular varieties, these Greek black olives are plump and juicy with a powerful flavor, bright acidity, and high salt content. They are delicious with soy products such as tofu and tempeh, and they work wonders with leafy greens and cruciferous vegetables such as broccoli and cauliflower, tempering bitterness with acidity.

Moroccan oil-cured: These black olives have a wrinkled, leathery surface, the result of a dry-salt curing process; later, a long, luxurious olive oil bath softens and enriches them. Because they retain more of their natural bitterness, oil-cured olives are best when cooked. These little olives marry particularly well with tangy tomatoes, celery, eggplant, citrus, and sweet root vegetables.

Picholine: A slender, full-flavored green olive from the south of France, the picholine is mildly bitter, faintly sweet, and tart with a nice, crunchy texture. Olives à la Picholine are steeped in a solution of lime and wood ashes before marinating in salty brine.

Niçoise: These small, tart, red-brown olives have a light salty taste. They are interchangeable with Italian gaeta olives, which are plump, brine-cured olives packed in oil.

Salsa

Low in fat and calories, salsas are heaven-sent for light cooking, giving foods a spirited kick. Although most people think of salsas as those chunky hot sauces that accompany Tex-Mex food, they can take many other forms, too. There's no law saying that salsas must be limited to the usual ingredients: tomatoes, onions, and chile peppers. And they don't even have to be hot. When you consider that salsa is the Spanish word for "sauce," be it cooked or uncooked, a whole world of possibilities unfolds. In addition to more traditional tomato-based salsas, fruit salsas add flavor to foods with a marvelous combination of sweet and hot ingredients.

"I like to make bean soup in the winter. And to add flavor, I often stir in a jar of salsa." Vanessa Johnson, Test Kitchens Director

Mango and Roasted Corn Salsa

Here's an example of a tangy fruit salsa that we recommend serving with grilled chicken or pork.

1½	cups fresh corn kernels (about 3 ears)
1	teaspoon vegetable oil
1½	cups diced peeled mango
¼	cup fresh lemon juice
2	tablespoons diced sweet onion
2	tablespoons minced fresh mint
2	tablespoons minced fresh cilantro
1½	teaspoons grated peeled fresh ginger
¼	teaspoon salt

1. Preheat oven to 400°.
2. Combine corn and oil, tossing well. Place on a baking sheet, spreading evenly. Bake at 400° for 15 minutes. Cool. Combine corn, mango, and remaining ingredients; toss. Yield: 2½ cups (serving size: ¼ cup).

CALORIES 43 (17% from fat); FAT 0.8g (sat 0.1g, mono 0.2g, poly 0.4g); PROTEIN 0.9g; CARB 9.4g; FIBER 1.2g; CHOL 0mg; IRON 0.2mg; SODIUM 63mg; CALC 5mg

Pesto

Basic pesto is an uncooked sauce made with fresh basil, garlic, pine nuts, Parmesan cheese, and olive oil. (See page 377 for more information on using fresh basil in recipes.) You can make your own pesto (see page 45) or buy it either refrigerated or in a jar. Simple dishes take on an easy sophistication as you swirl the bold sauce into penne pasta or use it to spruce up pizza, chili, or omelets. Add pesto to mayonnaise to enliven a sandwich of roasted bell peppers, tomato, and feta; drop a spoonful or two into a tomato and chickpea soup.

We prefer the refrigerated pestos over the bottled versions because we think the refrigerated ones taste more like fresh pesto.

Because three of the primary ingredients in pesto—olive oil, Parmesan cheese, and pine nuts—are high-fat foods, use pesto judiciously. **You'll find that a little bit of pesto goes a long way because it's such an intensely flavored condiment.**

Freezing Pesto	Test Kitchen SECRET

Thanks to olive oil, pesto retains its bright color when frozen. Just drop a tablespoon of pesto into each section of an ice cube tray, and freeze. Remove the frozen cubes, and transfer them to a heavy-duty zip-top plastic bag.

Or skip the ice cube tray, and spoon the pesto directly into a plastic bag or container to freeze. Let the pesto thaw for a few hours before you use it. Pesto will keep in the freezer for up to 3 months and in the refrigerator for up to 5 days.

Vinegars

Without adding fat, vinegar can add depth and brightness to recipes, from salads to desserts. Use it to deglaze pan drippings and add a little acidity to balance a sauce, or reduce it into a syrup for drizzling over fruit or vegetables. Add it to cooking liquid, and then braise to subdue the bite, or simply use is in a vinaigrette. Here's a roundup of the vinegars we recommend that you keep in your healthy-cooking pantry.

Vinegars We Use	Cooking Light Recommends

These are some of the vinegars that we use in testing.
Balsamic vinegar: We use a middle-of-the-road balsamic: Alessi 4-year Balsamic Vinegar. We also recommend Fini Condimento, a balsamic aged in casks of juniper, chestnut, and mulberry; Gaeta Condimento, aged 4 years in antique barrels; and Cavalli Condimento of Reggio Emilia.
Cider vinegar: We like Heinz Cider Vinegar.
Rice vinegar: We use Marukan and Nakano vinegars, standard supermarket brands.
Sherry vinegar: We prefer Columela Reserva Solera and Gran Capirete.
Tarragon vinegar: We like Maître Jacques Tarragon Vinegar.
White vinegar: We use Maître Jacques White Wine Vinegar.

When buying vinegar, read the label to see how long the vinegar has aged; some are aged 6 years, others for as long as 30 years. The longer the aging, the more complex the flavor.

Red and White Wine Vinegar The stalwarts in the kitchen, these vinegars are versatile and work well in just about any dish. Wine vinegars, like wine itself, vary in flavor according to the type of grape from which they are made, where the grapes are grown, and how the vinegar is stored and aged.

Use red wine vinegar in Greek and Italian vinaigrettes, drizzled over hot soups, or as a part of wine sauces. Use white wine vinegar with foods that you would pair with white wine, such as chicken and fish. Champagne produces a light, mild white vinegar, which is excellent for seafood salads.

Wine vinegars that don't refer to a particular wine on the label are often made from undistinguished wine blends or grape juice. These are what you'll usually find at the supermarket and are fine for most recipes.

Balsamic Vinegar For cooking, the best balsamic vinegars are labeled *condimento balsamico* and are reasonably priced. These have a slightly more acidic, but no less complex, nature. Aged for shorter periods and by slightly different methods, these vinegars are still quite tasty.

Some traditionally produced balsamic vinegars (*balsamico tradizionale*) are aged for decades and become increasingly concentrated and syrupy over time. These are the equivalents of vintage port or a perfectly constructed, well-aged wine, and they're phenomenally expensive—sometimes more than $100 per bottle. The best are made on a small, artisanal scale in and around Modena in northern Italy. Reserve these for drizzling over berries and vegetables, as they stand on their own and don't need other ingredients to mask their intense flavor.

Buying Balsamic
Cooking Light
Recommends

Look for the words *condimento* or *tradizionale* on the label. Though most of the balsamic vinegars you'll find at the supermarket are just a mixture of grape juice, vinegar, and caramel coloring, Alessi's Balsamic Vinegar Aged 20 Years is an exception.

Cider Vinegar Made from the juice of apples (or apple cider), it is light brown in color and has a sweeter fruit flavor and a gentler acidity than most white wine vinegars, though it is still quite sharp. It's an excellent everyday vinegar to use in pickling, salad dressings, and barbecue sauces. **Unlike other vinegars, which have begotten many gourmet siblings, cider vinegar remains simple and true to its roots. Unadorned Heinz Cider Vinegar works just fine.**

Rice Vinegar Colorless and very mild, vinegar made from fermented white rice is essential to many Asian recipes. **White rice vinegar is a key ingredient in the seasoned rice (sushi meshi) that gives Japanese sushi its name.** The sweet-and-sour mildness makes it suitable for Asian dipping sauces and salad dressings. Because it's not harsh, rice vinegar is excellent for making quick pickles.

Dark Chinese and Japanese rice vinegars are very different. They have complex, savory, and smoky flavors, and they are excellent in braised meat dishes or in dipping sauces for bland foods such as tofu, noodles, and steamed dumplings. Combine dark rice vinegars with a little sweet soy sauce or with salty tamari or miso to use in dressings for rice or cooked vegetable salads.

Rice Wine Vinegar Rice wine vinegar is made from fermented rice wines like sake and mirin, and it's sweeter than rice vinegar. It's a good choice when you want a combined sweet-and-sour flavor without the acidic "heat" of a stronger vinegar such as white wine vinegar.

Use rice vinegar in fruit and vegetable salsas and with cucumber or seafood salads when you want a little acidity but not the citrus flavor of lemon or lime juice.

Sherry Vinegar Sherry vinegar has a sour-sweet flavor and deep notes of oak. The best ones age in oak barrels and have rounded, distinct notes of hazelnut.

It's a great everyday vinegar for salad dressings and marinades or for drizzling over cooked vegetables. A dash of sherry vinegar is traditionally used in gazpacho, but the vinegar also works well in salad dressings, especially ones with nut oils. Use it when making Spanish or Mexican nut-based salsas or moles (dark, reddish-brown Mexican sauces containing onion, garlic, chiles, ground seeds, and a small amount of bitter chocolate). It's also good for deglazing the pan after cooking poultry or game, and it's delicious on grilled vegetable salads, especially those with zucchini, bell peppers, and chiles.

> The flavors of sherry vinegar and balsamic vinegar are very different, so they're not interchangeable; cider vinegar is a closer match to sherry vinegar.

The Best Vinegars
Cooking Light Recommends

Generally, the more expensive the vinegar, the better the flavor. If you want to try a more expensive vinegar, try fine, well-aged vinegar made from the Cabernet Sauvignon grape, Italian Chianti or Barolo vinegars, or a robust Spanish Rioja vinegar, all of which have more rounded flavors than other varieties.

If you really want to splurge, look for wine vinegar made by the ancient Orleans process, named for the French town most commonly associated with producing fine vinegar. Aging in barrels adds smoky, nutty, and woodsy flavors.

Storing Vinegars
Test Kitchen SECRET

To store vinegar, keep it in a tightly capped container in a cool, dark place at room temperature. Vinegar keeps indefinitely when stored properly.

Vinegar can corrode metals because it's acidic by nature, so you'll need to use glass or nonmetal containers and lids if you're making your own vinegar.

It can become murky or cloudy over time, and you may notice sediment in the bottom of the bottle. None of this makes it unusable, just unattractive. If it bothers you, pour the vinegar through a coffee filter to catch the sediment.

Because of its high acid content, vinegar is an unfriendly environment for bacteria, so you don't need to worry about vinegar spoiling. If you buy unpasteurized vinegar, don't be alarmed if a white film forms on top. It's the harmless "mother" used to ferment vinegar. Just peel it off, and discard.

Versatile Vinegar

If a recipe you've prepared tastes flat, stir in 1 or 2 teaspoons of vinegar to perk it up.

Add a little vinegar to the water when you're poaching eggs to keep them compact. It also makes the egg whites whiter.

To check if baking soda is still active, combine ¼ teaspoon baking soda with 2 teaspoons vinegar. If the baking soda bubbles, it still works.

Dissolve hard deposits in a teapot by steeping a solution of one part vinegar to six parts water in the pot overnight.

Making Flavored Vinegars

1. Add bruised herbs, slices of fresh fruit, or other flavoring ingredients to a widemouthed jar containing plain vinegar.

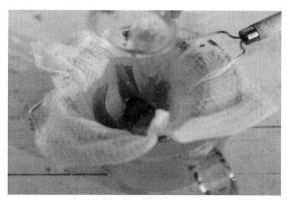

2. After 1 to 2 weeks—depending on how strong you want the flavor—strain mixture through a cheesecloth-lined sieve into a glass measure or medium bowl.

3. Pour filtered vinegar into a decorative bottle. (You can find bottles such as these at kitchenware or craft stores.)

Making Herb Vinegars Use good white wine or cider vinegar to make delicious herb or fruit-flavored vinegars at home. To make an herb vinegar, steep a handful of washed, well-dried herbs in a sterilized bottle of vinegar placed in a cool, dark place for 2 weeks. Strain the vinegar into sterilized bottles, and add a fresh herb sprig for decoration and identification.

Making Fruit Vinegars Make homemade fruit vinegars with raspberries, blackberries, blueberries, or black currants. Use about 4 ounces of fruit to a pint of vinegar. Place the cleaned fruit in a jar, crush it a little with a spoon, and pour in hot vinegar. Seal and leave in a cool, dark place for 1 week. Repeat using another batch of fresh fruit and leaving for 2 to 4 more weeks, then strain into sterilized bottles.

> "Use fruit-flavored vinegar to deglaze the pan after cooking chicken, salmon, scallops, or lobster."
> Kathleen Kanen,
> Food Stylist

Herbs

We use fresh herbs to pull a recipe together and infuse the dish with unparalleled aromas and flavors.

Herbs are the fragrant leaves (or stalks, as with chives) of plants whose stems are not woody like those of trees or shrubs. For refined and delicate dishes, a hint of herbs is enough; at other times, handfuls are required. Here are descriptions of fourteen of the herbs that we use most often in our Test Kitchens. These are the ones that we recommend that you keep on hand.

Keeping Fresh Herbs Fresh	Test Kitchen SECRET

Whether you've snipped fresh herbs from your garden or bought them at the supermarket, here's how to keep them fresh.

- To keep herbs fresh for up to 1 week, trim about ¼ inch from the stem, and rinse with cold water. Loosely wrap herbs in a damp paper towel, then seal in a zip-top plastic bag filled with air. Refrigerate. Check herbs daily, as some of them lose their flavor after a couple of days.

- Place herbs stem-down in a glass with water (let water cover about 1 inch of the stem ends); change the water every other day. Most herbs will keep for up to a week this way.

- Many supermarkets carry herb plants in their produce sections. After you bring the plant home, snip off as much as you need, and the plant will last for weeks or even months.

- To revive limp herbs, trim ½ inch off of the stems, and place in ice water for a couple of hours.

- Wash herbs just before using; pat dry with a paper towel.

To chop herbs easily, place the leaves in a measuring cup, and snip with kitchen scissors. If your recipe calls for a large amount, do this in several batches.

Although we generally use our knives, another effective tool for chopping herbs is a mezzaluna, which is a curved blade that chops as you rock it from side to side on a cutting board.

Recipes often call for a chiffonade of herbs—especially basil. To make a chiffonade, stack the leaves, roll them cigar-style, and cut the roll into thin slices.

Ask the *Cooking Light* Cooks

Must I always use fresh herbs in recipes?
The flavor of fresh herbs is generally much better than that of dried because most herbs lose significant flavor when they are dried. However, herbs such as rosemary, dill, and thyme dry well and maintain a good flavor. We almost always prefer to use fresh, but sometimes fresh is not practical, so quality dried herbs are an important part of a basic pantry, especially when it comes to convenience and last-minute meal preparation.

How much do I use if I'm substituting dried herbs for fresh in a recipe?
Fresh herbs are not as strong or concentrated as their dried counterparts. The standard substitute of dried herbs to fresh is one to three (one part dried herbs to three parts fresh). This translates into 1 teaspoon dried for 1 tablespoon fresh. The exception is rosemary; use equal amounts of fresh and dried.

Basil Basil is one of the most important culinary herbs.

Sweet basil, the most common type, is redolent of licorice and cloves. Basil is used in the south of France to make pistou; its Italian cousin, pesto, is made just over the border. Used in sauces, sandwiches, soups, and salads, basil is in top form when married to tomatoes.

Measuring Basil	Test Kitchen
	SECRET

When cooking with basil, don't stuff the basil leaves into the measuring cup; instead, pack them loosely. Then tear them in half.

Chives Add chives at the last minute, as heat

destroys their delicate onion flavor. Thinly slice them to maximize their taste, or use finely snipped chives as a garnish. They are great in dips and quesadillas and on baked potatoes.

Cilantro Also called coriander or Chinese

parsley, this native of southern Europe and the Middle East **has a pungent flavor with a faint undertone of anise.** The leaves are often mistaken for flat-leaf parsley, so read the tag. If you don't like cilantro, you can sometimes substitute flat-leaf parsley, equal parts parsley and mint, or parsley plus a dash of lemon juice.

Dill Since ancient Roman times, dill has been a

symbol of vitality. In the Middle Ages, it was thought to provide protection against witches and was used as an ingredient in many magic potions. In the kitchen, its feathery leaves lend a fresh, sharp flavor to all kinds of foods: gravlax, cottage cheese, cream cheese, goat cheese, omelets, seafood (especially salmon), cold yogurt soups, potato salads, and all kinds of cucumber dishes (including, of course, pickles).

Lavender You won't find lavender in super-

markets, so you probably haven't used it unless you've gone to specialty stores, ordered it, or grown your own.

But it's worth an acquaintance. **Fresh lavender brings a delicate, unique quality to certain foods—particularly baked goods such as biscotti, tea cakes, and rolls.** Cooking with lavender is actually pretty straightforward. In most cases, you simply pull the leaves from the stem (toward the flowers, not the roots), chop the leaves, and add them directly to the recipe. In some uses, you'll steep the leaves in water, then strain out the leaves—similar to brewing a cup of tea. And don't forget the blossoms. Put them in a vase on the table to let their fragrance fill the room.

While some people use lavender's blossoms and even the stems, we think the leaves deliver more and better flavor. You'll only need a little each time, though, because the leaves are relatively potent—too much may result in a perfumy, soapy taste.

Lemongrass Lemongrass is one of the most important flavorings in Thai cooking, and one that has found its way into other cuisines as well. It's a long, thin, light green stalk, not unlike a green onion. As its name implies, it has a distinct lemon flavor with herbal undertones. **To use, discard the tough outer leaves and about 2 to 3 inches of the thick root end. This will leave the tender stalk, which can be sliced or chopped.**

Marjoram Also known as "sweet marjoram," this herb is a member of the mint family and is very similar in flavor to oregano. In fact, "wild marjoram" is another name for oregano. Marjoram has a very delicate flavor, so it's best to add it toward the end of cooking so that its flavor does not disappear.

Mint Mint isn't just a little sprig that garnishes your dessert plate. It is extremely versatile and can be used in both sweet and savory dishes. In the Mediterranean, it is treasured as a companion to lamb and is used in fruit and vegetable salads. You can add it to a bevy of dishes and drinks—lamb, peas, carrots, ice cream, tea, mint juleps, and mojitos. In addition to spearmint, other varieties of mint include chocolate, ginger, grapefruit, pineapple, lemon, and orange mint.

Though there are many varieties, spearmint is preferred for cooking. Its bright green leaves are fuzzy, making them very different from the darker stemmed, rounded leaves of peppermint.

Oregano Oregano grows wild in the mountains of Italy and Greece; its Greek name means "joy of the mountain." The Greeks love it sprinkled on salads, while the Italians shower it on pizza and slip it into tomato sauces. Add chopped oregano to vinaigrette, or use it in poultry, game, or seafood dishes when you want to take them in a Greek or Italian direction.

Which Is Which? **Test Kitchen SECRET**

Oregano and marjoram are so similar in looks and flavor that they are often confused. Oregano, however, has a more potent taste and aroma; marjoram is sweeter and more delicate.

Parsley No refrigerator should be without parsley. It's the workhorse of the herb world and can go in just about every dish you cook.

Flat-leaf parsley is preferred for cooking, as it stands up better to heat and has more flavor, while the more decorative curly parsley is used mostly for garnishing.

Parsley's mild, grassy flavor allows the flavors of other ingredients to come through. Curly parsley is less assertive than its brother, flat-leaf parsley (often called Italian parsley). Reach for either when a dish needs a little burst of color. Sprinkle a little persillade, a mixture of chopped parsley and garlic, on roasted lamb, grilled steaks, fish, chicken, and vegetables, as they do in France. Add lemon or orange zest, and you get gremolata, a blend used in Milanese cooking, especially as a final garnish on osso buco.

Rosemary In Latin, rosemary means "dew of the sea"—appropriate since it is indigenous to the Mediterranean. Rosemary is one of the most aromatic and pungent of all herbs. Its needlelike leaves have a pronounced lemon-pine flavor that pairs well with olive oil, garlic, and roasted lamb. Rosemary is also a nice addition to focaccia, tomato sauce, pizza, and pork, **but because its flavor is strong, use a light hand.**

Sage Native to the northern Mediterranean coast, sage is used often in the region's cuisine. Sage's long, narrow leaves have a distinctively fuzzy texture and a musty flavor redolent of eucalyptus, cedar, lemon, and mint. There are some other varieties of sage that boast a slightly different flavor: purple, pineapple, peach, and honeydew melon.

Italians love it with veal, while the French add it to stuffings, cured meats, sausages, and pork dishes. Americans, of course, associate it with turkey and dressing. **Use it with discretion; it can overwhelm a dish.**

Tarragon This herb is native to Siberia and western Asia, though it is primarily used in France. It's often added to white wine vinegar, lending a sweet, delicate licorice-like perfume and flavor. It pairs well with fish, omelets, and chicken cooked with mustard, and it's a crucial component of béarnaise sauce. Fresh tarragon isn't always easy to find, but when you get it, you'll love the bittersweet, peppery taste it imparts. **Heat diminishes tarragon's flavor, so add tarragon toward the end of cooking, or use it as a garnish. A little goes a long way.**

Thyme Thyme comes in dozens of varieties, but most cooks use French thyme. This congenial herb pairs well with many other herbs—especially rosemary, parsley, sage, savory, and oregano. Its earthiness is welcome with pork, lamb, duck, or goose, and it's much beloved in Cajun and Creole

cooking. It's also the primary component of Caribbean jerk seasonings. **Because the leaves are so small, they often don't require chopping.**

Preserving Fresh Herbs

If your herb garden is full at the end of the summer, preserve that freshness into winter with these two freezing techniques:

- Blanch the leaves by placing them in boiling water for 15 seconds. (If you don't blanch them, the leaves will turn black.) Remove from water with a slotted spoon; immediately place in a bowl of ice water to prevent them from cooking any further. Drain and pat dry with paper towels. Arrange whole or chopped leaves in a single layer on a baking sheet; freeze. When frozen, transfer to a heavy-duty zip-top plastic bag.
- Blanch 1 cup packed herbs. Place in a blender with ½ cup water; pulse until finely chopped. Pour into an ice cube tray; freeze. Remove frozen herb cubes from tray; store them in the freezer in a heavy-duty zip-top plastic bag. Toss cubes into soups, stews, or braises.

What to Do About Those Stems

Test Kitchen SECRET

- Don't worry about stemming cilantro, dill, or parsley; their stems are tender and can be chopped and used with the leaves.
- Strip rosemary and thyme leaves from their tough, inedible stems by pulling in the opposite direction of the way the leaves grow.
- Basil, mint, oregano, sage, and tarragon leaves are large enough to pick off their stems one by one.
- Don't throw those stems away. Use them to flavor soup, or throw them on the coals to flavor a grilled dinner. If rosemary stems are straight and long enough, you can use them as skewers for chicken, lamb, or beef to impart wonderful flavor into the center of the meat.

Spices

Spices, derived from the bark, buds, fruit, roots, seeds, or stems of plants and trees, are a key flavor component of *Cooking Light* recipes.

Some spices, such as allspice, cinnamon, and cloves, are associated with sweet dishes—yet spices can also enhance a variety of savory dishes. In the following descriptions and recipes, you'll find ideas to further explore their versatility.

First, we'll give you some general tips on selecting, storing, and using spices. Then we'll highlight the spices that we use most often in our Test Kitchens.

Buying and Storing Spices

Ground spices have a shelf life of about 1 year. Of course, you probably have spices that are older than that. A good rule of thumb is the smell test: If ground spices don't emit an aroma when the jar is opened, they'll be lackluster in food, too.

Buy your spices from a store that sells lots of them. Otherwise, the spices you buy may have been sitting on the shelves for months. Nothing bad happens to spices that sit on the shelf for a long time—they just lose some of their potency, so you have to use more to get the desired flavor.

Buy spices in the smallest size possible, especially those that you won't use often.

Store spices in a cool, dark place, like the freezer. Don't store your spices in decorative wall spice racks because heat and sunlight hasten flavor loss.

How to Get the Best from Spices
Test Kitchen SECRET

For the subtlest effect, use spices whole. For more flavor, bruise or crush them lightly. For the most impact, grind them finely. The finer you crush, grind, or mill spices, the more powerful and pervasive their effect on the finished dish will be. *Freshly ground spices have a fresher, "sweeter" flavor than off-the-shelf ground spices. This is especially true with cinnamon, cloves, and nutmeg.*

A mortar and pestle are the best tools for coarsely crushing spices, and many people think using this method releases a better, gentler flavor than using an electric mill. But it is difficult to crush such hard spices as cinnamon and cloves in a mortar. *A small, deep mortar is better than a wide, shallow one, from which the spices tend to shoot out.*

A coffee grinder crushes most spices, especially tough, woody ones, such as cinnamon and cloves. Clean the mill afterward by grinding a small piece of bread or 2 tablespoons of raw rice. For cardamom- or cinnamon-flavored coffee, grind a cardamom pod or a 1/2- to 1-inch piece of a cinnamon stick with the coffee beans.

Bruising (barely breaking the outer seed coat or husk) enhances flavor and aroma by allowing the flavor of the inner seed to work its magic. Bruise soft spices like cardamom pods and juniper berries by pressing down with the blade of a chef's knife.

To make spice pastes, roast and grind the dry spices first before adding the wet or fresh ingredients. This lets the spices properly incorporate.

Allspice Allspice grows primarily in Jamaica, where it is called "pepper" and is featured prominently in jerk seasoning paste. As the name suggests, its flavor and aroma are a mixture of cinnamon, nutmeg, and a touch of clove. It is a delicious but underused spice that adds deep, warm flavor to pork, bean, onion, and tomato dishes, as well as pickles, salsas, relishes, and ketchup. Add a few whole berries to marinades, and use ground allspice in gingerbread and other cakes and cookies. **Buy whole rather than ground. Whole allspice stores almost indefinitely in an airtight jar and will grind in a pepper mill. Cooking brings out its sunny flavor.**

Anise Two spices give us anise flavor in the kitchen. The first—*sweet anise*—is related to dill and caraway and is used in European cakes, biscuits, breads, and the production of aniseed liqueurs, such as Pernod. Warm gently before use to release its aroma.

The second and more familiar spice is *star anise*, probably the world's prettiest spice, and it's used widely in Asian cookery. Star anise is a principal ingredient in Chinese five-spice powder and is indispensable for Chinese duck, pork, and beef. It makes an unusual but delicious flavoring for poached fruits such as pears and plums. **Buy star anise whole. One or two "stars" usually impart sufficient flavor to infuse an entire dish. To substitute star anise for aniseed in a recipe, reduce the quantity to half or a third of the recipe's recommendation.**

Caraway People either love or hate caraway, which has a pungent aroma and a slightly lemony, anise flavor. It is popular with meat and in central and eastern European cabbage and cheese dishes. Caraway is also good with various types of smoked and pickled fish. Pumpernickel and other rye breads usually feature caraway.

Caraway seed is soft and easy to grind, but it loses its scent quickly once it's ground. Buy it whole, and warm or toast lightly before using to bring out the flavor.

Cardamom Cardamom comes from the same family as ginger and turmeric and is the seed pod of a tropical plant. The best pods will be pale sage green and have sticky black seeds inside. They are intensely aromatic and have an orangy, slightly camphorated flavor that works well in sweet and savory dishes. In India, cardamom is important in many spice mixtures, especially garam masala, and some Arabic countries add ground cardamom to coffee. Scandinavians use cardamom in cakes and sweet breads. Try cardamom in rice dishes; with orange, lemon, or lime; and with fish, chicken, and pork. It's delicious with such root vegetables as carrots, parsnips, and sweet potatoes. **Cardamom's essential oils are volatile, so ground cardamom's flavor dissipates quickly. Bruise whole pods before using them to allow the flavor to escape—press down on them with the blade of a knife until the pod opens. If the seeds are dry and light brown, they are old and have lost their flavor and aroma. Discard those pods.**

Roasting and Toasting Spices

Heat whole spices in a dry pan to release their natural volatile oils and bring out optimal aroma and flavor. Use a small, heavy skillet. Add the whole spices (roasting ground spices tends to turn them bitter and is best avoided), and place over gentle heat. Either shake the pan or stir with a wooden spatula to keep the spices on the move, and toast gently for 1 to 3 minutes.

Some spices—like mustard and poppy seeds—"pop" when they are ready; others darken. *The essential sign is that the spice becomes aromatic and smells toasty.* Tip into a bowl to cool before grinding.

Cinnamon Although cinnamon may be more familiar in dishes such as toast, sweet rolls, mulled cider, or pumpkin pie, its distinctive notes blend with meats and fish and perk up grains and vegetables in a surprising way. Moroccans and Persians use it often with lamb and chicken. And in Indian food, cinnamon is typically paired with cardamom and used in rice pilafs.

Cinnamon comes from the aromatic bark of a tree native to Sri Linka, India, and Burma. Buy it as sticks (or quills) or ground. **Cinnamon sticks have a sweeter, subtler flavor and a longer shelf life than ground. Whole cinnamon is best ground in a clean coffee mill. Make cinnamon sugar to sprinkle on French toast and pancakes by processing a ½- to 1-inch piece of cinnamon stick and sugar in a coffee mill until fine.**

Real Cinnamon
Test Kitchen SECRET

Technically, what we Americans buy in the supermarkets, whether ground or in sticks, is not "true" cinnamon, but it's a close cousin, produced by a similar tree. The flavor of the two is very similar, although the kind we buy here is slightly coarser and stronger than "true" cinnamon. Most of the cinnamon we buy in the United States comes from Indonesia, but another type from Vietnam known as Saigon cinnamon is considered to be the best cinnamon.

Cloves Cloves are an ancient spice, used for millennia in China and imported by the Romans from the Moluccas (now part of Indonesia). Today, Zanzibar and Madagascar are important producers. Cloves, which have an intensely sharp, slightly bitter taste, are the dried flower buds of a tree. Use sparingly because they can overpower other flavors. In holiday cooking, cloves traditionally appear ground in gingerbread and fruitcake and whole in mulled wine or studded into baked and glazed hams. **Use whole or ground. Cloves work well with onion dishes, in pickles, and in braised beef or pork stew, especially when cooked with beer. If you use whole cloves to flavor a dish, make sure to remove them before serving. Cloves don't need toasting before use.**

Ginger Ginger is the rhizome of a tropical plant, and its warm, slightly woody flavor makes it one of the world's favorite spices. You'll find ginger in many guises. Botanically speaking, it's a distant relative of the banana, and the plant, a perennial, bears glossy, green, spear-shaped leaves and highly perfumed blossoms of white or yellow. Virtually all of the plant possesses ginger's signature spicy fragrance, although cooks look solely to the pungent root for their purposes.

Fresh ginger, with its gnarled root and papery brown skin, is available in almost any grocery's produce department near the specialty-ingredients section. Sushi lovers recognize *pickled ginger*, preserved in sweet vinegar, as a side dish as traditional as the daub of fiery wasabi paste. Accomplished bakers and chefs often use *crystallized (or candied) ginger* as another way to warm and mellow their creations. Though its powerful scent and peppery flavor are

Fresh Ginger
Test Kitchen SECRET

Look for fresh ginger in the produce section of your supermarket. Choose the freshest, youngest-looking ginger you can find. Old rhizomes are fibrous, tough, and flavorless.

Store fresh ginger tightly wrapped in plastic wrap in the vegetable crisper section of the refrigerator for up to 3 weeks. Or store whole fresh ginger in a refrigerated jar of sherry, and use both ginger and sherry in Asian dishes. Ground ginger loses its aroma and flavor quickly, and it should be used within 2 or 3 months.

smoothed in cooking, ginger adds a fresh, herbal liveliness to both sweet and savory dishes.

Ginger is delicious partnered with honey and saffron and works well with pears, apples, and quinces. **In Asian and Indian cookery, fresh ginger forms a holy trinity with garlic and chili and works very well with lime, soy, and seafood.**

Preparing Fresh Ginger

1. Use a vegetable peeler or paring knife to remove the tough skin and reveal the yellowish flesh.

2. Cut the peeled ginger into slices, then stack the slices, and cut into strips. Line up the strips, and cut crosswise into small pieces to mince.

3. To grate fresh ginger, peel, then cut a piece big enough to hold comfortably while using a fine grater.

Nutmeg Nutmeg is the kernel of the fruit of a tropical evergreen tree. Each kernel comes wrapped in a lacy covering that we use separately as the spice mace. They both share a warm, sweet, musky flavor suited to desserts, cookies, and cakes. Nutmeg has an affinity with dairy, too—it is excellent in milky desserts and drinks. In Britain, nutmeg is widely used in fruitcakes, often in combination with ginger and cinnamon. Italians, however, prefer nutmeg in savory cooking—they find it works well with spinach, cauliflower, broccoli, pasta, chicken, and veal. **Use nutmeg freshly grated or milled. Nutmeg mills pass the spice over a sharp blade, shaving off minute amounts. Except in cakes, add nutmeg toward the end of cooking to retain its evanescent aroma and warm, spicy flavor.**

Peppercorns Most peppercorns are harvested in southwestern India from the same type of vine, and some peppercorns aren't really pepper at all.

- *White peppercorns* are fully ripe berries that have been soaked in water and hulled, which produces a slightly fermented taste. Some cooks use white pepper as an alternative to black in light-colored dishes like mashed potatoes. It also stands up to high heat better than black pepper.
- *Black peppercorns* are the strongest in flavor and bite and are the world's most popular spice. Black peppercorns are picked when slightly underripe, then air-dried, which results in their dark color.
- *Pink peppercorns* are papery in texture and slightly sweet. They're not real peppercorns; they're actually the dried berries of the Brazilian pepper tree grown mostly on an island in the Indian Ocean. They are aromatic but not peppery and are usually included in mixes only for the color.
- *Green peppercorns* are pickled unripened berries. They have a fresh taste that's less pungent than other types of peppercorns.

Saffron Saffron has always been the world's most expensive spice, but you need only a few dried stigmas from the saffron crocus to color a dish golden yellow and impart a warm, aromatic, and slightly bitter quality. In Sweden, saffron is used in buns and cakes for the December 13th festivities of St. Lucia's Day. Fruited saffron bread is a specialty of Cornwall and Devon in England, too. But it is best known today for its use with rice (in paella or risotto). Its tangy flavor works well in sauces for fish and in Mediterranean-style seafood soups. Saffron also combines well with honey, pears, rosemary, garlic and onions, and ginger and cardamom.

For most dishes, saffron is best soaked in a few tablespoons of warm liquid to allow the color and flavor to develop fully before adding to the rest of the ingredients. You can also "toast" saffron very gently in a small dry pan to release its aroma, but saffron tastes bitter if overheated. It is easy to use too much, which gives an unpleasant medicinal tang to the dish.

Spice Blends

Here's a sampling of some blends that we think are useful for home cooks who want to experiment with flavors.

Ground Ancho Chile Powder Ancho chiles are dried poblano peppers. Most chili (with an "i") powders are a blend of spices, including ancho chiles, cumin, garlic, and oregano. Chile (with an "e") powders are finely ground dried chiles and nothing else. Tex-Mex dishes use chili powder; true Mexican dishes uses chile powder for pure flavor with mild heat.

Ground Chipotle Chile Powder Chipotle chiles are dried, smoked jalapeño peppers, previously available only in cans with adobo sauce. The adobo packaging presents two problems: The flavor of the tomato-based adobo sauce sometimes takes over, and most recipes use just a single pepper, leaving you the rest of the can to deal with. The powder is much easier to use. Blend it with other ingredients; it gives a pure smoky chipotle flavor.

Garam Masala This Indian spice blend's ingredients typically include black pepper, cardamom, cinnamon, cloves, and cumin. Commercial versions are usually milder than homemade, but they certainly save time. (See recipe on page 449.)

Red Curry Powder This spice mix is the basis of many Thai and Malaysian dishes. The mainstream version is milder than its ethnic counterpart. It has a softer edge, making it more versatile and easier to incorporate into a variety of dishes.

Wasabi powder This intensely hot green powder, made from a ground root, is used anywhere horseradish would be. Like red curry powder, wasabi powder is milder than the pure wasabi you buy in Asian markets, and it's also more versatile.

Rubs and Pastes

You can prepare rubs and pastes in advance so when it's time for dinner, preparation is minimal.

Rubs Rubs are merely mixtures of dried herbs and spices. **Many rub recipes call for whole spices to be crushed; to do this, a mortar and pestle are the tools of choice.** But for an alternative method, place whole spices in a plastic bag, and pound with a rolling pin or meat mallet. You can store the dry rubs indefinitely in an airtight container in a cool, dry place. Although the amount of rub you use is up to your taste buds, **a general rule is 3 tablespoons to cover 1 pound of food.**

Make sure you apply the rub to a food that is completely dry. The most effective way to apply a rub is to place the mixture in a zip-top bag, put the food inside, and shake.

For a crisp coating sauté the coated foods in a little oil. This also brings out the flavors of the spices in the rub.

Create complex taste sensations by applying simple herb-and-spice mixtures to fish, poultry, meats, or vegetables.

Pastes Pastes are similar to rubs, but they get their consistency from the addition of a liquid such as honey, juice, oil, or vinegar. **When using pastes, a general rule is ¼ cup paste to cover 1 pound of food.** Don't be timid when applying a paste; it needs to be rubbed in so that the flavors penetrate the food. For maximum flavor, chill foods for 30 minutes to an hour after rubbing. Broiling is the best method for these foods because it caramelizes any sugars in the paste, resulting in deep, rich flavors. This cooking method also helps prevent the paste from coming off the food. Pastes will keep in the refrigerator in an airtight container for up to a week.

Spicy Bayou Rub

A combination of red and black pepper gives this rub a kick; nutmeg and oregano balance the heat.

2	tablespoons paprika
2	teaspoons garlic powder
1½	teaspoons dried thyme
1	teaspoon ground red pepper
¾	teaspoon dried oregano
½	teaspoon salt
½	teaspoon freshly ground black pepper
¼	teaspoon ground nutmeg

1. Combine all ingredients. Rub on fish, chicken, beef, or pork. Yield: ¼ cup (serving size: 1 tablespoon).

CALORIES 20 (32% from fat); FAT 0.7g (sat 0.2g, mono 0.1g, poly 0.4g); PROTEIN 0.9g; CARB 4g; FIBER 1.1g; CHOL 0mg; IRON 1.7mg; SODIUM 295mg; CALC 24mg

Sweet Curry Paste

Omit the mango chutney, if desired, but increase the orange marmalade to ¾ cup.

½	cup mango chutney
¼	cup orange marmalade
1	tablespoon dark sesame oil
½	teaspoon ground red pepper
½	teaspoon curry powder
¼	teaspoon salt

1. Combine all ingredients, and stir well with a whisk. Rub on fish, chicken, beef, or pork. Yield: ⅔ cup (serving size: 1 tablespoon).

CALORIES 65 (20% from fat); FAT 1.4g (sat 0.2g, mono 0.6g, poly 0.6g); PROTEIN 0.2g; CARB 13.8g; FIBER 0.1g; CHOL 0mg; IRON 0.2mg; SODIUM 90mg; CALC 8mg

Fiery Herb Rub

The fire comes from the black pepper.

2	tablespoons cracked black pepper
2	tablespoons grated Parmesan cheese
2	teaspoons dried basil
2	teaspoons dried rosemary
2	teaspoons dried thyme
¼	teaspoon garlic powder
¼	teaspoon salt

1. Combine all ingredients. Rub on fish, chicken, beef, or pork. Yield: ⅓ cup (serving size: 1 tablespoon).

CALORIES 20 (12% from fat); FAT 0.8g (sat 0.4g, mono 0.2g, poly 0.1g); PROTEIN 1.3g; CARB 2.7g; FIBER 0.9g; CHOL 2mg; IRON 1.8mg; SODIUM 156mg; CALC 64mg

Salt

A little salt at the right time is more flavor-enhancing than a downpour at the wrong time.

We know that salt, in part because it dissolves slowly, enhances the ability of an ingredient to taste more like itself and creates harmony among surrounding ingredients. A dull soup or a flat sauce often needs nothing more than a sprinkling of salt to become irresistible.

Seasoning with Salt It's not difficult to master the use of salt in the kitchen. Think of your recipes as construction projects: You are not simply cooking ingredients—you are carefully building flavors. For example:

• Season onions with salt after they've been sautéed.
• Salt rice before adding liquid when preparing risotto.
• Season meat with salt after it's been browned.

Using salt carefully, a pinch and a step at a time, means the final dish will be close to perfectly seasoned. **This is how professional chefs make food taste so good; they know that salt added after cooking cannot make up for a lack of it during the process.**

Which Salt to Use? Taste and texture are the main reasons to use the salt you prefer. Sodium can vary significantly: from 230 to 580 milligrams per ¼ teaspoon. It's all a matter of density: Some salts are fluffed so that the crystals contain more air; others are created as hollow pyramids to increase their flavor surfaces. Lower sodium generally indicates less density in the crystals, but it doesn't necessarily have anything to do with flavor.

> **Kosher and sea salts actually taste saltier than the same amount of table salt—so you get more flavor with less sodium.**

Sodium Guidelines
Cooking Light Recommends

The Institute of Medicine, which sets the nutrition standards for food labels, recently dropped the recommended sodium intake from 2,400 to 1,500 milligrams per day for adults from 19 to 50. The institute is trying to address a major health problem facing 50 million Americans: high blood pressure. Cutting sodium can help most of those people lower their risk of heart attacks, strokes, and kidney disease. For those who are not on a sodium-restricted diet, we simply recommend a moderate use of salt in cooking. To help you keep an eye on your sodium intake, we list the sodium content per serving in the nutrient analysis that appears with each recipe.
Krista Montgomery, Food Editor, Registered Dietitian

All salt is sea salt. Salt only comes from two sources: seawater and inland deposits from ancient seas. That which is made from seawater can be labeled "sea salt," but it's frequently identical to table salt—both are more than 99 percent sodium chloride (plus various trace minerals).

The one distinction may be naturally evaporated sea salt. These salts are evaporated by sun and wind, harvested, and sold without processing; they contain the minerals present in seawater. If you're paying more for sea salt, check the label to see how it's manufactured.

Whatever its source, sea salt is best used as a condiment (instead of in cooking). The crystals offer a pleasant crunch and the distinct flavor of the sea.

Salt Selections

It's not all the same. Salt comes in dozens of textures, colors, and tastes. In our recipes, we generally use the three most popular varieties—kosher, sea, and table. But you might be interested in some of the other choices you may have encountered.

Type	Qualities	Recommended Uses	Availability	Price
Table salt (plain)	small, hard, dry cubes; pours easily; dissolves slowly; sharp-tasting on front of palate, otherwise mild	general cooking, household cleaning	widely available	cheap
Table salt (iodized)	same as plain table salt, with iodine added	prevents goiter (an iodine-deficiency disease common where seafood is not available)	widely available	cheap
Kosher (Diamond Crystal)	dry, hollow pyramids; dissolves quickly; moderately salty; delicate	general cooking, baking, brining, preserving, finishing; all-purpose	regional	cheap
Kosher (other brands)	flattened cubes and fused flattened cubes, very dry and hard, dissolves slowly, mild	general cooking (except baking), good for salt crusts and salt doughs	generally available	cheap
Sea salt	any salt from sea water, often the same as table salt	finishing	varies widely	varies widely
Sel gris	hard, moist gray crystals of solar-evaporated salt from the northern Atlantic coast of France; briny; sweet; delicate; dissolves slowly	baking and roasting, finishing	mail-order, gourmet shops	expensive
Fleur de sel	hard, slightly moist white crystals of solar-evaporated salt from the northern Atlantic coast of France; briny; sweet; delicate; dissolves slowly	finishing (condiment)	mail-order, gourmet shops	expensive
Hawaiian Alae	pale orange crystals; hard, dry; slight taste of iron; silky from natural clay	finishing	regional, mail-order	cheap
Black salt (*Kala namak*)	large rocks or fine powder, pale violet to purple-black, strong sulfuric aroma, earthy	Indian cuisine	mail-order, ethnic markets	moderate

Vanilla

Because of vanilla's rarity, price, and delicacy, it pays to know when to use the bean and when to use the extract.

Vanilla is the fruit of an orchid variety whose blossoms open for just hours one day a year. In that brief time, most vanilla orchids are hand-pollinated. Then, after the long, thin bean forms over the course of 6 weeks, it must be hand-picked and cured in a complex process taking 3 to 6 months.

Vanilla Beans These beans have a fruity, rich flavor, and there are more than 250 identified flavor components in vanilla. The sweet, seductive fragrance and flavor of vanilla are so familiar that you might not even notice them—unless they were taken away. It is, of course, the favorite flavoring for ice cream, but just about any dessert would taste flat without a little vanilla added.

Cooking with vanilla beans—as opposed to the commercial extract—adds a profound flavor to many dishes. The difference is well worth the trouble, and that trouble is slight. (Most supermarkets carry vanilla beans in the spice section; if yours doesn't, consult our list of mail-order sources.) Extracting the pulp from the pod is simple; just follow our step-by-step instructions on page 389.)

- Vanilla beans freeze well; just pop them into the microwave for 15 to 30 seconds to plump and thaw.
- Revive a dry vanilla bean by wrapping it in a damp paper towel and microwaving it at HIGH 5 to 8 seconds.
- When moist, the bean is easier to cut and more seeds can be scraped, so scrape the seeds after steeping in liquid.

Choosing top-quality vanilla beans can be difficult, especially since they're often hermetically sealed in glass jars. Look for shiny, black beans that don't rattle or clank but thud against the glass. Also, white crystals on the beans are a sign of good quality. You can expect to pay around $2 to $3 a bean.

Vanilla Extract Extract is made by macerating chopped vanilla beans in an alcohol-water solution to extract the flavor. Then it's aged for several months. Pure vanilla extract must contain 13.35 ounces of vanilla bean per gallon during extraction and 35 percent alcohol. Pure vanilla extract is a richly fragrant clear brown liquid. It costs more than imitation, but there's no comparison when it comes to flavor and quality. Imitation vanilla extract is made of artificial flavorings and leaves an aftertaste.

> When using vanilla in recipes, you can substitute 1 tablespoon of vanilla extract for 1 (6-inch) vanilla bean. The flavor won't be exactly the same, but it will be close, and the recipe will be fine.

If you make your own vanilla extract, it will be more fragrant and flavorful than any you can buy. Basically, all you do is store split vanilla beans—about 4 or 5 beans, whole or in pieces—in 2 cups of vodka. The vanilla mixture will get better and better as time goes on. As you use it, continue adding more vodka and bean pieces (with the seeds removed) to maintain an even consistency of vanilla flavor.

Beans vs. Extract

Use the whole bean:

• In lightly cooked sauces and syrups

• When the presentation of a dish calls for proof of the bean (the speckle of vanilla's black seeds in crème brûlée tells guests they're worth the expense)

• If you object to the alcohol used in extract but still want vanilla's rich complexity

• To flavor coffee (drop a small piece of the hard, dry bean in with coffee beans before you grind them, or store a vanilla bean in your coffee canister for a little extra zip)

Use vanilla extract:

• When baking and cooking, where the vanilla will be exposed to heat for long periods of time (since heat somewhat weakens vanilla's fruitlike flavor, there's no point in using the more expensive bean)

• As an emulsifier in sweet and savory egg batters (in waffle and pancake batters, it helps smooth the mixture; a drop or two is all you need)

• When you need vanilla's flavor quickly and don't have time to steep a bean in the recipe's liquid

Although imitation extracts are less expensive, we think pure extract (instead of artificial flavoring) is a better choice in terms of flavor and quality. Imitation vanilla is made from paper-manufacturing by-products treated with chemicals. Its flavor is one-dimensional and often has a harsh finish. We occasionally use extracts such as almond, maple, or lemon, but we don't often because of the artificial flavor.

Even Sweeter Sugar

After using a vanilla bean, let it dry at room temperature, then drop it into a container of granulated sugar. One bean will permeate up to 5 pounds of sugar and will keep it flavorful for up to a year.

Vanilla beans can also add flavor to powdered sugar. Dry several beans at room temperature, then grind them in a food processor with 1 cup powdered sugar. Strain the mixture through a fine sieve to remove the vanilla bean pieces. This mixture can be used in whipped cream, to sprinkle on cakes, or to coat candies.

Scraping Seeds from a Vanilla Bean

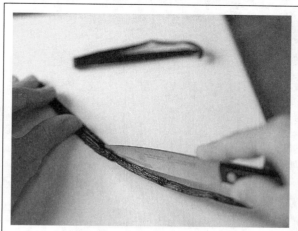

1. Using a small knife with a tip, cut vanilla beans in half lengthwise.

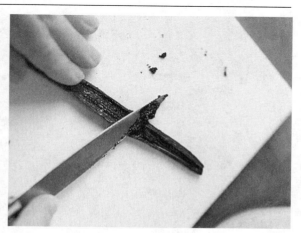

2. Scrape seeds out with knife blade, or push them out of vanilla bean half with thumbnail.

CHAPTER 12

Sugars & Chocolate

At *Cooking Light*, we believe that healthy eating is all about balance, so we see no reason to cut sweets out of your life. When you learn to use sugars and chocolate wisely, they can benefit your body as well as your soul.

Sugars

Common white sugar has many cousins, from brown sugar to corn syrup. Here's a guide for knowing the characteristics and the best uses for each type. See the chart below for a comparison of calories between different types of sweeteners.

Calories in Sugars

(per tablespoon)			
Brown sugar	52	Maple syrup	52
Corn syrup	58	Molasses	54
Granulated sugar	45	Powdered sugar	29
Honey	64	Turbinado sugar	46

Granulated Sugar

Granulated, or white, sugar is the most refined type of sugar. Granulated sugar contributes sweetness and moisture to baked goods, helps them brown, and gives them structure. Granulated sugar makes pastries tender, gives crunch to some cookies, and is essential in cake batters for aeration. When beaten with butter, sugar granules create tiny bubbles that expand during baking, causing cakes to rise, even without chemical leaveners.

At the market you'll find two kinds of granulated sugar: cane, derived from sugarcane, and beet, made from sugar beets. They're chemically identical (they're the same sucrose molecule), and they sell equally well in American markets.

Powdered or Confectioner's Sugar

Powdered sugar is pulverized granulated sugar. **Older cookbooks call it 10x sugar, meaning it's 10 times finer than granulated sugar.** It's used mostly to make icings and frostings (since it dissolves quickly) and to dust over baked cookies, cakes, and cupcakes.

Because of its powdery nature, it tends to attract water, so a small amount of absorbent cornstarch is usually added before packaging to keep the sugar dry.

Taking Appropriate Measures

To measure both granulated and powdered sugar, lightly spoon into a dry measuring cup, and level off the excess with a knife.

Brown sugar is moist and clumpy; measure by packing it into a dry measuring cup. The sugar should hold its shape when unmolded.

Brown Sugar

Brown sugar owes its moist, pliable texture and caramel-like flavor to molasses, a small amount of which is added to granulated sugar to create brown sugar. For a delicate molasses-like flavor, use light brown sugar in recipes. Dark brown sugar has more molasses and therefore has a deeper, richer, more assertive taste than light brown sugar. For a stronger toffeelike flavor, use the dark variety. Many recipes that call for brown sugar specify which to use.

For any *Cooking Light* recipe that calls for brown sugar, use light brown sugar.

As a general rule, the darker the sugar, the deeper the flavor.

Molasses

Molasses is a by-product of the sugar-refining process. **Boiling the juices extracted from sugarcane and sugar beets transforms them into a syrup from which sugar crystals are extracted. The liquid left behind is molasses.** *Light molasses,* as its name implies, is light in both color and flavor; it's often used to top pancakes. *Dark molasses*—used in gingerbread, shoofly pie, barbecue sauces, and Boston baked beans—is darker, thicker, stronger in flavor, and less sweet than light molasses. *Blackstrap molasses* (also called

black treacle) has a strong bitter flavor. Popular with some health-conscious people because of its mineral content (which is actually only slightly higher than that of other types of molasses), blackstrap is more commonly used as cattle feed.

Raw Sugar

Raw sugar comes from the residue left after sugarcane has been processed to remove the molasses (further refining of that residue creates granulated sugar). Some familiar names are Demerara and turbinado, which are both coarse, dry, and golden, and Muscovado and Barbados, both fine, moist, and dark brown. **In general, raw sugar is coarser in texture than granulated or brown sugar; use it when you want extra crunch—atop cookies and muffins or in a crisp or crumble.**

Corn Syrup

Available in light and dark varieties, corn syrup is created by combining cornstarch with an enzyme that converts the starch to sugar. Pancake syrups are often made with corn syrup and flavoring.

Corn syrup contributes silky smoothness and adds moisture and chewiness to such baked goods as cakes and cookies. When cooked with granulated sugar to make syrups and fondants, it helps prevent crystallization.

Dark corn syrup is a mixture of light corn syrup and a darker syrup produced during the refining of sugar; it's often used in pecan pie fillings to provide a deep butterscotch taste. *Light corn syrup* has a more neutral flavor than dark.

See page 91 for our Test Kitchen Secret on reducing the fat in cookies by adding corn syrup to the dough.

Honey

Moist, spreadable, and abundant, honey adds more than sweetness to your cooking—it adds a rich, unique flavor to foods. And although honey has no nutritional advantages over sugar, it does add moistness to baked goods. It also spreads easier than sugar as a glaze on fish and meats, and dissolves in liquids like vinaigrettes.

Because honey is produced in so many places and in such different strengths and flavors, it's important to choose the best blend. Orange blossom, clover blossom, sage blossom, and buckwheat are some of the most common types. **The general rule states the lighter the color, the milder the flavor. We usually use mild-flavored honeys, such as alfalfa and clover.** Should you wish, you can use a stronger variety, such as buckwheat. Like corn syrup, honey adds moisture to cakes and cookies. Unlike corn syrup, which is fairly neutral, honey imparts a distinctive flavor.

Honey Hints

When measuring honey, lightly coat your measuring cup or spoon with cooking spray first, and all of the honey will slide out easily.

If your honey crystallizes, you can soften it by simply placing the open jar in the microwave on HIGH for 2 to 3 minutes, stirring periodically.

Honey (22 calories per teaspoon) is sweeter than granulated sugar (16 calories per teaspoon), so you won't need as much of it to sweeten foods.

The Taste of Honey — Test Kitchen SECRET

Be sure to taste honey before you use it in a recipe to make sure the flavor is appropriate. A strong buckwheat honey, for example, might overwhelm a delicately-flavored dish.

Honey Gelato

We like mild clover and lavender honeys in this recipe.

½   cup honey
⅓   cup nonfat dry milk
1   (12-ounce) can evaporated fat-free milk
⅛   teaspoon salt
4   large egg yolks
1   cup 2% reduced-fat milk

1. Combine first 3 ingredients in a medium, heavy saucepan. Heat mixture over medium heat until honey dissolves, stirring frequently (do not boil). Remove from heat.

2. Combine salt and egg yolks in a large bowl, stirring with a whisk. Gradually add honey mixture to egg mixture, stirring constantly with a whisk. Place honey mixture in pan; cook over medium heat until mixture reaches 180° (about 3 minutes), stirring constantly (do not boil). Remove from heat; stir in 2% milk. Cool completely.

3. Pour mixture into the freezer can of an ice-cream freezer; freeze according to manufacturer's instructions. Spoon gelato into a freezer-safe container. Cover and freeze 2 hours or until firm. Yield: 8 servings (serving size: ½ cup).

CALORIES 153 (19% from fat); FAT 3.3g (sat 1.2g, mono 1.2g, poly 0.4g); PROTEIN 6.7g; CARB 25.4g; FIBER 0g; CHOL 111mg; IRON 0.5mg; SODIUM 121mg; CALC 208mg

---

Honey in Frozen Desserts

Test Kitchen SECRET

- Honey is a natural choice for gelato because its resistance to freezing ensures creaminess.
- Store the gelato in an airtight container in the freezer for up to a week; it won't freeze solid but will maintain a soft, stretchy texture.

Maple Syrup

We use maple syrup for both sweet and savory dishes. It adds moisture and a unique flavor to cakes, cookies, and frostings; it also adds a depth of flavor to tangy marinades, brines, and vegetables. **Sugar and honey actually may be used more commonly to add another layer of flavor to savory dishes, but neither contributes the clean, distinct flavor and subtle maple bouquet that maple syrup delivers.**

Maple syrup comes in different grades (see "Making the Grade" on the next page), ranging in color from light golden to dark brown, almost like molasses. As with honey, the lighter the syrup, the milder the flavor. Use light syrups for anything from pouring over waffles or pancakes to baking in cookies and cakes. The darker grades—more amber in color—are also suitable for eating and baking, but the darkest kind is best used in baking when you want to add intense maple flavor—it works wonderfully in soft ginger cookies and in gingerbread.

Always refrigerate maple syrup after opening to ensure freshness.

Whatever maple syrup you buy, be sure the label says "pure maple syrup"; syrups labeled "maple flavored" are usually just corn syrup with artificial maple flavoring.

Stocking Up
Cooking Light Recommends

Because maple syrup is produced in the early months of the year, that's a good time of year to stock up. Most grocery stores offer either Grade A Medium or Dark Amber, but if you can't find any locally, try these sellers: Christie's Maple Farm at 800-788-2118 (www.christiesmaplefarm.com) or Vermont Maple Outlet at 800-858-3121 (www.vermontmapleoutlet.com).

Making the Grade The deep, clean character of pure maple syrup can't be copied—or beat.

In our recipes, we use Grade A, Dark Amber.

Flavored syrups, often based on corn syrup, tend to be overly sweet. Pure maple syrup comes in different grades based on color and flavor. Each syrup-producing state uses its own grading system, but generally you'll find these grades:
- Grade A (3 versions)

  Light Amber: a mild-flavored syrup

  Medium Amber: still mellow, but slightly more caramel-like

  Dark Amber: a hearty, dark liquid
- Grade B

  This grade is less common and is a very dark syrup with a robust taste, almost like molasses. The stronger, darker syrups are excellent for cooking.

Syrup Partners
Test Kitchen SECRET

Some strongly flavored foods go especially well with maple syrup. Its sweetness would overwhelm a delicate sole, for instance, but it's ideal for salmon. Or brush maple syrup on pork, blend it with vegetables, or stir it into soups.

Maple-Glazed Salmon
Hoisin sauce and five-spice powder can be found in the Asian-food sections of large supermarkets.

2	tablespoons maple syrup
1½	tablespoons apple juice
1½	tablespoons fresh lemon juice
2	teaspoons hoisin sauce
1½	teaspoons grated peeled fresh ginger
1½	teaspoons country-style Dijon mustard
¼	teaspoon five-spice powder
4	(6-ounce) salmon fillets (about 1 inch thick)

Cooking spray

1. Preheat broiler.

2. Combine the first 7 ingredients in a large heavy-duty zip-top plastic bag. Add the salmon to bag; seal. Marinate in refrigerator 15 minutes.

3. Remove the salmon from the bag, reserving the marinade. Place the salmon fillets, skin sides down, on a broiler rack coated with cooking spray. Broil for 12 minutes or until the fish flakes easily when tested with a fork, and baste the salmon occasionally with the reserved marinade. Yield: 4 servings (serving size: 1 fillet).

CALORIES 316 (41% from fat); FAT 14.4g (sat 2.5g, mono 6.9g, poly 3.2g); PROTEIN 35g; CARB 9.3g; FIBER 0.1g; CHOL 111mg; IRON 0.9mg; SODIUM 184mg; CALC 18mg

Chocolate & Cocoa Powder

All you need to make magnificent light chocolate desserts are the best ingredients, a good technique, and a little bit of knowledge.

Chocolate Defined

The various forms of chocolate are defined by the amount of unsweetened baking chocolate (also known as chocolate liquor) in the product. Here are the most common types.

Unsweetened Baking Chocolate This is pure chocolate liquor—ground, shelled, and roasted cocoa beans without added sugar or any other ingredients—and despite the reference to liquor, it contains no alcohol. Baking chocolate is quite bitter and is not meant to be eaten by itself.

Sweet Dark Chocolate This category includes all chocolates, bittersweet and semisweet, that have at least 35 percent chocolate liquor.

The terms bittersweet and semisweet are often used interchangeably, since there is no official distinction between them. Generally (but not necessarily), bittersweet chocolate is less sweet than semisweet, because bittersweet often contains more chocolate liquor. Semisweet and bittersweet chocolate are commonly used in baking, but both are also delicious eaten out of the package.

Sometimes, packaging prominently indicates the percentage of chocolate liquor on the label. Although 35 percent is the required minimum, American bittersweet and semisweet chocolates found in supermarkets—such as Hershey's or Baker's—usually contain at least 50 percent

---

> ### Using Chocolate in Recipes
> **Test Kitchen**
> **SECRET**
>
> In our Test Kitchens, here's how we make sure that all of our chocolate desserts turn out great every time.
> - Choose the best-tasting and freshest ingredients.
> - Use small amounts of the real thing rather than fat-free or sugar-free substitutes.
> - Use cocoa powder—it delivers a strong punch of chocolate flavor, alone or in conjunction with other types of chocolate.
> - Always check the dessert 5 minutes before the recipe directs because oven temperatures can vary, and low-fat baked goods dry out easily.

---

chocolate liquor. It's not uncommon to find chocolate liquor contents from 60 percent or more in such premium chocolates as Valrhona and Scharffen Berger. These have intense chocolate flavor and are excellent in low-fat desserts.

Milk Chocolate America's favorite snacking chocolate, milk chocolate is often used for making candy bars. It's lighter in color and has a milder, creamier flavor than dark chocolate. It must contain at least 10 percent chocolate liquor, at least 12 percent milk solids, and no less than 3.66 percent butter fat. **Because of the milk solids, high sugar, and low chocolate liquor, milk chocolate doesn't usually substitute for dark chocolate in recipes.**

White Chocolate White chocolate isn't really chocolate, since it contains no chocolate liquor. It may contain cocoa butter, however, which is derived from chocolate liquor. Look for cocoa butter on the ingredient listing for quality white chocolate; if it contains palm kernel oil, it's white confectionery coating and should not be labeled as white chocolate.

To officially be labeled as white chocolate, products must include cocoa butter, milk solids, milk fat, and such sweeteners as sugar or high-fructose corn syrup.

Storing Chocolate Semisweet and bittersweet chocolate keep remarkably well for at least a year. Because chocolate absorbs flavors and odors, wrap it securely in plastic, and store it in a cool, dry place. Milk and white chocolates lose freshness more quickly, so if you purchase more than you will use within a couple of months, freeze the extra chocolate. Wrap it securely in plastic and enclose in a zip-top plastic bag. Before using, thaw the chocolate completely at room temperature without removing it from the bag. This will prevent condensation, which will damage the chocolate, from forming.

If your chocolate has a grayish-white coating, don't worry. This is called "bloom" and does not affect flavor or cooking quality. It will go away when the chocolate is heated. Bloom develops when chocolate is stored in warm or humid conditions.

Cocoa Powder

Cocoa powder is made from roasted, ground cacao seeds that have had much of their fat removed. There are two types of cocoa: *natural* (nonalkalized) and *Dutch process* (alkalized). Both are unsweetened, but their flavors differ subtly. Natural cocoa tastes fruity, tart, and acidic, and is simply untreated cocoa. Rarely labeled "natural," its package usually reads "cocoa." Dutch process cocoa is named for a Dutchman who invented a method for treating cocoa with an alkali to reduce its harshness and acidity. "Dutching" gives the cocoa a rich, dark color and a mellow toasted flavor that contains some coffee notes.

It's best to store cocoa away from herbs, spices, and other aromatic substances: It picks up other flavors relatively easily.

If a recipe calls for cocoa and is leavened with baking soda, use the natural variety of cocoa. Because Dutch process cocoa is more alkaline, it may alter the recipe's chemistry by reacting differently than natural cocoa. In recipes with no leaveners, either type may be used successfully.

Do Brands Make a Difference?

Cooking Light Recommends

Normally, the *Cooking Light* Test Kitchens use national supermarket brands of chocolate, such as Hershey's, Nestlé, or Baker's. But we wanted to know if premium chocolate would improve some of our top-rated recipes. The outcome of our side-by-side test? The vote was split. Some staffers couldn't detect a difference, while others thought that seeking out premium chocolate was well worth the extra time and money. The fat and calorie content will be the same either way, so the choice is up to you.

Measuring Cocoa

Test Kitchen SECRET

Measure cocoa just as you would flour: Lightly spoon the cocoa into a dry measuring cup, then level off the excess with a knife.

CHAPTER 13

Tea, Beer & Wine

These beverages aren't just for drinking—they play a key role in cooking, too.

Tea

Whether it's green or black, tea is a source of disease-fighting antioxidants. Each type of tea has its own health claims (see below), although the scientific evidence supporting them is limited. But when something tastes good and has potential health benefits, why not enjoy it regularly?

Cooking with Tea Go beyond your afternoon cup of tea and try cooking with a spot of tea. Every cake batter contains liquid—milk, buttermilk, or water—and replacing some or all of that with strong brewed tea (stronger than you'd drink) infuses the cake with delicate flavor. You can toss loose green tea into a stir-fry; add a cup of strong tea to soup stock, sauces, and marinades; or used minced tea leaves like an herb for seasoning. Just about any tea will work, but those with pronounced flavors, such as English breakfast or Darjeeling, are best. Many herb and spice teas also make good flavorings.

Using Tea in Recipes	Test Kitchen SECRET

We use tea bags for some recipes and loose tea for others. Tea bags are convenient and easy to use, while loose tea results in a stronger brew, which we prefer in a few recipes. If you can't find loose tea, cut tea bags open, and measure out the amount specified. We test with supermarket brands—no need to visit a specialty shop.

Healthy to a Tea — *Cooking Light* Recommends

Tea	Health Claim	Staff Favorites for Sipping
Black	There is some evidence that 2 cups a day may improve survival rates among heart attack victims.	Peet's Pride of the Port—a smooth, slightly nutty blend
Green	Histamine-blocking compounds may fight allergies; regular consumption may help prevent Parkinson's disease.	Teavana's Japanese Wild Cherry Sencha, which has a mild sencha flavor and a delicate aroma
White	Minimal processing leaves more antioxidants intact than what is found in green tea.	Emperor's White Tea—a subtly sweet tea that's a nice pick-me-up
Red	This is not really tea—it's the dried needles of the African rooibos herb. It's caffeine-free and antioxidant rich.	The Republic of Tea's Cedarberg Organic, a rich but mellow red-tinged brew

Black Currant Pound Cake

Black currant tea's naturally sweet fruity flavor and aroma stand out in this cake but don't overpower it.

Cake:

⅔ cup boiling water
6 black currant tea bags (such as Twinings)
⅓ cup fat-free sour cream
3 cups all-purpose flour
1 teaspoon baking powder
¼ teaspoon salt
2 cups granulated sugar
¾ cup butter, softened
3 large eggs
2 teaspoons vanilla extract
Cooking spray

Glaze:

¼ cup boiling water
1 black currant tea bag (such as Twinings)
¾ cup powdered sugar
½ teaspoon fresh lemon juice

1. Preheat oven to 350°.

2. Pour ⅔ cup boiling water over 6 tea bags in a bowl; steep 10 minutes. Remove and discard tea bags; cool tea to room temperature. Stir in sour cream.

3. Lightly spoon flour into dry measuring cups; level with a knife. Combine flour, baking powder, and salt, stirring with a whisk. Place granulated sugar and butter in a large bowl; beat with a mixer at medium speed until well blended. Add eggs, 1 at a time, beating well after each addition. Beat in vanilla. Add flour mixture and brewed tea mixture alternately to sugar mixture, beginning and ending with flour mixture; mix after each addition. Spoon batter into a 10-inch tube pan coated with cooking spray. Bake at 350° for 1 hour and 10 minutes or until a wooden pick inserted in center comes out clean. Cool in pan 15 minutes on a wire rack. Remove from pan; cool completely on wire rack.

4. Pour ¼ cup boiling water over 1 tea bag; steep 5 minutes. Remove and discard tea bag. Add powdered sugar and juice to brewed tea, stirring well with a whisk. Drizzle glaze over cake.
Yield: 16 servings (serving size: 1 slice).

CALORIES 300 (29% from fat); FAT 9.8g (sat 5.7g, mono 2.8g, poly 0.5g); PROTEIN 3.9g; CARB 49.6g; FIBER 0.6g; CHOL 63mg; IRON 1.3mg; SODIUM 171mg; CALC 35mg

English Breakfast Angel Food Cake

English breakfast tea imparts full-bodied flavor to this classic angel food cake and turns it tan.

½ cup boiling water
¼ cup loose English breakfast tea leaves
1 cup plus 2 tablespoons sifted cake flour
1½ cups sugar, divided
12 large egg whites
1 teaspoon cream of tartar
¼ teaspoon salt

1. Preheat oven to 325°.

2. Pour boiling water over tea leaves in a bowl; steep 5 minutes. Strain through a fine sieve into a bowl; cool tea to room temperature.

3. Lightly spoon flour into a dry measuring cup; level with a knife. Combine flour and ¾ cup sugar, stirring with a whisk. Place egg whites in a large bowl; beat with a mixer at high speed until foamy. Add cream of tartar and salt; beat until soft peaks form. Add ¾ cup sugar, 2 tablespoons at a time, beating until stiff peaks form. Beat in brewed tea.

4. Sift about ¼ cup flour mixture over egg white mixture; fold in. Repeat procedure with remaining flour mixture, ¼ cup at a time.

5. Spoon batter into an ungreased 10-inch tube pan, spreading evenly. Break air pockets by cutting through batter with a knife. Bake at 325° for 50 minutes or until cake springs back when lightly touched. Invert pan, and cool completely.

Loosen cake from sides of pan using a narrow metal spatula. Invert cake onto a plate. Yield: 12 servings (serving size: 1 slice).

CALORIES 147 (1% from fat); FAT 0.1g (sat 0g, mono 0g, poly 0.1g); PROTEIN 4.3g; CARB 32.5g; FIBER 0.2g; CHOL 0mg; IRON 0.7mg; SODIUM 105mg; CALC 3.6mg

Green Tea

Research shows that green tea may contribute to the prevention of heart disease, cancer, and rheumatoid arthritis. This tea also contains polyphenols, which are effective and powerful antioxidants. Some researchers recommend that to maximize tea's overall health benefits, a person should consume the equivalent of at least 4 cups of green tea per day, which would total about 300 to 400 milligrams of polyphenols. But to actually drink that amount might prove a bit difficult for many people, which is why learning to cook with green tea is such a wonderful idea.

Getting the Most from Green Tea

Use the highest-quality green tea for maximum flavor. But when you're first getting started, you'll probably find that the standard supermarket brands work fine.

Loose or bagged tea can be interchanged in many dishes, but not all; it's a good idea to have both types on hand. One tea bag contains about 1 teaspoon tea leaves.

Once it's opened, store green tea in a sealed container in a cool, dark place for no more than 6 months.

Don't use green tea that is more than 6 months old for cooking. Most of its flavor will have been lost beyond that point.

Save used tea leaves, and spread them around the bases of plants as the Chinese do. Because used tea leaves contain organic matter, they make a good fertilizer.

Green Tea Types

Loose or bagged, green tea comes either pure or flavored with flowers (such as jasmine) or fruit (such as lemon). Use lemon- or ginger-flavored teas for seafood dishes. Fruit- and flower-flavored teas work well in desserts and drinks. Because availability varies in the United States, we use common commercial types easily found in the tea section of your supermarket. But if you want to experiment a little more, try some of these other varieties.

Type	Description
Gunpowder	This makes a dark green tea with a strong, pleasant flavor and a long-lasting aftertaste. One of the first teas exported from China to Europe, it derives its name from its resemblance to the gunpowder used during the seventeenth century. Each leaf is rolled tightly into a pellet shape, but the leaves unfurl when brewed in hot water.
Dragon Well	When brewed, this is a light green, fresh, and mellow tea with a flowery aroma. The tea leaves are flat, long, and vibrant green. When the highest grades of Dragon Well brew, the leaves open to reveal intact buds.
New Mist	This is not really a tea type, but if you find this on a label, get it. The name refers to the highest-quality grade of any tea and is based on the time of day the tea is harvested. Only the youngest leaves are used; they're handpicked before dawn and processed the same day.

Tea Sauce

This sauce is great with a variety of dishes. Brush it on pork loin or salmon before baking, use it as a dipping sauce for pot stickers, or try it as a salad dressing.

    ¾   cup boiling water
    2   teaspoons loose green tea or 2 green tea
         bags, opened
    3   tablespoons minced fresh chives
    2   tablespoons extra-virgin olive oil
    1   tablespoon fresh lemon juice
    1   tablespoon low-sodium soy sauce
    1   teaspoon minced peeled fresh ginger
    1½   teaspoons honey
    ¼   teaspoon minced seeded hot red chile
    ⅛   teaspoon salt
    3   garlic cloves, minced

1. Combine boiling water and green tea in a bowl; cover and steep 3 minutes. Remove tea bags, strain mixture through a fine sieve into a bowl; discard leaves. Add minced chives and remaining ingredients. Cover and chill 30 minutes. Yield: 1 cup (serving size: 2 tablespoons).

CALORIES 38 (81% from fat); FAT 3.4g (sat 0.5g, mono 2.5g, poly 0.3g); PROTEIN 0.3g; CARB 1.9g; FIBER 0.1g; CHOL 0mg; IRON 0.1mg; SODIUM 97mg; CALC 5mg

---

Best Ways to Brew

Test Kitchen SECRET

- For recipes, we brew green tea to the boiling point (212°) using standard tap water. Among some connoisseurs, the tea (especially for drinking purposes) is considered best when brewed to 160° to 170°.
- We found it best to brew the tea, either as loose leaves or in bags, for 3 to 5 minutes for cooking purposes. If you are using the leaves, you'll notice them fully unfurl and soften.
- Avoid aluminum or plastic containers for brewing, as they will affect the flavor.

Pan-Fried Udon Noodles with Teriyaki Sauce

    1   (12.3-ounce) package extra-firm tofu,
         drained and cut into 1-inch cubes
    2   tablespoons low-sodium teriyaki sauce
    1   tablespoon rice vinegar
    1   tablespoon vegetable oil
    2   teaspoons loose green tea or 2 green tea
         bags, opened
    1   tablespoon minced peeled fresh ginger
    2   large garlic cloves, minced
    1   cup (2-inch) julienne-cut peeled radish
    1   cup thinly sliced leek (about 1 large)
    ½   cup (2-inch) julienne-cut carrot
    3   cups hot cooked udon noodles (about
         9 ounces uncooked)

1. Combine first 3 ingredients in a large zip-top plastic bag; seal and marinate in refrigerator 15 minutes. Remove tofu from bag, reserving marinade.
2. Heat oil in a large nonstick skillet over medium-high heat. Add tea; sauté 30 seconds. Add tofu, ginger, and garlic; sauté 2 minutes. Add radish, leek, and carrot; sauté 1 minute. Add noodles and reserved marinade; cook 2 minutes or until thoroughly heated. Yield: 4 servings (serving size: 1½ cups).

CALORIES 335 (18% from fat); FAT 6.6g (sat 1.1g, mono 1.6g, poly 3.3g); PROTEIN 12.8g; CARB 56.3g; FIBER 3g; CHOL 0mg; IRON 5.6mg; SODIUM 152mg; CALC 87mg

"Once you start to use green tea for extra flavor, you'll see how adaptable and useful it can be." Alison Ashton, Food Editor

Beer

As we explore more adventurous cuisines, we discover that the most appropriate beverage for many foods is beer.

Although you may usually think of wine as the libation for fine dining, with many dishes, the flavor of beer is a better complement to the food.

Pairing Foods with Beer Beer's slightly sweet malty flavors (with undertones of bitter hops and bready yeast) complement many foods. That said, beer pairs particularly well with strong flavors. Hence, beer is the beverage of choice for foods with vinegary, smoky, spicy-hot, and pungent tastes. It's no accident that beer is popular with Mexican, Thai, Indian, and German cuisines. Usually the best beer to enjoy with these dishes is one from the country where the food originated.

When choosing beer to pair with a particular dish, match like with like—mild lagers and lighter ales with delicate and subtle foods, and full-flavored ales with stronger foods.

Cooking with Beer If you overbought beer for your last party, don't worry. Beer doesn't actually go bad, so you can save it for the next gathering, or you can use it to add low-fat flavor to recipes. (For one example, see our recipe for Beer-Battered Onion Rings on page 293.)

Remember that when you cook with beer, most of the alcohol evaporates, leaving only the great flavor behind. The flavor beer adds to the recipe will be similar to the flavor you get when you drink it: Dark beers add a more pungent, rich flavor; light beers will add a very mild beer flavor.

> "To achieve an ideal paring, beer and food should taste better together than either would separately. Neither the food nor the beer should overpower the other; the flavors should balance."
>
> Mike Wilson, Test Kitchens Staffer

How to Taste Beer

Test Kitchen
SECRET

Notice the appearance of the beer before you taste it. The head should hold for a while, indicating good body and malty character. As you drink, the foam should cling to the glass. Carbonation varies based on beer style and producer, but some beers—such as typical American pilsners—can be overly fizzy from high levels of carbon dioxide. Aromas should be hoppy, malty, or fruity, depending on the beer.

Beer Primer Beer is made with malted grain (usually barley), water, yeast, and a flavoring. The flavoring is usually hops (the dried cone-shaped flowers of a vining plant), whose bitterness counters the sweetness of the malt.

Different flavors and beer styles are achieved by using malts that have been roasted to various degrees, by choosing different types of yeasts and hops, and by controlling when the hops are added. The flavor of beer also can be changed by using other grains, such as wheat, in addition to barley. Beer is divided into two main types: lagers and ales. However, there are many styles of both.

- *Lagers* are made with special strains of yeast that sink to the bottom of the brewing tank. Lagers are fermented and stored at cold temperatures. They tend to be light in color, with a subtle crisp, clean taste.
- *Ales* often are fermented with yeasts that sit atop the tank and prefer warmer temperatures. These yeasts ferment more quickly and produce beer with fruitier flavors and more yeasty and malty aromas. Ales are made with more hops and have an earthier, stronger, more complex taste than lagers.

Although every region in the country offers a variety of uniquely flavored beers, the lagers and ales we list below and on page 405 are made in common styles that can be matched to certain kinds of foods. We'll tell you what those different styles of beer taste like and what foods are generally the best to pair them with.

Lager Styles

Type	Description
Bock	These German-style dark beers are often high in alcohol. Full-bodied with low-to-medium hoppiness and a good malty taste, they're usually made in the spring to be served in the fall. Serve bock with smoked meat, sausages, and sauerkraut. Try Aass Beer or Shiner Bavarian Bock.
Doppelbock	Stronger and even more intense than regular bock, doppelbocks are high in alcohol (7.4 percent). They taste great with strong cheese, pickled herring, and raw onions. Celebrator Doppelbock is a good choice.
Lambic	Brewed only in Belgium, lambics are made with wild, rather than brewer's, yeast. These beers are less hoppy and can be sour, sweet, or fruity. Often, they are infused with cherry or raspberry extract. Fruited lambics are ideal with fruity desserts like pies, compotes, and fresh berries. Traditional lambics also go well with dark chocolate.
Märzenbier / Oktoberfest	Originating in Germany, these lagers were historically brewed in March to last until the next brewing season. They have an amber color, full malt flavor, and medium hoppiness. Oktoberfest beer is an example of a Märzenbier; it goes well with smoked meats and vinegary potato salad. Try Samuel Adams Oktoberfest and Paulaner Oktoberfest-Märzen.
Pilsner	Originally brewed in Plzen, Czech Republic, pilsners have a golden color with a flowery aroma, lots of malt flavor, and a dry finish with a bitter taste. American pilsners, such as Budweiser, are light in color and have less hoppiness and malt flavor than European pilsners like Pilsner Urquell. Pair these with pork or seafood.

Ale Styles

Type	Description
American Ale	Pale to amber in color, American ales have medium body, medium to high hops, and are not high in alcohol. Nuts and slightly sweet foods such as coleslaw, roast lamb, and beef are good with American ales. Try Sierra Nevada Pale Ale.
Bitter	These English ales have lots of malt and hops, low carbonation, and good body. Extra special bitter (ESB) is higher in alcohol and has more body than other bitters. Try a bitter with roast duck, roast beef, and well-aged Cheddar and Stilton cheeses. Try Boddington's Pub Ale, Fuller's ESB, and Redhook ESB.
India Pale Ale (IPA)	Because this ale was originally made in England for shipping to India, it needed high alcohol content and lots of hoppiness to survive the long trip. It has a pleasing malty flavor with a full-bodied taste. The high bitterness balances slightly sweet foods. Try it with barbecued ribs or glazed ham. Victory Hop Devil IPA and Harpoon IPA are good choices.
Pale Ale	Ales made with lighter roasted malt have a pale to amber color, medium hops, and maltiness with a drier taste. Try them with steak, salmon, or other fatty fish. Bass makes a good English-style pale ale.
Porter	Dark brown and full-bodied with high alcohol and chocolate tastes, porters are moderate-to-high hoppiness beers that can be enjoyed with bittersweet chocolate desserts. Try Samuel Smith, the Famous Taddy Porter.
Stout	Very dark and made with toasted malt, stouts are full bodied and hoppy. Ireland's Guinness is the most famous stout. Bitter coffee and chocolate flavors make stout great with oysters, rich meats such as braised short ribs, and game such as grouse.
Wheat Beers (Hefeweizen, Weissbier, Weizen, Weizenbock)	Beers containing wheat are often cloudy and slightly tart with high carbonation. They're also very refreshing and are ideal with spicy foods like curry. The tartness and wheaty flavors go well with fried food such as fish and chips. Try Sierra Nevada Wheat Beer and Pyramid Hefeweizen.

How to Serve Beer

Serve beer in glasses large enough to hold a 12-ounce bottle so you can pour the entire contents at once. Sloping pilsner flutes are nice, as are the large, slightly tapered English-style pint glasses. Begin pouring with your glass slightly tilted, and gradually straighten it as you pour, carefully building the head.

The head on beer, especially lagers and bubbly ales, is important. A good inch to inch-and-a-half head of foam is ideal.

Serve most beer well chilled but not icy (about 40° to 45°). Stouts and British-style ales such as ESB can be served at cellar temperature (about 50°).

Wine

Whether you are cooking with wine or serving it with your meal, it can enhance the flavors of the food.

The advice "Don't cook with wine you wouldn't drink" is not always good advice. If you're a good cook but an indiscriminate drinker, perhaps the advice should be, "Don't drink anything you wouldn't cook with." The criteria for drinking wine and cooking with wine are not the same. For wine-centric dishes like Beef Bourguignonne (page 408) or Coq au Vin (page 58), feel free to splurge a bit. But for dishes like risotto, soup, or pasta sauces, in which wine is one of many flavors, less expensive wines work fine. Keep in mind that price is not the sole indicator of quality; there are many inexpensive high-quality wines on the market.

Wine for cooking anything other than desserts should generally be dry because the high sugar content in sweet wines can change the balance of flavors. For desserts, sweet or fortified wines offer sweet, rich flavor.

Cooking with Wine

Test Kitchen SECRET

Here are some basics for cooking with wine.

- While the wine you cook with does not have to be expensive, it needs to be of good quality because it will contribute its flavors to the final dish.
- The type of recipe will determine when in the cooking process the wine should be added. For the most impact, add the wine at the end of the cooking process to evaporate some of the water and alcohol and concentrate the acidity, sugar, and flavors. But if you're cooking a stew, it's best to add the wine at the beginning to allow the wine time to blend with the other ingredients and flavors.

- You don't need a lot of wine in a dish to get big flavor. If you decide to add wine to a recipe that does not call for wine, substitute the wine for one of the other liquid ingredients rather than overpowering the dish with the wine.
- The longer the cooking time, the more alcohol that evaporates. (Note that not all of the alcohol evaporates; after simmering for $2\frac{1}{2}$ hours, 5 percent of the alcohol will still remain.)
- High temperatures can cause some of the flavor elements to disappear from the wine, so it's a good idea to limit cooking time and temperatures.

Selecting Wines for Cooking

Here are some general guidelines for pairing wines with recipes.

Type	Description
Desserts	Madeira, Marsala, port, and sweet sherry are good basics for dessert recipes. For poached fruits, either a red or white wine can be used, depending on the other ingredients in the recipe.
Marinades	Use either red or white; it's the acid in the wine that you need for the marinade.
Meats	A robust red wine is usually the best choice for meat and game recipes.
Poultry	The wine choice will depend on the other flavors in the dish. If the flavors are mild, white is best; for a spicy or strong-flavored dish, a red wine is best. Keep in mind that red wine will add color that may or may not be desirable.
Sauces	Again, the best wine for a sauce will depend on the other flavors. Mild sauces need white wine; strong sauces need red. If the sauce will be reduced after the wine is added, avoid highly acidic wines because the acidity will get more intense.
Seafood	Usually, seafood dishes need white wine, but there are some spicy seafood stews and other strongly flavored fish dishes that would require a red.

Leftover Wine

What can you do when a recipe calls for ½ cup of wine and you don't want to drink the wine with your meal? You can store the wine to use again for either drinking or cooking if you limit the wine's exposure to air. Below are some storage options. We don't really have a preferred method—it depends on how long you plan to store the wine.

- Replace the cork, and store the wine in the refrigerator. The wine will stay fresh for 1 to 3 days.
- Replace the cork with a bottle stopper.
- Transfer wine to glass containers or plastic water bottles, seal, and store in the refrigerator. The wine will stay fresh for 3 to 4 days.
- Use a pumping device (available at most wine stores) that sucks air from the bottle. The pump fits over a rubber stopper inserted into the mouth of the bottle.

Wine Picks

Cooking Light Recommends

Here are some guidelines for selecting wines for cooking from *Cooking Light* contributor, Karen MacNeil.

If a recipe calls for dry white wine, the best all-around choice is a quality American Sauvignon Blanc. This wine will be very dry and offer a light herbal tilt that will enhance nearly any dish.

If the recipe has bold or spicy flavors, go for a more aromatic white wine such as a Riesling. Its fruity flavors and floral aromas will counterbalance the heavy spices.

If a recipe calls for dry red wine, consider the heartiness of the dish. A long-simmered lamb or beef roast calls for a hearty red wine such as a Petite Syrah or a Zinfandel. A lighter dish might call for a less powerful red—a Pinot Noir or Chianti.

> "It's worth the investment to buy a quality wine for cooking. Just don't forget to sip a little as you stir."
>
> Karen MacNeil, *Cooking Light* Contributor

The Right Amount

For the best results, remember that whatever spirit you use should act as a flavor enhancer—add too much, and you can easily overwhelm a dish. If tasters say they hardly know it's there, you've added just the right amount.

Beef Bourguignonne

Red wine and mushrooms mark this dish as a classic from the Burgundy region of France. This recipe is cooked in a pressure cooker. (See page 84 for more information on pressure cookers.)

1½	pounds boned chuck roast, cut into 1-inch cubes
¼	cup all-purpose flour
½	teaspoon salt
½	teaspoon pepper
2	bacon slices, diced
½	cup dry red wine
1	(10½-ounce) can beef broth
3	cups baby carrots (about ¾ pound)
3	cups sliced shiitake mushroom caps (about ½ pound)
2	tablespoons chopped fresh or 2 teaspoons dried thyme
6	shallots, halved (about ½ pound)
4	garlic cloves, thinly sliced
7	cups hot cooked medium egg noodles (about 5½ cups uncooked pasta)

1. Combine first 4 ingredients in a large, heavy-duty zip-top plastic bag. Seal and shake to coat.
2. Cook half of bacon in a 6-quart pressure cooker over medium heat 30 seconds. Add half of beef mixture; cook 5 minutes or until browned. Remove beef from cooker. Repeat procedure with remaining bacon and beef mixture. Return beef to cooker. Stir in wine and broth, scraping pan to loosen browned bits. Add carrots, mushrooms, thyme, shallots, and garlic. Close lid securely; bring to high pressure over high heat (about 6 minutes). Adjust heat to medium or level needed to maintain high pressure; cook 20 minutes. Remove from heat; place pressure cooker under cold running water. Remove lid. Serve stew over noodles. Yield: 7 servings (serving size: 1 cup stew and 1 cup noodles).

CALORIES 376 (30% from fat); FAT 12.5g (sat 4.5g, mono 5.4g, poly 1.3g); PROTEIN 24.7g; CARB 40.9g; FIBER 3.3g; CHOL 44mg; IRON 5mg; SODIUM 525mg; CALC 53mg

> "We don't recommend using cooking wines because of their inferior flavor and the fact that they have salt and food coloring added."
>
> Vanessa Johnson, Test Kitchens Director

PART THREE

The Global Kitchen

Many of us at *Cooking Light* are passionate about eating in our favorite ethnic restaurants, but we think it's even more fun to create those authentic dishes in our own homes. Some ethnic cuisines are naturally light, as they emphasize fresh, natural foods flavored with local herbs and spices. Other traditional favorites from other cultures are not light, but we've figured out how to make them healthier without reducing their flavor or their authentic nature. We've grouped the cuisines of specific countries into general geographic regions because of the similarities in ingredients and cooking methods in that particular part of the world.

CHAPTER 14

The Mediterranean

Beginning with Spain and moving through France, Italy, the Greek isles, and the Middle East, we'll show you how the Mediterranean diet is a model for healthy eating. These classic cuisines feature quality ingredients and simple cooking methods that we admire in our Test Kitchens.

Spain

The foods of Spain are infinitely appealing because they are linked to Mediterranean ingredients such as olive oil, garlic, dried legumes, grains, tomatoes, and peppers. Plus, freshness and quality are paramount. Meals typically end with fresh fruits; sweets, although occasionally enjoyed, are not daily necessities.

Regional Cooking

While certain dishes are common across Spain, each of its regions offers particular culinary pleasures.

Andalucía Hillsides in this region are lined with the olive trees responsible for the exceptional oils essential to Spanish cooking. Andalusians still accent their cooking with Eastern spices inherited from the Moors. Chilled gazpachos are refreshing in the sunny climate, as are the shellfish vinaigrettes drizzled with the region's superb sherry vinegar. Iberian ham is revered for its singular texture and nutty flavor. (Devotees will recognize the name *Jabugo*, the town where thousands of hams are cured in cool mountain caves.)

> ### How We Lightened It
> **Test Kitchen SECRET**
>
> Spanish cooks tend to have a lavish hand with olive oil. While we decreased the oil considerably, some of these recipes still contain more than 30 percent fat. We hesitated to trim more because we wanted to preserve the authenticity and flavor of the cuisine. Happily, most of the fat is the heart-healthy monounsaturated variety.

Aragón The highest peaks of the Spanish Pyrenees offer a dramatic backdrop for this region. Navarra is renowned for its trout streams and the legendary running of the bulls; La Rioja is celebrated for its wines. Both border the fertile valley of the Ebro River. The peppers that grow here are essential to such regional dishes as *chilindrón* stews of lamb or chicken and traditional vegetable medleys. Delicate fire-roasted *piquillo* peppers, sautéed or stuffed, have recently captured the attention of the wider culinary world for their versatility and flavor.

Asturias The cuisine of this land of spectacularly abrupt green mountains and rugged coastlines features *fabada* bean stew, Cabrales blue cheese aged in mountain caves, salmon, trout, and hard apple cider.

411

Basque Country Food is preeminent in Basque culture, where traditional male-only gourmet clubs still flourish. Dishes made with the freshest fish coexist with classic preparations based on the traditional salt cod.

Castilla Although Madrid is at the center of landlocked Castilla (comprising Castilla y León to the north and Castilla La Mancha to the south), the freshest seafood is rushed overnight from every coast to satisfy the locals' demanding palates. Other gastronomic pleasures from the region: chorizo, Spain's typical sausage spiced with garlic and paprika; *manchego*, sheep's milk cheese; garlic soups and bean stews; and suckling pig and baby lamb, roasted in wood-burning brick-vaulted ovens.

Cataluña This privileged region encompasses the Pyrenees and its valleys, the agricultural lands of La Cerdanya and L'Empordà, the stunning Costa Brava, and Barcelona, where fine eating is a way of life. Catalan cooks are fond of sweet and savory combinations and of sauces flavored and thickened with almonds, pine nuts, and hazelnuts.

Spanish Pantry

Type	Description
Chorizo	This is Spain's traditional sausage, seasoned with paprika and garlic. When chorizo is hard-cured, it's often sliced and served as a tapa; when soft-cured, it becomes an important component of Spanish bean stews.
Olive Oil	Spain's olive oils, used generously in much of the cooking, are noted for their exquisite quality and fine flavors, ranging from smooth and subtle to fruity and robust.
Paprika	Unlike the sweet and hot paprikas in American supermarkets, the highest-quality Spanish paprika is smoked and very strong, so a little goes a long way. Spain's best is *pimentón de La Vera*, which is slowly smoked to give it a most distinctive flavor and aroma. It brings simple grilled foods to life and gives an exciting lift to paellas and stews. There are several varieties of smoked paprika. *We use La Chinata's bittersweet smoked paprika, available from Tienda.*
Rice	Spanish rice, sometimes called Valencia rice, is a short-grain variety with a firm texture that readily absorbs flavors from other ingredients, making it ideal for paellas. *We use white Calasparra rice, although any brand of Italian Arborio will work.*
Saffron	An essential ingredient in Spanish cooking, most of the world's finest saffron is produced in Spain. Painstaking to harvest, it takes more than 10,000 flowers to yield an ounce of dried saffron.
Serrano Ham	One of the secrets to the richly robust flavors of Spanish cuisine is pork—specifically, cured ham, or *jamón*. This air-cured ham is used in traditional tapas when thinly sliced and is an exceptional addition to stews and sautéed vegetables.
Sherry Vinegar	One of the world's most prized and potent vinegars, it's made from the finest sherry wine, then aged in sherry barrels for an average of 6 years.

Galicia This region is known for savory empanadas made with meat and fish; hearty *caldo gallego* (Galician soup) made with greens, beans, and meats; wonderfully moist country breads; and bountiful seafood, including scallops still attached to their shells.

Valencia The orange groves of this region alternate with vast, swampy rice fields. *Paella valenciana,* the classic rice dish, was created here.

Gazpacho Andaluz

Olive oil and bread are typical components of gazpacho, but as this recipe shows, you can eliminate the bread and cut down on the oil.

1½	pounds ripe tomatoes, each cut into quarters
1	cup coarsely chopped peeled cucumber
½	cup coarsely chopped Vidalia or other sweet onion
½	cup coarsely chopped red bell pepper
½	cup coarsely chopped green bell pepper
3	tablespoons sherry vinegar
2	tablespoons extra-virgin olive oil
½	teaspoon salt
¼	teaspoon sugar
¼	teaspoon ground cumin
5	garlic cloves, coarsely chopped

1. Combine all ingredients in a food processor; process until smooth. Press tomato mixture through a sieve over a bowl, pressing solids through with the back of a spoon; discard any remaining solids. Cover and chill. Yield: 6 servings (serving size: ½ cup).

CALORIES 80 (51% from fat); FAT 5g (sat 0.7g, mono 3.4g, poly 0.6g); PROTEIN 1.5g; CARB 9g; FIBER 2g; CHOL 0mg; IRON 0.8mg; SODIUM 207mg; CALC 18mg

Tortilla Española (Spanish Potato Omelet)

Tortilla Española (its relation to Mexican tortillas comes solely from its round shape) is one of the most popular dishes in Spain. The potatoes are normally fried, but roasting them provides excellent results. *Unlike an American omelet, this one's best made several hours ahead, then served at room temperature.*

6	cups thinly sliced peeled baking potato (about 3 pounds)
2	cups thinly sliced sweet onion
	Cooking spray
2	tablespoons olive oil, divided
¾	teaspoon kosher salt, divided
4	large eggs
	Oregano sprigs (optional)

1. Preheat oven to 350°.
2. Place potato and onion in a roasting pan coated with cooking spray. Drizzle with 1 tablespoon plus 2 teaspoons oil; sprinkle with ½ teaspoon salt. Toss well. Bake at 350° for 1 hour or until potatoes are tender, stirring occasionally with a metal spatula to prevent sticking.
3. Combine eggs and ¼ teaspoon salt in a large bowl. Stir in potato mixture; let stand 10 minutes. Heat 1 teaspoon oil in an 8-inch nonstick skillet over medium heat. Pour potato mixture into pan (pan will be very full). Cook 7 minutes or until almost set, gently shaking pan frequently. Place a plate upside down on top of omelet; invert onto plate. Carefully slide omelet, cooked side up, into pan; cook 3 minutes or until set, gently shaking pan occasionally. Carefully loosen omelet with a spatula; gently slide omelet onto a plate. Cool. Cut into wedges. Garnish with oregano, if desired. Yield: 6 servings (serving size: 1 wedge).

CALORIES 315 (23% from fat); FAT 8g (sat 1.7g, mono 4.6g, poly 1g); PROTEIN 9g; CARB 52.6g; FIBER 4g; CHOL 142mg; IRON 1.4mg; SODIUM 345mg; CALC 36mg

How to Make Paella

1. Dissolve saffron in the wine and clam juice. Keep warm because cold broth can keep the rice from cooking completely.

2. Sauté bell peppers, onion, garlic, and paprika. Add rice, and stir to coat with the oil. This "seals" the rice, preventing it from releasing its starch and keeping it firm.

3. Stir in clam juice mixture, and bring to a boil. Add reserved seafood mixture and mussels. Bake at 400° for 15 minutes or until shells open and the rice is slightly underdone.

Seafood Paella

Paella is one of the most famous and beloved of all Spanish dishes. Paellas are as varied as the cooks who make them, but the constants are good broth, short-grain rice, Spanish smoked paprika, and a paella pan—although a 13-inch skillet will work, too. Saffron is traditional in paella, but it's not crucial.

½	cup dry white wine
3	(8-ounce) bottles clam juice
¼	teaspoon saffron threads, crushed (optional)
¼	pound large shrimp
½	pound grouper or other white fish fillets, cut into 1-inch pieces
½	pound cleaned skinless squid, cut into ½-inch-thick slices
¼	teaspoon kosher salt
3	tablespoons olive oil, divided
½	cup chopped green bell pepper
½	cup chopped red bell pepper
½	cup chopped onion
4	garlic cloves, minced
2½	teaspoons Spanish smoked paprika or regular paprika
1	cup chopped tomato
1½	cups uncooked short-grain rice
1	pound small mussels, scrubbed and debearded

1. Preheat oven to 400°.

2. Bring wine, clam juice, and, if desired, saffron to a simmer in a small saucepan (do not boil). Keep warm over low heat.

3. Peel and devein shrimp, leaving tails intact. Combine shrimp, grouper, and squid in a bowl; sprinkle with salt, and let stand 5 minutes. Heat 1 tablespoon oil in a 13-inch paella pan or large skillet over medium-high heat. Add fish mixture, and sauté for 1 minute (the mixture will not be completely done). Remove fish mixture and any liquid from pan, and place in a bowl.

4. Heat 2 tablespoons oil in pan over medium-high heat. Add bell peppers, onion, garlic, and paprika; sauté 3 minutes. Stir in tomato; cook 2 minutes. Stir in rice, and coat well. Add clam juice mixture; bring to a boil, and cook 3 minutes. Add reserved fish mixture; cook 2 minutes. Add mussels to pan, nestling them into rice mixture.

5. Bake, uncovered, at 400° for 15 minutes or until shells open; discard any unopened shells. Remove from oven; cover and let stand 10 minutes. Yield: 8 servings (serving size: 1 cup).

CALORIES 179 (32% from fat); FAT 6.3g (sat 0.9g, mono 3.9g, poly 0.9g); PROTEIN 15g; CARB 15g; FIBER 1.3g; CHOL 97mg; IRON 2.1mg; SODIUM 322mg; CALC 44mg

Underdone Rice	Test Kitchen SECRET

For paella, the rice should be slightly underdone when you remove the pan from the oven. It should be firm in the center, similar to Italian risotto. Let the paella stand for 10 minutes, covered with a dish towel. This lets the rice continue cooking.

The different regions in Spain are what give Spanish cuisine its complexity. Each region is almost a culinary world unto itself.

Chorizo a la Llama (Flamed Chorizo)

Chorizo is Spain's typical sausage. Hard-cured chorizo is simply sliced and eaten; soft-cured chorizo is sautéed first, as in this tapas recipe.

½   pound soft-cured sweet chorizo
¾   cup dry white wine
1   tablespoon brandy
1   small whole jarred pimiento, cut into thin strips (such as Goya)
16 (½-inch-thick) slices diagonally cut French bread baguette

1. Remove sausage from plastic casing. Place in a small skillet; add wine, and bring to a boil. Reduce heat, and simmer 20 minutes or until wine almost evaporates. Add brandy. Ignite brandy with a long match, and let the flames die down. Continue cooking for 2 minutes or until liquid evaporates and chorizo is lightly browned.

2. Remove chorizo from pan, and cool slightly. Carefully cut sausage crosswise into 16 slices. Place 1 sausage slice and 1 pimiento strip onto each bread slice; secure each with a wooden pick. Yield: 16 servings (serving size: 1 appetizer).

CALORIES 127 (43% from fat); FAT 6g (sat 2.1g, mono 2.9g, poly 0.7g); PROTEIN 5.4g; CARB 12g; FIBER 0.7g; CHOL 13mg; IRON 0.9mg; SODIUM 313mg; CALC 18mg

Touting Tapas	Test Kitchen SECRET

Appetizers called tapas are both a food and a way of life in Spain. Neighborhood tapas bars are plentiful, and their setups are always the same: dozens of appetizers in earthenware casseroles and on platters displayed along the bar. Between sips of chilled dry fino sherry and bites of tapas, food and drink combine to create an atmosphere of instant camaraderie. According to Food Editor Krista Montgomery, eating tapas—small portions of highly flavored foods—is a very healthy way to eat.

France

Fabulous dishes from surprisingly commonplace ingredients characterize real French cooking.

French cuisine is most commonly associated with sophisticated, complex, and sometimes fussy dishes, the sort of food you'd get in starred restaurants. But the simple, hearty cooking presented here is the real basis of all French cuisine, for it is the cuisine of the hearth and of the land.

French cuisine actually is based on a few simple tenets, **the most important being a total devotion to using the finest possible ingredients at their peak of freshness.** The use of ingredients is also based on the belief that less is more. For instance, French cuisine is not a matter of adding more butter and cream, but in knowing when to add a bit of either to elevate the flavor of the dish.

Regional Cuisine

France is divided into 22 political regions, each of which has its own character and landscape. But when it comes to food, the fats used to prepare signature dishes serve best to divide the country. In Lyon and all areas to the north, butter is the fat of choice. The Southern region, divided between Provence and the Côte d'Azur, is devoted to olive oil, while the southwest (the area that borders Spain) is known for its use of goose and duck fats. Several of the areas are known for specific dishes or for a specific style of cooking, especially Alsace, Lyon, and Provence.

Alsace Sharing a border with Germany, this region is in the northeastern part of France. This area's German heritage is reflected in the cuisine, so when you hear the term *Alsatian,* it is usually referring to a dish featuring braised meat, sauerkraut, potatoes, or sausage. The wines of this area are known for their delicate flavors and dryness. Some examples of Alsatian wine grapes are Gewürztraminer, Pinot Blanc, and Riesling.

Lyon Located in central France, this city is known for its excellent food. The term *Lyonnaise* means "in the style of Lyon," and it usually refers to foods prepared with or garnished with onions.

Provence This region is located in the southeastern part of France, and foods prepared in the style of the region are termed *Provençal.* The trademark ingredients are garlic, tomatoes, and olive oil, plus onions, olives, mushrooms, anchovies, and eggplant.

How We Lightened It	Test Kitchen SECRET

Aside from removing a teaspoon or two of oil or butter, we're able to keep French recipes as authentic as any you might find in a French home or bistro. Though it may be surprising, no artifice, stretching, or extreme efforts were necessary to make these recipes low in fat because of their fresh and simply prepared seasonal ingredients.

Savory Onion Tart

Savory tarts are an integral part of French cuisine. They range from simple, rustic bread-dough tarts, such as this one, to rich egg, butter, and cream confections. Variations on this tart can be found in just about every region of France: from the Côte d'Azur to Burgundy to Alsace.

½ teaspoon dry yeast
½ teaspoon sugar
¾ cup warm water (100° to 110°)
2¼ cups all-purpose flour, divided
1 teaspoon kosher or sea salt, divided
Cooking spray
1½ teaspoons olive oil
6 cups thinly sliced onion
2 tablespoons half-and-half
1½ tablespoons chopped fresh thyme, divided
¼ teaspoon pepper

1. Dissolve yeast and sugar in warm water in a large bowl; let stand 5 minutes. Lightly spoon flour into dry measuring cups, and level with a knife. Stir in 2 cups flour and ½ teaspoon salt until smooth. Turn dough out onto a floured surface. Knead until smooth and elastic (about 5 minutes), and add enough of remaining flour, 1 tablespoon at a time, to prevent dough from sticking to hands (dough will feel tacky).

2. Place dough in a large bowl coated with cooking spray, turning to coat top. Cover and let rise in a warm place (85°), free from drafts, 1 hour or until doubled in size. (Press two fingers into dough. If an indentation remains, dough has risen enough.) Punch dough down; cover and let rest 5 minutes. Roll the dough into a 12-inch circle on a floured surface. Fit dough into a 10-inch round removable-bottom tart pan. Press dough against bottom and sides of pan.

3. Preheat oven to 425°.

4. Heat oil in a large nonstick skillet over medium heat. Add the onion; cover and cook 20 minutes or until golden brown, stirring frequently. Remove from heat; stir in ½ teaspoon salt, half-and-half, and 1 tablespoon thyme. Spread mixture over dough in pan. Bake at 425° for 25 minutes or until crust is golden brown. Sprinkle with 1½ teaspoons thyme and pepper. Let stand 5 minutes. Cut into 6 wedges. Yield: 6 servings.

CALORIES 238 (10% from fat); FAT 2.7g (sat 0.7g, mono 1.2g, poly 0.6g); PROTEIN 6.6g; CARB 46.7g; FIBER 3.7g; CHOL 2mg; IRON 2.7mg; SODIUM 327mg; CALC 39mg

French Pantry

Contrary to popular belief, one of the best things about French cuisine is its lack of pretense. What are really very commonplace ingredients come together for extraordinary results. See the list below for some of the ingredients that lie at the heart of French cooking. (Most of these have been presented in detail elsewhere in the book.)

Type	Description
Artichokes	globe artichoke—the true artichoke
Chicken Stock	information on pages 37-39
Curry Powder	usually associated with Indian cooking; a blend of over 20 spices, herbs, and seeds
Dijon Mustard	famous French mustard made with brown or black seeds
Flat-leaf Parsley	has a stronger flavor than regular curly-leaf parsley
Garlic	information on page 296
Gruyère Cheese	the assertive, nutty flavor is similar to that of Swiss cheese
Leeks	information on page 295
Rosemary	information on pages 378-379
Sea Salt	information on pages 386-387
Shallots	information on page 294
Unsalted Butter	often preferred for baking because of the lack of salt
Wine	information on pages 406-408

French Cooking Terms and Techniques

Here are some basic terms and techniques that are commonly used in French cooking.

Type	Description
Aïoli	a strongly flavored garlic mayonnaise from the Provence region of southern France
Beurre Blanc	butter sauce, a reduction of white wine and butter
Bouquet Garni	an assortment of whole herbs and spices secured in a cheesecloth bag and used to flavor soups, stews, and stocks; typically includes fresh thyme, bay leaves, and parsley stems, but can also include other aromatics like celery and leeks
Cassoulet	classic bean dish that includes duck or goose and usually pork
Deglaze	to add a small amount of liquid (usually water or wine) to a pan after sautéing food, then stirring to loosen the browned bits; mixture then used to make a sauce or reduced and served with the food
Gâteau	cake
Gratin	any dish topped with cheese and/or breadcrumbs, then heated in the oven or broiler until melted and browned
Haricots Verts	a variety of tender, thin green beans, cousins to pole and bush green beans; usually refers to tender, small green beans in general
Haute Cuisine	a style of cooking that emphasizes elaborate meals with many courses; usually refers to fancy, fussy French fare
Herbes de Provence	an assortment of dried herbs that usually includes thyme, bay leaves, rosemary, basil, and savory
Poivre	pepper; in France, almost always freshly ground black, but occasionally white or pink
Pommes	apples
Pommes Frites	French fries
Potage	pureed vegetable soup
Poulet	chicken
Roux	a combination of cooked butter and flour that is used to thicken soups and sauces
Sauté	to cook food quickly in a small amount of fat in a skillet
Scalloped	prepared by layering food with cream or a creamy sauce (usually applies to potatoes)
Vinaigrette	one of what the French refer to as the five "mother sauces;" traditionally, a combination of three parts oil to one part vinegar, seasoned with salt and pepper

> "French dishes are typically made with the freshest seasonal ingredients, used as carefully and simply as possible." Ann Pittman, Food Editor

Baekeoffe (Alsatian Meat Stew)

This savory, richly flavored dish comes from the Alsace region of eastern France, where the cuisine reflects a strong German influence. After marinating, the meats and vegetables cook together slowly in the marinade and emerge filled with flavor.

4	cups thinly sliced onion
1½	cups (1-inch) sliced carrot
1	cup thinly sliced leek (about 1 large)
1	(1-pound) boneless beef shoulder roast, trimmed and cut into 2-inch cubes
1	(¾-pound) pork blade steak, boned, trimmed, and cut into 2-inch pieces
12	thyme sprigs
10	parsley stems
4	whole cloves
3	bay leaves
2	garlic cloves, halved
1½	cups Riesling or other white wine
1½	teaspoons kosher or sea salt, divided
½	teaspoon pepper
1	pound small red potatoes, quartered

Cooking spray

1. Combine first 5 ingredients in a large nonreactive bowl. Place thyme, parsley, cloves, bay leaves, and garlic on a double layer of cheesecloth to form a *bouquet garni*. Gather edges of cheesecloth together; tie securely (see Test Kitchen Secret at right). Add bouquet garni, wine, ½ teaspoon salt, and pepper to bowl. Toss well to coat. Refrigerate 8 to 24 hours, stirring occasionally.
2. Preheat oven to 375°.

3. Place one-third of the potatoes in a 3-quart casserole coated with cooking spray. Top with half of the meat mixture, and sprinkle with ¼ teaspoon salt. Repeat the layers with one-third of the potatoes, remaining meat mixture, and ½ teaspoon salt. Top with the remaining potatoes, and sprinkle with ¼ teaspoon salt. Pour any remaining marinade (including the bouquet garni) over meat mixture. Cover and bake at 375° for 2½ hours. Remove the bouquet garni, and discard. Yield: 6 servings (serving size: 1⅓ cups).

CALORIES 376 (29% from fat); FAT 12.1g (sat 4.4g, mono 5.3g, poly 0.9g); PROTEIN 40g; CARB 25.7g; FIBER 3.9g; CHOL 110mg; IRON 5.3mg; SODIUM 592mg; CALC 61mg

How to Make a Bouquet Garni
Test Kitchen SECRET

A bouquet garni is used to season French dishes. Place thyme, parsley, cloves, bay leaves, and garlic on a double layer of cheesecloth. Gather edges of cheesecloth, and secure with a string. Tie tightly; you don't want the bag to break and disperse its contents into the stew.

For additional recipes that are French in origin, see Béchamel Sauce on page 40, Crème Anglaise on page 53, Coq au Vin on page 58, and Beef Bourguignonne on page 408.

Italy

Italian food is all about using the freshest ingredients available and bringing out their flavors.

Italian cooking is healthful, and so is the Italian way of eating. It's a cuisine that one does not tire of easily because it runs the gamut from rich and complex to light and simple.

A typical meal consists of several courses. No one course dominates the meal, so portion sizes need not be as large. The first course (*primo piatto*) is usually a soup, pasta, or risotto. The second course (*secondo piatto*) is a meat, fish, or chicken dish that's accompanied by a vegetable and followed by a salad. The meal often ends with fruit rather than a dessert (although occasionally, Italians do like to indulge in something sweet).

Basic Techniques

Cooking Pasta Pasta should be cooked in a generous amount of boiling water. It is not necessary to add oil to prevent it from sticking. Simply follow these rules.
- Use at least 4 quarts of water for 1 pound of pasta.
- Stir as soon as the pasta goes in and periodically while it is cooking, and make sure the water is always at a rolling boil.
- Drain the pasta when it's *al dente* (firm and chewy but not crunchy); don't rinse it.
- Toss pasta with the sauce right away to prevent it from sticking, and allow it to absorb as much flavor from the sauce as possible. (See pages 265-271 for more information on pasta.)

Pan Roasting Until not too long ago, many Italian kitchens did not have ovens, so most cooking was—and still is—done over the stove. Meats are more often pan roasted than oven roasted. Most recipes that involve roasting follow a basic technique: **Meat is first browned in either olive oil or butter, and a cooking liquid (usually a dry white or red wine) is added to the pan.** Once the alcohol has evaporated and the tasty brown bits have been loosened from the bottom of the pan, the heat is lowered, and the meat cooks under a cover that is slightly ajar until it is very tender.

Dressing an Italian Salad According to an Italian proverb, it takes four people to dress a salad well: a wise person for the salt, a generous person for the olive oil, a stingy person for the red wine vinegar, and a patient person to toss it together. (Sometimes the proverb calls for a wealthy person adding balsamic vinegar.)

Sautéing The purpose of sautéing is to intensify and draw out flavor. **Unlike most recipes that tell you to heat the oil until hot, with Italian cooking, you want the onions and garlic, for example, to cook very slowly.** Not only does this minimize the chances of burning the garlic, but you'll also get a richer flavor with a slower, more patient approach.

Turn to pages 44-48 for authentic Italian sauces including Clam Sauce, Pesto, Marinara Sauce, and Mushroom Sauce. For additional pasta recipes, see Farfalle Carbonara and Spaghetti Aglio e Olio (page 268).

Italian Pantry

High-quality ingredients are essential to Italian cooking—the better your olive oil, tomatoes, and cheese, the better the food.

Type	Description
Dried Porcini Mushrooms	Look for packages that have large slices of whole mushrooms. They add a wonderful rich flavor to risottos, pasta sauces, and stews, and they can infuse cultivated white mushrooms with their robust flavor.
Garlic	Use garlic judiciously so it's not an overwhelming presence.
Olive Oil	An essential ingredient in Italian cooking, olive oil is used not simply as a cooking oil but for the flavor it adds to a dish. (See pages 361-362 for more information on using olive oil.)
Parmigiano-Reggiano	Only cheese that is produced according to strict guidelines in a limited area surrounding Parma may be sold as Parmigiano-Reggiano. Its incomparable flavor, texture, and richness make it not only an excellent grating cheese but also one of the world's great table cheeses.
Pasta	Use pasta imported from Italy or domestic pasta. Premium brands of artisanal production will have a satisfying texture and the subtle flavor of semolina flour. *For egg pasta, avoid the "fresh" pasta sold in refrigerated cases. Either use homemade or buy the dried noodles packaged in nests.*
Rice	Arborio is the most common rice used in making risotto, but other varieties—such as *carnaroli* or *vialone nano,* which are just now becoming available in America—are perhaps even better. One characteristic they all share is a translucent, starchy exterior that melts away in cooking to give risotto its distinctive creamy consistency.
Tomatoes	When fresh, ripe tomatoes are not available, use good canned tomatoes (unless the recipe specifically calls for fresh). *Choose whole peeled tomatoes rather than chopped or crushed. Use imported Italian San Marzano tomatoes if you can find them; they're the best.*

Spaghetti Alla Norma

This is the classic Sicilian pasta sauce. The combination of eggplant and tomato is quintessentially Italian.

- 2 tablespoons olive oil
- 3 garlic cloves, minced
- 1½ pounds coarsely chopped peeled tomato
- 1 teaspoon salt
- 1 pound eggplant, peeled and cut into ½-inch cubes (about 4 cups)
- ¼ cup thinly sliced fresh basil
- 1 (12-ounce) package spaghetti
- 6 ounces fresh mozzarella cheese, cut into ¼-inch cubes (about 1 cup)

1. Place oil and garlic in a large skillet; cook over medium-high heat 30 seconds or until garlic begins to sizzle. Add tomato and salt; cook 15 minutes or until liquid has evaporated. Add eggplant; cover, reduce heat, and cook 15 minutes or until eggplant is tender. Stir in basil; set aside.
2. Cook pasta in boiling water 9 minutes; drain. Toss with sauce and cheese. Serve immediately. Yield: 7 servings (serving size: 1 cup).

CALORIES 329 (29% from fat); FAT 10.5g (sat 3.9g, mono 4.6g, poly 1g); PROTEIN 12.2g; CARB 47.3g; FIBER 4.1g; CHOL 19mg; IRON 2.8mg; SODIUM 444mg; CALC 149mg

Greece

Delicious regional produce forms the basis of everyday Greek cooking.

The foods of the Greek isles are not elaborate and complicated. They are based on humble but delicious regional produce: seasonal vegetables; leafy greens, wild or cultivated; grains, mainly in the form of homemade bread; fruity olive oil; home-cured olives; beans and other legumes; local cheeses; yogurt; sometimes meat; and occasionally, fresh or cured fish. These form the basis of everyday Greek cooking.

Olive oil, the primary fat used in Greek cooking, is basic to every Greek's life and identity. It's also tied to rituals, both folk and religious, that mark the crucial events in the cycle of life.

Seasonal Culture Food follows the seasons, and the seasons are dotted with religious holidays, some of which have evolved from ancient celebrations. In fact, many dishes are still closely related to religious holidays. The rules of the Greek Orthodox Church have shaped eating habits to the extent that even nonreligious Greeks abstain from foods derived from animals, such as meat, dairy products, and eggs, during religious holidays. Until recently, **Greeks have had a mainly vegetarian diet because it was not possible to pasture the large herds needed to provide meat for everybody.**

Ingenuity Every day, the Greek cook creates an interesting and delicious dish from the same few humble ingredients. Take *horta*—wild or cultivated greens—as an example. They are steamed or blanched and made into salad dressed with lemon juice and olive oil. When meat or poultry is available, greens can be added to either and finished with *avgolemono*, a delicious sauce of egg and lemon. And of course, a mixture of various greens is the basis of many baked or fried pies.

Seafood has never been plentiful enough to become a staple because, while the seafood of the Aegean is exceptionally delicious, it's also scarce.

Olives are one of the hallmarks of Greek cuisine. Rich and meaty, they add distinctive flavor to many Greek dishes. (See pages 370-371 for more information on olives.)

How We Lightened It
Test Kitchen SECRET

Because of the emphasis on healthy ingredients such as fresh greens, herbs, tomatoes, grains, lemon juice, and olive oil, Greek food is not hard to lighten. You can reduce the amount of olive oil and cheese and keep the regional flavors authentic. You can also reduce the fat without changing the flavor by replacing whole-milk yogurt with a low-fat or fat-free version.

Greek Pantry

Type	Description
Aleppo Peppers	These dried crushed red peppers from the Middle East are milder and more flavorful than Mexican chile peppers. Their taste is closer to that of indigenous Greek hot peppers. You may substitute a smaller amount of crushed red pepper.
Cinnamon	On the islands, in the Peloponnese, and in other parts of Greece, most tomato-flavored sauces for vegetables (as well as for meat dishes) are spiced with cinnamon sticks.
Feta Cheese	Probably the most familiar Greek cheese, feta is a slightly pungent, crumbly cheese made primarily from sheep's milk, with the addition of goat's milk. *Greek feta packed in brine tastes stronger than that wrapped in plastic. Either kind will work well in most recipes.*
Horta	Various sweet, bitter, sour, and fragrant greens are gathered from the hills and fields after the first rains of fall and throughout the winter; some greens are also cultivated. Horta are used in myriad combinations—different in each part of the country—to make *hortopites* (greens pies), stews, and salads. A delicious mixture of different wild greens (either boiled, blanched, or sometimes raw), horta used to be the center of poor peasants' meals. The greens, simply dressed with olive oil and freshly squeezed lemon juice, were complemented with olives, home-baked bread, and maybe some cheese, cured pork, or salted fish. Many city folks dream of this frugal meal and drive many miles on weekends to get it.
Kalamata Olives	These are probably the best-known and most-loved olives in the world. Kalamata olives take their name from a city in the southern Peloponnese and are the most flavorful olives from that region. These black, firm, and juicy olives are almond-shaped with a pointed tip. Authentic Kalamata olives are cured in brine, which contains high-quality local red wine vinegar.
Lemon	*Freshly squeezed lemon juice is the most commonly used flavoring in savory and many sweet dishes.* Lemon vinaigrette stars in most boiled or raw salads and in grilled or barbecued meat or fish.
Olive Oil	*Greek olive oils are a great bargain in American markets.* Many small olive groves, mainly on Crete and in the Peloponnese, now produce excellent organic olive oils.
Oregano	*Dried oregano is used in traditional Greek cooking.* It is gathered in the summer from mountains and hills, where it grows wild. Densely fragrant, imported Greek oregano is often mixed with domestic varieties when packaged in the United States because it is considered too potent for unaccustomed users. *We use Spice Hunter's Greek oregano, which is in the spice sections of some supermarkets.*
Phyllo	These paper-thin sheets of pastry dough—usually made with flour and water, some olive oil, and maybe a little lemon juice or vinegar—wrap all sorts of fillings: greens or vegetables with or without cheese; meat, fish, or seafood with rice; or bulgur, herbs, and spices. Phyllo is also used in many sweets, like baklava and *galatomboureko,* a luscious milk custard. *Kataifi,* used in our baklava recipe (page 424), is shredded phyllo pastry that comes frozen in one-pound packages.
Yogurt	Greeks love sweet, creamy yogurt made from sheep's milk, but it's not available in most American markets. *We use drained plain low-fat yogurt in all of our Greek-style recipes that call for yogurt.*

Rolled Baklava

This baklava is rolled in a jelly-roll fashion instead of assembling it in flat layers and cutting it into triangles. The traditional butter is replaced with olive and vegetable oils, which, along with the almonds, make this dessert very high in heart-healthy monounsaturated fats.

Rolls:
2	tablespoons olive oil
2	tablespoons vegetable oil
2	lemon wedges
¾	cup whole almonds (5 ounces), toasted
1½	tablespoons sugar
½	teaspoon ground cinnamon
¼	teaspoon ground nutmeg
12	sheets frozen phyllo dough, thawed
8	ounces frozen shredded phyllo dough (*kataifi*), thawed

Cooking spray

Syrup:
1⅓	cups sugar
1⅓	cups water
1⅓	cups honey
4	lemon wedges
1	(3-inch) cinnamon stick

1. Preheat oven to 350°.

2. To prepare rolls, combine first 3 ingredients in a small saucepan. Cook over medium-low heat 5 minutes. Cool; discard lemon. Place almonds, 1½ tablespoons sugar, ½ teaspoon cinnamon, and nutmeg in a food processor; process until coarsely chopped.

3. Place 2 phyllo sheets on a large cutting board or work surface (cover remaining dough to keep from drying); lightly brush with 1½ teaspoons oil mixture. Top with 2 phyllo sheets, and lightly brush with 1½ teaspoons oil mixture. Sprinkle about 2½ tablespoons almond mixture evenly over phyllo stack, leaving a 1½-inch border on 1 short edge. Crumble one-third shredded phyllo over almond mixture; top with 2½ tablespoons almond mixture.

4. Starting at short edge without border, tightly roll up phyllo stack, jelly-roll fashion. Lightly brush border and outside of roll each with 1½ teaspoons oil mixture. Cut roll evenly into 10 pieces. Repeat procedure twice with remaining sheets of phyllo, oil mixture, almond mixture, and shredded phyllo. Place all 30 rolls on a jelly-roll pan or baking sheet coated with cooking spray. Bake at 350° for 30 minutes.

Making Rolled Baklava

1. After the phyllo is brushed with lemon oil and almonds, the kataifi is sprinkled over it.

2. Tightly roll up the phyllo, jelly-roll fashion.

3. Then slice with a serrated bread knife into 1¹/₂-inch pieces.

5. To prepare syrup, combine 1⅓ cups sugar and remaining ingredients in a large saucepan. Cook over medium heat 5 minutes or until sugar dissolves; discard lemon and cinnamon stick.

6. Carefully place baked baklava rolls, cut sides up, in a 13 x 9-inch baking pan coated with cooking spray (rolls will fit snugly). Pour syrup over rolls; let stand at room temperature for 3 hours. Carefully turn rolls; cover and let stand 8 hours. Yield: 15 servings (serving size: 2 rolls).

CALORIES 343 (27% from fat); FAT 10g (sat 1.3g, mono 5.7g, poly 2.6g); PROTEIN 4.2g, CARB 61.8g, FIBER 1.8g, CHOL 0mg, IRON 1.5mg, SODIUM 147mg, CALC 29mg

> **We first tasted the baklava rolls** just 2 hours after we made them, and they were delicious. Letting them stand for the full 11 hours, however, allows them to soak up more flavor, making them even better.

Greens and Cheese Pie (*Hortopita*)

In this recipe, sweet spinach and pungent mustard greens combine with plenty of green onions and fennel, parsley, dill, and oregano. Feta cheese adds a sour, salty component to the pie's filling.

1	tablespoon olive oil
2	cups thinly sliced green onions
1½	cups minced fennel (about 1 large bulb)
10	cups fresh spinach (about 5 ounces)
8	cups thinly sliced mustard greens (about 8 ounces)
1¼	cups (5 ounces) feta cheese
¼	cup chopped fresh parsley
¼	cup chopped fresh or 1 tablespoon dried dill
1	teaspoon dried Greek oregano
½	teaspoon salt
½	teaspoon pepper
8	sheets frozen phyllo dough, thawed

Cooking spray
Flat-leaf parsley sprigs (optional)

1. Preheat oven to 375°.

2. Heat oil in a large nonstick skillet over medium-high heat. Add onions; sauté 4 minutes. Add fennel; sauté 3 minutes. Remove onion mixture from pan; cool. Add spinach to pan; sauté 30 seconds or until spinach wilts. Place spinach in a colander, pressing until barely moist. Add mustard greens to pan; sauté 30 seconds or until greens wilt. Place greens in a colander, pressing until barely moist. Combine onion mixture, spinach, greens, feta, and next 5 ingredients in a large bowl.

3. Working with 1 phyllo sheet at a time (cover remaining dough to keep from drying), place 2 sheets in a 13 x 9-inch baking pan coated with cooking spray. Gently press sheets into bottom and up sides of pan, allowing the ends to extend over edges of pan. Coat top sheet with cooking spray. Fold 1 sheet of phyllo in half crosswise; place on sheets in bottom of pan, and coat with cooking spray. Top with 1 sheet of phyllo, gently pressing sheet into the bottom and up sides of pan; coat with cooking spray. Spread greens mixture evenly over top of phyllo. Fold a sheet of phyllo in half crosswise; gently press on the greens mixture in pan, and coat with cooking spray. Top with the remaining 3 sheets of phyllo, coating each with cooking spray. Cut ends extending over pan. Fold edges of phyllo to form a rim; flatten rim with fork. With a sharp knife, cut 4 slits in top of phyllo. Bake at 375° for 50 minutes. Cool 30 minutes. Garnish with parsley sprigs, if desired. Yield: 6 servings.

CALORIES 194 (44% from fat); FAT 9.4g (sat 4.1g, mono 3.2g, poly 1.3g); PROTEIN 8.1g; CARB 20.8g; FIBER 2g; CHOL 21mg; IRON 3.6mg; SODIUM 622mg; CALC 234mg

> **"Don't worry about having fresh herbs on hand—dried oregano is typically used in traditional Greek recipes."** Alison Ashton, Food Editor

Meat, Bulgur, and Rice Dolmades

Once the grape leaves are rolled, they're braised in broth and lemon juice. Their fragrant, slightly tart taste adds flavor to the broth, which is thickened with cornstarch to form a dipping sauce for the dolmades. They make great appetizers. Look for grape leaves in the Mediterranean section of your supermarket.

1	cup coarsely chopped fennel (about 1 bulb)
½	cup coarsely chopped onion
¼	cup coarsely chopped green onions
½	pound ground round
2	tablespoons uncooked medium-grain rice
2	tablespoons uncooked bulgur
1½	teaspoons olive oil
1	large tomato, cored and cut in half crosswise (about 1 pound)
½	teaspoon Aleppo pepper or dash of crushed red pepper
¼	teaspoon salt
30	bottled large grape leaves

Cooking spray

1	(14-ounce) can fat-free, less-sodium chicken broth
¼	cup fresh lemon juice
1	tablespoon cornstarch
1	tablespoon water
3	tablespoons chopped fresh or 1 tablespoon dried dill

Lemon wedges (optional)

1. Combine first 3 ingredients in a food processor, and process until minced. Combine fennel mixture with beef, rice, bulgur, and oil. Grate tomato halves over mixture; discard skin. Sprinkle beef mixture with pepper and salt; stir to combine.
2. Rinse grape leaves under cold water; drain and pat dry with paper towels. Remove stems, and discard. Spoon 1 rounded tablespoon of beef mixture onto the center of each grape leaf. Bring 2 opposite points of leaf to center, and fold over filling. Beginning at 1 short side, roll up leaf tightly, jelly-roll fashion. Repeat procedure with remaining grape leaves.
3. Place stuffed grape leaves close together, seam sides down, in a Dutch oven coated with cooking spray. Add broth and juice; bring to a boil. Cover, reduce heat, and simmer for 30 minutes. Carefully remove dolmades from pan. Combine cornstarch and water. Stir cornstarch mixture into broth; bring to a boil, and cook for 1 minute. Stir in dill. Serve with dolmades. Garnish with lemon wedges, if desired. Yield: 6 servings (serving size: 5 dolmades and ¼ cup lemon broth).

CALORIES 132 (23% from fat); FAT 3.3g (sat 0.8g, mono 1.5g, poly 0.4g); PROTEIN 11.2g; CARB 14.3g; FIBER 3g; CHOL 22mg; IRON 2.1mg; SODIUM 255mg; CALC 81mg

Tomato Shortcut
Test Kitchen SECRET

Greek cooks don't peel or seed tomatoes. Instead, they cut the tomatoes in half and grate them. While it seemed a bit odd to us at first, it's really quite clever. It's much quicker than a water bath and peeling. If the tomato is ripe, the skin will just fall away, leaving the pulp. We use the largest holes on a box grater to do this, and it works like a charm.

The Middle East

From Iran to Morocco, Middle Eastern cuisine is sensuous, full of rich flavors and aromas, and quite heart-healthy.

The Middle East includes many countries and cuisines, but we will focus on Lebanon, Iran, Turkey, and North Africa. While there are specific regional and cultural differences, the foods of these areas share some commonalities. Kebabs, savory pies made with paper-thin pastry, stuffed vegetables, pilafs, cake-like omelets, rice puddings, and pastries filled with nuts and soaked in syrup are common throughout the region. Lamb is the favorite meat; eggplants, zucchini, artichokes, okra, and bell peppers are the favorite vegetables. Also popular are chickpeas, fava beans, lentils, and navy beans. Meat stews are cooked with legumes and vegetables or fruits. Pine nuts, almonds, walnuts, and pistachios are ubiquitous garnishes, sauce thickeners, and pastry fillings. Sweet dishes are perfumed with orange blossom water and rose water.

How We Lightened It
Test Kitchen SECRET

Middle Eastern recipes, in most cases, already meet the standards for heart-healthy cooking. For the traditional recipes that we did need to modify a bit, in most cases, all we had to do was decrease the amount of oil.

Lebanon
The cooking in Lebanon is similar (with the exception of local specialties) to that of Jordan, Syria, and Egypt. A combination of tastiness and healthfulness is a persistent theme in Lebanese food. With the usual benefits of the Mediterranean diet, Lebanese cooking emphasizes such ingredients as olive oil, onions, garlic, nuts, lemons, oranges, and fresh vegetables (raw and pickled carrot and cucumber slices are especially popular in Lebanon) rather than butter and red meat. Also intriguing is the Lebanese habit of grazing on various dishes throughout the day, which research is showing to be a healthy way to dine.

Key Characteristics of Lebanese Food
- City cooking is based on rice, while the country staple is cracked wheat.
- A variety of *kibbeh*—pies with shells made from cracked wheat and lamb pounded to a paste, and fillings of fried onion, ground meat, and pine nuts—are Lebanese (and Syrian) specialties.
- Pomegranate syrup (recipe on page 357) and tamarind lend a delicate sweet-and-sour taste to certain dishes.
- Lemon juice and sumac add sharpness.
- Mint and flat-leaf parsley are favorite herbs.
- Cardamom and turmeric also predominate.
- Crushed coriander seed, also a distinct flavor of Egypt, is fried with garlic or mixed with cumin.

"It's easy to incorporate Lebanese dishes into American kitchens because most of the ingredients are widely available in most supermarkets. In addition to our grocery stores, we're lucky at *Cooking Light* to have access to several local Middle Eastern markets, which is where we go for the freshest and best ingredients for these types of dishes." Vanessa Johnson, Test Kitchens Director

Iran

The most exquisite and refined dishes of the Middle East are prepared in Iran, although they are little known abroad. Here, the cuisine is based on long-grain rice, which grows near the Caspian Sea—it's mixed with meats, vegetables, fruits, and nuts, or served plain and accompanied by sauces.

Key Characteristics of Iranian Food
- Gentle spices: cinnamon, allspice, and saffron
- Fresh herbs and yogurt
- Meat dishes served with raisins and fruits such as dates, quinces, cherries, apples, and peaches
- Sweet-and-sour flavors, combining vinegar or lemon juice with sugar
- The distinct flavor of dried limes or dried sumac (a dark wine–colored berry) in stews and soups

Turkey

The Turkish Ottoman Empire left its influence on the tables of many countries in the region, including Bulgaria, Romania, Yugoslavia, Hungary, Greece, Cyprus, Crete, Syria, Lebanon, and Egypt, as well as parts of Russia and North Africa.

Key Characteristics
- Favorite spices for meat: cinnamon and allspice
- Favorite herbs: dill, mint, and flat-leaf parsley
- Common garnishes: toasted pine nuts and dribbles of red paprika mixed with oil
- Kebabs
- Pilafs
- Stuffed vegetables
- Yogurt dishes
- Nut sauces
- Extraordinary variety of *boreks* (savory pies) filled with cheese, spinach, minced meat, or mashed pumpkin

North Africa

The fourth distinctive cooking style is found in North Africa, the most refined and delicious of which is that of Morocco. Here, cooking is derived from the old court cuisines of the great dynasties, when Morocco was the center of an empire that extended throughout Spain, Tunisia, and Algeria.

Key Characteristics
- Cumin and chiles: used to flavor cold vegetable appetizers as well as fish dishes
- A blend of flavors—including cinnamon, ginger, saffron, mint, and cilantro—which may be very delicate or peppery hot, and where savory may be married with sweet
- Couscous
- *Harissa,* a paste of garlic and chile peppers
- Olives and preserved lemons
- Meat partnered with vegetables or with such fruit as prunes or quinces
- Paper-thin pancakes
- Savory stews called *tagines*
- Steamed dishes

Yogurt-Tahini Dip

You can find tahini in most grocery stores on the shelves with the peanut butter.

1	cup plain low-fat yogurt
3	tablespoons tahini (sesame-seed paste)
2	tablespoons fresh lemon juice
1	tablespoon chopped fresh flat-leaf parsley
½	teaspoon salt
1	garlic clove, crushed

1. Combine all ingredients in a large bowl; cover and refrigerate 30 minutes. Yield: 1 cup (serving size: 1 tablespoon).

CALORIES 27 (60% from fat); FAT 1.8g (sat 0.4g, mono 0.6g, poly 0.6g); PROTEIN 1.3g; CARB 1.9g; FIBER 0.3g; CHOL 1mg; IRON 0.3mg; SODIUM 87mg; CALC 41mg

Falafel

This Middle Eastern speciality is generally served in a pita half, but you can also serve the patties as appetizers.

1½   cups dried chickpeas (garbanzo beans, about 12 ounces)
2   cups chopped fresh cilantro
1   teaspoon ground cumin
1   teaspoon ground allspice
¼   teaspoon salt
¼   teaspoon black pepper
⅛   teaspoon ground red pepper
5   garlic cloves, peeled
1   onion, quartered
1   leek, trimmed and cut into 3 pieces
6   tablespoons olive oil, divided
Yogurt-Tahini Dip (page 428)
8   (6-inch) pitas, cut in half

1. Sort and wash chickpeas; place in a large bowl. Cover with water to 2 inches above beans. Cover; let stand 8 hours. Drain.
2. Combine chickpeas and next 9 ingredients in a food processor; process until mixture resembles coarse meal. Divide mixture into 16 equal portions, shaping each into a ½-inch-thick patty.
3. Heat 2 tablespoons oil in a large nonstick skillet. Add 5 patties; cook 3 minutes on each side or until golden. Repeat procedure twice with remaining oil, ending with 6 patties.
4. Spread 1 tablespoon Yogurt-Tahini Dip in each pita half; fill with 1 patty. Yield: 8 servings (serving size: 2 pita halves).

CALORIES 430 (29% from fat); FAT 13.9g (sat 1.8g, mono 8.3g, poly 2.5g); PROTEIN 14.6g; CARB 63.3g; FIBER 5.3g; CHOL 0mg; IRON 5.7mg; SODIUM 398mg; CALC 140mg

Fool (or Fül) Medammes (Fava Bean Salad)

Fava beans are large, flat beans that resemble big lima beans. They come in large pods that are not edible unless the pod is very, very young. Fava beans are very popular in Mediterranean and Middle Eastern dishes.

1⅓   cups dried fava beans (about 9 ounces)
¼   cup chopped fresh flat-leaf parsley
2½   tablespoons extra-virgin olive oil
2   tablespoons fresh lemon juice
½   teaspoon kosher salt
½   teaspoon ground cumin
3   garlic cloves, crushed
1   hard-cooked large egg, finely chopped

1. Sort and wash beans; place in a large saucepan. Cover with water to 2 inches above beans. Cover; let stand 8 hours. Drain beans.
2. Return beans to pan. Cover with water to 2 inches above beans. Bring to a boil; cover, reduce heat, and simmer 45 minutes or until tender. Drain well. Place beans in a medium bowl. Stir in parsley and next 5 ingredients; toss gently. Sprinkle with egg. Yield: 8 servings (serving size: ½ cup).

CALORIES 160 (30% from fat); FAT 5.4g (sat 0.9g, mono 3.5g, poly 0.7g); PROTEIN 9.3g; CARB 19.5g; FIBER 4.8g; CHOL 28mg; IRON 2.5mg; SODIUM 134mg; CALC 42mg

Baked Kibbeh

This popular dish has many variations, but the standard ingredients are ground meat (usually lamb), bulgur, and various seasonings. Traditionally, the meat may be raw or cooked; we cook ours because of food-safety issues for ground meats.

Stuffing:

1	teaspoon butter
3	cups chopped onion
½	pound lean ground lamb
⅓	cup pine nuts, toasted
2	teaspoons ground cinnamon
2	teaspoons ground allspice
½	teaspoon salt
½	teaspoon pepper
1	teaspoon pomegranate molasses (optional)

Kibbeh:

2	cups uncooked bulgur
2	cups minced fresh onion
2	teaspoons ground cinnamon
2	teaspoons ground allspice
½	teaspoon salt
½	teaspoon pepper
1	pound lean ground lamb

Cooking spray

2	teaspoons butter

1. Preheat oven to 350°.

2. To prepare stuffing, melt 1 teaspoon butter in a large nonstick skillet over medium-high heat. Add 3 cups onion; sauté 3 minutes. Add ½ pound lamb, and cook until browned, stirring to crumble. Remove from heat. Stir in pine nuts, next 4 ingredients, and pomegranate molasses, if desired. Set stuffing aside.

3. To prepare kibbeh, combine bulgur and next 6 ingredients in a large bowl. Press half of kibbeh into bottom of an 11 x 7-inch baking dish coated with cooking spray. Spread stuffing over kibbeh. Press remaining kibbeh over stuffing. Cut kibbeh into quarters. Press thumb into center of each quarter, leaving an indentation. Place ½ teaspoon butter into each indentation. Bake at 350° for 20 minutes. Let stand 5 minutes. Cut each quarter in half. Yield: 8 servings.

CALORIES 335 (29% from fat); FAT 10.7g (sat 3.4g, mono 3.8g, poly 3.1g); PROTEIN 25g; CARB 38.4g; FIBER 9.1g; CHOL 60mg; IRON 3.9mg; SODIUM 376mg; CALC 68mg

---

Making Kibbeh — **Test Kitchen SECRET**

Moistening your fingers helps in assembling this layered pie. Pomegranate molasses is available in Middle Eastern markets or in a supermarket's international-food section.

Tabbouleh (Parsley, Tomato, and Bulgur Salad)

The amount of bulgur used varies according to family tradition. We've included less here to allow the flavors of the tomato and parsley to come through.

4	cups diced tomato
⅔	cup chopped fresh flat-leaf parsley
⅓	cup thinly sliced green onions
¼	cup uncooked bulgur
¼	cup chopped fresh mint
2½	teaspoons extra-virgin olive oil
2	tablespoons fresh lemon juice
½	teaspoon kosher salt
½	teaspoon ground allspice
¼	teaspoon ground cinnamon
¼	teaspoon freshly ground black pepper
5	large iceberg lettuce leaves

1. Combine first 5 ingredients in a large bowl. Cover; let stand 30 minutes. Stir in oil and next 5 ingredients; toss well. Serve with lettuce leaves. Yield: 5 servings (serving size: 1 cup salad and 1 lettuce leaf).

CALORIES 83 (31% from fat); FAT 2.9g (sat 0.4g, mono 1.8g, poly 0.5g); PROTEIN 2.6g; CARB 14g; FIBER 3.6g; CHOL 0mg; IRON 1.6mg; SODIUM 255mg; CALC 31mg

Hummus Bi Tahina

Hummus is a traditional Middle Eastern sauce made from mashed chickpeas and seasoned with lemon juice, garlic, and olive or sesame oil. It's usually served as a dip for pita bread. When you add tahini (sesame-seed paste), it becomes Hummus Bi Tahina.

2	(15½-ounce) cans chickpeas (garbanzo beans), undrained
3	small garlic cloves
¼	cup plus 1 tablespoon tahini (sesame-seed paste)
¼	cup fresh lemon juice
3	tablespoons water

1. Drain chickpeas, reserving ¼ cup liquid, and set aside.
2. Drop garlic through food chute with food processor on; process 10 seconds or until minced. Add chickpeas, reserved ¼ cup liquid, tahini, lemon juice, and water; process 3 minutes or until smooth, scraping sides of bowl occasionally.
3. Spoon tahini mixture into a serving bowl. Serve immediately, or cover and chill. Yield: 3 cups (serving size: 2 tablespoons).

CALORIES 44 (37% from fat); FAT 1.8g (sat 0.3g, mono 0.6g, poly 0.7g); PROTEIN 2.4g; CARB 5.5g; FIBER 1.1g; CHOL 0mg; IRON 0.7mg; SODIUM 74mg; CALC 28mg

---

Tahini Substitute | Test Kitchen SECRET

See "Nut Butters" on page 365 for a tip on using cashew butter as a replacement for tahini when you're making hummus.

Burghul bi Jibn wal Batinjan (Bulgur with Cheese and Eggplant)

Combining bulgur with eggplant and *halumi* cheese, this Syrian favorite (pronounced boor-GHOUL bee jeebn wal bet-in-JAN) makes a lovely vegetarian entrée. Coarse- or medium-ground bulgur works best. Halumi is a firm, chewy, rather salty cheese. To reduce its saltiness, soak the cheese in a bowl of fresh water for half an hour. You can also substitute mozzarella.

1½	cups (6 ounces) diced halumi cheese
6	cups (1-inch) cubed eggplant (about 1 pound)
¾	teaspoon salt, divided
4	teaspoons olive oil, divided
4	cups vertically sliced onion
2	cups uncooked coarse-ground bulgur
3¼	cups boiling water
¼	teaspoon pepper

1. Soak cheese in a bowl of water for 30 minutes. Drain.
2. Place eggplant in a colander; sprinkle with ½ teaspoon salt. Toss well. Drain 30 minutes. Rinse and pat dry with paper towels.
3. Heat 1 teaspoon oil in a large nonstick skillet over medium-high heat. Add onion; sauté 15 minutes or until golden brown, stirring frequently. Add ¼ teaspoon salt, bulgur, boiling water, and pepper; bring to a boil. Cover, reduce heat to medium low, and simmer 15 minutes or until liquid is absorbed.
4. Heat 1 teaspoon oil in a large nonstick skillet over medium-high heat. Add eggplant; sauté 10 minutes or until browned. Combine cheese, bulgur mixture, eggplant, and 2 teaspoons oil in a Dutch oven. Toss well to coat; place over medium heat 5 minutes or until cheese is soft. Serve hot. Yield: 6 servings (serving size: 1½ cups).

CALORIES 325 (30% from fat); FAT 11g (sat 4.8g, mono 2.3g, poly 0.6g); PROTEIN 13.5g; CARB 47.1g; FIBER 12g; CHOL 21mg; IRON 1.6mg; SODIUM 622mg; CALC 306mg

CHAPTER 15

Asia & India

Asian-style foods are inherently low in fat yet full of bold
and daring flavors and interesting textures. Although the different cuisines
share some common bonds, each has its own distinct characteristics.
And in Indian cooking, the focus is on spices instead of fat,
making this way of cooking inherently healthy.

China

China is home to more than a fifth of the world's population—a country so vast and ancient that unique regional styles were bound to develop. **Shaped by climate, geography, and ingredient availability, "Chinese cooking" is not one but many different cuisines.** The varied styles have had millennia to thoroughly define themselves, gaining adherents, experts, and enthusiastic diners along the way.

Modern times have blurred some of the regional lines, and it is now not unusual to find specialties from one area prepared in all parts of the country. But the traditions of each area endure, so a devotee of Chinese cooking is always aware of a dish's origin—and the flavors, ingredients, and techniques that go with it. Because of that, **it helps to understand the four primary regions, or schools, of Chinese cooking.**

The Northern School The Northern School includes Beijing, the northern provinces, and Inner Mongolia. Its cuisine is the most eclectic, incorporating the refined cooking of palace kitchens and the Shandong province (where

> ### How We Lightened It
> **Test Kitchen SECRET**
>
> Most classic Chinese cuisines are inherently healthful because of their reliance on vegetables, vegetable oils, stir-frying, and fat-free condiments. But sodium levels can get pretty high because many condiments, such as soy sauce, oyster sauce, and hoisin sauce, are high in sodium. Our solution? We used low-sodium soy sauce. We also kept the fat down by using less vegetable oil than traditional recipes call for.

classic Chinese cuisine originated), as well as Mongolian and Muslim dishes.
- *Claim to fame:* noodles, steamed breads, and pancakes (served instead of rice)
- *Cooking style:* stir-frying, pan-frying, braising, and barbecuing
- *Favorite seasonings:* garlic, chives, leeks, star anise, and sweet bean sauces
- *Signature dish:* Moo Shu Pork with Mandarin Pancakes

The Eastern School The Eastern School encompasses two centers, Shanghai and Fuzhou, along with the eastern provinces. Nicknamed "Heaven on Earth" and "The Land of Fish and Rice," it's renowned for its vegetarian specialties and subtle, refined flavors.

- *Claim to fame:* source of China's best soy sauces and some of the best rice wines
- *Cooking style:* red-cooking (braising in soy sauce-based mixture), stir-frying, steaming, and quick simmering
- *Signature dishes:* Cinnamon-Beef Noodles and Steamed Vegetarian Dumplings

The Western School The Western School, acclaimed for its spicy dishes, includes Sichuan, Hunan, and Yunnan provinces. Its sultry, sub-tropical climate may be one reason it is also known as "The Land of Abundance."

- *Claim to fame:* known for tongue-tingling heat
- *Cooking style:* combining flavorings and condiments for intricate blends of hot, sour, sweet, and salty in one mouthful
- *Favorite seasonings:* chiles—fresh, dried, and in pastes; peppercorns; ginger; garlic; water chestnuts; bamboo shoots; mushrooms; and nuts
- *Signature dishes:* Sichuan-Style Stir-fried Chicken with Peanuts

The Southern School The Southern School includes Canton—praised by some as the haute-cuisine capital of China—and Hong Kong, known for combining Cantonese cooking with contemporary techniques and ingredients from the West. The Cantonese are considered some of China's most adventurous diners, relishing all sorts of exotica.

- *Claim to fame:* masters of *dim sum* (snacks)
- *Cooking style:* ingenious blending of superb ingredients and refined techniques
- *Signature dishes:* Steamed Salmon with Black Bean Sauce, Hoisin Barbecued Chicken, Stir-fried Broccoli with Oyster Sauce, and Shrimp Fried Rice

Long-Grain Rice

In America, most people don't normally rinse rice before cooking, but it's routine in China. Rinsing removes the white powder caused by polishing and allows the grains to separate during cooking, creating a fluffier effect. (See page 260 for more information on rice.)

2¼ cups uncooked long-grain rice
4 cups water

1. Place rice in a fine sieve, and rinse with cold running water, stirring with fingers, until water runs clear.
2. Combine rice and 4 cups water in a saucepan; bring to a boil. Cover, reduce heat, and simmer for 17 minutes or until liquid is absorbed. Fluff rice with a fork. Yield: 6 cups (serving size: 1 cup).

CALORIES 253 (2% from fat); FAT 0.5g (sat 0.1g, mono 0.1g, poly 0.1g); PROTEIN 4.9g; CARB 55.5g; FIBER 0.9g; CHOL 0mg; IRON 3mg; SODIUM 3mg; CALC 19mg

For additional Chinese-style dishes, see Asian Vegetable Stir-fry (page 86), Shrimp and Broccoli in Chili Sauce (page 87), and Chicken-Cashew Stir-fry (page 89).

Chinese food is not one but many different cuisines from several different regions.

The Chinese Pantry

Lovers of Chinese cooking will want to keep these ingredients on hand. Many are in well-stocked supermarkets; most are available in Asian markets or at www.ethnicgrocer.com or other similar sites. Unless otherwise specified, all condiments should be refrigerated after opening.

Type	Description
Black Vinegar	This kind of rice vinegar tends to be lighter and sweeter than Western vinegars. It has a mellow flavor and is used in sauces and dressings. ***A good substitute is Worcestershire sauce.***
Chile Paste or Sauce	This is a spicy seasoning of crushed chile peppers, oil, vinegar, garlic, and other flavorings. You can substitute crushed red pepper, but start with one-third the amount and add more to taste.
Dark Sesame Oil	Nutty and rich, it's made from roasted or toasted sesame seeds and is not interchangeable with the pressed sesame seed oil found in health-food stores. Because it smokes at high temperatures, it's primarily used as a seasoning and not for stir-frying.
Dried Chile Peppers	These are available in a range of sizes in Asian markets. The smaller the pepper, the more intense its heat. While both fresh and dried peppers are used in Chinese cooking, the dried ones are used to infuse oils, sauces, and dressings with their spicy flavor. They're normally left whole, cut in half lengthwise, or finely ground. Seeds may be left in or discarded, but they will increase the intensity or hotness of the chile flavor.
Dried Chinese Mushrooms	Pungent dried shiitake mushrooms (also called black mushrooms) impart a strong smoky flavor. Another variety, dried wood ear mushrooms, is relished for its crunchy texture.
Fermented or Salted Black Beans	Used to season sauces, these are black soybeans that have been fermented with seasonings like ginger, orange peel, and licorice, then dried. The beans should be rinsed and drained before using; they refrigerate indefinitely. Look for dried beans in packages or plastic bags rather than in cans or jars.
Ginger	It's one of the most widely used seasonings in Asian cooking. When buying fresh ginger, look for hefty, smooth, shiny knobs. Ginger also comes in crystallized and pickled forms for other applications.
Hoisin Sauce	A sauce made with soybeans, sugar, vinegar, and spices, it's sweet and fairly thick. The main uses are in dipping sauces and in marinades for barbecuing and roasting.
Oyster Sauce	This is a Cantonese staple that's made from oysters, salt, and seasonings. It's often used in sauces for seafood, meat, and vegetables. You can substitute an equal amount of soy sauce.
Plum Sauce	Also known as duck sauce, it's made from plums, apricots, vinegar, and sugar. In China, it's often served with roasted goose or duck; in the United States, it's the table sauce in American-Cantonese restaurants.
Rice Wine	This is an all-purpose cooking wine made from fermented rice. You can substitute sake or Japanese rice wine or a high-quality dry sherry (but not cream sherry). The best variety of rice wine is Shaohsing.
Soy Sauce	Made from fermented soybeans and wheat, its flavor varies by manufacturer and aging process. Regular soy sauce contains 1,030 milligrams of sodium per tablespoon; light or low-sodium versions have 484 milligrams.

Shrimp Fried Rice

Fried rice is an extremely versatile dish that can be made with all kinds of meat, seafood, and vegetables.

2   tablespoons fat-free, less-sodium chicken broth
2   tablespoons rice wine or sake
1   tablespoon low-sodium soy sauce
1   teaspoon dark sesame oil
½   teaspoon salt
¼   teaspoon freshly ground black pepper
2   tablespoons vegetable oil
2   large eggs, lightly beaten
2   cups chopped green onions
1   tablespoon minced peeled fresh ginger
5   cups cooked long-grain rice, chilled
1   pound medium shrimp, cooked, peeled, and coarsely chopped
1   (10-ounce) package frozen green peas, thawed

1. Combine first 6 ingredients in a bowl; set mixture aside.
2. Heat vegetable oil in a wok or large nonstick skillet over medium-high heat. Add eggs; stir-fry 30 seconds or until soft-scrambled. Add onions and ginger; stir-fry 1 minute. Add rice, shrimp, and peas; stir-fry 3 minutes or until thoroughly heated. Add broth mixture; toss gently to coat. Yield: 6 servings (serving size: 1⅓ cups).

CALORIES 380 (19% from fat); FAT 7.9g (sat 1.7g, mono 2.5g, poly 3.1g); PROTEIN 20.8g; CARB 53.3g; FIBER 1.7g; CHOL 184mg; IRON 4.8mg; SODIUM 527mg; CALC 83mg

---

Chilled Rice

Test Kitchen SECRET

In this and other fried-rice recipes, the cooked rice must be chilled to prevent its grains from sticking. To chill, spread the cooked rice on a jelly-roll pan; cover and refrigerate 8 hours or overnight.

Steamed Vegetarian Dumplings

Dumplings have a prominent place in Chinese cuisine and are prepared in many different ways for holidays and festivals. They vary by region, and the ingredients depend on area availability.

½   pound firm tofu, drained and cut into ½-inch slices
1   cup boiling water
½   cup dried wood ear mushrooms (about ½ ounce)
½   cup drained, sliced water chestnuts
¾   cup shredded carrot
1   tablespoon minced peeled fresh ginger
1   tablespoon minced green onions
4   teaspoons cornstarch
1   teaspoon salt
2   teaspoons low-sodium soy sauce
½   teaspoon dark sesame oil
1   large egg, lightly beaten
50   won ton wrappers or gyoza skins
1   teaspoon cornstarch
Cooking spray
½   cup low-sodium soy sauce
¼   cup water

1. Place tofu on several layers of paper towels, and cover with additional paper towels. Let stand 30 minutes, pressing down occasionally. Place tofu in a large bowl, and mash with a fork until smooth. Set tofu aside.
2. Combine boiling water and mushrooms in a bowl; cover and let stand 20 minutes or until soft. Drain. Place mushrooms and water chestnuts in a food processor; pulse 5 times or until minced. Add mushroom mixture, carrot, and the next 7 ingredients to tofu; stir well.
3. Working with 1 won ton wrapper at a time (cover remaining wrappers to keep them from drying), spoon 1 teaspoon tofu mixture into center of each wrapper. Moisten edges of wrapper with water; bring 2 opposite corners to center,

pinching points to seal. Bring remaining 2 corners to center, pinching edges together to seal. Place dumplings, seam sides up, on a large baking sheet sprinkled with 1 teaspoon cornstarch (cover loosely with a towel to keep them from drying).

4. Arrange one-third of the dumplings in a single layer in a vegetable steamer coated with cooking spray. Steam dumplings, covered, for 15 minutes. Remove the dumplings from steamer; set aside,

and keep warm. Repeat the procedure with the remaining dumplings.

5. Combine ½ cup soy sauce and ¼ cup water in a small bowl. Serve with dumplings. Yield: 50 appetizers (serving size: 1 dumpling and about ¾ teaspoon sauce).

CALORIES 35 (15% from fat); FAT 0.6g (sat 0.1g, mono 0.1g, poly 0.2g); PROTEIN 1.5g; CARB 5.8g; FIBER 0.2g; CHOL 5mg; IRON 0.6mg; SODIUM 179mg; CALC 10mg

How to Make Steamed Vegetarian Dumplings

1. Working with 1 won ton wrapper at a time, spoon 1 teaspoon tofu mixture into the center of each wrapper (keep remaining wrappers covered to prevent drying).

2. Moisten edges of wrapper with water, and bring 2 opposite corners to the center, pinching points to seal. Bring the other 2 corners to the center, pinching points together.

3. Place on a large baking sheet sprinkled with cornstarch (cover loosely with a towel to keep them from drying).

4. Arrange one-third of dumplings in a single layer in a vegetable steamer coated with cooking spray. Steam, covered, for 15 minutes.

Dim Sum

In Chinatowns across America, dim sum is the rage. Now you can make these fun finger foods at home. Cantonese for "heart's delight" or "a bit of heart" (depending on the translation), dim sum includes an exotic variety of small, mouth-watering snacks.

Four-Flavor Dumplings

Gyoza (ghe-O-za) skins are round wrappers available at Oriental food stores. Won ton wrappers cut into circles can be substituted.

1	cup boiling water
½	ounce dried shiitake mushrooms
¼	pound ground chicken or turkey
¼	cup thawed, drained, and squeezed dry frozen chopped spinach
¼	cup minced green onions
1½	teaspoons cornstarch
1½	teaspoons dry sherry
1½	teaspoons oyster sauce
½	teaspoon dark sesame oil
⅛	teaspoon salt
32	(3-inch) gyoza skins
⅓	cup frozen tiny green peas, thawed
¼	cup finely diced carrot
8	medium shrimp, peeled and quartered
2	teaspoons cornstarch

Steamed green cabbage leaves

1. Combine boiling water and mushrooms in a bowl; cover and let stand 30 minutes. Drain; discard stems, and mince caps.

2. Combine chicken and next 7 ingredients in a large bowl; add 3 tablespoons minced mushrooms (set remaining mushrooms aside), and stir well. Set chicken mixture aside.

3. Working with 1 gyoza skin at a time (cover remaining skins to keep them from drying), moisten 4 equally spaced points around edge of skin with water. Spoon about 1 teaspoon chicken mixture into center of each circle. Bring 4 moistened points over filling to center, pressing fingers together. Push fingers toward center of circle to form 4 pockets (if pockets do not open enough for chicken mixture to be visible, use the tip of a knife to separate the dough and open pockets).

4. Working with 1 dumpling at a time, fill first pocket with minced mushrooms, second pocket with peas, third pocket with carrot, and fourth pocket with 1 piece of shrimp. Place filled dumplings on a large baking sheet sprinkled with 2 teaspoons cornstarch (cover loosely with a towel to keep them from drying).

5. Line a bamboo steamer with steamed cabbage leaves. Place filled dumplings ½ inch apart in steamer, and cover with steamer lid. Add water to a large skillet to a depth of 1 inch; bring to a boil. Place steamer in skillet, and steam dumplings 10 minutes; remove dumplings from steamer. Serve dumplings with dipping sauces. Yield: 32 appetizers (serving size: 1 dumpling).

CALORIES 31 (12% from fat); PROTEIN 2.2g; FAT 0.4g (sat 0.1g, mono 0.1g, poly 0.1g); CARB 4.5g; FIBER 0.2g; CHOL 8mg; IRON 0.4mg; SODIUM 63mg; CALC 10mg

Shaping Four-Flavor Dumplings — Test Kitchen SECRET

Moisten 4 equally spaced points around edge of gyoza skin. Bring 4 moistened points together, pressing with fingers. Push fingers toward center of gyoza skin to form 4 pockets.

Korea

Korean cuisine has its own distinct flavor combinations and quintessential dishes.

Associate Food Editor Ann Taylor Pittman's mother is from Korea, and Ann says that she has taken what she learned from her mother's kitchen into adulthood and basically stayed true to the way Koreans eat—using just a little meat for flavoring, adding generous amounts of garlic and chiles to intensely season dishes, and enjoying little nibbles of relish- or salad-type sides with meals. Ann has shared some of the dishes from her Korean kitchen with us, so we'll share them with you.

"I transform leftover ham or bits of pork into a fried rice dish that I serve in an egg crêpe. I often soak meat in a sweet-salty or sweet-spicy marinade that has all the flavors of traditional *bulgogi*. And now, I even crave *kimchi* (which, to my mother's chagrin, I rejected as a child), frequently sitting down to a simple supper of steamed rice, lettuce leaves, toasted seaweed, and the pungent relish." Ann Pittman, Food Editor

Note: Kimchi is a spicy-hot condiment that is served at almost every Korean meal. It's made of a fermented vegetable, such as cabbage, that has been pickled and stored tightly in sealed pots or jars and buried in the ground.

Korean Pantry

These recipes use mostly everyday ingredients, but there are a few authentic items you may have to get by going to an Asian market.

Type	Description
Sambal Oelek	Sambal oelek or crushed red pepper supplies the heat in Korean recipes. Sambal oelek, unlike some other chile sauces, is neither sweetened nor seasoned with garlic, so the pure taste and fiery heat of chiles really come through. If you'd like to tame the flame, start by using only about half the amount of chile sauce or crushed red pepper called for. You can always add more, but it's hard to take it back.
Toasted Sesame Seeds	Many Korean recipes call for toasted sesame seeds. Save yourself the time and trouble of toasting your own by purchasing pretoasted seeds, available in most Asian markets.
Rice Cakes	Sliced rice cakes can be found either in the freezer case or vacuum-packed on the shelves of your local Asian market. (They're sometimes labeled "rice ovaletts.") Sliced rice cakes are about the size and shape of sliced water chestnuts. Thawed and tossed into soup, they become soft but retain a pleasant resilience.
Mirin	Mirin is a low-alcohol, golden-hued rice wine that adds subtle sweetness to some of these dishes. Many large supermarkets carry it in the Asian foods section.

Korean Barbecue Tips

Bulgogi, Korean barbecue, is one of Korea's most famous dishes. At Korean restaurants and in many Korean homes, you'll find people seated around the tabletop grill, which is used to quickly sear thin slices of marinated meat. The meat is often wrapped with short-grain rice in red leaf lettuce leaves with fresh *shiso* (perilla leaves).

Paper-thin slices of beef or pork are bathed in a sweet-salty or sweet-spicy marinade, then quickly seared on a hot grill.

Great Bulgogi
Test Kitchen SECRET

Here are some tips on making great Korean barbecue.

- Slice the meat paper-thin so it absorbs the flavors of the marinade and cooks quickly. Freezing it briefly first makes this task easier. Use a very sharp knife or mandoline to create 1/16-inch-thick slices.
- Although Koreans cook bulgogi on tabletop grills, we've developed these recipes for standard backyard grills. Because the meat is sliced very thinly, you'll need to cook it on a wire grilling basket. For best results, allow the basket to heat on the grill a few minutes before adding the meat.
- The raw meat tends to clump on the basket. Just spread it out as best you can, and toss with tongs.
- You can also cook the meat in a large, heavy skillet (cast iron works great) or grill pan over high heat for 3 to 5 minutes.

Bulgogi (Korean Beef Barbecue)

"Korean barbecue" is a bit of a misnomer because the meat is grilled quickly instead of being cooked the way true barbecue is done—covered and grilled over low heat for a long period of time.

- 1 pound top sirloin steak, trimmed
- 1 tablespoon brown sugar
- 3 tablespoons low-sodium soy sauce
- 1 tablespoon mirin (sweet rice wine)
- 1 teaspoon minced peeled fresh ginger
- 1 teaspoon dark sesame oil
- 3 garlic cloves, minced

Cooking spray

1. Wrap beef in plastic wrap; freeze 1 hour or until firm. Remove plastic wrap; cut beef diagonally across grain into 1/16-inch-thick slices.
2. Combine beef, sugar, and next 5 ingredients in a large zip-top plastic bag. Seal and marinate in refrigerator 1 hour, turning bag occasionally.
3. Prepare grill.
4. Place a wire grilling basket on grill rack. Remove beef from bag; discard marinade. Place beef on grilling basket coated with cooking spray; grill 5 minutes or until desired degree of doneness, turning frequently. Yield: 4 servings (serving size: 3 ounces).

CALORIES 208 (33% from fat); FAT 7.6g (sat 2.7g, mono 3.2g, poly 0.7g); PROTEIN 26.1g; CARB 6.4g; FIBER 0.2g; CHOL 76mg; IRON 3.1mg; SODIUM 457mg; CALC 19mg

"I remember having this dish for the first time in a Korean restaurant in Memphis, Tennessee, when I was 4 years old. There was something miraculous about those tender, superthin slices of beef. After that trip, I repeatedly begged my mother for the 'Korean salty beef,' which she often prepares on the stovetop."
Ann Pittman, Food Editor

Pork and Kimchi Dumplings

Serve this as an appetizer—the recipe doubles easily if you're expecting lots of guests. You can use won ton wrappers in place of gyoza skins.

Dumplings:

½	cup finely chopped shiitake mushroom caps
½	cup finely chopped Shang Kimchi (right)
¼	cup finely chopped green onions
1	teaspoon cornstarch
1	teaspoon minced peeled fresh ginger
2	teaspoons mirin (sweet rice wine)
2	teaspoons low-sodium soy sauce
½	teaspoon dry mustard
½	teaspoon dark sesame oil
4	ounces ground pork
24	gyoza skins
1	teaspoon cornstarch

Cooking spray

Sauce:

1	tablespoon minced green onions
3	tablespoons low-sodium soy sauce
1½	tablespoons mirin (sweet rice wine)
1½	tablespoons rice vinegar
1	teaspoon sesame seeds, toasted
½	teaspoon dark sesame oil

1. To prepare dumplings, combine first 10 ingredients. Working with 1 gyoza skin at a time (cover remaining skins to prevent drying), spoon about 1½ teaspoons pork mixture into center of each skin. Moisten edges of skins with water. Fold in half, pinching edges together to seal. Place dumplings, seam sides up, on a baking sheet sprinkled with 1 teaspoon cornstarch (cover loosely with a towel to prevent drying).

2. Arrange half of the dumplings in a single layer in a bamboo or vegetable steamer coated with cooking spray. Steam dumplings, covered, for 10 minutes. Remove dumplings from steamer; keep warm. Repeat with remaining dumplings.

3. To prepare sauce, combine 1 tablespoon onions and remaining ingredients. Serve sauce with dumplings. Yield: 8 servings (serving size: 3 dumplings and about 2 teaspoons sauce).

CALORIES 131 (24% from fat); FAT 3.5g (sat 1g, mono 1.4g, poly 0.8g); PROTEIN 5.8g; CARB 17.7g; FIBER 1.2g; CHOL 12mg; IRON 1.3mg; SODIUM 466mg; CALC 29mg

"My mom always keeps a jar of spicy, garlicky kimchi in the refrigerator. She often buys it from an Asian market, but sometimes she makes her own."
Ann Pittman, Food Editor

Shang Kimchi (Summer, or Raw, Kimchi)

Most kimchi is fermented for days or weeks to develop a pungent flavor. Although this recipe skips the fermentation step, it tastes authentic. Save some for the Pork and Kimchi Dumplings (left).

14	cups coarsely chopped napa (Chinese) cabbage (about 2 pounds)
3	tablespoons kosher salt
1	tablespoon sesame seeds, toasted
2½	tablespoons sambal oelek or Thai chile paste
2	tablespoons minced fresh garlic
2	teaspoons dark sesame oil

1. Place cabbage and salt in a large bowl, tossing gently to combine. Weigh down cabbage with another bowl. Let stand at room temperature 3 hours, tossing occasionally. Drain and rinse with cold water. Drain and squeeze dry.

2. Combine cabbage, sesame seeds, and remaining ingredients. Cover and refrigerate at least 4 hours before serving. Yield: 4 cups (serving size: ¼ cup).

CALORIES 19 (47% from fat); FAT 1g (sat 0.2g, mono 0.4g, poly 0.4g); PROTEIN 0.9g; CARB 2.5g; FIBER 1.9g; CHOL 0mg; IRON 0.3mg; SODIUM 302mg; CALC 51mg

Cambodia

The cuisine of Cambodia is complex in flavor, simple to prepare, and exceptionally lean.

The appeal of Cambodian cooking is linked to the country's scarred history—it's a hybrid cuisine that combines some of the best traditions of the Chinese, Vietnamese, French, Thai, and Indian people who have invaded or influenced Cambodia through the centuries. **Cambodians do have one distinguishing feature with regard to their taste in food: a strong aversion to fat.**

How We Lightened It	Test Kitchen SECRET

Cambodian food is, by nature, low in fat. The focus is on the flavor and the cooking methods instead of fat, so you don't have to do anything to traditional Cambodian dishes other than keep portion sizes reasonable.

Cambodian Pantry

We are able to find most of these ingredients in our local Asian markets, though many are available at supermarkets, as well. Some of them might not be labeled consistently, so ask a clerk for help if necessary.

Type	Description
Bean Threads or Cellophane Noodles	Made from the starch of green mung beans, they have a different texture from traditional noodles. They can also be found labeled as "transparent" or "shining" noodles, "pea-stick noodles," or "mung bean sticks."
Daikon	This is a large Asian radish, similar in appearance to a parsnip. Carrot can be substituted.
Dried Jellied Fungus	Available only in Asian stores, it's similar in appearance to dried wood ear mushrooms.
Fine Rice Vermicelli	Unlike traditional vermicelli, these Asian noodles are wide and flat (more similar in shape to fettuccine). You can also find them labeled as "rice-stick noodles."
Fish Sauce	Made from water, anchovies, and salt, this sauce is very potent—a little goes a long way. It's also very high in sodium: 1 tablespoon contains the sodium of 1 teaspoon of salt. Use it sparingly.
Oyster Sauce	This concentrated sauce made from oysters, brine, and soy sauce is a commonly used Asian condiment.
Rice Paper	This edible, translucent paper is similar to phyllo dough in texture. Rice paper can also be found labeled as "dried pastry flake."
Udon Noodles	These thick Japanese noodles are similar to spaghetti. They come round or square and are typically made from either wheat or corn flour.

Lort Cha (Short Rice Noodles)

This is a quick-and-easy stir-fry, and most of the ingredients are quite familiar in American kitchens.

- 2 tablespoons low-sodium soy sauce
- 1 tablespoon oyster sauce
- ½ teaspoon sugar
- 1 pound uncooked udon noodles or spaghetti
- 1½ teaspoons vegetable oil
- Cooking spray
- 2 (4-ounce) lean, boned center-cut loin pork chops (about ¾ inch thick), cut into thin strips
- 2 garlic cloves, minced
- 1 large egg, lightly beaten
- 1½ cups fresh bean sprouts
- 1½ cups thinly sliced green cabbage
- 1½ cups julienne-cut green onions

1. Combine first 3 ingredients in a bowl. Stir well, and set aside.
2. Cook noodles in boiling water 10 minutes (discard noodle seasoning packet). Drain; rinse under cold water. Set aside.
3. Heat oil in a wok or large skillet coated with cooking spray over high heat. Add pork and garlic, and stir-fry 2 minutes. Add soy sauce mixture, and stir-fry 30 seconds. Add egg, and stir-fry 30 seconds. Add cooked noodles, bean sprouts, sliced cabbage, and green onions; stir-fry 3 minutes or until vegetables wilt and udon noodles are thoroughly heated. Yield: 4 servings (serving size: 1½ cups).

CALORIES 326 (23% from fat); FAT 8.2g (sat 2.3g, mono 3g, poly 1.8g); PROTEIN 21.9g; CARB 40.4g; FIBER 3.8g; CHOL 91mg; IRON 3.4mg; SODIUM 411mg; CALC 65mg

Chap Chai (Seafood-Vegetable Soup)

Fish balls are available in the frozen food section of most Asian markets. If you can't find them, use 7 ounces of firm white fish, cut into pieces.

- 1½ ounces dried wood ear mushrooms
- 2 cups boiling water
- ½ pound cleaned skinned squid
- ½ cup water
- 12 small clams in shells, scrubbed
- 1 teaspoon vegetable oil
- 2 large garlic cloves, minced
- 2 cups thinly sliced peeled daikon radish
- ½ pound medium shrimp, peeled and deveined
- 5 (14-ounce) cans fat-free, less-sodium chicken broth
- 1 (7-ounce) package fish balls
- 3 cups thinly sliced napa (Chinese) cabbage
- 1 cup (1½-inch) julienne-cut green onions
- ¼ cup fish sauce
- ¼ teaspoon pepper

1. Combine mushrooms and 2 cups boiling water; cover and let stand 30 minutes or until soft. Drain; cut into ¼-inch-wide strips.
2. Cut squid into ¼-inch-thick rings; set aside.
3. Bring ½ cup water to a boil in a Dutch oven. Add clams; cover and cook 3 minutes or until shells open. Discard any unopened shells. Remove clams with a slotted spoon; set aside. Pour cooking liquid into a bowl; set aside.
4. Heat oil in pan over medium-high heat. Add garlic, and sauté 2 minutes or until golden. Add reserved cooking liquid, radish, shrimp, and broth. Bring to a boil; cook 2 minutes. Add fish balls; cook 1 minute. Add mushrooms, squid, clams, cabbage, and remaining ingredients; cook 1 minute. Yield: 13 servings (serving size: 1 cup).

CALORIES 85 (24% from fat); FAT 2.3g (sat 0.5g, mono 0.6g, poly 0.7g); PROTEIN 11.6g; CARB 4.5g; FIBER 0.7g; CHOL 75mg; IRON 2mg; SODIUM 730mg; CALC 42mg

Thailand

Thai food is known for its aromatic herbs and spices, which enhance flavors as well as offer healthful benefits.

Its sensuality is what makes Thai food so special. With the first bite, you're instantly rewarded with an unexpected surprise, perhaps an accent or spice, a jolt of sweet or sour flavoring, or a combination of textures—soft, chewy, creamy, and crunchy—that intrigue and tease the palate.

Yet regardless of the individual recipe or the complexity of the ingredients, **Thai food gets its distinct flavors from four basic seasonings: salt, garlic, cilantro, and Thai or white peppercorn.** These, in turn, are supported by a cast of chiles and fish sauce. Most dishes taste best when accompanied by long-grain Thai jasmine rice.

Adapting Thai Flavors

Test Kitchen SECRET

Here are some ways you can adapt Thai flavors to your American kitchen.

Peppers: Authentic Thai cooking is very spicy. If you don't like hot food, decrease the chiles and peppercorns that are in the recipe.

Coconut milk: To see just how much trouble extracting fresh coconut milk is, we tried it in our Test Kitchens. Although it's not hard, it is time-consuming. We tasted the fresh milk side by side with diluted canned coconut milk and found the two almost identical in taste.

Palm sugar: Palm sugar is made from the sap of the sugar palm tree. In Thai markets, it's displayed in large mounds, scraped up with a paddle, and smeared onto the fresh banana leaves used to transport it. In Asian markets in the United States, it's sold in small, round crystallized blocks. Light brown sugar is an acceptable substitute.

Coconut Soup with Chicken

Galangal will give you the most authentic Thai flavor, but we liked it just as well with the fresh grated ginger.

4	cups water
1	(14-ounce) can coconut milk
½	cup sliced peeled lemongrass, crushed
20	pieces sliced peeled galangal or 15 pieces sliced peeled fresh ginger, crushed
4	serrano chiles, slightly crushed
5	kaffir lime leaves, slightly torn or 1½ teaspoons grated lime rind
1¾	pounds skinless chicken breast quarters
¾	pound skinless chicken thigh quarters
¼	cup Thai fish sauce
3	tablespoons fresh lime juice
6	tablespoons chopped fresh cilantro

1. Combine water and coconut milk in a Dutch oven; bring to a boil over medium heat. Stir in lemongrass, galangal, chiles, and lime leaves; bring to a boil. Add chicken; cover, reduce heat, and simmer 50 minutes or until chicken is done.
2. Remove chicken from broth; chill chicken 15 minutes. Strain broth through a colander into a bowl; discard solids. Return broth to pan.
3. Remove chicken from bones; discard bones. Cut chicken into pieces; return to pan. Stir in fish sauce; cook 1 minute over medium heat. Stir in lime juice. Remove from heat. Garnish with cilantro. Yield: 6 servings (serving size: 1 cup).

CALORIES 298 (51% from fat); FAT 17.0g (sat 13.3g, mono 1.4g, poly 0.9g); PROTEIN 33.3g; CARB 3.2g; FIBER 0.2g; CHOL 93mg; IRON 3.7mg; SODIUM 1,038mg; CALC 38mg

Thai Pantry

Type	Description
Bird Chiles	Although bird chiles are often identified with Thai cooking, they're actually from South America and have been embraced by Thai cooks only recently. Bird, or chiltepín, chiles are small, red or green, and very hot. Thai chiles, which look similar but are a bit larger, are just as hot and can be used in the same capacity. We call for milder serranos rather than Thai chiles as a substitute, though, because they're easier to find. In general, 2 bird chiles yield 1 teaspoon minced.
Coriander	Thais use every part of this aromatic herb for seasoning. The root is pounded with other ingredients into pastes; the seeds are ground and used to impart their grassy, peppery flavor to soups and curries. The stems and leaves, known as cilantro, are used as garnishes and in stir-fries, soups, and stews. While coriander root is important for Thai seasoning, it's not readily available, so we've substituted cilantro stems instead.
Fresh Mint	Mint is used often in combination with cilantro to flavor and garnish salads. Thais tear mint by hand instead of slicing it. Once bruised, the leaves release a potent and refreshing aroma.
Galangal	Also called Laos ginger, galangal (found in Asian markets) is that distinctive Thai flavor most Americans can't identify. We found it to be stronger, more astringent, and spicier than ginger, but you can substitute the latter.
Garlic	Most recipes incorporate garlic, a seasoning familiar to Thai cooking since ancient times.
Ginger	This aromatic and pungent rhizome has an unmistakable peppery flavor and adds a layer of spiciness.
Kaffir Lime Leaves	Kaffir lime leaf is closely identified with Thai cooking for its distinct citrusy aroma. Fresh leaves are hard to come by, but you can purchase them frozen at most Asian markets. If you can't find them, substitute lime zest.
Lemongrass	Thai cooking has brought fame to this tart herb. Its white bulb is pulverized for seasoning pastes or added to soups and stews, while the tender green stalk is thinly sliced for salads. Steeped in hot water, lemongrass also makes a refreshing tea. Look for it in the produce section of your supermarket or in Asian markets.
Shallots	Shallots have a peppery taste and an earthy scent. Thinly sliced fresh shallots are added to salads; minced shallots are used for seasoning pastes.
Thai Basil	Thais use many varieties of basil, and they taste more like licorice than the Italian kind. To retain Thai basil's fresh flavor, add it to stir-fries, soups, or stews at the last minute.
Thai Fish Sauce	This condiment has gained favor over the use of fermented fish in many parts of Thailand and in the United States because of its versatility and less intense taste and scent. It's still plenty potent, though—just a small spoonful makes a world of difference in Thai dishes.
Thai White Peppercorn	An indigenous spice, Thai white peppercorn was used to add heat long before Westerners introduced chiles. You can use white peppercorn, commonly available in supermarkets, in place of the spicier Thai variety.
Turmeric	Related to ginger, it gives food a golden color and a slightly pungent flavor. In Thai cuisine, turmeric root is grated or pounded to release its color and aroma. Since raw turmeric is not widely available in the United States, we've used the ground variety.

India

Indian cooks are masters at using spices to lend an aura of richness and depth to food. The cuisine is uncomplicated and quick, and it provides deliciously healthy meals.

While other cuisines use spices strictly as aromatics, in Indian cooking, they're also used for coloring, cooling, heating, souring, thickening, and creating texture.

Regional Styles

Typically, Indian food can be grouped according to two broad regional categories.

Northern Region In the north, near the snow-capped mountain ranges of the Himalayas, fertile plains yield grains, vegetables, and fruits, such as wheat, millet, chickpeas, lentils, walnuts, and pomegranates. **Here, the signature flavors include cumin, garlic, mint, cilantro, onion, and tomato.** Bread is a staple eaten with grilled or braised lamb, goat, chicken, and dairy products. Northeastern India is home to the lush slopes of Darjeeling, where the famous Darjeeling Orange Pekoe tea grows.

In the desert regions of northwestern India, smoke-roasted venison and wild boar are enjoyed, along with spicy yogurt-braised vegetables, millet, and chickpea breads.

Southern Region The predominantly tropical south, with its heavy monsoon rains, is the rice bowl of India. In this region, rice accompanies virtually every seafood meal. If one is vegetarian (and 60 percent of all Indians are),

| How We Lightened It | Test Kitchen SECRET |

Because of the emphasis on flavoring with spices instead of fat, the frequent use of high-fiber lentils, and the fact that most of the dishes are vegetarian, Indian food is inherently healthy. And in Indian cooking, the chicken is always skinned to allow the flavoring to penetrate the meat. If it's a lamb recipe, we make sure to use a lean cut of lamb—a cut from the leg or the loin.

One especially gratifying aspect of Indian cuisine is that its famous dishes can be successfully prepared using pots and pans found in the average American kitchen; no special equipment is required.

lentils substitute for fish. Rice is also transformed into crêpes, pancakes, noodles, dumplings, and flatbreads. Seafood or legumes served with local produce—coconut, plantain, banana, and ginger—make up the diet of those living along the southern coast.

Although black pepper, cardamom, and turmeric are indigenous to southern India, the region is best known for the hot red chiles introduced by the Portuguese in the 16th century. Therefore, southern foods tend to be hotter than their northern counterparts.

Spices: The Foundation of Indian Food

With the exception of cinnamon, cloves, and saffron, most spices need to be ground or crushed to release their fragrance. Like perfume, ground spices should be kept in airtight containers. But even under the best of conditions, ground spices retain their fragrance for only about 2 months.

Since spices are so important in Indian cooking, it's best to buy only whole spices and grind them in a spice or coffee grinder as needed. (See page 380 for more information about grinding whole spices.) **When stored in a cool cupboard, away from light, whole spices will keep for up to 2 years. After** 2 years, they don't really go bad—they just lose some of their flavor.

In Indian cooking, some spices are roasted to lend them a distinct caramelized, smoky fragrance. However, cooking removes some of the volatile and essential oils. Raw spice, in pure ground form, has far more fragrance.

Roasting Spices	Test Kitchen SECRET
When roasting spices, keep them moving in the skillet to prevent burning.	

Indian Pantry

Only a handful of spices and seasonings—black pepper, cardamom, turmeric, and ginger—are indigenous to India. Other spices were introduced by traders and migrating ethnic groups, so some of these spices are also prevalent in other cuisines.

Type	Description
Cardamom	Small green or white pods enclose fragrant seeds. Use either the whole pod or the ground seeds to add a warm, spicy-sweet flavor to foods.
Cilantro	This annual herb with green, lacy leaves looks like parsley but has a distinct pungent odor and flavor.
Coriander Seeds	The dried, round fruit of the cilantro herb, about the size of a black peppercorn, is most often used in the ground form. It has a warm, fruity aroma.
Cumin	The bitter taste of this crescent-shaped seed mellows to a nutty flavor during cooking. Use cumin whole or ground.
Curry Powder	This mixture of pungent spices comes in varying degrees of heat—mild, medium, or hot. It may contain over 20 spices, including cardamom, chiles, cloves, cumin, fennel seed, and red and black pepper. The longer the list of ingredients, the more complex the flavor.
Garam Masala	Meaning "hot spices," this spice blend is so named because it is believed to raise body temperature. Although not spicy, the mixture adds a fragrant warmth to dishes. It's readily available from Indian grocers, but you can also make it yourself. (See recipe on page 449.)
Turmeric	This bright yellow powder adds both color and a slight bitter flavor to dishes.

Making Chapatis

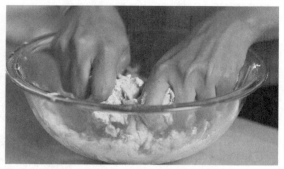

1. Combine water and flour in a large bowl, and mix, gathering and pressing until the flour stays together. If the dough becomes too dry, add a tablespoon or two of water (but no more or the dough will become too soft and sticky to roll).

2. Knead the dough lightly for 3 minutes; divide into 12 portions; roll each into a ball. With a rolling pin, roll each ball into a 5-inch circle (they'll be very thin). Cook each chapati in a skillet for 15 seconds; turn and cook 15 more seconds.

3. With tongs, remove and place on a cooling rack over the eye of a gas burner, or hold directly over eye until chapati is puffed and brown. Don't be discouraged if all of your chapatis don't puff; about half of ours did.

Whole Wheat Chapatis

A typical north Indian flatbread, *chapati* is traditionally made with just two ingredients—flour and water. Its plain flavor complements spicy Indian dishes.

¾ cup all-purpose flour
¾ cup whole wheat flour
½ cup water

1. Lightly spoon flours into measuring cups; level with a knife. Combine flours and water in a large bowl. Press mixture together using a rubber spatula or your hands (mixture will be dry but will stay together). Turn dough out onto a lightly floured surface. Knead for 3 minutes. Cover and let rest 15 minutes. Divide dough into 12 equal portions, shaping each into a ball. Roll 1 ball into a 5-inch circle (circles will be very thin) on a lightly floured surface (cover remaining dough while working to keep it from drying).
2. Heat a large nonstick skillet over medium-high heat until very hot. Place 1 dough round in pan, and cook 30 seconds or until brown spots appear, turning after about 15 seconds. Place bread on a cooling rack over eye of a gas burner. Hold bread over flame with tongs, turning until both sides of bread are puffed and brown spots appear (some chapatis will puff more than others). Repeat with remaining dough. Yield: 6 servings (serving size: 2 flatbreads).

CALORIES 108 (3% from fat); FAT 0.4g (sat 0.1g, mono 0.1g, poly 0.2g); PROTEIN 3.7g; CARB 22.8g; FIBER 2.3g; CHOL 0mg; IRON 1.3mg; SODIUM 1mg; CALC 7mg

If you prefer, you can skip the gas eye step and cook the chapatis completely in the skillet, though they won't puff as well. Cook them 30 seconds on each side.

Classic Lamb Curry

Lamb curry, a classic dish from northern India, is the most popular of all curries.

Cooking spray
2 pounds boneless leg of lamb, trimmed and cut into 1-inch pieces
1 teaspoon vegetable oil
1½ cups chopped onion
5 whole cloves
3 cardamom pods
2 bay leaves
1 (3-inch) cinnamon stick
1 tablespoon ground coriander seeds
1 tablespoon paprika
2 tablespoons minced peeled fresh ginger
2 teaspoons Garam Masala (right)
½ teaspoon ground red pepper
½ teaspoon ground turmeric
2 garlic cloves, minced
2 cups finely chopped plum tomato
1½ cups water
½ teaspoon salt
½ cup chopped fresh cilantro, divided
4 cups hot cooked long-grain rice

1. Heat a large nonstick skillet coated with cooking spray over medium-high heat. Add lamb; cook for 5 minutes on all sides or until browned. Remove from pan.
2. Heat oil in pan over medium-high heat. Add onion and next 4 ingredients; cook for 4 minutes or until onion is browned. Stir in coriander and next 6 ingredients; cook 1 minute. Add lamb, tomato, water, and salt; bring to a boil. Cover, reduce heat, and simmer 1½ hours or until the lamb is tender. Stir in ¼ cup cilantro. Serve over rice; sprinkle with ¼ cup cilantro. Yield: 4 servings (serving size: 1 cup lamb and 1 cup rice).

CALORIES 457 (22% from fat); FAT 11.2g (sat 3.5g, mono 4g, poly 1.8g); PROTEIN 40.4g; CARB 46.8g; FIBER 4.5g; CHOL 112mg; IRON 5.7mg; SODIUM 477mg; CALC 70mg

Garam Masala

This is darker and more flavorful than commercial blends.

1 tablespoon cumin seeds
1 tablespoon coriander seeds
2 teaspoons black peppercorns
12 cardamom pods
8 whole cloves
1 (2-inch) cinnamon stick, broken into pieces
½ teaspoon ground nutmeg

1. Place first 6 ingredients in a skillet over medium-high heat; cook until spices smoke, become fragrant, and turn dark, shaking pan constantly (about 5 minutes). Stir in nutmeg. Remove from heat; cool. Place in a spice grinder; process until finely ground. Store in an airtight container. Yield: ¼ cup.

CALORIES 69 (46% from fat); FAT 3.5g (sat 0.5g, mono 1.6g, poly 0.3g); PROTEIN 2.5g; CARB 11.7g; FIBER 5.9g; CHOL 0mg; IRON 6.3mg; SODIUM 19mg; CALC 149mg

Curry Powder

This curry powder is dark, slightly bitter, and salt-free.

1½ tablespoons coriander seeds
1 teaspoon cumin seeds
1 teaspoon yellow mustard seeds
1 teaspoon fenugreek seeds
1 teaspoon white peppercorns
6 whole cloves
1 tablespoon ground turmeric
1 teaspoon ground red pepper

1. Combine first 6 ingredients in a spice grinder; process until finely ground. Place in a bowl; stir in turmeric and red pepper. Store in an airtight container. Yield: ¼ cup.

CALORIES 99 (38% from fat); FAT 4.2g (sat 0.5g, mono 2.2g, poly 0.7g); PROTEIN 4.1g; CARB 15.8g; FIBER 7.5g; CHOL 0mg; IRON 7.3mg; SODIUM 17mg; CALC 127mg

CHAPTER 16

Central & South America

The explosive flavors of the cuisines of the Caribbean, Mexico, and Central and South America are perfectly suited for healthy eating.

Latino Cooking Terms and Techniques

Here are some dishes and flavors that are part of the culinary traditions of Central and South America.

Type	Description
Adobe	a spiced marinade
Ceviche	a dish and a technique, originally from Peru; a method of cooking fish or other seafood without heat, letting it marinate in lime or other citrus juice
Chimichurri	a condiment for beefy churrasco that's made with parsley, garlic, and olive oil; similar to pesto
Chipotle	smoked jalapeño, both dried or canned in adobo sauce
Churrasco	in Argentina and Brazil, marinated and grilled skirt steak; in Nicaragua, the treatment given to filet mignon
Empanada	Spanish-inspired pastry turnover, usually stuffed with spiced meat or seafood
Fufu	African dish of mashed plantains with garlic, onion, and bacon
Guajillo	dried chile with overtones of sweet fruit
Mesclun	a mix of baby greens
Mojo	spicy Caribbean sauce; a mixture of garlic, citrus juice, oil, and fresh herbs
Picadillo	spicy ground beef, usually cooked with olives and capers; served with rice, black beans, and fried plantains
Poblano	fresh green chile used in Mexico and Central America; when dried, it's called ancho
Sofrito	a foundation of many stews and meat dishes; a sauté of onion, garlic, bell pepper, tomatoes, herbs, and spices
Tamal	as in "tamale," a cornmeal-based appetizer or snack, usually steamed in a corn husk
Yuca	African root vegetable; also know as cassava and manioc; different from *yucca,* a plant belonging to the agave family, which gives the world tequila

The Caribbean

Cultures and seasonings from around the world collide in this spicy, flavorful island cuisine.

The Caribbean is a patchwork of islands, cuisines, and cultures, ranging from Jamaica's jerk pork to Trinidad's curries, from Puerto Rico's plantain fritters to the refreshing conch salads of the Bahamas. Each successive wave of immigrants has added its own unique flavors to the pot.

Caribbean Pantry

Type	Description
Allspice	Also known as *pimiento* or Jamaican pepper, it's made from the aromatic berries of a Caribbean tree. One of the defining ingredients in Jamaican jerk and French West Indian fish soups, allspice seems to encompass the tastes of cinnamon, nutmeg, and cloves—hence its name.
Annatto Seed	Known as *achiote* in Spanish, this is a rust-colored, earthy-flavored seed. Considered the poor man's saffron by some, it's used in Spanish Caribbean rice dishes and French West Indian stews.
Calabaza	This large, round Caribbean pumpkin has a dense, bright orange flesh. The flavor is similar to that of butternut squash, which makes a good substitute.
Coconut Milk	The "cream" of the tropics, produced by blending freshly grated coconut with hot water. Taste of Thai makes a canned light coconut milk that's great to use in healthy Caribbean cooking.
Conch	This giant sea snail's delicate, mild, white flesh is used in dishes ranging from salads to stews to steaks. You can substitute bay scallops if you can't find conch.
Guava	An egg-shaped tropical fruit with a musky, perfumy flavor. Because it contains numerous seeds, it's generally enjoyed as juice or jelly.
Pigeon Pea	This brown, oval bean originally hails from Africa; in the Caribbean, it's also known as the *gunga* (Congo) pea and the *pois d'Angole* (Angola pea). Endowed with a nutty, earthy flavor, the pigeon pea is often paired with rice.
Plantain	This jumbo cooking banana can be eaten at every stage of ripeness. When green, it tastes starchy, like a potato; when ripe, it tastes sweet, like a banana.
Scotch Bonnet Chile	This chile, shaped like a Chinese lantern, is one of the world's hottest—50 times hotter than a jalapeño. Behind all that heat is a complex flavor that's earthy, floral, and apricot-like all at once. If you can't find the Scotch bonnet, you can substitute its Mexican cousin, the habanero.

Jamaican Jerk Pork Tenderloin

Use one Scotch bonnet pepper for a mildly spicy dish and four for a very spicy dish. (An authentic jerk marinade has about 12 peppers.) We butterfly the pork to increase the surface area for the marinade to penetrate.

2	cups coarsely chopped green onions
½	cup coarsely chopped onion
2	tablespoons white vinegar
1	tablespoon soy sauce
1	tablespoon vegetable oil
2	teaspoons kosher salt
2	teaspoons fresh thyme
2	teaspoons brown sugar
2	teaspoons chopped peeled fresh ginger
1	teaspoon ground allspice
¼	teaspoon ground nutmeg
¼	teaspoon black pepper
⅛	teaspoon ground cinnamon
2	garlic cloves, minced
1	to 4 Scotch bonnet or habanero peppers, seeded and chopped
1	(1½-pound) pork tenderloin, trimmed

Cooking spray

1. Place first 15 ingredients in a blender or food processor, and process until smooth.
2. Slice pork lengthwise, cutting to, but not through, other side. Open halves, laying each side flat. Slice each half lengthwise, cutting to, but not through, other side; open flat. Combine pork and green onion mixture in a dish or large zip-top plastic bag. Cover or seal; marinate in refrigerator 3 to 24 hours. Remove pork from dish or bag; discard remaining marinade.
3. Prepare grill.
4. Place pork on grill rack coated with cooking spray; grill 8 minutes on each side or until meat thermometer registers 160° (slightly pink). Yield: 4 servings (serving size: 3 ounces pork).

CALORIES 248 (27% from fat); FAT 7.5g (sat 2g, mono 2.8g, poly 2g); PROTEIN 36.9g; CARB 7.1g; FIBER 1.5g; CHOL 111mg; IRON 3.1mg; SODIUM 1,126mg; CALC 52mg

Making Jamaican Jerk Tenderloin

1. To butterfly the pork, cut it lengthwise, cutting to, but not all the way through, the other side. Open up the halves; cut each half the same way. Open the pork so that it lies flat.

2. To make the jerk marinade, combine the marinade ingredients in a blender or food processor. (The marinade will be thick and pasty.) Pour over the pork, and marinate for up to 24 hours. The longer you marinate the pork, the more flavorful it will be.

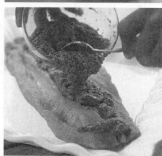

3. Keep as much marinade on the pork as possible, and grill until done. To serve, cut horizontally across the grain into thin slices.

Regional Caribbean Dishes

Here's our guide to some of the most popular and authentic dishes that you'll find throughout the islands.

Type	Area	Description
Accras	French West Indies	spicy salt-cod fritters
Adobo	Cuba	a mixture of sour orange juice, cumin, and garlic used to marinate meats and fish; dishes made with it are often served with *mojo,* a sauce prepared from the same ingredients
Arroz Con Leche	Spanish islands	creamy rice pudding
Arroz Con Pollo	Spanish islands	a sort of landlubber's paella made with chicken and annatto
Asopao	Puerto Rico and the Dominican Republic	a soupy seafood-rice stew flavored with annatto
Blaff de Poisson	French islands	pan-fried fish served in a broth flavored with lime juice, allspice berries, and Scotch bonnet chiles; name of dish is said to echo the sound the fish makes as it hits the frying pan
Boka Dushi	Dutch islands	"sweet mouth" in the Papamiento dialect; refers to Indonesian-style chicken satés
Bolo Pretu	Curaçao and other islands	black fruitcake
Christophene Farcie	French Islands	chayote squash stuffed with cheese and chiles
Choka	Trinidad	a grilled-vegetable dip
Court-Bouillon	French islands	a delicate fish stew flavored with lime juice and allspice
Cutters	Barbados	sandwiches that are traditionally made with flying fish
Jerk	Jamaica	fiery barbecued pork that's smoked over allspice wood
Keshi Yena	Curaçao	hollowed-out Edam cheese filled with olive- and caper-spiced beef
Pepperpot	Barbados and other islands	a soulful beef-and-vegetable stew enriched with *callaloo* (spinachlike *malanga* leaves) and *cassareep* (cassava vinegar)
Pika	Dutch islands	pickled onion-and-chile sauce
Pindasaus	Dutch islands	spicy peanut sauce
Poulet Boucane	Guadeloupe	"buccaneer chicken," seasoned with island spices and smoked over sugarcane
Rotis	Trinidad, Tobago, and other islands	flatbreads filled with split peas; the tortillas of the southern Caribbean and are served filled with everything from stewed vegetables to curried goat
Run Down	Jamaica	a stew made with smoked fish and coconut milk
Salmagundi	Jamaica	spicy potted fish
Sauce Chien	French islands	"dog sauce" is the literal translation; a fiery vinaigrette
Souse	Barbados	pickled pig ears and tails
Yuca Frita	Cuba	fried yuca (cassava) with garlic sauce

Cuba

Cuban food reflects both Spanish and African cuisines, but it's heavily influenced by native island ingredients.

There is no such thing as Cuban haute cuisine, and there never has been. Cuban cooking is simply the fortuitous result of Spanish and African influences combined with native ingredients. **The zest for life that comes across in Cuban music comes across in the cuisine.** The people are open, friendly, honest, and approachable—and so is the food. Onions, garlic, tomatoes, peppers, lime juice, and spices and herbs such as cumin, oregano, parsley, and cilantro make the dishes come alive. *Sofrito,* a mixture of minced vegetables sautéed in olive oil,

is an aromatic building block for many dinners. Rice and plantains, either ripe or green, serve as backdrops for bolder flavors.

Acceptable Shortcuts
Test Kitchen SECRET

Using a few handy shortcuts, you can prepare authentic Cuban cuisine in a snap. However, some shortcuts that speed preparation are fine, while others are not. Viviana Carballo, contributing editor, offers these tips:

- Canned broth is an excellent time-saver. Though canned beans, bottled roasted peppers, bottled *sofrito,* and commercial *mojo* marinade are fine shortcuts, bottled garlic is absolutely not.
- Powdered garlic and onion salt won't do, either.
- Fresh lemon juice is a must, and fresh herbs such as cilantro and parsley are crucial.

Picadillo

This classic Cuban dish remains popular because it's so easy to make, and because of its appealing sweet and savory flavors. Although picadillo is traditionally made with ground beef, using ground turkey offers a great lower-fat alternative. Other renditions of picadillo include cinnamon and cloves, but this is the standard Cuban version. Typical accompaniments are white rice and ripe plantains.

1	teaspoon olive oil
1	cup finely chopped onion
1	pound ground turkey
3	garlic cloves, minced
1	cup low-salt beef broth
⅓	cup raisins
⅓	cup coarsely chopped pimiento-stuffed olives
3	tablespoons capers
1	tablespoon tomato paste
¼	teaspoon freshly ground black pepper
3	cups hot cooked rice

1. Heat oil in a large nonstick skillet over medium-high heat. Add onion; sauté 5 minutes. Add turkey and garlic; cook 5 minutes or until browned, stirring to crumble. Add broth and next 5 ingredients; stir well. Bring to a boil. Cover, reduce heat, and simmer 25 minutes. Serve with rice. Yield: 4 servings (serving size: 1 cup picadillo and ¾ cup rice).

CALORIES 423 (29% from fat); FAT 13.5g (sat 3.2g, mono 6.2g, poly 2.8g); PROTEIN 26.1g; CARB 48.9g; FIBER 2.7g; CHOL 90mg; IRON 3.9mg; SODIUM 782mg; CALC 62mg

"Under no circumstances would we give up flavor, and many of us would rather do without a certain dish than compromise authenticity." Viviana Carballo, *Cooking Light* Contributor

Cuban Pantry

Some of the ingredients used in Cuban cooking—specifically *calabaza,* cilantro, plantains, and *sofrito*—are the same ones that are used frequently in several other cuisines.

Type	Description
Adobo	a seasoning for meats and poultry; the dry version is a rub consisting of salt, pepper, garlic, oregano, and cumin; a wet version, used as a marinade, contains sour orange juice, garlic, seasonings, and various herbs and spices
Arroz	rice (plain white is used most often)
Beans	a daily staple, from chickpeas to black beans, or red, white, and pink beans
Bijol	bright orange powder used for coloring and made with *achiote* (annatto) seeds and flavorings, often used with saffron
Bitter Orange	a component of marinades and *mojos* with a flavor between lime and orange (also known as *naranja agria*)
Calabaza	type of pumpkin from the Caribbean with a mild but distinctive flavor; a good substitute is butternut squash
Cilantro	herb used in *sofrito*, either as a garnish or to punch up the dish
Coconut	refreshing juice used in alcoholic drinks or taken plain; white flesh is eaten from the hand or—when harder—used to make sweets; canned is usually used
Mojo	juice-based (usually bitter orange) sauce served cold or hot; used cold as a marinade; hot, garlic is sautéed in olive oil, and juice and flavorings are added to the pan and then poured over meats or tuber vegetables
Plantain	green or ripe, boiled, mashed, fried, or baked; also known as a cooking banana
Saffron	its deep, earthy flavor has no substitute, but its color can be reproduced with Bijol
Sofrito	the linchpin of Caribbean cooking; a mix of onion, pepper, garlic, herbs, and seasonings sautéed in olive oil; tomatoes, tomato sauce, or cilantro may be added

Mexico

Real Mexican food is about fresh, high-spirited ingredients and flavors that come to life in bright and bold dishes.

Over the years, we've learned a great deal about Mexican cooking and have developed easy-to-follow guidelines for combining commonly available ingredients to make classic dishes. In this section, we offer a few recipes for real Mexican food—way beyond such Mexican-American inventions as cheese-covered nachos, and U-shaped tacos stuffed with ground beef and iceberg lettuce.

The Fundamentals

Fresh corn tortillas are absolutely essential. They form the all-important foundation of Mexican cuisine.

Roasted fresh chile peppers are also a staple of the Mexican kitchen. The dozens of chiles used in Mexico are relied on more for their taste than for heat. And woven into a luscious guacamole or lively salsa, roasted chiles provide a flavor stamp of authenticity.

Crunchy, zesty fresh ingredients such as cilantro, raw onions, and radishes play a big role as well, especially when used as garnishes for snack foods and the street fare that's so popular throughout Mexico.

Mexico has lots of seafood offerings. At the top of the list is a dish from the port town of Veracruz: *pescado a la veracruzana. Pescado* is Spanish for "fish" (red snapper is most popular); *a la veracruzana* refers to a sort of Mediterranean-Mexican blend of tomatoes, capers, olives, herbs, and pickled jalapeño chiles.

Fire-roasting fresh chiles; griddle-toasting dried chiles, garlic, and tortillas; blistering tomatoes or tomatillos under a broiler or in a skillet—all of these are basic cooking steps that add rustic sweetness and depth of flavor to traditional recipes for salsas, marinades, spicy condiments, and stew bases.

Mexican Pantry

Type	Description
Ancho Chile	When fresh poblano chiles are dried, they're called anchos. Mildly spicy, like their fresh counterparts, anchos give a rich sweetness to marinades or a simmering pot of chili.
Cilantro	This familiar Mexican herb is used only when fresh; it loses all flavor when dried. It provides an explosive sprinkle over lots of street foods, mostly as a component of salsa and guacamole. Store it wrapped in barely damp paper towels in a plastic bag, in the warmest part of the refrigerator.
Guajillo Chile	These smooth-skinned, brick- or cranberry-red dried chiles are a little spicier than anchos and not nearly as sweet. They're often ground into a powder that gives a tangy jolt to fresh fruits and vegetables; teamed with anchos, they lend multilayered flavor to stews and soups.
Jicama	This root vegetable is the color of a potato, and it's not much bigger. Sliced or julienned, it adds a slightly sweet, juicy crunch to chicken salads or coleslaw. You can also peel it, slice it, and eat it as a snack, as Mexicans do.
Masa Harina	Corn tortillas are made from dried grain (field) corn cooked with mineral lime, then ground into a paste called masa. Several decades ago, a method to dehydrate and powder the perishable masa was discovered; the result became known as masa harina, or masa flour.
Poblano Chile	This mildly spicy, dark green fresh chile resembles a small bell pepper, but it has a pointed end, tougher skin, and more compact flesh. The flavor is also similar to that of a bell pepper, only more concentrated and complex.
Queso Añejo	This hard, aged cheese made from cow's milk adds a salty kick to whatever it touches. Dishes that always get a dusting of grated queso añejo, such as enchiladas, grilled corn on the cob, and street snacks made from corn masa, would be naked without it—like pasta without Romano or Parmesan.
Serrano Chile	These bullet-shaped, hot green chiles are about 2 1/2 inches long and 1/2 inch wide. They have a punchy flavor that is much less sweet than a jalapeño and is pure heaven to green-chile lovers.

"From the ancho's sweetness to the serrano's punch, chiles supply more than just heat—they supply earthy, rich flavor." Krista Montgomery, Food Editor

Roasted-Poblano Guacamole with Garlic and Parsley

In this guacamole, roasted poblanos add spark to the creamy, almost nutty-tasting avocados, especially when bolstered with roasted tomato and flat-leaf parsley.

2	poblano chiles (about 6 ounces)
2	plum tomatoes (about 6 ounces)
2	garlic cloves, unpeeled
1⅓	cups ripe peeled avocado, seeded and coarsely mashed (about 3)
3	tablespoons chopped fresh flat-leaf parsley
2	tablespoons fresh lime juice
¼	teaspoon salt
2	tablespoons grated queso añejo or Parmesan cheese
2	tablespoons sliced radishes
7	ounces baked tortilla chips

1. Preheat broiler.
2. Cut poblanos in half lengthwise, and discard the seeds and membranes. Place poblano halves (skin sides up), tomatoes, and garlic on a foil-lined baking sheet. Broil 12 minutes or until poblanos are blackened, turning the tomatoes once. Place the poblanos in a zip-top plastic bag, and seal. Let stand 10 minutes. Peel poblanos, tomatoes, and garlic.
3. Place the poblanos and garlic cloves in a food processor, and pulse until coarsely chopped. Combine the poblano mixture, tomato, avocado, parsley, juice, and salt in a bowl. Sprinkle with cheese and radishes. Serve with tortilla chips. Yield: 8 servings (serving size: ¼ cup guacamole and ¾ cup chips).

CALORIES 179 (38% from fat); FAT 7.5g (sat 1.3g, mono 4.1g, poly 1.5g); PROTEIN 3.6g; CARB 27g; FIBER 4.8g; CHOL 2mg; IRON 1mg; SODIUM 280mg; CALC 57mg

Salsa de Molcajete (Roasted Tomato and Green Chile Salsa)

More than a mere mix of ingredients, this salsa uses centuries-old techniques to combine flavors, bringing out the best of each. Though it's typically done in a *molcajete* (Mexican lava rock mortar), you can also make this salsa using a marble mortar and pestle (as we did). Finely chopping the garlic and chiles in a food processor, then adding the tomatoes and pulsing until coarsely pureed will yield great results as well.

6	plum tomatoes (about 1 pound)
3	garlic cloves, unpeeled
2	jalapeño peppers
⅓	cup chopped fresh cilantro
¼	cup finely chopped onion
1	teaspoon fresh lime juice
¼	teaspoon salt

1. Preheat broiler.
2. Place tomatoes, garlic, and jalapeños on a foil-lined baking sheet. Broil for 16 minutes, turning after 8 minutes. Cool and peel tomatoes and garlic. Combine garlic and peppers in a molcajete, mortar, or bowl; pound with a pestle or the back of a spoon to form a paste. Add tomatoes, and coarsely crush using the pestle or spoon. Combine tomato mixture, cilantro, and remaining ingredients in a small bowl. Yield: 6 servings (serving size: ¼ cup).

CALORIES 23 (12% from fat); FAT 0.3g (sat 0g, mono 0.1g, poly 0.1g); PROTEIN 0.9g; CARB 5g; FIBER 1.2g; CHOL 0mg; IRON 0.5mg; SODIUM 106mg; CALC 10mg

---

Full-Flavored Salsa
Test Kitchen SECRET

Roasting tomatoes gives them a sweet and complex taste. Rinsing the onion under cold water makes it crisp, and crushing roasted garlic and chiles in a mortar releases their full flavor.

"There's just no comparison between a fresh corn tortilla and one of those frozen ones that comes in a plastic bag." Susan Stone, Food Editor

Tortillas de Maíz (Corn Tortillas)

One of life's most delicious experiences is enjoying the elemental flavor of a just-baked corn tortilla. Once you learn how to press and griddle-bake tortillas, you'll see that they're really quite easy and rewarding.

1¾ cups masa harina (such as Maseca or Quaker)
1   cup plus 2 tablespoons hot water

1. Lightly spoon masa harina into dry measuring cups; level with a knife. Combine masa harina and water in a large bowl; stir well. Turn dough out onto a surface lightly sprinkled with masa harina; knead lightly 5 times or until soft (the consistency should be like soft cookie dough but not sticky). Divide dough into 12 equal portions. Shape each portion into a ball.
2. Working with 1 portion at a time, place dough between 2 sheets of plastic wrap (cover remaining balls to prevent drying). Place ball, still covered, on a tortilla press. Close press to flatten dough, moving handle from side to side. Open press; turn dough one-half turn. Close press to flatten. Remove dough. Carefully remove plastic from dough.
3. Place a nonstick skillet over medium heat. Add dough, and cook 15 to 30 seconds or until tortilla releases itself from the skillet. Turn tortilla; cook 30 seconds or until brown spots form. Turn again; cook another 30 to 45 seconds (at this point, most of the tortillas will puff like pita bread). Remove from pan. Keep warm. Repeat procedure with remaining dough. Yield: 12 tortillas (serving size: 2 tortillas).

CALORIES 129 (11% from fat); FAT 1.6g (sat 0.3g, mono 0.3g, poly 1g); PROTEIN 3.3g; CARB 27.7g; FIBER 3g; CHOL 0mg; IRON 1mg; SODIUM 99mg; CALC 67mg

---

Market-Fresh Tortillas
Test Kitchen SECRET

If you'd rather not make your own, search out a locally made brand of tortillas (they'll usually be fresher) in your grocery, and heat them, wrapped in a clean kitchen towel, in a vegetable steamer. Steam 1 minute, turn off heat, and let stand 15 minutes.

Tortilla Presses
Cooking Light Recommends

Tortilla presses are available at fine cookware stores and through the Santa Fe School of Cooking and Market (www.santafeschoolofcooking.com) for approximately $27. You can find them for a fraction of that cost at Mexican markets, though. Or you can use a rolling pin.

Homemade tortillas are simple to make and well worth the effort.

How to Make Tortillas de Maíz (Corn Tortillas)

1. Combine the masa harina and water in a bowl, and stir well. Knead the dough until it becomes soft, like cookie dough, but not sticky. The softer the dough, the more moist and tender the tortillas. But don't make it so soft that more than a bit sticks to your hands.

2. Divide dough into 12 equal portions. Shape each portion into a ball. Working with 1 portion at a time, place dough between 2 sheets of plastic wrap (cover remaining balls to prevent drying). Place ball, still covered with plastic wrap, on tortilla press. Thicker plastic from food storage bags is easiest to work with and is great for beginners.

3. Close press to flatten the ball into a 5-inch disk, moving the handle from side to side. Open press; turn dough one-half turn. Close press to flatten. Remove dough from press; carefully remove plastic wrap.

4. Place dough in a nonstick skillet over medium heat (make sure skillet is hot). Cook 15 to 30 seconds or until tortilla releases itself from pan. Turn tortilla (with spatula or tongs); cook 30 seconds or until brown spots form. Turn tortilla again, and cook another 30 to 45 seconds. At this point, the tortilla may puff slightly (but you shouldn't worry if it doesn't).

South America

South America is a continent of explosive flavors and culinary sophistication that reflect the diversity of the people and the land.

In discussing South American food, it's best to separate the continent into four broad gastronomic regions.

Northwestern South America, especially the Andean Mountain nations of Ecuador, Bolivia, and Peru, boasts some of the most exotic food in Latin America. Potatoes and the highly nutritious grain quinoa (see page 260) originated here and still play major roles in the cuisine. Peru alone boasts more than 100 different potato varieties, including a blue (actually, it's lavender) potato that has become the darling of trendy chefs in North America. Peru also has some of the spiciest food in South America.

> Few regions of the world boast such a rich culinary tradition as South America. And if trends continue, more of its foods will go from humble to high chic as Americans discover just how incredible Latin flavors can be.

North Central South America The cuisine of this region displays a Spanish influence, especially in Columbia and Venezuela. Many of the most dominant seasonings of the region—cumin, oregano, cinnamon, and anise—came directly from Spain. For that matter, so did the local enthusiasm for fresh orange and lime juices and for the ancient Mediterranean flavors of wine and olive oil. Many dishes in northeastern South America feature a contrast of sweet and salty tastes (in the form of raisins, prunes, capers, and olives).

Southern South America comprises Argentina, Chile, Paraguay, and Uruguay. This is cattle country, and the locals enjoy luscious grass-fed beef in the form of *asados,* large cuts roasted in front of a campfire, and *parrilladas,* thick, juicy steaks grilled on a gridiron over blazing oak. And though the accompaniments are quite simple, they're intensely flavorful: A tomato, onion, and pepper relish known as *salsa criolla* and a pestolike parsley, garlic, and vinegar sauce called *chimichurri* are prime examples.

Brazil's cuisine is as diverse as its population. Portuguese settlers popularized such European ingredients as olives, onions, garlic, wine, and *bacalhau* (salt cod). The natives of Brazil's rain forests taught the Europeans how to enjoy such exotic tropical vegetables and fruits as *madioca* (cassava root), *maracuja* (passion fruit), and *caju* (cashew fruit). African slaves contributed okra, yams, peanuts, dried shrimp, and *dende* (palm oil) to the Brazilian melting pot, not to mention a passion for fiery *malagueta* chile peppers. Their influence lives on in the popular *moqueca de peixe,* a sort of bouillabaisse from the state of Bahia in northern Brazil, and *feijoada,* Brazil's most famous regional dish. There are many different versions of feijoada but it's typically a stewlike mixture with a variety of sausage and meats, black beans, greens, onions, and garlic.

Brazilian Fish Stew (*Moqueca de Peixe*)

From the state of Bahia in northern Brazil, *moqueca de peixe* (moo-KAY-ka duh PAY-shuh) is a tropical fish stew fragrant with garlic and peppers and enriched with coconut milk.

⅓	cup fresh lime juice
½	teaspoon salt
½	teaspoon freshly ground black pepper
2	garlic cloves, minced
1	(1½-pound) sea bass or halibut fillet, cut into ½-inch-wide strips
1½	pounds large shrimp, peeled and deveined
2	tablespoons olive oil
2	cups finely chopped onion
1	cup finely chopped green bell pepper
1	cup finely chopped red bell pepper
¾	cup minced green onions (about 1 bunch)
5	garlic cloves, minced
1	bay leaf
2	cups chopped tomato (about 2 large)
½	cup minced fresh cilantro, divided
2	(8-ounce) bottles clam juice
1	(14-ounce) can fat-free, less-sodium chicken broth
1	cup light coconut milk
¼	teaspoon ground red pepper

1. Combine first 6 ingredients in a large bowl; toss to coat. Marinate in refrigerator 30 minutes.
2. Heat oil in a large Dutch oven over medium heat. Add onion, bell peppers, green onions, garlic, and bay leaf; cook 6 minutes, stirring occasionally. Increase heat to medium-high; add tomato, and cook 2 minutes. Add ¼ cup cilantro, clam juice, and broth. Bring to a boil; reduce heat, and simmer 10 minutes. Discard bay leaf.
3. Place one-third of vegetable mixture in a blender, and puree until smooth. Pour pureed vegetable mixture into pan. Repeat procedure with remaining vegetable mixture. Add coconut milk and red pepper to pureed vegetable mixture. Bring to a boil over medium-high heat; cook 3 minutes. Add fish mixture; cook 3 minutes or until fish is done. Sprinkle with ¼ cup cilantro. Yield: 6 servings (serving size: 1½ cups).

CALORIES 309 (24% from fat); FAT 8.4g (sat 2.6g, mono 2.5g, poly 1.8g); PROTEIN 41.5g; CARB 15.9g; FIBER 3g; CHOL 178mg; IRON 3.8mg; SODIUM 733mg; CALC 102mg

How to Make Brazilian Fish Stew

1. To make the *sofrito,* sauté onion, garlic, and peppers together, which makes a flavorful base for the stew. Add remaining ingredients, and simmer for 10 minutes.

2. Puree one-third of the vegetable mixture to give the stew body.

Popular South American Dishes

Here's our guide to some of the dishes you might enjoy if you're dining somewhere in South America.

Type	Description
Ajiaco columbiano	Colombian chicken and vegetable stew
Anticuchos	Peruvian beef kebabs
Arepas	cornmeal flat cakes popular in Colombia
Arroz chaufa de mariscos	Peruvian fried rice with seafood
Arroz con camarones	Colombian rice pilaf with shrimp
Asado	Argentinean grilled beef, lamb, or pork roasted gaucho-style, in front of a campfire
Caldillo de congrio	Chilean fish stew made with conger eel
Cau-cau de mariscos	Peruvian seafood stew
Chimichurri	Argentinean garlic-parsley-vinegar sauce served with grilled beef
Chupe de camarones	Ecuadoran shrimp soup
Churrasco	a smorgasbord of grilled meats from Brazil, served on skewers and carved directly onto your plate
Couve mineira	garlicky Brazilian-style collard greens
Empanadas	chicken, meat, fish, or cheese turnovers, popular throughout South America
Ensalada de palmitos	Brazilian hearts of palm salad
Guasacaca	Venezuelan avocado sauce
Hallacas venezolanas	Venezuelan tamales
Humitas bolivianas	Bolivian corn tamales
Mariscada	Venezuelan seafood stew
Matambre	literally, "hunger killer": a stuffed, rolled, grilled flank steak from Argentina and Uruguay
Moqueca de peixe	brazilian seafood stew flavored with peppers and coconut milk
Pamplona de pollo	a colorful stuffed, rolled, grilled chicken breast from Uruguay
Parrillada	Argentinean grilled steak
Patacón	Colombian fried plantains
Pebre	a pickled onion relish served as a table condiment in Chile
Salsa criolla	a tomato, onion, and pepper relish
Saltenas	Bolivian meat turnovers
Seviche (Ceviche)	uncooked seafood marinated with lime juice and chiles (popular in Ecuador and Peru)
So'o-losopy	Paraguay's ground beef soup
Sopa paraguaya	Paraguayan corn bread
Tira de asado	a crosscut short rib steak from Argentina

South American cooks make extensive use of the four primal foods of the New World: corn, beans, squash, and chiles.

Lightening Sofrito

South Americans use prodigious amounts of onions, garlic, and bell peppers—the ingredients of a flavoring called *sofrito* in Spanish-speaking countries and *refogado* in Brazil. Sautéed in olive oil or lard until soft and fragrant, the sofrito is the foundation of hundreds of South American dishes. To keep sofrito healthier, we use olive oil instead of lard.

Chimichurri

Considered the barbecue sauce of Argentina, this emerald-colored condiment is built on garlic and parsley and is a pungent cross between vinaigrette and pesto.

2	cups coarsely chopped fresh flat-leaf parsley (about 2 bunches)
1	cup coarsely chopped onion
⅔	cup coarsely chopped carrot
¼	cup coarsely chopped garlic
½	cup vegetable broth
⅓	cup white vinegar
2	tablespoons extra-virgin olive oil
1	teaspoon dried oregano
½	teaspoon crushed red pepper
¼	teaspoon salt
¼	teaspoon black pepper

1. Combine first 4 ingredients in a food processor; pulse until mixture is finely chopped.
2. Combine the broth and remaining ingredients. With processor on, slowly pour broth mixture through food chute; process until well blended. Yield: 1½ cups (serving size: 2 tablespoons).

CALORIES 32 (68% from fat); FAT 2.4g (sat 0.3g, mono 1.7g, poly 0.2g); PROTEIN 0.5; CARB 2.5g; FIBER 0.5g; CHOL 0mg; IRON 0.4mg; SODIUM 94mg; CALC 15mg

Uruguayan Bean Salad

In Uruguay and Argentina, this salad belongs to a roster of side dishes that accompanies cocktails and steaks. It's traditionally made with *poroto*, a small, dark, rectangular bean with an earthy flavor. Fava beans come closest in flavor, but you can also use kidney or pinto beans.

3	cups canned fava or kidney beans, drained and rinsed
1	cup chopped seeded tomato
¾	cup finely chopped onion
¼	cup chopped fresh flat-leaf parsley
3	tablespoons red wine vinegar
2	tablespoons extra-virgin olive oil
1	teaspoon dried oregano
½	teaspoon crushed red pepper
½	teaspoon freshly ground black pepper
¼	teaspoon salt

1. Combine all the ingredients in a bowl, and toss gently. Yield: 6 servings (serving size: ⅔ cup bean salad).

CALORIES 167 (28% from fat); FAT 5.2g (sat 0.6g, mono 3.3g, poly 0.5g); PROTEIN 6.7g; CARB 23.7g; FIBER 6g; CHOL 0mg; IRON 2mg; SODIUM 353mg; CALC 34mg

Common Ingredient *Substitutions*

If you're right in the middle of cooking and realize you don't have a particular ingredient, use the substitutions in this list.

Ingredient	Substitution
Arrowroot, 1 teaspoon	1 tablespoon all-purpose flour or $1\frac{1}{2}$ teaspoons cornstarch
Baking Powder, 1 teaspoon	$\frac{1}{2}$ teaspoon cream of tartar and $\frac{1}{4}$ teaspoon baking soda
Chocolate	
Semisweet, 1 ounce	1 ounce unsweetened chocolate and 1 tablespoon sugar
Unsweetened, 1 ounce	3 tablespoons cocoa and 1 tablespoon butter or margarine
Cocoa, $\frac{1}{4}$ cup	1 ounce unsweetened chocolate (decrease fat in recipe by $\frac{1}{2}$ tablespoon)
Coconut, grated fresh, $1\frac{1}{2}$ tablespoons	1 tablespoon flaked coconut
Corn Syrup, light, 1 cup	1 cup sugar and $\frac{1}{4}$ cup water or 1 cup honey
Cornstarch, 1 tablespoon	2 tablespoons all-purpose flour or granular tapioca
Flour	
All-purpose, 1 tablespoon	$1\frac{1}{2}$ teaspoons cornstarch, potato starch, or rice starch
Cake, 1 cup sifted	1 cup minus 2 tablespoons all-purpose flour
Self-rising, 1 cup	1 cup all-purpose flour, 1 teaspoon baking powder, and $\frac{1}{2}$ teaspoon salt
Shortening	
Melted, 1 cup	1 cup vegetable oil (*do not use oil if recipe does not call for melted shortening*)
Solid, 1 cup	$1\frac{1}{8}$ cups butter or margarine (decrease salt in recipe by $\frac{1}{2}$ teaspoon)
Sugar	
Brown, 1 cup, firmly packed	1 cup granulated white sugar
Powdered, 1 cup	1 cup sugar and 1 tablespoon cornstarch (processed in food processor)
Honey, $\frac{1}{2}$ cup	$\frac{1}{2}$ cup molasses or maple syrup
Eggs	
1 large	2 egg yolks for custards and cream fillings or 2 egg yolks and 1 tablespoon water for cookies
1 large	$\frac{1}{4}$ cup egg substitute
2 large	3 small eggs
1 egg white (2 tablespoons)	2 tablespoons egg substitute
1 egg yolk ($1\frac{1}{2}$ tablespoons)	2 tablespoons sifted dry egg yolk powder and 2 teaspoons water or $1\frac{1}{2}$ tablespoons thawed frozen egg yolk
Milk	
Buttermilk, low-fat or fat-free, 1 cup	1 tablespoon lemon juice or vinegar and 1 cup low-fat or fat-free milk (let stand 10 minutes)
Fat-free milk, 1 cup	4 to 5 tablespoons fat-free dry milk powder and enough cold water to make 1 cup
Sour Cream, 1 cup	1 cup plain yogurt

Baking Products (side label)

Dairy Products (side label)

	Ingredient	Substitution
Fruits & Vegetables	**Lemon,** 1 medium	2 to 3 tablespoons juice and 2 teaspoons grated rind
	Juice, 1 teaspoon	$1/2$ teaspoon vinegar
	Peel, dried	2 teaspoons freshly grated lemon rind
	Orange, 1 medium	$1/2$ cup juice and 2 tablespoons grated rind
	Tomatoes	
	Fresh, chopped, 2 cups	1 (16-ounce) can (may need to drain)
	Juice, 1 cup	$1/2$ cup tomato sauce and $1/2$ cup water
	Tomato Sauce, 2 cups	$3/4$ cup tomato paste and 1 cup water
Miscellaneous	**Broth,** beef or chicken, canned, 1 cup	1 bouillon cube dissolved in 1 cup boiling water
	Capers, 1 tablespoon	1 tablespoon chopped dill pickles or green olives
	Chili Sauce, 1 cup	1 cup tomato sauce, $1/4$ cup brown sugar, 2 tablespoons vinegar, $1/4$ teaspoon ground cinnamon, dash of ground cloves, and dash of ground allspice
	Chili Paste, 1 teaspoon	$1/4$ teaspoon hot red pepper flakes
	Gelatin, flavored, 3-ounce package	1 tablespoon unflavored gelatin and 2 cups fruit juice
	Ketchup, 1 cup	1 cup tomato sauce, $1/2$ cup sugar, and 2 tablespoons vinegar (for cooking, not to be used as a condiment)
	Tahini (sesame-seed paste), 1 cup	$3/4$ cup creamy peanut butter and $1/4$ cup sesame oil
	Vinegar, cider, 1 teaspoon	2 teaspoons lemon juice mixed with a pinch of sugar
	Wasabi, 1 teaspoon	1 teaspoon horseradish or hot dry mustard
Seasonings	**Allspice,** ground, 1 teaspoon	$1/2$ teaspoon ground cinnamon and $1/2$ teaspoon ground cloves
	Apple Pie Spice, 1 teaspoon	$1/2$ teaspoon ground cinnamon, $1/4$ teaspoon ground nutmeg, and $1/8$ teaspoon ground cardamom
	Bay Leaf, 1 whole	$1/4$ teaspoon crushed bay leaf
	Chives, chopped, 1 tablespoon	1 tablespoon chopped green onion tops
	Garlic, 1 clove	1 teaspoon bottled minced garlic
	Ginger	
	Crystallized, 1 tablespoon	$1/8$ teaspoon ground ginger
	Fresh, grated, 1 tablespoon	$1/8$ teaspoon ground ginger
	Herbs, fresh, 1 tablespoon	1 teaspoon dried herbs or $1/4$ teaspoon ground herbs (*except rosemary*)
	Horseradish, fresh, grated, 1 tablespoon	2 tablespoons prepared horseradish
	Lemongrass, 1 stalk, chopped	1 teaspoon grated lemon zest
	Mint, fresh, chopped, 3 tablespoons	1 tablespoon dried spearmint or peppermint
	Mustard, dried, 1 teaspoon	1 tablespoon prepared mustard
	Parsley, chopped fresh, 1 tablespoon	1 teaspoon dried parsley
	Vanilla Bean, 6-inch bean	1 tablespoon vanilla extract

Low-Fat *Substitutions*

Here are a few simple reduced-fat substitutions for high-fat ingredients.

	Ingredient	Substitution
Fats & Oils	Butter	Light butter, reduced-calorie margarine (*except for baking*)
	Margarine	Light butter, reduced-calorie margarine (*except for baking*)
	Mayonnaise	Fat-free, light, or low-fat mayonnaise
	Oil	Polyunsaturated or monounsaturated oil in a reduced amount
	Salad Dressing	Fat-free or reduced-fat salad dressing or vinaigrette
	Shortening	Polyunsaturated or monounsaturated oil in a reduced amount
Meat & Poultry	Bacon	Reduced-fat bacon; turkey bacon; lean ham; Canadian bacon
	Ground Beef	Ground round, extra-lean ground beef, or ground turkey
	Sausage	50%-less-fat pork sausage; turkey sausage
	Luncheon Meat	Sliced turkey, chicken, lean roast beef, or lean ham
	Tuna Packed in Oil	Tuna packed in water
	Egg, whole	2 egg whites or $1/4$ cup egg substitute
Dairy	Sour Cream	Fat-free or reduced-fat sour cream; fat-free or low-fat plain yogurt
	Cheese, Cheddar, Swiss, Monterey Jack, Mozzarella	Reduced-fat cheeses (or use less of the regular cheese)
	Cottage Cheese	Fat-free or 1% low-fat cottage cheese
	Cream Cheese	Fat-free or light cream cheese; Neufchâtel cheese
	Ricotta Cheese	Part-skim ricotta or fat-free ricotta
	Whole Milk	Fat-free or skim milk; 1% low-fat milk
	Evaporated Milk	Fat-free evaporated milk
	Half-and-Half	Fat-free half-and-half or fat-free evaporated milk
	Whipped Cream	Fat-free or reduced-calorie frozen whipped topping
	Ice Cream	Fat-free or low-fat ice cream or frozen yogurt; sherbet; sorbet
Other	**Soups,** canned	Low-fat, reduced-sodium soups
	Fudge Sauce	Fat-free chocolate syrup
	Nuts	A reduced amount of nuts (one-third to one-half less)
	Unsweetened Chocolate, 1 ounce	3 tablespoons unsweetened cocoa and 1 tablespoon butter

Alcohol *Substitutions*

Liqueurs, spirits, and wines add special flavors to food that are difficult to replace. Alcohol itself evaporates at 172°, leaving only its flavor behind. However, this chart gives ideas for substitution of alcoholic ingredients, should you choose to change the recipe.

Ingredient	Substitution
Amaretto (2 tablespoons)	$1/4$ to $1/2$ teaspoon almond extract
Grand Marnier or other orange-flavored liqueur (2 tablespoons)	2 tablespoons orange juice concentrate or 2 tablespoons orange juice and $1/2$ teaspoon orange extract
Kahlúa, coffee- or chocolate-flavored liqueur (2 tablespoons)	2 tablespoons strong brewed coffee and 1 teaspoon sugar
Rum or **Brandy** (2 tablespoons)	$1/2$ to 1 teaspoon rum or brandy extract for recipes in which liquid amount is not crucial (add water if it is necessary to have a specified amount of liquid)
Sherry or **Bourbon** (2 tablespoons)	1 to 2 teaspoons vanilla extract
Port, Sherry, Rum, Brandy, or fruit-flavored liqueur ($1/4$ cup or more)	equal measure of orange juice or apple juice and 1 teaspoon of corresponding flavored extract or vanilla extract
White Wine ($1/4$ cup or more)	equal measure of white grape juice or apple juice for dessert recipes; equal measure of fat-free, less-sodium chicken broth for savory recipes
Red Wine ($1/4$ cup or more)	equal measure of red grape juice or cranberry juice for dessert recipes; for soups, stews and other savory dishes, sometimes may substitute an equal measure of beef broth

Index

Recipe titles are in italics.

Chapatis, Whole Wheat, 448
Cheese. *See also* Cheesecakes.
    Bread, Two-Cheese Oregano, 119
    grating, 238, 240
    Parmesan, 239, 421
    Pizza Bianca, Three-Cheese, 116
    Popovers, Parmesan, 105
    Potato, Fontina, and Cremini au
      Gratin, 303
    ricotta, 102, 103, 142
    Sauce
      Alfredo Sauce, 44
      Asiago Cheese Sauce, 43
      Classic Cheese Sauce, 42
      Easy Cheddar Cheese
        Sauce, 43
      Gruyère Cheese Sauce, 43
      Sauce, Smoked Gouda
        Cheese, 43
      Swiss Cheese Sauce, 43
    slicing, 239
    storing, 238, 239, 240
    substitutions, 241
    varieties of, 238-239
    yogurt cheese, 235
Cherries
    Pie, Chocolate Chip-Cherry, 167
    removing pits from, 344
    selecting, 344
    storing, 344
    varieties of, 344
Chicken. *See also* Poultry.
    Breasts, Artichoke and Goat
      Cheese-Stuffed Chicken, 211
    Coq au Vin, 58
    Fricassee with Orzo,
      Chicken, 237
    Oven-Fried Chicken, 71
    Pad Thai, 89
    Pecan Cream and Mushrooms,
      Chicken with, 365
    Roasted Chicken, Garlic-
      Rosemary, 78
    Roasted Chicken, Lemon-
      Herb, 79
    Salad, Mango Tango
      Chicken, 353
    Steamed Chicken with Black
      Bean Salsa, 83
    Stir-Fry, Chicken-Cashew, 89
    Stock, Brown Chicken, 39
    Stock, White Chicken, 38
    Thighs with Garlic and Lime,
      Chicken, 212

    Tips and techniques
      breasts, 209, 210
      buying, 207
      cuts of, 207-209
      food safety, 207
      free-range, 208
      organic, 208
      precooked, 209
      removing skin from, 208
      roasting, 74, 78, 79
      rotisserie, 208
      serving size, 207, 209, 210
      stuffing, 211
      thighs, 209
      using in recipes, 210
Chile peppers, 298-299, 457, 458,
Chinese cooking, 433-438
Chimichurri, 465
Chives, 296, 377
Chocolate. *See also* Cocoa.
    Biscotti, Espresso-Chocolate
      Chip, 127
    brands of, 397
    Brownies, Chocolate-Mint, 124
    Cake, Devilish Angel Food, 145
    Cake, Mocha Crumb, 142
    Cake, Texas Sheet, 148
    Cheesecake, Chocolate, 152
    Cheesecake, Zebra-Stripe, 155
    Cookies, Chocolate Icebox, 132
    forms of, 396-397
    Fudge Sauce, 54
    grating, 163
    Pie, Chocolate Chip-Cherry, 167
    Pie, Double-Chocolate
      Cream, 163
    Smoothie, Chocolate-Peanut
      Butter, 26
    Soufflé, Hot Chocolate, 180
    storing, 397
    using in recipes, 396
Chutney, 369-370
Cilantro, 377, 445, 447, 456, 458
Cinnamon, 382, 423
Clams
    buying, storing, 221
    Clam Sauce, 45
    cleaning, 221, 222
    types of, 222
Clay-pot cookers, 79
Cocoa
    measuring, 397
    types of, 397
    using in baking, 397

Coconut
    Cake, Coconut Triple-Layer, 138
    coconut milk, 352, 444
    cracking a coconut, 352
    Frosting, Fluffy Coconut, 139
    Macaroons, Chewy Coconut, 129
    Pie, Coconut Cream, 160
    processed, 352
    selecting fresh, 352
    Soup with Chicken, Coconut, 444
Colanders, 13
Condiments, 369-375. *See also*
  specific types.
Cookies, 91, 122-133. *See also*
    Biscotti.
    Bars, Two-Layer Caramel-
      Pecan, 125
    Brownies, Chocolate-Mint, 124
    Crisps, Spicy Oatmeal, 129
    Drop Cookies, Lemon-
      Honey, 128
    Gingerbread Little Cakes, 131
    Icebox Cookies, Chocolate, 132
    Icebox Cookies, Peanut
      Butter, 133
    Icebox Sugar Cookies, Basic, 132
    Macaroons, Chewy Coconut, 129
    Squares, Easy Lemon, 125
    Sugar Cookies, 130
    Tips and techniques
      baking, 123
      bar cookies, 124, 125
      cooling baked, 129
      drop cookies, 128, 129
      equipment for baking, 122
      fat in, 123
      freezing, 123
      lightening, 91
      measuring dough, 128
      rolled cookies, 130, 131
      slice-and-bake, 132, 133
      storing, 123
      sugar cookies, 133
Cooking methods. *See* specific
  types.
Corn
    cooking, 276
    Creamed Corn with Bacon and
      Leeks, 277
    cutting off the cob, 277
    Grilled Corn on the Cob,
      Cajun-, 277
    grilling, 277
    selecting and storing, 276

Recipe titles are in italics.

Recipe titles are in italics.

Recipe titles are in italics.

Recipe titles are in italics.

Recipe titles are in italics.